Bloodless Victories
The Rise and Fall of the Open Shop in the Philadelphia Metal Trades, 1890–1940

This book examines how a group of manufacturers of metal products – "everything from buttonhooks to battleships" – in America's third biggest city helped each other to meet the challenges of organized labor (and sometimes an interventionist state) in the half-century between the "second industrial revolution" and the Second World War. After thirty years of success, the employers were finally overwhelmed by a resurgent labor movement backed by New Deal politicians and administrators. Their story offers the broadest and most detailed account available of the industrial relations problems and policies of small and mid-sized firms in this period. This book analyzes labor issues by means of a careful local case study, but its conclusions about the interplay of labor, organized capital, law, and the state in determining the fate of workers' rights and employers' interests have broad relevance to the history and politics of twentieth-century industrial relations.

Howell John Harris is a Reader in History at the University of Durham, England. He was educated at Jesus and Nuffield Colleges, Oxford, and at the New York State School of Labor and Industrial Relations at Cornell University. He has been a Senior Fulbright Fellow at Princeton University as well as a Woodrow Wilson Center Fellow. He won the Taft Prize in Labor History for his book *The Right to Manage* (1992).

Bloodless Victories
The Rise and Fall of the Open Shop in the Philadelphia Metal Trades, 1890–1940

HOWELL JOHN HARRIS

University of Durham

CAMBRIDGE
UNIVERSITY PRESS

PUBLISHED BY THE PRESS SYNDICATE OF THE UNIVERSITY OF CAMBRIDGE
The Pitt Building, Trumpington Street, Cambridge, United Kingdom

CAMBRIDGE UNIVERSITY PRESS
The Edinburgh Building, Cambridge CB2 2RU, UK   http: //www.cup.cam.ac.uk
40 West 20th Street, New York, NY 10011-4211, USA   http: //www.cup.org
10 Stamford Road, Oakleigh, Melbourne 3166, Australia
Ruiz de Alarcón 13, 28014 Madrid, Spain

First published 2000

Printed in the United States of America

Typeface Sabon 10/12 pt.   *System* QuarkXPress [BTS]

A catalog record for this book is available from the British Library.

Library of Congress Cataloging in Publication Data
Harris, Howell John, 1951–
Bloodless victories : the rise and fall of the open shop in the Philadelphia metal trades,
1890–1940 / Howell John Harris.
p. cm.
Includes index.
ISBN 0-521-58435-3
1. Metal-workers – Labor unions – Pennsylvania – Philadelphia – History.   2. Industrial
relations – Pennsylvania – Philadelphia – History.   I. Title.
HD6515.M5.H37 2000   331.88′169′0974811 – dc21   99-057408

ISBN 0 521 58435 3   hardback

[T]he mission of the National Metal Trades Association is to enable the manufacturers of this country to win a bloodless victory upon the great battlefield where are marshalled the forces of capital and labor. Today each side is armed to the teeth, and from time to time we smell the smoke from skirmishes upon the outskirts; but the carnage of a great conflict may still be avoided. It is for us to work toward a peaceful outcome.

[Howard P. Eells, President, Bucyrus Co., Milwaukee, and National Metal Trades Association, in NMTA, *Synopsis of Proceedings of the Twelfth Annual Convention* (New York, 1910), p. 5]

Contents

Figures and Tables

Acknowledgments

This book has taken far too long to research (1983–94), write (1991–95), and unwrite (1996–99). My great regret is that this has meant that, by the time it appears, death has deprived two old friends who helped me with it of their chance to criticize the result. Bill Adam, a master patternmaker, and one-time electrical appliance assembly worker Haldor Reinholt introduced me to what little was left of industrial Philadelphia in the 1980s, and to their old Communist and United Electrical Workers comrades. Both of them had kept the faith, and they disapproved of my interest in the wrong side of the class war. But they were unfailingly generous and welcoming, and shared their own understanding of the labor revolt of the 1930s and the vanished world of Philadelphia's skilled working class. This book is dedicated to them because I promised, and I know they would have appreciated it – the gesture, though not the argument.

I have also accumulated debts of gratitude to people and organizations still around to be paid off. First stands David Brody, who wrote me when I was planning to do something completely different from this, and told me that the records of the Metal Manufacturers' Association of Philadelphia (hereafter MMA) had come into the public domain, and I had better take a look. Seven years later, he told me that I must not finish this project before I had dealt with the collapse of the Open Shop employment system in the 1930s as well as with its creation and maturity in the 1900s through 1920s. Dave was right, as usual. This book is not up to his standards of economy, lucidity, and originality, but Dave, it's the best I can do.

Philip Scranton's contributions to this book have also been fundamental. We have researched together, swapped drafts and ideas, and visited ever since we met in 1983. The historiographical and methodological framework into which this book fits is largely of Phil's creation. He has done more than anyone else to rediscover and interpret the experience of those specialized yet flexible manufacturers of skill-intensive products who used to sit beyond the margins of histories of business and its development. He has also pioneered in the writing of *industrial* history, which pays its respects to business and labor history and other genres, but hopes to breach some of the artificial boundaries separating them.

Jonathan Zeitlin also played a key role in getting this project off the ground. He introduced me to the literature that he and others – most notably Phil – were creating, which highlighted the historical importance of the nonmanagerial firm, of the collective organizations that they built to help themselves achieve a variety of objectives that they were too weak to attain separately, and of the industrial districts into which they clustered and which facilitated their cooperation. All of this helped make sense of the MMA and its members, and provided their story with a context. Jon is a facilitator of other people's work as well as being a very original scholar himself. His seminars and conferences in Cambridge, England, in 1984–87, provided critical venues within which I could develop and display my early ideas. By providing deadlines, he then *forced* me into print. So too did another friend, Sandy Jacoby, whose own work on the historical development of U.S. industrial relations, and in particular on employers' contributions to it, has been extremely influential, on me and others.

A mass of other friends, colleagues, and acquaintances have helped, too. If Fred Miller and Ken Fones-Wolf, then at Temple University Urban Archives, had not been so active and persuasive, the records of the MMA might have ended up in the trashcan, not the public domain, and this book would have been impossible. Ken also shared his unparalleled knowledge of the MMA papers with me, often as we commuted by rattly train back through Philadelphia's miles of postindustrial devastation to our leafy suburban destinations – through the places where metal manufacturers used to work, to those where they used to live. In the long years of researching and writing, many other fellow-historians have listened politely as I rambled on about my work, have read draft material, and have made many valuable suggestions and criticisms. The only fair way of settling my accounts is to thank, in particular, Tony Badger, Gerry Berk, Manfred Boemeke, Jack Brown, Mel Dubofsky, Dan Ernst, Nando Fasce, Shel Garon, Roger Horowitz, Stan Katz, Tom Klug, Mike Lacey, Marj Lasky, Walter Licht, Nelson Lichtenstein, Joe McCartin, David Montgomery, Dan Nelson, Dan Raff, Dan Rodgers, Ron Schatz, Jon Sumida, Chris Tomlins, Gerald Zahavi, and Bob Zieger.

Librarians and archivists are the historian's indispensable allies. Some materials for this book have been conjured up by the Inter-Library Loan service at the University of Durham, or drawn from the collections of the Borthwick Institute and Joseph S. Rowntree Trust in York, Rhodes House and the Bodleian Library, Oxford, and the British Library, London. But most of them have been gathered in America, in particular from the New York Public Library and the American Management Association, New York

City, the Rockefeller Archives Center, Pocantico Hills, and the Kheel Center and Catherwood Library at Cornell University's School of Industrial and Labor Relations, Ithaca, New York; from the Firestone Library, Princeton, New Jersey; in Philadelphia from the Urban Archives and Paley Library, Temple University, the Federal Records Center, the Historical Society of Pennsylvania, the University of Pennsylvania Archives and Van Pelt Library, the Quaker Collection at Haverford College and from D. Robert Yarnall, Jr.,'s collection of his father's papers; elsewhere in Pennsylvania, from the United Steelworkers archives at Penn State University, and the United Electrical Workers collections at the University of Pittsburgh; from the Hagley Library in Wilmington, Delaware; and, in Washington, from the Department of Labor's superb holdings, the Library of Congress, including its Manuscripts Division, and the National Archives, particularly the old Suitland Record Center and downtown Modern Military Records branch. Finally, Bob Breese, his staff at the MidAtlantic Employers' Association (the MMA's direct descendant), and their colleagues from other big associations, brought my understanding of the tradition of collective action among American employers up to date, supplying copies of privately circulated material and other confidential information which could not have been obtained from any other source.

Research requires other inputs besides ideas, books, and records. It needs money. The principal underwriter for this book has been my employer since 1980, the University of Durham, England, which has given me a decent salary, provided research leave or leave of absence, and paid for much else that has gone into it, including a substantial fraction of the production costs. It has had to be very patient to see much return on this investment, and it has been very trusting that eventually something of value would appear. The Fulbright Commission and the Woodrow Wilson International Center for Scholars at the Smithsonian granted me six-month fellowships in 1982–83 and 1986 for other purposes, but did not object to my diversion of part of the time they had paid for into this project, not theirs. The Rockefeller Archives Center and the Center for the History of Business, Technology, and Society at the Hagley Museum have also been generous. I hate to think what the real cost of this book will have been, but it would have been even higher – and the research process would have been far less agreeable – if I had not enjoyed so much hospitality from friends in Ithaca, Princeton, Philadelphia, Washington, and elsewhere while working on it.

I thought that this book was finished in 1995, but Cambridge University Press's readers and my editor, Frank Smith, had other ideas. Not all of them were welcome, nor have I been able to incorporate all of their suggestions, but I should like to thank them for their constructive criticism. It proved impossible to discard, rearrange, and rewrite as much material as they required, but the book is better for the cuts and other changes that I have managed to make at their behest. I should also like to thank my copy editor, Elise Oranges, for all of her indefatigable efforts to make me write American. Any surviving errors of grammar and style are, I hope, the results of my reluctance to accept every correction.

My wife, Wendy Harris, knew me even before I knew anything about the MMA. More to the point, she also knew Bill Adam and Hal Reinholt and their comrades. If Dave Brody hadn't told me to go to Philadelphia, this book would never have been begun. But if I hadn't known that a warm welcome awaited me there, I might well have ignored him. So she shares the credit for getting the project going. And thanks to her, our relationship has survived the periods of obsessiveness and despair without which no book would be complete. She's hardly read a word of it, but she has done everything more important.

Durham, England, September 1999

Abbreviations

AALL	American Association for Labor Legislation
AFL	American Federation of Labor
AFSC	American Friends Service Committee
AHIT	*American Heritage of Invention and Technology*
ALLR	*American Labor Legislation Review*
Annals	*Annals of the American Association for Political and Social Science*
ARCLR	Advisory Research Committee on Labor Relations
BHR	*Business History Review*
BIR	Bureau of Industrial Research
BSR	B. Seebohm Rowntree (Papers)
Bull. NMTA	*Bulletin of the National Metal Trades Association*
CIO	Committee for Industrial Organization
DRY	D. Robert Yarnall, Sr. (Papers)
ECM	Executive Committee Minutes
FMCS	Federal Mediation and Conciliation Service [Records]
G.E.	General Electric Corporation
HML	Hagley Museum and Library
IA	*Iron Age*
IAM	International Association of Machinists
IMJ	*Iron (later International) Molders' Journal*
IMU	Iron (later International) Molders Union
DIR	Department of Industrial Research (Wharton School)
ITR	*Iron Trade Review*
J. ECP	*Journal of the Engineers Club of Philadelphia*
JAH	*Journal of American History*
JFI	*Journal of the Franklin Institute*
JHBS	*Journal of the History of the Behavioral Sciences*

JPR	*Journal of Personnel Research*
JSRT	Joseph S. Rowntree Trust
L&N	Leeds & Northrup Co.
LCMD	Library of Congress Manuscript Division
LMDC	Labor-Mangement Documentation Center
LSRM	Laura Spellman Rockefeller Memorial
MID	Military Intelligence Division, U.S. Army
MMA	Metal Manufacturers' Association (of Philadelphia)
MMAP	Metal Manufacturers' Association Papers
MMJ	*Machinists' Monthly Journal*
MTFWU	Machine, Tool, and Foundry Workers' Union
N-B-P	Niles-Bement-Pond Corp.
NAM	National Association of Manufacturers
NCF	National Civic Federation
NFA	National Founders Association
NIRA	National Industrial Recovery Act
NLB	National Labor Board (under NRA)
NLRB	National Labor Relations Board
NMTA	National Metal Trades Association
NRA	National Recovery Administration
NWLB	National War Labor Board
PADEP	Philadelphia Association for the Discussion of Employment Problems
PCC	Philadelphia Chamber of Commerce
PEB	*Philadelphia Evening Bulletin*
(E)PL	[Philadelphia] (*Evening*) *Public Ledger*
PMA	Pennsylvania Manufacturers' Association
PMHB	*Pennsylvania Magazine of History and Biography*
PP	*People's Press*
PR	*Philadelphia Record*
Procs. ECP	*Proceedings of the Engineers Club of Philadelphia*
QC-HC	Quaker Collections, Haverford College
QJE	*Quarterly Journal of Economics*
RAC	Rockefeller Archives Center
RCA	Radio Corporation of America
RG	Record Group (U.S. National Archives)
(P)RLB	(Philadelphia) Regional Labor Board (under NRA)
SOC	Social Order Committee (of Philadelphia Yearly Meeting, Religious Society of Friends)
SWOC	Steel Workers Organizing Committee
Trans. ASME	*Transactions of the American Society of Mechanical Engineers*
TUUA	Temple University Urban Archives

UE	United Electrical, Radio, and Machine Workers
ULR	*Union Labor Record* (Philadelphia)
USCIR	U.S. Commission on Industrial Relations
USIC	U.S. Industrial Commission

1

Introduction

This is a book about power. It is an examination of how and why American employers were so successful for so long in their campaign to construct and maintain a system of industrial relations in which unions would play no part. The creation, persistence, and sudden collapse of the resulting Open Shop order define the chronological limits of this work, c. 1890–1940. This periodization allows us to study the vicissitudes of organized class relations through successive booms and depressions, the systemic crises of the First World War and New Deal, and across two generations of change in the structures of industrial enterprises themselves and, to a lesser extent, in the ideologies of those who controlled them.

This book is therefore about some of the main industrial relations issues confronting American employers and their workers, the public, and the state, through five decades. It aims to illuminate these large national realities, but does so from a particular local standpoint. It is rooted in the experiences and behavior of one self-selected group of employers, in one industry, in one city. The city is Philadelphia; the industry is secondary metal manufacturing, the heart of the Open Shop movement there and elsewhere;[1] and the group is the Metal Manufacturers' Association of Philadelphia (MMA), set up in December 1903 to fight the good fight against organized labor, and doing so with considerable success throughout the next thirty years. The focus will be on the association, on the employers' collective endeavor to remain non-union, rather than on the individual firms that made it up.

---

[1] That is, the production and fabrication of a variety of goods from a range of metals, rather than the refining of those materials from ores and scrap. See esp. Grace H. Stimson, *Rise of the Labor Movement in Los Angeles* (Berkeley, 1955) and sources cited in note 3 for this industry's leading role among anti-union manufacturers.

I

By the early 1980s it was clear that the New Deal Order of relatively strong and legitimate unions was a historical anomaly in the development of organized class relations in the United States. That system was falling apart, shattered by politico-legal assaults, industrial restructuring, ideological change, and other fatal blows. American employers were confidently shaping and taking advantage of these circumstances to rebuild the union-free environment that they had almost always preferred. The Open Shop order that flourished from the 1900s until the 1930s began to seem well worth a fresh examination. It was a set of ideas and relationships whose time had come again. Employers' structural strength, what Selig Perlman called their " 'effective will to power,' " their determination and ability to exercize unilateral authority relatively unfettered by outside intervention from unions and the state, was evidently the great continuing explanation in the history of U.S. industrial relations. This was the heart of the matter. This was the foundation of "American exceptionalism." This was what deserved scrutiny.[2]

There was much to be done, and not enough to build on. Although we had several serviceable monographs on the "peak associations" of the business community that claimed to speak for it in national politics, we had hardly any worthwhile studies of the industry- and community-based employers' organizations through which the Open Shop war was prosecuted at the grass roots.[3] And while we had some excellent studies of large-

---

[2] See Steve Fraser, "The Labor Question," in Steve Fraser and Gary Gerstle, eds., *The Rise and Fall of the New Deal Order, 1930–1980* (Princeton, 1989), pp. 55–84; Kim Moody, *An Injury to All: The Decline of American Unionism* (London, 1988). For the literature of "employer exceptionalism" see Larry G. Gerber, "Shifting Perspectives on American Exceptionalism: Recent Literature on American Labor Relations and Labor Politics," *Journal of American Studies* 32 (1997): 253–74, esp. pp. 265–71; Sanford M. Jacoby, ed., *Masters to Managers: Historical and Comparative Perspectives on American Employers* (New York, 1991), pp. 1–15, 173–200; Selig Perlman, *A Theory of the Labor Movement* (New York, 1949 ed., first published 1928), p. 4 [quote] and Ch. 5, esp. Sec. 1; Steven Tolliday and Jonathan Zeitlin, eds., *The Power to Manage? Employers and Industrial Relations in Comparative-Historical Perspective* (London, 1991), pp. 273–343.

[3] For literature on peak associations, see Richard W. Gable, "A Political Analaysis of an Employers' Association: The National Association of Manufacturers" (Ph.D. diss., University of Chicago, 1950); Howard Gitelman, "Management's Crisis of Confidence and the Origins of the National Industrial Conference Board," *Business History Review* (hereafter BHR) 58 (1984): 153–77; Albert K. Steigerwalt, *The National Association of Manufacturers 1895–1914: A Study in Business Leadership* (Grand Rapids, 1964); Allen M. Wakstein, "The Open-Shop Movement, 1919–1933" (Ph.D. diss., University of Illinois, 1961); Robert Wiebe, *Businessmen and Reform* (Cambridge, Mass., 1962), esp. Chs. 2, 7. Daniel Ernst's *Lawyers Against Labor: From Individual Rights to Corporate Liberalism* (Urbana, 1995), is a splendid account of the American Anti-Boycott Association, closely allied with the NAM and other

scale, anti-union corporate employers, we knew and could know very little of the tactics and strategy of the smaller firms that made up the bulk of the recruits in the Open Shop cause.[4] For these firms, and the associations that they supported, were rarely represented in public archive collections – the firms, because of the usual problems afflicting the creation and preservation of the records of small, private organizations; the associations, for similar reasons and because much of their work was necessarily clandestine, and somewhat questionable if not actually illegal, so that it resulted in as few records, kept for as short a time, as possible. As the National Metal Trades Association's president explained on the retirement of the key staff officer responsible for its anti-union victories, "the greater part of his work, the more intimate, far-reaching and important part, has never been written, will never be written, can never be written."[5]

Open Shop organizations in fighting organized labor in the courts; and Sidney Fine's definitive *"Without Blare of Trumpets": Walter Drew, the National Erectors' Association, and the Open Shop Movement, 1903–57* (Ann Arbor, 1995) is the only, very welcome, study of a national metal trades employers' association. Apart from those recent additions to the literature, one has to rely on near-contemporary studies that had at least the advantage of being able to use many records and publications that have not survived, and interviews with association executives – William Franklin Willoughby, "Employers' Associations for Dealing With Labor in the United States," *Quarterly Journal of Economics* (hereafter QJE) 20 (1905): 110–50; F. W. Hilbert, "Employers' Associations in the United States," in Jacob H. Hollander and George E. Barnett, eds., *Studies in American Trade Unionism* (London, 1906), Ch. 7; Margaret L. Stecker, "The National Founders Association," *QJE* 30 (1916): 352–86; and particularly Clarence E. Bonnett, *Employers' Associations in the United States: A Study of Typical Associations* (New York, 1922). Literature on state and local associations is even sparser – significant exceptions are Alfred H. Kelly, "A History of the Illinois Manufacturers' Association" (Ph.D. diss., University of Chicago, 1938); J. Roffe Wike, *The Pennsylvania Manufacturers' Association* (Philadelphia, 1960); and Thomas Klug, "The Roots of the Open Shop: Employers, Trade Unions, and Craft Labor Markets in Detroit, 1859–1907" (Ph.D. diss., Wayne State University, 1993), which complements this work.
[4] Pioneering works in industrial relations history with a big-business focus include David Brody, *Steelworkers in America: The Non-Union Era* (Cambridge, Mass., 1960) and Robert Ozanne, *A Century of Labor-Management Relations at McCormick and International Harvester* (Madison, 1967). Histories of personnel management have also tended to concentrate on the behavior of the larger and more prominent firms – see Daniel Nelson, *Managers and Workers: Origins of the New Factory System in the United States, 1880–1920* (Madison, 1975) and Sanford M. Jacoby, *Employing Bureaucracy: Managers, Unions, and the Transformation of Work in American Industry, 1900–1945* (New York, 1985). The development of these literatures is discussed in Jonathan Zeitlin, "From Labour History to the History of Industrial Relations," *Economic History Review* 40 (1987): 159–84; by Jacoby himself in "Masters to Managers: An Introduction" in *idem*, ed., *Masters to Managers*, pp. 1–15, 201–5, and by Tolliday and Zeitlin in "Employers and Industrial Relations Between Theory and History" in their ed. *The Power to Manage?* pp. 1–31.
[5] NMTA, *Synopsis of Proceedings of the 15th Annual Convention* (New York, 1913), p. 4. The Wagner Act, National Labor Relations Board (NLRB), and La Follette Com-

No evidence = no history, so without a paper trail of primary sources the prospects of exploring the Open Shop seemed bleak indeed. But the MMA had survived into the 1980s; it had preserved many of its records rather than casually discarding them when they were no longer of use, or deliberately shredding them when they became an embarrassment; most unusually, it had been prepared to deposit them in a public archive. For these reasons, if for no others, it was worth careful examination.

But how much could its story matter? I was still operating under the common misapprehension that Philadelphia was, as the English visitor John Foster Fraser put it in 1903, "the joke-town of America," where nothing much ever happened, and then very slowly. It did not feature much in the bloody battle honors of American labor. It was not the center of any great industry, or so I thought – not a Pittsburgh, Akron, Detroit, or Chicago. In addition to being in the wrong place to be interesting, the MMA also seemed to have the wrong kind of members to weigh very much in the scales of history. Although I understood that smaller firms were the backbone of the Open Shop movement, I still shared the usual prejudices of American business historians of my generation, which led me to underestimate their collective importance. As Mira Wilkins summed up the conventional wisdom laid out by Alfred Chandler and those who followed in his wake, "In dealing with modern business history from the late nineteenth century ... the significant actors are not the small, single product, single plant, single function, local market enterprises, but rather ... the multiproduct, multiplant, multifunctional, multidivisional, multinational enterprises administered by a managerial hierarchy."[6]

Fortunately, the MMA papers, even at first reading, were sufficiently fascinating that I determined not to be put off the attempt to understand the reality that they described by the fear that this might end up as no more than a trivial pursuit. The decision was made easier by some fine and pioneering scholarship which showed me that, in business history as elsewhere, the conventional wisdom is rarely the whole truth, and that the provincial world of the proprietary capitalist was worth a closer look.[7]

mittee in the 1930s were also very bad for the survival of those records of the Open Shop movement that they did not manage to expose.

[6] Fraser, *America at Work* (London, 1903), pp. 76–77; Wilkins, "Business History as a Discipline," *Business and Economic History* 17 (1988): 4.

[7] See Mark Granovetter, "Small Is Bountiful: Labor Markets and Establishment Size,"*American Sociological Review* 49 (1984): 323–34; Charles Sabel and Jonathan Zeitlin, "Historical Alternatives to Mass Production: Politics, Markets, and Technology in Nineteenth-Century Industrialization," *Past and Present* 108 (1985): 133–76 and, as eds., *Worlds of Possibility: Flexibility and Mass Production in Western Industrialization* (New York, 1997); Philip Scranton, *Proprietary Capitalism: The Textile Manufacture at Philadelphia* (New York, 1983), *Figured Tapestry: Production, Markets, and Power in Philadelphia Textiles, 1885–1940* (New York, 1989), and *Endless Novelty: Specialty Production and American Industrialization, 1865–1925* (Princeton, 1998).

1.3 HOW THE PROJECT GREW

The MMA papers, although quite extensive, only offered material for a thin institutional narrative, with many gaps.[8] Given that there was so little secondary literature on the kind of organization of which it was an example, it was hard to tell where it fitted, where its history was representative, where it was exceptional, and why. So one of the first tasks had to be to construct an account of the national institutional setting within which it was formed and functioned. This involved an exploration of the critical period in American industrial relations, particularly in the metal trades, which began about a century ago and saw rapid growth in the power of skilled workers' unions, followed by counter-organization by employer communities, including Philadelphia's.

The primary sources for retelling this story were participants' accounts – in trade union journals and the business press, publications and proceedings of the new employers' associations themselves, and testimony given before public tribunals investigating the labor problem. Out of the exploration of the complex interactions between skilled workers' unions and national and local employers' associations in the metal trades I emerged confident that the MMA was indeed a fairly typical member of a well-integrated family of businessmen's organizations, responding to a common challenge in commonplace ways. Its story was particular but not exceptional; it could serve as a basis for general observations on the dynamics of middle-sized, anti-labor employers' collective behavior in the Open Shop era.

One stage in contextualizing the MMA's institutional history was therefore relatively easily accomplished. The next stage was much harder. The MMA was a voluntary organization that existed to serve its members' needs; it did not have much of an independent existence. Those members were firms of a particular type – mostly proprietary in character, run by their controlling owners in person – and the entrepreneurs and senior managers who represented them in the association. Companies and individuals were therefore the principal historical actors, and the MMA was mostly an institutional reflection of their interests and priorities. But I had no idea about what and who those historical actors really were, and the MMA papers were not very helpful. There was no comprehensive list of association officers, or much information about which firms they came from, or what their status was in them. There was no consistent and continuous list of member firms either, nor data about what they made, how large they

---

[8] The only record series donated to Temple University's Urban Archives (hereafter TUUA) were those of the most obvious historical importance. A dumpster full of memorabilia and routine administrative material was discarded at about the same time – interview, John H. Shelsy (Senior Vice President, MidAtlantic Employers' Association), Valley Forge, 12 Sept. 1998.

were, where they were located, who owned and ran them, or what were the economic conditions of their industries.

And even if such information about member firms and association activists had been readily available, it would only have provided part of the picture. The MMA was merely a self-selected minority of the large and very diverse Philadelphia metal-manufacturing community. To know how it fitted into its immediate context, to understand where and why it gathered its strength, and to appreciate the changing relationships between the MMA's sample and its local universe, required exhaustive research into the socio-economic fabric of the whole of Philadelphia's metal trades.

Fortunately, rapid advances in the power, usability, and affordability of personal computers and their software over the last decade have made it quite easy for the artisan historian to gain some command over the masses of scraps of data that are the essential ingredients in any community-based case study. These have been collected from city directories, state surveys, and federal censuses, as well as from archival sources. They have been related to one another, and have been used to reconstruct a reasonably solid basis for this book.

Once the bug bites, gathering, linking, and interpreting quantifiable data can become dangerously addictive. The process and the results may fascinate the researcher, but they may have little appeal for anybody else. In this book, this type of data is usually kept in the background, and I have avoided extensive discussion of data-gathering and analytical techniques in the interests of economy and accessibility. What remains, as well as a trace of the data itself, is the confidence that that which can be measured has been, and that the innumerate historian's usual resort to implicit quantification, in the desperate attempt to claim that what s/he has come across is typical or important, has been minimized. When quantitative data are included in the text, they are reported using data graphics rather than tables, wherever appropriate, following the wisdom of William Playfair, that "Information, that is imperfectly acquired, is generally as imperfectly retained; and a man who has carefully investigated a printed table, finds, when done, that he has only a very faint and partial idea of what he has read; and that like a figure imprinted on sand, is soon totally erased or defaced."[9]

---

[9]   The resulting databases will be referred to in footnotes in CAPITALS. Full descriptions and sources are given in the Appendix. Playfair quote from Edward Tufte's bible of style, *The Visual Display of Quantitaive Information* (Cheshire, Conn., 1983), p. 32, which I have attempted to follow. Data graphics are also used to provide some visual variety, in preference to photographs of dead white males and dirty old machines. They offer concrete information that the latter often don't. Readers with a hankering for good pictures and revealing text should look at Philip Scranton and Walter Licht's excellent *Work Sights: Industrial Philadelphia, 1890–1950* (Philadelphia, 1986).

On this half-submerged empirical foundation I have erected a description of the changing Philadelphia metal-manufacturing community through four decades, of the men and the firms composing it, and of these employers' culture and practices. Satisfying my and, I hope, readers' interest in these aspects of the MMA's membership, and placing them in context, also required a considerable amount of qualitative research – in local histories, company histories, biographical compendia, local magazines, and, to a small and disappointing extent, in archives. Hardly any of the MMA's member firms or their executives have been so considerate as to leave collections of their papers. Even so, it has proved possible to reach some conclusions about the character of the firms, and the values of their proprietor-managers, which help explain the determination and methods with which they prosecuted the anti-labor struggle.

The third stage in the effort to broaden the research base of this study required moving outside the semiprivate world of Philadelphia employers, their employees, and their everyday affairs, to find out what trace their interactions left on the public record – particularly when their relations broke down and conflict spilled onto the streets. The local and labor press were some help here. Much more useful were the records of federal dispute-settlement and investigative agencies that became involved in metal trades labor relations during the two great systemic crises of 1916–21 and 1933–38 that tested, and then destroyed, the Open Shop. The richness of these official sources makes up for the absence of surviving documentary evidence from almost all of the companies and unions that were parties to the disputes.

1.4 THE FINAL STRUCTURE

Chapter 2 begins with a description of the metal-manufacturing community in the 1900s in terms of the industries and firms that made it up. It explores the nature of these firms – almost all locally owned and controlled, regardless of size, prime examples of proprietary capitalism and hands-on management. It examines, principally by means of short biographical sketches, distinctive features of the local entrepreneurial class – how and where they were recruited, the ways in which they pursued their careers, and their strategies for ensuring the survival and growth of their companies. The purpose of the chapter is to introduce the setting and the historical actors, and to explain something of the challenge that labor unions would pose when they tried to organize and bargain within an intensely competitive business community such as this. The chapter attempts to get inside these firms, and inside the heads of the men who owned and ran them. It explores the reasons for their belief in the necessity of simple, direct, personal management and unfettered control over their subordinates. Most of the source material is drawn from the 1900s and 1910s, but there is little evidence that the original, uncomplicated set of anti-labor convictions that prevailed at the outset of the Open Shop era altered much through succeeding decades. There was change in the ideology and practices of some Philadelphia metal manufacturers toward their employees – some movement toward more sophisticated forms of personnel management and welfare capitalism – but this is best thought of as supplementing more traditional attitudes and behavior, not displacing them.

Chapter 3 moves away from describing the composition and character of the business community among whom the MMA would recruit, toward a narrative account of the association's origins. This requires attention to both the local and national contexts. Philadelphia sustained dense networks of informal contacts among like-minded businessmen with shared interests and traditions of self-organization for common ends. These were some of the ties that bound together a group of possessive-individualistic entrepreneurs into a working community, and provided resources and models on which the MMA would be able to draw.

But the decision to mobilize these resources and build on these and other organizational experiences required some external stimulus. Between 1897 and 1904 there was a crisis in relations between employers and their skilled workers that affected metal-manufacturing communities like Philadelphia's right across the U.S. industrial belt. Craft unions were making the running; proprietary capitalists were forced to respond, and to decide how to meet this new challenge. Chapter 3 goes on to explain what courses they took, and why. It draws the connections between local employers' uncertain route through an unhappy experiment in collective bargaining with the most strongly organized of their skilled men – which ended in a decision to join forces to confront them – and the wider national developments that Philadelphia mirrored.

The chapter is almost as much about what happened outside the city as what went on within it. Philadelphia employers acted as members of national associations, their skilled workers were members of nationwide unions, and the strategies of both parties were largely determined by these outside affiliations rather than by local circumstances. Toward the end of 1903, local activists within the National Founders' and National Metal Trades Associations decided both to implement the Open Shop program developed at the national level since 1901 and to build a permanent local association complementing the national organizations' work and borrowing tactics as well as strategy from their brethren elsewhere.

Chapter 4 brings the focus back to the local level, and offers a straightforward narrative of the opening engagements in the long Open Shop war, c. 1904–15. Philadelphia metal manufacturing was convulsed by large strikes involving hundreds, and eventually thousands, of skilled workers, particularly in 1904–5, 1906–7, and 1910–11. The MMA and its members were in the thick of these conflicts, many of which they provoked and almost all of which they won. The chapter is an examination of the methodology of union-busting in the critical period when the Open Shop became securely established. It is a picture of tactical innovation in the service of a staunchly reactionary strategy. The chapter argues that coordinated labor replacement and the employers' ability to exploit the recurrent depressions of the prewar decade were central to the success of the Open Shop. Labor was weak and divided, serious violence was rare, and the employers' victories were quite easy and cheap to achieve and, as the book's title suggests, almost bloodless. The active support of the forces of order – particularly the judiciary, whose anti-labor decisions have received so much recent scholarly attention – was of secondary importance. Indeed, by the late prewar years, Open Shop employers regarded elected politicians as being almost as much of a threat to their freedom to manage as were the whipped trade unions. So the MMA extended its field of operations beyond the effective, economical deployment of resources for industrial conflict to include the political representation of the employers' interests against unwelcome intrusions from progressive state and federal governments.

Chapter 5 interrupts the flow of the narrative to describe the MMA as an institution and explain some of the internal reasons for its rapid attainment of stability and success. It analyzes the MMA in terms of its membership – which kinds of firms joined, which did not, and why; its political culture and financing – how this voluntary association reconciled the conflicting imperatives of the collective discipline required for the prosecution of the Open Shop war with the tight-fisted egoism that motivated its members; and of the routine functions it performed, which helped explain members' commitment as well as its overall achievement. The perspective of Chapter 5 is that employers' collective action, particularly in a culture that is as strongly individualistic as that of the United States, and one where interest groups enjoyed such feeble institutional endorsement by the state, was almost as complicated a project as the efforts of successive generations of industrial workers to transform their kind of class-consciousness into durable organization. The means that the MMA adopted to build its own culture of commitment, to construct a consensus in support of the evolving strategy of a stable leadership group, and to deliver demonstrably useful services to its members add to our understanding of the ways in which comparable voluntary organizations coped with these universal problems.

At the heart of the services that the MMA routinely delivered was an institution neglected by historians, but key to employers' success in the metal trades' Open Shop war – the Labor Bureau, a central office serving the specialized recruitment needs of a group of cooperating firms, of which dozens were created in the major manufacturing cities of the 1900s and 1910s, and which flourished until the 1930s. Since the late 1970s, labor historians have explored and debated employer–employee conflicts in terms of contests for control of the labor process within the enterprise. The intention of Chapter 5 is, in part, to refocus our attention onto contests for control of the labor markets on which both employers and employees depended.

The narrative resumes with Chapters 6 and 7, which deal with the MMA's greatest crisis before the 1930s – the years of overfull employment, workers' insurgency, and federal intervention unprecedented in terms of its potential power and pro-labor intentions, which characterized the war boom of 1915–18; and then the years of uncertainty, turmoil, chronic and acute unemployment, and a renewed conservatism, that followed. The Open Shop was challenged more than it ever had been; and it emerged triumphant.

In these chapters, the MMA does not always take center stage. Labor relations changed from an uneven but relatively straightforward contest between employers and workers, which was decided at the local level, into a more complicated but still unequal conversation between the traditional protagonists and the federal government. The lines connecting local developments with national organizations and tendencies were much more tightly drawn than ever before. Both chapters accordingly pay more attention to the world of labor and to the political economy of industrial relations than the story of the Open Shop's initial victories required. In addition, the MMA was spared the worst of the conflicts in war and postwar Philadelphia by the simple fact of its earlier success. The most important new developments in metalworkers' power and ambitions took place among other local employers' workforces. But it was the ability of those large firms to crush the workers' insurgency that allowed the MMA to continue to enjoy its relatively undramatic existence. For this reason, Chapters 6 and 7 focus on the city's metalworking industries as a whole rather than just on the MMA itself.

Chapters 8 and 9 deal with the Open Shop at its zenith, between the success of local and national employers' anti-union offensives, the recovery from the postwar recession, and the collapse of prosperity and Republican hegemony during Herbert Hoover's troubled presidency. During these years there was a near-total absence of labor unionism and overt industrial conflict among the Philadelphia metal trades, and the MMA faced the paradoxical consequences of victory: What else was there left to do, once the craft unions had been defeated, and state and federal governments no longer represented the threats to employer interests that they sometimes had in the Progressive Era? The answer to this question was offered by new leaders, members, and their associates from outside of the business community, who remade the MMA in the mid- to late 1920s. The rational, systematic development and use of industry's human resources offered a large new field for constructive activity. Personnel management and welfare capitalism – employer-initiated measures designed to provide workers with an increased measure of dignity and security in their lives – became the MMA's new program. The association grew to its interwar peak in terms of membership, employment, influence, and prestige on this basis.

The new model MMA of the 1920s was at the forefront of managerial progressivism. Its leaders were tied into a variety of national corporate, academic, reformist, and governmental networks. Their program represented the local implementation of the advanced agenda of socially conscious, quite self-confident élites. It met with limited support and some resistance from the local business community, and there was – as with managerial progressivism in general – a large gap between intention and achievement. But it is hard not to be impressed by the leaders' vision and sincerity, and their sense of the possibilities and the necessity for change within the capitalist employment relationship even during a period when they faced no external threat from labor and the state or internal challenge from their employees. It is difficult not to share their feelings of shock and despair when their dreams of reason collapsed in 1931–33.

The story of the MMA in the 1920s and early Depression has a heroic and tragic dimension. It represents in microcosm the flawed promise and the fate of even the most enlightened business leadership in the last traditional Republican era. It also has one unique feature. The men who were the principal architects of the MMA's liberal capitalism were no ordinary entrepreneurs. They were a small, tight group of Orthodox Quakers – committed pacifists, opponents of war in 1917–18, founding members and lifelong supporters of the American Friends Service Committee. Encountering them was one of the bonuses of engaging in a historical case study focused on Philadelphia, one of whose names for itself was, after all, the Quaker City. Their work allows us to appreciate the blurred boundaries between secular and religiously inspired reformism in early twentieth-century America, and to understand business decision making in such a value-laden area as industrial relations in all its human complexity.

Chapters 10 and 11 complete this account of the birth, early struggles, and enlightened maturity of the Open Shop in the Philadelphia metal trades, by attending to its death and transfiguration. The story of economic collapse, political upheaval, state intervention, and workers' self-organization in the 1930s is full of drama, but essentially familiar. What happened in Philadelphia happened in most mid- to large-sized manufacturing centers in the United States, at about the same time, in much the same way, and for many of the same reasons. The Philadelphia metal trades, almost free of trade unionism at Franklin Roosevelt's accession, although home to small, powerless groups of isolated Communists, Socialists, and other radicals, became a site of wholly unanticipated battles. A tradition of working-class Republicanism collapsed. City, state, and federal governments turned hostile to the Open Shop. Businesses proved increasingly unable, or unwilling, to resist. Eventually, in 1936–37, the new unions that joined the

Committee for Industrial Organization (CIO), fortified by success at the polls, confident of their political backing, officered by battle-hardened veterans and younger militants, overwhelmed the MMA. It did not give up without a fight; but it did give up.

Philadelphia metal trades labor relations in the 1930s were undeniably turbulent, but they were not particularly violent – whether compared with the city's strife-torn, strongly unionized textile industry or with the bloody martyrdoms still occurring elsewhere in the nation. In the MMA's territory, at least, labor achieved the second almost bloodless victory in this book. Workers and their allies destroyed the social order of the Open Shop, but they were assisted in so doing by the fact that businessmen increasingly appreciated both that it had outlived its viability and usefulness, and that by conceding they could help create a tolerable new order on the rubble of the old. By the end of the 1930s the MMA and most of its members had navigated the rapids of the transition. Labor's moment of insurgency had passed. In the new world of formalized collective bargaining and state regulation, the MMA would find growing reasons to persuade its members that there were many things it could do for them – that their businesses had many needs for expertise, information, and advice in the management of human resources, which they could satisfy best, or most easily, or most efficiently, if they continued to act together.

This book closes almost sixty years ago. The MMA – in the shape of its successor organization, the MidAtlantic Employers' Association – has not closed its doors yet. It has adapted to the suburbanization of industry, and then to regional de-industrialization, by abandoning the city and moving beyond its roots in manufacturing; it has outlived its union opponents, and it has been far more successful in adjusting to changes in members' needs and the composition of their workforces. When this book is published, it and many of its fellow associations in other cities and regions, most of them also rooted in the metal trades' Open Shop war, but now moved far beyond it, will be poised confidently at the threshhold of their second century.[10]

1.5 WHAT THIS BOOK IS NOT ABOUT

Reducing the results of a dozen years' research and writing to fit within the confines of a publishable book took much effort, and some sacrifices. This surgery was in the interest of emphasizing and clarifying the institutional narrative. But there will doubtless be readers, particularly from a labor or social history background, who are struck by what is not included in the following analysis, not because it was taken out, but because it never was

[10] See http://www.maea.org for a description of current services.

there in the first place. The second half of this introduction is designed to alert them to what they will not find, and to offer some explanations for why they will not find it.

A. Gender (that is, Women)

In 1900, Philadelphia's labor force was 26 percent, and its "manufacturing and mechanical" component 25 percent, female. The latter were mostly young – 59 percent of them under twenty-five, as against 26 percent for their male counterparts – and single: Only 15 percent of them were married, widowed, or divorced, as against 66 percent of male industrial workers. Their earnings were only 55 percent as high as men's.[11]

At the time there was nothing unusual about this pattern of women's industrial employment.[12] One further feature of it was also quite commonplace. Their world of work did not include the metal trades, save for a few low-wage, light manufacturing occupations – clock and watch making, engraving, jewelry, cutlery – often conducted on a workshop scale and under sweatshop conditions. Production areas of most factories were closed to them. They were not admitted to apprenticeships, so they had no regular route to adult skilled status, or supervisory positions, or executive and entrepreneurial opportunities. In 1900, more than 98 percent of all "manufacturers and officials" were male. The situation in the companies on which I focus was no different, and it did not change over time: Of the 1,045 proprietors, partners, and executive officeholders whose careers I have pursued through 250 companies and across four decades, 98.5 percent were men. The few exceptions were mostly partners' widows or younger family members in junior positions. None of these women is recorded as ever having taken part in any of the activities of the MMA, which was, among other things, a gentlemen's club.[13]

The industries that were at the center of the Open Shop movement, in Philadelphia as elsewhere, were the most male-dominated even among the metal trades. In 1902, for example, the fifty-seven companies that provided

---

[11] U.S. Department of Commerce and Labor, Bureau of the Census, *Special Reports: Occupations at the Twelfth Census* (Washington, 1904), pp. 672–78, lines 47, 75, 108, 112, 113, 118, 137–38, 144, for this and subsequent data on the 1900 workforce, unless separately noted; U.S. Department of the Interior, Bureau of the Census, *Twelfth Census of the United States, 1900, Vol. 8: Manufactures, Part 2* (Washington, 1902), pp. 784–91, lines 1, 11, 15, 25, 30, 33, 37–38, 42, 45–47, 49, 52, 65, 69, 70–71, 76, 80, 89, for earnings information.

[12] Leslie W. Tentler, *Wage-Earning Women: Industrial Work and Family Life in the United States, 1900–1930* (New York, 1979), Chs. 1 and 2 esp.; Julie A. Matthaei, *An Economic History of Women in America: Women's Work, the Sexual Division of Labor, and the Development of Capitalism* (New York, 1982), esp. Chs. 7 and Ch. 9, pp. 209–18.

[13] PHILCHAP (*sic*) database.

the MMA with its early recruits employed 7,881 people, literally 99 percent of them male. In forty-two of those firms, there was not a single female employee; and even in the other fifteen, one cannot usually tell from surviving data whether their ninety-one women were actually engaged on production work. In most cases, probably they were not. George Vaux Cresson, founder in 1859 and chief executive until his death in 1908 of the power-transmission machinery builder that bore his name, employed the third-largest number – 10 women out of 410 workers. As he told the U.S. Industrial Commission in 1900, "we have a few young ladies in the office as clerks, stenographers, and typewriters." The small handfuls of women recorded elsewhere were probably similarly employed. Two manufacturers of plumbing fittings, whose workforces were more than 10 percent female (33 of 312), were probably the only significant exceptions to the rule of exclusion from the shop floor.[14]

The MMA did not even count women *as* workers until acute labor shortages in 1918 forced it, and more of its members, to take that desperate measure in their search for recruits. Until then, members paid no dues in respect of the few women in some production jobs, and the association took no official notice of them. Then the proportion of women workers roughly doubled (to 5 percent) within a few months, entering their factories as laborers, inspectors, plain core makers, small machine operators, and light assembly workers, and getting paid about 60 percent as much, on average, as males. (Revealingly, the highest paid women were paid less than all but the very lowest paid men, the watch-keepers – a job that was usually a disguised pension for old and/or disabled employees.)[15]

The small but lasting change in the makeup of MMA members' workforces that the war produced did not involve any detectable shift in their attitudes toward women's employment. At first, the MMA charged

---

[14] 1902FACT database; Cresson testimony in U.S. Industrial Commission (hereafter USIC), *Report of the Industrial Commission on the Relations and Conditions of Capital and Labor Employed in Manufactures and General Business* (Washington, 1900), Vol. 14, p. 266. Women made up about 4 percent of the workforce of Philadelphia metal manufacturing industries altogether, but less than 2 percent of those at the heart of the Open Shop movement – U.S. Department of the Interior, Bureau of the Census, *Twelfth Census of the United States, 1900, Vol. 8: Manufactures, Part 2*, pp. 784–91, lines 1, 11, 15, 33, 37, 42, 52, 65, 80, 89 (Open Shop core) and 25, 30, 38, 45–7, 49, 69–71, 76 (others).

[15] Earl Sparks, Report of the Secretary, Dec. 1917, pp. 1, 5. The secretaries' reports to the annual membership meetings are the most complete, and among the most rewarding, of record series in the MMA papers (hereafter MMAP), Series I, Box 1, Folders 12-25 (hereafter, e.g., I-1-12/25), Accession URB 44, TUUA, and are referred to hereafter as [Name], SEC [date]. Sparks, SEC 1918, pp. 2–5; Executive Committee Minutes (the other main continuous source run, MMAP I-2/3-26/56; hereafter ECM), 13 Feb., 13 March, 10 Apr., 7 May, 12 June, 19 Nov., 11 Dec. 1918; "General Wage Report: Philadelphia and Vicinity, Aug. 1918," MMAP II-4-42; employment figures from PID16-40 database.

TABLE I.I The Philadelphia Metal Trades Labor Force, 1900–1930

	1900[a]	1910	Male[b]	1920	Male[b]	1930	Male[b]
Blacksmiths	4,382	4,090	100%	4,042	100%	2,193	100%
Boilermakers	1,631	1,903	100%	2,457	100%	1,109	100%
Metal Polishers	n.a.	1,623	94%	1,668	95%	1,216	96%
Machinists	15,050	19,772	100%	30,466	100%	20,432	100%
Molders	n.a.	3,007	100%	2,483	100%	1,797	100%
Patternmakers	817	947	98%	911	100%	651	100%
Apprentices	n.a.	n.a.		1,336	100%	501	100%
Semiskilled[c]	n.a.	1,233	96%	15,840	98%	3,473	96%
Laborers	n.a.	582	98%	7,687	99%	1,508	100%

[a] Data for 1900 use some different job categories (e.g., molders are grouped with stove workers and iron and steel workers), but no women are included in these groups either.

[b] Rounding conceals one woman machinist in 1910–30 and a handful of other craftswomen in 1910 (possibly misallocated, like 1910's lady patternmakers, who are likely to have worked in paper and cloth rather than wood and metal; they had all disappeared by 1920).

[c] Semiskilled operatives and laborers include agricultural and transportation equipment only – those in the electrical equipment industries were not consistently reported separately, and those from other industries not at all.

Source: Bureau of the Census, *Occupations 1900*, pp. 672–78; U.S. Department of Commerce, Bureau of the Census, *Thirteenth Census of the U.S. 1910* (Washington, 1914), Vol. 4, pp. 181–93; U.S. Department of Commerce, Bureau of the Census, *Fourteenth Census of the United States 1920* (Washington, 1923), Vol. 4, pp. 304–20; U.S. Department of Commerce, Bureau of the Census, *Fifteenth Census of the United States 1930* (Washington, 1931), Vol. 4, pp. 1384–1400.

members half-rate dues in respect of their female employees, putting women on a par with young boys or the lowest of the unskilled. But within months firms protested that their women workers were nothing like so difficult to recruit or control, and therefore should not cost as much to service, so the association dropped the dues level to one-tenth as much as it charged on a regular (adult male) employee.[16]

That policy endured through the interwar years, reflecting the fact that the focus of the association's concerns remained, as it always had been, the skilled component – wholly male – of its still overwhelmingly male workforce (see Table 1.1). Except for those few months in 1918–19, women workers were not even a slightly important issue for metal trades employ-

[16] ECM 19 Nov. 1918, 11 Feb. 1919.

ers. If they wanted them for clerical or light manufacturing jobs, "girls" were always available; they came cheap; they were not given any extensive training, because they were not expected to have any long-term future among the workforce; and they were not a problem. They were not a problem for my principal historical actors, so they are no concern of mine.

One of the reasons they were not a source of difficulty, of course, is that the skilled workers' unions – which were the problem – were also exclusively male, reflecting and reinforcing the character of the trades they claimed to represent, and wished to control. Once again, this should come as no surprise: Philadelphia's metal tradesmen, just as much as their employers, behaved in ways and believed in things that were normal, and seemed natural, at their time. The only thing that contemporaries found remarkable enough to deserve comment was the rare exception who proved the rule that skilled metal work was a male preserve. In 1919 there were more than 30,000 machinists in Philadelphia, and their union was at the peak of its strength. It had just one woman member, Hannah Black, a recent immigrant Scot who had learned her trade in the more liberal setting of a Glasgow munitions factory. She was sufficiently unusual that the *Philadelphia Bulletin*, which rarely dealt with the world of labor, unless labor was making a noise in the streets, devoted a story to her. She stood alone in her union, as her trade's representative at a Women's Trade Union League conference, and in the 1920 census.[17]

However, although women continued to have no place among skilled metal workers, they did find increasing numbers of entry-level jobs in light manufacturing (see Figure 1.1). They continued to experience job segregation, pay discrimination, and limited opportunities, even where they did not suffer total exclusion, and the ratio of women's wages to men's scarcely shifted from its apparently predestined 60 percent. The big growth area was the radio and electrical appliance industries, the city's success stories of the 1920s and 1930s.[18]

Women therefore had a substantial presence in the territory of the new mass production industrial unions of the depression decade. But it was a presence that the – generally male – local leaders of those unions slighted or ignored. As far as most of the city's craft and industrial unionists were concerned, working-class Philadelphia remained, as it always had been, the city of *brotherly* love.

Few concessions were made by the skilled male leadership and social democratic activists of the radio and electrical workers' unions – the heart

[17] "Woman Machinist in Union," *Philadelphia Bulletin*, 9 June 1919.
[18] Information on changing employment patterns from database PHIL1439. For the radio industry, see esp. Gladys M. Palmer and Ada M. Stoflet, *The Labor Force of the Philadelphia Radio Industry in 1936* (Philadelphia, 1938).

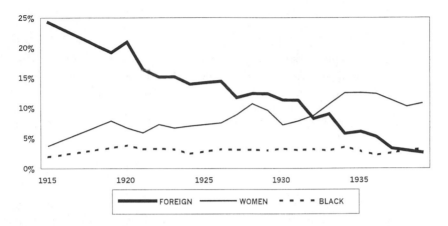

Figure 1.1. The Philadelphia Metal Trades Labor Force, 1915–1939. *Source:* PHIL 1439 database. Years 1916–18 and 1925 estimated by interpolation.

of the city's dynamic new labor movement – to the fact that the membership was about 50 percent female. There were "girls'" jobs, "boys'" jobs, and "men's" jobs, somewhat arbitrarily distinguished from one another, after the great upheaval, just as much as before – if not more so, in that the categories were now entrenched and legitimized by collective contract. The members were "the boys" who would go "back on the firing line" and "put [their] shoulders to the wheel." Even when some of the "boys" on the picket line just happened to be "girls" led by their own lady stewards, their leader, Martin Cassidy – a former railroad Brotherhood officer – plowed on regardless in his sensitive and encouraging way: "Keep it up, brothers, and we'll be going places."[19]

Historians have recently wondered whether the industrial unions might not have gotten more and better places if they had noticed a bit more clearly than Cassidy that there were members who were not "brothers," and unorganized workers who were not "chaps." Potential recruits to the armies of labor were not necessarily just the beefy young white men in overalls of the

[19] Patricia Cooper, "The Faces of Gender: Sex Segregation and Work Relations at Philco, 1928–1938" in Ava Baron, ed., *Work Engendered: Toward a New History of American Labor* (Ithaca, 1991), pp. 320–50; "Workers Wages Boosted, Union Closed Shop, Employment Gains; Company Wins Much Too," *People's Press* (hereafter *PP*) (7 March 1936): 8; Martin Cassidy, "Local 102 Ramblings," *PP* (2 May 1936): 8; "Philco Workers See Craft Union in Action," *PP* (16 May 1936): 4; cf. Ruth Meyerowitz, "Organizing the United Auto Workers: Women Workers at the Ternstedt General Motors Parts Plant," in Ruth Milkman, ed., *Women, Work and Protest: A Century of US Women's Labor History* (Boston, 1985), Ch. 11.

labor cartoonists' stereotype. It was all very well to thank Pauline at Brown's Café for keeping up the moral pressure on scabs by refusing to serve them; but Pauline's sisters in their dead-end, low-paid, light machining and light assembly jobs might perhaps have been better served by their unions, and might therefore have become more attached to them.[20]

However, that is not my concern. This is not primarily a work of labor history, so this book will not even be adopting the inadequate " 'add women and stir' " formula for "gendering" the working-class past that Ava Baron has castigated.[21] Most of the time, in most of the places and relationships I investigate, women were just not there to be added and stirred. Instead, I will be dealing with the world of Philadelphia metal working as I found it, and as the proprietors, executives, and mostly skilled workers, who are my concern, lived it. For that reason, I will be using gendered language, outside quote marks, in writing about my historical actors. I will be doing this in the interests of descriptive accuracy and fidelity to their outlook and experience.

Hang on a minute, some readers may be exclaiming: Don't men exist in a world of women? Aren't people's experiences at work and as workers embedded in their family and community contexts? When skilled men speak up and fight for a "living wage," when they cite their status and responsibilities as breadwinners and heads of households to justify their actions, shouldn't that remind us that work is not separable from other areas of life, and that men have gender identities too? Also, women may have been absent from the shop floor in most metal plants, but they were at the center of the homes that working lives supported, and that made men's work possible. And, in times of crisis, women were on the streets too – on picket lines, shaming and assaulting scabs, raising funds, organizing cooperatives, enabling strikers to hold out longer before, in Philadelphia until the 1930s, they succumbed to the almost inevitable defeat. All of that was undeniably true but, for the purposes of this telling of this story, it remains beside the point.[22]

[20] "Philco Notes: Local 102 Ramblings," *PP* (16 May 1936): 6; "Come And Get It!" *PP* (27 March 1937): 1; "Pauline Takes Care of Scabs," *PP* (23 May 1936): 5. Elizabeth Faue, *Community of Suffering and Struggle: Women, Men, and the Labor Movement in Minneapolis, 1915–1945* (Chapel Hill, 1991), offers a more sweeping indictment.

[21] Ava Baron, "Gender and Labor History: Learning From the Past, Looking to the Future," in her ed. *Work Engendered*, pp. 1–46 at p. 8.

[22] Works that ask and answer these questions include Jay Kleinberg, *The Shadow of the Mills: Working Class Families in Pittsburgh, 1870–1907* (Pittsburgh, 1989) and Dana Frank, *Purchasing Power: Consumer Organizing, Gender, and the Seattle Labor Movement, 1919–1929* (New York, 1994). For a Philadelphia metal-working strike that was a classic, if temporary, community mobilization like the one Frank studied, see the account of the 1920–21 Cramp's conflict below, Chapter 7, Section 2.

B. *Race (that is, African Americans)*

Philadelphia had the largest African-American community of any major northern industrial city in 1900, and their numbers continued to grow rapidly thereafter. But its members scarcely figure in this book. Their exclusion is not my choice; it was decided upon – or, more accurately, it was taken for granted – by most members of the majority community, irrespective of class. Their contemporaries counted African Americans out, so I can scarcely work them in. (Black women were doubly excluded from the metal trades, although not from the labor force in general; the discussion that follows accordingly confines itself to their menfolk.)[23]

In 1900, African-American and "colored" men made up 5 percent of the city's male labor force. In manufacturing and mechanical pursuits, their representation fell to just over 1 percent. In skilled and semiskilled metal trades occupations, they made up a mere 0.7 percent of the total. For them, too, neither apprenticeship nor anything it might lead to was generally an option.[24]

This pattern of exclusion was not accidental. It resulted from a consensus among most employers and their employees that African Americans had no place in industrial work, except perhaps for those jobs that were so hot, heavy, dirty, dangerous, health- and life-destroying, and/or poorly paid, that no white men, not even recent immigrants, wanted them. In 1927 company president Frank Sutcliffe reported

employing negroes in a department where there were acid fumes so that nobody else would work there. Later we found a way to remedy the fumes. Then the union men came and said, You have an agreement to employ our men. These negroes must be discharged. Is it not a great waste to tell colored men they can not enter any trade, and then build jails for them because they have nothing to do?[25]

---

[23] Catherine Golab, *Immigrant Destinations* (Philadelphia, 1977), p. 19; William E. B. Du Bois, *The Philadelphia Negro: A Social Study* (New York, 1967 ed.; first published New York, 1899), Ch. 9; Ray Stannard Baker, *Following the Color Line: American Negro Citizenship in the Progressive Era* (New York, 1964 ed.; first published New York, 1908), Ch. 7; Roger Lane, *William Dorsey's Philadelphia and Ours: On the Past and Future of the Black City in America* (New York, 1991), esp. Ch. 3.

[24] U.S. Bureau of the Census, *Occupations at the Twelfth Census*, pp. 672–78.

[25] Philadelphia Labor College, *Trade Union Conference: Elimination of Waste in Industry, April 9–10, 1927* (Philadelphia, 1927), p. 64; cf. Roger Lane, *Roots of Violence in Black Philadelphia* (Cambridge, Mass., 1986), p. 39. Cf. Philadelphia's sister city – John Bodnar, Roger Simon, and Michael P. Webber, *Lives of Their Own: Blacks, Italians, and Poles in Pittsburgh, 1900–1914* (Urbana, 1982), pp. 58–59, 61–62, 133–134 esp.; Peter Gottlieb, *Making Their Own Way: Southern Blacks' Migration to Pittsburgh, 1916–1930* (Urbana, 1987), esp. p. 89, pp. 90–94, 96, 97, 99.

For African Americans before the First World War, menial jobs were their only narrow openings into most metal-working plants, where small numbers worked as janitors, stokers, and the like. In the highest paying metal industries – firearms, locomotive manufacture, and machine repairing (the stronghold of the Machinists' union, as racist as it was sexist) – even these were reserved for white adult males only. The only exceptions to this bleak picture were companies making iron and steel forgings, pipes and tubing, and structural shapes, where African Americans found jobs in numbers much larger than their share of the working population.[26]

This, too, was not accidental, and did not simply result from the fact that such all-male heavy industries offered plenty of jobs deemed suitable for the least regarded categories of less-skilled workers. Two-thirds of all African-American metal-working jobs in the city, and a far higher proportion of those in production work, were to be found in just one company – Midvale Steel. As William E. B. Du Bois reported in 1899, Midvale began hiring black workers in about 1890 at the suggestion of "a manager whom many dubbed a 'crank'; he had a theory that Negroes and whites could work together as mechanics without friction or trouble." His purpose in introducing African-American men into Midvale's mostly skilled Irish, German, British, and (white) American workforce was not charitable; it was to break down the ethnic work gangs that were one barrier to managerial control.[27]

There were 200 African Americans among Midvale's 1,200 workers when Du Bois's field investigator called in 1896 or 1897, and 800–1,000 "colored men" out of 3,400 when its president testified before the Industrial Commission in 1900. Charles Harrah praised his black workers as thrifty, sober, and tough – "They are men of strong animal energy" – who were both "intelligent and docile," and made "very good citizens." Midvale recruited most of them directly from Fairfax County, Virginia – it was reluctant to employ city-bred men, whom the company thought too accustomed to servile work. Although they "come in as laborers unskilled (*sic*) they gradually become skilled." About half of them were reported as skilled by the late 1890s, and Midvale claimed to pay them as much as whites in the same jobs. White workers initially resented them, but by 1900 they had accepted African Americans' presence, and even socialized with them out of working hours, in their own homes.[28]

---

[26] All calculations about labor force shares 1914–39 are from PHIL1439 database unless otherwise noted. According to Stanley Lieberson's calculations, blacks were already overrepresented by a factor of nine among Philadelphia's iron and steel workers in 1900, as compared with how many there "should" have been in a city with a labor force that was 5 percent African American – *A Piece of the Pie: Blacks and White Immigrants Since 1880* (Berkeley, 1980), p. 318.

[27] Du Bois, *Philadelphia Negro*, pp. 129–31.

[28] Harrah in USIC, *Report*, Vol. 14, p. 353.

Unfortunately, after that brief flurry of interest around the turn of the century, Midvale's African-American workforce almost vanished from the public record. Their numbers and their prospects declined, relatively and absolutely, until the war. It seems likely that the same thing happened in Midvale's Nicetown works as in other Pennsylvania steel communities: the increased availability of southeast European "new immigrants," preferred employees in an increasingly racist society, crowded out established black workers, limited the opportunity to progress of those that remained, and closed the door on newcomers. But the beach-head Midvale had helped African-American men establish in the hot, heavy end of the Philadelphia metal trades, although beleaguered, was not all lost: In 1915 blacks still made up 700 (16 percent) of the 4,492 workers in the forgings industry (mostly Midvale), where they were outnumbered two to one by unnaturalized immigrants. They had begun to diffuse into other industries with similar labor requirements. And the war would bring more new similar openings – particularly in foundry work.[29]

But then change ground to a halt. Throughout the interwar period, African-Americans' share (about 3 percent) of the metal trades labor force was never more than about half as big as their share of the total industrial workforce, where, of course, they were always grossly underrepresented (see Figure 1.1). Even where they did get, and keep, jobs, they faced segregation, discrimination, and severely restricted opportunities to advance into any desirable positions. The industries to which they did gain freer admission were stagnating or experiencing secular decline, which may partly explain their readiness to employ a cheap and exploitable stream of job-seekers in lower level positions, and their unattractiveness to white workers. In contrast, the new growth sectors, offering many relatively well-paid semi-skilled mass production jobs — automobile bodies, bearings, electrical equipment, and radio manufacturing – were as lily-white as the old domains of skill ever had been.[30]

So things did not get any better over time. African Americans' best chances of getting metal trades jobs occurred in 1920, on the brink of the

[29] William P. Barba (Midvale's manager) in U.S. Commission on Industrial Relations (hereafter USCIR), *Industrial Relations: Final Report and Testimony, Submitted to Congress by the Commission on Industrial Relations . . . 64th Congress 1st. Session* (Washington, 1916), Vol. 3, p. 2876, makes no mention of any African Americans among his workforce in his 1914 testimony, although he discusses ethnicity quite extensively, and they were undoubtedly there; cf. later photographs of segregated workcrews in Scranton and Licht, *Work Sights*, pp. 197–213 (blacks work together at furnace-mouth and forge; whites operate machines); Bodnar et al., *Lives of Their Own*, pp. 133–34, and Gottlieb, *Making Their Own Way*, pp. 89, 90–94, 96, 97, describe similar processes at work in Pittsburgh.
[30] The only apparent exception, Westinghouse, was a heavy machinery plant with a large foundry, which is probably where most African Americans worked. Walter Licht, *Getting Work: Philadelphia, 1840–1950* (Cambridge, Mass., 1992), p. 46.

postwar recession; thereafter, the situation tightened once again, and during
the Depression unemployment became devastating, and exclusion near-
total. In 1932–33, for example, all of the jobless machinists who applied
to the state's Philadelphia employment office were white males – African
Americans had never been let into the ranks of the skilled, so they did not
even have a chance to join them in the same unemployment queue. Almost
all job openings bore explicit racial labels, and black unemployment (particularly among young men) soared. For African Americans' job opportunities in the metal trades, relatively the worst interwar year was 1936,
which, for their white working-class non-neighbors, was the best that the
Depression had to offer.[31]

The new unions of the CIO were not semiofficially exclusionist like those
of the American Federation of Labor (AFL), but in Philadelphia they did
not have to be: African Americans were scarcely present as potential
recruits. The CIO's Philadelphia heartland – the United Electrical Workers'
terrain – was an almost uncontested white dominion. And even where
African Americans did squeeze into the city's burgeoning labor movement,
they were ignored.

In the spring of 1934 Local 697 of the Lead, Oil, Varnish & Paint Makers
Union demanded and secured recognition from the Girard Smelting &
Refining Co. Blue-collar workers voted 92 percent pro-union, and, with the
help of the Regional Labor Board (RLB), they won a wide-ranging agreement with their hard-boiled proprietor. They began to construct a workplace rule of law in place of their boss Axelrod's previously unrestricted
authority. He agreed to do his hiring through the union, and workers won
protection against arbitrary dismissal. Incentive pay was replaced by
straight-time wages, which were raised for all – particularly for the lowest
paid – and employment and earnings security were improved by a scheme
to share available work rather than laying anybody off. (Layoffs, in seniority order, would only be made when part-time wages dropped below a
poverty level.)[32]

What is interesting about these events is not just the high degree of solidarity that the workers displayed, the effectiveness of their organization,
and the (for their time) wide-ranging and advanced employment rights they
achieved; it is who they were. For the employees of Girard were some of
the lowest of the low among Philadelphia's metal workers, and most of
them were black. They worked for peanuts in a hellish industry, which

---

[31]   Pennsylvania Department of Labor and Industry, State Employment Commission,
       Thirty Thousand in Search of Work (Harrisburg, 1933), pp. 15, 64, 66; Gladys
       Palmer, *Depression Jobs: A Study of Job Openings in the Philadelphia Employment
       Office 1932–1933* (Philadelphia, 1934) p. 6.
[32]   National Labor Board (hereafter NLB) Case 580, Record Group 25, U.S. National
       Archives.

explains why, even during the Depression, the jobs were theirs to hold. Echoing the conditions in Southern agriculture that many of them must have hoped to leave behind, they lived in debt to the firm, with most of their small and irregular wages swallowed by their company store accounts. But these workers, deemed unskilled, sustained one of the city's earliest and largest new unions.[33]

These men were members of a community that was already on the move from a passive, dependent position within the local Republican party toward Democratic activism. It was using its increasing influence to contest systematic segregation in public education and other spheres. And they, too, were ready to assert themselves in novel ways to demand rights long denied. On 10 July 1934, to secure their union, to force Axelrod to live up to his agreement, and to make him reemploy a brother "who had lost his job because of illness contracted while at the mill," they struck without notice. But they did not walk out. Perhaps they calculated that the Philadelphia police, who had a deserved reputation for brutality even against skilled white workers, would not spare them the most savage treatment. Instead, they simply stopped work and stood at their positions for a couple of hours until Axelrod gave way. Lead smelting and refining was not just a filthy business, it was a vulnerable one – any extended period of neglect of furnaces and mills would result in great loss and damage. In the next two weeks, they did the same thing again twice, but this time their "strikes" only lasted minutes until the company conceded and finally agreed to settle future differences of opinion through the grievance procedure.[34]

These strikes followed close on the heels of the General Tire sitdown in Akron, which Daniel Nelson called the "first important sit-down strike in American industry," but there is no evidence that they were inspired by its example or understood as a similar phenomenon. The local press, including the labor press, did not know what to make of this behavior, any

[33] Ibid.; PHIL1439 for industry data; David Brody, "Workplace Contractualism in Comparative Perspective," in Nelson Lichtenstein and Howell J. Harris, eds., *Industrial Democracy in America: The Ambiguous Promise* (New York, 1993), Ch. 8, for the larger context.

[34] Nathan Shefferman Memorandum, 12 July 1934 [quote] in NLB Case 580; Frank Donner, *Protectors of Privilege: Red Squads and Police Repression in Urban America* (Berkeley, 1990), pp. 41–42; Vincent P. Franklin, *The Education of Black Philadelphia: The Social and Educational History of a Minority Community, 1900–1950* (Philadelphia, 1979), Chs. 5 and 6; and John Shover, "The Emergence of a Two-Party System in Republican Philadelphia, 1924–1936," *Journal of American History* (hereafter *JAH*) 60 (1974): 985–1002 at p. 1000, for the local political context; "Lead Workers Gain Closed Shop at Girard," "Seven Minute Strike Keeps Girard Closed Shop," "Third Stoppage Forces Girard Closed Shop, " and "Grievance Body Named by Lead Workers Union," *Union Labor Record* (hereafter *ULR*) 7:13 through 16 (13 July–3 Aug. 1934) – all page one news.

more than did Axelrod or the RLB. These were not strikes as they knew them, so they reported them safely wrapped within inverted commas. At first neither they nor the strikers had a word for what they were doing, as this was about two years before the start of the sit-down era proper. The term the men eventually employed to describe their actions indicates where they got some of their tactical inspiration: These were "Gandhi strikes," pioneering examples of the kind of nonviolent direct action more usually associated with the Civil Rights Movement of two to three decades later.[35]

The Girard workers then disappeared from view. Always marginal to the city's white working class, they were quickly forgotten by it. When, in January 1937, sit-downs came to Philadelphia in force, and were participated in by masses of white, skilled, and by now solidly unionized workers, their points of reference were their fellows in Akron, Ohio, and, more immediately, Flint, Michigan. They made no connections with and learned no lessons from the precocious, isolated, and short-lived success of a few hundred of their despised and excluded African-American brethren two and a half years earlier.[36]

C. Ethnicity

Unlike gender and race, this was an important dimension of difference among metal workers. It was something that they and their employers recognized, and that mattered to them, but it too is not very significant for the purposes of this book. This is because, particularly in the pre–First World War years, metal workers were mostly drawn from the same few ethnic groups, among which there were skill and status differences, but that had a great deal in common with one another. Their employers and foremen also came from the same groups. Thus labor relations crises in the Philadelphia metal trades were mostly arguments between groups of men divided from one another by class and status, rather than by ethnicity or religion.

Philadelphia was the most ethnically homogeneous of America's big cities, with 47 percent of its population native-born, of native parents, and only 23 percent foreign-born, at the very height of the New Immigration. Furthermore, a large part of Philadelphia's recent immigrant population was culturally indistinguishable from its host community. British, Irish (including Ulster Protestant), and German incomers moved into settled working-class neighborhoods, "mill towns" within the city's built-up area

[35] Daniel Nelson, *American Rubber Workers and Organized Labor, 1900–1941* (Princeton, 1988), pp. 133, 138 [quote]–139, on the origins of the sit-down phenomenon; "Third Stoppage Forces Girard Closed Shop."
[36] William Leader, "New Strike Plan Solidifies Union," *Philadelphia Daily News,* 27 Apr. 1937.

like Kensington and Spring Garden that their ethnic forebears had staked out several generations earlier. The pietistic Protestantism of the native and newcomer, middle- and working-class majority helped account for one of Philadelphia's enduringly important peculiarities, the strength of the deeply rooted, popular, and notoriously corrupt political machine that kept it the "Gibraltar" of Republicanism until the early 1930s.[37]

In 1900, two-thirds of the skilled labor force in metal manufacturing were native-born, while 31 percent had at least one foreign-born parent, and 32 percent were foreign-born. Ethnic origins of those born abroad or with one foreign-born parent were overwhelmingly Irish [26 percent], German [17 percent], and British [12 percent]. These and native white Americans of native parents made up more than 90 percent of the total.[38]

Ethnicity and occupation overlapped because of differential recruitment into skilled and less-skilled work. This resulted from a combination of varying opportunities to acquire training among the major ethnic groups; the fact that personal and family contacts were the main channels into all jobs, which further reinforced ethnic segregation; and prejudice by employers and their foremen, who took the hiring and promotion decisions.[39]

Ethnicity and the opportunity to acquire a skill were connected in part because boys' familiarization with the metal crafts often began in the home, and one of the best introductions to an apprenticeship, particularly in the unionized trades, came from a father, uncle, or older brother who was already an established journeyman. But it also resulted from the fact that Philadelphia did not meet all of its own training needs, and – until the 1920s was partly dependent on migration from those great reservoirs of skill – Britain, Germany, Austria, and Scandinavia.[40]

[37] Golab, *Immigrant Destinations*, esp. Ch. 1, explains Philadelphia's limited appeal to "new immigrants" – essentially, its (i) relatively slow growth; (ii) low proportion of unskilled, entry-level jobs; and (iii) the competition for those jobs from the poorer members of its huge Irish community and from African Americans. For the cultural and political consequences of Protestant hegemony, see Marian L. Bell, *Crusade in the City: Revivalism in Nineteenth-Century Philadelphia* (Lewisburg, 1977); Ken Fones-Wolf, *Trade Union Gospel: Christianity and Labor in Industrial Philadelphia, 1865–1915* (Philadelphia, 1989), esp. Chs. 1, 7; Peter McCaffery, *When Bosses Ruled Philadelphia: The Emergence of the Republican Machine 1867–1933* (University Park, 1993); Lincoln Steffens, *The Shame of the Cities* (New York, 1957 ed.; originally published 1904), esp. pp. 2, 10–11, 134–36; and J. T. Salter, *Boss Rule: Portraits in City Politics* (New York, 1935), esp. pp. 21–22, 179, 212, 216 – quote at p. 54.

[38] Data from U.S. Department. of Commerce and Labor, *Occupations at the Twelfth Census*, pp. 672–78.

[39] For a detailed exploration of the working of these processes in the Philadelphia labor market in general, see Licht, *Getting Work*, esp. Chs. 2–5.

[40] Helen M. Herrmann, *Ten Years of Work Experience of Philadelphia Machinists* (Philadelphia, 1938), pp. 13, 15–18, 27.

The top of the occupational hierarchy among Philadelphia metal workers therefore overlapped with the bottom of the supervisory and managerial ranks, 54 percent of whom were also first- or second-generation "old immigrants" (17 percent German, 15 percent Irish, and 12 percent British).[41] Almost all of the foremen, and many managers and even entrepreneurs, had started out as skilled workers. So in many plants the distinctions between skilled workers and their bosses were matters of age and achieved status, not of culture and values.

Ethnic and religious loyalties often divided skilled workers from one another, at the same time as they provided vertical connections across class and status hierarchies. Until 1913, for example, the Machinists' union's small "Anglo-Saxon" membership was split into six lodges, divided by neighborhood, trade, and language. The Molders' and Boilermakers' unions were heavily Irish and Catholic in membership and leadership, which distinguished them from the higher status crafts, such as pattern-making, and also introduced another source of social distance into their relations with their rather WASPish engineer-entrepreneur employers.[42]

Ethnicity was therefore one of many divisions of labor among skilled workers, and more rarely between them and their bosses. But one thing they could generally agree about was the lesser eligibility – as employees or as fellow unionists – of the newer southern and eastern European immigrants who were arriving in Philadelphia, although in relatively smaller numbers than in most other large industrial cities, in the prewar decades. These "new immigrant" workers were generally thought to be destined for laboring jobs and came cheap. They were not often candidates for unionization, not because of any presumed Slavic passivity or despised Southern Italian peasant ways, but because their lack of recognized skill denied them entry to those unions that did exist. They were useful

---

[41] These data refer to manufacturing industries as a whole. The metal trades were probably less Irish, particularly above supervisory level, and more "Anglo-Saxon" and native.

[42] "Local Machinists Will Combine," *Trades Union News* (22 May 1913): 1. The 1900 Census report shows clear ethnic differences among the skilled and semiskilled occupational groups – e.g., only 11 percent of pattern-makers were first- or second-generation Irish (including Ulster Protestants), as against 40 percent of blacksmiths, and 44 percent of boiler-makers. For more impressionistic data, cf. Henry Roland, "Effective Systems of Finding and Keeping Shop Costs," *Engineering Magazine* 15 (1898): 610–20 at p. 619; Monthly Report, Local No. 15 (machinery molders), *Iron Molders Journal* (hereafter *IMJ*) 36 (1900): 98–99; *Core Makers' Journal* 4:12 (Dec. 1900): 11 – these sources are lists of names of employees in machine-tool works, mostly British and German, and unionized foundry workers, mostly Irish. Golab, *Immigrant Destinations*, pp. 212–15, identified occupations of 4,464 of Philadelphia's Poles in 1915 – all of those listed in the city directory. 486 were skilled or semiskilled metal workers, and only two were *possibly* foundry craftsmen. Almost half were machinists – a designation covering a wide range of skills – and most were probably from the German zone of Poland.

to employers rather than valued or feared by them; they could be hired any day off the street and were replaced with little trouble. William Barba of Midvale well expressed the combination of objective fact and nativist or "Anglo-Saxonist" prejudice that resulted in employers' hiring preferences:

In fine work, . . . there are no better mechanics than some of the foreign peoples, especially the North European peoples. . . . [I]f we were to choose of the foreign-born peoples whom we would like to employ we would, of course, take the English-speaking people; second, the North European peoples, and last of all, the south European peoples, and I think that the grading of efficiency goes exactly in that proportion.[43]

Given their objective lack of skill, and the patterns of prejudice impeding their acquisition of it, new immigrant workmen were part of the Philadelphia metal trades' reserve army rather than of its core labor force – above the African Americans, to be sure, but below everyone else. Between the depression year of 1914 and the start of the wartime boom in 1915, for example, their labor force share increased from 16 to 24 percent. That turned out to be an all-time high; after 1920, a combination of layoffs, the end of mass immigration, the passage of time, and increasing pressures toward naturalization "Americanized" the labor force, in Philadelphia as in other industrial centers (see Figure 1.1).

Metal trades unions never addressed a specific appeal to potential recruits from outside of their old immigrant core before the 1930s, and by then they did not need to. Their problem, even then, in winning members to the cause was not a matter of overcoming the cultural inhibitions, if any, of second-generation ethnics and the less skilled; it was dealing with the skilled, settled, old-immigrant working classes themselves.[44]

D. The Working Classes and Their Culture

By now, readers may have noticed that the effort to define what this book is not about is becoming increasingly artificial, the closer we get to the

[43] Caroline Golab, "The Immigrant and the City: Poles, Italians, and Jews in Philadelphia, 1870–1920" and Richard A. Varbero, "Philadelphia's Southern Italians in the 1920s" in Allen F. Davis and Mark H. Haller, eds., *The Peoples of Philadelphia: A History of Ethnic Groups and Lower-Class Life, 1790–1940* (Philadelphia, 1973), Chs. 10 and 12; USCIR, *Final Report*, Vol. 3, p. 2876.

[44] For revealing evidence of the cautious, calculating, individualistic, and even cynical, but sometimes enthusiastic, attitude of skilled metal workers toward unionization, see interviews with a sample of 683 machinists, millwrights, and tool-makers conducted by Gladys Palmer's fieldworkers in 1936, the very midst of the labor revolt – Machinists Study, Palmer Papers, TUUA, esp. Respondents 067, 106, 451, 460, 601.

kernel of the relationship between masters and workmen, and managers and employees, who shared the same gender and its assumptions, the same unquestioned pride of race, and the same status-conferring ethnic, religious, and sometimes, indeed, craft identities. Gender, race, and ethnicity will therefore receive little further attention in this book, but the skilled white working class, its actions, and its values must; they are so integral to the story that discussion of them must be woven into it, not isolated out.

Nevertheless, the attention that Philadelphia's metal workers receive will be that which is due them, not as subjects in their own right, worthy of the most detailed analysis, but as objects of their employers' attempts to influence and control them. They only become interesting and important in this scheme to the extent that their behavior and aspirations assist or impede the strategies of the class that does interest me. The labor or social history in this book is therefore very much a secondary theme that is present because it is unavoidable, given that the employment relationship involves two groups, often as partners, sometimes as antagonists.

In attending to the owning and employing class, my approach is more that of an institutional than a social historian. I am most interested in formal organization and overt, public behavior. For the most part, metal-working employers and the MMA will speak through their authorized representatives, their elected leaders, the journals that they controlled, and the actions that they took. This is partly a matter of methodological bias, but more a reflection of the availability of worthwhile evidence. The same will be true of my approach to their workers and their unions. Surviving contemporary data on the private convictions of the rank-and-file will be used, where appropriate, but only with due caution. No claims can be made that it is fully representative, or indeed much better than anecdotal and suggestive. The labor history in this book will be as institutional and élitist as the rest of it.

Readers may think that this results in missed opportunities; that there are tantalizing hints of what this book might have turned into, had it been written by another hand. But it wasn't. The book ranges far and wide already in its efforts to contextualize and explain the behavior as employers of Philadelphia metal manufacturers through four decades. It has been, more or less, a pleasure to research, and even to write. But all things must come to an end, and this one has. We each have some right to write our own book; and now every reader has the right to read into it what he or she wishes, and the opportunity to criticize it with as much vigor as seems fitting.

2

The Iron Masters

The first aim of this chapter is to describe the structure of the metal-manufacturing community of the great and grimy industrial city of Philadelphia at the dawn of the twentieth century. Examining some of the men and the companies that composed it, we will then explore the proprietary capitalist nature of business enterprise in Philadelphia metal working, and go on to investigate their owners' managerial philosophies. We will discover that most of them favored tradition, simplicity, and direct, personal control just as much as they believed in the absolute rights of ownership. This bundle of values would have significant implications for the type of labor relations strategy that they decided to pursue. When unionized skilled workers attempted to assert a claim to share in decision making about wages, hours, and working conditions in firms such as these, they would be seen as trespassers in other men's houses, in many cases houses that their proprietor-managers had built at their own risk and with their own sweat. This fact, and the threat that craft unions posed to enterprises' viability as well as enterprisers' freedom, would help sustain the Open Shop creed for a long generation.[1]

2.1 THE WORLD'S GREATEST WORKSHOP[2]

Philadelphia was America's first big city, its oldest manufacturing rather than commercial metropolis, and in 1900 only New York and Chicago –

[1] For an unselfconscious reference by a manufacturer to his company as "his House," see ECM, 31 March 1925, p. 6.
[2] For examples of this boastful cliché, see Herman Leroy Collins and Wilfred Jordan, *Philadelphia: A Story of Progress* (New York, 1941), Vol. 3, pp. 121, 122; Philadelphia Chamber of Commerce, *1917 Philadelphia Yearbook* (Philadelphia, 1917), pp. 11, A1; Thomas D. Richter, *Philadelphia: Its Contributions – Its Present – Its Future*

which had surpassed it in the 1880s – outranked it in population and output. These three cities were in a different league from other American industrial centers – the value of the goods that Philadelphia produced exceeded that of forty-five states and territories. The city prided itself on the breadth of its industrial base, but its prosperity still rested on two great foundations: textiles and metal products. Philadelphia established a lasting reputation for quality and versatility in an enormously wide range of different branches of these trades well before the Civil War. The essential shape of its industrial economy was hammered out by the 1850s, and it endured with remarkably little change until the 1920s.[3]

In Philadelphia in 1900, almost 284,000 people were employed in manufacturing – about 18,000 proprietors and officials, 19,000 salaried employees, and 246,000 wage earners. These were distributed among almost 16,000 separate establishments, and made up about one-half of the city's labor force. About one-fifth of them were engaged in making metal goods of all kinds – everything from buttonhooks to battleships, according to the local boast. They toiled in about 700 factories and workshops scattered around the sprawling city's neighborhoods.[4]

Philadelphia's largest metal manufacturers in the early 1900s were its giant transportation equipment makers. The Baldwin Locomotive Works (founded 1831), the J. G. Brill Co. (1869–   ), and the William Cramp Ship and Engine Building Co. (1830–   ) anchored this capital goods sector.

(Philadelphia, 1929), p. 29; Arthur Shadwell, *Industrial Efficiency: A Comparative Study of Industrial Life in England, Germany and America* (London, 1920 ed.; first published 1906), p. 247.

3   U.S. Department of the Interior, Bureau of the Census, *Twelfth Census of the United States, 1900, Vol. 7: Manufactures, Part I* (Washington, 1902), p. ccxxx; Gladys Palmer, *Philadelphia Workers in a Changing Economy* (Philadelphia, 1956), esp. Ch. 2. J. Leander Bishop, *A History of American Manufactures from 1608 to 1860* (Philadelphia, 1868), Vol. 3, pp. 18–45, 64–71, gives capsule accounts of many of the leading machine-building and transportation equipment manufacturers in the 1860s; most of the companies, and some of the individuals, that he mentions were still on the scene forty years later. See also Bruce Laurie and Mark Schmitz, "Manufacture and Productivity: The Making of an Industrial Base, Philadelphia, 1850–1880," in Theodore Hershberg, ed., *Philadelphia: Work Space, Family, and Group Experience in the Nineteenth Century. Essays Towards an Interdisciplinary History of the City* (New York, 1981), pp. 43–92.

4   U.S. Department of the Interior, *Twelfth Census, Vol. 8, Part 2*, pp. 784–91, categories as in Introduction, note 11; 1902FACT database; Stephanie W. Greenberg, "The Relationship Between Work and Residence in an Industrializing City: Philadelphia, 1880" in William W. Cutler, III, and Howard Gillette, Jr., eds., *The Divided Metropolis: Social and Spatial Dimensions of Philadelphia, 1800–1975* (Westport, 1980), pp. 141–68; cf. Eugene P. Ericksen and William C. Yancey, "Work and Residence in Industrial Philadelphia," *Journal of Urban History* 5 (1979): 147–78, for similar 1930 pattern.

Baldwin was America's largest producer of steam engines for the railroads of the United States and the world; Brill was its biggest streetcar maker; and Cramp had helped turn the Delaware River into the "American Clyde" and make Philadelphia the shipbuilding capital of the United States and itself "the greatest naval arsenal in the Western Hemisphere," in its own proud words.[5]

The transportation equipment builders were responsible for at least 36 percent of local metal trades employment directly, and a further large slice indirectly, through helping to create a local market for suppliers of specialized equipment, goods, and services. By 1900, some of the suppliers had grown to be giants in their own right, and their markets, too, had become nationwide. Midvale Steel's (1867–) huge output of steel castings and forgings was principally destined for the railroad and shipbuilding industries. Hoopes & Townsend (1851–), one of the country's largest makers of bolts, nuts, and rivets, shared the same orientation. And Philadelphia's early emergence as a center for the production of the heaviest and most sophisticated of capital goods had also induced some of its machine-building firms to concentrate on making metal-working equipment. Beginning in the 1840s William Bement, William Sellers, and their lesser brethren made it nineteenth-century America's first, and for a long time preeminent, machine-tool manufacturing center; but it was the market provided by the railroad and shipbuilding industries that made them.[6]

---

[5] Paul T. Warner, *History of the Baldwin Locomotive Works: 1831–1923* reprinted in Fred Westing, *The Locomotives That Baldwin Built* (Seattle, 1961); David B. Tyler, *The American Clyde: A History of Iron and Steel Shipbuilding on the Delaware from 1840 to World War I* (Wilmington, Del., 1958); Charles H. Cramp testimony in U.S. Industrial Commission (hereafter USIC), *Report of the Industrial Commission on the Relations and Conditions of Capital and Labor Employed in Manufactures and General Business* (Washington, 1900), Vol. 14, p. 411. Important recent monographs on Philadelphia's biggest firms are John K. Brown, *The Baldwin Locomotive Works, 1831–1915: A Study in American Industrial Practice* (Baltimore, 1995) and Thomas R. Heinrich, *Ships For the Seven Seas: Business, Labor, and New Technologies in the Philadelphia Shipbuilding Industry* (Baltimore, 1996).

[6] The Midvale Steel Co., *The Midvale Steel Co. Fiftieth Anniversary 1867–1917* (Philadelphia, n.d.), pp. 11, 32–33 [Midvale was also renowned for its heavy guns and armor plate, but was not primarily a munitions maker]; W. R. Wilbur, *History of the Bolt and Nut Industry of America* (Cleveland, 1905), pp. 109–113 esp.; Robert M. Gaylord et al., "The Machine Tool Industry," in John G. Glover and William B. Cornell, eds., *The Development of American Industries: Their Economic Significance* (New York, 1932), Ch. 26, esp. pp. 507, 519–22; Joseph W. Roe, *English and American Tool Builders* (New Haven, 1916), Ch. 19; Ross M. Robertson, "Changing Production of Metalworking Machinery, 1860–1920," in Conference on Research in Income and Wealth, *Output, Employment, and Productivity in the U.S. After 1800* (New York, 1966), pp. 479–95 at pp. 485–89; Bruce Sinclair, *Philadelphia's Philosopher Mechanics: A History of the Franklin Institute 1824–1865* (Baltimore, 1974), esp. pp. 290–94.

The second main group of industries was the machine-shop and foundry sector, employing about 16 percent of the total. Unlike those in the first group, firms in this sector were numerous – there were at least 200 of them in the city – and typically quite small. Their products were highly diverse, so generalization about them is difficult, but steam-engine builders and makers of boiler-room, power-transmission, materials-handling equipment, and textile machinery were among the larger companies. Most had well-established product lines and, like the transportation equipment and machine-tool makers with whom they interacted, they traded on their reputations for quality manufacture, engineering expertise and innovation, and the ability to satisfy the specific needs of demanding industrial customers.[7]

Philadelphia's third great metal industry was the manufacture of hand tools and hardware, which was different from the first two in that much of its output was destined for consumer markets. Here, too, there was one giant firm, Henry Disston & Sons (1840–   ), and a number of smaller ones, which benefitted from Philadelphia's status as America's greatest hardware trading center and from their ability to collaborate with Disston in national marketing efforts.[8]

If we examine the structure of the metal-manufacturing community in terms of companies rather than industries, we can see that most of its constituent parts were very small enterprises. But the big firms had the lion's share of the local economy. From Tables 2.1 and 2.2 and Figure 2.1, we can appreciate (i) the predominant importance of the giant transportation-equipment makers and of the large machinery, hardware, and tool-makers as job-providers within the metal trades; and (ii) the highly skewed distribution of employment opportunities that resulted. We should also notice (iii) the solid middle ranks – the 147 companies with 50 to 500 employees that were responsible for one-third of local metal-working jobs. These would turn out to provide the hard core of the MMA, particularly during its first two decades.

[7] See Charles T. Porter, *Engineering Reminiscences Contributed to "Power" and "American Machinist"* (New York, 1908), p. 333, and testimony of George Cresson in USIC, *Report*, Vol. 14, pp. 276, 270.

[8] For Disston, see esp. Henry Disston & Sons, Inc., *The Saw in History* (Philadelphia, 1926); for hardware in general, see Merchants and Travelers Association, *Tales of the Trades: A Presentation of Facts Concerning the Making of Articles in Everyday Use* (Philadelphia, 1906), pp. 81–84; William H. Becker, "American Wholesale Hardware Trade Associations, 1870–1900," *BHR* 45 (1971): 179–200; "Philadelphia-Made Hardware: How Five Manufacturers Have Joined Forces to Carry on a Novel Publicity Campaign," *Commercial America* 3 (Apr. 1906): 5. Between 1921 and 1923 Ax and Edge Tool, File, and Saw manufacturers sold 83 percent (by value) of their products beyond state boundaries, against a city average of 64 percent for all metal products firms. They therefore had a particularly strong need to develop this marketing initiative – figures from PHIL1439 database.

TABLE 2.1 Philadelphia Metal Manufacturing, 1902: Major Industries and Firms

INDUSTRY	FIRMS	EMPLOY	SHARE	CUMULATIVE
Railroad Engines (*Baldwin*)	1	11,024	18.3%	
Shipbuilding	2	8,640	14.4%	33%
(*Cramp 7,400, Neafie & Levy*)				
Machinery & Parts	133	5,984	9.9%	43%
Iron & Steel Forgings	5	3,145	5.2%	48%
(*Midvale 3,000*)				
Saws (*Disston 2,425*)	3	2,443	4.1%	52%
Iron Castings	32	2,396	4.0%	56%
Machine Tools	6	1,868	3.1%	59%
(*Niles-Bement-Pond 1,037,*				
Wm. Sellers 796)				
Railroad Cars & Parts	2	1,862	3.1%	62%
(*Brill 1,670*)				
Hardware & Specialties	32	1,856	3.1%	65%
(*Enterprise 800*)				
Lighting Fixtures	30	1,594	2.6%	68%
Electrical Machinery &	36	1,501	2.5%	70%
Equipment				
Stoves, Heaters & Ranges	24	1,330	2.2%	72%
Brass & Bronze Products	35	1,179	2.0%	74%
Watches & Clocks	1	1,147	1.9%	76%
Bolts, Nuts & Rivets	1	1,100	1.8%	78%
(*Hoopes & Townsend*)				
Industries Employing <1,000	327	13,136	21.8%	
TOTALS	670	60,205		

Source: 1902FACT database.

The Philadelphia metal-manufacturing complex can thus be visualized as a cluster of large- and middle-sized companies with national and even international markets, embedded in a matrix of smaller firms with which they were interdependent.[9] "The great plants" were, as the Chamber of

[9] Philadelphia also contained three great federal industrial facilities – the Navy Yard, Frankford Arsenal, and the Mint. The first two had 1,500–2,000 employees each, making them among the largest employers of skilled metal workers in the transportation equipment and machine-building sectors (and, in Frankford's case, the

TABLE 2.2 Metal Trades Firms and Employees, 1902

Range		Firms	Employees	Proportion	Cumulative
10,000+	(*Baldwin*)	1	11,024	18.3%	
5,000-9,999	(*Cramp*)	1	7,579	12.6%	31%
2,500-4,999	(*Midvale*)	1	3,000	5.0%	36%
1,000-2,499		6	8,619	14.3%	50%
500- 999		4	2,944	4.9%	55%
250- 499		16	5,193	8.6%	64%
100- 249		62	9,955	16.5%	80%
50- 99		69	4,960	8.2%	88%
25- 49		95	3,254	5.4%	94%
10- 24		149	2,390	4.0%	98%
1-- 9		265	1,287	2.1%	100%
TOTALS[a]		669	60,205		

[a] The apparent discrepancy in the count of Firms is because Cramp operated a brass foundry, which is returned separately under its Industry heading in Table 2.1 but is here amalgamated with the parent company.

Source: 1902FACT database.

Commerce explained, "the backbone of Philadelphia's industrialism," but networks of local suppliers were essential components, even of some of the larger firms' production strategies. Most parts they manufactured for

largest employer of women – about one-half of the total in 1905 – given the machine-tending nature of many of its mechanized processes); the Mint, while smaller, was an important center for research in precision manufacture and a market for local suppliers who could meet its quality standards. These federal facilities play no direct role in this book, although the Navy Yard, in particular, was important as the only large work site where skilled metal workers' unions could organize in safety before the 1930s, setting limits on the success of the Open Shop and guaranteeing that there would always be a trade-union nucleus. See U.S. Department of Commerce, Bureau of the Census, *Thirteenth Census of the United States 1910, Vol. 9: Manufactures: Reports by States, with Statistics for Principal Cities* (Washington, 1913), p. 1053, and U.S. Department of Commerce, *Census of Manufactures 1914*, Vol. 1, p. 1290; John Milner Associates, *Historical and Archaeological Survey of Frankford Arsenal Philadelphia, Pennsylvania* (processed report prepared for the Department of the Army, Baltimore District Corps of Engineers, May 1979), esp. pp. 126, 129–41; James Rankin Young, *The United States Mint at Philadelphia* (Philadelphia, 1903), esp. pp. 26, 50, 92, and Midvale Co., *1942: The 75th Anniversary of the Midvale Co.* (Philadelphia, 1942), p. 34.

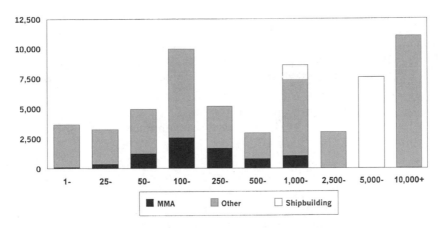

Figure 2.1. Distribution of the Philadelphia Metal Trades Labor Force, 1902, by Size of Firm and Early MMA Membership. *Note:* The MMA series shows 1902 employment for those companies that joined between 1904 and 1907 and could be traced back. Cf. Figures 5.2 and 9.3. *Source: 1902*FACT database.

themselves, but many they brought in and assembled. Integration of all stages of production within a single enterprise was not common, and in the smaller ones it was impossible. So Philadelphia metal manufacturers did a great deal of business with one another. Typical products of smaller companies in the machine-shop and foundry sector included specialized processes and services, and semifinished manufactures, sold to other local firms, as well as finished goods destined for narrow but nationwide industrial markets.[10]

Philadelphia metal manufacturers in aggregate were therefore capable of an enormous "scale and scope" of output, but not in Alfred Chandler's

[10] Philadelphia Chamber of Commerce, *1917 Philadelphia Yearbook*, p. A3; Ericksen and Yancey, "Work and Residence in Industrial Philadelphia," esp. p. 156; Palmer, *Philadelphia Workers*, pp. 23–24. This typology is similar to that recently elaborated by Philip Scranton in *Endless Novelty: Specialty Production and American Industrialization, 1865–1925* (Princeton, 1997), p. 21 – the giant firms (Baldwin, Cramp, Disston, Midvale) are the "integrated anchors," while the smaller local businesses are "networked specialists" or "specialist auxiliaries." Even among the latter, the pattern shops, jobbing iron foundries, and machine repairers were distinguished by their extreme local-market orientation: in 1921–23 only 8, 10, and 13 percent, respectively, of their output was sold across state lines (which would have included "exports" to parts of the metropolitan region just across the New Jersey and Delaware borders) – figures from PHIL1439 database. These were the only industries where craft unionism clung on. Cf. C. Lawrence Christenson, *Collective Bargaining in Chicago: 1929–30 – A Study of the Economic Significance of the Industrial Location of Trade-Unionism* (Chicago, 1933), for a similar metropolitan pattern.

terms. Instead, most of them pursued the alternative strategy characterized by Philip Scranton as one of "proximity and profusion." For the smaller firms, the fact that they were massed together in an industrial district underpinned their ability to thrive. They constructed formal and informal mechanisms for bringing together their single-function or single-process enterprises' productive capacities in versatile, kaleidoscopically changing combinations. As Gladys Palmer put it, the "'external economies' of localization and specialization would, in combination, yield the kind of advantages associated with large-scale, integrated enterprises." In Oliver Williamson's language, most Philadelphia manufacturers depended far more on "markets" – their intricate and informal contractual networks – than on "hierarchies" permitting the internalizing of investment, production, scheduling, and pricing decisions, and the integration of related functional activities within a single omnicompetent enterprise.[11]

Control over the resources necessary for constructing and marketing an extraordinary variety of goods was therefore broken down into a large number of discrete but interdependent units that were not so large as to be beyond the capacity of their owners to manage, and their managers to own. Most of them were single-plant enterprises, generally of quite modest size, run by their founders or the latter's descendants. Philadelphia metal manufacturing, just as much as Philadelphia textiles, was therefore still organized on a proprietary capitalist basis, which we will now explore.

2.2 FAMILY FOUNDATIONS

Philadelphia in 1900 was a mature manufacturing metropolis with a relatively stable industrial base. In terms of their products, technology, and organization, most of its metal-manufacturing firms remained fixed in their "first industrial revolution" molds within a familiar world of steam, iron, and railroads, and they continued to enjoy a modest prosperity on that basis. The turn-of-the-century metal-manufacturing community's present was therefore continuous with its past. The same was true of many of its constituent parts. They were not simply proprietary firms, they were dynastic in character. The commemorative history of a Philadelphia carriage builder, the Alexander Wolfington Co., which evolved into an auto and bus body maker, describes the ethos of the durable proprietary firm quite precisely – "Through the years, business success to the Wolfingtons has meant,

[11] Alfred D. Chandler, Jr., *Scale and Scope: The Dynamics of Industrial Capitalism* (Cambridge, Mass., 1990), esp. Ch. 2; Philip Scranton, "Diversity in Diversity: Flexible Production and American, Industrialization, 1880–1930," *BHR* 65 (1991): 27–90; Palmer, *Philadelphia Workers*, p. 24; Oliver E. Williamson, *Markets and Hierarchies: Analysis and Antitrust Implications: A Study in the Economics of Internal Organization* (New York, 1975).

simply, the ability to direct their companies in the direction they have wanted them to go, the capacity to provide a worth-while and dependable livelihood for their employees, and the means to raise their families adequately." It was a common sentiment.[12]

Philadelphia businesses prided themselves on their longevity. Many that survived into the twentieth century could trace unbroken histories back through the decades. The oldest was Job T. Pugh, auger bit makers, founded in 1774 and still going strong in the 1920s. But many were only a generation or so younger. The James Yocom iron foundry first fired up its furnace in 1804. Yocoms still owned and managed it into the 1920s. William and Harvey Rowland started making steel springs in 1805. The firm they established continued to do so into the automobile age. Silversmith Jacob Stockman opened for business in 1814. City surgeons soon discovered his skill as a precision metal-worker and turned to him to help them transform their ideas into instruments. As his manufacturing business grew, he took an immigrant weaver's son, George Pilling, as his apprentice. Pilling eventually became a partner, gave one of his sons his old master's name, and on the latter's death gave the firm his own. Pillings remained in charge of a successful company maintaining the same productive relationship with local medical professionals until 1969. Textile machinery manufacturers Proctor & Schwarz opened for business in 1812. Proctors and Schwarzes were still at the helm a century later, a record bettered by H. W. Butterworth & Sons, whose management included nobody but Butterworths at the same time. Other textile-machinery firms, for example, Smith & Furbush or Schaum & Uhlinger, were almost as old, and their founders' descendants remained as closely involved in running them.[13]

Proprietary capitalism prevailed irrespective of firm size. The Cramp Shipyard and Disston Saw Works were still family-run, Disston keeping up the useful tradition of bringing new generations of family members into the company by starting them at manual work and rotating them through several departments. Baldwin Locomotive was still a partnership, as it had been for most of its life, controlled by a slowly changing group of

---

[12] William Sheppard, *Careers on Wheels* (New York, 1954), p. 89. Cf. Geoffrey Jones and Mary B. Rose, "Family Capitalism," *Business History* 35:4 (Oct. 1993): 1–16 at pp. 2–3.

[13] John J. Macfarlane, *Manufacturing in Philadelphia 1683–1912* (Philadelphia, 1912), p. 56; Edwin T. Freedley, *Philadelphia and Its Manufactures: A Hand-Book Exhibiting the Development, Variety, and Status of the Manufacturing Industry of Philadelphia* (Philadelphia, 1859), p. 293; Collins and Jordan, *Philadelphia*, Vol. 3, pp. 185–87; "The Pilling Company," "Pilling Co. History," and Pilling Genealogy, copies in author's possession, supplied by the firm; Sylvester K. Stevens, *Pennsylvania: Titan of Industry* (New York, 1948), Vol. 2, pp. 150–52; advertisement, *The Manufacturer* 3 (1921): 51; Roe, *English and American Tool Builders*, p. 247; PHILCHAP database.

proprietor-managers. It remained so in effect if no longer in form even after 1909, when the five men then holding the firm incorporated it to ease the problems of buying out a deceased partner's widow's share and raising the formidable capital their expansion program demanded. The J. G. Brill Co., which started life as a horsecar builder in 1869 and achieved massive success in the age of electric traction, stayed in the hands of the families of the founding partners throughout.[14]

Both of Philadelphia's two leading heavy machine-tool manufacturers, Bement & Dougherty (latterly Bement-Miles) and William Sellers, remained under their founders' direct personal control until the turn of the century. Bement then became consolidated with the Philadelphia Engineering Works, the Niles Tool Works of Ohio, and the Pond Machine Works of New Jersey and was run thereafter – with a notable lack of success – as a branch of an out-of-town corporation. This was an unusual fate for a firm in a city scarcely involved in the Great Merger Movement of those years. Even after the death of the towering figure of William Sellers in 1905, his company remained in family hands for another generation. Smaller but still nationally or internationally renowned firms found it yet more natural to maintain their status as proprietary firms even as they acquired employees by the hundreds – the Abram Cox Stove Co. (1847–   ), Stanley G. Flagg (1854–   , pipe fittings), Fayette R. Plumb (axes, hammers, and hatchets, 1856–   ), the McCaffrey File Co. (1863–   ), the Asbury family's Enterprise Mfg. Co., producers of domestic hardware, and the North Bros. Mfg. Co., who originated the famous "Yankee" range of ratchet-operated screwdrivers and other hand tools.[15]

---

[14] John Thomas Scharf and Thompson Westcott, *History of Philadelphia, 1609–1884* (Philadelphia, 1884), Vol. 3, pp. 2267–68; Stevens, *Pennsylvania*, Vol. 1, p. 317; Frank H. Taylor, ed., *The City of Philadelphia: A Compilation of Facts Supplied by Distinguished Citizens for the Information of Businessmen, Travellers, and the World at Large* (Philadelphia, 1900), pp. 182–83; Jacob S. Disston, Jr., *Henry Disston (1819–1878) Pioneer Industrialist Inventor and Good Citizen* (New York, 1950), esp. pp. 8, 15, 22; Frank Disston, "How We Hold Our Men," *System* 31 (1917): 114–21, picture at p. 114 captioned "Starting a Staff Officer's Training in the Trenches"; Harry C. Silcox, *A Place to Live and Work: The Henry Disston Saw Works and the Tacony Community, of Philadelphia* (University Park, 1994), esp. Chs. 1–2; Philip Scranton, "Build a Firm, Start Another: The Bromleys and Family Firm Entrepreneurship in the Philadelphia Region," *Business History* 35:4 (Oct. 1993): 114–51 at pp. 135–37; Stevens, *Pennsylvania*, Vol. 2, pp. 2–5.

[15] PHILCHAP database; Stevens, *Pennsylvania*, Vol. 3, pp. 716–19; Cecil E. Fraser and George F. Doriot, *Analyzing Our Industries* (New York, 1932), pp. 185, 207 esp.; "Obituary: William Sellers," *Journal of the Franklin Institute* (hereafter *JFI*) 159 (1905): 365–81; John N. Ingham, *Biographical Dictionary of American Business Leaders* (Westport, 1983), Vol. 3, p. 1729; Taylor, ed., *City of Philadelphia*, p. 193; Macfarlane, *Manufacturing in Philadelphia*, pp. 53–56; David N. Keller, *Cooper Industries 1833–1983* (Athens, Ohio, 1983), Ch. 30; Stanley G. Flagg & Co., Inc., *One Hundred Years of Leadership 1854–1954* (n.p., 1954); PHILCHAP database.

A company's survival was not utterly dependent on the availability of competent male heirs. The established firm was an institution representing a fruitful combination of capital, expertise, and reputation, which could cheat fate even when its founder(s) failed to provide for a dynastic succession. Bement "graduate" George Cresson set up his own machine shop in 1859, when he was twenty-three. By 1870 it had turned into the first company in America exclusively devoted to the manufacture of power-transmission machinery; by 1900 it was a world leader, selling on quality, like Disston, and never cutting its prices. The company was incorporated in 1892, but Cresson retained control until his death in 1908, at which time the firm was reorganized with another family partnership assuming power.[16]

Thus a break in proprietary control, or even a company's acquisition of the status of an incorporated business under Pennsylvania's laws, did not necessarily entail any fundamental alteration in its character. For example, the Harrison Safety Boiler Works was established in 1879 by Joseph L. Wharton, who had been set up in the foundry business by his grandfather eight years earlier. Wharton bought the special tools, machines, and manufacturing rights required to produce the patent Harrison Safety Boiler from the estate of the late Joseph Harrison, Jr., a pioneer locomotive engineer. Wharton employed Harrison's brother-in-law as superintendent, a foreman, David Cochrane, and a bookkeeper, William Satterthwaite Hallowell, whom he made his junior partner.

These four men organized a simple division of functions among themselves. Wharton was the "capitalist" rather than an active manager; his superintendent used his connections in the worlds of railroading and heavy mechanical engineering to solicit orders; Hallowell provided them both with administrative backup; and Cochrane ran the works and developed new steam specialties to help the firm maintain its position as the Harrison patents expired and the original designs became outdated. John C. Jones, who joined the firm straight from college in 1889 and "systematized" the growing company's operations, was added to the partnership in 1917. The three partners acquired formal titles after incorporation in 1920, but all stayed in the saddle. Hallowell retired in 1926; Wharton remained president until 1931, after sixty years in business; Jones succeeded him and soldiered on until 1938, serving a modest forty-nine years with the same firm. The firm kept the Harrison name because of the reputation it enjoyed, until

[16] "George Vaux Cresson," *Proceedings of the Engineers' Club of Philadelphia* (hereafter *Procs. ECP*) 25 (1908): 206; Taylor, ed., *City of Philadelphia*, pp. 244, 192; Cresson testimony, USIC, *Report*, Vol. 14, pp. 266–67; PHILCHAP database; cf. the takeover of the city's oldest and most famous heavy engineering plants, the Port Richmond Iron Works (1828–) and Southwark Foundry (1836–) by Cramps and Baldwin in 1891 and 1912, respectively – Stevens, *Pennsylvania*, Vol. 2, pp. 79–86.

Cochrane's patents displaced the founder's in importance, at which point the partners renamed the firm in honor of its inventive foreman. H. S. B. W.– Cochrane Corporation was a dynamic business – unusually for a capital-goods producer, it advertised extensively, established out-of-town sales and service offices, and even had product development and research departments. But in ownership form and management structure it long maintained the typical Philadelphia pattern of the durable proprietary, partnership, or family enterprise.[17]

2.3 THE ROYAL ROAD[18]

Philadelphia's industrial fabric was impressively stable, but it accommodated great dynamism too. The city offered ambitious journeymen and clerks many opportunities to turn themselves into managers and capitalists in their own right. Philadelphia metal manufacturers believed that industry offered careers open to talent, because they had experienced success themselves or witnessed it among their peers. Local folklore emphasized how many business leaders had worked their way up, among them Henry Disston, who set up in business (or so one story went) after taking his saw-maker master's tools in lieu of the wages he was due when his employer went bankrupt; Alba Johnson, who advanced from junior clerk at Baldwin to partner, president, and finally, in semi-retirement, chairman of its associated Southwark Foundry; and his partner and successor at Baldwin, Samuel Vauclain, whose path led upward from a machinist's apprenticeship at the Pennsylvania Railroad's Altoona shops.[19]

Of course, success on this scale was exceptional. But the lives of founders of more modest enterprises who were pillars of the metal-manufacturing

---

[17] *Cochrane Environmental Systems: Manufacturers of a Diversified Line of Water and Waste Water Treatment and Control Equipment* (brochure, 1981) and typewritten "History of Cochrane Corporation," n.d. (copies in author's possession, supplied by firm); Stevens, *Pennsylvania*, Vol. 3, pp. 936–40; "Resolution Unanimously Adopted at the Twenty-third Annual Meeting of the Association Held in the Manufacturers' Club Wednesday Evening, December 8th.," ECM 8 Dec. 1926 – marking Hallowell's retirement.

[18] I. L. Vansant, ed., *The Royal Road to Wealth: An Illustrated History of the Successful Business Houses of Philadelphia* (Philadelphia, 1869), is the classic exposition of the "opportunity" theme, including from the metal trades the stories of Baldwin, Chambers Bros. (machinery foundrymen), the Port Richmond Iron Works, and Sellers.

[19] For Disston, see Stevens, *Pennsylvania*, Vol. 2, p. 203, Ingham, ed., *Biographical Dictionary of American Business Leaders*, Vol. 1, pp. 277–78; for Johnson, "Nothing For Ourselves, Everything for Country," *Engineers and Engineering* 40 (1923): 177–81 at p. 177; for Vauclain, see his memoir, *Steaming Up! The Autobiography of Samuel M. Vauclain* (San Marino, Calif., 1973; original ed. New York, 1930).

community in 1900 illustrate the processes by which ambitious men came to realize common dreams – winning independence and prosperity, and creating their own enduring businesses.[20]

John E. Lonergan was born in County Tipperary in 1841, migrated to Vermont in 1852, and started his working life in a sawmill before going on to train as a railroad machinist in Massachusetts. He invented locomotive devices in his spare time while working as a "boomer" in California until, at the age of twenty-eight, he moved to Philadelphia to manufacture what he had patented.

Philadelphia was an attractive place for Lonergan to set up in business. The Pennsylvania and Reading Railroads and the Baldwin and Norris Locomotive Works gave him an unparalleled concentration of potential customers within a few blocks. His skilled labor needs could be met from the apparently bottomless well of the city's labor market, which by then gave Philadelphia an additional locational advantage for firms producing quality capital goods. As the Chamber of Commerce later boasted, Philadelphia "presents perhaps one of the best examples in economic history of the demonstration of the law which compels industries to follow labor." "[K]indred manufacturing enterprises" were pulled toward the city to draw on the "skilled and trained" workforce that Philadelphia's early development as a center of metal-working had created. Finally, the prevalent "room with power" system allowed him to rent space and equipment in an existing brass-manufacturing plant, minimizing his initial capital requirements. (In due course Lonergan extended the same facility to Henry Brinton, a knitting machine manufacturer, to whom he leased spare floorspace and probably loaned venture capital. When Brinton formed his own company, Lonergan became its president.)[21]

---

20 Cf. Herbert G. Gutman, "The Reality of the Rags-to-Riches Myth: The Case of Paterson, New Jersey, Locomotive, Iron, and Machinery Manufacturers, 1830–1880," in his *Work, Culture and Society in Industrializing America* (Oxford, 1977), pp. 211–33; James H. Soltow, *Origins of Small Business: Metal Fabricators and Machinery Makers in New, England, 1890–1957* (Philadelphia, 1965) [*Transactions of the American Philosophical Society*, n.s. Vol. 55, pt. 10].

21 Typewritten "J. E. Lonergan Co. History" (1975?), "John E. Lonergan Early Company History," *JELCO News Release* 1:1 (September 1981): 1–2, and "John E. Lonergan The Later Years," *JELCO News Release* 1:2 (Oct.–Nov. 1981): 1, copies in author's possession, supplied by firm; on skilled labor supply and industrial location, see Freedley, *Philadelphia and Its Manufactures*, pp. 72–73, Philadelphia Chamber of Commerce, *Philadelphia Yearbook 1917*, pp. B7–8 [quote], and Arthur D. Graeff, ed., *A History of Steel Casting* (Philadelphia, 1949), pp. 28–33; for "room with power" system and Brinton, see Taylor, ed., *City of Philadelphia*, p. 212; Hartwell Stafford, ed., *Who's Who in Philadelphia in Wartime* (Philadelphia, 1920), p. 120; PHILCHAP database; cf. Flagg, *One Hundred Years of Leadership*, p. 11.

Lonergan's own firm grew modestly but steadily by emphasizing quality and producing a broadening range of railroad and stationary steam engine safety devices and ancillary appliances. Lonergan remained in control well into his eighties, at which point he passed the presidency on to his nephew, John Cavanaugh (he and his wife had no children of their own, but they brought up eight orphaned relatives). Cavanaugh served until 1956, when a non-family member who had, like many employees, made his life in the firm, starting as a turret lathe operator straight out of high school, succeeded him.

Lonergan was unusual in the very WASP metal-manufacturing community in being a pious Irish Catholic, but his career was in other respects unexceptional, save in the degree of its success. His epitaph could stand for many of his fellows: "a man of great force and determination of character, his breadth of idea (*sic*), and consistency of purpose were supplemented by the foundation traits of firmness, thrift and industry. He was known as a man of great energy of action. One of those who achieve success by indomitable force of character, and concentration of purpose."[22]

Lonergan was a self-educated journeyman, as were numerous other metal-manufacturing executives whose route into management or ownership led through foremanship or striking out on their own. But Philadelphia's metal-manufacturing community also included many professionally trained engineers. Some of them experienced the same dissatisfactions that skilled workers felt with their lack of independence, and had a better chance of identifying a gap in the market that a small, specialized, single-product firm could fill.[23]

Tinius Olsen, for example, the son of a gunstock maker, was born in Kongsberg, Norway, in 1845. He began to learn metal-working at home, and design skills at drawing school. He started his career as a machinist in the naval yard at Horten, and acquired a proper engineering training at the local technical college and by private study. On graduating at the head of his class, he became foreman at a large jobbing foundry and machine shop in Trondheim. But he did not enjoy bossing resentful older skilled men, and felt he needed broader experience. So he obtained a government grant to seek it abroad, and never looked back, traveling first to Newcastle, England,

22 "Lonergan Early Company History," p. 2.
23 For more examples of successful artisans, see Stevens, *Pennsylvania*, Vol. 3, pp. 734–36 (Smith, Drum & Co.), 752–54 (Steel Heddle Mfg. Co.), 877–79 (Wicaco Machine Corp.); biographies of David C. Hitchner (H. B. Underwood Corp.), E. J. Rooksby and Jesse G. Haydock (H. B. Underwood and later E. J. Rooksby Cos.), and Alfred Crook (Philadelphia Roll & Machine Co.), in Stafford, ed., *Who's Who in Philadelphia in Wartime*, pp. 52, 47, 48, 228.

and then on to Philadelphia in 1869. Why Philadelphia? The magnet for a young mechanical engineer was the William Sellers works, whose reputation was already international, and where a succession of young Norwegian machinists and engineers, including former Horten instructor Carl Barth, later one of Frederick W. Taylor's leading collaborators, helped one another find employment.

Olsen felt out of his depth in the big city, and he frequented Lutheran Sunday schools and Bible classes in his free time to find himself a community of the like-minded. There he met two Bible teachers, the brothers Riehlé, who had just bought a small commercial scale works. Mechanical engineers were beginning to be concerned about improving their knowledge of the physical characteristics and serviceability of the materials that they worked with. To increase the safety of their boilers, a local firm had awarded the Riehlés a contract to design and build a machine for testing boiler plates under load. They had no idea how – the one brother whose background is recorded had made his money as a wholesale grocer's bookkeeper – and turned to their young acquaintance for help. So shortly after coming to Philadelphia Olsen left Sellers to become director of the Riehlé works, where he spent the 1870s designing a pioneering line of increasingly heavy, versatile, and accurate testing machines.

Despite or perhaps because of his achievements, Olsen grew restive. The Riehlés denied him the income and authority to match his contribution to the firm; finally, in 1879, the year his son was born, they refused his request for a partnership and showed him the door. The Riehlés had lost their designer but found a competitor. Olsen had no capital save the quality of his innovative ideas and the backing of his Swedish wife, a doctor of medicine who pawned her jewelry to finance the venture and supported his bid for independence. The Riehlés' resources and established reputation – which, after all, Olsen had established for them – could not prevent his success. The city's prestigious Franklin Institute gave the unknown firm's machines its seal of approval, and Olsen's company went from strength to strength. Olsen made increasingly precise, ever-larger capacity customized equipment for client companies and government agencies that were not price-sensitive buyers. If they needed a machine protected by the net of Olsen patents, or which he alone could produce to specification, they had to turn to his firm.

Olsen was the sole proprietor until 1912, when he incorporated the business and began to share control with his only son, Thorsten, who joined the firm after completing an engineering degree – a necessary qualification for an intended successor in a technically demanding family business. Thorsten became a skilled machine designer in his own right, and successively a partner, vice-president, treasurer, and in 1920 "directing manager." Tinius remained president until 1929, when Thorsten succeeded him.

Thorsten's only son, Tinius II, took over in 1955, and the fourth generation followed in 1973.[24]

Hugo Bilgram, born in Bavaria in 1847, and a graduate of the Augsburg
Maschinenbau Schule, had a similar career to Olsen's. Arriving in Philadelphia in 1869, he found employment as a machinist at the Southwark
Foundry, a renowned heavy engineering works, and at the Franklin Institute as a drawing instructor. By 1883 he had perfected "a highly ingenious
and thoroughly practical" device that cut bevel gears quickly and accurately. His "beautiful machine" demonstrated his advanced understanding
of geometry and engineering design and produced equipment for which
there was keen demand from the booming bicycle industry. This was
Bilgram's chance to set up as an independent manufacturer, incorporating
his tiny Machine Works in 1884 and going on to design and make a wide
range of customized cogs for complicated tasks.[25]

Bilgram was an agnostic, a theoretical socialist – not that unusual among
the Philadelphia engineering community, particularly its German element –
and an intellectual. He stopped his works at lunchtime to regale his well-
paid but nonunion employees with his radical views on politics and economics; he was a correspondent of the renowned anarchist Joseph Labadie,
and he published four books about the defects of capitalism. He was also
a "joiner," an active member of the Franklin Institute and in particular of
its Committee on Science and the Arts, which scrutinized new devices like
Olsen's, and a faithful supporter of the MMA from the beginning.

[24] "A Philadelphia Story" in Kenneth O. Bjork, *Saga in Steel and Concrete: Norwegian
Engineers in America* (Northfield, Minn., 1947), pp. 84–104; *Tinius Talks* 7:1 (1955)
and 30:1 (1980), copies in author's possession, supplied by firm; biographies of the
Olsens, Barth, and Frederick Riehlé in Stafford, ed., *Who's Who in Philadelphia in
Wartime*, pp. 21, 120, 127, 227; Barth's memoir in his testimony before U.S. Con-
gress, House, Special Committee To Investigate the Taylor and Other Systems of Shop
Management, *The Taylor and Other Systems of Shop Management: Hearings . . .
Under Authority of HR 90* (Washington, 1912), Vol. 3, pp. 1539–57 (hereafter
Taylor System Hearings). The story of the Olsen-Riehlé relationship is nice but apoc-
ryphal: According to the Riehlés, their first contract – with a local cast-iron pipe
founder, to settle a lawsuit with a disgruntled customer – was won in 1867, before
Olsen even left Norway. F. A. Riehlé, "Testing Machines," *Iron Trades Review* (here-
after *ITR*) 32:10 (8 March 1898): 8–9. For a picture of a working Olsen machine,
see Frederick Allen, "They're Still There: The Hurdy-Gurdy," *American Heritage of
Invention and Technology* (hereafter *AHIT*) 10:1 (Summer 1994): 4–5.

[25] History and Heritage Committee, American Society of Mechanical Engineers,
Mechanical Engineers in America Born Prior to 1861: A Biographical Dictionary
(New York, 1980), pp. 59–60; *Bilgram Gear Company Catalog* (Philadelphia, c.
1985), copy in author's possession, supplied by firm; Robert S. Woodbury, *Studies
in the History of Machine Tools* (Cambridge, Mass., 1972) for "History of the Gear-
Cutting Machine" (1958), p. 91; Henry Roland, "The Geometrical Generation of
Irregular Surfaces in Machine Construction," *Engineering Magazine* 19 (1900):
83–97 at p. 93 [quotes]; advertisement, *Engineers and Engineering* 37 (March 1920):
civ.

Bilgram ran his firm as a tight family business: In 1913 the executive force, that is, Hugo and three other Bilgrams, all lived in the same house! Hugo died in 1932, but his family remained in active control until 1959. The company was then sold to another proprietor, and a generation later it was still in the same business and the same hands. Like the Lonergan and Olsen firms, it combined continuing modest size, family ownership, and personal management with technological innovation in the production of a limited range of high-value, specialized equipment for industrial consumers.[26]

New firms of similar character continued to join the ranks of Philadelphia metal workers well into the twentieth century, taking advantage of the opportunities that the new technologies and markets of the "second industrial revolution" opened up. In 1916, for example, immigrant craftsmen Theodore Wiedemann and his brother-in-law, Henry Bockrath, set themselves up as jobbing machinists and heat-treaters, bringing their sons and cousin into the business as soon as they could. By the 1920s they had specialized in die-making and punch-press production to take advantage of the growing importance of sheet-metal-forming in the automobile and domestic appliance industries. Wiedemann Machine Co. continued as a family firm until the third generation sold it in 1964, and as a division of a large national corporation it survived into the 1980s.[27]

Latter-day successors of Olsen and Bilgram, engineering professionals and would-be entrepreneurs, still found Philadelphia a congenial environment too. Albert Kingsbury, for example, started out as a Yankee machinist but went on to study at Cornell. Robert Thurston, his major professor, was impressed by the ex-craftsman's practicality, so he used him as a research assistant and thereby introduced him to tribology, the newly scientific study of friction and its reduction, in which Thurston was the leading figure. Kingsbury made it his speciality, too, pursuing a twin-track career of professor of engineering and inventor thereafter, and developing in the

[26] Respondent No. 618, Machinists Study, Palmer Papers, TUUA; PHILCHAP database. For "socialism" in the turn-of-the-century engineering community, see Barth testimony, U.S. Congress, *Taylor System Hearings*, Vol. 3, pp. 1563, 1566; "Memoirs: Max Livingston" and John C. Trautwine, Jr., "Socialism As Illustrated By Papers Recently Presented to the Engineers' Club of Philadelphia," *Procs. ECP* 23 (1906): 202–04 and 25 (1908): 109–13; for an exploration of the origins and meaning of this "engineers' collectivism," see Donald Stabile, *Prophets of Order* (Boston, 1984). Bilgram's books were *Involuntary Idleness: An Exposition of the Cause of the Discrepancy Existing between the Supply of, and the Demand for Labor and its Products* (Philadelphia, 1889), *A Study of the Money Question* (New York, 1894), *The Cause of Business Depressions* (Philadelphia, 1914), and *The Remedy for Overproduction and Unemployment* (New York, 1928).

[27] Leaflet, "Story of a Family," (1979), Wiedemann Division, Warner & Swasey Co., Cross & Trecker Group, in author's possession, supplied by firm.

1890s and early 1900s revolutionary air-lubricated and thrust bearings. The introduction of the steam turbine in marine propulsion and electric power plants, and of unprecedentedly large water turbines for power generation, created an imperative demand for them to satisfy. So Kingsbury abandoned academe in favor of an industrial career, becoming a general engineer at the Westinghouse Electrical & Manufacturing Co. from 1903 to 1914, and licensing firms to produce his patent devices. Relying on Westinghouse to manufacture the large bearings he contracted to produce after going into business on his own account eventually proved unsatisfactory – Westinghouse gave his orders a low priority, and it charged too much – so eventually he set up his own manufacturing operation.

Westinghouse established a big marine turbine and turbo-generator plant in Philadelphia as a result of the First World War, locating its operations there for reasons of proximity to the country's largest shipbuilding region and what *Iron Age*, the leading metal trades journal, called "the best technical labor market in the country." Kingsbury followed suit in search of craftsmen and customers, and trod in the steps of countless less eminent predecessors by taking an old factory in the Frankford mill district of northeast Philadelphia, filling it with a mixture of new and serviceable old equipment, and creating a firm that has continued to occupy its small but profitable market niche from that day to this.[28]

The Wiedemann family and Kingsbury were and remained small fry. But the enterprise-creating engines characteristic of nineteenth-century Philadelphia were still capable of producing larger new businesses, too. The city had other resources besides a skilled labor force and a broad and diverse customer base to help them on their way; it had venture capital. Established businessmen continued to finance promising new starts. George Cresson, for example, was one of four original partners in, and first president of, the American Pulley Co., set up in 1895 as an innovative one-product firm in a field closely related to his own. Cresson's firm dominated traditional cast-iron pulley manufacture, while the new firm complemented its output with lighter forged and pressed-steel equipment.[29]

The firms mentioned so far were suppliers of producers' goods, albeit to the new industries of the second industrial revolution. But the really big success stories of early twentieth-century Philadelphia oriented themselves toward the new consumer durables markets themselves. Still, their founders'

[28] Duncan Dowson, *History of Tribology* (London, 1979), pp. 328, 370–71, 552–83; *Iron Age* (1915) quoted from Gerald G. Eggert, *Steelmasters and Labor Reform, 1886–1923* (Pittsburgh, 1991), p. 97; Richard F. Snow, "They're Still There: Bearing Up Nobly," *AHIT* 4:1 (1988): 5; http://www.kingsbury.com.
[29] Committee on Science and Arts, "The All-Wrought Steel Pulley," *JFI* 145 (1898): 272–80, Stevens, *Pennsylvania*, Vol. 2, pp. 35–37 and cf. Vol. 3, pp. 523–25 [Nice Ball Bearing].

careers remained very similar to those of their smaller manufacturing neighbors and predecessors.

Edward G. Budd (b. 1870) served his machinist's apprenticeship at Sellers and moved on in 1892 to become successively a journeyman, then the drafting office foreman, and finally head of the hydraulic press design group at Bement-Miles. He took evening classes at the Franklin Institute and The University of Pennsylvania like countless other ambitious craftsmen who appreciated the value of formal training and scientific knowledge. After perfecting the revolutionary "all-wrought steel pulley" at Bement-Miles, he left to join Cresson's new American Pulley company as its factory manager. His command of the new technology of heavy production presswork won him an even bigger job in 1902, as general manager of Hale & Kilburn Co., producers of streetcar seats and railroad car fittings. Under his management the firm began to make automobile body panels in 1909, but the directors would not accept his advice to reorient the company toward the manufacture of all-steel auto bodies and away from its stagnant traditional markets. So Budd took his own advice instead; he removed his equity stake and a cadre of skilled workers, and with the backing of local capitalists formed his own company in 1912. It immediately acquired big contracts from auto manufacturers and, on the brink of the Great War, was poised for dramatic growth.[30]

Eldridge Johnson (b. 1867) was also a journeyman machinist who improved himself by night classes (in his case, at the Spring Garden Institute), and became the foreman of a machine shop across the Delaware River in Camden, New Jersey, in his early twenties. In short order he became his boss's partner, soon buying the old man out and carrying on with a small-scale jobbing business, repairing machines and constructing experimental models and prototypes for other designers. But it was an idea of his own – in 1897, for a spring-driven gramophone – that made his fortune. On the strength of it he founded the Victor Talking Machine Co. in 1901, whose 1906 Victrola became the best-selling model in a booming American and world market. In 1929 Victor was taken over by a national firm, Radio Corporation of America (RCA), and remained at the leading edge of the consumer durables revolution through the interwar period.[31]

It was on the backs of dynamic local entrepreneurial firms like Budd, RCA-Victor, and radio manufacturers Philco and Atwater Kent that the Philadelphia metropolitan area's metal trades would continue to prosper through the interwar period, even as the local giants of the first industrial

---

[30] Edward G. Budd, Jr., *Edward G. Budd (1870–1946) "Father of the Streamliners" and the Budd Company* (New York, 1950) and Mark Reutter, "The Life of Edward Budd Part I: Pulleys, McKeen Cars, and the Origins of the Zephyr" and "The Life of Edward Budd Part II: Frustration and Acclaim," *Railroad History* 172 and 173 (1995): 5–34, 58–101.

[31] Ingham, ed., *Biographical Dictionary*, Vol. 2, pp. 668–69.

revolution like Baldwin, Cramp, or Niles-Bement-Pond closed their doors or entered irreversible decline.[32]

These stories underline the points about the nature of Philadelphia's capitalists, and the processes of business formation in which they engaged, made by contemporaries as well as by astute commentators from Gladys Palmer to Philip Scranton. They were a self-renewing and largely home-grown business class, made up of men who spent most of their working lives in the city and their executive lives in one or two companies. The mature economy of turn-of-the-century Philadelphia was a mixture of well-established firms that retained the same structures of local ownership and management as they grew, and multitudes of new starts, a small minority of which added themselves to the lists of intergenerational survivors.[33]

2.4 THE CULTURE OF ENTERPRISE

Now that we have made the acquaintance of the proprietary firms and engineer-entrepreneurs who are this book's *dramatis personae*, it is time to explore their codes of values and managerial practices, and the effects that

[32] For Atwater Kent, see Ingham, ed., *Biographical Dictionary*, Vol. 2, pp. 707–08; for Philco, see Philco Corporation, *The Story of Philco Progress* (Philadelphia, c. 1940) and William Balderston, *"Philco": Autobiography of Progress* (New York, 1954). See also Philip Scranton, "Large Firms and Industrial Restructuring: The Philadelphia Region, 1900–1980," *Pennsylvania Magazine of History and Biography* (hereafter *PMHB*) 116 (1992): 419–65 and Chapter 7, Section 3, on changing industrial structure.

[33] There was little change over the next two decades. In 1922, the first year for which reasonably full data exist, 892 of the city's metal trades establishments (shipbuilding excepted), employing 43,281 people (51 percent of the sectoral total), were still proprietary businesses, even though many of them were quite large close corporations. Another 24 firms employing 33,480 (39 percent) did have "outside" bond- or shareholders, but here, too, there was no effective separation of management and controlling ownership, which was usually still in the hands of their founding families or partners, or their descendants. Few of these companies had diversified beyond their original product-lines or established manufacturing plants outside of the Philadelphia region, so the city remained the center of their continuing traditional interests and the locus of their decision making. Finally, 11 plants, with 8,045 employees (9 percent), were divisions of national corporations, the largest of them – Westinghouse and General Electric – recent arrivals. So for the first quarter of the twentieth century, at least, most firms, even the largest, remained proprietary in fact. Data from *Moody's Industrials* (New York, 1922 ed.), PHILCHAP and PID-1640 databases. William M. Hench, "Trends in the Size of Industrial Companies in Philadelphia From 1915 through 1930" (Ph.D. diss., University of Pennsylvania, 1938), esp. pp. 22–23, 30, 39, 41, 54, is a crude but suggestive study of rates of company foundation and survival.

these had on relations between masters and workmen. We will discover a complex and contradictory picture.

Philadelphia metal-manufacturing companies were very nonbureaucratic in their managerial practices and ethos. Most of them were not large enough to sustain any elaborate administrative hierarchy, even supposing that their proprietor-managers had perceived the need. Engineer-entrepreneurs ran their own businesses directly and quite informally, with the aid of partners, family members, and a few subordinates. In 1900, the Census Bureau counted scarcely more "proprietors and officials" than there were plants, emphasizing the fact that most of the latter were one-man bands, and that even the larger enterprises only had a handful of managers. The average executive was assisted by three salaried employees, and oversaw the work of forty-one wage earners. Ninety percent of employees in Philadelphia's metal-working industries were blue-collar; the "supervisory overhead ratios" and "administrative capacities" of constituent firms were correspondingly small.[34]

But Philadelphia was also the site of path-breaking innovations in the theory and practice of rationalized – "systematic" and "scientific" – management. Frankford Arsenal was where Captain Henry Metcalfe developed his "Shop Order System of Accounts" in the 1870s. Most famously, the city was the home of Frederick W. Taylor, and its engineer-entrepreneur community was his peer group, supplying the family, friends, and business associates who gave him the opportunity to develop and apply his ideas. His "Uncle Billy" Sellers was a patron of most of his classic experiments, at Midvale Steel and the Sellers plant itself, and in 1903 his fellow Unitarian and Germantown neighbor, James Mapes Dodge, president of materials-handling specialists Link-Belt (c. 300 employees), became the first client for his complete system of "scientific management." Link-Belt and another smaller Philadelphia metal trades firm, molding machinery makers Tabor

---

[34] Arthur L. Stinchcombe, "Bureaucratic and Craft Administration of Production: A Comparative Study," *Administrative Science Quarterly* 4 (1959): 168–87, for the classic typology of management styles; Seymour Melman, "The Rise of Administrative Overhead in the Manufacturing Industries of the United States, 1899–1947," *Oxford Economic Papers* 3 (1951): 62–112, for national and long-run contexts; W. Paul Strassmann, *Risk and Technological Innovation: American Manufacturing Methods during the Nineteenth Century* (Ithaca, 1959), p. 9, for the "engineer-entrepreneur"; U.S. Department of the Interior, Bureau of the Census, *Twelfth Census of the United States, 1900, Vol. 8: Manufactures, Part 2* (Washington, 1902), pp. 784–91, for data. Roughly comparable figures for 1905 are five salaried employees and thirty-nine wage-earners per proprietor and/or official – the ratio of salaried employees probably rose because of the exclusion of the smallest establishments after 1900. U.S. Department of Commerce and Labor, Bureau of the Census, *Census of Manufactures 1905 Part 2: Reports for Selected Industries and Detail Statistics For Industries, By States* (Washington, 1907), pp. 978–83, lines 21, 59, 68, 73, 78, 80, 90, 99, 101, 109, 141, 151, 165, 169, 173, 181.

(with about eighty employees), of which Taylor was a part owner, became pilgrimage sites for students of Taylorism by about 1906, and other, much less prominent, local equipment builders also joined the exclusive company of officially recognized "Taylorized" firms.[35]

There is an apparent paradox here, but only if we ignore some of the best modern scholarship on "scientific management" that stresses its limited general impact, and that its practice differed very substantially from the way many contemporaries, and most subsequent interpreters, came to understand it. Taylor and his followers were better as self-publicists than at applying their theories of management in undiluted form. Examining the small practical meaning of Taylorism even in its Philadelphia heartland, and the reasons for its limited local appeal, will help us to appreciate it better and illuminate the managerial culture and practices of the metal-manufacturing community's majority.[36]

The second principal area of contradiction within the culture and practice of Philadelphia metal-working enterprises concerns the opinions that proprietors and managers expressed about their employees and their roles, and the relations that should exist between them and their superiors. The difficulty here was that they thought of their workers both as subordinates, from whom they required obedience, and as co-workers, from whom they desired loyalty. Employees were both factors of production, a vital yet costly resource whose use must remain under strict control if it were to be effective, and they were independent human agents, with interests, wills, and acknowledged rights of their own. Devising and justifying – to themselves and others – appropriate strategies for dealing with these workers would be one of the great challenges of the early twentieth century, and vital for the shaping and success of the Open Shop movement that was their answer to this problem.

[35] Henry C. Metcalfe, "The Shop Order System of Accounts," *Transactions of the American Society of Mechanical Engineers* (hereafter *Trans. ASME*) 7 (1886): 440–88; Frank B. Copley, *Frederick W. Taylor: Father of Scientific Management* (New York, 1923), Vol. 1, pp. 124, 221–22, 438, Vol. 2, pp. 170–02, 175–85; Robert Kanigel, *The One Best Way: Frederick Winslow Taylor and the Enigma of Efficiency* (New York, 1997), is particularly fine for its description of Taylor's milieu – Sellers and Taylor's patron at Bethlehem Steel, Joseph Wharton, were both from the Hicksite Quaker community, like Taylor's father; Daniel Nelson, *Frederick W. Taylor and the Rise of Scientific Management* (Madison, 1980), esp. pp. 142, 149, 233. Pennsylvania – mostly Philadelphia – harbored a fifth of known applications of Taylorism in its first decade and a half – C. Bertrand Thomson, *The Theory and Practice of Scientific Management* (Boston, 1917), pp. 37–38. Employment from 1902FACT database.

[36] Nelson, *Taylor and Scientific Management* and "Scientific Management and the Workplace, 1920–1935" in Sanford M. Jacoby, ed., *Masters to Managers: Historical and Comparative Perspectives on American Employers* (New York, 1991), Ch. 3.

2.5 CAPITALISM WITH A HUMAN FACE

If I am running a business I know all about it . . . . [W]hen a business gets too big for one head to manage it is not managed . . . . I think business should be done as it has been done . . . , certainly with modern improvements . . . , but the old story will hold good, as it always did. You want to get a business done by men of average intelligence, strength, and health, so as to stand the racket; then you can run the business right. (George Cresson, 1900)[37]

Informal and personal control was not just a reflection of company size. Taylor acolyte Morris Ll. Cooke remembered Cramps in the 1900s as a scene of uncoordinated, undermanaged chaos.[38] And Baldwin Locomotive, which its works manager described as "probably as good an example of a modern industrial works as we have in this country," with its pioneering all-electric-drive machine shop and relentless pursuit of efficiency and economy, boasted of the simplicity of its line management – himself, four assistants, and twenty foremen. Baldwin held to this Victorian structure even as it grew explosively to a labor force of 19,000 in 1907 on the back of the last great railroad boom (see Figure 2.2).[39]

Baldwin could get by with these few supervisory staff because it still relied on a supposedly antiquated management system, in which detailed responsibility for production was devolved to "inside contractors" who bid for the right to carry out jobs at a predetermined price, using company-supplied facilities, materials, and labor. They organized the work and pressurized the hourly paid and piece-workers under them to produce to strict time, quality, and price standards. They, not the firm, held on to the profit that represented the margin between costs and contract price; although if the contractor made too much money, he could expect his price to be knocked down next time around.[40]

---

[37] USIC, *Report*, Vol. 14, p. 272.

[38] Kenneth E. Trombley, *The Life and Times of a Happy Liberal* (New York, 1954), pp. 88–89. Cramps may well have been the big East Coast shipyard that management specialist Forrest E. Cardullo described as "the most disgusting exhibition of shiftless management that I have ever seen in my life," where there was "a dearth of foremen, and as in the time of the Judges in Israel, 'every man did that which was right in the sight of his own eyes' " – "Industrial Administration and Scientific Management" in Clarence B. Thompson, ed., *Scientific Management: A Collection of the More Significant Articles Describing the Taylor System of Management* (Cambridge, Mass., 1922), pp. 40–102 at pp. 54–55. Cramp, like Baldwin, classified just 4 percent of its workers as clerical and administrative employees in 1915 – PID-1640 database.

[39] J. Wilmer Henzey, "The Organization and Methods of a Modern Industrial Works," *JFI* 158 (1904): 401–09, quote from p. 401; E. L. Walker, "Electric Drive," *Procs. ECP* 22 (1905): 41–56 at pp. 44–45. Baldwin also had subforemen, "track foremen," and gang bosses, but Henzey did not count these as managers.

[40] E. A. Bingham, "No Unions, No Strikes," *Bulletin of the National Metal Trades Association* (hereafter *Bull. NMTA*) 2 (1903): 361–66; John W. Converse, "Pro-

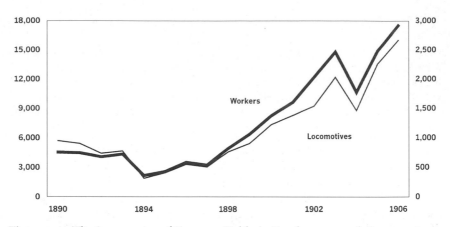

Figure 2.2. The Locomotive of Progress: Baldwin Employment and Output, 1890–1906. *Note:* Any apparent falloff in labor productivity – read from the way in which employment increased faster than units of output, 1897–1903 – is an illusion. Baldwin's locomotives were becoming much larger, more powerful, and more complex. *Source:* "The Development of the American Locomotive," *JFI* 164 (1907): 233–72 at p. 269.

Baldwin's high labor productivity depended on heavy capital investment, incentive payment for workers and contractors, very long working hours (two shifts covering the whole day), and a strict "drive" system backed up with heavy fines for poor work and bad timekeeping. It built locomotives to order, not standard designs for stock, and adapted itself to the instability of demand for its products by laying off and rehiring its mostly skilled workers as required. It retained a cadre of designers, contractors, and long-service employees as a permanent core around which its huge nonunion labor force could be expanded and trimmed down at will. As soon as work picked up, *esprit de corps* and high wages brought back those who were laid off.[41]

Baldwin's objection to the Taylor and other systematic management and payment systems in vogue by the 'teens was the same as that of

gressive Non-Union Labor: Some Features of the System and Management at the Baldwin Locomotive Works," *Cassier's Magazine* 23 (1903): 656–66; John Foster Fraser, *America at Work* (London, 1903), Ch. 4. On the inside contract system, see Dan Clawson, *Bureaucracy and the Labor Process: A Study of US Industry 1860–1920* (New York, 1980), esp. Ch. 3, and Ernest J. Englander, "The Inside Contract System of Production and Organization: A Neglected Aspect of the History of the Firm," *Labor History* 28 (1987): 429–46.

[41] Converse testimony, pp. 230–31, Harrah testimony, p. 350, in USIC, *Report*, Vol. 14.

Midvale's general manager, William Barba – "too much overhead." It was even less prepared than Midvale to accept that there was any constructive role for "efficiency experts" to play. Barba thought that a certain amount of system was "absolutely essential in order to secure the shortest way to the production of the work,"[42] but, in Baldwin president Alba Johnson's opinion,

The essence of successful management is to keep down . . . the unremunerative labor, and to keep to a maximum the remunerative labor. . . . Every process of accounting must be kept to the maximum simplicity. . . . Every premium system and every efficiency system . . . involves a large number of nonproducers, and the question is whether, by reason of those nonproducers, you can so spur the men on to increased production as not only to pay the cost of their maintenance but in addition thereto increase the produce of labor over and above the additional load that you have put on his back.[43]

Baldwin's practice reflected Johnson's wisdom. In 1916, Baldwin's white-collar and administrative employees were only 4 percent of its labor force, against an average by then of 15 percent for the rest of the secondary metalworking industry.[44]

Similarly detailed qualitative evidence for practice in other large Philadelphia businesses is lacking, but there are useful indicators in contemporary accounts of a few companies. In the bigger plants outside of the transportation equipment sector, like Sellers with its maximum of 1,100 employees in the late 1890s, Bement Miles, Enterprise (800), the Newton Machine Toool Works, and Cresson (about 400), management methods were more up-to-date. Careful cost-accounting prevailed – as Cresson explained, "The main thing about running a business is something like water coming out of a spigot. If you stop it off anywhere, it does not run out" – together with individualized incentive wages involving simple piecework or more elaborate bonus systems.[45]

These systems did not, however, rest on attempts at exact work mea-

---

[42] Barba testimony in U.S. Commission on Industrial Relations (hereafter USCIR), *Industrial Relations: Final Report and Testimony, Submitted to Congress by the Commission on Industrial Relations . . . 64th Congress 1st Session* (Washington, 1916), Vol. 3, p. 2855. Taylor had left Midvale a quarter-century before, and his extreme systematization had quickly been attenuated.

[43] Johnson testimony, Ibid., pp. 2819–31, quote at p. 2831.

[44] Brown, *The Baldwin Locomotive Works*, Ch. 4 esp., for a wonderful exploration of this idiosyncratic system; PID1640 database.

[45] Henry Roland, "Cost-Keeping Methods in Machine-Shop and Foundry" and "Effective Systems of Finding and Keeping Shop Costs," (in two parts), *Engineering Magazine* 14 (1897): 225–38 at pp. 225, 236–38 and 15 (1898): 395–400 and 610–20; Cresson in USIC, *Report*, pp. 268, 271; "Factory Cost System of Enterprise Mfg. Company," *Iron Age* (hereafter IA) 72 (1903), 17 Sept. pp. 55–58; 24 Sept. pp. 57–59; 1 Oct. pp. 45–46; 8 Oct. pp. 51–52.

surement: At Enterprise, the smallest unit in which time records were kept
in 1903 was the quarter-hour; at Sellers, Bement-Miles, and Newton, rates
for a job, and time allowances, were arrived at by the usual processes of
guesstimating, making comparisons with existing jobs and tasks, and haggling between the foreman and the workman. This was what Carl Barth
called "the old, rotten way," which he and Taylor and their associates found
at Link-Belt too, and struggled to replace. As James Dodge later admitted,
his firm operated piece-work in the same way as other Philadelphia machinery builders: "We made mistakes, and the way we adjusted them was to
take it out of the hide of the workman."[46]

What was also lacking, even in large and, by the standards of the day,
well-managed plants, was central coordination or planning of production
– something to which the Taylorites became utterly committed. According
to Dodge, Link-Belt, before its Taylorization, ran "on the same principle
that a sausage stuffer works. We would dump orders in one end and squeeze
them out at the other; . . . if there was a special rush, we would make a
special case of it, and everybody would go up in the air to try to get it out."
Tabor was the same: Its president, Taylor's friend and Sellers "graduate"
Wilfred Lewis, followed the conventional wisdom that "success . . . was
mainly a matter of keeping down the number of clerks or 'non-producers'
and having one good superintendent to lay out the work and keep it moving
through the shop." Gang boss Charles Cox recalled what that meant in
practice: "We simply had nothing more than a bill of material to guide us,
and it was my duty to look after the stock and the castings and everything
in general, to see whether it was there." This was what John Rhcinfeldt,
Link-Belt machinist and later assistant in Taylorizing Tabor, called "the old,
happy, go-as-you-please system, come day, go day, God may send some
day."[47]

Taylorites mocked, but their managerial contemporaries were strongly
attached to this lack of formality. At Williamson Bros. Co., for example –
a middle-sized machinery manufacturer – William Hemmerly, clerk and
assistant to Taylor, recalled that its proprietary managers and powerful
foremen "didn't recognize the planning department as being the source
from which all orders entering the shop should come." So the attempt to

[46] U.S. Congress, *Taylor System Hearings*, Vol. 3, p. 1546; USCIR, *Final Report*, Vol.
      1, p. 870. One thing well-run Philadelphia piecework employers like Baldwin, Link-
      Belt, Midvale, and Sellers did *not* do was to cut rates unless the job changed – Nelson,
      Taylor and Scientific Management, pp. 9, 143. Dodge meant that rates were often
      inexact, and on a "tight" rate the workman lost; on a "slack" rate, however, the
      reverse was true.

[47] U.S. Congress, Senate, *Evidence Taken by the Interstate Commerce Commission in
      the Matter of Proposed Advances in Rates by Carriers, August to December, 1910,*
      61st. Cong., 3rd. Sess., 1911, Senate Document Vol. 50, 4: 2698–99 (Washington,
      1911) (hereafter *Eastern Rate Case*); Copley, *Taylor*, Vol. 2, p. 175; U.S. Congress,
      Taylor System Hearings, Vol. 3, pp. 1529, 1595.

Taylorize their shop failed, the efficiency consultants withdrawing in the face of this stubborn opposition.[48]

Normal practice was for a handful of proprietor-executives to determine, and attempt to implement, corporate strategy and tactics. Firms did not hire additional managers in direct proportion as employee numbers grew: Rather, they added to their existing managers' burdens and broadened their "span of control" over clerks and wage-earners. They thereby committed themselves to a degree of organizational overload resolved by improvisation, informality, and the devolution of decision-making responsibility to foremen and craftsmen.[49]

Senior executives did not see their style of overstretched personal management as a problem, but rather as a competitive advantage – it looked cheap and fit in well with their strongly individualistic outlook. Bureaucratic management limited the entrepreneur's freedom to treat the firm as an extension of his personality and property, family and household. At Link-Belt, before Taylor's arrival on the scene, there was some systematization, but nothing that could confine Dodge's "very impulsive" nature. As Taylor's biographer, Frank B. Copley, put it, "never . . . was a man who believed less in red tape and . . . more in self-expression."[50]

Taylorism necessarily involved severe disruption of traditional ways of running a business. Employers were also concerned that it might harm one of the chief sources of their firms' productive efficiency. Dodge, like many of his contemporaries, feared that an excessive system, as well as proving costly, would "destr[oy] . . . all individual initiative" including what the Sellers company's Justus Schwacke called "the wonderful individuality of the American workingman, his resourcefulness."[51] Most

---

[48] U.S. Congress, *Taylor System Hearings*, Vol. 3, p. 1589.

[49] The 1914 Census of Manufactures distinguishes between officials and clerks rather than lumping them all together as salaried, demonstrating a strong inverse relationship between mean establishment size and the ratio of proprietors and officials to clerks and wage earners. U.S. Department of Commerce, Bureau of the Census, *Census of Manufactures 1914, Vol. 1: Reports by States with Statistics for Principal Cities and Metropolitan Districts* (Washington, 1918), pp. 1348–57; calculations involved all Philadelphia secondary metal trades data for industries with more than twenty persons per establishment.

[50] Copley, *Taylor,* Vol. 2, p. 177 [quote]. Link-Belt was, however, an engineer-driven company, and Dodge was committed to experimentation and technical improvement – Link-Belt Co., *The Story of Link-Belt 1875–1925* (Philadelphia, 1925), p. 31; George P. Torrence (Pres., Link-Belt Co.), *James Mapes Dodge (1852–1915): Mechanical Engineer Inventor Pioneer in Industry* (New York, 1950), esp. pp. 8–9, 12–13; Kathy Burgess, "Organized Production and Unorganized Labor: Management Strategy and Labor Activism at the Link-Belt Company, 1900–1940" in Daniel Nelson, ed., *A Mental Revolution: Scientific Management Since Taylor* (Columbus, 1992), pp. 130–55 at p. 133.

[51] Copley, *Taylor,* Vol. 2, p. 77; USCIR, *Final Report,* Vol. 3, p. 2898.

Philadelphia metal manufacturers do not seem to have gone along very far with the Taylorites' theoretical belief (not always carried into practice) in the possibility of increasing productivity by limiting skilled workmen's capacity for creative autonomy on the job. Barba of Midvale believed, on the contrary, that "most efficiency is obtained by careful thought, planning, and laying out in his own mind, in his own way of the operations that are required by his machining sketch, so that he makes as few retracements, as few miss trips, and as many short cuts to the desired end as it is possible to do."[52]

Bureaucratic management systems, including Taylor's, were considered particularly inappropriate in the light of Philadelphia firms' products, markets, and processes. Even Link-Belt's vice president, Staunton Blood-good Peck, acknowledged that "relatively few plants may advantageously adopt comprehensively the Taylor system." Schwacke explained why: "Much of our work is not what you call manufacturing – that is repetition – much of our work is single units." One consequence was that, even at the Taylorite showpiece Link-Belt, "deskilled" jobs and workers of narrow competence did not prevail. Dodge emphasized that "No duplicate work is done, and no package article made or sold." Link-Belt produced conveying equipment for specialized applications, most of it to specific customer order. President Charles Piez explained that there was "very little repetition," although installations did include some standardized components, and much of the work was in the nature of jobbing.[53] Dodge stressed that

We do not do competitive [i.e., merely price-sensitive] work in our shops, and we have to develop all-around workers, and we frequently change men from a lathe to a boring mill, or from a boring mill to a drill press, or something like that, so as to have them ambidextrous, so that when we want men to stick in on one thing we have got them. We do not need specialists. Specialists are detrimental to a shop. Of course that may be so [sic] in a chewing gum factory, or something like that, but we do not need them in our company.[54]

Link-Belt, like Tabor, could bear the heavy administrative burden required to operate under the Taylor system in part because of the high-value, patent-protected, and customized nature of its products. Between 1916 and 1922, 34 and 41 percent of these two design-intensive companies' workforces

---

[52] Ibid., p. 2860.
[53] Staunton B. Peck, "Efficiency," *Proceedings of the 16th Annual Convention of the National Founders' Association* (New York, 1912), pp. 146–53 at p. 147; USCIR, *Final Report*, Vol. 3, p. 2895; James M. Dodge, "A History of the Introduction of a System of Shop Management," in Thompson, ed., *Scientific Management*, p. 226; USCIR, *Final Report*, Vol. 1, p. 867.
[54] USCIR, *Final Report*, Vol. 4, p. 3189; cf. testimony of Hollis Godfrey on Tabor, U.S. Congress, *Taylor System Hearings*, Vol. 3, p. 1834.

were white-collar and administrative staff, two to three times the local sectoral average.[55] But to make quality goods, and to respond quickly to shifts in the mix and volume of demand, they, just as much as their more traditional neighbors, also required versatile skilled workers whose powers of independent decision were limited but not eliminated by their innovations in management.

The great advantage of Taylorism to Piez was not that it freed his firm from dependence on its skilled workmen, but that it gave him and his team a way of producing order and predictability within a business with an extremely "heterogeneous product," and improved coordination between departments. Taylorism, in Dodge's view, boiled down to "Prompt shipments. Keeping our promises," which had previously been "practically valueless." It was simply a perfected form of systematic management in a world as far away from "Fordist" mass production as it is possible to imagine.[56]

To Tabor's chief of time study, ex-Link-Belt and "boomer" machinist Hudson Reed, "The whole essence of scientific management as I see it, as a practical man in the shop, is the careful preparation of the work before it enters into the shop; and . . . following up of the work to see that it is done according to [plan]." Link-Belt superintendent Adams thought that "It is systematized knowledge of your processes of manufacture. . . . [T]he feature which distinguishes it most is . . . the routing and planning from a central office." These elements were fundamental.[57]

According to Link-Belt's vice president Peck, the payment system, which attracted so much attention, was "*relatively* unimportant"; what mattered most was the promotion of "a spirit of friendly co-operation." From the workers' point of view, Taylorism meant – in the opinion of another sympathetic observer – that "they had to work steadily; they had to pay strict attention to business; they had to follow the instructions given them; but they made more money than they could in any other shop; the management helped them; the company treated them 'square,' and you could not drive them out of the shop with a club." This was not to deny that men who could not meet exacting output standards made low pay, and left. But what remained was a select body of workmen, working swiftly, doing well, and proud of their work and their élite status as Link-Belt employees, with the sort of trust in management and organizational commitment that other

[55] PID-1640 database. Cf. Frank W. Sterling, "The Successful Operation of a System of Scientific Management," in Thompson, ed., *Scientific Management*, pp. 296–366 at p. 297, on prewar conditions.
[56] USCIR, *Final Report*, Vol. 4, p. 3179, Vol. 1, p. 872; U.S. Congress, *Eastern Rate Case*, p. 2699. Cf. John W. Carter, "The Production Control Method of the Tabor Mfg. Company," *Annals of the American Association of Political and Social Science* (hereafter *Annals*) 118 (1923): 92–96.
[57] U.S. Congress, *Taylor System Hearings*, Vol. 3, pp. 1520, 1652.

Philadelphia firms also sought to inculcate, albeit by less modern and bureaucratic methods.[58]

The proof of the pudding was in the eating: Dodge believed that "Our men do not see any reason why they should pay dues to a union to insure them less wages than they are getting now." Adams saw friends and relatives of existing workers voting for the Link-Belt system with their feet: "Where they get a chance, they usually come to us." They came, and they stayed: The average machineshop worker in 1912 had started out in 1904, and most would have served right through Link-Belt's "Taylorization."[59]

In this discussion of organizational cultures and practices among Philadelphia metal-working firms, Tabor and Link-Belt have received far more than their fair share of attention. But they did so at the time, and have continued to since, given the degree of interest in, and controversy about, the "Taylor System," of which they were the showcases. What needs to be stressed here is both that they were exceptional among their contemporaries for the degree to which they invested in administrative staff as a solution to problems of management; and that, in most other respects, they were quite ordinary. They shared the Philadelphia norms of ownership and active control by the same small groups of men, and a complex interdependence between managers and the skilled workmen at the heart of the production process. They also had little obvious impact on their neighbors' practices. The general prejudices against "red tape" and anything that stood in the way of managerial freedom were formidable barriers to the broader diffusion of the new bureaucratic techniques in Frederick Taylor's home town, among the metal-working community of engineers and businessmen of which he was an honored member.

But these prejudices also undergirded a common determination to resist any infringements by skilled workers and their unions on what proprietor-managers thought of as the necessary, indeed natural, ordering of industrial life. This theme in Philadelphia's turn-of-the-century business culture would run right through the Open Shop era, without significant

---

[58]   Peck, "Efficiency," p. 148, emphasis in original; "Scientific Management and the Workers," *Engineering and Industrial Management* 1 (1919): 111–12, derived from Robert T. Kent's "Scientific Management as Viewed from the Workman's Standpoint," *Industrial Engineering and the Engineering Index* 8 (1910): 378.

[59]   USCIR, *Final report*, Vol. 1, p. 872; U.S. Congress, *Taylor System Hearings*, Vol. 3, pp. 1642, 1655. Tabor was also, according to its part owner, Frederick Taylor, a high-wage shop – "It aims to be at least 35 per cent higher than the same man doing the same work could get in any other establishment right around us" – *Scientific Management: Comprising Shop Management, the Principles of Scientific Management, Testimony Before the Special House Committee* (New York, 1947), p. 275. Doubtless this, and the companies' humane managerial style, explained workers' organizational commitment and acceptance of high output norms.

challenge from within the employing community until the 1920s. This "proper relationship" between managers and workers is next on the agenda for exploration.

2.6 TOUGH LOVE: ENTERPRISE AND AUTHORITY

The great sin at Midvale is insubordination. . . . That is not forgiven. . . . Lying is looked upon with less severity. Drunkenness is glossed over. And then that other thing, in which a man keeps two or three market baskets, while we look upon that as an amiable foible, very few can afford it and it brings its own end very quickly. (Charles J. Harrah, 1900)[60]

The managerial style of these Philadelphia firms relied on the personal and direct exercize of authority, which affected both relations between executives and their administrative subordinates, and labor relations. The predominant tone that employers struck when speaking about their underlings was much more severe than Harrah's. Frank Copley reported of William Sellers that "in him Quaker thrift was manifested so excessively as to make him often insensible to the just claims of others," and that he was "not only one of the greatest engineers of his age, but also one of its grandest disciplinarians," believing that "to spare the damn is to spoil the man." His guiding principle was that "every organization must have a directing head, some one who embodies the organization's common will or purpose" and that its "success . . . naturally depend[ed] on the readiness of the parts to obey those orders. Should they be in the habit of starting a debate whenever an order reaches them, the organization of course will not get anywhere. . . . [A] subordinate should do his best to follow out his instructions before he tries to improve on them." The remedy for disagreement or failure in this sometimes benevolent dictatorship was discharge; adequate performance at every level was guaranteed by fear. As Baldwin superintendent Samuel Vauclain explained in 1903, "we are not running a philanthropic institution and we demand results. The slothful, the careless, the vicious suffer; every man's work must be right up to the notch, and by treating our

---

[60] USIC, *Report*, Vol. 14, p. 352. "Market baskets" – the idiom is obscure, but Harrah is probably referring to extramarital relationships. Note the tolerance of working-class masculine behavior, so long as it does not impinge on production and workplace relationships. However, this accepting attitude did not survive long. Harrah told how "a wedding with us means sometimes fifteen days before it can be considered consummated; and then again we have to bury an Irishman, and that takes about a week," but fourteen years later his manager Barba reported "the abuse of liquor, appearing in the works under the influence of liquor" and "quarreling or fighting" as the commonest sacking offences. USCIR, *Final Report*, Vol. 3, p. 2853. With his usual modesty and accuracy, Taylor claimed to have solved Midvale's drinking problems a generation earlier – Kanigel, *One Best Way*, p. 197.

employees as men we expect the best service they can give. And I assure
you that we get it."[61]

Underlying this strict disciplinary creed was a primitive pleasure/pain psychology, well exemplified by Philadelphia Engineers' Club president Henry
H. Quimby's statement in 1908, that "if we resist temptation it is only
because we prefer to abstain, whether it be through fear of consequence or
hope of reward." This theory inspired the Sellers company's method of persuading its molders to wear the leg and foot protectors that the company
provided against bangs and burns: It was made clear to them that, if injured,
they would only receive financial help on condition that they had been using
the guards supplied. From the metal manufacturer's perspective, this was
not a severe philosophy, but simply one that was in line with fundamental
truths about human motivation, the contractual obligations of master and
servant, and the freedoms and responsibilities of adult men, most of whom
were American citizens.[62]

The older generation of employers and managers were dedicated to the
gospel of work – as a moral imperative and the road to self-realization. As
Coleman Sellers put it in 1903, "To me, work has been my life. An indus-
trious mental and physical employment is the pleasure of life." Carl Barth
similarly spoke of work as "an outlet for my natural energy" and boasted
of his "love of work for its own sake" and his adult lifetime in America
spent "Working like the devil."[63] Such an attitude, combined with a realistic appreciation that metal manufacturers had a heavy investment in capital
equipment, which they needed to utilize as intensively as possible, translated into a commitment to retaining a working schedule of ten or more
hours a day, and fighting any reduction. James Dodge could "not admit
that there is any grind of the day." This was not to deny "that a man, when
he gets through a piece of work, . . . should feel wholesomely tired." Hard
manual labor might exhaust a man's vital resources, and justify a cut in
hours, but Philadelphia metal manufacturers denied that most of their jobs
were of that character. Midvale's manager, William Barba, thought that "in
the mechanical jobs, such as the machine-shop work, . . . a man really does
little work, all he has to do is to set a piece and see to it that the machine
does the work." So, as Dodge put it to the U.S. Industrial Relations Commission in 1914, "if you were one of us and were down there working along
and saw the men happy and . . . wanting to work that long and make the

[61] Copley, *Taylor*, Vol. 1, pp. 121, 133, 135–36, 152–53, 191; cf. Logan Pearsall Smith, *Unforgotten Years* (London, 1938), pp. 134–35; Bingham, "No Unions, No Strikes," p. 366.

[62] Quimby, "President's Address," *Procs. ECP* 25 (1908): 66–82 at p. 76; Alexander E. Outerbridge, Jr., "Safety First for Foundrymen," *Journal of the Engineers Club of Philadelphia* (hereafter *J. ECP*) 35 (1918): 300–12.

[63] "25th. Anniversary Banquet at the Union League," *Procs. ECP* 20 (1903): 18; U.S. Congress, *Taylor System Hearings*, Vol. 3, p. 1539.

wages they can, and not wanting the time reduced, I think you would say, 'Let them work.' "[64] Maximizing useful, but not exhausting, labor was further justified by an ideology of productionism – an unquestioning belief in the virtue of output. Dodge believed that it was "a truism; that a man that makes two blades of grass grow where only one grew before is a benefactor of his race," for "increase in production . . . has got to go on to the end of time."[65]

Nothing should stand in the way of efficient production. But how was it to be achieved? It all depended on creating a satisfactory company environment. This did not mean one that was utterly safe – in 1900, Midvale reckoned to injure about 1 percent of its workers a day, and to "hurt" – presumably more seriously – about a quarter of them every year; in 1914, Baldwin Locomotive's president Johnson accepted that there was "a certain percentage of fatalities below which it seems impossible to get" because of the "misfortune, carelessness, and incapacity which is inseparable from the employment of human labor." In 1911–12 Baldwin inflicted about one death, 20 serious injuries, and 200 lesser injuries for its approximately 12,000 employees every month.[66]

But the factory, although admittedly a dangerous place, ought not to be heavily regulated by the state. Link-Belt's Charles Piez was concerned that excessive governmental concern for employees' welfare might "shatter the fiber of the workman," in a moralistic rather than literal sense. To Johnson,

anything which tends to take away the personal responsibility of the workman, which tends to make him a child rather than a citizen, is unwise. . . . [E]verything should be done that can properly be done to recognize the manhood of the workman, to recognize his responsibility as a citizen, as the father of a family, and as an individual.[67]

A satisfactory organizational environment was one that allowed individuals proper opportunities for the responsible performance of their allotted roles within a manly relationship bounded by freedom of contract and insulated against outside interference. But what were the limits on the employer's right to lay down the rules, and what freedom was there for the workman in this situation? The sphere within which obedience and

[64] Ibid., p. 1703; USCIR, *Final Report*, Vol. 3, p. 2853; Vol. 1, p. 870.

[65] USCIR, *Final Report*, Vol. 3, p. 2853; Vol. 1, p. 870; U.S. Congress, *Taylor System Hearings*, Vol. 3, p. 1700.

[66] USIC, *Report*, Vol. 14, p. 352; USCIR, *Final Report*, Vol. 3, pp. 2866, 2835, 2924. Midvale's men paid for their own medical attention through a compulsory levy and the proceeds of fines for spoiled work; Baldwin had no in-plant first aid (p. 2825) despite its "slaughterhouse" reputation, for which see testimony of the Machinists' business agent, Edward Keenan, USCIR, *Final Report*, Vol. 3, p. 2881.

[67] USCIR, *Final Report*, Vol. 4, p. 3184; Vol. 3, p. 2864.

conformity were required was not all-encompassing. Employers recognized and respected their men's status as independent adult citizens, which gave them rights as well as duties. Harrah stressed that Midvale

ma[d]e it a rule never to interfere with the religion or the politics or the economics of any of our men but we insist upon it in the same manner that they respect the rules that are laid out for the government of the works and to which all of us are subject. . . . Outside of our fence they can do anything they please.[68]

The great problem for turn-of-the-century manufacturers was how to rec- oncile this republican ideology with their ingrained anti-unionism. Harrah's was the usual solution – to emphasize the distinction between workers' freedom "outside of our fence" and duty of obedience within it – but there were obvious weaknesses in this formula. The essence of labor organiza- tion was the workers' collective demand for the freedom to exercize their citizenship rights inside the fence, too, to affect the terms of the employ- ment relationship. Leaders of the metal-manufacturing community recog- nized the resulting tension within their formula in 1900, but could not quickly resolve it.

George Cresson claimed not to know whether his men were organized, and not to care: "We are willing to have it either way, just so they attend to their business. We do not bother them much, and they do not bother us much." He blustered that he "never interfered with my men in anything they wanted to do. I considered they were American citizens and knew better than I did what they wanted." He recognized "Absolutely" their "right to have some voice in fixing the wages" – "they are Americans." He was even prepared to see advantages in dealing with organized labor: "It would depend how they did it; how much it bore on us in the way of arbi- trarily and unjustly interfering with our business." He was "not at all" opposed in principle, and even feared practical disadvantages if employers opposed their men's wishes: "If the employers are fair about the matter the men will see that they are fair about as soon as anybody"; organized anti- unionism would sour the good relations that both sides desired.[69]

Charles Harrah also acknowledged the legitimacy, and even saw some advantages, of trade unionism, and he too claimed neither to recognize nor to fight it in his works: It was

decidedly beneficial to the employer. The natural trend of an employer is to protect his interests regardless of the interests of others. For several years of my life I lived

[68]   USIC, *Report*, Vol. 14, pp. 349, 351; cf. President A. C. Dinkey to John F. Perkins (employer member), 23 Aug. 1918, pp. 4, 7–10 esp., Executive Session Minutes, 26 Aug. 1918, in Melvyn Dubofsky, ed., *Research Collections in Labor Studies: The Wilson Administration and American Workers: Papers of the National War Labor Board* (Frederick, 1985), microfilm ed., Reel 8, justifying Midvale's continuing oppo- sition to an "outside" union.
[69]   USIC, *Report*, Vol. 14, pp. 266–67, 269, 272.

in a slave country, in Brazil, and I found there what was afterwards confirmed by my experiences in this country, that it is a most unfortunate thing when a man has unlimited power.[70]

Collective bargaining offered much, in theory. In addition to being in accordance with American democratic principles, and more practically, it could take wage rates out of competition. As Harrah explained, "[s]tability is of great importance to us – stability of prices and stability of wages.... [L]abor should be fixed in such a manner that everybody should be on the same footing, and it is of very little moment to us what price we pay for labor provided we all start alike." Second, it offered the prospect of a responsible, disciplined bargaining partner – partly because, as Cresson said, "It creates intelligence in the men.... [A] body of men has a great deal more principle in it than any one man"; and partly because of the character and caliber of the men craft unions had at their head. (Harrah cited Samuel Gompers as "a thinking man, a student.")[71]

Cresson and Harrah in 1900 offered many of the same arguments as those that underlay other businessmen's readiness to enter into social relations with "moderate" and "responsible" union leaders under the aegis of the National Civic Federation (NCF) at the same time, and even to experiment with the recognition of labor organizations. Their rhetorical evasions of the fact that, whatever they might say in general and theoretical terms, in practice their aim was to avoid the necessity of dealing with unions in their own plants, seemed to satisfy their Industrial Commission interlocutors in 1900, and was equally typical of many of the NCF's early supporters. But such confused thinking would not provide satisfactory guidance over the next few years of labor relations crisis, out of which emerged both the organized Open Shop movement and a more coherent rationale for it, born of hard thinking and bitter experience.[72]

[70] Ibid., p. 349.

[71] Ibid., pp. 350, 272, 350. There was, however, a contradiction in this view of labor leaders – remote, national ones might be admirable; but local organizers were viewed according to the normal pejorative stereotype as "men who will want to create trouble.... whose business it it is to stir up the workmen and get them dissatisfied with what they are doing" – Cresson, p. 269.

[72] For the NCF, Marguerite Green, *The National Civic Federation and the American Labor Movement 1900–1925* (Washington, 1956) and Gordon M. Jensen, "The National Civic Federation: American Business in an Age of Social Change and Social Reform, 1900–1910" (Ph.D. diss., Princeton University, 1956), esp. Ch.5, have not been bettered. James Weinstein, *The Corporate Ideal in the Liberal State* (Boston, 1968) added little. The thinking of the NCF's business supporters is best studied through the transcripts of its conferences rather than in the work of its secretary, Ralph M. Easley. See esp. *Industrial Conciliation: Report of the Proceedings of the Conference Held Under the Auspices of the National Civic Federation ... 16–17 December 1901* (New York, 1902). Proceedings of the October 1903 conference,

A satisfactory organizational environment came to be defined as one that was free of unionism. Unionization was always open to many objections. Most basically, it threatened to upset the proper relations of superior and subordinate. To Justus Schwacke of the Sellers firm, it encouraged workers to "attempt to assume conditions to which they are not entitled as employees." For Link-Belt's Piez, it "practically relieves you of all control over the discipline of the shop." In the opinion of Midvale's Barba, unionization forced the employer to "yiel[d] the control of his business to people possibly not in his employ, ... to a small group of men who are then placed in a position to control features of his business that must remain in his grasp if he is going to succeed and get more work for more men."[73]

If employers were vulnerable to being overruled by their subordinates or outsiders, the necessary rules of effective business operation would be violated. Employees did indeed have rights as men and citizens, which employers continued to acknowledge, but during working hours their principal role was as order-takers in naturally hierarchical organizations. Cresson's and Harrah's attempts to square the circle were abandoned, their reservations forgotten.

A firm was a unified structure of authority relationships in the service of profitable production. It was *not* a microcosm of a democratic commonwealth. Baldwin's general superintendent Sykes thought of the employee's obligations in this context rather conservatively – "All that we ask of a man is that he conform to the rules of the establishment, that he produce according to the position in which he is placed and paid for to produce, and that he be a law-abiding workman." But some of his peers were not content with this narrowly contractual version of the workman's duties as the subject of a corporate state. Link-Belt's president Piez went so far as to claim that he "would sooner be elected president by the men under me than by the board of directors of the company." He both believed that his men were "absolutely loyal to me, to such an extent that they would elect me to-morrow the business agent of their union" (which would have been difficult, as he had smashed it), and required them to be so. "I don't refer to discipline as military discipline, but a sort of cooperative spirit that must exist." However, whether it actually existed or not, organizations must be free to function as if it did. "How do you suppose it would affect the effec-

which was an attempt to patch up the conciliatory approach, were not published, because they were too embarrassing – all of the employer spokesmen were vehement for the Open Shop. See editorial, "The Open Shop as an Issue" and Henry C. Hunter [Secretary, New York Metal Trades Association], "The Open Shop," *IA* 79:17 (29 Oct. 1903): 26–27, 29–32. Hunter's was one of the suppressed contributions. This indicates that the ideological development that went on among Philadelphia metal manufacturers between 1900 and 1903 paralleled that which occurred more generally.
[73] USCIR, *Final Report*, Vol. 3, p. 2898; Vol. 4, p. 3179; Vol. 3, p. 2873.

tiveness of an army to have the men ... disloyal to the man at the head?
The men at the head of the various labor organizations insist on loyalty to
them, and I have the same right to insist on loyalty to me. I can not get the
best work out of the men unless I have their cooperation."[74]

Workmen owed obedience to the firm in general and to its managers and
foremen in person – to Baldwin's contractors, whom President Johnson
thought of as "small proprietor[s]" within their territories, with all the
accompanying rights that the status implied; to Midvale's ten departmental
superintendents, "Each of [whom] ... has within reason the final right to
discipline the men who are employed under him, and who (*sic*) he knows,
meets face to face, and can name every one of them; and he is the best judge
as to the fitness of the discipline which he is called upon to impose."[75]

This commitment to maintaining line managers' personal standing meant
that, however well-intentioned patriarchal proprietors might be about preserving access for aggrieved individuals to the "top boss" – the celebrated
"open door" policy that was central to their rationale for the lack of a need
for labor unions – in practice enterprises operated in a generally authoritarian manner. Dodge might claim that "When they do come to me I take
it up as if it was my son," and as his superintendent, Willis Adams, explained, he could do what he liked to give justice, because "Mr. Dodge,
naturally, being the highest authority, is the final authority." But Michael
Donnelly, a former employee, was realistic about the consequences of
making a complaint: "If you do not get along with the foreman, you must
look for a job elsewhere and get out of there." Even in a firm like Link-
Belt, the "foreman's empire" survived to this extent, that he could confidently expect not to be overruled by his superiors in the event of arguments
and difficulties with the men he had to control. If he was overruled, he had
his ways of getting back at, and getting rid of, his objectionable subordinates and showing higher management that it was in their interests to
support him.[76]

Higher management generally agreed that if the foreman's authority
were undermined, efficiency must surely suffer, and the foremen themselves
would have a justifiable grievance. They were a vital managerial stratum
who could take a walk themselves if their manhood were attacked in this
fashion, and were highly valued accordingly. Adams backed his men up all
the way: "The superior should do it, or he does not want to keep the men
under him."[77]

The resulting blockage of upward communication was a recognized
pathology of the authoritarian firm, and something that both Tabor and

[74] Ibid., Vol. 3, p. 2869; Vol. 4, pp. 3178, 3192, 3180, 3179.
[75] Ibid., pp. 2832, 2877.
[76] U.S. Congress, *Taylor System Hearings*, Vol. 3, pp. 1704, 1707, 1644, 1685.
[77] Ibid., p. 1657.

Link-Belt, as pioneers in bureaucratic rationalism, tried to overcome. Tabor's revolutionary approach was to remove the foreman's firing power, which change, or so superintendent Leroy Tabor claimed, brought about freedom of speech in the workshop, including freedom to criticize, and improved levels of cooperation. Link-Belt more conservatively depended on keeping formal personnel records, with regular reports on each man's performance. These would hopefully act as a restraining influence on the foremen's exercize of their power by providing objective data on each man's past behavior against which their rulings might be tested.[78]

2.7 ONE BIG HAPPY FAMILY

Q: How do you deal with your men usually? A. The men have largely been boys under me. My superintendent was a boy of fourteen when he came to me. I am the oldest one in the place now, and I was pretty near the youngest when I started out. . . . I manage my men very successfully. I can handle my men better than anybody else, because the men have confidence in me. (George Cresson, 1900)[79]

Thus far I have emphasized the hard edge to employers' thinking and behavior in dealing with their employees, as individuals and if they had the temerity to form a union. But while managers always required obedience from their subordinates, they also wanted and encouraged them to be loyal, committed, and to exercize initiative on their employers' behalf. They recognized that neither obedience nor the other virtues could be created by severity alone; they had a decent respect for their men's independence, and a more complex understanding of what motivated them than the calculus of pleasure and pain offered. As Cresson put it, "Philadelphians have a considerable amount of blood in them. . . . [I]f a man is treated right he will stay with you; if not, he will not." Loyalty and commitment depended on reciprocity, but the relationship was never entirely equal. Dependence and obedience were never quite lost sight of. "[M]en appreciate what you do for them; but if a man does not, I do not want him."[80]

Employers set a high value on what they thought of as their close-knit enterprise communities, embedded in settled working-class neighborhoods and recruiting most of their foremen and managers from within the firm. Harrison Safety Boiler's William S. Hallowell was confident in the "pleasant and good" social conditions at his firm, helped by the fact that "Our works

---

[78]   Ibid., pp. 1627, 1707.
[79]   USIC, *Report*, Vol. 14, pp. 269–70.
[80]   Ibid., p. 270.

are located in a section having comfortable small houses, which our men generally occupy."[81] Midvale's president, Alva C. Dinkey, emphasized that most of the management, from bottom to top, "have grown up from the rank and file of the Company's employees. They are a consolidated body, have confidence in each other, have a long history of cooperation and intercourse."[82] Cramp Shipbuilding's general manager, Harry Hand, who had started out there as a draftsman, similarly stressed that

the closer the actual head of the establishment gets to the workmen, the better success he has. It is rather peculiar – the conditions that exist around our place. Almost all the people in the plant have been apprentices, and have grown from the apprentice boy up to positions of great authority. . . . Consequently, men like myself and my assistants under me, know these [long-service work]men by their first names and call them so, and they call us by our first names.[83]

Cramp, too, had its own neighborhood, as did the Disston family's Keystone Saw Works, located on the city's northeastern fringe, surrounded by the houses its workers bought with the aid of the "building society" (cooperative savings and loan institution) that the firm sponsored. Link-Belt was also a neighborhood company: Three generations of some Nicetown families were to be found in its machine shop, and the firm, like most others, relied on its foremen's and workers' personal contacts for recruitment.[84]

Philadelphia firms therefore depended on their core groups of long-service, skilled employees, which widespread home ownership, relatively stable employment, and ample opportunities for advancement fostered. To Midvale's Barba, "a satisfied body of men is the best asset that any manufacturing plant can have," and long service was one indicator of such satisfaction.[85] Harrah explained why he "tr[ied] to make the place attractive to the men," apart from the sentimental reason that "I do not like to see new faces around me. I like to see old faces":

[81] Ibid., pp. 267, 270; USCIR, *Final Report*, Vol. 3, p. 2926.
[82] Dinkey to Perkins, 23 Aug. 1918, p. 10, in Dubofsky, ed., *Papers of the NWLB*, Reel 8.
[83] USCIR, *Final Report*, Vol. 3, pp. 2887–8; cf. Charles Cramp in USIC, *Report*, Vol. 14, pp. 415–16.
[84] Greenberg, "Relationship Between Work and Residence in an Industrializing City: Philadelphia, 1880," p. 153; Silcox, *A Place to Live and Work*, Chs. 1, 2 ; U.S. Congress, *Taylor System Hearings*, Vol. 3, pp. 1642, 1650–51. By the mid-1920s, Link-Belt was also strongly supporting home ownership by its employees: about one-third of them were mortgage holders in the "building society" that it backed. "Notes on the American Tour of Messrs. Northcott and Hawksby, September 1926," p. 13, in file America 1923–8, B. Seebohm Rowntree (hereafter BSR) Papers, Joseph S. Rowntree Trust (hereafter JSRT), York, England.
[85] USCIR, *Final Report*, Vol. 3, pp. 2860–61.

it is for a very selfish reason. There is no philanthropy in it. We invest a great deal of capital in the education of a man. You must be patient with a man; you must explain how things are done; he wastes a lot of your material in doing it; after you have a man thoroughly educated you can not afford to lose him. It is not because you love the man; it is not because you want to be a philanthropist, it is from pure common business sense; that is all there is in it.[86]

Such settled, committed employees had to be made, not simply wished for. However, metal manufacturers did not support employee benefit plans for this purpose – there were none of the formal schemes for motivating and retaining workers that came to be known as "welfare capitalism"; as Frank Disston later argued, "the men are too independent for that – they are given the means for doing their own welfare work," by paying them well. Companies did establish employee-run benevolent associations to assist sick and disabled workmen, but these operated on a strictly contributory basis. To Baldwin's Johnson they involved the same relationship "as a journeyman to his employer, who hands his savings to his employer to hold for him."[87]

Instead of practicing welfare capitalism, Philadelphia patriarchs preferred to demonstrate the kind of informal, personal charity that rewarded loyalty, stressed dependence, and gave the man granting it a nice warm feeling inside. Link-Belt would loan "any employee . . . what we deem is an amount which he will be able to pay easily" to meet emergencies. "Of course, a man must have been with us long enough to establish confidence." Disston thought this man-to-man approach far preferable to "any humiliating red tape or investigations."[88]

Although there was thus no systematic provision for needy or superannuated employees, there was a sort of imperfect, implicit contract that workers should not be discharged simply on grounds of age or disability, so long as there was some kind of job that they could perform. At Midvale, the "faithful servant" could expect to be "continued in our employ as long as he is able to come to the works. When he is physically unable to get within the gates he is pensioned off." This sort of "pension" was a gift whose size and duration were strictly matters for the employer to determine, and with no better guarantee than his generosity and his word. Link-Belt, similarly, found "bench work" for "old men . . . who have gotten

[86] USIC, *Report*, Vol. 14, pp. 350–51.
[87] Disston, "How We Hold Our Men," p. 120; USIC, *Report*, Vol. 14, p. 352; USCIR, *Final Report*, Vol. 3, p. 2826; cf. "The Open Shop Creates Community of Interest: Some Features of the Welfare Work in the John B. Stetson Plant," *The [Open Shop] Review* 13 (1916): 3–11. Stetson, however, had a large female workforce. See also Howard M. Gitelman, "Welfare Capitalism Reconsidered," *Labor History* 33 (1992): 1–31.
[88] USCIR, *Final Report*, Vol. 4, p. 3193; U.S. Congress, *Taylor System Hearings*, Vol. 3, p. 1645; Disston, "How We Hold Our Men," p. 120.

so old that they are not very active." Employees came to expect this benevolence from the better sort of employer: A Tabor machinist could look forward to continuous employment even in the bleak years of the 1930s as his reward for the loss of an eye at work.[89]

Veteran employees were pointed to with pride. Disston, the firm most successfully committed to promoting job tenure, had so many veterans that its president felt he had to answer the question whether he was "running a saw works or an old men's home." In 1917, the company employed aproximately 2,700 men and 200 women. Nineteen men had "served us continuously" for more than fifty years, ninety for forty to fifty years, 238 for thirty to forty years, 320 for twenty to thirty years, and 763 for ten to twenty years – altogether, half the payroll. They "add[ed] stability to the establishment," eliminated the need for "constant supervision which an irresponsible working force requires," and passed on the strong company culture to young workers, often their sons and grandsons.[90]

But Disston was exceptionally placed, as a world market leader enjoying fairly stable demand for quality products. Elsewhere, veterans were less numerous – so employers could afford to be demonstratively generous to them, because the need did not arise too often. At the Harrison Safety Boiler Works, for example, the average age of shop employees in 1914 was thirty-four – at Baldwin it was just twenty-six – and the average length of service was four to five years. Building commitment among such a workforce required more than the indefinite promise that, if men managed to stay with the firm until they were old, they would be taken care of. The greatest risk – actually a near-certainty – in the working lives of most turn-of-the-century Americans was irregular and discontinuous employment. Manufacturers had to do something to minimize this risk and deliver on their side of the bargain, if they wanted loyalty and commitment in return.[91]

That something could involve, as at Baldwin, the more or less formal division of the workforce into a skilled, dependable core – about a third of the peak workforce – who could expect continuous employment, or at least preferential access to job opportunities in a recession, and a periphery of "floaters," to whom the company owed nothing other than an attractive wage, for as long or as short a time as they were required (see Figure 2.3 for the changing numbers and proportions of these groups, 1911–14). It might also entail a readiness to try to keep the organiza-

[89] USCIR, *Final Report*, Vol. 3, p. 2853; U.S. Congress, *Taylor System Hearings*, Vol. 3, p. 1653; Respondent 178, Machinists Study, Gladys Palmer Papers, TUUA; cf. William Graebner, *A History of Retirement: The Meaning and Function of an American Institution, 1885–1978* (New Haven, 1980), pp. 121–24.

[90] Disston, "How We Hold Our Men," pp. 116–18; PID-1640 database.

[91] USCIR, *Final Report*, Vol. 3, pp. 2925–26, 2819; cf. Alex Keyssar, *Out of Work: The First Century of Unemployment in Massachusetts* (New York, 1986).

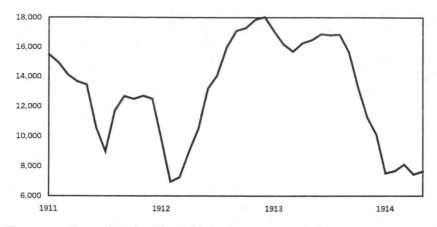

Figure 2.3. Unsteady Jobs: The Baldwin Locomotive Workforce, January 1911–May 1914. *Note*: The rapid but brief recovery after the strike in 1911, and the huge layoffs after midsummer 1913. *Source*: Johnson Exhibit No. 3 in USCIR, *Final Report*, Vol. 3, pp. 2923–24.

tion together in hard times by cutting hours and producing standardized items for stock, taking orders at or below cost, or chasing unfamiliar markets. To Midvale's Barba, it made sense to "striv[e] to hold our best men in our employ during these times, hoping that something will come up that will enable us to put more of them to work. . . . [O]ur investment in those men in their training and ability and equipment, is like an investment in machines and tools, . . . and you might just as well break up your tools as to break up your organization." To keep together its organization, Link-Belt even developed a semiformal seniority system, whereby newer or less-skilled employees were let go first, and their jobs taken by older hands, albeit at a lower rate of pay than they had been receiving in their previous positions.[92]

But even the best-intentioned capital goods maker could not altogether avoid the consequences of the irregularity of demand for its products, and "working for stock" was a strictly limited option where most output consisted of nonstandard, even customized, goods, and where recessions prompted firms to cut inventory along with other costs. The ability of a firm to protect more than a large fraction of its employees against layoff was therefore highly problematic. So the essential bargain between a firm

[92]   USCIR, *Final Report*, Vol. 3, pp. 2825, 2827, 2829; USIC, *Report*, Vol. 14, pp. 268, 351; USCIR, *Final Report*, Vol. 3, p. 2857; Vol. 4, p. 3184; U.S. Congress, *Taylor System Hearings*, Vol. 3, p. 1706.

and most of its workmen had to revolve around shorter term commitments that were more consistent with the nature of its markets.[93]

The basic promise boiled down, in most cases, to the provision of a chance to make money, and better money than in most other kinds of industrial work in Philadelphia. At Midvale, the fundamental employment policy was to "creat[e] an opportunity for a good man to earn more with us than he can with anyone else, with the education and upbuilding of the less efficient to a point of greater efficiency, up to their capacity.... We believe utterly in the creation of the opportunity for every man to earn as much as he wishes to earn. We make no high limit on the amount of money that a mechanic earns." For Baldwin, too, "The best efficiency is to encourage men to make high wages. ... [W]e believe that our contract with labor is that of buying its services, and paying them the highest price for it." Baldwin lived up to its side of this contract. Even during the savage 1914 recession its men received at least 15 percent more than the city's average industrial earnings, while metal workers generally enjoyed a 23 percent advantage. The next year, with the return of prosperity, Baldwin workers were back in their normal privileged position, earning 22 percent more than the average metal worker, leave alone the rest of the city's employees.[94]

Given that firms stressed the fundamental economic motivations of their employees, and believed that the cash stimulus was most effective when the individual workman could see a direct connection between his effort, his output, and his reward, their commitment to piece-rate and other incentive schemes followed naturally. One of the objections to unionism was that it sought to break this connection by pursuing time wages, minimum rates, shorter hours, and "arbitrary" limitations on output. For all of these reasons it was morally as well as economically unacceptable.[95]

Thus even within the supposedly familial relationship of masters and men, in the end the market ruled, and the cash nexus mattered most, both ways.

[93] "The Philadelphia Machinery Market in 1904," *IA* 75 (5 Jan. 1905): 100–102 at p. 100. Cf. Committee on Industrial Relations, National Metal Trades Association, *Stabilizing Metal Trades Employment* (Chicago, 1931), pp. 17–19 – among firms surveyed then, almost two-thirds of their output could not be manufactured for stock; half thought that variations in employment were completely beyond their control, the rest mostly.

[94] USCIR, *Final Report*, Vol. 3, pp. 2858, 2821, 2824; PHIL1439 database. The metal worker's margin over other industrial workers shrinks if male earnings are examined separately – in 1900, from about 21 percent to just over 3 percent; 1905 results are broadly comparable – U.S. Department of the Interior, *Twelfth Census*, Vol. 8, pp. 784–91; U.S. Department of Commerce and Labor, *Census of Manufactures 1905 Part 2: States and Territories* (Washington, 1907), pp. 978–83.

[95] USCIR, *Final Report*, Vol. 3, p. 2898.

Most skilled workers (particularly the younger ones) chased the highest paying jobs, so their commitment to any particular employer was conditional, and any loyalty was, in Gerald Zahavi's terms, "negotiated." And employers could never afford to forget that labor was their biggest cost, after materials and fuel, and the only one whose price and value to them were potentially controllable. In this context, their labor strategies would always be shaped by their strong inclinations toward encouraging mutualistic relations with their workmen. But their behavior would also be driven and limited by the fact that, as Thomas E. Durban of the Erie City Iron Works put it, "Stripped of all sentimentality, it is a fact beyond dispute that labor is a commodity." They would never lose sight of this fundamental truth.[96]

2.8 CONCLUSION

Readers may acknowledge that our *dramatis personae* and their opinions were often quite fascinating but be inclined to write them off as possessing little greater significance. Perhaps Philadelphia was indeed a peculiar place, in business-historical terms – unusual for its continuing attachment to proprietary capitalist enterprise and rather antiquated managerial mores. In the words of one commentator, who ought to have known better and had best be left with a decent protective anonymity, were not its huge textile- and metal-manufacturing complexes mere "nooks and crannies" in American industrial development, outside of the main drift toward managerial capitalism, and therefore of merely antiquarian interest?

Some nooks; some crannies. It would be more accurate to think of Philadelphia as prototypical of a kind of industrial community generally neglected by business historians until recently, its metal-working firms and their owner-managers as representative of an entire class that lay at the foundation of the Open Shop movement. Philadelphia was certainly older, bigger, and more diverse than most other metal-manufacturing cities, but there was little else about its employer class, their beliefs, or the companies that they ran, that was exceptional.

---

[96] For workers' behavior, see Nelson, *Taylor and Scientific Management*, p. 145; Respondents 067, 079, Machinists Study, Palmer Paper; Zahavi, "Negotiated Loyalty: Welfare Capitalism and the Shoeworkers of Endicott Johnson, 1920–1940," *JAH* 70 (1983): 602–20; Rowland C. Berthoff, "The 'Freedom to Control' in American Business History," in David H. Pinkney and Theodore Ropp, eds., *A Festschrift for Frederick B. Artz* (Durham, N. C., 1964), pp. 158–80; Durban, "The Erie Strike Situation," in National Founders Association, *Proceedings of the 17th Annual Convention* (New York, 1913), pp. 40–55 at p. 46; cf. his "The Attitude of Employers Towards Hours and Wages," *The [Open Shop] Review* 13 (1916): 18–23, a reprint of an address originally made in 1902. Durban's analysis ran counter to the central thesis of the AFL's anti-injunction campaign.

If we look below the commanding heights of Baldwin, Cramp, Midvale, Disston, and Brill, what we see is a large group of middle-sized durable goods producers much like those that one could find in many other city-regions of the old American manufacturing belt. Their owners were recruited from the same ethno-religious backgrounds, increasingly they or their sons went to the same engineering colleges, they pursued similar career patterns, they joined the same professional bodies, they read the same trade papers, and they had the same problems, which they dealt with in similar ways. They were members of well-defined local business communities and of more amorphous regional or national groupings striving for coherence and expression around the turn of the century. Their individual companies had limited administrative and other resources, a weakness that they were in the habit of addressing by cooperative action. There were obstacles to success in these collective endeavors – localism, competitive rivalries, and the rampant pursuit of immediate self-interest. But these could be overcome, under the right circumstances. Heightened conflict with their skilled workmen was commonly the vital external stimulus that their organization-building efforts required. And this is what we will proceed to explore.[97]

[97] My understanding of this national context is largely derived from the work of Philip Scranton, esp. "Diversity in Diversity" and *Endless Novelty*. But see also Monte A. Calvert, *The Mechanical Engineer in America, 1883–1910: Professional Cultures in Conflict* (Baltimore, 1967) and Fred H. Colvin, *Sixty Years With Men and Machines: An Autobiography* (New York, 1947), for the engineer-entrepreneur and his ethos; Gutman, "Reality of the Rags-to-Riches Myth," John N. Ingham, *Making Iron and Steel: Independent Mills in Pittsburgh, 1820–1920* (Columbus, 1991), and Soltow, *Origins of Small Business*, for career patterns; Robert H. Wiebe, *Businessmen and Reform* (Cambridge, Mass., 1962), on the organizational impulse.

3

Laying the Foundations: Peace and War in the Metal Trades, c. 1890–1904

The aim of this chapter is to give an account of the origins and early development of the MMA both in its local context and as an illustration of the organizing process among American metal trades employers that was provoked by the labor relations crisis that began about a century ago. Just as Philadelphia metal manufacturers, for all their local peculiarities, were actually quite like their fellows in other industrial cities, so too the MMA that they created would take its place in the nationwide employers' anti-union movement that emerged. The MMA would have some exceptional features. It would also be unusually large and successful. But its beginnings, membership, structure, purposes, strategy, and tactics were very similar to those of the dozens of other local metal trades employers' associations, formed at about the same time, that made up the grass roots of the Open Shop movement for the next three decades. Addressing his members at their annual banquet in 1921 Staunton Bloodgood Peck, Link-Belt's Philadelphia manager and the MMA's newly elected president, spoke of "these associations, of which ours is typical." Nobody contradicted him then. Nor should we now. None of the other associations has a history that is as thoroughly documented as the MMA's, but there is no reason to believe that Peck was wrong.[1]

---

[1] Peck, Presidential Address 1921. Presidential addresses to the annual meetings in early December make up one of the major record series in the MMA Papers, I-1-5/11 and are referred to hereafter as [Name], PRES [Date]. Local metal trades associations were established in Chicago, Cincinnati, Cleveland, Columbus, Milwaukee, and Greater New York in 1900; Bridgeport, Buffalo, Dayton, Detroit, Kansas City, Minneapolis–St. Paul, Moline and Rock Island, Paterson, St. Louis, and Springfield [Ohio] in 1901; Denver, Pittsburgh, and Worcester in 1902; Boston, Elmira, Grand Rapids, Indianapolis, Rochester, Syracuse, Toronto, and Youngstown by 1903; Baltimore, Philadelphia, and Pittsfield by 1904; Toledo, Springfield [Massachusetts], and Hartford by 1907. NMTA, "Proceedings of the Fifth Annual Convention, New York, 1–2 April 1903," *Bull. NMTA* 2 (1903): 449–631, esp. pp. 466, 483, 487, 496, 502, 508,

3.1 BONDS OF ASSOCIATION

As we have seen, Philadelphia metal manufacturers were an independent-minded, individualistic bunch, and most of their companies operated in quite competitive markets. But they were also linked together in a variety of ways – by the facts that they were located in the same industrial neighborhoods and shared the same local labor markets; through networks of deals and contracts; less frequently, by the multiple directorships in a number of companies, or in the manufacturers' banks that met Philadelphia firms' needs for working capital, held by executives whose interests were not confined to a single firm[2]; and through shared activity in a wide variety of local organizations. The men and their businesses thus depended on, and sustained, a high degree of cooperation among themselves to solve common problems. There was a habit of collaborative behavior and the institutions to support it. These would provide the MMA with patterns to follow and solid foundations on which to build.

Metal manufacturers, like the rest of the Philadelphia bourgeoisie, were great "joiners." They were mostly members of the same few high-status Protestant churches and of a multitude of cultural societies, downtown social clubs, suburban sports and country clubs, fraternal associations, and other similar groups.[3] Affiliations such as these demonstrated the breadth and balance of businessmen's recreational interests, and the consequences of the growing suburbanization of bourgeois residence and leisure. But they did not necessarily bring metal manufacturers together often or in large numbers with those whose business interests were closest to their own. There were a few societies, however, that were much more central to Philadelphia's strictly manufacturing élite, and some to the metal manufacturers within it in particular.

514–15, 592; E. F. D[u Brul]., "The Labor Bureau," *Bull. NMTA* 3 (1904): 28; "Proceedings of the Sixth Annual Convention of the NMTA, Philadelphia, PA, 23–24 March, 1904," *Bull. NMTA* 3 (1904): 268; "Report of Acting Commissioner," *The Open Shop* 6 (1907): 216. The literature on the employers' movement is small but growing – see works cited in the Introduction, note 3.

[2] Cf. biographies of Godfrey Rebmann, pp. 125, 233, William Sauter, p. 184, and J. Henry Scattergood, p. 190, in Hartwell Stafford, ed., *Who's Who in Philadelphia in Wartime* (Philadelphia, 1920).

[3] Charles R. Deacon, "Clubs in Philadelphia," and Horace S. Fogel, "Sports of All Sorts," in Frank H. Taylor, ed., *The City of Philadelphia: A Compilation of Facts Supplied by Distinguished Citizens for the Information of Businessmen, Travellers, and the World at Large* (Philadelphia, 1900), pp. 125, 162–67; Thomas D. Richter, *Philadelphia: Its Contributions – Its Present – Its Future* (Philadelphia, 1929), pp. 57–61; *Boyd's Philadelphia Blue Book Élite Directory 1914* (Philadelphia, 1913); Stafford, ed., *Who's Who in Philadelphia in Wartime.* Cf. John S. Gilkeson, Jr., *Middle-Class Providence, 1820–1940* (Princeton, 1986), Ch. 4.

The clubs that drew the city's men of business together – to socialize and to take stands on issues of local "good government" and national high-tariff Republican politics – were the Union League and the Manufacturers. The latter especially provided an important downtown meeting place for metal manufacturers whose firms were scattered around the expanding periphery of the city. Its members organized themselves into sections – of which the most important were textiles and the metal trades – that gathered together regularly to discuss matters of common interest. This was one place where the idea of a separate Metal Manufacturers' Association grew: In 1900, George Cresson, one of its founders and early leaders, was the club's president.[4]

Even more central to the metal-manufacturing community were the Franklin Institute and the Engineers' and Foundrymen's Clubs. The Franklin Institute was first historically, and also in status. Metal manufacturers and other members of the city's community of applied scientists and engineer-entrepreneurs supported, financed, and directed the institute from the 1860s on, when Sellers, Bement, and others had saved it from collapse. They played a particularly important role in its Committees on Science and the Arts, which certified and diffused information about new technologies like Tinius Olsen's testing machines, and on Instruction, which oversaw the institute's schools of machine design, naval architecture, and technical drawing, with their hundreds of students. These schools, together with other local institutions like the city Board of Education's Manual Training Schools, the Drexel and Spring Garden Institutes, the Southwark Mechanics' Institute, and the Williamson Free School of the Mechanical Trades recently established in the suburbs, helped provide Philadelphia with the home-grown component of the technically educated skilled working class from which draftsmen, supervisors, and future managers and entrepreneurs could be recruited.[5]

---

4   Union League, *Chronicle of the Union League of Philadelphia 1862 to 1902* (Philadelphia, 1902); Maxwell Whiteman, *Gentlemen in Crisis: The First Century of the Union League of Philadelphia* (Philadelphia, 1975); for the Manufacturers' Club, see Philip Scranton and Walter Licht, *Work Sights: Industrial Philadelphia, 1890–1950* (Philadelphia, 1986), pp. 133–36 and testimony of John G. Gray (its secretary) and Cresson in U.S. Industrial Commission (hereafter USIC), *Report of the Industrial Commission on the Relations and Conditions of Capital and Labor Employed in Manufactures and General Business* (Washington, 1900), Vol. 14, pp. 205, 266.

5   Bruce D. Sinclair, *Philadelphia's Philosopher Mechanics: A History of the Franklin Institute 1824–1865* (Baltimore, 1974), esp. Chs. 10, 12; A. Michal McMahon and Stephanie A. Morris, eds., *Technology in Industrial America: The Committee on Science and the Arts of the Franklin Institute, 1824–1900* (Wilmington, Del., 1977); Committee Membership and "Annual Report of the Committee of Instruction," *JFI* 153 (1902): 78–80, 160, 148–49; Henry W. Spangler, "Training in the Engineering Trades in Philadelphia," *Procs. ECP* 26 (1909): 113–34, and J. W. Ledoux, "Educational," *J. ECP* 34 (1917): 212–28.

The Franklin Institute also continued to serve as a center for applied research in its own right and in collaboration with supporting companies – most notably the Sellers firm and its close associate, Midvale, of which Sellers had been president in the 1870s and early 1880s. These firms invested heavily in data collection and problem solving in areas like power transmission, metal cutting, and foundry technology, which were of general interest to metal manufacturers. The institute was also a focus for the collation of relevant research from the whole industrial world and the dissemination of this useful knowledge to its surrounding community.[6]

The Engineers' Club was established in 1877, and was among the first of its kind in the country. It started out as a kind of junior section of the Franklin Institute, which was dominated by the pioneer generation of engineer-entrepreneurs. As one of its founder members, Tabor's Wilfred Lewis, recalled in 1903, they were mostly "young men just out of college, striving to find chinks in the blank wall of industry on which to place their feet and begin to climb." The club was centered in West Philadelphia, just off the Penn campus where many of its members had studied, and was full of Baldwin's and Sellers's staff, who met regularly at one another's homes to exchange hospitality and ideas.[7]

By the turn of the century the club had grown to a membership of hundreds, including architects, civil, electrical, mining, and military engineers, and a minority of out-of-town members. But its core consisted of city-based mechanical engineers, many of them, like Lewis, members since the start of their careers and by then middle-aged entrepreneurs or managers themselves. It had acquired an attractive downtown clubhouse where professional and social meetings were held, and become an umbrella organization for local sections of the national engineering societies. It also accommo-

---

[6] For Sellers- and Midvale-sponsored research in the 1880s and 1890s, see Wilfred Lewis, "Experiments on the Transmission of Power By Gearing," *Trans. ASME* 7 (1885): 273–310, and "Experiments on the Transmission of Power By Belting," *Trans. ASME* 7 (1886): 549–97; H. L. Gantt, "Steel Castings," *Trans. ASME* 12 (1890): 710–24; and Frank B. Copley, *Frederick W. Taylor: Father of Scientific Management* (New York, 1923), Vol. 1, pp. 124, 221–22, 237–38, 438 and Vol. 2, pp. 114, 162–63, 170–71. Frederick Taylor's work on belting, shop management, etc., was an aspect of the Sellers and Midvale firms' commitment to the support of research, for which see also the Company's 1942 *The 75th Anniversary of the Midvale Co.* (Philadelphia, 1942), pp. 13, 15–16, 19–20, 29. For examples of the Franklin Institute's continuing role in the communication of knowledge, see A. E. Outerbridge, Jr., "Recent Progress in Metallurgy," *JFI* 160 (1905): 413–20. Outerbridge was both Professor of Metallurgy at the Franklin Institute and works manager at Sellers.

[7] "Addresses Presented at the Fortieth Anniversary Engineers' Club of Philadelphia," *J. ECP* 34 (1917): 234–40; "Twenty-Fifth Anniversary Banquet at the Union League," *Procs. ECP* 20 (1903): 3–41 at pp. 33–34; Ray M. Fuller, *"Through The Years": A Historical Outline of the Engineers' Club of Philadelphia. Founded December 17, 1877* (Philadelphia, 1970), p. 1.

dated other, smaller and less formal engineers' groups within the city – the T-Square Club for draftsmen, the Technische Verein for Germans, and the alumni associations of the out-of-town engineering schools where a minority of members had been trained. As for The University of Pennsylvania's own engineering school itself, the Junior Section of the club effectively was its alumni association, reflecting the close and mutually supportive relationship between the university and its city, which we will encounter later in this book.[8]

Finally, even more distinctively a metal manufacturers' association than either the Franklin Institute or the Engineers' Club came the Foundrymen's Association (later Club), established in 1891. It was similar in spirit to the many "guilds" formed by the city's small-scale merchants and manufacturers, whose concerns were trade regulation, the promotion of common interests, and the provision of a central place to meet and do business.[9]

One of these bodies, the Builders' Exchange, established in 1886, was a particularly important inspiration for Philadelphia foundrymen as they united to address the challenges of the 1890s. The key feature of the exchange was that it was both a trade guild and an association of organizations of master craftsmen with labor problems that they could only hope to solve together. This strategic necessity for collaboration resulted from the small size of individual firms, the ability of a strike against any subcontractor to tie up a job, and their journeymen's annoying combination of cross-craft solidarity, on the one hand, and a readiness to fight fellow workers and their employers in defense of conflicting claims to particular jobs, on the other. The exchange was also rooted in the social clubs of urban artisans and the lower middle class – the Freemasons and the Grand Army of the Republic in particular – of which most of its leaders were members. They seem to have shared the mutualistic and producerist ethos common among their generation and milieu. So, rather than uniting simply to fight their organized journeymen, they also hammered out collective agreements within the trade community that, their leader John S. Stevens boasted, were "an example of (*sic*) the trade in other cities. . . . Agreements to arbitrate and not to strike, to remain at work pending contracts, and for stated periods, were generally respected; so, also, were masters' agreements as to time, pay and treatment of men." The Philadelphia Builders reached out to

[8]   Carl Hering, "Address by the Retiring President," *Procs. ECP* 22 (1905): 87–113; Engineers' Club of Philadelphia, *Directory of the Engineers' Club of Philadelphia* (Philadelphia, 1903); "The New Club House," *Procs. ECP* 24 (1907): 349–55; "The Junior Section of the Engineers' Club of Philadelphia," *Procs. ECP* 25 (1908): 86–87; "Twenty-Fifth Anniversary Banquet," pp. 30, 32; "Editorial," *J. ECP* 34 (1917): 379.

[9]   Taylor, ed., *City of Philadelphia*, pp. 69–90, 197–98, 221, 225.

their fellows in other eastern cities, helping to create and lead the National Association of Builders that looked after the employers' interests by encouraging similar agreements elsewhere.[10]

Many Philadelphia metal manufacturers were Builders' Exchange members in the 1890s, particularly stove foundrymen, ornamental and structural iron workers, and brass foundrymen who made gas and water plumbing, and gas and electric lighting, fixtures. They were evidently impressed by its success in "elevating" its members' interests "by virtue of concentrated action, influence judiciously exercised, and a determination to maintain their rights, freely expressed."[11]

The Foundrymen's Association that they created fulfilled a variety of social and business functions similar to those that the Builders' Exchange discharged, looking after common problems of the trade – for example, relations with raw material suppliers and railroad rate-setting. The principal ostensible purpose of its monthly meetings was the reading and discussion of technical papers that made innovations in foundry practice and management methods available for the members' consideration. But the association had other less obvious although no less important functions, too. In times of threat or crisis, it was the place where employers met to plan their course of action. And at all times it was a focus for purposeful sociability among foundrymen, who operated in an industry laced together by countless more or less formal contractual relations between entrepreneurs and firms.[12]

These businesses were as often one another's customers as their competitors, for foundries contracted out specialized molding and pattern-making, or that which was beyond their production capacity, to their neighbors. In 1899, for example, North Bros. Mfg. Co.'s foundry was struck, tieing up a range of castings including parts for its own ice-cream freezers and meat choppers, and for at least nineteen other local firms, some of which had their own foundries too, producers of items as various as cigarette machines, lighting fixtures, textile machinery, plumbing fittings, and

[10]   Clement Tilman Congdon, *History of the Master Builders' Exchange of the City of Philadelphia from Its Organization in the Year 1886 to 1893* (Philadelphia, 1893), esp. pp. 1–11, 22–23, 28–30, 35, 117–21, 134–35 and "Portraits and Biographies"; Stevens (president), "The Sympathetic Strike: A Warning to Labor," *The Independent* 55 (1903): 1493–97, quote at p. 1496. For the National Association, see Robert M. Jackson, *The Formation of Craft Labor Markets* (Orlando, 1984), esp. Ch. 10.

[11]   William W. Morgan, "The Builders' Exchange," in Taylor, ed., *The City of Philadelphia*, pp. 89–90 at p. 89.

[12]   For examples of different sorts of meetings, see "Philadelphia Foundrymen's Association," *IA* 71 (15 January 1903): 16 (technical); same title, *IA* 85 (1910): 1397 (coordinating).

machine tools.[13] So the foundrymen needed to interact continuously with one another and with the local suppliers, equipment dealers, analytical chemists, and other independent businesses that together made for the ability of an industry of small-scale units to operate efficiently and flexibly. The association's regular social gatherings helped promote that everyday interaction, as well as encouraging the male bonding that promised to make its members' anti-labor solidarity more effective.

Meetings were usually accompanied by a meal, and on special occasions socializing became the primary objective. At the "vaudeville dinner" at the Manufacturers' Club on 4 May 1904, for example, the Philadelphia foundrymen entertained their Pittsburgh and New England fellows to a drink and a song, a joke and a smoke. According to Secretary Evans's account in *The Foundry* (the national trade journal), a good time was had by all. "[T]he blast went on at 6:30 and the pouring off [drinking and speechifying] continued for several hours and more," with twenty-eight toasts in quick succession, as "one of the shop rules provided that no molder [which was how the foundrymen referred to themselves at their leisure] was allowed more than three minutes to pour off, and no slopping over was permitted under any circumstances." ("Pouring off" was the trade term for filling a mold with molten metal, which had to be done quickly and safely. Given the foundrymen's frequent complaints about their workmen's chronic drunkenness, it is ironic to see association members apply the term to filling their own bellies with alcohol, and emptying their mouths of wind.)

The toasts were announced as " 'Pickings from the scrap pile' " and were interspersed with "a number of excellent vaudeville acts" and "satirical songs" including " 'World's Fair Foundry Exhibit Committee,' with music to 'Bedelia'," and " 'The Foundry Exhibit at the World's Fair, 1904,' music to 'When Johnnie Comes Marching Home'," of which the *libretti* unfortunately have not survived. The association's officers acted out parts in skits humorously depicting everyday foundry life: "Thomas Devlin appeared as 'The Old Man'; Howard Evans presided in the capacity of 'Cupola Boss'; Josiah Thompson, 'Labor Agitator'; George C. Davis, 'Original Alchemist'."

Even on an evening such as this bacchanalian frolic, the Foundrymen gave semiserious attention to the trade issues that bedevilled them and brought them together. "Stanley G. Flagg, Jr., explained why a foundryman was justified in taking orders at cost in order to keep his plant running. . . . S. G. H. Fitch was rather embarrassed in being requested to answer for the necessity of opening a keg when the foundry runs the first heat. . . . W. S. Hallowell told why foundrymen should agree on prices." One par-

[13] Committee of IMU Local No. 111 to North Bros. Mfg. Co., July 1899 (typed price list and grievances), in North Bros. Mfg. Co. Papers, Hagley Museum and Library (hereafter HML).

ticipant went so far as to lower the tone of the evening by being altogether sober, reminding his audience of the real breaches in the trade community of their fond imaginings, which they had recreated with booze and good fellowship and by the exclusion of the journeyman molders who caused them so many headaches:

He asked how many foundrymen took sufficient interest in their molders to extend sympathy and assistance in time of trouble. How many visited their men at their homes who were kept in on account of illness, and how many sent around the pay envelope every week when their faithful employes (*sic*) were unable to earn a livelihood. . . . [A] little more of this sort of attention on the part of employers would greatly minimize strikes if not preventing their occurrence entirely and the National Founders' Association would not be a necessity.[14]

But of course, they believed it was. After all, they had helped to create it. Their Foundrymen's Association had not confined its work to its own locality. Like the Builders' Exchange it had stimulated the creation of, first, other local associations and, second, a national body. During the depression of 1893–97 they had become seriously concerned about the "machine question" – that is, the difficulty of getting skilled men to operate the new molding machines then coming into use efficiently or at all, thereby denying foundrymen one means of cutting costs. Realizing that no purely local solution was possible for a problem that was national in scale, the Philadelphia foundrymen set about spreading the gospel, and the burden, of entrepreneurial self-defense. Cincinnati, rapidly replacing Philadelphia as the most important machine-tool producer, was the site of the International Molders Union (IMU)'s headquarters. Its foundrymen were the first to follow Philadelphia's lead in 1893. By 1896, there were three further active associations in the midwest, the New England machine-tool district, and Pittsburgh. Their representatives met in Philadelphia that May and set up the American Foundrymen's Association (AFA), which immediately focused on "plans for protecting the members from the unfair exactions of labor organizations" as well as its longer term business, the encouragement of managerial and technological innovation in a traditional industry.[15]

The National Founders' Association (NFA) was the product of those plans, dedicated single-mindedly to handling those labor relations matters that gave the foundrymen their most pressing common interest. Philadelphians were key activists within it from the beginning. William Pfahler, of the Abram Cox Stove Co., was its first president, and chief strategist. They

14 Howard Evans, "The Philadelphia Foundrymen's Association," *The Foundry* 24 (1904): 189–90.
15 "A Foundrymen's Association," *Journal of the Independent Brotherhood of Machinery Molders* 4:12 (Dec. 1891): 3; Clarence E. Bonnett, *History of Employers' Associations in the United States* (New York, 1956), pp. 344, 357, 379, 389, 398, 405–06.

lived in a city where they and their forebears had been clashing with their organized journeymen since the 1850s, within their individual firms and through collective action. They had forged temporary alliances as the need arose, which formed and dissolved as the tide of labor flowed and ebbed. Organized class conflict was just as much a tradition of the Philadelphia metal-manufacturing community as was the ambitious journeyman's pursuit of the royal road to a foremanship or independence, or the patriarchal employer's concern for his men.[16]

By the time the Philadelphia Foundrymen heard their speaker's homily, they had more than a decade of permanent local organization behind them, and five years' experience working through the NFA to deal with the latest and most threatening uprising of their skilled workers. They were prominent in both bodies – the NFA and its offspring, the National Metal Trades Association (NMTA) – that middle-sized American metal manufacturers like themselves had created to respond to that challenge. Locally and nationally they had experimented with a negotiatory strategy like that of the Builders' Exchange, and by 1904 they had concluded that it would not serve their purposes.

Because of the nature of the firms that they ran, and of their product markets, metal manufacturers could not – nor did they wish to – escape dependence on their skilled men. But they believed that they could not afford the consequences if the ground rules of that relationship were no longer to be set by themselves. Self-interest and shared convictions about their rights as owners, employers, and managers inclined them to abandon compromise at the earliest opportunity. Experience in organization-building and the ties of belonging that bound their community together gave them the resources for successful self-assertion.

In the next section of this chapter, we will strengthen the connections between local developments and the national institutional context sketched out above, and maintain that interplay through the remainder of this account of Philadelphia's metal-manufacturers' road toward lasting engagement in the Open Shop war.

3.2 THE CHALLENGE OF LABOR

The opening years of the twentieth century witnessed an aborted revolution in labor relations in American manufacturing. Aided by low unemployment and booming product markets, workers organized to extract a collective advantage from an unprecedentedly strong bargaining position. Their opportunistic aggression, demanding and increasingly often winning

[16] See Edgar Edgar B. Cale, "The Organization of Labor in Philadelphia" (Ph.D. diss., University of Pennsylvania, 1940).

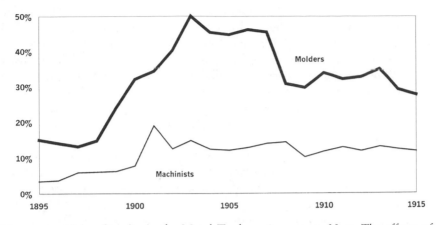

Figure 3.1. Union Density in the Metal Trades, 1895–1915. *Note:* The effects of the end of the NMTA–IAM relationship in 1901, the New York Agreement in 1904, and the 1907–08 and prewar recessions. *Source:* As in footnote 18.

higher wages, shorter hours, and employer recognition of their organizations and acceptance of their working rules, threw employers onto the defensive. The number of strikes and strikers about tripled from 1896 to 1903; the total number of union members about quadrupled.[17]

At the center of this "amazing storm" lay the metal-working industries, terrain that was contested in many manufacturing cities between some of America's strongest, most dynamic craft unions and employer communities quite like Philadelphia's. Between 1897 and 1903, the IMU's membership grew from 11,544 to 52,059, or from about one-seventh to more than one-half of the skilled foundry labor force. The International Association of Machinists (IAM)'s numbers increased from about 15,000 to roughly 50,000, the latter figure representing more than one-sixth of their much larger, more rapidly growing organizational territory among the country's machine shops (see Figure 3.1). Overall, union membership in the metal and metal products sector more than quadrupled, and it actually doubled between 1900 and 1902 alone.[18]

---

[17] U.S. Department of Commerce, Bureau of the Census, *Historical Statistics of the United States, Colonial Times to 1970* (Washington, 1976), Series D 86, Unemployment (p. 135), D 795 (p. 169) and D 845 (p. 172), Earnings in Manufacturing, D 940, Union Membership (p. 177), D 977–985, Industrial Conflict (p. 179); Paul K. Edwards, *Strikes in the United States 1881–1974* (Oxford, 1981), esp. pp. 86–91; Bruno Ramirez, *When Workers Fight: The Politics of Industrial Relations in the Progressive Era, 1898–1916* (Westport, 1978), pp. 9–11.

[18] Frederick W. Smith, *The Amazing Storm: Business Answers to the Labor Question 1900–1920* (New York, 1986). IMU membership from William Huston Chartener, "The Molders' and Foundry Workers' Union: A Study of Union Development"

How were employers to meet this challenge? Proprietary capitalists were in the front line of the fight, not giant corporations like International Harvester, U.S. Steel, or – in Philadelphia – Baldwin, Cramp, and Disston. Middle-sized and smaller businesses were both more vulnerable to their skilled workers and much less well endowed with the resources needed to pursue an aggressive, autonomous anti-union strategy. Their owners and managers, like George Cresson or even Charles Harrah, were also uncertain how to react, unsure about the attractions and pitfalls of the various policies on offer.

In this difficult situation, they drew together for mutual support and looked around for working models to imitate, so that 1898–1903 witnessed a profoundly interesting period of policy experimentation by proprietary firms in metal-manufacturing centers across the United States. They were seeking answers to two great, interconnected questions: How could they build durable, effective employers' associations on a membership base of competitive, individualistic companies? And how should the members of those associations deal with the challenge of labor – by cooperating, not just with one another, but, for a limited range of purposes, with skilled workers' unions too, in search of a *modus vivendi*; or by combining to beat the latter just as thoroughly as the giant firms had already managed? Belligerency seemed dauntingly difficult and even dangerous; compromise was more immediately attractive. Middle-sized employers therefore joined together defensively to reestablish equilibrium between themselves and their skilled workers. On the basis of a balance of organized strength they could go on to create an edgy, temporary "armed truce" relationship at the least, or ideally a civilized, durable mutual accord based on reciprocal recognition, identification of shared interests, and two-way trading of favors and concessions.[19]

There were persuasive precedents for what came to be known as the "trade agreement" system and "collective bargaining," the process at its heart. In the United States, agreements regulated relations between masters and men in the building and printing trades in many cities; they had brought the promise of peace and stability to the heart of the bituminous coal industry since 1897; and they governed wages, hours, and working conditions in a few skill-dependent national-market industries.[20]

(Ph.D. diss., Harvard University, 1952), p. 339; IAM data from Mark Perlman, *The Machinists: A New Study in American Trade Unionism* (Cambridge, Mass., 1961), pp. 31, 33, 206, 215; skilled labor force numbers from the U.S. Department of Labor, Bureau of Apprenticeship, *The Skilled Labor Force: A Study of Census Data on the Craftsman Population of the United States, 1870–1950: Technical Bulletin No. T-140* (Washington, 1954), pp. 15–16. Overall sectoral data from U.S. Bureau of the Census, *Historical Statistics*, Series D 955, Union Membership, p. 178.

[19] Jeffrey Haydu, "Trade Agreement versus Open Shop: Employers' Choices before World War One," *Industrial Relations* 28 (1989): 159–73.

[20] Jackson, *Formation of Craft Labor Markets*; John R. Bowman *Capitalist Collective Action: Competition, Cooperation, and Conflict in the Coal Industry* (New York,

"Machinery foundrymen" – proprietors of machine-building plants that included both foundries and machine shops, and whose employees therefore included the foundry crafts (molders, core-makers, and pattern-makers) as well as machinists and other skilled metalworkers – followed the example of one of these pioneers when they set up the NFA in 1898, and the NMTA in 1899. Both organizations tried to reproduce the relationship constructed in the 1890s, after a generation of conflict, between the Stove Founders National Defense Association and the IMU.[21]

Both failed. The attempt to create, almost at the outset of their relationship, the basis for stable compromise between dynamic, antagonistic organizations that had to deliver immediate benefits to their recently acquired, results-oriented memberships, was doomed to disappointment. The objectives of the parties were wholly incompatible. Employers looked to the NFA and NMTA for protection of their traditional freedom to manage, to which they sought the IMU's and IAM's consent in return for some economic concessions, limited recognition, and lessened hostility. Molders and machinists meanwhile pursued higher wages, shorter hours, shop-level recognition of their unions, job reservation for union members only, and the right to a voice – even a veto – on a wide range of vital work-related issues. These included the number of apprentices, the employment of semiskilled helpers, the utilization or manning of equipment, the operation of payment systems, the determination of a "fair day's work," the hiring and firing of workers, and the settlement of workplace grievances.

The NMTA's celebrated "Murray Hill" agreement with the IAM only lasted from May 1900 until May 1901. It ended when the Machinists struck and the employers, educated by their short but unhappy experience of the impossibility of dealing with a booming, democratic, job-controlling union as bargaining-partner, decided to assert and defend their right to run their own factories without further interference from it. The NMTA's 1901 Declaration of Principles was the ideological foundation of what the association rapidly turned into a crusade for the "open shop" – that is, one where, in theory, employees could find work irrespective of union

1989); David Brody, "Market Unionism in America: The Case of Coal," in his *In Labor's Cause: Main Themes on the History of the American Worker* (New York, 1993), pp. 131–74; Ramirez, *When Workers Fight*, Part I; George E. Barnett, "National and District Systems of Collective Bargaining in the United States," *QJE* 26 (1912): 425–43.

[21] John P. Frey and John R. Commons, "Conciliation in the Stove Industry," *Bulletin of the Bureau of Labor,* Vol. 12, No. 62 (Jan. 1906): 124–96; George E. Barnett, "Report on the Agreement Between the Molders' International Union and the Stove Founders National Defense Association," (21 Dec. 1914), in Melvyn Dubofsky, ed., *Research Collections on Labor Studies: The Wilson Administration and American Workers: U.S. Commission on Industrial Relations* (hereafter USCIR) *1912–1915: Unpublished Records* (Frederick, 1985), Reel 9; and Russell Bauder, "National Collective Bargaining in the Foundry Industry," *American Economic Review* 24 (1934): 462–76.

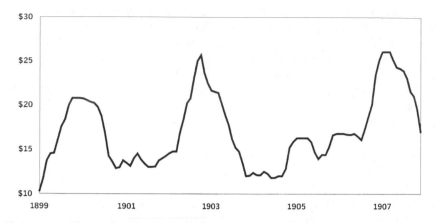

Figure 3.2. The Roller Coaster of Prosperity: The Foundry Sector, 1898–1907 – Southern Foundry Pig, per Ton. *Note:* The price of the basic raw material bought on short contracts is the best business barometer for the foundry sector. The Philadelphia Molders made their breakthrough at a cyclical peak in 1900, reached their two "acceptable" agreements during a mild recession in 1901–02, made the gains that soured Foundrymen on the relationship at the next peak in 1903, and were whipped in the next two recessions. *Source:* "Fluctuations in the Prices of Iron and Steel Products 1898–1907," *Iron Age* 81 (1908): 144.

affiliation, their relations with their employers grounded in freedom of *individual* contract.[22]

The NFA's road to the same destination was longer and more tortuous. This was not because its members were any less committed to the defense of their interests, rights, and authority than their machine-shop brethren. Machinery foundrymen were at the heart of both organizations, whose outlooks and strategic preferences overlapped even more than did their membership. It was principally because the IMU was so much stronger than the IAM. The costs of an open breach with it during a period of low unemployment and tight product markets (see Figures 3.2 and 3.3) would therefore have been much higher. The arguments for caution, delay, and persistence with the negotiatory approach, if only to buy time and peace,

[22] For the Murray Hill Agreement, see esp. Marguerite Green, *The National Civic Federation and the American Labor Movement 1900–1925* (Washington, 1956), pp. 21–23; Jeffrey Haydu, *Between Craft and Class: Skilled Workers and Factory Politics in the United States and Britain, 1890–1922* (Berkeley, 1988), pp. 78–85; David Montgomery, *The Fall of the House of Labor: The Workplace, the State, and American Labor Activism, 1865–1925* (Cambridge, 1987), Chs. 4–6, esp. pp. 210–13, 259–69; Perlman, *Machinists,* pp. 24–27; Ramirez, *When Workers Fight,* Ch. 6.

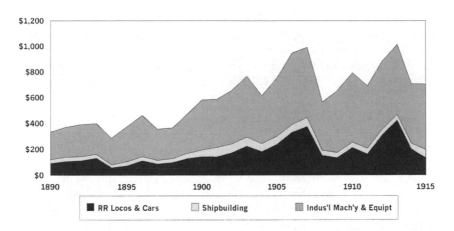

Figure 3.3. Output of the Heavy Capital Goods Industries, in Millions of 1913 Dollars, 1890–1915. *Note:* These three sectors provided the major national markets for Philadelphia metal working before the war. The severity of the 1907–08 and 1914–15 recessions is very evident. *Source:* U.S. Department of Commerce, *Historical Statistics*, series P359, P360, P353, adjusted using price index P373.

were commensurately powerful. For this reason their "New York Agreement" of 1899 remained in place until 1904.[23]

Philadelphia metal manufacturers were involved with both national employers' organizations from the very outset. They shared the same labor relations problems as their fellows in other cities, tried the same solutions, experienced the same frustrations, and were gripped by the same anxieties. Finally, in the early winter of 1903, as the NFA–IMU relationship stumbled, deadlocked, toward its final collapse, they decided to take advantage of the return of unemployment to shake themselves free of the Molders and other, weaker unions. They followed the lead of the NMTA, and in particular of its members in other skill-dependent machine-building communities (Cincinatti, Ohio, and Worcester, Massachusetts), creating a local association to complement the work of the national bodies and to prepare to wage industrial war.

3.3 THE ROAD TO REACTION

Philadelphia foundrymen, as we have seen, were active organization-builders even before the labor relations crises of the long boom, 1897–1903.

---

[23] The best source is Margaret L. Stecker, "The New York Agreement: A Study of Collective Bargaining Between the Iron Molders' Union and the National Founders' Association, March, 1899–November, 1904," (Jan. 27, 1915), in Dubofsky, ed., *USCIR Unpublished Records*, Reel 2.

Philadelphia was also, not accidentally, the site of the NFA's first and most serious attempt to handle locally the contentious questions that national negotiations repeatedly addressed but never settled. The intention was to provide uniform local wages, hours, and working conditions; to reach compromises on those substantive issues where national agreement was presently impossible; and to complement the New York Agreement's inadequate grievance procedures.[24]

The first, tentative deal between the Philadelphia members of the NFA and the IMU came in 1900. The IMU's Local 15 (machinery molders) was growing rapidly, recovering members and strength lost in the depression and the internecine strife that had preceded it. Philadelphia had been a center of "dual unionism" while the Knights of Labor existed, and the IMU's rival Brotherhood of Machinery Molders, a Knights national trade district, had recruited heavily. But by 1900 Local 15 had put those troubles behind it, and it could no longer be ignored.

Philadelphia Molders and Founders reached a truce serving both sides' immediate interests. It provided for a ten-hour day, overtime, and a $2.75 minimum daily rate for molders. According to the union journal, "Many of the foundrymen had but recently joined the ranks of the N.F.A., they were unfamiliar with trade agreements, and in several instances were bitterly opposed to any form of negotiation ... which recognized the [union] as a factor." Still, a strike was avoided, and NFA officers prevailed upon their members to get them to pay the agreed minimum. Some refused, but still the IMU did not strike them, partly because of a lack of confidence in its own recently and imperfectly organized members, but also "in view of the efforts being made by officers of the N.F.A. to establish a better understanding and work of education among their members which they had undertaken with a view of making the trade agreement a success in Philadelphia."[25]

In March 1901 the parties met again. Their aim was to build on the previous contract and to give local effect to the spirit of a recent compromise agreement ending a big, long, costly, and bloody strike in Cleveland, Ohio. This had been a trial of strength and a test of principle for the IMU and the NFA; William Pfahler and Antonio Pessano, of the George V. Cresson Co., leaders of the Philadelphia founders, had helped settle it. Back in Philadelphia, and with the help of a conciliatory IMU vice president, John P. Frey, they then produced a remarkably long and detailed agreement, with no changes in hours or wages – only this time, most NFA members paid up without difficulty – in return for which the founders secured important

24   Stecker, "New York Agreement," esp. pp. 119–20.
25   "Chronicler,"*IMJ* 36 (1900): 86–87; L. M. Shalkop, "Philadelphia and Vicinity," *IMJ* 36 (1900): 146–47; J. M. Williams, "Marching Onward," *IMJ* 36 (1900): 213–14; "The Philadelphia Strike," *IMJ* 42 (1906): 32–35 at pp. 32–33 [quotes].

concessions. Pfahler was proud of the resulting accord, which "involve[d] so many points of imaginary difference, and show[ed] the possibility of arranging even the smallest difference by conference." The NFA agreed: Philadelphia's was "[p]robably the first approach towards an agreement which carried with it fair play to everyone."[26]

The agreement traded off most of the IMU's claims to job control in exchange for extensions to workers' and the union's recognized rights. The Molders won guaranteed overtime pay, at time and a half, or double time on Sundays and four legal holidays; some hope that the Founders would play ball by paying the agreed minimum wage, and not chisel away at piece-rates, or make excessive demands for output; a grievance procedure whose first stage was a personal interview with the employer, and then local union intervention, which gave the business agent a clear role within the shop; and a rule that a warning should precede disciplinary dismissal, with investigation by the NFA as a further safeguard. In return, skilled workmen gave up their attempt to include any but themselves within the scope of the agreed uniform minimum wage, abandoning their less-skilled co-workers. They abandoned their traditional claims to regulate conditions of work unilaterally. They specifically undertook to deliver a "fair and honest day's work," and to impose no "[a]rbitrary limitations" of output, against the customs of their trade. They further accepted management's right to install new machinery, to staff it with less-skilled workers and otherwise to run it as they wished, and to introduce and control incentive payment systems.[27]

However advantageous to the founders on questions of working practices it might appear, there was real mutuality in this agreement. The Molders were starting out from a weak position. A period of stability, even under an apparently unsatisfactory contract, would give their insecure organization time to grow and become entrenched. Their leaders, at least, saw the benefit of formalized collective bargaining, particularly in the way that it laid down ground rules for holding combative union and employers' association members in check. Both sides "deprecate[d] strikes and lock-outs, and desire[d] to discourage such drastic measures among the members

---

[26] "The Cleveland Conference," *IMJ* 37 (1901): 144–50 at p. 144; Stecker, "New York Agreement," pp. 119–20, 247–48; "Chronicler," *IMJ* 37 (1901): 689–90; William H. Pfahler, "Co-operation of Labor and Capital," *Annals* 20:1 (July 1902): 45–58 at p. 51; NFA, *Food for Thought* (Detroit, 1903), p. 3.

[27] NFA, *Food for Thought*, pp. 56–59 [quote p. 58]; for the national context of IMU-NFA bargaining, see F. W. Hilbert, "Trade Union Agreements in the Iron Molders' Union," in Hollander and Barnett, eds., *Studies in American Trade Unionism*, Ch. 8, pp. 252–53; Margaret L. Stecker, "The Founders, the Molders, and the Molding Machine," *QJE* 32 (1918): 278–308 at pp. 288, 296–97; Frank T. Stockton, *The International Molders Union of North America* (Baltimore, 1921), esp. p. 147; U.S. Commissioner of Labor, *Regulation and Restriction of Output: Eleventh Special Report* (Washington, 1904), pp. 149–78, esp. pp. 149–50.

of their respective associations." Both "agreed that all unfair or unjust shop practices" were "to be viewed with disfavor" by both the NFA and the IMU, "and any attempt on the part of either party . . . to force" any such practice "upon the other" was "to be the subject of rigid investigation by the officers of the respective associations; and if upon careful investigation such charges are sustained against the party complained of, then such party is to be subject to discipline." Any unresolved disputes – but only those – could be left to the New York Agreement procedures. For the next three years both sides tried to make their relationship work and, give or take a few inevitable troubles, it did.[28]

The message from Philadelphia seemed to be that the Founders could get much of the substance of the NFA's desired relationship with the molders through local negotiation. But the agreement was silent on two crucial issues: union membership and the control of entry to the trade. Looking backward seven years later, and four years after the Philadelphia Founders cut loose from the IMU's restrictions, William S. Hallowell, in 1902 the NFA's district chairman, and by 1908 president of the MMA, reminded his members of what those silences had meant: "In all iron foundries, with the exception of the Baldwin Locomotive Works, Midvale Steel Company, and Cramp's Ship Yard, every molder and core-maker employed was compelled to be a member of the Iron Molders Union." Having an all-union shop meant accepting some union rules and customs, whatever the agreement said. And the one to which the Philadelphia molders clung most tenaciously was their limitation on numbers of apprentices. National union "law" only permitted one for every eight journeymen, plus one for the shop.[29]

Apprentices represented the challenge of low-wage labor: They worked alongside journeymen, on the same work, but at lower rates, whether paid by the piece or by the day. If trained in excessive numbers, they threatened to oversupply the labor market and make it that much harder to maintain and enhance molders' pay and conditions. The founders wanted the freedom to dilute the skilled component of the labor force at will, to give themselves a cheap and adequate labor supply in rush times, and to gain an improved bargaining position vis-à-vis their journeymen at all times. This, understandably, the IMU was not prepared to accept.[30]

The Philadelphia molders were protected against this scourge. The local Founders, on the other hand, were strapped for labor in a time of rising demand. The result? Evidently, for all of the apparent concessions of the

[28] NFA, *Food for Thought*, p. 59; "The Philadelphia Strike," p. 33.
[29] Hallowell, "Your Association – What It Has Done to Improve Industrial Conditions," Banquet Address, 9 March 1908, p. 2, MMAP II-3-5.
[30] Frey and Commons, "Conciliation in the Stove Industry," p. 163; Stockton, *International Molders Union*, Ch. 12.

agreement, a powerful union voice in the shops and a nice, tight labor market, permitting continuing advances toward shorter hours, higher wages, and the goal of pay equality for all journeymen, over the next two years.

The Philadelphia Agreement lasted from 1901 until 1904. During its life, the Molders' minimum wages advanced one-sixth, and their standard working hours declined from ten to nine. There were no other changes in the contract, although Local 15 opposed the continued inclusion of the objectionable clauses formally recognizing employers' rights. Nevertheless, despite the machinery molders' increasing strength, they could not negotiate, and did not fight for, any concessions.[31]

These were comparatively good, if not untroubled, years for Philadelphia foundrymen. They invested in new premises and equipment to increase their production capacity. Few disputes with their molders went as far as a strike, and those that occurred were quickly settled by the intervention of IMU national officials. Employers grumbled about informal but nonetheless effective IMU job controls, but on one issue of contract interpretation they prevailed. In the 1903 bargaining round, the one local that had maintained a formal limit on piece-workers' earnings, something utterly inconsistent with the letter and spirit of the agreement, abandoned it, after its president was promoted to the foremanship of a prominent local foundry.[32]

So, while tight labor and product market conditions persisted, and the NFA continued its fruitless pursuit of IMU acceptance of its terms for a lasting national relationship, the Philadelphia Agreement endured, and local foundrymen learned to work together in new ways for common ends. This experience built on, and strengthened, the numerous social and business links that they already had among themselves.

The NFA operated through a district committee responsible for handling disputes and negotiations for the city and its hinterland. Philadelphia was the heart of the NFA's District Three: It made up about two-thirds of the membership, a reflection of its size and of the strength of the Molders' organizations that it had to face. After the negotiation of their first local agree-

[31] "The Philadelphia Strike," *IMJ* 42 (1906): 32–35; "The Chronicler," *IMJ* 38 (1902): 475, 551.

[32] See regular weekly reports "Philadelphia Machinery Market" in the *Iron Age*, e.g., 71:10 (5 March 1903): 40–41, and annual review, "The Philadelphia Machinery Market in 1903," Ibid., 73:1 (7 Jan. 1904): 24–25; "Philadelphia and Vicinity," *IMJ* 38 (1902): 860–61; for strike reports, see "The Chronicler," *IMJ* 37 (1901): 152–53 (at the William Sellers foundry, against an "offensive" timekeeper); "The Chronicler," *IMJ* 38 (1902): 82–83 (at the Philadelphia Roll & Machine Co., where molders refused to work on patterns sent in from a – struck – out of town foundry); Ibid., p. 305 (at Stanley Flagg & Co., to enforce the molders' right to control "a device which the company called a molding machine"); NFA, *Food for Thought*, inside back cover; "Correspondence," *IMJ* 39 (1903): 205.

ments, its NFA members discovered that they had to collaborate ever more closely with one another to administer the contract and work out and defend a common position at the annual bargaining sessions.[33]

In preparation for the 1902 negotiations, Philadelphia NFA members pooled information on the size and distribution of their workforces, methods of payment, and actual wages paid, "[i]nasmuch as the Molders will doubtless present various reasons to sustain their position," and employers needed to be ready to reply in kind. To counter the Molders' demands, which they deemed "without precedent and unfair," and to judge the likely effect of any concessions, the foundrymen's negotiators needed data about members' labor costs that the latter had previously jealously protected, even from one another. So they took a step away from competitive secrecy and toward employer solidarity, which paid off immediately. They managed to shave the 10 percent wage increase the IMU requested down to an acceptable level of between 5 and 6 percent. Evidently mutual trust, thorough organization, and collective action were worth the effort. More than twenty years later, William Hallowell looked back on this episode as the beginning of the movement that led to a permanent local employers' association.[34]

The 1902 survey helps us to see what kind of local firm joined the metal trades employers' vanguard. There were about thirty of them, in a city with at least twice that number of foundries, and more than three times as many if machine-building establishments with molding departments are added to the total. Twenty-two companies replied to the questionnaire. They employed just under 600 skilled bench and floor molders, almost equal numbers of each class. Two-thirds of the former were piece-workers, two-thirds of the latter (producing smaller numbers of heavier and more complex castings) day-workers. Only two companies paid day-workers less than the minimum agreed with the IMU ($2.75), indicating that the local agreement had largely succeeded in putting a floor below wage-rates. But, despite employers' accusations about the leveling effect of standard or minimum wages, there was still a wide variation in earnings within and between firms. Most piece-workers earned substantially above the minimum, up to $4.75 a day for the highest paid men. Respondents employed about twenty-seven skilled foundry craftsmen, on average – ranging from about a dozen to roughly ninety.[35]

---

[33]   NFA membership figures from NFA9905 database (see Appendix), supplemented by typewritten list in MMAP II-4-41.

[34]   Hallowell to Earl Sparks, 6 Oct. 1924, enclosing copy of NFA circular of 12 June 1902, in MMAP II-4-43.

[35]   Handwritten table, MMAP II-4-41; foundries and firms with molding departments from 1902FACT database and *Penton's Foundry List* (Cleveland, 1908). This average is very close to the mean number of molders (29) in the 1,588 plants involved in 273

TABLE 3.1 The NFA's Philadelphia Membership, 1902

Sector	Members	Employ	Ave.	Others	Employ	Ave.
Brass & Bronze	2	266	133	31	793	26
Iron & Steel	11	1,122	102	19	1,166	61
Durable Goods	16	4,938	309	193	6,869	36
TOTALS	29	6,326	218	243	8,828	36

Source: As in footnote 35.

The NFA's questionnaire results are actually somewhat misleading, partly because only about three-quarters of its Philadelphia members replied, but mostly because those that did just gave information about the skilled component even of their molding workforces. This was all that interested the NFA (and the IMU). Supplementing these data with recorded employment figures for 1902, we get a better impression of the importance of NFA members among the city's heavy metal manufacturers. NFA members' skilled molders only made up a minority, in some cases a very small one, of their total blue-collar payroll: The smallest association foundry had 40 employees, while the largest machine-builder (Niles-Bement-Pond) had 1,037; the mean employment for NFA members stood at 218, and the median firm had 120.

Only two of them were brass foundries, both marine engineering shops employing at least one-quarter of the city's nonferrous molding workforce (see Table 3.1). The NFA, like the IMU, was primarily an organization for the iron trade; in the brass trade, both shared (or, in the IMU's case, contested) their jurisdiction – with the NMTA and the Brass Workers' Union, respectively. The NFA members were two of the largest nonferrous foundries in the city; the average size of their establishments was more than five times greater than that of the average nonmember's. Among jobbing iron and steel foundries, the NFA's eleven members employed almost one-half of the city total. Here, too, the NFA's were the larger enterprises, on average – more than one-half as big again as nonmembers. Finally, sixteen were producers of durable goods and machinery – boilers, steam engines, elevators, hardware, hand tools, machine-tools, and machinery for paper-making, wood-working, and the textile industry, amongst others – rather

recorded strikes between 1903 and 1913–NFA, *Summary of Union Molders' Strikes: 1904 to 1909 Inclusive* (Detroit, 1910), *Summary of Union Molders' Strikes: 1910–1911* (Detroit, 1911), NFA, *Proceedings of 16th Annual Convention* (New York, 1912), p. 29 and *Proceedings of 17th Annual Convention* (New York, 1913), p. 11. These data included non-NFA firms. NFA members were generally larger, employing an average of about 50 foundry workers each between 1904 and 1914 – see Figure 3.4.

than foundry operators per se. Their foundries were parts of establishments employing 42 percent of the total labor force in their respective industrial categories. They were the heart of the NFA, and were, in Philadelphia terms, large businesses – they were almost nine times bigger than nonmembers in the same sectors.

Clearly, employers' association membership, even in this most strongly organized trade, attracted only a minority of potential recruits, including neither the whales nor the minnows of their respective industries. As Sellers treasurer Justus Schwacke – by then its president – said of the NMTA's very similar profile in 1911, "the most sympathy and co-operation is at present to be expected . . . from what may be conveniently termed the middle class of employers which form the bulk and mainstay of like associations."[36]

No local metal-working giants joined, except the foundry departments of the Cramp Ship & Engine Building Works and the Neafie & Levy Ship-yard. The fact that the two shipyards felt it worthwhile to join the NFA testifies to the threat that the IMU, alone among the metal crafts, posed to their open-shop status. Possibly a recent strike at Cramp's – the only one it suffered before the plague of stoppages during World War I – had affected their attitude toward the benefits of employers' collective action.[37]

In general, companies that counted their workers by the thousand had the strength to remain nonunion without needing to cooperate formally with the middle-sized and smaller local firms – if any – in their industries. Large enterprises that were already "open shops" did not share the same labor relations problems as unionized establishments. So why should they bear the lion's share of the operating costs of an association whose raison d' être at the time was to spread and lighten the burden of working under union conditions? Why should they subject their corporate policy-making to a measure of collective control, and thereby dilute their cher-ished autonomy?

Thus their decision not to throw in their lot with their neighbors made eminently good sense. Alba Johnson of Baldwin insisted in 1914 that "we never affiliate with any other employers of labor for any purpose what-ever." William Barba of Midvale explained why: "We have refrained from membership in every organization which could in any way be construed as

---

[36] NMTA, *Synopsis of Proceedings of the 13th Annual Convention* (New York, 1911), p. 8. Cf. Table 5.1.

[37] "Philadelphia Strike," p. 33; Harry Hand and Edward Keenan testimony in USCIR, *Final Report*, Vol. 3, pp. 2887, 2878; Thomas R. Heinrich, *Ships For the Seven Seas: Business, Labor, and New Technologies in the Philadelphia Shipbuilding Industry* (Baltimore, 1996), pp. 145–47. As many as 8,640 of the shipbuilders' 8,819 em-ployees have been excluded from the above totals: The Cramp brass foundry, with 179 men, was a geographically separate establishment making its own return, but Neafie & Levy's was not.

united to operate collectively." It had briefly joined the NFA, but "They sought to use collective means to influence a group of employers with reference to labor and labor matters. We prefer to be absolutely independent from any such association." Even Schwacke's company had "never been favorable to entering employers' organizations, and we did not do so until the very last minute."[38]

The ideology of the Open Shop required individualism on the part of employees; the practice of the large, autonomous, proudly nonunion firm displayed a fine example of corporate individualism for them to follow. It was also good public relations: The power of large firms was suspect in the Progressive Era in any case. The common suspicion that their iron resolve to remain nonunion underpinned the Open Shop movement could be partly allayed by steadfast denials that they had anything to do with it.[39]

Small-scale foundrymen, who did not have the resources to resist IMU pressure, even with the concerted assistance of their middle-sized brethren, were similarly unlikely to join the NFA. One-half of the jobbing foundries in Philadelphia, employing about one-eighth of the total labor force, were smaller than the smallest local firm that joined the NFA (forty employees). The very smallest were simply ineligible: NFA membership was not open to firms capitalized at less than $50,000, which in Philadelphia metal-working in the early 1900s implied an employment threshold (including other classes of workers besides molders) of about twenty. If they were eligible – just – they were further dissuaded by the NFA's setting a minimum dues level, regardless of a firm's foundry payroll.[40]

No more than about six-tenths of the jobbing foundries with more than forty employees became members either. Association membership had hidden costs as well as the high initiation fees, regular dues, and special assessments for strike-breaking costs, which dissuaded many of these middle-sized firms from joining. From 1901 until 1904, NFA membership at every firm other than Cramp's also involved recognition of the IMU, and adhering to contract terms, rather than just putting up with it as a reality

---

[38]   USCIR, *Final Report*, Vol. 3, p. 2821 (but cf. p. 2862: "not affiliating" did not exclude other forms of cooperation, e.g., the exchange of references – the basis for blacklisting), 2851–52, 2899.

[39]   President, Hess-Bright Mfg. Co. to IAM District Lodge No. 1, 28 May 1918, in Case 63, Records of the National War Labor Board, Record Group 2, U.S. National Archives – hereafter cited as NWLB Case –. Cf. Sidney Fine's discussion of the relationship between the NEA and U.S. and Bethelehem Steel in *"Without Blare of Trumpets": Walter Drew, the National Erectors' Association, and the Open Shop Movement, 1903–57* (Ann Arbor, 1995) – neither the NFA, NMTA, nor MMA would have any such dominant members.

[40]   Stecker, "The National Founders' Association," p. 373; 1902FACT database; data on capitalization calculated from U.S. Department of the Interior, Bureau of the Census, *Twelfth Census of the United States, 1900, Vol. 8: Manufactures, Part 2* (Washington, 1902), pp. 784–91.

on a par with the weather. Independent foundrymen could calculate that the weather would certainly change in the future, as it had in the past. Unemployment would return some day, and employers would regain an advantage in the labor market. But the IMU–NFA contract implied a formal and permanent relationship that would protect molders' wages and working conditions against downward adjustments otherwise unavoidable in recurrent recessions.

Many foundrymen therefore came to think of the New York Agreement as having turned the NFA into the IMU's ally in a joint assault on their freedom of action. But even when the NFA intervened to help them, it had its own agenda. It evolved into a centralized organization under the strict control of its national officers, responsive to their strategic vision and tactical approach. Members wanting its assistance were pressured to accept its guidance, however unwelcome and intrusive. The collective discipline required for the careful management of a national employers' association, and the habits of self-direction of the independent local proprietor, fit together rather awkwardly.[41]

Thus there was a distinct downside to NFA membership. On the one hand, it promised valuable assistance in times of strikes and, until 1904, offered a bargaining procedure that was supposed to minimize conflict. On the other, it was expensive, and resulted in the certainty of infringements on entrepreneurial freedom by both the association and – until 1904 – the IMU, and the possibility of higher and stickier labor costs. This was not what the NFA's original leaders had envisaged or intended. As membership was a matter of voluntary action and egocentric calculation on the part of employers, no association that delivered such a very mixed bag of costs and benefits could hope to grow, or even survive. By late 1903, the NFA nationally began to respond to members' dissatisfaction and the perceived drawbacks of its strategy, preparing to pursue a more confrontational policy. This was partly inspired by the successful example of the NMTA, and partly designed to meet the challenge posed by the blatantly anti-union American Foundrymen's League. Philadelphia foundrymen, too, embarked on a new course in harmony with this new departure.[42]

The successful outcome of the 1902 bargaining round had taught them the benefits of intelligent preparation and mutual aid, and strengthened their

---

[41]   NFA Commissioner O. P. Briggs reported in *ITR* 37 (25 Feb. 1904): 36–37 at p. 37, answering the charge of NFA–IMU collusion; correspondence between Briggs and F. M. Cresson, 24/29 Nov. 1905, in MMAP II-4-32. The NFA had helped Cresson defeat its molders in 1904, and was warning the company not to take advantage of its victory by cutting piece rates, which might stimulate another strike or reorganizing drive. Cresson responded very vigorously.

[42]   "American Foundrymen's League," *IA* 76 (10 Aug. 1905): 337, and "An Increasing Number of Open Foundries," (17 Aug. 1905): 414–15.

links with one another. It also seemed to underline the continuing value of negotiating with the Molders. Hallowell believed that "a very fair compromise was effected," and was still wholeheartedly committed to the New York and Philadelphia Agreements: They had worked "so satisfactorily" in ensuring that "the interests of employer and employe (*sic*) [had been] seriously, impartially and fairly considered by the representatives of [their] two organizations . . . , pending which no cessation of business nor of labor ha[d] occurred."[43]

But 1903's results were much less agreeable, eroding Philadelphia foundrymen's support for the trade agreement experiment. The Molders pursued the objectives of narrowing differentials between more and less skilled men, and shorter hours, with determination and success in a very tight labor market where delivery times for machinery were long and getting longer. The Founders could afford a bad settlement more than a strike, so the resulting agreement was very much on the Molders' terms. The foundrymen were forced to accept a reduction in the standard working day from ten to nine hours immediately, without any cut in pay. Hourly rates were thereby increased 11 percent, and employers were required to raise the actual daily wage by one-sixth if they wanted to hold to old production schedules at the expense of paying overtime. They also had to promise further increases of 10 percent on the less-skilled core-makers' daily minimum, and 3.5 percent for the molders, which would come into force in June 1904, at which time the differential between the molders' and the core-makers' wages was set to decline from 16 to 9 percent. The contract was supposed to run until June 1905. This costly deal turned out to be the last local agreement that the NFA's Philadelphia members and the IMU would make.[44]

1903 was a disturbed year for Philadelphia labor relations. A general strike tied up the all-important textile industry, but the Manufacturers' Club-based Textile Manufacturers Association emerged almost unscathed. More directly affecting the metal trades, construction workers' boycotts prevented the installation of nonunion ironwork and equipment in large downtown building projects. Metal manufacturers therefore had instructive local examples of the advantages of employer organization, on the one hand, and of the costs of disunity and inactivity in the face of a union threat permitted to grow too powerful, on the other.[45]

In November 1903 the NFA convention decided that no further local deals would be concluded unless and until the IMU accepted its minimum terms for a continuing relationship – recognition of the employers' author-

---

[43] Hallowell to North Bros. Mfg. Co., 28 June 1902, in North Bros. Papers, HML.

[44] Editorial, "The Philadelphia Strike," p. 33.

[45] Philip Scranton, *Figured Tapestry: Production, Markets, and Power in Philadelphia Textiles, 1885–1941* (New York, 1989), pp. 210–25; "President Plumb's Address," *IA* 72 (16 July 1903): 50–51.

ity in all disputed work-related issues. The proposed standard national contract, to which a committee including Hallowell and other Philadelphia activists attempted to secure IMU agreement in fruitless negotiations continuing through the winter, would have built on the strongest pro-employer terms in the 1901 Philadelphia and other local settlements. These talks continued at the same time as the Founders were making preparations for getting rid of the IMU if it balked at their surrender terms.[46]

The MMA was set up just after the NFA convention issued its ultimatum, but while the outcome of this challenge was uncertain, and the New York Agreement was still theoretically in force. Its creation was precipitated by growing dissatisfaction among the larger Philadelphia machinery foundrymen about their relationship with IMU locals whose strength had increased under the cover of an agreement that apparently favored the employers. But it was not solely a response to local circumstances. It was also inspired by the example of pioneering local metal-trades employers' associations in other cities, and was encouraged by both of the national bodies with which its members were affiliated. The NMTA had already worked out and implemented its own combattive strategy; the NFA was preparing to follow it. In this situation, the NFA's Philadelphia members were free to take the lead in setting up a body that was in line with the NMTA's confrontational policy without encountering opposition from their own parent organization.[47]

Experience had taught the NMTA, led by Cincinnati machine-shop operator Ernest Du Brul, that labor wars were won or lost at the community level, which was therefore where employer solidarity had to be organized. National employers' associations had to extend their central and district structures downward, so that they could fight labor toe-to-toe. Craft unions were built up from strong grass roots; employers' associations had to match them. So the NMTA deliberately mimicked the tactics and even the language of the labor movement, which one of Du Brul's activist allies, with permissible exaggeration, termed "probably the most perfect organization known." The NMTA's president backed him up: "Steal a leaf from organized labor . . . and apply it to our own case. . . . [W]e should organize from the bottom up."[48]

---

[46] Bauder, "National Collective Bargaining," p. 471; Stockton, *International Molders Union*, p. 132; Willoughby, "Employers' Associations," pp. 131–32; "The Detroit Conference," *IMJ* 40 (1904): 317–18.

[47] McPherson, "Organization of the Metal Manufacturers Association of Philadelphia PA.," SEC 1907, p. 1; Hallowell, "Your Association," p. 1.

[48] "National Metal Trades Association: Fourth Annual Convention," *IA* 69 (17 April 1902): 12–13, for Du Brul's program; J. C. Hobart, "The Employment Department of Employers' Association Work," *IA* 71 (28 May 1903): 30–32 at p. 31; "Address of President H. N. Covell," *Bull. NMTA* 3 (1904): 248–53 at p. 251.

And this is exactly what they did. Commissioner Du Brul took to the road in 1902–3, traveling around the industrial states to all of the major metal-working centers. He recruited new members and attempted to persuade them to follow Cincinnati's lead and form a "local" wherever they were strong and numerous enough. In 1903–4, the association hired a small corps of organizers for the same purpose. What happened in Philadelphia was therefore no isolated event, it was the local implementation of a conscious and coherent national program.[49]

Through the summer, moves began that would result in the formation of a broader based, continuously active local employers' association not limited in recruitment to any one sector of the metal trades, nor functioning principally as a bargaining organization. As Hallowell later reported, "meetings of foundrymen [were] called to discuss labor conditions and to take some united action in reference to the demands made by the Iron Molders' Union; and as the necessity frequently arose to call together those interested in the manufacturing business in the metal lines, it was considered advisable that an organization be formed." Those meetings started the process of bringing NFA members and nonmembers together.[50]

In November the NFA convention charted its collision course with the IMU, and highlighted the need to prepare for the coming battle by establishing what George Cresson would describe as "a closer organization and interest of employers" in the metal trades. Hallowell and Stanley Flagg, a medium-sized manufacturer of plumbing fittings with recent experience of union opposition to mechanization in his own foundry, were the Founders' local leaders. They were instructed by their members to correspond with people experienced in setting up local associations, and convened a preliminary private meeting of men who were active in the NFA and the NMTA on November 21st.[51]

Who were these men, all of whom would play major roles in the MMA and form the core of its leadership group for the next twenty years? We met them and their like in the previous chapter. George Cresson had been the vice president of the NFA in 1901. Justus Schwacke, long-serving treasurer of the William Sellers firm, sat on the NMTA's administrative council in 1900–01 and had gone on to chair that association's district committee. His successor in the latter office was Arthur Falkenau, a respected inventor-entrepreneur with a small hydraulic equipment and testing machine

[49] NMTA, "Proceedings of the Fifth Annual Convention," pp. 490–92, 499–500, 527; "The Metal Trades Convention," *IA* 71 (2 Apr. 1903): 38; "The Organization of the Employer," *IA* 71 (14 May 1903): 31–36.
[50] McPherson, "Organization of the MMA," p. 1; Hallowell, "Your Association," p. 1.
[51] "Notes for Order of Business," [9 Dec. 1903], MMAP I-1-35; Hallowell, PRES 1908, p. 3.

plant who was an active member of the Engineers' Club and Franklin Institute.[52]

The activists' conversations were quickly followed by a larger and more open meeting on the 27th, clearly designed to spread the gospel of organization beyond the ranks of the already converted, and to draw local NMTA and NFA members, and unaffiliated firms, closer together. NMTA commissioner Du Brul made his pitch on behalf of that association's strategy. Cincinatti and other metal-working centers had already demonstrated that local organization was "not only badly needed but could be successfully and most advantageously carried out."[53]

The manufacturers who attended agreed unanimously, and sent out a circular letter on 4 December with 22 signatures, representing firms employing about 3,500 workers. They called about 100 "business principals" to an invitation-only meeting at the Manufacturers' Club to discuss "the advisability of forming an Association of Metal Workers, which would be entirely independent of and in no way interfere with national or other organizations now existing." Most of the leading firms among the signatories were large machinery foundries – William Sellers, with 796 employees in 1902; George Cresson, with 410; Schaum & Uhlinger, textile machinery builders, with 194; and the Harrison Safety Boiler Works, with 146. Also represented were other major local foundries, including the Foundrymen's Association chairman Thomas Devlin's (330 employees) and the Belfield family's (150), and big lighting- and plumbing-fixture manufacturers Horn & Brannen (230) and Haines, Jones & Cadbury (162).[54]

In response to their invitation about fifty employers of foundry workers, machinists, brass workers, metal polishers, pattern-makers, and others met in the Manufacturers' Club on 9 December. All had union problems. The Pattern makers were about 90 percent organized, and had forced the jobbing pattern shops to accept a written agreement and pay a high minimum wage. Most skilled brass workers in the "chandelier" (gas and electric light fixture) shops were union members, too, and although the manufacturers "had never recognized the Union to the extent of making agreements with them, they were frequently subjected to labor troubles of one kind or another."[55]

The Machinists were weak in Philadelphia, and NMTA members accord-

---

[52]   NFA9905, NMTA0036, PHILCHAP databases; Schwacke testimony, USCIR, *Final Report*, Vol. 3, p. 2889.

[53]   Circular Letter, 4 Dec. 1903, MMAP II-3-11. The framed original of this founding document of the MMA languished on the floor at the back of the coat closet of MidAtlantic Employers' Association CEO Bob Breese's office in September 1998 – a fate emblematic of such organizations' historical consciousness; at least it was spared the dumpster.

[54]   Ibid. for quotes and attendees; 1902FACT for employment and industrial location.

[55]   Hallowell, "Your Association," pp. 2–4.

ingly few, which explains why they were unable to form an NMTA branch of their own. There were just nine NMTA members in Philadelphia in 1903, of which at least five – Adams & Westlake (brass founders and marine engineers, 87), Cresson, Harrison Safety Boiler, Link-Belt (290), and Sellers – were also in the NFA. Men from these firms would hold the MMA's presidency for the next two decades. Philadelphia NMTA members reported fewer "assessable operatives" in 1903 than those in Boston, Chicago, Detroit, Milwaukee, or Toronto, and only about half as many as in Cincinnati or metropolitan New York, the two largest city branches. So only the NFA was well enough organized to serve as a focus for the rest of the metal trades' associational efforts. Because so many of its members were machinery foundrymen with heterogeneous workforces and diverse labor relations problems, it made sense for them to ally themselves with other local employers of the fractious skilled workers on whom they all depended. They wanted the greater strength that broader alliances would bring, and were "convinced that a closer relationship of the manufacturing interests was a necessity in order to protect their mutual interests in labor troubles." Their best option was to establish a citywide organization for, in principle, the whole metal-working sector, where similar labor problems and business interests should form a firm foundation for unity.[56]

The activists' rationale was clear: "There has long been recognized the desirability of a local organization of employers whereby they may become acquainted with each other, and . . . be in a position to act in harmony upon questions affecting the welfare of all." But the "manufacturing interests of Philadelphia [were] too extensive and diversified to make it practicable to have one association of employers of all industries," along the lines of the burgeoning Open Shop associations of the smaller cities of the midwest. Nevertheless, "those having had some experience in handling labor problems have realized the possibilities of a combination of manufacturers of metal products in their various forms." Such an association would not be blazing a trail through uncharted territory, or embarking on an enterprise of uncertain outcome. Employers who had already joined together in other manufacturing cities had "found most encouraging and gratifying results."[57]

At the Manufacturers' Club meeting, local proprietor-managers endorsed the recommendations of their emerging leaders, and accepted the advice of distinguished visitors – Du Brul again, and the secretary of the Pittsburgh Manufacturers' Association speaking for the NFA. "It was the consensus of opinion that a Local Association was a necessity," and thirty-five of the fifty firms present agreed to join immediately. A committee was appointed

[56] NFA9905 and NMTA0036 databases; "Secretary's Report," *Bull. NMTA* 2 (1903): 462; McPherson, "Organization of the MMA," p. 1.
[57] Circular letter.

to draw up a constitution and by-laws, reporting back within the week; on 17 December, the constitution was accepted, and a nominating committee was appointed to recommend an executive committee. On the 21st, the nominees were endorsed, Falkenau becoming the first president. So within a month of the original summons from Flagg and Hallowell the Metal Manufacturers' Association of Philadelphia had come into being – to the extent, at least, of having a name, a constitution, leaders, and members. It had no funds, no premises, no staff, and a still-unclear plan of action. In 1904, it would quickly remedy all of these defects.[58]

3.4 PREPARATIONS FOR BATTLE

The MMA's lack of a home was the least of its problems. Thanks to the Foundrymen's Association president, Thomas Devlin, who was also vice president of the Manufacturers' Club, it was able to use the latter's premises for meetings and doing business until it could rent and equip its own small downtown office. Its lack of staff was equally easily solved. D. H. McPherson, one of the small corps of traveling organizers that Commissioner Du Brul had hired in his successful attempt to boost NMTA recruitment, became the MMA's secretary. He and a male stenographer made up the whole of the MMA's minuscule staff.[59]

Strategy and tactics were also borrowed from the NMTA, whose breach with the IAM in 1901 had plunged its members into a rash of strikes. The key to successful strike-breaking was the ability to replace quickly the men who had walked out. Cincinnati showed how. It had a very cohesive metal-manufacturing community and one of the first local metal trades employers' associations (hereafter MTAs), founded in 1900. In 1901 its members cooperated closely with one another against striking machinists, mobilizing their collective resources to pick off and reopen struck plants one by one. Over the next couple of years they consolidated their strength by locking out men who struck and tried to gain temporary work with other local metal trades firms until their own employers conceded. Most strikers normally expected to find temporary alternative employment locally, particularly in boom times, rather than to have no choice but to rely on their union's funds or to leave home looking for work. But in Cincinnati the easy option was closed, so the risk and expense of striking were sharply increased. As a result, although the labor market remained tight, and industrial guerrilla warfare continued, it was on a diminishing scale, and local

---

[58] McPherson, "Organization of the MMA," p. 1 and Hallowell, PRES 1908, pp. 3–4.
[59] ECM 17 Feb. and 17 March 1904. D. H. McPherson, "Experiences in Organizing Employers," *Bull. NMTA* 3 (1904): 41–43, on the frustrations of the job, which may have helped induce him to take a settled position.

IAM membership was whittled down by more than two-thirds over the next two years, from approximately one-sixth to less than one-twentieth of the labor force.[60]

Cincinnati employers attributed their success to the fact that they advanced beyond ad hoc strike-breaking and adopted a systematic, proactive policy to gain control of the local labor market. At the heart of this new approach was a novel institution, the cooperative employment department or labor (occasionally "information") bureau. This was an innovation in manpower management that represented the successful "adaptive imitation" of the behavior of large companies, like the major railroads and – more directly influential – the National Cash Register Company of Dayton, Ohio. Previously, companies the size and character of the Cincinnati MTA's members had generally left matters of hiring and firing under the decentralized, uncoordinated control of their foremen. Now, they were prepared to begin to bureaucratize it.[61]

The Cincinnati employment department was set up almost immediately after the local association's victory in the 1901 strike. The department was and remained a combination of an efficient centralized blacklisting agency, designed to facilitate the MTA's strategy of locking out strikers and mobilizing local strike-breakers, and a genuinely progressive development in employment management planned to be of some tangible benefit to employees as well as to employers. Its objects were "to secure and tabulate information concerning the character, ability, and previous record of every employee and to furnish such information on request to any of our members," to "find employment for deserving men in the shops of our members," to "prevent undesirable characters from securing employment" there, and "to prevent apprentices breaking contracts."[62]

It operated by hiring a secretary, renting downtown office space, and compiling a card file with personal details on all of the men in member firms' employ. This card file was continuously updated by firms supplying

[60] For the history of labor replacement, see Joshua Rosenbloom, "Strikebreaking and the Labor Market in the United States, 1881–1894," *Journal of Economic History* 58 (1998): 183–205; for Cincinnati, see "The Machine Tool Metropolis," *Machinery* 9 (1902): 26–28; "Organization of the Employer," pp. 32, 34; "The Cincinnati Machinists' Strike of 1901," *ITR* 35 (7 Aug. 1902): 50–51; NMTA, "Proceedings, Fifth Annual Convention," pp. 484, 496, 520, 629.

[61] Daniel Nelson, *Managers and Workers: Origins of the New Factory System in the United States, 1880–1920* (Madison, 1975), esp. Ch. 5; Paula V. Black, "An Experiment in Bureaucratic Centralization: Employee Blacklisting on the Burlington Rail Road, 1877–1892," *BHR* 51 (1977): 444–59; Julian V. Wright, "The Labor Department in Metal Working Industries," *ITR* 36 (7 May 1903): 89–90; Judith Sealander, *Grand Plans: Business Progressivism and Social Change in Ohio's Miami Valley* (Lexington, 1988), Ch. 2.

[62] Hobart, "Employment Department," p. 32; Hobart in NMTA, "Proceedings, Fifth Annual Convention," p. 573.

data on men they hired at the door, who quit or who were discharged. Men seeking employment were referred to the central office, required to fill in record forms (if their details were not already on file), and checked over by the secretary. If they were deemed suitable, they were sent to the plant superintendent or foreman, who retained the final power to hire and fire.[63]

What was the advantage to the employer of this system? The department's chief advocate and architect, machinery foundryman J. C. Hobart, argued that it was "certainly a convenience to be able by telephoning . . . to have men of good character sent us when needed. They may not always be as efficient as we desire . . . , but we are much better off than if we had advertised in the usual way." The Worcester MTA (which followed Cincinnati's lead in 1903) explained why. The employer using it would be protected against (i) the cost of the usual method of finding out whether applicants actually possessed the skills they claimed – just trying them out. Incompetents and men exaggerating their skills would be screened out before they even walked in the door, by checking on the positions they had actually filled in the past, even the specific tools they knew how to operate; (ii) apprentices leaving before their time, who would find other local shops closed to them, and be "persuaded" to work out their indentures; (iii) individual bargaining by skilled craftsmen, whose claims to have a better offer from another shop or to have made so much in their last jobs could be dented by the bureau's procedure. It would not offer places to men currently in work without getting in touch with their employers first, and recorded why a man had left his previous job and how much he had been paid; and of course (iv) the danger of hiring a known union activist would be much reduced. MTA members would be able, through cooperation, to "[get] a line upon those men whose influences in a shop are essentially vicious and disorganizing, and to exert upon them a powerful restraining influence, and at the same time to demonstrate to all those well disposed men and to the apprentices the value of a good record." As the *Iron Age* later emphasized, "The disciplinary feature inherent in this form of organization is seldom alluded to or employed, but that it is there is recognized by everyone."[64]

The Cincinnati MTA employment department's symbol was two clasped hands, the employer's and the employee's. What was there in this for the workmen that made Hobart believe that its operation would demonstrate to them the mutuality of interests between themselves and their employers?

---

[63]   Hobart, Ibid., p. 574.

[64]   Hobart, "Employment Department," p. 32; "The Worcester Metal Trades Association," *IA* 71 (30 Apr. 1903): 20–21 at p. 21. For further details on *modus operandi* see "The Worcester Labor Bureau," *IA* 72 (9 July 1903): 10–12 and Charles Perkins Adams, "The Worcester Labor Bureau," *Bull. NMTA* 3 (1904): 32–34); "Labor Bureaus and Workmen's Records," *IA* 81 (1908): 1709.

[I]t obviates the necessity of going from shop to shop, saves him car fare and time: he knows that if there is nothing against his character he can get a job any time he wants by applying to the Department and he appreciates this fact and makes use of it. The Department at the start is regarded with suspicion, but as soon as the workman is convinced that it is impartial, that it makes no distinction beyond demanding that the applicant's character be good and that he must be unemployed when making the application and when he finds that granted those conditions it can and does find him employment he endorses it and you have laid the foundation for winning the confidence of the employee and for a change of Public opinion regarding Employers associations.[65]

As the Worcester MTA further explained, an employment department would "enable good men, who may for any cause get out of a job, a quick opportunity to get work without expense" and therefore "tend to attract good workmen to the city . . . , and just as effectually tend to convince undesirable men, agitators and their ilk, that their proper sphere is elsewhere," because they would know that they would be excluded. Bureaus and their parent associations made a clear operational as well as rhetorical distinction between the ordinary workman – whom Hobart praised as "conservative, loyal American citizens, the backbone and sinews of this nation," although regrettably easily misled – and the "agitator," pejoratively equated with the classic outsider, " 'a tramp who comes and goes, leaving desolation and ruin in his path,' " the shatterer of a community's natural harmony. The labor bureau would filter out the latter at the same time as, within limits, serving the interests of the former.[66]

Thus the employment department was the instrument for a pioneer "union-substitution strategy" on the part of Cincinnati metal trades employers subscribing to it, not just a union-busting technique. Its aim was to "undermine union influence by showing [good men] that they can get what they most want without the necessity of paying anybody for it." What did a good man want? "[T]o better his condition, to elevate himself and to educate his family." This was why workers joined unions. There was nothing wrong with most workmen's motives, but they had become distanced from their employers as businesses grew and incorporated; and they too had learned the benefits of collective action. Both groups had an interest in a rising real standard of living for the consuming masses, but "ha[d] diverged merely on the means by which these objects are to be secured." Employers had abandoned the "education of the working classes" to union leaders and must now face the consequences.[67]

But, given that workers were, at bottom, sound, and could only get what they wanted from a productive capitalism – and that "[t]he suc-

[65] Hobart in NMTA, "Proceedings, Fifth Annual Convention," p. 574.
[66] "The Worcester Metal Trades Association," p. 21; Hobart, "The Employment Bureau," *Bull. NMTA* 2 (1903): 321–30 at pp. 326, 329.
[67] Hobart, "Employment Department," p. 30.

cessful employer is by nature endowed with the qualities of a leader. His opportunities for education, experience, and all that goes to make a sound, conservative, broad minded judge of industrial conditions are beyond comparison superior to those of the worker" – then the conclusion was obvious: Workers had to be led back into the natural paths of right-eousness. This should be done by isolating them from agitators' noxious influences, by propaganda, and by demonstrating to them that employers could and would deliver what they wanted – "higher wages and shorter hours" and "means by which employees can reach employers so that they can have their grievances heard without the necessity of joining a union to do so."[68]

The velvet glove on the employer's outstretched hand was as im-portant as the iron fist it did not quite conceal, perhaps more so. As Hobart put it, "we have sunk every appearance that we could of an effort to forcibly control the labor situation. We want our men to believe in us when we try to actually do what will be to the ultimate benefit of our employees."[69]

The good workman who used the bureau would find that the employer gave him preference over applicants at the door, a preference that was particularly valuable when the labor market slackened. One particular class of worker received extraspecial treatment: the NMTA's "certificate men." These were men who had "worked loyally" through a strike and were pas-tured out until their services were required again, at which time the bureau would help to mobilize them. This was a cheaper and less centralized way of maintaining a cadre of strike-breakers than the NFA's system of having a "flying squadron" of men under contract to the association itself, rather than in regular employment with its members.[70]

More surprisingly, the bureau's secretary would "Listen to any complaint of any workman regarding unjust or unfair conditions, and if, upon inves-tigation, such complaint is well founded, will correct such condition without divulging the name of the employee making the complaint." In practice, this meant that he acted as a "joint 'Social Secretar[y]'" for members, interceding between them and their employees, and discovering and remedying "overbearings" and abuses of power by foremen. He did this either by getting discharges reversed or by helping wrongly discharged men who could not be reinstated – because of the breakdown of personal

[68] Ibid., p. 31.
[69] "Organization of the Employer," p. 33; Hobart, "Employment Department," pp. 30–31; Hobart in NMTA, "Proceedings, Fifth Annual Convention," p. 486.
[70] "A Strike Against the Premium Plan," *IA* 71 (16 April 1903): 53; "N. M. T. A. Employe's Certificate," *ITR* 37 (25 Aug. 1904): 46–47; "Employers' Certificates," *IA* 75 (1905): 1093. Both the NMTA and NFA were formalizing, and making more efficient, the interregional labor market in strike-breakers which had existed for decades – see Rosenbloom, "Strikebreaking and the Labor Market."

relations with their foremen, and the necessity of saving the latter's face – to find employment in other member firms.[71]

So the employment department was the means by which firms supporting it could prosecute two complementary anti-union strategies at the same time, undermining the appeal of unions by a combination of improved everyday personnel practice and judicious, efficient discrimination.

The employment department could also fulfill an institutional need of the local association that set it up: to provide a regular service sufficiently important to persuade firms to join, cooperate, and keep paying their dues once the immediate threat of a strike or a union campaign had been overcome.[72] As Hobart explained,

when the exciting cause has been removed, there is danger of the interest failing, and of members dropping out. The reason for this is simply that employers have no time to spend or money to give to what is accomplishing no result that they can see. Let every local establish a labor bureau, and its members will see more than sufficient results to prevent their losing interest.[73]

Bureaus could do more than just hold existing members: They could also help local associations and the NMTA deal with the larger problem of their minority status within a largely apathetic employer community. The NMTA, which its president called "This little Association of ours," at this time was still smaller than the NFA, and a mere "drop in the bucket" (see Figure 3.4). The president of the Cleveland MTA explained why – it had a classic "free-rider" problem:

We find in every walk of life and business, certain individuals and firms perfectly willing to stand back and let others settle their labor troubles. They say to their help, "We will give you the same that you compel the other employers to give, so keep on working for us and you will not lose any time." This is the man who is willing to follow the trail that has been blazed by his fellows without expense to him of time, blood or money. Like flies, fleas and fevers, he is with us.

Hobart amplified the point that, "Although a minority, yet because we are a unit we will necessarily legislate for all, and the outsider will reap a

[71] Hobart, "Employment Bureau," p. 325; "The Metal Trades Association: The Buffalo Meeting," *IA* 71 (9 Apr. 1903): 6–13 at p. 10 "Organization of the Employer," p. 33; E. F. Du Brul, "An Open Letter to Mr. Ralph Easley, Editor, Monthly Review, National Civic Federation," *Bull. NMTA* 2 (1903): 270–75 at p. 273; E. F. D[u Brul]., "The Labor Bureau," 28.
[72] Cf. Daniel Ernst's discussion of the American Anti-Boycott Association's similar problem and solution, which he explains very persuasively in terms of Mancur Olson's classic work on interest group formation, *The Logic of Collective Action* (New York, 1968) – *Lawyers Against Labor: From Individual Rights to Corporate Liberalism* (Urbana, 1995), Ch. 3, esp. pp. 49–50, 59–61.
[73] Hobart, "Employment Bureau," p. 327.

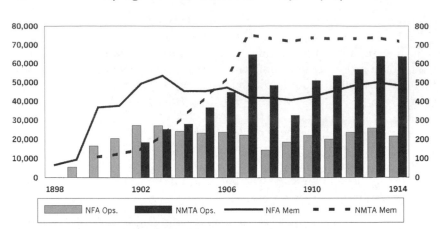

Figure 3.4. Growth of the NFA and NMTA, 1898–1914: Operatives (left-hand axis) and Members (right-hand axis). *Note:* The NFA's greater earlier growth, the NMTA's greater dynamism, and the stabilization of both associations by the mid-1900s. Data for 1905–06 and 1908 are interpolated, and probably exaggerate the reality for 1908. Some of these figures – e.g., the NMTA's 1907 and 1913 operative data – are approximations, and operatives do not include all employees. For the NFA, they were skilled foundry workers; for the NMTA, all other metalworkers. NFA and NMTA members' average employment per firm – 50 and 84, respectively, for 1899–1914 and 1902–14 (range 34–59 and 46–125) – was therefore in actuality higher than the above figures would indicate. Given that the two associations overlapped, there was also substantial double-counting of members, and a single company's foundry and machine-shop employees would be included separately within both operative totals if it joined both. *Source:* Stecker, "The NFA," p. 374, supplemented by "National Founder's Association," *ITR* 36:4 (12 Nov. 1903): 42–55 at p. 42. Figures for 1901, 1904, and 1906 are interpolations based on splitting the difference between the confirmed data for the years either side. NMTA: *Bulletin* 2 (1903): 460–61; 3 (1904): 267–68; "Synopsis of Proceedings of the 9th Annual Convention of the NMTA, Boston, Mass., 21–22 March 1907," *The Open Shop* 6 (1907): 213, 218; *Synopsis of Procedings of the 12th Annual Convention* (New York, 1910), pp. 12–13; *13th* (1911), p. 16; *14th* (1912), p. 14; *15th* (1913), pp. 27–28, 34, 214; *16th* (1914), pp. 7, 45, 47, 49, 234.

portion of the benefit of our work whether we or he will it or not. [But] . . . the lack of his support delays the date upon which we would be able to show the results he demands before joining us."[74]

A functioning local bureau could help to persuade "the large number of . . . noncombatants" of the benefits of association membership. If they

---

[74]   NMTA, "Proceedings, Fifth Annual Convention," pp. 527, 499–500, 576; cf. McPherson, "Experiences in Organizing Employers." See also George J. Stigler, "Free Riders and Collective Action: An Appendix to the Theories of Economic Regulation," *Bell Journal of Economics and Management Science* 5 (1974): 359–65.

joined, they could take advantage of centralization of some employment management functions. This was "a recognized part of the successful large, modern manufacturing establishment" but outside the experience and beyond the capacity of most middle-sized and smaller firms.[75]

How else could more employers be brought to see the necessity of defensive self-organization and to adopt the NMTA's preferred strategy? The association had two answers. First, it disseminated consciousness-raising propaganda through its monthly *Bulletin*, which was circulated to non-members as well as members. This was "chiefly devoted to saying the most offensive and altogether irritating things about organized labor," reporting on the dollars-and-cents consequences of giving way to unions and highlighting examples of successful business countermeasures. More concretely, it sent out its organizers to set up "locals," and offered their members technical and financial assistance, particularly with the tasks of establishing and running a labor bureau. It held a special convention for branch secretaries and district officers in Cincinnati, to demonstrate how the bureau worked, to bring them "in closer touch with one another and . . . all into closer relations with the national organization." The intended "practical result" was to be "a chain of employment departments located in the principal machinery producing centers of the country, which, through the national organization, will have means of inter-communication and co-operation." Arthur Falkenau, the MMA's first president, represented Philadelphia at that meeting, six months before his association came into being. By the spring of 1904, he and Secretary McPherson were prepared to add Philadelphia's link to the chain.[76]

Establishing an NMTA-style labor bureau was one of the MMA's first actions. Although it was not formally affiliated with the NMTA, the bureau was set up "in pursuance of [its] recommendation . . . , and in accordance with [its] plan." McPherson was sent to Cincinnati and Cleveland to study how their bureaus operated, and by March 1904 almost everything was ready. However, there was one small problem: The legality of an employer-operated labor bureau needed to be established first.[77]

This was a serious consideration in Philadelphia because Pennsylvania, in common with several other industrial states, had a law designed to

[75] Hobart in NMTA, "Proceedings, Fifth Annual Convention," p. 576; E. F. D., "Labor Bureau."

[76] "The Misuse of Organization," *Gunton's Magazine* 24 (1903): 471–80 at p. 475 [quote]; NMTA, "Proceedings, Fifth Annual Convention," pp. 490–92; "The Meeting of Metal Trades Representatives at Cincinnati," *IA* 71 (21 May 1903): 44 and 71:22 (28 May 1903): 53.

[77] ECM 1 and 8 March 1904. This was an obligation the NMTA laid on its branches – "The best legal advice obtainable shall be secured by the first employment department in a state . . . , and the department shall be conducted in conformity with the law as shown." – presumably because of variations in state legislation. "Employment Departments in the Metal Trades," *ITR* 36 (23 July 1903): 46.

protect workers' rights to join unions. Discharge or threats of discharge for membership in a "lawful labor organization," requirement of promises or agreements ("yellow-dog contracts") not to join or to remain in membership, or actions that would "in any way prevent or endeavor to prevent any employee from forming, joining or belonging" to such a union, or which would "interfere or attempt to interfere by any other means whatever, direct or indirect, with any employee's free and untrammeled connection" with a union, were misdemeanors punishable by a minimum $1,000 fine and/or up to a year in prison.[78]

What was unusual about the Pennsylvania law was not its sweeping provisions, but the fact that it had not yet been declared definitely unconstitutional by the state's highest court. The law's status was unclear because one superior court had ruled against it. But that employer-favorable judgment was only a controlling precedent for that particular bench of judges and within their jurisdiction, and it might at some time be reversed.[79]

Thus the MMA had to tread warily if it wanted to stay definitely within the law, as its constitution required, because the anti-union purpose of an NMTA-style bureau of the kind it was setting up was obvious. The details on present and former employees of member firms, and new applicants for employment, which it would keep in its card catalog, were to be confined to name, address, age, nationality, trade and speciality, references from previous employers, and dates of joining and leaving a member firm's payroll. According to its attorney, "No distinction is made between Union men or non Union men, and no record is made as to whether a man is or is not a Union man. The . . . Bureau does nothing to prevent a man from securing employment, but, on the contrary, aids him."[80]

It would not take any initiatives: It would only supply men if a member asked for them, but it would, "if requested, show to members of the association the record which it has." As far as the association's counsel was concerned, this *modus operandi* would guarantee its legality – dealing with members only, not keeping compromising information, and not requiring its members to take its advice about whom to hire. "[M]embers of the association do not bind themselves not to employ any one by reason of any

---

[78]   U.S. Commissioner of Labor, *Twenty-Second Annual Report, 1907: Labor Laws of the United States* (Washington, 1907), p. 1182 [quote]; Hyman Kuritz, "The Pennsylvania State Government and Labor Controls from 1865 to 1922" (Ph.D. diss., Columbia University, 1953), Ch. 5, esp. pp. 156, 176; Sargent Holland, "The Right of an Employee Against Employers' Blacklists," *American Law Register* 42 (1903): 803–09.

[79]   Felix Frankfurter and Nathan Greene, *The Labor Injunction* (Gloucester, Mass., 1963; first published 1930), pp. 146–47, lists other states with similar laws that had been found unconstitutional. I thank Daniel Ernst for his enlightening comments on the Pennsylvania law.

[80]   Copy of letter from attorney Frank P. Pritchard to president Arthur Falkenau, 25 Apr. 1904, in MMAP I-1-3.

information received. . . . No attempt is made to keep a blacklist which is binding on the members."[81]

Readers may be surprised at the extent to which an unenforceable pro-labor statute modified employers' behavior, or at least their original stated intentions, at the height of the judiciary's and business community's legal war against the unions. As we will see, the MMA's actual conduct would not be quite as simon-pure as its attorney's outline of its official policy suggested. There were ways of discouraging workers from joining unions, and warning employers not to hire union members, without keeping a formal blacklist. And within a decade the records did come to include information about men's "affiliation" as well as their experience. Nevertheless, the MMA would not depart dramatically from its early decision to stay within the margins of what the Pennsylvania anti-"yellow dog" statute might at some time be determined to mean.[82]

The law set some of the parameters for the MMA's action. The competition and opposition of the city's skilled trades unions, which were already in the field as employment agents, and on which MMA members and their skilled employees were somewhat dependent, determined the rest. Metal trades firms made little use of "help-wanted" advertising in the early 1900s, so the only formal agencies for satisfying their skilled labor needs, however imperfectly, were the unions. The business agents' resulting command of information on job openings also offered them an advantage in recruiting new members, and holding those they had, particularly during the 1904 recession. The MMA's hopes to exploit the return of unemployment to undermine organized labor depended on rapid success in displacing them from this strategic position.[83]

The creation of the MMA and the opening of its Labor Bureau did not pass unnoticed by the organization that was its most important rival and target – the IMU. Local unionists knew what to expect, because they also had the experience of other cities to draw on; and the launching of the bureau, even before its first test in a labor–management confrontation, was a very public affair.

[81] Ibid. The NMTA's rules similarly prohibited blacklisting – "Employment Departments in the Metal Trades," p. 46.
[82] For inclusion of labor–union membership status in Bureau records, see, e.g., McPherson, SEC 1907, p. 11; Attorney Thomas R. White's opinion, ECM 30 March 1920, p. 2; Memoranda for Special Committee on Study of Employment Department Methods (21 Feb. 1930), p. 2, MMAP II-3-46. The MMA opened Labor Bureau records to investigators from the U.S. Commission on Industrial Relations in 1914, and from the La Follette Committee in 1936, neither of whom discovered anything objectionable. See Schwacke and Henry Morgan testimony on Bureau procedure in USCIR, *Final Report*, Vol. 3, pp. 2890, 2892, 2903–13, Morgan, SEC 1914, p. 3, and Sparks, SEC 1936, p. 5.
[83] Memoranda for the Special Committee, p. 1.

The launch was timed to coincide with the holding of the NMTA's annual convention in Philadelphia, an important recruit for the Open Shop cause, and was accompanied by a large-scale leafleting exercize among metal trades employers and their employees. This was necessary because the MMA had to make the city's skilled workmen aware of the new facility for gaining employment and persuade them to use it. It had also, as a new organization striving to win members, to convince more firms that they should join. Fortunately for our purposes, the *Molders' Journal* obtained copies of both of the MMA's promotional pamphlets and reprinted them in full. They deserve extensive quotation, so that we can appreciate its rather two-faced appeal.

To employers, the MMA proclaimed that "your employees are in need of protection, which you cannot hope to secure for them except by membership" in the association. "A membership with us enables your employees to dispose of their labors at such prices and considerations as may be mutually satisfactory, not only to themselves, *but also to you* [emphasis in original]; all of this regardless of the insistence of the walking delegate" – the pejorative term for the union business agent or organizer, the employer's bogey. "[T]he fact that a mere membership with us will enable our members to withstand the unjust and uneconomic demands of the unions, should be sufficient argument for you to join." The promise of the bureau to employers, therefore, was a promise of freedom – for both businessmen and their employees – from union interference and dictation.[84]

Understandably enough, the MMA's pitch to workmen was somewhat different. It was adapted, and in some cases directly lifted, from J. C. Hobart's standard description of what a bureau was for, and how it should operate. It "aim[ed] to establish the principle of fair dealing between employee and employer, and to protect both in their exercise of their free rights as individuals given by the Constitution of the United States." After wrapping itself in the Stars and Stripes, the MMA proceeded to add an appeal to the independent workingman's interests and pocket to the somewhat-perfunctory appeal to his principles:

The main purpose of the Bureau is to make it easy for the employer to find men who want work, and for the men, when they want work, to find an employer. A plain, simple proposition, making it possible for men out of work to learn at one place which employers are in need of men, and by leaving their applications, make it possible for employers to learn at the same place what men want work. . . .

The operation of the Bureau is no secret, but is open to all. Our secretary will welcome you and give you as much of his time as you desire.

One of the principal objects of the Bureau is to show the employer and employee

---

84   Geo. D. Kemp (Business Agent), "Philadelphia and Vicinity," *IMJ* 40 (1904): 261–62.

that their interests are identical, and that the greatest good can be secured for both by their united efforts.

The Bureau keeps no black list.[85]

The die was cast, the gage thrown down, and the half-truthful claims made. Now all the MMA had to do was to prove its mettle in a trial of strength. The impending crisis must have been on foundrymen's minds that May evening when they drank, joked, and caroused before settling down to serious business.

The relationship between Philadelphia metal manufacturers and their fellows in other cities had at last become fully reciprocal. In the 1890s, Philadelphia had been the leader in machinery foundrymen's self-organizational efforts. It had remained deeply involved in the NFA's pursuit of "peace with honor" with the IMU from 1900 through 1903. It was scarcely affected by the great Machinists' strikes of 1901, and it played no major part in the NMTA's development of the Open Shop crusade in 1902–03. But by winter 1903–spring 1904 it was ready to take its place in the newly reunited ranks of foundrymen and machine-shop operators, hewing to the same ideological line, fighting with the same weapons. The great Philadelphia strikes of 1904 through 1907, and 1910–11, would be major victories in the Open Shop war. In the next chapter we will observe them, blow by blow.

[85]   Ibid.

4

Combat, Crisis, and Consolidation, 1904–1915

The structure and purposes of this chapter are simple. The MMA was born of and for conflict; this chapter is a narrative of a decade of employer–employee confrontation in the Philadelphia metal trades, where the MMA strove to implement the strategy of both of its parent organizations, the NFA and the NMTA. The MMA emerged victorious, its members' supremacy over their workers quickly, cheaply, and almost bloodlessly reestablished. The chapter's interest lies largely in the detail. When, how, and why did employers provoke, fight, and win strikes? How difficult was it to battle against organized labor, how much did it cost, and what were the results? How vital were violence and the law to achieving desirable outcomes? When, why, and with what effect did the MMA add political action to its defensive armory? At the end of the period, the MMA would be recognized by friend and foe alike as, in the words of its third president, Edward Langworthy, "one of the fixed and important factors in the business life of Philadelphia," which had "the respect of those whom it has opposed" and on whom it had exercised a "wholesome and restraining influence."[1] Behind the temperate language lay some drama.

4.1 EARLY VICTORIES, 1904–1906

The MMA went into business at a good time for a fledgling organization to confront its first major test. The year 1903 had been what the Philadelphia core-makers' business agent John Clarke called "the most successful ... in the past decade for the core maker, and ... his Brother molder," which was what had enabled the IMU to strike such a hard bargain with local NFA members that summer (see Figure 3.2). But in the fall the demand

---

[1] Langworthy, PRES 1913, p. 3.

for foundry products and molders' labor slackened. The trade went from what the *Iron Age*'s local correspondent termed "almost unprecedented activity during the early months of the year, to extreme dullness, . . . a change which was scarcely anticipated." What followed was a year of "extreme inactivity" and unrelieved gloom. Even the largest firms were affected. Baldwin Locomotive, for example, experienced a 30 percent decline in output (see Figures 2.2 and 3.3).[2]

Heavy unemployment resulted, in foundries as elsewhere. In bench molding, jobs were so scarce that the local closed the shops to nonunion men: It was a case of "no card, no work." The machinery molders reported trade "Very bad, with lots of idle molders."[3] Their business agent, George D. Kemp, complained about

the employers taking advantage of trade conditions and antagonizing the employees in changing about from one system to another, or . . . from better to worse conditions, which in our opinion, even though the employer is suffering from trade conditions as well as the employee, does not show a spirit of fairness.[4]

The foundrymen had begun to reverse years of enforced concessions on working practices that had raised labor costs, reduced productivity, and eroded managerial prerogatives. They were pleading pressure of competition, but were actually emboldened by the strong hand that the return of unemployment had served them. Kemp and his brother molders could only "sit and wonder what the outcome will be," while some foundries went out of business and the others chafed against union restrictions. They did not have to wait long to find out. Spring brought no upturn in the industry. Trade was "at a standstill" in February, with the city "full of core makers out of employment." By June, the bench molders reported trade "Never worse; men getting laid off everywhere," and the core-makers warned "Trouble pending; core makers, stay away."[5]

What transformed labor relations in the Philadelphia foundry industry from shop-level skirmishing into conflict on the streets in the summer of 1904 was the time bomb ticking away in the 1903 contract. Wages were supposed to be raised, and the core-maker/molder differential compressed. The IMU looked on that agreement as a definite promise to pay, but, as Clarke angrily wrote, "After waiting patiently a year for the manufacturers to make good their agreement, we find at this late day [24 June 1904] that we have no agreement with them; that for the representatives of two organization

---

[2]   See "Philadelphia Machinery Market in 1903," *IA* 73 (7 Jan. 1904): 24, and "The Philadelphia Machinery Market in 1904," *IA* 75 (5 Jan. 1905): 100–02 at p. 100.
[3]   "Local Union Reports for December 1903," *IMJ* 40 (1904), pp. 37, 47.
[4]   Kemp, "Philadelphia and Vicinity," *IMJ* 40 (1904), pp. 103–04.
[5]   Ibid.; "Local Union Reports for February," *IMJ* 40 (1904), p. 228, and "Local Union Reports for June," pp. 534, 539.

(*sic*) to sit for three long days to discuss a rate of wages, is no more after it is signed and agreed to than so much chaff."[6]

Implementation of the agreement stumbled up against two obstacles. The first was the economic condition of the industry, which removed the necessity, and in some cases the means, to pay a price for peace; the second followed a winter of fruitless national negotiations between the NFA and the IMU. Once it had concluded that the Molders would never willingly accept the provisions of the Founders' proposed Standard Form of Agreement, and that the costs and risks of a breakdown in relations were now tolerable, the NFA administrative council issued new instructions to its members in April 1904. They were advised to allow existing local agreements to expire if they did not conform to the association's terms, and introduce new open-shop working conditions unilaterally. The Philadelphia foundrymen followed this national guidance closely – after all, their leaders had helped to draw it up. So their condition for paying the wage rates agreed on in 1903 was IMU submission on working practices. For Clarke, "The little advance in wages is not the knife that cut, but the nefarious price or premium system that they would like to introduce in all the shops. If they can do this, why, there shall be no more day work; nothing but hog, hog, all the time."[7]

After an uneasy two-month lull during which the contract was neither honored nor abrogated, war was declared in George Cresson's foundry on the 4th of August. Cresson introduced piece work, against contract and custom, and provoked a strike in the middle of the slack summer season. He and his fellows had experimented with bargaining; now they would go back to the old ways he had described to the Industrial Commission in 1900: "If I found a man was making trouble so that we could not run our business, . . . I would say, We do not need your services any more, and that was the end of it." The result would be a return to the way things ought to operate, according to Charles Harrah's description of the way Midvale always had: "We make the scale [determine wages and output standards]. . . . They work accordingly."[8]

But Cresson's molders would not work at all under the new conditions, so the company introduced nonunion men to take the piecework jobs in their stead. The firm was not interested in avoiding a strike; and, thanks to the Labor Bureau, it was confident of being able to win. It had chosen the time, the place, and the issue: Secretary McPherson emphasized that,

[6] John G. Clarke to John P. Frey, in "Correspondence," *IMJ* 40 (1904), p. 30.
[7] NFA, *Proceedings of the 17th Annual Convention* (New York, 1913), pp. 7–9; "Standard Form of Agreement for Machinery and Jobbing Foundries," in MMAP II-4-41; John G. Clarke, "Agreements," *IMJ* 40 (1904): 605.
[8] U.S. Industrial Commission (hereafter USIC), *Report of the Industrial Commission on the Relations and Conditions of Capital and Labor Employed in Manufactures and General Business* (Washington, 1900), Vol. 14, pp. 269, 350.

"As it was a foregone conclusion that there would be a strike as soon as the non-union men were put to work, we were ... prepared for the trouble."[9]

The strike started with about sixty molders, machine operators, core-makers, and some laborers walking out. As George Cresson later reported, the Molders immediately established heavy pickets, "making it impossible for any person to come to, or from our works without being questioned. By moral pursuasion (*sic*) at first the pickets would prevent the men who were seeking employment from applying at our office. We immediately took the matter up with the NFA ... who have since rendered us every assistance, but they with us were glad to take advantage of the co-operation offered by the Local MMA."[10]

The Cresson strike was a precedent-setting battle for both the IMU and the NFA. Cresson was both the second largest member of the MMA, after Sellers, and very prominent in the NFA, whose new president, Antonio Pessano, had only recently left it to take control of a Detroit firm. The IMU believed that the strike was about more than conditions in Cresson's shop; it was about the whole future of their relations with the Philadelphia foundrymen. They were "unwilling" either "to pay the advance" or "to stand before the world as repudiators of their own agreement," and so had "cast about for some excuse which would give an appearance of justice to the step they had in contemplation." The Molders were right: As soon as the men walked out, the foundrymen tore up the agreement, declaring it violated, and celebrated the return of their freedom while Cresson, their leader, fought on their behalf.[11]

The strike was also a test of the Labor Bureau's potential. The bureau had to prove itself to the members, and it could do so only if it could provide strike-breakers quickly, cheaply, and of acceptable quality. To do this, it had to win the patronage of local skilled men. This was surprisingly easy. Union loyalties were usually recent, and no organization, not even the Molders, had total control over the local skilled labor force, even at the peak of its power in 1903. The large, strictly open-shop firms limited labor's coverage and penetration. The unions also faced the constant problem of migrant and immigrant workmen competing with their members for jobs. In these circumstances, union strength was critically dependent on the tightness of the labor market and the complaisance of the companies they dealt with. In 1904, when the MMA came on the scene, jobs were scarce and employers were justifiably confident that they could fill them without union help.

---

[9]   Cresson, PRES 1904, p. 1, and McPherson, SEC 1904, p. 3.
[10] Cresson, PRES 1904, p. 2. According to the NFA, the exact number was fifty-seven – *Summary of Union Molders' Strikes: 1904 to 1909 Inclusive* (Detroit, 1910), p. 1.
[11] "The Philadelphia Strike," *IMJ* 42 (1906): 32–35.

TABLE 4.1 Operations of the Labor Bureau, 1904–1918

Year	Apply[a]	Change[b]	Known[c]	Called[d]	Sent[e]	Placed[f]	Ops%[g]
1904	5,130					986	31%
1905	2,366	−46%				2,053	58%
1906	2,561	8%			2,947	2,374	47%
1907	1,842	−28%			1,976	1,670	27%
1908	7,436	304%	91%		780	429	12%
1909	5,037	−33%	89%	522	688		
1910	3,729	−26%	72%	1,125	1,791		
1911	5,699	53%	88%	531	1,007		
1912	5,117	−10%	90%	870	1,177		
1913	6,303	23%	92%	727	1,234	433	8%
1914	4,035	−36%	94%	242	415	194	4%
1915	6,453	60%	87%	635	1,291	479	12%
1916	7,970	24%	81%	892	1,946	615	10%
1917	5,633	−29%	68%	1,023	1,847	633	8%
1918	5,063	−10%	62%		2,105		

[a] *Apply* is the number of workmen who came to the bureau looking for employment.

[b] *Change* is the year-on-year increase or decrease in their numbers, which indicates the tightness or otherwise of the local labor market – the prosperity of 1905–07 shows through clearly, as do the recessions of 1907–08 and 1914–15.

[c] *Known* shows the proportion of applicants already known to the bureau. The highest prewar percentage of new applicants, revealingly, showed up in 1910 – a year of high employment and heavy recruitment for strike-breaking.

[d] *Called* – employees requisitioned by member firms.

[e] *Sent* – workmen sent from the bureau to fill those requests. These permit the calculation of a ratio of men hired as a proportion of those sent for employers to look over, which reached a high point of 85 percent in 1907, and fell to about 35 percent in the prewar years. Victory over the unions both reduced employers' dependence on the bureau and freed them to be pickier about the small number of men they continued to hire through it.

[f] *Placed* [placements] is the clearest measure of success in satisfying applicants' and members' needs.

[g] *Ops%*, the proportion of hires through the bureau to the average number of operatives in member firms, was at its highest in the MMA's early, critical years of active strike-breaking, 1904–07.

Source: Secretary's Reports 1904–18, MMAP.

Unemployment was the MMA's key strategic advantage. As Table 4.1 makes clear, more than twice as many applicants came to it looking for work in 1904 as in the semiprosperous year of 1905 or the boom year 1906. When the large open shops laid off workers, these nonunion men came onto the labor market. Unemployment made union men available, too, and cut them free from union discipline, since their membership and benefits lapsed after a period of prolonged worklessness and inability to pay their dues. In

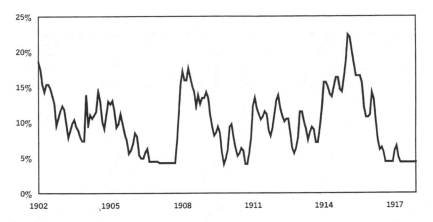

Figure 4.1. Estimated Unemployment in Major Cities, 1902–1917. *Note:* The compiler of this series estimated that the irreducible minimum of fricitional unemployment in the prewar urban labor market was about 4 percent. Compare this chart with Figures 2.2, 2.3, 3.1, 3.2, and 3.3, and Table 4.1, for a composite picture of the labor and product market contexts for industrial relations policy making. *Source:* Hornell N. Hart, *Fluctuations in Unemployment in Cities of the United States, 1902 to 1917* (Cincinnati, 1918), p. 48.

addition, union membership was supposed to deliver preferential access to jobs. When it no longer did, both because of the level of unemployment and because employers had organized their own labor market and severed their connection with the unions' business agents, then even union members in good standing found themselves torn between their loyalty to their craft and their immediate self-interest. In these circumstances the "practice of solidarity" was not easily reconciled with another aspect of the craftsman's "manly bearing," the ability to find that essential prerequisite for personal independence and family security, a job at one's trade. In the last analysis, employers, not unions, had control over the limited supply of such jobs, which gave them the whip hand. Recurrent recessions between the launching of the Open Shop movement, in Philadelphia and elsewhere, and the first positive impact of the First World War in the summer of 1915, only reinforced the employers' structural supremacy (see Figure 4.1).[12]

---

[12] For the key role of craft unions as employment agents in the United States, and the strategic significance of this power for their influence over members and employers, see Charles E. Edgerton and E. Dana Durand, *Labor Organizations, Labor Disputes, and Arbitration*, in USIC, *Reports*, Vol. 17 (1901), pp. LXI, 227; U.S. Commissioner of Labor, *Regulation and Restriction of Output: 11th Special Report* (Washington, 1904), pp. 21, 187–89. See also Robert Max Jackson, *The Formation of Craft Labor Markets* (Orlando, 1984), esp. pp. 210, 241, 275; Frances A. Kellor, *Out of Work:*

TABLE 4.2 Labor Bureau Operations, 15 Feb. 1904–15 Jan. 1905

OCCUPATION	APPLY[a]		HIRED[b]		RATIO[c]
Molders	379	7.4%	169	17.1%	2.2
Polishers & Buffers	247	4.8%	112	11.4%	2.2
Patternmakers	87	1.7%	39	4.0%	2.2
Coremakers	154	3.0%	64	6.5%	2.4
Machinists	915	17.8%	182	18.5%	5.0
Helpers & Laborers	1,138	22.2%	147	14.9%	7.8
Brass Workers	248	4.8%	32	3.2%	7.8
Machine Operators	692	13.5%	69	7.0%	10.0
Others[d]	1,270	24.8%	172	17.4%	7.4
TOTALS	5,130		986		5.2

[a] *APPLY* gives the number of men who applied to the bureau for work, which the next column expresses as a percentage of the total. It provides a measure of the voluntary supply of workers from the labor market.

[b] *HIRED* gives the number of men hired through the bureau, which the next column expresses as a percentage of the total. It offers a measure of the demand for workers from MMA members.

[c] *RATIO* is the ratio of *Apply* to *Hired*, and indicates the relative difficulty that the bureau had in filling positions in particular job categories – the higher the ratio, the easier the recruitment task; the lower the ratio, the better the chances an applicant of a particular skill had of getting a job from the MMA.

[d] "Others" included large numbers of "Boys" and carpenters, and small numbers of sheet iron workers, chippers, packers, tinsmiths, lacquerers, draftsmen, engineers (presumably stationary), and foremen.

Source: McPherson, SEC Feb. 1905.

Evidence for the inability of craft unions to control the labor market, and skilled men's behavior, is visible in Table 4.2. In 1904, bureau applicants were drawn from right across the metal trades labor pool. There is little sign that the unions' official boycott was successful, despite the Molders' and Brass Workers' initial confidence – one of their business agents promised Secretary McPherson that they "would put us out of business in six months." The skilled workers' readiness to come forward in numbers sufficient to meet the MMA's members' needs right from its very outset is especially impressive given that so high a proportion of the jobs that the bureau had to fill in its first year was indeed for strike-breakers, as business agents had warned, rather than regular replacements. Molders, core-makers,

A Study of Unemployment (New York, 1915), pp. 236–37; William O. Weyforth, *The Organizability of Labor* (Baltimore, 1917), p. 146. "Practice of solidarity" and "manly bearing" from David Bensman, *The Practice of Solidarity: American Hat Finishers in the Nineteenth Century* (Urbana, 1985) and David Montgomery, "Workers' Control of Machine Production in the Nineteenth century," *Labor History* 17 (1976): 485–509, on the skilled worker's ethical code and practices.

pattern-makers, and metal polishers, in particular, who came to the bureau and got jobs through it did so in defiance of their unions and often as volunteer scabs (or, as Secretary McPherson approvingly described them, men "who could do their own thinking").[13]

If such men were intent on looking after their individual interests and prepared to disregard their unions' definition of the common good, they had a strong chance of finding work. The MMA's members could not afford to be terribly selective about whom they hired from among this force of "independent workmen." They did not apply the criterion of job competence very strictly – half of the men from the strife-torn crafts who registered at the bureau were placed at work in 1904, as against one in five machinists, or one in ten machine operators, who were not usually looking for jobs that other men had vacated by the act of striking.

Unemployed skilled men who were prepared to take their striking or locked-out neighbors' jobs were therefore the MMA's key resource. In 1905–7, years of tight labor markets and even more strike-breaking, between 87 and 93 percent of applicants for employment at the bureau were placed in jobs, indicating that hardly any rejections on grounds of incompetence could have occurred. What mattered was the "independent" craftsman's readiness to cross a picket line and do what he was told. Such paragons might not be the cream of their crafts, but they were adequate and, even more important, they did not include the "agitator and troublemaker" who found it "impossible to secure employment through the Bureau."[14]

The MMA did not just sit back and wait for these men to respond to its leafleting and press advertising, walk in off the streets to register their availability for work, and assist this process of eroding union control. When molders were suspended from the IMU for disciplinary infractions or non-payment of dues, their names were published in the *Molders' Journal* to inform business agents that they were no longer in good standing and should not be allowed to work in union shops, even if they left their home towns and looked for jobs elsewhere. By October, George Kemp was complaining about the NFA and "kindred organizations" using this information, which the IMU was generous enough to supply gratis, for recruiting strike-breakers. Given that Kemp was locked in battle with the MMA at the time, it must have been among the organizations he had in mind.[15]

The IMU was outmaneuvered. The Labor Bureau was useful because of where it operated, as well as how. It was located in the heart of downtown, at 10th and Chestnut. The Cresson plant was miles away, at 18th and Allegheny, alongside the Reading Railroad tracks in the Tioga-

---

[13] McPherson, SEC 1904, p. 1, SEC Feb. 1905, p. 2.

[14] McPherson, SEC Dec. 1905, p. 2.

[15] George D. Kemp, "On the Question of Journal Reports," *IMJ* 40 (1904): 763–64. Previous practice had been to publish the names of new members, local by local, too – an open invitation to confrontation-minded foundrymen to fire them.

Swampoodle district of North Philadelphia. Effective picketing, for the IMU and other unions, depended in part on being assisted by neighborhood disapproval of scabbing in a working-class community, as well as on credible threats to prevent men from ever working again in union shops, and violently intimidatory words and deeds. However, the Labor Bureau recruited men in center city, far from the factory's local milieu but just a 5¢ streetcar ride from any other neighborhood. With the help of the NFA, it also brought in men from outside the city, who were even less susceptible to the social pressures of shaming and sending to Coventry, because they were complete strangers and often had no intention of staying on in the city after the strike anyway. And it offered locally recruited scabs – or "independent workmen," depending on one's viewpoint – a new channel of access to jobs even after a strike was over – and one outside of union control. Therefore, the MMA could now make a solid promise that if they stuck by their employers, their employers would stick by them.[16]

The MMA immediately made the Molders' pickets' jobs much harder, too, because job applicants no longer had to run the gauntlet at the factory door individually and unaided. They registered for work downtown, where the union did not control the streets. When they turned up for work, many of them were unknown to the strikers, and to that extent they were harder to persuade or coerce. Under those circumstances, picketing was more useful for maintaining the morale and solidarity of the strikers, and preventing a drift back to work by the less resolute brethren among them, than it was in keeping out strike-breakers. Pickets had to follow the new men back from the workplace "to their homes and boarding houses" and "around the city," as merely keeping watch outside the plant was no longer enough. When pickets did that, the MMA could use its influence with the Republican city council to get police protection so that men could be "escorted from shop (*sic*) to their homes."[17]

So the MMA allowed the struck employer to take the initiative in strikebreaking, and to do so on terrain that was unfavorable to the union. Nevertheless, the IMU was a hard nut to crack: It made strike-breakers' lives unpleasant, with the result that Cresson had to recruit more than 250 men to keep his 60 vacancies filled, because many of the replacements only lasted a day or two. Nor were strike-breakers especially skilled or otherwise desirable. Even Secretary McPherson admitted that "the men secured at the start were far from being first-class," and the Molders boosted their self-confidence in their irreplaceability by reporting on the poor-quality

---

[16]   NFA, *A Policy of Lawlessness: Partial Record of Riot, Assault, Murder, Coercion, and Intimidation Occurring in Strikes of The Iron Molders' Union During 1904, 1905, 1906 and 1907. Supplement to Report of O. P. Briggs, President of National Founders' Association, November, 1908* (Detroit, 1908), a compilation of affidavits testifying to the Molders' iron-fisted picketing tactics.

[17]   Cresson, PRES 1904, pp. 2–3.

output that the strike-breakers made. But they were missing the point: The aim of strike-breaking was more than to make profitable, saleable castings – it was to make an impression; to prove to the IMU "that they could not close the plant. . . . [T]here were but three days upon which a heat was not run off." The NFA assisted by sending in a few "professional" scabs who "stiffened up" the new men and "enabled us to hold them."[18]

The strike settled down into guerrilla warfare, with the union men on the outside and an increasingly competent strike-breaking crew inside. The Molders attempted to overcome their isolation from the new workforce by "getting a couple of Union spies to work," but the bureau checked out who they were, and they were discharged before they "had an opportunity to do any harm." This success depended partly on the routine checking of references, but also on access to the NFA's "list . . . of union spies and bad actors who endeavor to secure work in struck shops in order to create trouble and make bad castings." Eight of the new crew tried independently to win a nine-hour day (Cresson had reverted to a ten-hour schedule), but as McPherson "ke[pt] in close touch with the new men at our works," he found out about their plans, "and when they presented their demand, we were prepared for them and each man was discharged and paid up in full and not allowed to go back into the Foundry."[19]

Cresson pointed out how fortunate he had been to have the bureau to assist him with his intelligence work, by comparing his experience with that of the Worcester foundrymen at the same time. Worcester had a Metal Trades Association, but unlike Philadelphia's it did not take care of foundry labor problems; so "the Foundrymen," who "ha[d] no Local there . . . were depending entirely upon the [NFA] representative who could be there only part of the time, having the Utica strike to handle." Lucky Cresson, and lucky Philadelphia: In Worcester, the IMU had gotten its "spies" in, who had managed to "create a stampede . . . by getting the new men discontented and have them all quit in a body." Cresson was protected against having his new crew reorganized in this way, by McPherson wiring Worcester to check out a good skilled brass molder who applied for a scab job but who turned out to be one of the men who had led the "stampede" there! As far as Cresson was concerned, the wisdom of the MMA's inclusion of foundry workers under its protective umbrella, and its local supplementation of the NFA's centralized strike-breaking facilities, was proven.[20]

Cresson won his strike, or, as the machinery molders quite accurately termed it, lockout – the firm set the trap; the Molders merely sprang it and got caught in its jaws. And he won it on the cheap. NFA contract

[18]   McPherson, SEC 1904, pp. 3, 5. Cf. Editor, "Comment," *The [Open Shop] Review* 13 (1916): 278–89 – mocking the IMU's by then hoary claim that strike-breakers turned out scrap.
[19]   Cresson, PRES 1904, p. 3.
[20]   Ibid.

strike-breakers were too few in a year when the breakdown of the New York Agreement caused major strikes in Cleveland, Cincinnati, and St. Louis, as well as Worcester, Utica, and Philadelphia. They were expensive, both for the NFA and for the member firm using them. And by themselves they offered no long-term solution: While a struck firm had the benefit of their temporary presence, it still had to build up a regular replacement crew. The Philadelphia foundrymen, with the MMA's assistance, could begin that difficult process from the moment they were struck and build around locally recruited independent workmen who were not going to move on as soon as a strike, with its scabs' bonuses and relaxed work norms, was over.[21]

The strike cost the MMA the taxing sum of $157.47 – about ten weeks' wages for an average molder – over and above the ordinary costs of running the bureau, mostly in advertising expenses. No information had to be paid for, no guards hired, no lawyers retained, no injunctions sought – although McPherson did consult the American Anti-Boycott Association about the latter possibility, the strike was won without resorting to the courts. The NFA and the city authorities played their parts, but the MMA's contribution to breaking the strike was fundamental. Cresson's firm itself, of course, carried the main burden of the struggle, bearing the direct costs of a temporary lowering of output and quality. He was willing to do this, not only because a principle was at stake, but because these expenses could be considered as an investment that would bring a good return, after the IMU's control at the workplace had been broken, hours lengthened, piece work extended, and rates "adjusted."[22]

The network of cooperating national and local associations springing up gave metal trades employers a real strategic advantage, even with respect to their most strongly unionized workmen in the best-organized cities. Adams & Westlake Co., Edward Langworthy's company, had its main works in Chicago, a labor stronghold where, as late as 1903, even the NMTA was still advising members to negotiate rather than risk a strike. During the 1904 recession, the NMTA fought back. The company's Chicago brass foundry was struck in the resulting conflict, which ended in victory. Adams & Westlake was barely inconvenienced by the strike,

21   Geo. D. Kemp for Local 15 in "Local Union Reports for August," *IMJ* 40 (1904): 691; Editorial, "Our Strikes," Ibid., pp. 756–58.

22   "Treasurer's Reports of Receipts and Expenses for Year Ending 1905," MMAP III-4-1; ECM 13 Dec. 1904. The NFA's strike-breaking costs fell after the adoption of the Open Shop policy – from $400 per striker replaced during the great 1900–1901 Cleveland Strike, to $64 in 1906–07, and just $38 in 1912–13. By 1912 it only cost the NFA one-third as much to win most of its strikes as it cost the IMU to lose them. But its belligerent tactics, relying on a centrally mobilized and controlled "flying squadron" of professional strike-breakers, were always far costlier than the MMA's. See NFA, *Proceedings of the 17th Annual Convention* (1913), pp. 11–12.

because it was able to have its castings made in its Philadelphia plant instead, which was an open shop. No strike-breakers, in the strictest sense of the word, were required, but the firm did need to add to its regular labor force with more men prepared to work on "blacked" patterns. The union attempted to exploit this opportunity to infiltrate "agitators," but the Labor Bureau screened them all out. This small firm had acquired the same freedom to relocate production, and do an end run around a union whose industrial strength was patchy and concentrated, as was possessed by multiplant industrial giants like U.S. Steel. The company was not large enough to run its own employment department – it only had eighty-seven Philadelphia employees in 1902 – and in the ordinary course of affairs did not need to. But its membership in the MMA gave it access to this vital administrative resource during an emergency.[23]

Assistance did not simply flow from the national to the local association – it went the other way, too. Philadelphia was what employers thought of as a good labor market, that is, one that was usually well-supplied, and accordingly cheap, especially during a recession, because of the city's size, diversity, and role as a major port and railroad center. It was also a good recruiting ground for strike-breakers. Philadelphians who would not scab at home showed less compunction about breaking other people's strikes in cities where they were not known and did not intend to make a living once the strike was over. The MMA helped the NFA hire scabs for the Utica and Worcester molders' strikes, who were directed to go to the bureau, where they were interviewed and checked out, so that "Union spies, or hoboes looking for a railroad ticket" could not get through.[24]

It gave even more help to the NMTA, which set up a temporary office in Philadelphia to recruit machinists to break the 1904 strike that crippled the IAM in Chicago. The bureau cooperated by checking the records it held on the men who answered advertisements, so as to ensure that only "first-class Machinists" were sent. And to break a strike at the factory of an isolated NMTA member in the anthracite district of northeast Pennsylvania, the MMA sent men directly from its own employment register, sparing the NMTA the entire burden. (Workmen had to pledge their tools and clothing against the cost of transportation; their possessions were forfeited if they did not in fact take up the scab jobs on arrival!)[25]

In cases like these, the MMA operated in collaboration with national employers' associations just as the strategists behind the NMTA's local association/labor bureau plan had intended. The NMTA routinely supplied information about roving "agitators," and set up a League of Local

[23] "Proceedings of the Fifth Annual Convention of the National Metal Trades Association," *Bull. NMTA* 2:7A (July 1903): 471; McPherson, SEC 1904, p. 3; 1902FACT database.
[24] McPherson, SEC 1904, pp. 4–5.
[25] Ibid., p. 4.

Secretaries in 1905 to facilitate direct contacts between associations in major manufacturing centers "for assisting each other by furnishing men in times of trouble." But when a strike was a purely local affair, and the union opponent was small, weak, and isolated, the MMA, even in its first year, could handle the situation entirely unaided.[26]

In October, for example, the polishers and buffers made a straight wage-and-hour demand, and the chandelier manufacturers among the MMA's membership met with McPherson in the Manufacturers' Club to consider their response. They "decided to stand firm, and make no concessions whatever. Anticipating a strike, advertisements were placed in a number of out-of-town papers." When the polishers walked out of Horn & Brannen, the largest firm in the local industry (1902 employment 230, against an industry average of 53), because it had discharged its union-sympathizing foreman (through whom the union exercized effective control over hiring, firing, and shop administration), McPherson was ready. The record is silent on this, but here, too, as in the Cresson case, the suspicion that the MMA chose the strike's time and place seems reasonable: In all of these early strikes, the bellwether firms were members of the MMA's inner group of councillors and officers.[27]

In the Horn & Brannen strike, McPherson "immediately sent for the thirty-five Polishers registered at the Labor Bureau, and a number of them reported the following morning. The situation was explained to them, and seventeen agreed to start work. . . . [A]ll reported at the Labor Bureau at 6:45 A.M. . . . [and] such men as [Mr. Brannen] could use were escorted to the shop, and . . . are still working there. A few of the old employees who were forced to strike, were taken back and the strike collapsed in a few weeks." The plant was put on an open-shop basis, "while previous to the strike it was a case of 'no card, no work.' "[28]

If the Brass Workers' union had imagined that it was going to launch a strike-in-detail, concentrating its attention on companies one by one, it had a nasty surprise in store. What it encountered instead was a rolling lockout, as plant after plant declared for the open shop, was briefly struck, and filled from the Labor Bureau. This campaign to have "piece work or premium system started in all Brass Shops now employing Polishers and Buffers on the day work plan" continued for the next two years. It cannot have helped the men's confidence in their shrinking union's potency that in 1905 "one of their officers disappeared with the funds."[29]

By 1906, the MMA could winkle out remaining union shops where the

[26] "A Blacklist System," *The Trades Union News* (Philadelphia) 11 Aug. 1904, p. 1; McPherson, SEC Feb. 1905, p. 2.
[27] McPherson, SEC 1904, pp. 3–4; 1902FACT and MMAEXEC databases.
[28] McPherson, SEC 1904, pp. 3–4.
[29] ECM 14 Mar. 1906; McPherson, SEC 1906, p. 12.

men struck for an increased minimum wage by using the Cincinnati technique of borrowing skilled men from members already running open shops to serve as cadres around whom new nonunion workforces could be constructed. Other strike-breaking craftsmen and instructors were recruited from the smaller industrial cities of the hinterland – Lancaster, Reading, and Trenton – to break in "green hands on plain work." The battle was won, 80 percent of the union men were not rehired, and individual piece work, with no minimum wage, and as many "apprentices" – cheap adolescent labor rather than genuine trainees – as a manufacturer wanted to hire, introduced.[30]

The local union collapsed with the defeat: Most gratifyingly, "so many of the Union Polishers . . . refused to pay dues, that it was necessary for their business agent to secure employment," and he was not replaced. The international union abandoned its Philadelphia members and advised them "to secure employment wherever they can." As President Hallowell reported in 1908, "Since that time there has been no further trouble, and the attempts made to reorganize the shops have absolutely failed." The direct cost to the MMA of this successful union-busting campaign? $21.93 in 1905 and $134.43 in 1906, largely for out-of-town advertising for strike-breakers.[31]

The Philadelphia Machinists were even less well organized than the Brass Workers. Their only recorded strikes in these early years that affected the MMA took place in the summers of 1905 and 1906. The first did not even involve the IAM, but was instead an example of an informal, shop-level workers' action. A committee of his men called on Camden, New Jersey, steam-fittings manufacturer Warren Webster, giving him two days to cut their hours from sixty to fifty-four a week, with no reduction in pay. He called them together and explained that he would not, and could not, comply, "[o]n account of contracts which had several months to run," and which presupposed existing labor costs. All except his foreman and "two or three loyal workmen" walked out, and he advertised for replacements. On the third day he secured a few, and reopened the shop. "Each day the force was increased until a full quota of men were at work, and the former employees declared the strike a failure and discontinued their picketing, and about 20 percent of the old men were taken back as individuals. Inasmuch as these men were not organized, and consequently had nobody to direct and advise them, their fight from the start was a losing one, and it took them only a few days to realize this." The MMA gave Webster

<hr />

[30] McPherson, SEC 1906, pp. 12–13.
[31] Ibid., p. 13; William S. Hallowell, "Your Association – What It Has Done to Improve Industrial Conditions," Banquet Address, 9 March 1908, pp. 3–4, MMAP II-3-5; McPherson, SEC 1905, p. 2; "Treasurer's Reports 1905" and "Treasurer's Reports of Receipts and Disbursements for Year Ending 1906," MMAP III-4-1.

help and counsel even though he was not a member, and he joined in consequence.[32]

The strike at the Autocar Co. in May of the next year was similar, although much larger in scale. Autocar had 600 employees at its truck plant out in the suburbs, and 425 of them, including practically every machinist, took part. The IAM had a presence in the shop, holding meetings and openly appointing shop committees that called on the management to reduce hours from sixty-six to fifty-five a week. Autocar's superintendent Pollard replied with the same logic as Warren Webster, but offered to comply in three months' time. Nevertheless, the men immediately walked out. Autocar, like Webster, was not an MMA member, but its application to join and be helped was accepted "with the understanding that all expenses incurred as a result of the strike be paid by them." To win a battle, and a new member, of such significance, the association was prepared to bend its rules and act, effectively, as a fee-for-service strike-breaking agency.[33]

So as not to let such a big job "interfere with our regular routine work," the MMA opened a temporary hiring office in the inner city Spring Garden manufacturing district, and recruited 200 men in ten days. They were escorted out to the plant by "special officers," who were company employees that the firm had sworn in as deputies, and taken back to their homes in safety. There was absolutely no violence. The company's display of overwhelming force, official backing, and total determination swiftly undermined the strikers' morale. "[S]eeing their places being filled so rapidly, [they] asked to be taken back, and were informed that the men who had made themselves objectionable by picketing the shop would under no circumstances be allowed to return, and that any man who wished employment would have to file an application and return as an individual."[34]

The strike collapsed within a fortnight. Hundreds returned to work, but not a single one was a union member, and "not one man furnished by the Association was laid off to make room for a striker." The firm got rid of what it called "a lot of dead wood and disgruntled men, who undoubtedly would have given us considerable trouble in the future." Before the strike, the firm had operated on a day work basis. Afterwards, three-quarters of its men were put on piecework, earning higher wages, and apparently satisfied (or at least quiescent). Superintendent Pollard certainly was. His strike had been a very productive, and not very risky, enterprise.[35]

[32] McPherson, SEC Dec. 1905, p. 3.
[33] McPherson, SEC 1906, p. 11.
[34] Ibid., pp. 11–12.
[35] Ibid., p. 11; Board of Directors Minutes, 19 Dec. 1906, Autocar Company Records, Historical Society of Pennsylvania; ECM 11 Dec. 1906.

4.2 THE BIG FIGHT: THE 1905–1907 MOLDERS' STRIKE

Polishers and buffers were no problem, and machinists were a pushover, but foundry workers were another kettle of fish. In 1904, Cresson had demonstrated that they could be beaten. But his solitary victory was succeeded by an uneasy truce between the IMU and the rest of the MMA's foundryman members, who still operated union shops, although their formal contractual relationship had lapsed, and who were in no hurry to follow his example. The IMU waited "with patience, which the foundry-men construed as fear," for an upturn in business, which it detected in the summer of 1905 (see Figures 3.2 and 3.3), and resumed its struggle to win back official recognition and get the 1903 contract honored. The Pattern Makers' League, similarly, thought that the time was ripe to take the ini-tiative, which it did by formally requesting the MMA to bargain on behalf of its members.[36]

Faced with these two challenges, the MMA was forced to give a definite meaning to its labor relations policy rather than just making a series of ad hoc responses. By 1905, it had the experience of its early victories behind it, and was backed up by the solidifying open-shop, nonnegotiatory con-sensus in both the NMTA and the NFA. It decided to resolve any uncer-tainty by telling the Pattern Makers' business agent, politely but dishonestly, that "the rules governing the Association, do not comprehend any action by the Association as a whole upon questions raised by Labor Organiza-tions or their representatives."[37]

Behind this public fiction the MMA perfected techniques for coordinat-ing members' individual responses to union pressures so that they could present a united front. In the case of the Pattern Makers, members were asked to supply details of the wages that they paid these skilled men, and the hours that they worked them. They were then advised of the going rate, so that low-paying and long-day shops could consider coming into line.

---

[36] Editorial, "Philadelphia Strike," p. 34; "Sixteenth Convention Report," *Pattern Makers' Journal* 16 (1905): 34.

[37] Executive Committee to Samuel Thueson, ECM 14 June 1905. According to the MMA's Constitution, of which a copy survives in MMAP I-1-1, its objects included "The adoption of a fair basis for just and equitable dealings between the members and their employees, whereby the interests of both will be properly protected" and "The investigation and suggestion of means of adjustment, by the proper officers of the Association, of any question arising between members and their employees which may be referred to them." The constitution therefore seemed to envisage – it cer-tainly left open the possibility – that the MMA would continue to act as a negotia-tory and dispute-settlement agency like the NFA's district committee. This language reflected the MMA's origins in the trade agreement era, but was flexible enough to serve equally well throughout and beyond the Open Shop period.

There was no bargaining, but there was a measure of preemption here, as the association attempted to reduce the sense of grievance among the employees of the most exploitative member firms and minimize strike risks and the possibility of uninformed, shop-by-shop, "whipsaw" settlements.[38] This practice of preemption became settled policy, President Langworthy emphasizing to members "who are operating open or non-union shops" that it was

of vilat [vital] importance to so treat the independent workman that he will have no cause for desiring to join the ranks of union labor in order that through concerted action, and force of numbers, he can enforce conditions favorable to himself, to a degree which he could not otherwise obtain either through voluntary actions and regulation of the management, or after a straight-forward, man to man presentation of his desires.[39]

Once the Pattern Makers had been dealt with, all that remained was to sort out the Molders. They wrote, asking "in simple language" for just 25¢ on the core-makers' daily minimum, or on the daily wage of those who were already receiving more, and were turned down; they sent a delegation to talk to the foundrymen's representatives and were refused a hearing; committees in each foundry called on their employers and were told that there could be no separate settlements, everything was in the hands of the national and local associations; they tried to arrange meetings with the officers of the latter and ran up against a blank wall. The MMA and NFA stalled for time and tried to divide the workforce by "individual conference and increases for [the] more skilled," using what the IMU condemned as "tactics which would be a discredit to an organization of schoolboys" but which were nonetheless successful, up to a point. The strike was delayed until the end of October, as the "foundrymen were sure that winter would chill our members and send us all back to the sand heap." The employers' reluctance to hasten a strike was understandable, as McPherson noted that "at the time the demand was made upon them, they were all busy with plenty of work ahead, and realized that a strike could only be combatted at a tremendous financial loss."[40]

The strike began at the Harrison Safety Boiler Works, which, like all of the other MMA foundries, turned the core-makers down flat, stating that "under no circumstances would they grant their demands, which practically meant a recognition of the Iron Molders Union." As William Hallowell recalled, defending his strategy and tactics before the U.S. Commission on

---

[38] ECM 13 June 1905.
[39] Langworthy, PRES 1909, p. 3.
[40] "Philadelphia Strike," pp. 34–35; "Bad Faith of Foundrymen," *The Trades Union News* 20 Nov. 1905, p. 4; "Philadelphia Strike," *IMJ* 42 (1906): 474; McPherson, SEC 1906, pp. 6–11; A Striker, "The Philadelphia Strike," *IMJ* 42 (1906): 47–48. The "sand heap" was a name for the molder's workplace.

Industrial Relations nine years later, he did not think his men were worth the union minimum, "As we used a large number of very plain cores, for which (*sic*) it did not require the services of experienced journeymen core-makers to turn out." So he took the risk of provoking them to walk out, to test how loyal the molders would be to their less-skilled union brothers. (The molders had made no demands of their own at this stage, but they were waiting on the outcome of the core-makers' challenge.)[41]

He did not have long to wait: Attempts to use lower skilled labor, and to modify jobs so as to do without the core-makers, were countered by the molders' refusal to cooperate. They walked out, too, and for a month Hallowell's foundry was shut down. Hallowell's attempts to get his castings made in other foundries only succeeded in spreading the battle to include them as well. But he kept up the fight:

We eventually succeeded in starting our plant with a few men and gradually trained a number . . . who had been helpers in our shop before the strike . . . , and normal conditions were then gradually resumed. For months our efforts . . . were hampered by union pickets . . . who occupied a portion of a house opposite our plant, where they could sit on the front porch and observe all men, teams, etc., going in and out of our plant. They had several men with bicycles ready to follow our teams wherever they went with boxes and crates which appeared to contain patterns, presumably for the purpose of ascertaining where we were trying to have castings made.[42]

The strike was a big one, quickly involving over 500 molders and core-makers, and drawing in national officers of the NFA and the IMU to direct their members' efforts. The IMU sanctioned the strike, which meant that the molders got strike pay and other assistance, and their capacity to endure was increased. The MMA coordinated its members' behavior and also tried to draw in nonmembers, through the Foundrymen's Club. Foundry operators in the MMA subscribed $750 as a fighting fund, and the MMA provided whatever else was required from its collective resources.[43]

The NFA gave all of the help that it could: Its convention resolved that the strike was "a deliberate attempt . . . to force upon our members contracts contrary to the spirit of our approved policy and contrary to the Constitution of the United States and the civil rights of our members, in preventing the exercise of the right of individual contract between employ-

[41] Hallowell Exhibit No. 1, in U.S. Commission on Industrial Relations, (USCIR), *Industrial Relations: Final Report and Testimony, Submitted to Congress by the Commission on Industrial Relations . . . 64th Congress 1st Session* (Washington, 1916), Vol. 3, p. 2926; MMAEXEC and NFA9805 databases.

[42] USCIR, *Final Report*, Vol. 3, p. 2926.

[43] The NFA's records showed eleven plants and 636 workers involved, far and away the largest Molders' strike to begin in 1905 – almost a quarter of the national total of shops, and 43 percent of the workers. NFA, *Summary of Union Molders' Strikes* (1910).

ers and employees." So it decided to "use all the moneys, ways and means at our command and to further assess our members to the extent necessary to establish the principle which is so grossly assailed." In particular, it sent "special contract operatives," that is, seasoned strike-breakers, and with their help McPherson began to wage a war of attrition against the locked-out men. He rebuilt permanent skeleton crews plant-by-plant, reopening them one-by-one, with the foundry of William Sellers, a firm whose treasurer, Justus Schwacke, was an MMA and NMTA officeholder, as the flagship.[44]

The geographical scope of the 1905–07 strike was much larger than that of the Cresson strike (or lockout) of 1904. The foundries involved were scattered throughout the city's industrial districts, and, as Hallowell's account makes clear, foundrymen and molders played an elaborate game of tag with one another. Harrison Safety Boiler drew in other plants by sending its struck patterns to them to have castings run off, and the molders responded by extending the strike (which thereby became, technically, a boycott) to them. But then the MMA members went one better, by sending their patterns outside the city to nonunion foundries elsewhere in the region, and the IMU was forced to try to follow into this much less favorable territory, too. The IMU also involved the MMA directly in the strike, by picketing its Chestnut Street office and making the task of assembling strike-breakers more difficult.[45]

That task was harder in any case, because it was larger, and because the foundry labor market, in Philadelphia and nationally, was much tighter. The MMA had only half as many job applicants to draw on in 1905 and 1906 as in 1904, and it was trying to meet a demand from members that was two to two-and-a-half times as great. The ratio of applicants to placements declined from 4.2 to 1.1, indicating a greater proportion of unsatisfied requests and a sharply diminished ability to pick and choose between job-seekers (see Table 4.1).[46]

But McPherson worked away patiently – drawing in men from the smaller, more weakly unionized cities of southeastern Pennsylvania; and scouring through all the molders on his register, and sending them individual letters inviting them for interviews. He recruited a few men this way, including discouraged strikers and, through them, their friends; he placed them at work alongside inexperienced hands, "and by gradually weeding out the inferior workmen, the struck Foundries were filled with a force of

[44] "National Founders' Association: Record Attendance and Perfectly Harmonious Sessions," *ITR* 38 (23 Nov. 1905): 12–15 at p. 13; Editorial, *IMJ* 42 (1906): 27–29; MMAEXEC and NMTA9936 databases.

[45] D.M. Shalkop, "The Conference Board of Eastern Pennsylvania," *IMJ* 42 (1906): 150–52.

[46] IMU members only experienced about a fifth as much unemployment in 1906 as in 1904 – "Out-of-Work Stamps Issued," *IMJ* 59:11 (Nov. 1923): 132–33.

fairly competent non-union men." The new workforce that he constructed was markedly different from what it replaced: It was smaller, cheaper, and more productive. The secret was that it included almost as many handymen and apprentices as it did skilled journeymen. Before the strike, the IMU had limited these less-skilled men to a maximum of one-eighth of the number of journeymen molders and core-makers, restricting employers' freedom to train an adequate supply of new craftsmen or to substitute less-skilled, more specialized labor for them. After the MMA's victory, the time-honored ratio no longer had any force.[47]

The IMU matched the MMA's investment of effort. The NFA considered that the union gave "more marked attention" to the Philadelphia strike "than to any other which had taken place in several years, by detailing a large corps of business agents and vice-presidents to be constantly on the ground for the purpose of devising ways and means to harass the proprietors . . . and drive them to a capitulation." IMU President Valentine directed the opening stages of the campaign in person, telling McPherson that it was "a fight to the finish so far as the union [was] concerned." Vice Presidents O'Keefe and O'Leary were almost permanently in Philadelphia, at least in the first few months, and Valentine visited repeatedly. Clearly, this was no mere local dispute. As a Reading molder put it, it meant "life or death to one of the organizations."[48]

The tactics of the IMU and of the MMA and NFA mirrored one another. MMA firms sent out their patterns into nearby cities; the IMU followed with its organizers and "missionaries." The MMA and NFA paid skilled strike-breakers bonuses, and the IMU offered them bribes to leave town – promises of $50, rail fare, and a clean union card were reported – and sent "kegs of beer" and "gallons of whiskey" to their boarding houses in the evenings, in a subtle attempt to reduce their operational effectiveness. This was what the IMU called conducting a strike along "progressive and law-abiding lines."[49]

[47] McPherson, SEC 1906, pp. 8–9. This dilution strategy, first employed on a large scale in the 1906 strikes, quickly became standard practice – NFA, *Proceedings of the 16th Annual Convention* (New York, 1912), pp. 7, 22; Margaret L. Stecker, "The Founders, the Molders, and the Molding Machine," *QJE* 32 (1918): 278–308 at pp. 297–302, 305–07. Strike reports in the *Iron Trades Review* for May–November 1906 reveal foundrymen's genuine surprise – and relief – that a risky and untried strategy combining extensive work reorganization, intensive training, and an unprecedented degree of mechanization (with one new machine installed for every three or four molders who walked out) had finally freed them from their dependency on skilled workers. Their gamble paid off. See, e.g., "What Boys Can Do," *ITR* 39 (23 Aug. 1906): 15.

[48] NFA, *A Policy of Lawlessness*, p. 31; "The Chronicler," *IMJ* 41 (1905): 857–59, 928, 930; "The Chronicler," *IMJ* 42 (1906): 36–7, 104–05, 185; Frank Bendel, "A Suggestion," Ibid., p. 111.

[49] ECM 13 March 1906; NFA, *A Policy of Lawlessness*, pp. 31–34; "The Chronicler," *IMJ* 42 (1906): 105.

But the IMU's self-restraint did not help it. As McPherson reported, "Usually in a Molder's Strike with so many men involved, there is considerable violence." Rather than trust in the IMU, the MMA made sure that it was so hemmed in that it could not use iron-fisted tactics and get away with them. A "Legal Committee" was appointed, under the chairmanship of Justus Schwacke, "and arrangements made with the Director of Public Safety to furnish ample Police protection." In cities like Boston, New York, and particularly Chicago, with popular Democratic political machines, employers complained about the inadequacy of police protection during strikes, and about the sympathetic or lily-livered attitudes of grand juries and elected justices when unionists were hauled before them. But in Philadelphia, the citadel of Republicanism, such problems were rare. MMA members signified their satisfaction with the director's services by making him a featured guest at their annual banquet after the strike's successful conclusion.[50]

Strike-breakers were escorted to and from their homes and lodgings for the first few months, so the Molders shifted their tactics from picket-line threats and insults to the harassment of strike-breakers on streetcars and at their boarding houses, and a couple of freelance assaults on the streets and in saloons. The MMA gathered accusations and evidence, had warrants taken out, secured one conviction, and had a number of men put under bond to keep the peace. As a result of this legal attack, and the passage of time, the pickets became less "numerous and aggressive," some of them drifting away or back to work at non-MMA foundries, and the strike soon settled down to a level of IMU interference that was quite tolerable.[51]

The MMA's victory depended on more than its own resources and routine law enforcement. First, the strike enabled it to win a powerful new recruit, the Niles-Bement-Pond Co., larger even than Sellers, which had hitherto refrained from joining and which McPherson singled out as "the plant upon which the Union determined to concentrate its efforts," perhaps because of the mistaken belief that it was outside of the MMA's defensive ring. But N-B-P was intent on winning the open shop by all possible means, which included compromising its autonomy, joining the MMA, and resorting to the law. The MMA rested content with the service that it got from the police and petty criminal courts. But N-B-P went a long step further in January 1906 by initiating an injunction suit before the Federal District Court. The MMA's attorneys assisted it in drawing up the Bill of Complaint. Fourteen men, including both the IMU national vice presidents and a dozen local union activists, were enjoined from "interfering with [its] employes (*sic*)

50   McPherson, SEC 1906, p. 10; Banquet Program, 1907, MMAP II-3-4.
51   NFA, *A Policy of Lawlessness*, pp. 31–34; McPherson, SEC 1906, pp. 9–10.

... by the use of threats, intimidation, molestation, personal violence, or other unlawful means, or from obtaining (*sic*) the employes of the company by bribes, gifts of money, or other similar means from leaving their employ, and from obstructing or interfering by the boycott or otherwise with the business of the firm."[52]

This was a narrowly drawn injunction, by the standards of the time, and it was obtained after a preliminary hearing and testimony, not *ex parte*. It never came to a full hearing, although the proceedings dragged on for more than five years before they were discharged. No one was fined or imprisoned for violating it, which was, according to Cincinnati machine-builder B. B. Tuttle, the "ultimate object" employers sought when going to law – "to land [any violator] behind the bars where he belongs." Nevertheless, it was quite effective because, as so often happened, the workers and their union obeyed without needing this degree of coercion. When some of the named activists and both vice presidents were charged with contempt, they found all their time taken up with court appearances and preparing their case. Eventually the vice presidents judged their freedom of movement and action so restricted by the court's terms for permitting them their liberty that they left town and abandoned their striking members, who drifted on with no strategic direction and nothing more than strike pay and reassuring words. It might be emotionally satisfying to imprison leaders and activists, but, as Tuttle argued, "in times of labor trouble, it is results you want and it is not ethics or anything else." N-B-P got the results required. Pickets were withdrawn, and the firm also found it much easier to have its castings made elsewhere "without involving the concerns who were making these castings in labor trouble."[53]

---

[52] "Injunction May Be Issued," *ITR* 39 (15 Jan. 1906): 15, and "Philadelphia Strike," *ITR* 39 (22 Jan. 1906): 13; McPherson, SEC 1906, p. 10; "The Chronicler," *IMJ* 42 (1906): 185. Federal District Court for Eastern Pennsylvania, Equity Docket Vol. 16, pp. 439, 615, 622–23, Philadelphia Federal Records Center, charts the progress of the case; NFA, *A Policy of Lawlessness*, pp. 31–34, reprints excerpts from affidavits on behalf of the plaintiff.

[53] NMTA, *Synopsis of Proceedings of the 16th Annual Convention* (New York, 1914), p. 221 [Tuttle]; "The Chronicler," *IMJ* 42 (1906): 361, 438; McPherson, SEC 1906, p. 10.

Legal scholars have given a great deal of attention to labor injunctions – both contemporary advocates of the AFL's anti-injunction program [Felix Frankfurter and Nathan Greene, *The Labor Injunction* (New York, 1930); Edwin E. Witte, *The Government in Labor Disputes* (New York, 1932)] and recent historians [most notably William E. Forbath, *Law and the Shaping of the American Labor Movement* (Cambridge, Mass., 1991)]. What is striking in the primary sources studied is the *rarity* of injunctions and employers' understanding of their limited practical utility. According to the NFA's general counsel George F. Monaghan, the association and its members applied for injunctions in just 39 of the 525 strikes that they encountered between 1902 and 1912 ["Union Lawlessness," NFA, *Proceedings of the 17th*

The second big reason why the MMA won was that the IMU miscalculated. By the spring of 1906, with the union – as NFA President O. P. Briggs gleefully reported – facing "defeat in Philadelphia, one of the largest foundry centers on the continent, the very birthplace of the union," which "would so completely foretell the ultimate downfall of the radical, closed-shop principle," the Molders decided that "desperate means were necessary." Unfortunately for them, they were by this time thoroughly penetrated by the NFA's "secret service," so that their strategy of exploiting the tight national labor market, and overtaxing the NFA's resources, by spreading the strike simultaneously to all major foundry centers – including Boston, Buffalo, Pittsburgh, Cleveland, St. Louis, Kansas City, Minneapolis–St. Paul, Milwaukee, and Chicago – backfired. The IMU was overwhelmed by the employers' planned and concerted resistance, and the Philadelphia strike – the spark igniting the IMU's suicidal bonfire – became simply one defeat among many.[54]

The pressure was off. Thirteen months after the strike began, all but three of the MMA members who had started it had stuck the course, and were reporting output from their new crews restored to 90 percent of its pre-strike level. (Two of the foundrymen who had fallen by the wayside only employed about twenty men between them, and the third, larger foundry had been expelled, not for settling with the IMU, but for its unwillingness to submit to collective discipline and pay its share of defense costs.) The strikers comforted themselves with the news of small defections from the founders' ranks; successes in "encouraging" strike-breakers to leave the city; and reports and cartoons about the expensive, poor-quality castings that their replacements were alleged to be turning out. They held on grimly, and said that the strike was therefore continuing, and a moral victory. The MMA pointed to the fact that, whatever the expense involved in getting there (which, for the association, was not excessive – $760 net, just over 8

Annual Convention (1913), pp. 74–86 at p. 82]. Injunctions were not necessarily easy to enforce, either – everything depended on the attitude of the local police and courts [Thomas F. Durban, "The Erie Strike Situation," Ibid., pp. 40–55 at pp. 52–53; E. H. Sholar, "The Birmingham Strike," Ibid., pp. 56–58]. Nevertheless, they could serve, as in Philadelphia, a helpful tactical and psychological purpose – according to B. B. Tuttle, "[T]he injunction has its uses; very often it relieves a situation . . . ; [it] bolsters up the weak fellow who is beginning to feel timid and ready to jump with the union; he sees that bill on the wall and thinks to himself 'I've got the court behind me.' He doesn't know what he's got behind him, but he thinks he's got the court behind him." NMTA, *Synopsis of Proceedings of the 16th Annual Convention* (1914), pp. 221–22.

54   "National Founders' Association Convention," *ITR* 39 (22 Nov. 1906): 19–30, esp. officers' reports at pp. 19–22, 24–27 [quote p. 19]; "Strikes in Many Foundries Involving from Seven to Eight Thousand Employees," *ITR* 39 (10 May 1906): 12–13.

percent of total expenditure in the two years the strike continued), and the strains on members' loyalty, their foundries were operating at near-normal levels of output with cheaper, more tractable employees, according to conditions that the employers had dictated.[55]

From the MMA's standpoint, this was real success. As William Hallowell, by then its president, noted in 1908, "all of our members affected who steadily and continuously cooperated with the Association were enabled to open and operate their plants upon a strictly open-shop basis," which was "the best and most gratifying evidence of the value of membership." They were "operating with independent workmen, without agreements of any kind, free to introduce molding machines and other labor saving machinery, free to have as many apprentices as they may see fit to employ, – in fact, free to operate their plants . . . without fear of union interference." McPherson further emphasized that "Only four of the small iron foundries" still had written agreements with the IMU, and that MMA members did not "have to fear sympathetic strikes, and stand for no restrictions of output by the Officers of the Union." It would be 1909–10 before the IMU was able to begin to recover from this severe setback and try to improve on the 1903 contract's wage-and-hour terms in the few foundries where it was still recognized.[56]

In addition, other skilled crafts waited on the outcome of the Molders' struggle before launching their own, so that the MMA had little trouble from any other quarter through the prosperous year 1906. It was, as the president of the anti-union American Plan Association of Cleveland later put it, "axiomatic among Trade Unionists" that " 'If the molders can't win, nobody can.' " The incalculable "moral effect" of the struggle against the Molders brought MMA members generally peaceful labor relations when a strike wave might otherwise have been expected.[57]

The third and final nail in the Philadelphia IMU's coffin was one that cost the MMA and its members far more than strike-breaking and legal action, but was even more devastating to their union opponents: the economic collapse of 1907–08, which the Pattern Makers' president deemed "the worst

---

[55]   McPherson, SEC 1906, pp. 9–10; NFA, *Summary of Union Molders' Strikes* (1910), p. 1; ECM 14 Feb., 13 March, 18 Apr. 1906; "Iron Moulders Grit Still in Evidence," *Trades Union News* (17 Jan. 1907), p. 1; 'A Striker,' "The Philadelphia Strike," pp. 47–48, "The Chronicler," pp. 267, 361, cartoons, pp. 45, 195, all *IMJ* 42 (1906); Treasurer's Reports, 1905 and 1906, in MMAP III-4-1; Hallowell, "Your Association," pp. 2–3.

[56]   Hallowell, PRES 1908, p. 5; Hallowell, "Your Association," p. 2; McPherson, "Organization of the MMA," p. 2; NFA, *Philadelphia and Vicinity* (Detroit, 24 Nov. 1909), pp. 1–2; NFA, *Summary of Union Molders' Strikes: 1910–1911* (Detroit, 1911), p. 4.

[57]   Jacob D. Cox., Jr., 6 July 1922, in John P. Frey Papers, Box 13, F.182, Library of Congress; McPherson, SEC 1907, pp. 3–4.

depression that has been experienced since the birth of American industries," and the shallow recovery that followed. This really was the *coup
de grâce*.[58]

In 1907, after the great Molders' strike had been effectively defeated, all
of the labor unions began to show signs of a gradual revival of confidence.
This was because the foundry and machinery trades' labor and product
markets became ever tighter. Foundry pig reached $28 a ton in January and
February, and demand was so great that huge volumes of imports were
required to satisfy it. Foundries had full order books, and poured record
tonnages month after month. The demand for machine-tools was "unprecedented" during the first half of the year, and buyers were more sensitive to
prompt delivery than to price. In these circumstances, foundrymen who had
won the open shop, at some cost in terms of quality and output in 1906,
began to resume informal relations with the IMU, and rehire their old
skilled molders.[59]

Even the Machinists began to show signs of activity, winning a major
victory against Enterprise Manufacturing after a three-week strike by
twenty-one union toolmakers, the élite of the craft (the firm's machine-
operators were unorganized piece workers). They secured increases of up
to 30 percent on the minimum wage, an end to the firm's punitive time-
keeping and attempts to extend piece work into the toolroom, reinstatement of all strikers, and even a pledge to abolish piece work in the machine
shop. After this success, which showed how the most skilled workmen could
win victories on behalf of their less-skilled fellows, if the latter gave them
passive support, the Machinists' local lodges gained record numbers of new
members, and were emboldened to begin a general movement for the nine-
hour day with no reduction in pay. By midsummer, they were strong enough
to take on Eldridge Johnson's giant Victor Talking Machine Co., across the
Delaware in Camden, over cases of discriminatory discharges, and win
recognition and a grievance procedure for the toolmakers they represented.
Other unions were similarly active: The Pattern Makers resumed their
general wage increase campaign; the Molders demanded the right to operate
molding machines and for their business agent to have access to the shop,
in the handful of firms where they were still recognized; and the Metal Spinners petitioned chandelier manufacturers for shorter hours and an end to
piece work.[60]

What brought an end to this period of renewed labor pressure was the
recession, which set in with brutal and totally unexpected force in the fall,

[58] *Pattern Makers Journal* 20:7 (July 1909): 10.
[59] A. A. Miller, "The Philadelphia Iron Trade in 1907," *IA* 81 (2 Jan. 1908): 65–68;
      "Philadelphia Machinery Market in 1907," Ibid., 170–72; ECM 14 Jan. 1907.
[60] John M. Gilbert, "Philadelphia , Pa.," *MMJ* 19 (1907): 262, 371–72, 483, 591, 682;
      "Strike of Union Machinists," *Trades Union News* 14 Feb. 1907, p. 3; "Machinists
      Win Local Strike," Ibid., 7 March 1907, p. 1; ECM 14 Jan., 13 March, 9 Oct.
      1907.

cutting every indicator of the level of activity to ribbons. MMA firms laid off half their workers as their overflowing order books were emptied by cancellations and not replenished. As the *Iron Age*'s city correspondent remarked, "From a practical standpoint, business was at a stand-still during the last quarter of the year." Some Philadelphia manufacturers went bankrupt overnight. Over the next several years of recession and weak recovery others went to the wall, mostly in a process of orderly liquidation and withdrawal from business.[61]

But for every cloud there is a silver lining. When President Hallowell reflected in 1908 on "what was probably the worst financial panic during the business lives of most of our members," he pointed to the transformation in the labor relations climate in the metal trades: There was "a great excess of applications for employment . . . at any wage to supply the necessities of life; instead of labor leaders and walking delegates or business agents being active and ready to insist upon the most drastic Union conditions, they have seldom been seen or heard from." More than three times as many job-seekers came to the Labor Bureau as in 1907, and the ratio of applicants to placements improved from 1.1 to 17.3. In 1906 and 1907, firms had accepted four out of five men that the bureau sent them; in 1908 it could afford to be much more selective, and still they rejected almost half.[62]

The Machinists' business agent, Edward Keenan, waxed poetic about "the winter season of 1907–08, a winter in which the machinists have had their ambitions nipped in the bud by the frost of depression and their fondest hopes buried beneath the snow banks of industrial inactivity." Spring came, but no improvement. A sense of humor was the only defense against gloom: "Machinists, through no fault of their own are enjoying an eight-hour day." Summer brought a reversal of the previous year's gains at Enterprise, with piecework enforced through a lockout. A year into the depression, Keenan was reduced to that most futile of business agents' messages, telling craftsmen from elsewhere who were hoping to find employment in a big city not to come and make an oversupplied labor market worse: "Do not come around knocking at our doors for a job at present as some of the men have been out so long that they think you are joking if you say how is business." "Remember, according to the new mode of spelling, P-H-I-L-A-D-E-L-P-H-I-A spells stay away."[63]

Strikes occurred in MMA members' plants, even in these grimmest

[61] Miller, "Philadelphia Iron Trade," p. 65. Edgar A. Custer, *No Royal Road* (New York, 1937), pp. 284–86, is a powerful account of the impact of the depression on his northeast Philadelphia foundry.

[62] Hallowell, PRES 1908, pp. 6, 4; for Labor Bureau figures, see Table 4.1. According to IMU figures, molders experienced about ten times as much unemployment in 1908 as in 1906 – "Out-of-Work Stamps Issued," pp. 132–33.

[63] Edward Keenan, "Philadelphia, Pa.," *MMJ* 20 (1908): 340, 438–39, 815–16, 1007, 341.

months, but they were isolated protests against wage-cutting and management attempts to tighten up on working conditions, and were easily dealt with. This became the pattern of the next two years; 1907–08 therefore marked a watershed, the end of the first period in the MMA's existence. Three strenuous years of effective and uniformly successful strike-breaking had made the most of the shallow recession of 1904–05, and had held labor in check even during the strong recovery of 1905–07. They had established the MMA as a force in the city, and had brought it experience, allowing it to transform operations that were experimental in 1904 into an administrative routine. They had strengthened their members' commitment to an organization that had proved itself well capable of looking after their interests. And they had built up the association to a point where it could handle sporadic outbursts of labor trouble without assistance from the NFA and NMTA, which had been so characteristic of its early years.

So by 1907 the MMA was solidly grounded, and able to survive the subsequent years of recession and feeble recovery. It had extended the frontiers of the open shop beyond the giant firms to include the medium-sized machinery builders that were its core membership, and even some smaller consumer-durables makers. It had helped to stop the apparently inevitable rise of labor of 1899–1903 in its tracks, and had driven even the strongest union, the Molders, back toward the fringes of the local industrial economy. Reviewing its first five years, President Hallowell asserted, with a fair degree of accuracy:

Our Association did not start out with a "chip on its shoulder" and pursue an aggressive policy against labor organizations, but there is one important thing it has done, it has stood for the independence not only of the employer but of the employee as well, and working quietly along these lines, with the effective organization it has built up . . . it has been enabled to defend its members against all unjust attacks of labor unions, so that it is today recognized by them as a power to be reckoned with, and therefore we can all properly feel that membership in our organization is indeed a valuable asset.[64]

4.3   1910–1911: THE GREAT UPHEAVAL

While 1909 was what President Langworthy called "a year of hopeful expectation rather than . . . of profitable business," with the association "marking time and carrying on its routine work . . . without anything occurring of special moment," 1910 in contrast was "one of the most eventful in [its] history." Of the members' roughly 4,160 operatives, 2,300 went out on strike (mostly in short sympathetic walkouts). In this troubled

---

[64]   Hallowell, "Your Association," p. 4.

year of returning prosperity (see Figure 4.1), the Labor Bureau was almost as busy as it had been in 1907, and busier than it would be again until 1916, sending its members 750 strike-breakers and about 1,000 regular replacements.[65]

What also made 1910 special was that, as the MMA's new secretary, Henry Morgan, reported, "the cleverest organizers, most influential officials, and others conceded to have weight with the mechanic" had made Philadelphia "their objective point" in a determined campaign "to abolish the 'Open Shop.'" For the AFL had not been entirely passive in the face of the employers' offensive. The craft unions that the MMA's members encountered established a Metal Trades Department that had a local branch in Philadelphia and was supposed to coordinate their activities. (It was also designed to silence calls for industrial unionism that, its proponents argued, would enable labor to match the effectively organized class solidarity of its opponents by overcoming some of its internal divisions.) The Pattern Makers' general secretary was soon optimistically reporting "an awakening in the metal trades of Philadelphia" and predicting progress in organizing at "one large corporation which has long been a detriment to our own members and to the movement in general." He did not mention Baldwin by name, but events of the next year would make it clear that the AFL had set its sights as high as possible, aiming at cracking the open shop by hitting right at its heart. The AFL also began to support community-based, revivalistic organizing campaigns designed to tap into the diffuse pro-labor, anti-business sentiments of the working and some of the middle classes, and to translate them into recruits and local political sympathizers.[66]

Philadelphia was not all stony ground for sowing the seed of labor activism. Its building trades' and textile workers' unions, albeit weakened by recession and failed strikes, made it still, to some extent, a union town. The AFL was able to capitalize on this potential because of the acute grievances of the more than 5,000 streetcar men of the Philadelphia Rapid Transit Co. (PRT), which led to months of conflict that involved many workers, unionized and otherwise, in sympathetic action on the transit workers' behalf. This in turn produced unparalleled organizing and mobilizing opportunities for the city's labor movement, as workers gained a sense of their own power and asserted their particular claims against their employers once the sympathetic strike wave had begun.[67]

---

[65] Langworthy, PRES 1909, p. 1, and 1910, p. 2.

[66] Morgan, SEC 1909, p. 2; Edward Keenan, "Philadelphia, PA," *MMJ* 20 (1908): 626, 910; 21 (1909): 541, 821; "Report of the Twelfth Convention," *Pattern Makers' Journal* 20 (July 1909): 65; Ken Fones-Wolf, *Trade Union Gospel: Christianity and Labor in Industrial Philadelphia, 1865–1915* (Philadelphia, 1989), Ch. 6.

[67] The account that follows draws largely on John K. Brown, *The Baldwin Locomotive Works, 1831–1915: A Study in American Industrial Practice* (Baltimore, 1995),

The PRT was an inefficient organization that owed its monopoly status to celebrated episodes of political corruption. It was trying to get out of a profit squeeze caused by being caught between a fixed 5¢ fare, on the one hand, and its obligation to pay high rents to the original franchise owners it had bought out too dearly in its search for monopoly, on the other. Its strategy was to further reduce levels of service that were already a public scandal and major inconvenience to all classes, and to drive down operating costs by depressing its workers' wages, worsening their working conditions, and increasing their workloads. This was not a recipe for peaceful labor, or good public, relations.

The result was a succession of strikes in 1909–10, accompanied by large-scale strike-breaking and increasingly aggressive intervention by the city's and state's forces of order, provoking mass actions by strikers and a supportive public, and a short-lived upheaval in municipal politics and local class relations. A wave of sympathetic stoppages, called, with optimistic inaccuracy, a "general strike," engulfed the city's textile and metal-working industries in the first half of March 1910. As President Golden of the United Textile Workers reported these momentous events to his members, "Public opinion . . . ran high in favor of the men on strike, and every effort was made to take advantage of the unique situation," which was "a splendid opportunity to preach the gospel of trade unionism to thousands . . . who could never have been reached except for extraordinary conditions."[68]

The Philadelphia labor movement claimed to have won more than 20,000 new recruits as a result of the strike wave and its associated organizing campaign. The most important group among the newly unionized workers had to build an organization from scratch. These were the men of the Baldwin Locomotive Works itself, the strongest bastion of the Open Shop, which, as the MMA's secretary emphasized, "up to this time had been considered invulnerable." Hundreds of Baldwin workmen got caught up in an armed conflict between police and transit strikers in late February outside of the plant. And a large minority came out on sympathetic strike in early March in response to the Central Labor Union's call, despite the lack of a previous union presence in the plant for all of the Metal Trades Department's efforts.[69]

Although their wages were comparatively high, Baldwin workers had

pp. 217–23; Charles Cheape, *Moving the Masses: Urban Public Transit in New York, Boston, and Philadelphia, 1880–1912* (Cambridge, Mass., 1980), Ch. 7, esp. pp. 182–87, 205–06; Philip Foner, *History of the Labor Movement in the United States, Vol. 5: The AFL in the Progressive Era, 1910–1915* (New York, 1980), Ch. 6; and particularly Philip Scranton, *Figured Tapestry: Production, Markets, and Power in Philadelphia Textiles, 1885–1940* (New York, 1989), pp. 267–74.

[68]   Quoted in Weyforth, *Organizability of Labor*, pp. 34–35.

[69]   Morgan, SEC 1910, p. 2.

many grievances. Most of them were related to the company's "drive" system – favoritism and exploitation in the operation of inside contracting, low piece rates, long hours, and no overtime pay. The workers also resented the fact that a pay cut justified by the recession of 1907–08, when the company's output and employment fell by more than three-quarters, had not been fully restored with the return of prosperity.[70]

Baldwin's chieftains Samuel Vauclain and Alba Johnson handled the crisis masterfully, granting a Saturday half-holiday and taking back strikers without discrimination. They promised the returning men plenty of work as they built up their force from 12,000 to 16,000 men to cope with a rush of orders (see Figure 2.3), and even interceded with the authorities on behalf of an employee arrested during a demonstration.[71]

This apparent flexibility did the trick. The men ended their strike, the order backlog was dealt with, and the company added to its pool of trained men. But, while Baldwin seemingly tolerated the formation of locals of the Machinists, Molders, Pattern Makers, Boilermakers, Blacksmiths, and Metal Polishers within the plant; the open wearing of union buttons; and the enforced closure of the works on Labor Day, it was preparing to hit back.

It perfected its spy system; identifying union activists was in any case much easier when they thought they no longer had to hide. And it invested heavily in building up capacity at its brand new Eddystone plant a dozen miles away. Younger, less union-conscious workers were transferred there as soon as the suburban plant was ready. Business fell off in 1911, and Baldwin began to run its employment down, month after month, from 15,475 in January to a low of 8,981 in July. This series of massive, prolonged layoffs gave it the opportunity to punish and cleanse the workforce at the huge old inner-city plant, from which all known militants were weeded out. A large but hopeless strike ensued at the downtown works in the summer when the unions, already on the ropes, asked for layoffs in line with seniority and were refused.

Baldwin had all of the advantages. It continued operations at Eddystone

[70] Testimony of John M. Tobin and Alba Johnson, USCIR, *Final Report*, Vol. 3, pp. 2836–48, 2862.

[71] This account draws on the sources cited in note 67, supplemented by Ken Fones-Wolf, "Mass Strikes, Corporate Strategies: The Baldwin Locomotive Works and the Philadelphia General Strike of 1910," *PMHB* 110 (1986): 447–57; Johnson Exhibit No. 3, USCIR, *Final Report*, Vol. 3, p. 2923; Morgan, SEC 1911, p. 1; M. O'Sullivan, "Is There Opposition on the Part of Large Industrial Corporations to Labor Unions? If So, What Are the Reasons Therefor?" 12 Dec. 1914, pp. 3–5, in Melvyn Dubofsky, ed., *Research Collections in Labor Studies: The Wilson Administration and American Workers: U.S. Commission on Industrial Relations, 1912–1915 Unpublished Records* (Frederick, 1985), microfilm ed., Reel 12; and Commonwealth of Pennsylvania, Secretary for Internal Affairs, *39th Annual Report of the Bureau of Industrial Statistics* (Harrisburg, 1911), p. 419.

with younger workers for whom the strike represented an opportunity to break through into the core group of established employees enjoying preferential access to jobs. It also had the services of a minority of particularly loyal and experienced workers whom Blacksmiths' organizer John Tobin called "Keystoners – that they put gold buttons on and put a badge so that everybody would know them." These were probably recruited from the Employees' Beneficial Association, set up on the first of June, whose members were promised relative job security and whose privileged status made them most dependent upon the company. And it recruited out of town.[72]

The strike dragged on while the company "[let] a fellow sit down and let their hair grow long and starve to death – their wives and children – that terror and torture that they try to inflict in all such cases – 13 weeks." At the end of the dispute, the company required the men whom it permitted to return to work to tear up and hand in their union dues books as the price of reemployment and a sign of abject personal submission.[73]

The strategy was a complete success. Three years later, the Boilermakers' business agent, David Napier, thought it impossible to "put your hand on a union man in Baldwin's Locomotive Works." The Pattern Makers had kept their heads below the parapet during the strike, sensibly fearing for their jobs if they joined the walkout, but even so they had been singled out by their foremen and offered a choice between the union and the company. According to their business agent, John Watt, only one of his members was missed in this clean sweep. John Tobin thought that he had a dozen members left, out of several hundred union blacksmiths in 1911. Asked by a member of the Industrial Relations Commission whether this "betoken[ed] that the men are satisfied with present conditions, and do not care to organize," Tobin's reply was blunt: "No, sir; that is not true. The conditions are that if I am seen talking to a man he will lose his job." He was "ashamed to say I am afraid to talk to a man looking for a position there, so is every other man known to have union activities." The few old union men still there were working "under cover," fearful for their jobs if their divided loyalties became known, but staying on as wholly inactive members to maintain their entitlement to fraternal and insurance benefits. The situation was the same for the Machinists; business agent Keenan claimed that he still had a few members at Baldwin and Midvale (which had responded to the brief surge in union-consciousness in 1910 as vigorously as Baldwin). "I don't know whether the firm knows it or not, but we do, and that is all we think is necessary. . . . I don't know that they

---

[72] Testimony of John Tobin, USCIR, *Final Report*, Vol. 3, pp. 2843–84.
[73] Ibid. The unions' interpretation of the "dues books" affair was disputed by the company – see general superintendent Sykes's testimony, USCIR, *Final Report*, Vol. 3, pp. 2869–70.

are so secretive, but they don't parade it to any extent." Discrimination had become "a general feature of the machinist's industry in the city of Philadelphia."[74]

Company spokesmen, understandably, saw things differently. President Johnson claimed to be running a genuinely open shop, in that "If union men come into our works and are faithful [the important proviso!] and competent workmen, [a convenient excuse for any dismissal] the question as to their being union men is not raised." But his superintendent Sykes was more forthright, both in public, telling the commission that Baldwin "reserved the right to ourselves . . . to employ those we seek to employ and to reject those we do not care to take into our employ," and in private.[75]

Sykes had a staunchly individualistic view of labor relations, denying to the commission's investigator, Mark O'Sullivan, "that there ever was a strike in their works, simply stating that men had quit and that they were glad afterwards to return." Despite this theoretical reluctance to recognize the unions' very existence, Sykes knew how to deal with them in practice. O'Sullivan asked him what would happen to one of the small number of passive union members still at Baldwin's "in case one of them should carry on an agitation on behalf of his union." Sykes replied "by asking . . . what I would do if I found a mad dog in my house. Of course, I told him I very likely would shoot the dog, and asked if a similar punishment would be meted out to one of the Company's employees. . . . My question seemed to nettle him as I believe he felt that he had chosen an unfortunate illustration."[76]

Link-Belt's president, Charles Piez, was much more politic, but no less clear in justifying his firm's steadfast anti-unionism on the basis of its experiences with the IAM at its Chicago works: "If you have found it impossible to work in conjunction with a certain organization, and that organization sets about, without your knowledge, to reorganize your works, should you be compelled to submit to that sort of thing, or should you be free to select anywhere labor that is not so affiliated?" To Piez and his colleagues, the answer was obvious.[77]

Piez's and Sykes's unapologetic defense of the blacklist and the closed non-union shop was representative of the climate of Philadelphia labor relations in the aftermath of the 1909–10 streetcar and "general," and the 1910–11 Baldwin strikes. Baldwin reestablished its absolute authority and would not be troubled by its workers again until the 1930s. The PRT took a different course under its dynamic new manager, Thomas Mitten. It

[74] USCIR, *Final Report*, Vol. 3, pp. 2918, 2916, 2836, 2850, 2878, 2880; O'Sullivan, "Is There Opposition?" p. 5.
[75] USCIR, *Final Report*, Vol. 3, pp. 2824, 2869–70.
[76] O'Sullivan, "Is There Opposition?" pp. 6–7.
[77] USCIR, *Final Report*, Vol. 4, p. 3186.

exploited divisions within its labor force to enable it to back out of the settlement that it had been forced to accept, withdraw recognition from the
Amalgamated, and set up its own successful "cooperative" labor relations
system, the Mitten Men and Management – a pioneering company union
– in December 1910. In line with the time-honored custom among frustrated union officers in the "Siberia of Organized Labor," Amalgamated
organizers ended up blaming their wouldn't-be members for their problems.
General Executive Board member William Fitzgerald opined that "The men
of Philadelphia are peculiar in characteristics." Organizer O'Shea went
further: He was "disgusted" with them. "They are a lot of thick Micks
[stupid Irishmen] of the shanty-type and you can't tell them anything." But
Mitten seemed to be able to.[78]

4.4 STRENGTHENING THE FOUNDATIONS, 1910–1915

While the titanic battles to secure the Open Shop were going on among the
commanding heights of the local economy, the MMA was preoccupied with
helping its members escape union pressures down among the foothills.
These resulted from the backwash of pro-labor sentiment and activism
stirred up by the mass strikes, and the repeated organizing campaigns
mounted by the Molders, the Machinists, and the AFL in general under the
"Labor Forward" banner, in the next four years. To carry out this task, the
MMA needed to do little more than repeat and extend its use of the tactics
that it had relied on to roll back the Molders and others in 1904–07.

Although the Molders had been driven out of the big machinery foundries
in 1904–07, they had maintained a toehold in the jobbing sector through
the recession that followed. So in 1910, at the time of the second PRT
dispute and the wave of sympathetic walkouts that accompanied it, they
were in a position to stage a partial recovery. Foundrymen still employing
union labor were induced to grant a wage increase, without any formal bargaining, but "on the understanding that a like increase would be asked for
and obtained from all shops in surrounding territory," so that city jobbing
firms should not be disadvantaged in the struggle for business in their local
market. The IMU was unable to keep its side of the bargain; but, although
the Philadelphia foundry trade may have been harmed somewhat thereby,
the IMU was not.[79]

[78] Luke Grant, "Co-Operative Plan of the Philadelphia Rapid Transit Co.," in Dubof-
      sky, ed., *USCIR Unpublished Records*, microfilm ed., Reel 6; USCIR, *Final Report*,
      Vol. 3, pp. 2733, 2793; copy of letter to T. E. Mitten, 18 Feb. 1920, in File
      10634.741, Box 3648, Military Intelligence Division Correspondence (hereafter
      MID), RG 165, National Archives.
[79] The Molders in Your Employ to Gentlemen, 25 March 1910, in North Bros. Mfg.
      Co. Papers, HML.

The IMU was set on the road to partial recovery, but not yet among MMA firms. For the moment, they were able to hold out without too much difficulty. For example, while the IMU mounted the largest strikes it had attempted in four years, the MMA gave "moral and financial assistance" to textile machinery builder Schaum & Uhlinger to take "legal action against the person or persons guilty of coercing, persuading, or inducing the indentured apprentices to leave their employ." This was a way of ensnaring the Molders' Union in litigation and blunting its attack. And while some Philadelphia foundrymen capitulated to the strike wave, the MMA helped two members and, "for the good of the cause," two open-shop nonmembers, to ride out this squall by supplying strike-breakers from the Labor Bureau.[80]

Second, the MMA engaged in its own smaller scale equivalent of the industrial war being waged above its head. The trouble center was the chandelier trade, whose members had failed to capitalize on their succession of small victories over the Brass Workers and Metal Polishers in 1904–06. The problem was that another related craft, the Metal Spinners (who turned brassware on special lathes), had not been confronted and defeated but merely quieted by unemployment, so that a nucleus for reorganization remained. And, in the recessionary aftermath of the earlier strikes, firms had concentrated on exploiting their short-term advantage by employing more cheap labor, but had done nothing to train genuine apprentices. Proper training required serious investment in human capital, which had the annoying habit of moving on in search of better wages at or before the end of their learning period. It was a difficult and unattractive enterprise for the small firm at the best of times, and between 1907 and 1910 labor had been in surplus and firms' priorities had been cost-cutting, not providing for a coming boom.

The result of this short-sighted policy had been that chandelier manufacturers found themselves over a barrel in 1910. Their skilled men were in a strong bargaining position, there were no adequate supplies of replacement workers in Philadelphia, and it was difficult to recruit out-of-towners because local wage rates were so low – an ironic effect of the employers' earlier success. The men demanded a wage increase and the closed shop, with the eight-hour day to follow. The five MMA members affected saw no choice but to fight to defend their labor costs and their rights.[81]

The MMA prepared itself for the coming struggle by amending its constitution to give it tighter control over members, who pledged "not to make any agreement either written or verbal with organized or unorganized labor, without first obtaining the consent in writing of the Executive Committee." New members won as a result of the MMA's taking the lead in confronting the chandelier crafts had the meaning of the new rule made clear to them,

[80] ECM 13 June and 12 July 1910; Morgan, SEC 1910, p. 5.
[81] Langworthy, PRES 1910, pp. 2–3; Morgan, SEC 1911, p. 1.

right from the outset. The association's collective interest in maintaining a united front against labor had to take precedence over any particular firm's individual interest in cutting a deal to save it from strife.[82]

The secretary took what were by then "the customary steps" in a large strike "to obtain men to fill the places of the strikers," setting up a temporary hiring office so as not to interfere with the Labor Bureau's normal business and to minimize the danger of its being tied up by picketing. Five firms that were not MMA members at the outset of the strike in October joined its struggle. Once again, a strike turned into an organizing opportunity, as the MMA decided to "render any assistance advisable to any chandelier manufacturer making application for membership, and supply them with any available help after the shops of the members had their full complement." The MMA voted up to $1,500 to cover extraordinary costs, "providing the defense of the strike is conducted in a manner satisfactory to our Executive Committee," and providing the nonmembers matched it dollar for dollar. The probationary members were admitted to full membership once they had fought through to a successful conclusion in 1911 and paid their full share of the defense costs that the MMA had assumed on their behalf.[83]

The strike was completely won, the "first break in the strikers' ranks" occurring when the MMA succeeded in reopening one of the large shops. It was more expensive than even the 1905–06 Molders' strikes, involving fewer men (about 400) but requiring the recruitment of more strike-breakers (650) without any assistance from a national employers' association. The MMA spent $3,510 gross, $1,048 net of the nonmembers' contributions, in 1910 and 1911. Most of this sum of almost $9 per striker – about four days' wages – was for the costs of advertising for and hiring replacements, and transporting them. A little ($5) was for "Information," and $180 paid for securitymen who were recruited to protect strike-breakers until adequate police protection could be obtained. The strike lasted three months, and ended in "a very signal victory" with the "men ... ordered to return to their respective shops by their Officials and if possible to secure their positions *as individuals*" (emphasis in original). The MMA celebrated by returning the unexpended balance in the defense account to cooperating firms for the payment of bonuses to the loyal workmen who had seen them through this difficulty.[84]

However, even successful strike-breaking was not unproblematic. The MMA's strikes were not bloody affairs – the hiring of a few guards in 1910

[82] Membership Applications, MMAP II-4-28.
[83] ECM 17 Oct. 1910.
[84] ECM 17 Oct., 31 Oct., 8 and 9 Nov., 14 Dec. 1910, 11 Jan., 18 Oct. 1911; Morgan, SEC 1909, p. 5; Chandelier Strike final account, ECM 8 March 1911; Treasurer's Reports for 1910 and 1911, MMAP III-4-2; Morgan, SEC 1911, p. 3.

and the payment of $11 to a strike-breaker, Carl Lutz, "which represented two and half days' time and replacing a tooth" damaged in a picket-line brawl in 1912, were the only pale reflections of the "age of industrial violence" it recorded during all these years of strenuous struggle. Nor were they costly for the association. But for individual affected members they could be disastrous.[85]

For the chandelier manufacturers in general, "The year 1910 would have been a banner year . . . but for the disturbances among mechanics," as one of them complained. For the Lawrence Gas Fixture Mfg. Co., already weakened by three years of below-normal business, and managerial incompetence and fraud, fighting the good fight pushed it over the precipice into bankruptcy. Lawrence Dickey represented the industry on the MMA executive committee, so his large firm was in the front line during the strike. As he told the bankruptcy examiner in 1912, "We were obliged to conduct that strike and were paying hands such as they were . . . which was constantly pouring out the funds without getting any direct results. . . . [W]e lost in addition to that some of our very best customers. . . . In fact we would have been better off closed down . . . than if we attempted to run." Even when the strike had been won, its disturbing, productivity-damaging effects lingered on, as "the help was coming in one day and going out the next and we were not settled for months afterwards."[86]

Continuing conflict with the Molders caused even more difficulty than with the Brass Workers. After 1910's small victory they slowly rebuilt their organization from its foundations in the jobbing sector, spreading back into some of the smaller machinery foundries, too, until by prosperous 1913 they were in a position to exploit favorable conditions, including the Labor Forward campaign. The MMA as usual helped members to resist, and nonmembers who were willing to take the heat. Secretary Morgan boasted that "the strikers' places filled so easily that it caused hardly a ripple in the usual conduct of the office," and that grateful nonmembers "operating satisfactorily with men furnished by the Bureau on 'Open Shop' basis" had accordingly joined the association. But from the perspective of one of those new members, Edward Hitzeroth, who ended up in bankruptcy court a little later than Lawrence Dickey, this glorious victory was decidedly pyrrhic. He

---

[85] ECM 20 June and 10 July 1912. In the Lutz case, "absolute 'Police' protection had been promised," and "there was no trouble to be anticipated" because the strike involved unorganized, unskilled workers. Thus the MMA executive committee did not consider the assault on Lutz to be among the risks he could fairly have been expected to know that he was assuming by volunteering to scab.

[86] Commonwealth of Pennsylvania, Secretary for Internal Affairs, *38th Annual Report: Report of the Bureau of Industrial Statistics for 1910* (Harrisburg, 1911), pp. 347–48 (pp. 329–441 record the impact and dimensions of the sympathetic strike wave); Bankruptcy Records, Case No. 4323, pp. 8, 11, 26–27, 81, Philadelphia Federal Records Center, explain the company's collapse.

had felt compelled to resist the effort to unionize his shop, as "that is a little expensive." But the replacement molders that Morgan supplied, although "good for moral effect," were "not exactly good for making good castings." Unlike Dickey, he did not blame his failure on his men and their quarrels – "there is a fine line between success and failure and I got the bum end of the stick" – but he was sure that they were a part of his problem.[87]

In fact, Morgan's sanguine report was misleading, and not just from the perspective of Hitzeroth, who had not thought that he could afford to lose to the IMU, but who – it turned out – could not afford to "win" either. The IMU's patient fightback reestablished union shop conditions at about thirty firms with almost 3,000 employees. Thirty-seven firms with foundry departments, employing over 23,000 workers, remained definite "open shops" at the same time, so the scale of the Molders' recovery should not be exaggerated. But they were strong enough that, during 1913's campaign, they succeeded in getting a resumption of formal local bargaining through the Philadelphia Foundrymen's Club (PFC), of which several MMA machinery foundries were also members. The standard contract that resulted covered about twenty companies with a 1915–16 employment of over 2,100. It dealt with recognition, working practices, and the establishment of a grievance procedure, as well as hours and wages. Its effect was wider than its coverage: It set employment conditions for the non-PFC foundries that were union shops, and it strongly influenced the basic wage at open shops, too.[88]

The success of the Molders' campaign raised two crucial issues for the MMA. The first was how far it was prepared to go for the sake of winning and holding onto control. Justus Schwacke, MMA and NFA vice president at the time, and NMTA president in 1910–11, asked the executive committee's opinion "regarding employment of operatives for inside work [a euphemism for spies] to be known to only one person connected with the Association, and reports to be furnished to the individual, and copy without signature of the operative to be furnished the management in whose employ the party may be." Former president Hallowell, a Hicksite Quaker, opposed the idea, which would have represented a revolutionary departure from the

---

[87] Morgan, SEC 1913, p. 9; Bankruptcy Records, Case No. 5498, Testimony 15 Nov. 1915, p. 10.

[88] Lists of Concerns Represented at the Meeting of The Philadelphia Foundrymen's Club, 22 Apr. 1913 and of Philadelphia Foundries 1913, in MMAP II-3-14; testimony of Charles B. Torpy (business agent, Molders), in USCIR, *Final Report*, Vol. 3, p. 2920; Philadelphia Foundrymen's Club, "To the Moulders (*sic*) in our employ," 25 Apr. 1913; Philadelphia Foundrymen's Club to Gentlemen, 26 June 1913; "Phila. Foundries Recognize Molders in Great Contract," *Trades Union News* (3 July 1913): 1; all employment data from PID-1640 database.

MMA's style of confrontational but clean anti-unionism; so no "sense of the meeting" developed and the proposal was shelved.[89]

The second question was, What should the MMA do about members who failed to hold the line against organized labor? But it was decided instead that tactical compromise was inevitable or even desirable. The MMA's formal constitutional rule, after the 1910 Chandelier Strike, required members to submit any proposed verbal or written union contract for prior approval, and there was no way in which the PFC–IMU relationship satisfied its principles or NFA and NMTA standards. Any member entering into an unacceptable deal was to be disciplined; any applicant for membership who showed signs of feebleness of will was to be excluded.

But it was one thing to enforce these stern rules against members employing brass workers or machinists, who – experience had shown – could easily be whipped; it was quite another to apply them to a fraction of the MMA's core membership who had fought the IMU for almost a decade and had finally decided to throw in the towel. The MMA had a choice: adhere to its principles, or recognize the difficulty of the situation in which otherwise-loyal members found themselves. Sensibly it chose the latter course.

The result was that after 1913 the MMA once again contained a minority of members who dealt with the IMU by making contracts with it rather than by fighting – 7 firms with an aggregate employment of 1,166 (mean: 167) as against 19 foundry operators employing 4,174 (mean: 220), which remained open shops. This was not a situation that the executive committee approved of, or wished to see deteriorate any further, but it was one with which, as pragmatists, they were prepared to live until an opportunity to rid themselves of contracts with the IMU, and one which did not involve expelling existing members, might arise. Two alternative systems of labor relations therefore coexisted in the prewar and wartime Philadelphia foundry trade, and within the MMA itself. Total victory for the Open Shop would not become possible for another decade.[90]

Conditions in the foundry trade were peculiarly difficult, and the MMA's uneasy compromise with some of its members did not need to be replicated elsewhere. All unions other than the IMU had been utterly defeated – by the MMA's own actions, by recurrent unemployment, and by the giant open shops. The MMA's strike-breaking tactics were honed to perfection, but they had been so successful, and the context was so favorable, that they

[89] ECM 16 Apr. 1913.
[90] For the PFC's continuing preference for a collective contract against the MMA's official position, see discussion in ECM 18 Oct. 1921.

rarely needed to be deployed any more. In this unfavorable setting it was, as the Machinists' Vice President Wilson complained in 1913, "awful hard to get [nonunion men] started," that is, interested in joining. But, as one of his members wrote, "Hand wringing doesn't organize the Philadelphia nonunion machinist" in this "stronghold of the Manufacturers' Association." Another bitterly denounced "machinists . . . who report initiations etc. to local agencies," and described how MMA members "directed you to the [Labor Bureau], where you gave your history before getting a job." As Wilson summarized the situation, "it is a real union man that carries a card in a city like this." In June 1914, the Industrial Relations Commission's sympathetic field investigator O'Sullivan asked local business agents to tell him, in confidence, how things stood. They were uniformly pessimistic, and with good reason. Their private estimates of the extent of local union membership in their trades were 2.5 percent for the Blacksmiths, 5 percent for the Boilermakers, 5.5 to 11 percent for the Machinists, depending on whether less-skilled machinists were counted as potential recruits, and 35 percent for the Molders, mostly in stove and job shops. The employers had "absolute control of the situation. . . . There is nothing left for the men to do other than to accept the terms offered. . . . The Unions . . . are in no position to help themselves."[91]

Employers held all of the advantages including, crucially, the renewed ability to exploit a weak labor market. MMA members' employment fell by 27 percent between the spring of 1914 and the summer of 1915; the decline in payrolls was even steeper, as short-time working became the norm. The recession was all the worse for being unexpected; according to Link-Belt's James Mapes Dodge, testifying before the Industrial Relations Commission in June 1914, when the collapse was at its steepest, business was "falling off like smoke." The labor market touched bottom in the second quarter of 1915, its year-long decline having overwhelmed the AFL's Labor Forward membership drive as effectively as the Crash of 1907 had stilled an earlier campaign. The IAM complained in 1915, to Secretary Morgan's satisfaction, that Philadelphia had become "the 'Scab City' of the country." Morgan thought of it differently, as "the Mecca for the independent workmen. . . . The no-card man leaves the city where there is strife and comes to Philadelphia, and stays at least until the trouble is over at home. 'Open Shop' principles, combined with the usually fair treatment accorded

[91] See regular reports of IAM vice president Wilson and business agent Keenan, and members' correspondence – *MMJ* 25 (1913): 573, 671–72, 779, 1036, 1142, 1259–60; 26 (1914): 83; 27 (1915): 1021, 1137, 1138, quotes from pp. 573 (1913), 83 (1914), 1137 (1915); O'Sullivan, "Interviews with Union Leaders on Efforts to Organize Metal Trades in Phliadelphia," June 1914, in Dubofsky, ed., *USCIR Unpublished Records*, microfilm ed., Reel 8, figures pp. 7–13, quotes pp. 7, 10.

the employees in our City, make our pleasant relations with them possible." Both of them were right, but only one of them was happy.[92]

5.5 THE CHALLENGE OF POLITICS

Although in the short term there were few threats to the Open Shop in Philadelphia in the last prewar years, there were stormclouds on the political horizon. The MMA's leading role in erecting the Open Shop's defenses exposed it to public scrutiny. By 1913–14, try as it might, the MMA was unable to prevent some unwelcome intrusion in its own and its members' private affairs. The AFL's metal trades unions might have lacked members in Philadelphia, but by 1913 they had influential friends in the Pennsylvania legislature in Harrisburg, in the Wilson Administration in Washington, and with the U.S. Commission on Industrial Relations, which held hearings in Philadelphia in 1914 in the midst of the AFL's Labor Forward organizing campaign. Schwacke (by then president) and Secretary Morgan were subjected to critical questioning along with representatives of the giant firms that had also done so much to win Philadelphia its notoriety in labor circles. It was just as well that the MMA had decided to keep its hands clean in 1913, because that meant that there was nothing embarrassing in its records for the commission's investigators to discover.[93]

The threat of legislation in workers' interests emanating from the Pennsylvania or federal legislatures had already provoked it to get involved in lobbying on its members' behalf. Meeting this new danger added to the range of the MMA's usefulness as the labor problem receded in immediate importance. As President Langworthy put it in 1910,

If this Association had no labor bureau, and if it made no effort to assist its members in their times of need, it would still be worth its cost in time and money if its only office were to scrutinize the labor bills submitted to the Legislature of the state, and to effectively assist in preventing the passage of those which are harmful or vicious.[94]

The politicization of industrial relations, and therefore the countermobilization of the employing community, had begun in 1907, as far as the MMA was concerned. The problem was that Pennsylvania's largest, most concentrated, and best organized group of industrial workers – coal miners – was a potent political force, compelling candidates and legislators of both

---

[92] ECM 11 March 1914, 9 June 1915; Morgan, SEC 1914, p. 1; USCIR, *Final Report*, Vol. 1, p. 866; Philadelphia Emergency Aid Committee, *Special Report* (n.p., c. 1915), esp. pp. 3–13; Morgan, SEC 1915, p. 1.

[93] USCIR, *Final Report*, Vol. 3, pp. 2889–2914; Morgan, SEC 1914, p. 3.

[94] Langworthy, PRES 1910, p. 3.

parties to pay attention to their interests, and returning sympathizers to Harrisburg and Washington. With this voting bloc behind him, former United Mine Workers officer William B. Wilson became a Democratic Congressman, the leader of labor's friends in Congress, and, in 1913, Woodrow Wilson's Secretary of Labor. Pennsylvania workers therefore had an influential ally in high places.[95]

At the head of labor's political agenda, in a state littered with health- and life-destroying industries, was the issue of employers' liability for fatal or merely injurious occupational accidents. Pennsylvania employers had grown used to enjoying unusually thorough protection against compensation suits brought by injured employees or late employees' grieving and destitute relatives. The rules of contributory negligence, assumption of risk, and fellow-servant liability meant that employers had little to fear in court if they failed to buy off damaged workers or their bereft dependants on the cheap beforehand. Metal trades employers were particularly vulnerable if any breaches were made in these legal defenses, because their industries were responsible for the greatest number of accidents – relatively and absolutely – in the state.[96]

The threat of the removal of their protective screen persuaded the MMA to take the initiative. They called on employers' associations throughout the state to pool their resources and employ permanent counsel to lobby at Harrisburg on their behalf against what the National Association of Manufacturers (NAM)'s counsel James Emery, speaking at the MMA's annual banquet, denounced as the danger of "Class Domination in Government." The coal miners had secured the pledges of both Republicans and Democrats to introduce a reformed liability law, and legislators brought in six bills of varying degrees of breadth and severity in response.[97]

The employers' coalition that the MMA helped to coordinate fought back. They realized that some sort of change in the law, however undesirable in principle, was inevitable; so they decided to throw their weight behind the mildest of the measures that the AFL supported, and to oppose the rest. This action had the desired effect – labor's lobbyists backed down when they "realized that the employers were thoroughly in earnest" and withdrew all of their bills except the least radical, which, after further

[95]   For Wilson, see John Lombardi, *Labor's Voice in the Cabinet* (New York, 1942), esp. Ch. 3; for the national context, see Julie Greene, *Pure and Simple Politics: The American Federation of Labor, 1881 to 1917* (New York, 1998).

[96]   Albert S. Bolles, *The Legal Relations Between the Employed and the Employers in Pennsylvania Compared With the Relations Existing Between Them in Other States* (Harrisburg, 1901), p. 178; Commissioner of Labor and Industry, Commonwealth of Pennsylvania, *First Annual Report* (Harrisburg, 1913), Pt. II, p. 25; *Third Annual Report* (Harrisburg, 1915), Pt. II, p. 253.

[97]   ECM 20 Feb., 13 March, 10 Apr., 12 June 1907; Banquet Program, MMAP II-3-4; Philadelphia Trades League, *17th Annual Report* (Philadelphia, 1907), pp. 88–94.

watering-down, passed into law. The only common-law defense that Pennsylvania employers lost was the fellow-servant doctrine; in other respects they were still well protected by a law whose conservative inspiration was the 1880 English statute, not any wider ranging recent American precedent.[98]

The state's employers did not follow up on their victory by establishing a permanent lobby, as the MMA had recommended; but nevertheless the MMA had cut its first legislative teeth, and would rarely be uninvolved in politics thereafter. In 1908, it collaborated with the NAM in lobbying against federal Eight-Hour and Anti-Injunction bills, and tried to persuade Pennsylvania members of the Republican Party's Committee on Resolutions against the inclusion of pro-labor planks on these issues in the national party platform. And in 1910, at the invitation of Pittsburgh NMTA branch leader, George Mesta, the MMA sent representatives to a joint meeting of manufacturers' associations "in our line of business" called to discuss a collective response to the renewed threat of pro-labor legislation. Pittsburgh, Erie, Lehigh County (Bethlehem and Allentown), and Philadelphia – all storm centers of union–employer confrontations in the metal trades – joined forces.[99]

As in 1907, the heavy industrial employers' priority was the limitation of their liability for industrial accidents. But by 1910 they found influential collaborators among the state's textile industry, centered in Philadelphia, whose major fear was tighter regulation of child labor and women's working hours, which would restrict their labor supply and their freedom to utilize it, and raise their labor costs. Both groups were also concerned about proposals for higher business taxes, and out of their defensive alliance grew the Pennsylvania Manufacturers' Association (PMA). Its first successful political skirmish in 1911 resulted in reference of the compensation issue to a state Industrial Commission, heading off the immediate legislative threat and giving the PMA time to marshal its forces and its arguments.

The context in which the PMA was created seemed multiply threatening. Pennsylvania's basic industries were meeting severe competition from newer, more dynamic regions within the United States and from abroad. Business confidence and prospects were in any case low between the recession of 1907–08 and that of 1914–15. And now, the last straw, Pennsylvania manufacturers already suffering from excess capacity and poor profitability were surrounded by a sea of uncomprehending domestic enemies – Democrats threatening the tariff and the labor-progressive coalition trying to restrict employers' freedom and increase

---

[98]   McPherson, SEC 1907, pp. 6–8.
[99]   ECM 19 May 1908; Hallowell, PRES 1908, p. 10; ECM 17 Oct. 1910; Langworthy, PRES 1910, p. 4.

their costs. The PMA was a direct response to the efforts of these "enemies within."

Its basic assumptions were productionist and strongly individualistic. Manufacturing was, in PMA President Joseph Grundy's words, "the very foundation of civilization." Therefore manufacturers were not a political "special interest" on a par with organized labor; instead, theirs was the true public interest: "We could not be accused of selfishness because we were . . . the advocates for all the State and for all the people of the State." The "great enemy" was "government and labor leaders who interfere with 'natural' economic forces. Government . . . should either be 'friendly' or indifferent." "The laboring man . . . need[s] no leader . . . other than himself and his employer with whom he share[s] a congenial interest."[100]

The MMA was the PMA's largest single affiliated organization, accounting for one-seventh of the original membership and collaborating with it very closely from the start. Two members of the MMA's executive committee, Justus Schwacke and lighting equipment manufacturer Robert Biddle, became a "Committee on Law and Legislation" and the contact men between the two associations. The MMA also subscribed funds that helped enable the PMA to "retain the services of an 'Expert,' and . . . inaugurate a campaign of education in what would be undesirable features, and eventually draft an improved bill for the approval of the Commission on Workmen's Compensation." The MMA's contribution was relatively large, whether measured against its own revenue or the PMA's, amounting to about one-tenth of both.[101]

The commission's own tentative draft was "very materially" amended to meet the requirements of the PMA, the Builders' Exchange, the Manufacturers' Club, and other interested bodies. The PMA fought hard and cleverly, relying partly on its excellent relations with Senator Boies Penrose's state Republican machine, and partly on its tactical skill in proposing "acceptable," that is, weaker and cheaper, alternative measures, rather than just saying no. As in 1907, the manufacturers were prepared to deal with the State Federation of Labor by demonstrating that neither side had the political clout to secure everything they wanted, although they could block their rivals' schemes, so they had better compromise.[102]

Eventually, in 1915, Harrisburg produced a system that freed the manufacturers from the disturbing prospect of generous awards granted by

[100]   J. Roffe Wike, *The Pennsylvania Manufacturers' Association* (Philadelphia, 1960), Ch. 1 and quotes pp. 84, 89, 103, 86; Ann H. Hutton, *The Pennsylvanian: Joseph R. Grundy* (Philadelphia, 1962), esp. Chs. 9–11, is a highly sympathetic yet revealing portrait of the man, his ideas, and his methods. Cf. Alfred H. Kelly, "A History of the Illinois Manufacturers' Association" (Ph.D. diss., University of Chicago, 1938), esp. pp. 8–13, for a broadly similar story of mobilization on the workmen's compensation issue.

[101]   Morgan, SEC 1911, p. 4; ECM 17 Apr., 12 June, 28 Aug., 11 Dec. 1912, 8 Jan. 1913; Wike, *PMA*, p. 58.

[102]   ECM 11 Sept. 1912; Wike, *PMA*, p. 20; ECM 8 Dec. 1915; Wike, *PMA*, pp. 35–36.

sympathetic juries once the remaining common-law defenses were removed, and also protected them against any open-ended "no fault" compensation law. It substituted a fixed tariff – so much for an arm, a leg, or a life. Compensation payments under the new system were not large, quick, or automatic, and their real value was soon eroded by wartime inflation. They were also predictable, so the PMA was able to establish a Casualty Insurance Company to provide its members with inexpensive protection against the acceptable risks involved in paying the price of industrial accidents. The law made insurance carriers the administrators of the scheme, so employer control further undermined claimants' rights. The MMA's members, men who were never inclined to ignore an opportunity for economy, bought into this excellent mutual insurance arrangement. Schwacke and Biddle doubled up as its Committee on Insurance, reinforcing the ties between the MMA and the PMA, which had helped stave off something much worse.[103]

The labor-progressive alliance was at its strongest during the 1913 General Assembly. By that time the PMA, which President Langworthy called "the manufacturers' legislative watch-dog," was a "powerful organization" that won "national prominence and drew a hot fire of abuse and vilification from political interests which resented its interference with the well-laid plans to ride into popular favor at the expense of the manufacturers." It opposed "pernicious" legislation, particularly the "theoretical propositions advanced by the alleged up-lifters looking toward different hours of labor for different classes of help" (that is, limits of fifty hours for women and forty-eight for children). It was a "great industrial army, which in the present unsettled condition of popular sentiment, is the chief hope and bulwark of the men who invest their money in private enterprises." One of those "up-lifters," Pennsylvania Child Labor Association President Jasper Brinton, agreed that they were "probably the most able representatives of (sic) any legislature . . . in the country today."[104] Secretary Morgan reinforced Langworthy's message, arguing that

No thinking man can doubt that [the 1913 session] . . . has demonstrated more clearly than ever before the absolute necessity of Associations of Employers. If there be a doubt in the mind of any member of this Association, a calm review of the continued encroachments and advances of Organized Labor from a legislative standpoint, both Federal and State, should convince him of the fallacy of his reasoning,

---

[103] John P. Horlacher, "The Results of Workmen's Compensation in Pennsylvania: A Study of the Pennsylvania System from the Point of View of the Injured Worker," Commonwealth of Pennsylvania Department of Labor and Industry, *Special Bulletin* No. 40, Pt. I-b (Harrisburg, 1940); cf. Robert Asher, "Business and Workers' Welfare in the Progressive Era: Workmen's Compensation Reform in Massachusetts, 1880–1911," *BHR* 43 (1969): 452–75, and "Failure and Fulfillment: Agitation for Employers' Liability Legislation and the Origins of the Workmen's Compensation in New York State, 1876–1910," *Labor History* 24 (1983): 198–222.

[104] Langworthy, PRES 1913, pp. 4–5; Brinton testimony in USCIR, *Final Report*, Vol. 3, p. 2955.

and be an object lesson. The Legislation endorsed by Organized Labor, and enacted because of their active interest as organized bodies, voiced as organizations when conditions seem to warrant it, has now become a force that only concerted opposition expressed by organized employers can successfully combat.[105]

The danger of "political interference," and the resulting necessity for political action, gave the MMA a new function, a new raison d'être. It evolved into what President Langworthy called "a strike insurance agency, a strike breaking agency, a labor bureau . . . [and] a body to guard (*sic*) labor legislation," all rolled into one. Members could buy all of their necessary protection and, after 1915, their liability insurance, too, through one organization, for a low and, in real terms, declining cost. The manufacturer's search for economy, control, and predictability in an uncertain political environment helped the MMA to retain the loyalty of its members, even when the recession of 1914–15 forced many to retrench, and shattered the organizing prospects of their union antagonists.[106]

The MMA, like the PMA, learned a new political sophistication. It did not just fight against the legislative menace from Harrisburg; it worked with it, understanding that politicians and administrators were prepared to cut deals with the powerful interests that they were attempting to regulate, in the interests of minimizing opposition. Thus, for example, when in 1915 a bill to tighten the hitherto-negligible controls over employment agencies was introduced, the MMA, with the PMA's assistance, lobbied its draftsman and the commissioner of the Commonwealth Department of Labor and Industry, John Price Jackson. As a result, "departments or bureaus maintained by persons, firms, or corporations, or associations, for the purpose of obtaining help for themselves, where no fee is charged the applicant for employment," were left completely free of the new law's restrictions.[107]

Commissioner Jackson, a politically sensitive man, proved ever ready to lend an ear to manufacturers' arguments. Short of staff and funds, and unsure of the solidity and permanence of his agency's political backing, he resolved to proceed by consultation with all the interests that his sincere desire to reduce "our enormous accident toll" affected. His corporatist, consensus-seeking approach gave employers, equipment builders, and craft unions representation on the industry committees that were to develop health and safety standards, and relied on voluntary cooperation, not legal action, to get those standards accepted.[108]

---

[105]   Morgan, SEC 1913, p. 8.
[106]   Langworthy, PRES 1910, p. 2.
[107]   Morgan, SEC 1915, p. 4.
[108]   Commissioner of Labor and Industry, *First Annual Report* (1913), Pt. I, p. 279, Pt. II, pp. 1–5, 25, 257–69, 322–27, 343, 355, 459; *Second Annual Report* (1914), Pt. I, pp. viii–xi; *Third Annual Report* (1915), Pt. II, pp. 7 (quote), 253.

In a state with as conservative a political culture as Pennsylvania's, and such strongly organized manufacturers, Jackson's caution was understandable. But giving a spokesman for the law-breakers, like MMA Secretary Morgan, who was made a member of the Foundry Safety Committee, a voice in determining what the law should be, and when and how it should be applied, did not guarantee the swift promulgation or strict enforcement of the safeguards that Pennsylvania workers badly needed. The Foundry Safety Committee, for example, was still debating the necessity of prohibiting boys from carrying heavy ladles of molten metal through the foundry's smoky gloom, across rough earth floors littered with obstructions, eleven years after it was established. Secretary Morgan and his colleagues did a fine job of representing their members' interests, but giving the poachers the biggest say in writing the game laws was not good for the pheasants' health.[109]

4.6 CONCLUSION

The MMA's first eventful decade had demonstrated its founders' wisdom. The structure, strategy, and tactics that they adopted all worked extremely well. The secretaries that the officers chose were competent and committed, making the members' interests their own, and showing ingenuity and even relish in the anti-labor battles. Resources were always sufficient for the tasks that the MMA set for itself. The members understood that it was better to hang together than to be hung separately, so they rarely tried to pursue immediate self-interest when that conflicted with the costs and discipline of collective self-defense. The MMA worked because its members wanted it to, not because it had much control over them. They displayed a high degree of class-consciousness, solidarity, and organizational sophistication, and were well rewarded for it.

In a larger sense, the MMA succeeded because almost everything it encountered in its working environment favored it rather than its opponents, not because of its own efforts and virtues. It received more useful assistance from state and national employers' associations than the fragile local labor movement ever got from international unions or the AFL. It had powerful allies in the shape of the giant local open shops, particularly Baldwin. It could usually rely on a favorable hearing from city and even state authorities, and the intervention of the local police, the state militia, local justices, and federal judges, while rarely decisive in strikes, was always helpful. Finally, the establishment of the Open Shop depended on the interaction between the employers' always dominant position in the labor

---

[109] ECM 23 Feb., 26 March, 27 Apr., 5 Oct., 23 Nov., 28 Dec. 1926.

market and their ability to exploit recurrent recessions in 1903–04, 1907–08, and 1914–15 (see Figures 3.2, 3.3, and 4.1).

In these and other respects, the local victories of the MMA depended on the normal structural advantages of capital in the American political economy rather than on anything special about its own behavior. They paralleled what was happening in the metal trades more generally. Nevertheless, it is worth examining key features of the way in which the MMA organized itself and its relations with its members' employees to make the most of its resources and opportunities. This will be the purpose of the next chapter, which will temporarily abandon narrative in order to anatomize the MMA as a working example of the kind of local employers' association that undergirded the Open Shop movement.

5

"The Largest, Strongest, and Most Valuable Association of Metal Manufacturers in Any City"[1]

This chapter examines the internal sources of the association's strength and success – patterns of membership and recruitment, leadership and cohesion, revenue and expenditure – particularly during its first two decades, when it was a classic local employers' organization (see Table 5.1). Following the money trail will lead to a consideration of what the MMA did, year in and year out, to serve its members' interests and retain their loyalty – in particular, of its Labor Bureau's role in assisting them with the management of their everyday employment relations during times of industrial peace.

5.1 A "COMPACT LOYAL BODY OF MANUFACTURERS" WITH "NO STRANGERS AMONG US"[2]

The MMA grew rapidly during its first two years and thereafter its membership stabilized at about fifty-five firms (plus or minus a handful) until the war, their numbers fluctuating in response to the ebb and flow of prosperity, although more slowly and less dramatically than their total employment (see Figure 5.1). Nor was there much change in their character. Qualitative and quantitative evidence demonstrates that, throughout its first two decades, the MMA continued to recruit best among the middling sort of locally owned and controlled metal-working firms, drawn from the same few industries. They were generally the bigger enterprises within those industries, but none of them employed more than some hundreds of

---

[1] Hallowell, PRES 1908, p. 3. NMTA figures for 1912 just about support this claim – if the MMA is measured in terms of its aggregate workforce rather than its membership. The MMA was actually about as big as the larger NMTA branches. But, unlike them, it also covered its members' foundry workforces, so a comparable employment total would have been somewhat smaller. See Table 5.1.

[2] Langworthy, PRES 1909, p. 5, and 1911, p. 4.

TABLE 5.1 The MMA and NMTA City Branches Compared, 1912

NMTA CITY BRANCH	Firms	Operatives	Mean
Boston	37	1,748	47
Chicago	88	3,525	40
Cincinnati	64	3,127	49
Cleveland	46	4,682	102
Hartford, CT	16	1,222	76
Indianapolis	25	1,789	72
New Haven	27	2,795	104
New York & New Jersey	66	4,695	71
Pittsburgh	18	710	39
Rhode Island	28	4,704	168
Springfield, MA	26	2,723	105
St. Louis	38	1,505	40
Tri-City	12	1,280	107
Worcester	55	3,656	66
Average			70
PHILADELPHIA	63	4,848	77

Source: NMTA, *Synopsis of Proceedings of the 14th Annual Convention* (New York, 1912), p. 21, and sources for Figure 5.1.

workers, and most of them far fewer. Chronic concerns about the threat posed by the same few craft unions welded this group together.

One of the sources of the MMA's strength was the way in which it united the advantages of having outside affiliations – particularly with the PMA, NFA, NMTA, and NAM – on which it could rely for specialized advice and assistance, and deep roots in its own community. The MMA limited its recruitment to the twin cities of Philadelphia and of Camden, New Jersey. Camden was part of the same labor market, and its mid-sized metal trades firms served the same product markets as their brothers across the Delaware. The huge, modern New York Shipbuilding and Victor Talking Machine Corporations stood in the same relation to them – as important local customers and guarantors of the open shop character of the common labor market – as Cramp's or Baldwin's did to their Philadelphia peers. Their owner-managers were also members of the same churches, clubs, and societies as their Philadelphia brethren, and lived in the same suburbs. Given these numerous ties, and Camden's proximity, membership applications from a part of the metropolitan area that just happened to be in a differ-

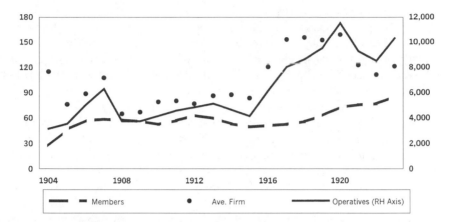

Figure 5.1. Growth of the MMA, 1904–1923. *Note:* These time series show clearly the various phases of the MMA's growth: rapid increase in 1904–06; stabilization and slow erosion by recession in 1907–10; resumed growth in 1911–12; shrinkage in 1913–15 in response to economic uncertainty and the MMA's own policy of shedding smaller members; and sustained growth thereafter. Year-on-year change in mean firm size reflects both cyclical variations in the labor force of firms that maintained their membership, and (in 1904–05, 1911–12) the effect of recruiting additional members, smaller on average than the original firms. Between 1912 and 1913 introduction of the minimum dues level "purges" small firms, and increases average firm size markedly, though nothing like as much as the war boom. *Source:* MMAYEARS database; reports on operatives in MMA Minutes, Secretaries', Treasurers', and Presidents' reports for respective years.

ent state met with none of the objections that induced the MMA to turn down firms from the smaller cities in Philadelphia's southeastern Pennsylvania hinterland.[3]

MMA members were Philadelphia institutions in terms of their ownership and control, as well as just their location. A survey of all 180 firms that were members at some time before 1925 reveals just three pure out-of-towners. One, Savage Arms, was a bird of passage, only present in Philadelphia and the MMA during the war. The other two, General Electric and Westinghouse, only built their Philadelphia factories and joined up after the war. All of these branch plants were large, and the latter two would in time become influential members, but they were scarcely significant exceptions to the MMA's rule of localism. They were marginal to it during most of the period in question. There were a few other members that were either (1) Philadelphia enterprises taken over by out-of-town corporations,

---

[3] ECM 12 June 1906; for Camden, see J. Frederick Dewhurst, *Commercial Survey of the Philadelphia Marketing Area* (Washington, 1925), p. 59.

but whose local executives (usually the previous proprietors, who had probably exchanged ownership for an equity stake) remained in place for long
periods thereafter, and continued to enjoy substantial autonomy; or (2)
Philadelphia branches of close corporations headquartered elsewhere, but
whose managers stayed put for years or decades on end and were well integrated into the local entrepreneurial community; or (3) Philadelphia firms
that grew by merger and acquired out-of-town plants themselves, but which
still had their primary locus of operations, ownership, and decision making
in the city. Each of these categories contributed some of the MMA's largest
and most influential members, and strengthened the MMA's connections
with national employers' associations and other business communities. But,
even taken together, they did not fundamentally challenge the MMA's essentially provincial character.[4]

The great bulk of the MMA's pre-1925 members were therefore typical
of that home-grown, proprietary capitalist business community introduced
in Chapter 2. The 170 of them (95 percent) that could be traced in local
business directories on at least one of three survey dates (1903, 1913, and
1925) were almost all sole proprietorships and partnerships; or family firms
with several men sharing the same surname active in senior management at
the same time and/or intergenerational succession; or close corporations
with a stable group of stakeholding senior executives, who were often
related to one another. Firms moved both ways along this spectrum from
simpler to slightly more complex forms of ownership and control across
the decades, but they rarely moved outside of its limits.[5]

It is therefore plain that MMA member firms, almost irrespective of size,
were examples of "traditional" rather than "modern" ways of organizing
a business. The men at their head made up the group of "business principals" who were active within the MMA. It was an association of employing capitalists, rather than of firms represented by their professional
managers, who were quite thin on the ground.

Surveys conducted by the association and by the state permit us to get a
rough idea of the distribution of employment among members, and of
members and employment among industries, in its early years. Within the
context of the highly skewed distribution of employment among companies
in the Philadelphia metal trades as a whole (see Figures 2.1 and 5.2), most
MMA firms ranked as middle-sized. But it also had its own internal
dualism, with a small number of members employing the bulk of the aggregate workforce and dominating the association's affairs. In January 1905,

---

[4]   Category 1 – Hess-Bright Bearing (later SKF), Niles-Bement-Pond, Otis Elevator;
       category 2 – Adams & Westlake, Link-Belt (both Chicago-based), and Autocar Co.
       (Pittsburgh); category 3 – Williamson Bros./American Engineering. All data from
       MMAYEARS, MMAEXEC, PHILCHAP, 1902FACT, and PID-1640 databases.
[5]   PHILCHAP database, supplemented by *Moody's Industrials* (New York, 1922).

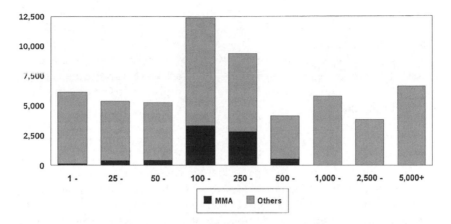

Figure 5.2. Distribution of Metal Trades Employment, by Size of Firm – Philadelphia, 1915–1916. *Note:* These data, unlike those for Figure 2.1, do *not* include the shipbuilding industry, i.e., Cramp. There is no 10,000+ category because Baldwin was shrunken by recession. *Source:* PID-1640 database.

for example, nine of the association's forty members employed more than half of the reported "operatives." William Sellers, the largest of all, accounted for an eighth of the total. These were the firms that provided the association with most of its leadership, consisting primarily of machinery foundrymen and the larger machine-shop operators who were also members or activists within the NFA and NMTA.[6]

The MMA's close identification with the *mittelstand* of the metal-manufacturing community was partly a result of deliberate policy. It set a minimum dues level (raised in 1913) to discourage membership from very small firms, which cost more to service than they paid in contributions, were chronically vulnerable to craft union pressure, and brought few worthwhile resources to the anti-labor fight. And it had no maximum dues level, or graduated scale, until the mid-1920s either, so that larger recruits would have found themselves paying heavily for services that they were well able to provide for themselves, and were understandably reluctant to join on these terms.[7]

---

[6] Assessment for Quarter Beginning Jan. 1. 1905, MMAP II-4-30; MMAEXEC database for "active minority"; NFA9805 and NMTA0036 databases. Using employment data from 1902FACT for the same firms, we find that those with over 100 employees made up just over 40 percent of the members but employed almost 80 percent of the recorded labor force; firms with more than 250 people made up about one-eighth of the members, but employed almost half of the total workers.

[7] MMA Constitution, Article III, MMAP I-1-1; ECM 11 Dec. 1912, 19 Feb. 1913.

The MMA therefore occupied a reasonably well-defined ecological niche within the metal trades – essentially the same one as the NFA had before it, minus the shipbuilders and plus middle-sized firms of similar character to the original NFA membership, save that they employed no foundry craftsmen. As we have seen, machinists and brass workers were also capable of causing quite enough trouble for their employers to make the latter appreciate the necessity of collective self-defense.[8]

The MMA's overall share of local metal trades employment in the last prewar year was not large – about 13 percent. But this apparently small share was significant because of the fact that it was concentrated, and of where it was concentrated. The MMA was not thinly spread across the city. Its recruitment was doubly selective. It drew disproportionately on particular industries, as well as on companies of a particular size within them. Companies with 100 to 500 employees were responsible for 80 percent of its aggregate labor force, and its members accounted for 37 percent of the city's total metal trades employment among these mid-sized enterprises. Most of them that joined the MMA were makers of machinery, machine tools, hardware, plumbers' supplies and steam fittings, and lighting fixtures. These were the cornerstones of the MMA – and also, not coincidentally, the terrain contested most vigorously by the skilled trades unions.

In 1914, the MMA's largest element still consisted of machinery foundries. Not quite a quarter of the membership, these integrated, multidepartmental firms employed about half of the MMA's workforce (see Table 5.2).[9] Setting the membership within the overall context of the city's metal trades, we can see the effects of the association's selective recruitment even more clearly (see Table 5.3). There were whole industries and groups of industries where there was no MMA presence at all – notably among the giant open shops, the light metal-trades employing low-wage, often female labor, and those with entrenched craft unions and established bargaining systems, for example stove-making and structural ironwork. But in its key industries, it had quite a high density of organization – 39 percent among machinery builders, 42 percent in plumbers' supplies and steam fittings (largely machined castings), and 48 percent in lighting fixtures, rising to 75 percent in machine tools.

---

[8]   Almost half of the MMA's members, responsible for 70 percent of their total labor force, employed some molders in 1915–16. But in most cases their foundries were only divisions of their enterprises, not their raison d'être. *Penton's Foundry List* (Cleveland, 1908 and 1918), List of Philadelphia Foundries 1913 in MMAP II-3-14, for identification of foundry departments in firms not classified as foundries by the state; all others, and all employment figures, from PID-1640 database.

[9]   Morgan Exhibit No. 2, in U.S. Commission on Industrial Relations (USCIR), *Industrial Relations: Final Report and Testimony, Submitted to Congress by the Commission on Industrial Relations . . . 64th Congress 1st Session* (Washington, 1916), Vol. 3, pp. 2924–25.

TABLE 5.2 Industrial Distribution of MMA Membership, 1914

	Number	Operatives	Ave. Firm	Percent	Range
Machinery Foundries (*Ferrous*)	11	2,676	251	42%	84–292
Machine-Shops	30	2,333	78	38%	10–505
Chandelier M'frs	9	509	57	8%	No Data
Machinery Foundries (*Nonferrous*)	4	342	86	5%	68–127
Jobbing Iron Foundries	4	245	61	4%	32–93
Brass-Novelty M'frs	3	114	38	2%	33–40
Jobbing Pattern Shops	3	43	14	1%	14–15
TOTALS	64	6,346	99		

Source: USCIR, *Final Report*, Vol. 3, pp. 2924–25.

The MMA dominated its core sectors not because it recruited the majority of firms within them, but because its members were usually among the biggest in their respective fields. As a result, in machine tools, for example, the average member firm employed more than sixteen times as many workers as the average nonmember; in machine repairing, the scalar difference was almost as great. In these two sectors, nonmembers were generally small jobbing firms, tool- and die-makers and repair mechanics serving purely local markets rather than machine builders and rebuilders. Many of these small fry had disappeared by the time of the next survey in 1919, only to be replaced by a multitude of similarly fragile and short-lived entrepreneurial outfits; while the MMA enjoyed the strong support of firms oriented toward regional and national or even international markets that were "durable producers" in more ways than one. In other sectors where it had a significant presence – plumbers' supplies, hardware, lighting fixtures, and machinery manufacture – the mean size of MMA firms was four or five times greater than that of nonmembers. And in several smaller industries where the MMA had only one member, that one was the single largest firm. The resulting density ratings were impressively high – 71 percent among gas engine builders, 60 percent in agricultural equipment, and 54 percent in beds and bed springs, the latter two firms (the last of them really a foundry operator with a specialized product) making quite a

TABLE 5.3 Metal Manufacturing Industries, 1915–1916, Ranked in Order of Total Employment

NAME	FIRMS	TOTAL	MMA	EMPLOY	%MMA[a]	SHARE[b]	SIZE[c]
Locomotives	1	6,581					
Machinery & Parts	127	6,540	16	2,563	33%	39%	4.5
Forgings	10	3,994					
Elec'l Machinery	38	2,699	3	268	3%	10%	1.3
Hardware	62	2,411	5	708	9%	29%	4.7
Nonstructural Shapes	21	1,947					
Saws	4	1,870					
Pulleys & Bearings	11	1,698	2	286	4%	17%	0.9
Automobiles & Parts	26	1,607					
Railroad Cars	2	1,474					
Stoves &c.	28	1,412					
Electroplating	53	1,398					
Plumbers' Supplies	25	1,298	4	549	7%	42%	3.8
Machine Tools	19	1,274	3	960	12%	75%	16.3
Castings – Iron	28	1,273	3	349	5%	27%	3.1
Machine Repairers	88	1,197	2	286	4%	24%	13.5
Metal Stampings	26	1,168					
Nonferrous Products	48	1,146	7	341	4%	30%	2.5
Instruments – Prof. & Scientific	36	1,104	2	111	1%	10%	1.9
Wire Products	37	1,057					
Lighting Fixtures	33	1,027	5	492	6%	48%	5.1
43 Other Industries <1,000 incl.	303	12,126	5	821	11%	7%	4.1
Pipes & Tubing	10	898	1	74	1%	8%	0.8
Shapes, Structural	8	557	1	141	2%	25%	2.4
Agric'l Implements	3	525	1	315	4%	60%	3.0
Beds & Bed Springs	9	438	1	235	3%	54%	9.3
Gas & Gasoline Engines	3	79	1	56	1%	71%	4.9
TOTALS:	1,026	56,301	57	7,734	100%	14%	2.7

[a] %MMA = employment in MMA member firms as a percentage of industry total.
[b] SHARE = employment by member in this industry as a percentage of MMA total.
[c] SIZE = ratio of mean size of member firms to nonmembers.
Source: PID16-40 database.

big contribution to aggregate MMA employment and playing an active role within it.

What else did middle-sized, proprietary firms in these industries have in common, apart from a troublesome, though not insuperable, union presence, that explained their unusual degree of commitment to the Open Shop? A tentative answer to this question can be offered on the basis of economic data about the MMA's core sectors contained in other state and federal surveys.[10]

Among the many distinctive features of the industries that made up the MMA's heartland, four stand out in successive federal censuses between 1900 and 1914. They do so even when compared with other local metal industries that were also non- or anti-union, and most of whose firms were also proprietary in character and middling in size, but which did not produce many MMA recruits at the time. This infertile territory included makers of electrical apparatus and supplies; professional and scientific instruments; high-value, often patent-protected durable goods, including gas and water meters, locks and safes, and scales; and files, saws, and other tools.[11]

First, the MMA's home industries were outstandingly dependent on highly paid, almost all-male, blue-collar labor. In 1914, their average wage was 13 percent above that in the rest of the metal trades and 22 percent above the rest of Philadelphia manufacturing. Second, the cost of that labor made up an unusually large share of their value added by manufacture – 47 percent in 1914, as against 41 percent for all other Philadelphia manufacturers outside the metal trades, and just 39 percent for the metal

[10] Only tentative, because (i) industrial categories used, and data gathered, by federal (in 1900, 1905, 1910, and 1914) and state (in 1914 and after) statisticians were neither closely compatible with one another nor even (in the federal case) altogether consistent over time; and (ii) more fundamentally, all the data are aggregated at the industry level. Given that MMA membership rarely accounted for more than a fraction of an industry's employment, and that member firms were so much larger, on average, than the nonmembers that contributed most of the aggregate data, it would be wrong to read too many inferences about the situation and the possible motivation of MMA members from the census evidence. The dangers of getting mired in ecological fallacies are too great, and in any event the decision to join the MMA was influenced by the personal values of a company's senior executives, their connections with existing members, and their guesstimates of costs and benefits. It was not the rigidly determined outcome of the economic circumstances of a company, and still less of its industry. However, the latter do seem to have provided part of the setting within which executives made their choices, so it would be foolish not to explore them. As this aggregate data is all that is available for the purpose, it is better to use it with care than not to use it at all. But as it is so problematic, sophisticated quantitative analysis is inappropriate, and modest conclusions are the most that can be offered.
[11] Cf. Chapters 7 and 9 for the different picture in the 1920s.

industries where the MMA did not recruit. Third, companies from the MMA's core industries also had to back their high-priced labor with ample capital – 13 percent more per head than in the rest of Philadelphia manufacturing, and 22 percent more than in the more favored metal trades. But, fourth, they achieved a disappointing rate of return on it – 72 percent of that attained by Philadelphia's other industries, and a bare two-thirds of that observed in the more profitable metal trades.[12]

Therefore what companies in the industries where the MMA recruited had in common included a set of chronic economic problems. They were peculiarly exposed to what they thought of as the exactions of their skilled workers. They bought raw materials and fuel – their other main inputs – in markets that they could not control. They sold their output under conditions of fierce competition and great and unpredictable seasonal and cyclical instability. Given their size, the nature of their product markets, and their limited managerial resources and anti-bureaucratic ethos, they could not dispense with their expensive, although not especially efficient, craft labor force. But they had every incentive to do what they could to limit its bargaining power, and to keep its price and behavior at work under tighter control than might have prevailed if their workers had been allowed an organized, collective influence over their wages, hours, and working conditions.

Material interest, not just ideology, therefore underpinned the commit-

---

[12]   *Data:* 1900 Census data as in Introduction, note 14; U.S. Department of Commerce and Labor, Bureau of the Census, *Manufactures 1905, Part II: States and Territories* (Washington, 1907), pp. 978–83; U.S. Department of Commerce, Bureau of the Census, *Thirteenth Census of the U.S. 1910: Vol. IX: Manufactures: Reports by States, with Statistics for Principal Cities* (Washington, 1912), pp. 1086–89; U.S. Department of Commerce, Bureau of the Census, *Census of Manufactures 1914 Vol. I, Reports by States with Statistics for Principal Cities and Metropolitan Districts* (Washington, 1918), pp. 1327–28, 1348–56, line 6, pp. 1350–51, lines 3, 17–19, 27, 35, 36, 63; pp. 1352–53, lines 29, 58; pp. 1354–55 [MMA] vs. lines 5–6; pp. 1348–49, lines 1, 26, 28, 46, 48–49; pp. 1352–53, lines 45, 47; pp. 1354–55, lines 4, 5, 9, 12; pp. 1356–57 [non-MMA].

   Procedure: the same steps were followed for the 1900, 1905, 1910, and 1914 Censuses. As the results did not change much, those for the latest date are used here. Briefly, a set of measures of labor force demographic characteristics and economic input/output performance indicators was calculated for all of the enumerated durable metal goods manufacturing industries in the Philadelphia returns. Industries were then sorted into two groups on the basis of whether or not they were part of the MMA's core territory, using the data underlying Table 5.3 and a similar exercize drawing on the 1902FACT database, which tracked the MMA's early (1904–06) recruits back to the last published state factory inspectors' report, in 1902. Data for the two groups of constituent industries were then aggregated and the same sets of measures calculated for the groups as for the several industries themselves. There were quite large differences among industries within core and peripheral groups along some of the parameters, but the differences between the groups remained even greater and probably more meaningful.

ment of companies from these skill-dependent, low-return, market-sensitive, old-technology industries to the Open Shop cause, in Philadelphia and elsewhere, through the troubled early years of this century. Even among the industries where the MMA did recruit, the best predictor of the association's density of organization was an industry's average wage rate. The more an industry paid its workers, the less they produced in return, and therefore the larger the share their wage bill took of the value of its product, the more inclined were its constituent companies to see the virtues of anti-labor collective action.[13]

Thus far, the argument of this chapter is in favor of an essential continuity in the character of the MMA's membership and the structural conditions underlying their behavior, right through its first dozen years and indeed, in most respects, its first two decades. It remained dominated by the same kinds of firms that had set it up, which contributed the lion's share of its labor force and hence its funds, which bore the brunt of its union-busting activities, and whose representatives filled most of the decision-making offices within it.

However, this argument for stability cannot be pushed too far. In particular, it does not necessarily mean that the members, although they continued to be recruited from the same industrial sectors and size-categories within the Philadelphia metal trades, were the same firms throughout. For the MMA did experience considerable turnover: Companies withdrew on account of bankruptcy or retrenchment, retirement from business, or relocation away from the city; a few resigned as a result of policy disagreements or dissatisfaction with services rendered. And, on the other hand, it was quite a vigorous and successful recruiter, particularly in its formative years, 1904–06, and in the aftermath of the labor relations crises of 1910–11 and 1916–18.

As a result, between 1904 and 1924, on average almost a fifth of the firms that were members of the association at some time during any particular year were either entering or leaving it (see Figure 5.3). Peak turnover was largely a product of unusually active recruiting, generally in years of labor relations crisis (1904–06, 1911–12, 1916–20; 1923 saw the only

---

[13]   *Data:* Density of organization as in Table 5.3; labor force demographic and economic performance indicators for 1914 and 1915 from PHIL1439 database.

   Procedure: Density of organization was tested against a number of other parameters (labor force makeup – proportions under 16, female, African American, noncitizen; economic performance – average wage, wages as a proportion of product value, output per head, i.e. proxies for skill-dependence, labor intensity, and productivity or "efficiency"). None of the parameters apart from average wage and wage bill/product value offered a very good fit with the varying density of organization among MMA industries. These findings are consistent with those in Larry J. Griffin et al., "Capitalist Resistance to the Organization of Labor Before the New Deal: Why? How? Success?" *American Sociological Review* 51 (1986): 147–67.

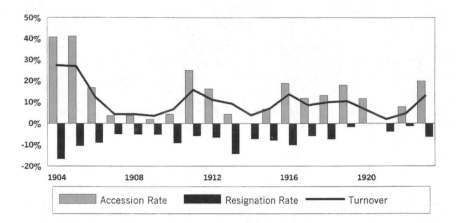

Figure 5.3. Year-on-Year Changes in MMA Membership, 1904–1923. *Note:* The *Accession Rate* (positive values) is the percentage of member firms at the end of a year that had joined during it; the *Resignation Rate* (negative values) is the percentage of members at the start of a year that left by December; *Turnover* is the percentage of a year's average membership that was *not* in the MMA for the whole year. *Source:* As for Figure 5.1.

noncrisis membership boom), when as many as two-fifths of the members at the end of a year might be new to the association. These periods also, apparently paradoxically, included the years of heaviest losses (1904–05, 1913, 1916), when between a tenth and a sixth of the January members would have departed by December. The association had its lowest turnover – down to between 4 and 8 percent – in and after years of economic depression (1907–09, 1914, 1921–22), as the decision not to join was one of the immediate savings potential members made. The MMA also cut down on recruitment activities in bad times, instead concentrating straitened resources on servicing current members. The winnowing of existing members by retrenchment or business failure was a lagged effect, so the association continued to contract slowly after the worst had passed, and even once the economy began to recover.

Turnover such as this might be thought to undermine the picture of stability presented earlier. But if we examine the membership careers of individual firms, it is largely restored. It turns out that the MMA was not just divisible into a body of larger firms and a diminishing tail of smaller ones. It was also an organization in which there was a stable core of committed members, surrounded by an unstable periphery of firms that flitted through the organization for a handful of years, or fewer. This is why above-average accession and resignation rates occurred in the same or neighboring years, when an unusual amount of membership "churning" was going on, the "revolving door" effect resolving the above apparent paradox.

For example, if we look at the cohort of firms that joined during the MMA's first five years – seventy-seven in number – and then see which were still members in 1916, we find thirty-six of them remaining. These firms would go on to accumulate, on average, twenty-five years of unbroken membership between 1904 and 1940; indeed, sixteen of them would still be there in 1940, their commitment surviving war, depressions, industrial restructuring, and intergenerational changes in management and even ownership. In contrast, the forty-one firms that did not remain members by 1916 only accumulated five years of membership each, on average.

So the MMA, in its first decade, rapidly developed into a quite stable organization, recruiting from a coherent group of interrelated industries, all of which shared common or comparable labor relations problems. Almost all of its member firms were of similar character, locally owned and personally managed, although they were of quite widely varying sizes. Leadership within the association was generally but not exclusively the prerogative of senior proprietor-managers recruited from the larger firms within the several industries at the heart of the MMA's organizing territory, and particularly from the machinery foundrymen among them.

5.2 "ON THE MATTERS FOR WHICH WE ARE ORGANIZED OUR MEMBERS ARE PRACTICALLY A UNIT" – GOVERNANCE AND COHESION IN THE MMA[14]

The MMA was a simple organization, dependent on a small number of long-serving committee members and on successive secretaries – three men in its first decade; and a fourth, Earl Sparks, who joined its small staff in 1910 while still at Temple College, became secretary in 1916 and served it for the whole of his career, and the rest of the MMA's life as an independent organization, until the 1950s. It was as personally managed as, and no more administratively complex than, most of its member firms, and it functioned like the other clubs and voluntary associations that their owners joined and supported.

Its 1903 constitution gave little hint of what its character would become, because it presupposed that the MMA would operate much more formally and bureaucratically than it ever did. For example, in a thirty-five-year period there was only one issue pressed to a vote on the executive committee, and not a single membership referendum, so the men who wrote in rules governing voting rights, letter ballots, and required majority levels

[14] ECM 22 March 1921.

could have saved their time. Similarly, other official procedures – such as those dealing with the "blackballing" of candidates for membership and the expulsion of miscreants – were rarely implemented. In these and other matters, the MMA proceeded by informal soundings and social pressure, rather than open consultation and formal discipline. Elections were even avoided in the appointment of the association's leaders. An active minority, which was supposed to be fairly representative of the several industries from which membership was drawn, renewed itself gradually by a process of uncontested cooptation. After its first half-dozen years, when there was some turnover among the key personnel, the MMA settled down under a team that changed little for the next decade.[15]

In these as in other respects, the MMA functioned like the national employers' associations in which some of its leaders played important roles. They displayed a similar preference for consensual decision making, a similar lack of membership participation, and were equally happy to leave policy and administration to stable oligarchies and full-time officers.[16]

The MMA was profoundly attached to the object of preserving its internal consensus. It went about achieving this aim in a number of ways. Perhaps the most important was by discouraging or refusing membership applications from firms that were too union-friendly. The MMA always contained a minority of unionized members, but it became increasingly reluctant to see that group increase. This was because their presence compromised its attempts to maintain a united front against organized labor, and to hold the line against the extension of collectively bargained wages, hours, and working practices. It also made problematic the confidential discussion of labor relations strategy and information about the local unions' internal affairs. The more union-busting successes the MMA racked up, the more careful it became about whom it admitted. In 1912, for example, an application by a jobbing pattern shop was refused because one of the firm's partners had been the local Pattern Makers' League business agent; and in 1916 a jobbing iron foundry was excluded because it was about to sign a closed shop agreement with the IMU, despite the fact that its managers collaborated closely with the MMA by informing its secretary of the progress of negotiations.[17]

A second policy designed to foster unity was the MMA's refusal even to take under consideration any subject that was likely to prove divisive among

---

[15] For a rare disciplinary expulsion, see ECM 18 Apr. 1906; on elections, see "Notes for Order of Business," [9 Dec. 1903], MMAP I-1-35, p. 2; ECM 8 Nov. 1905; MMA Constitution, By-Laws; MMAEXEC database.

[16] NMTA *Synopsis of Proceedings of the 14th Annual Convention* (New York, 1912), pp. 100–01, and NFA, *Proceedings of the 17th Annual Convention* (New York, 1913), p. 15.

[17] ECM 12 June 1912 and 8 March 1916.

the membership. It steadfastly declined any invitation from local or national business associations, inside or outside of the metal trades, to collaborate with them on matters that were not directly connected with the MMA's central purpose of keeping its members' labor costs under control and "freedom to manage" intact. For example, it refused to affiliate with the Philadelphia or U.S. Chambers of Commerce because they were "not within the prescribed limits of the work as carried on by the Association."[18]

These sensible rules of self-limitation helped underpin the MMA membership's homogeneity of character and outlook. And the very stability of Philadelphia's industrial structure until the postwar period meant that the city continued to host few branch plants of out-of-town, professionally and bureaucratically managed, technologically innovative corporations, so that the character of the business population among which it recruited experienced little change. For all of these reasons there were few forces at work disturbing the MMA's internal unity.

Three elected officers (a president, vice president, and treasurer) and three to five councillors made up the MMA's executive committee. After the association began to broaden its functions to include lobbying and group insurance in 1912–14, up to five subcommittees operated, including some nonexecutive members. A small number of volunteers filled all of these posts, with men typically being tried out as representatives on the nominating committee, advancing to the rank of councillor if willing and suitable, and then being given office. The MMA ran on the principle of rotating a limited supply of eligible candidates around all of its posts and not parting with a man's services, once he had been found acceptable, unless and until he was no longer able or willing to give it his time. The MMA, like most voluntary associations, was not overprovided with competent volunteers.[19]

The MMA's leadership group, broadly defined as officeholders and those who served as committee members for more than a single term, consisted of no more than about forty men during the whole of its first two decades. The largest member firms were included on the association's committees almost as a matter of course, but not always by the same man, so that American Engineering (formerly Williamson Bros. Co.), the Autocar Co., and Link-Belt together contributed eight of the forty key players. Smaller firms whose managers were particularly respected were also well represented – Leeds & Northrup (scientific instruments and industrial control systems) and Stokes & Smith (packaging machinery), for whose Orthodox Quaker proprietors office-holding in voluntary associations was a habit and

[18] ECM 17 Apr. 1912, 22 March 1921.
[19] All information in this section is from the MMA-EXEC database, unless otherwise noted.

a commitment, provided two men apiece. Altogether, about 20 of the 180 firms that were members at some time during the period provided the whole of the association's leadership from 1904 to 1924.

The inner group among the active minority was even smaller than the above total implies. If just the men who filled one of the three key offices, or had at least three periods as officeholders or committee members, are singled out, the MMA's directorate is whittled down to about sixteen names from a dozen firms, nine of them "present at the creation" in 1904–06 (the other three joined in 1911–15). Of these men, about ten gave the association almost continuous service once they had been elected for the first time. Lighting fixture manufacturer Robert Biddle, for example, was successively vice president, councillor, vice president, and councillor again, with important committee assignments; he enjoyed only one brief respite between 1904 and 1922. Brass founder Thomas Evans was treasurer for a gruelling thirteen-year stint from the association's beginnings until 1916. William Hallowell served without a break from 1904 until 1922, as councillor, vice president, president, councillor again, and finally Evans's replacement as treasurer. His successors as president, Edward Langworthy and Justus Schwacke, gave similar service from 1905 to 1920 and 1904 to 1922, respectively. Apart from one brief interruption in 1932–33 (from a Disston, whose company only joined in 1924), the association's presidents were exclusively recruited from firms within this inner group between 1903 and 1937.

The fact that the leadership hardly changed for decades resulted only in part from the lack of alternative candidates. It reflected a similar stability among the MMA's core membership and the low turnover among their senior managers. Men who owned large, even controlling, interests in the firms that they ran did not make career moves – until they retired or died, they were fixtures. Men who were willing to give their time to a voluntary association like the MMA, who were trusted and respected because of their track records and the prestige of the firms to which they belonged, who directed its affairs with skill and dedication, and who acquired special expertise in the difficult arts of strike-breaking and lobbying thereby – were similarly unlikely to be challenged or displaced.

The stabilization of its leadership group entailed some cost to the MMA. Outsiders and new members did not get a look in. Active participation in the association's affairs, gauged by attendance at the ordinary quarterly meetings, came to involve the same dozen or so companies, a handful of which could provide the necessary quorum (25 percent of the total workforce) because of their size. But there was a perceived advantage in terms of the quality of service that the association could deliver, which more than compensated for the decline in its political vitality.[20]

---

[20] Lack of willing candidates, ECM 23 July and 13 Aug. 1913; lack of participation, Langworthy, PRES 1910, p. 2, 1911, p. 4, and ECM 10 Sept. 1913.

The small size and stability of the active minority, together with rank-and-file members' acceptance of that leadership, helped maintain the association's cohesiveness and continuity of policy. Within the executive committee, unity was further preserved by a decision-making technique that the MMA borrowed from the Religious Society of Friends, to which several prominent members belonged. Of the roughly forty key players, c. 1904–24, at least nine were Quakers; and four of these, the Hicksites Robert Biddle and William Hallowell, and the Orthodox Morris Evans Leeds and Charles Evans, were members of the inner group of ten men who really ran the association. Although they were only a minority within a minority, the imprint that they left on the MMA's policy and procedures was larger than their mere numbers would suggest.[21]

The executive made its mind up in a way similar to that found in other Philadelphia civic groups, in which the language and methods of Quaker self-government were used in voluntary organizations even where members of the Society of Friends were no more than an influential and concerned fraction of the membership. They discussed matters freely and temperately until the "sense of the meeting" emerged. All decisions had to be consensual, which was how and why voting was avoided.[22]

The MMA employed the Quakers' useful political technique to help preserve its all-important united front, taking no decisions that did not enjoy broad backing, and as a result containing most of the frictions and disagreements among its members with minimal argument and very few resignations by the discontented. Delay or even inaction were better than fission. In this respect, too, the MMA's inner politics were not unlike those of the NFA and NMTA, which had their own ways of confining and resolving arguments without provoking open debate and secession within voluntary organizations that were ever conscious of the need to maintain unity, and of their limited hold over their members. The MMA's cultural and linguistic peculiarities made it somewhat distinctive, but only as a minor local variation on a common national theme.[23]

Consensual decision making was an entirely practical means of running an employers' association of moderate size, whose activists got to know one another very well, and which had to be careful not to trample on the interests or prejudices of its strong-willed members. Reading the MMA's

---

[21] Presidents Langworthy and Schwacke also came from companies with definite or probable Hicksite Quaker senior officers, Adams & Westlake and William Sellers, respectively – but I have been unable to determine their own religious affiliations. Still, it is safe to say that the majority of the MMA's leadership was recruited from a "Quakerly" milieu. See discussion in Chapter 8 on the Hicksite/Orthodox distinction.

[22] Howard H. Brinton, *Friends for Three Hundred Years: The History and Beliefs of the Society of Friends Since George Fox Started the Quaker Movement* (New York, 1952), Ch. 6; Kirk R. Petshek, *The Challenge of Urban Reform: Policies and Programs in Philadelphia* (Philadelphia, 1973), p. 5.

[23] Cf. references in note 16.

executive committee minutes, it is initially startling for a historian who associates the Friends with an honorable liberal tradition to find anti-union strategies settled by the "sense of the meeting." But at the time there was nothing incongruous about it, even for the Quaker minority among the MMA's activists; their common paternalistic approach to their own employees was quite compatible with partaking of much of the ideology, and most of the practices, of anti-unionism.[24]

5.3   "THE CHEAPEST LOCAL METAL MANUFACTURERS' ASSOCIATION IN THE EASTERN STATES"[25]

One of the predictable strains on membership commitment to voluntary organizations is the need to pay to maintain them. Leaders have to tread a fine line between making sure that they have enough resources to deliver an attractive package of services, and not overburdening the members with demands to contribute. The MMA always aimed to keep the costs of membership as low as possible, understanding that at the margin even a few dollars could make a difference to companies' decisions to join or stay. In particular, it kept its dues well below those of the national employers' associations, the NFA and the NMTA, thereby opening itself to members for whom those two militant bodies were too remote and too expensive.[26]

The MMA could operate on a shoestring (average 1905–15: c. $5,500 per annum) partly because it limited its scope, and because its activists gave their executive time free of charge and kept a sharp eye on expenditures – for example, buying a second filing cabinet for $34 in 1909 to cope with the increasing volume of records was a decision considered too important to leave to the staff. The result was that the financial burdens that it placed on members were, as Secretary Morgan emphasized, "trifling."[27]

The constitution provided for dues of up to 20¢ per assessed operative per month, but in practice they were kept at half that figure for the next two decades. This meant that MMA membership cost firms less than one-quarter of one percent of their wage bill in the prewar years. Initiation fees

---

[24]   For example, ECM 11 Sept. 1905. See also Chapter 8, Section 2.

[25]   McPherson, SEC 1905, p. 1.

[26]   The association also lightened the already small burden that it placed on members during recessions, when any overhead expense was a tempting target for cash-strapped companies seeking economies, and the MMA did not need the revenue as mass unemployment provided sufficient insurance against strikes. In the 1907–08, 1914–15, and 1920–21 recessions, dues were waived or halved, with the desired effect of minimizing resignations. See ECM 9 Dec. 1907, 11 Nov., 9 Dec. 1914, 10 Feb. 1915, 23 Aug. 1921.

[27]   ECM 11 Aug. 1909, 10 Dec. 1913; Morgan, SEC 1913, p. 8.

were limited to the equivalent of three months' dues, and sometimes were waived altogether. Firms did not have to buy into their share of an accumulated warchest, as in the NFA. Special assessments were only levied on and with the agreement of firms directly affected by an expensive strike involving a distinct interest group among the membership. In the NFA, "special" assessments were a routine way to fund its costly battles; they were levied compulsorily on all members, even though disputes were geographically confined.[28]

What did the members get in return for their minuscule dues? Strike-breaking services, one might expect, particularly after reading the previous chapter. But in fifteen of the association's first twenty strenuous years its accounts recorded no separately identifiable strike-breaking costs. In the other five years, major efforts against Molders, Brass Workers, and Machinists were largely defrayed by assessments levied on the firms directly involved. The result was that the costs of strike-breaking – 5 percent of expenditure in 1905, 13 percent in 1906, 22 percent in 1910, 31 percent in 1911, and 27 percent in 1916; average 1905–24: 4 percent – were exceeded by about a half by the costs of one of the MMA's two major regular expenditures – dinners.

Every year between 4 and 17 percent (average 1905–24: 6 percent) of the MMA's budget went on trying to persuade members to come to its annual or semi-annual meetings, by subsidizing the costs of the rich food, emphatically alcoholic drink, fine cigars, and entertainment that accompanied them. Attractions laid on included speakers who were amusing, informative, and consciousness-raising, and live music, some of it as a background to community singing from specially printed songsheets. Announcing the program for the 1911 Annual Banquet to be held in the prestigious Bellevue-Stratford Hotel, for example, Secretary Morgan

---

[28]   MMA Constitution, By-Laws; average wages from PHIL1439 database; cf. Margaret L. Stecker, "The National Founders' Association," *QJE* 30 (1916): 352–86 at pp. 378–82; NFA, *Proceedings of the 17th Annual Convention* (1913), p. 12 [Assessments]. NFA expenditure in 1912 was c. $96,000, or more than $4 per operative – NFA, *Proceedings of the 16th Annual Convention* (New York, 1912), p. 21. The MMA's unit cost in 1908–12 was a third of that figure. The NMTA's was even lower – its operating budget in the same period was c. $40,000 a year, or c. 80¢ per operative – NMTA, *Synopsis of Proceedings of the 12th Annual Convention* (New York, 1910), pp. 12–13, *13th* (1911), p. 16, *14th* (1912), p. 14. But, unlike in the MMA's case, this did not include defense costs: 30 percent of dues, plus any surplus on the operating budget, went into the defense fund – NMTA, *History – Methods – Facilities* (Cleveland, c. 1913). The unit cost of the Open Shop was therefore about the same in both cases, at c. 0.2 percent of payroll. But MMA dues were still a bargain, as members were covered against foundry labor troubles too, at a fraction of the NFA cost, and NMTA membership entailed paying *twice* – local branch dues, which were higher than the MMA's, came on top of national subscriptions.

introduced NAM president John Kirby, Jr., and National Council of Industrial Defense counsel James Emery, "who can not fail to interest you," discoursing on the business community's political priorities, particularly workmen's compensation legislation. These heavyweight speeches were accompanied by "a menu to tempt an epicure . . . [and] music [to] entertain those musically inclined and everyone will have the opportunity to help with the popular airs."[29]

To explain the importance that the MMA attached to its banquet meetings, it should be stressed that the association's explicit objectives included the promotion of "better acquaintance and a closer social relation between its members." The MMA built on the practice of the local businessmen's organizations to which its members also belonged, like the Manufacturers' and Foundrymen's Clubs, for which the deliberate encouragement of group loyalties and the provision of opportunities for purposeful sociability had proved highly functional. It was more formal than some similar groups, like the city's Women's Garment Manufacturers' Association, which its president described as "a club, with no set rules" that had "little meetings for the purpose of saying 'How do you do' to each other, and we remain in that tranquil condition until we are aroused again." But its conviviality had the same solidarity-building purpose.[30]

Drinking, eating, and singing together provided ways of "infusing the spirit of cordiality" into occasions that were the MMA's leaders' most important opportunities to meet and influence their members. Ordinary quarterly meetings were very sparsely attended, but annual and semi-annual dinner meetings drew together a majority of the membership. The officers reported on their stewardship and on current problems, and almost ritualistically urged members to cooperate more fully with the association's work. The featured speakers kept provincial-minded Philadelphia manufacturers in touch with important national issues. Members brought clients and

[29]   Expenditure data in Treasurer's Reports, MMAP II-4-1 to 3; menu and program details 1907–10 in MMAP II-3-4 to 7; ECM 10 Jan. 1912; Henry Morgan to "Gentlemen," *Bulletin* No. 155 (9 February 1911), MMAP II-3-8. NFA and NMTA annual conventions were similarly bonhomous affairs, with "Get Together" periods, "Alumni Reunions" for former officers, the "old 'war horses'," to discuss strategy and share "a loving-cup of wine," members referred to as "Brother" (or, for the graybeards, "Uncle"), and reminiscences and rituals to build a sense of history and what the NFA's president called its "wonderful cohesion." No NMTA convention was complete without a performance at the closing banquet of Cincinatti machine-tool builder "Uncle Billy" Lodge's "The Smoke Goes Up the Chimney Just the Same," with new topical verses sung by the composer and members joining in the chorus – See NFA, *Proceedings of the 16th Annual Convention* (1912), p. 39, *17th Annual Convention* (1913), pp. 6–16, 138; NMTA, *Synopsis of Proceedings of the 12th Annual Convention* (1910), pp. 165, 167, *15th* (1913), p. 213, *16th* (1914), p. 239, *17th* (1915), p. 94, *20th* (1918), p. 91.
[30]   Article II, MMA Constitution; Morris Bernstein testimony, USCIR, *Final Report*, Vol. 3, p. 3121.

valued subordinates whom they wanted to reward or impress to these stimulating and enjoyable occasions, as each firm had an allotment of free places to use as it wanted, and could buy extra tickets for less than the dinner's cost. So the members saw, indeed swallowed, something tangible in return for their dues, and strengthened the personal bonds that underpinned both the MMA and the contractual networks in which its members were enmeshed.[31]

The MMA invited its own guests, too, particularly representatives of the larger firms whose assistance it valued, and of prospective members. It was "the policy of [the] Association to look more to the character of our membership rather than merely seeking to increase our numbers," as President Langworthy put it. But the MMA was nonetheless interested in winning over businessmen who would add to its strength and meet its criteria – that they should "believe in the objects of our Association, and are ready and willing to support its principles and co-operate in its plans." Heavy investment in entertainment to draw such men in 1910–11, when the MMA was particularly intent on increasing its membership in the aftermath of the great strikes of those years, was justified by results. The star speaker whom it used to pull its audience in off the sidewalk was that celebrated Philadelphia storyteller, Frederick W. Taylor, who gave them his well-worn and semi-factual self-promotional spiel about how he had discovered something called "Scientific Management."[32]

The MMA's status as a businessmen's club consumed a significant fraction of its disposable revenues, but as President Schwacke admitted to the Industrial Relations Commission in 1914, after claiming that "considerable" stress was laid on the "social feature" of the organization, it would not have been "alone . . . sufficient to call [it] into being."[33]

Drawing attention to the small and irregular nature of the MMA's strikebreaking costs is to a degree misleading, in that the chief purpose of the MMA's, and of its parent bodies', activities was strike prevention by undermining labor unions. Most of its resources, year in and year out, including the huge uncosted contributions that members made in time, administrative support, and their readiness to bear the major burdens of the occasional strikes that could not be avoided, were devoted to this object. The MMA's rationale of strategic preparedness was made clear by President Langworthy in 1910:

---

[31] ECM 22 Apr. 1910.
[32] Langworthy, PRES 1909, p. 5; ECM 13 Sept. 1911. Presumably this was a version of Taylor's famous "Boxly talk" – Robert Kanigel, *The One Best Way: Frederick Winslow Taylor and the Enigma of Efficiency* (New York, 1997), pp. 390–99.
[33] Schwacke testimony and Commissioner Busiek's questions, USCIR, *Final Report*, Vol. 3, p. 2890.

the manufacturing industries of this country and the rights of the individual
workman must be guarded as never before, and it is only through national and local
organizations of manufacturers that this can be [done].

Every manufacturer must realize that he has no more important business duty
than safeguarding his labor.

Experience has taught the bitter lesson that the individual manufacturer cannot
single-handed and alone protect his own interests and the rights of his loyal employees from the unjust, and often unreasonable demands of organized labor. Hence it
seems clear that it is his plain duty, even when viewed from a selfish standpoint, to
join with his fellow employers in building up and maintaining organizations through
which he can accomplish that which he cannot accomplish alone. It is not expected
that organized labor is to be done away with, but for the good of all it must be held
in due bounds, and in *organizations* of manufacturers *only* is to be found the necessary corrective and restraining influence.[34]

But how were labor unions to be restrained? Not, as we have seen, by the
more unsavory kinds of union-busting. Secretary Morgan claimed, and the
Industrial Relations Commission's investigators' trawl through his records
confirmed, that there were "no inside operatives of any kind connected with
the Metal Manufacturers Association of Philadelphia. We keep tabs on
nobody. We are not . . . an offensive organization – and when it comes to
the defensive proposition we are only passively defensive."[35]

For the MMA, as Chapter Four demonstrated, successful strike-breaking
revolved around labor replacement, and this in turn depended on the existence, the everyday work, and the growing strength of its Labor Bureau,
running which was its secretary's routine employment and its own major
financial commitment. Salaries for the secretary and his assistant ate up
between two- and three-fifths of the association's annual budget; rental and
operating expenses (particularly help-wanted advertising) consumed most
of the remainder that did not disappear down the members' throats or into
their lungs.

In the next section we will examine the Labor Bureau's everyday work
in detail. It stood at the center of the MMA: Most members took little active
part in running the association; a sizeable fraction did not even attend the
annual banquets; and only a minority ever benefited directly from its strike-
breaking services, because strikes were infrequent and never affected more
than a section of the membership at any one time. But all members were
continually hiring workers and firing them or just "letting them go," setting
their wages, and assessing their competency. And many of them cooperated
more or less closely with the Labor Bureau and its secretary in carrying out
these vital tasks, so that for members and their workers it was the MMA's
public face and their most important point of contact with it.

[34]   PRES 1910, pp. 1–2 (emphases in original).
[35]   Morgan testimony in USCIR, *Final Report*, Vol. 3, pp. 2912, 2910.

5.4 "THE PRIMARY FUNCTION OF THE ASSOCIATION"[36]

Reconstructing how the bureau actually operated is problematic. Almost all of the MMA's routine administrative records were discarded after five years because the executive committee thought, incorrectly as it turns out, that "they were never likely to be of interest to anybody." Only one issue survives of the bulletins that the association sent to members about once a fortnight to keep them informed of current developments. Hardly any records of the frequent correspondence or everyday conversations between members and the secretary exist either. Most regrettably, the index cards with detailed occupational histories of tens of thousands of metal trades-men, which it accumulated in three decades of successful and sustained effort to maintain the Open Shop, also ended up in the trashcan, not the public domain.[37]

But the task of partial reconstruction is not impossible. Successive presidents and secretaries commented on the bureau's functioning within the privacy of the association, where they had no reason and little opportunity to falsify their reports. Officeholders testified before the U.S. Industrial Relations Commission in 1914, whose pro-labor investigators verified their stories by checking the association's records, a process that the La Follette Committee's staff, also armed with subpoenas, repeated two decades later. In the 1920s and 1930s, researchers from The University of Pennsylvania's Wharton School collaborated with the bureau in their studies of the Philadelphia labor market, and produced further independent evidence about the manner and scale of its operations. Finally, incomplete statistical reports do survive that allow us to study the bureau's changing role as it responded to labor market pressures, on the one hand,

---

[36] Earl Sparks, "The Metal Manufacturers Association of Philadelphia: A Review of Activities 1903–53," p. 2, in MMAP I-1-2. This was Sparks's own MMA history and personal memoir.

[37] ECM 28 Feb. 1922, p. 3. There are evidence problems with the surviving MMA records, too. First, successive secretaries took care to keep references in the Minutes to questionable matters, like collusion in wage-setting or price-fixing, or anti-unionism, as brief and ambiguous as possible, probably because there was always the possibility that they might enter the public domain via a court case or a Congressional investigation (as occurred in 1914 and 1936–37). Second, the telephone was in any case the vital means of everyday communication with members. It is not just that no record of these conversations survives, but also that managers took advantage of the fact that they could identify one another by voice alone to talk anonymously about applicants for employment. In other words, to prove that blacklisting had occurred, even at the time, would have required the resources of a well-equipped police department with wiretaps and recording equipment. See Industrial Relations Association of America, *Annual Convention Proceedings* (Chicago, 1920), p. 251.

and the dynamics of management–worker relations in a de-unionizing city, on the other.

First and foremost, the Labor Bureau was a deadly rival of the skilled trades unions in a zero-sum game. Their business agents – particularly those of the Molders and Brass Workers – did all that they could to oppose and subvert it, and were originally confident of success. They told their members "that a black-list against Union men was being kept, and the only jobs they could secure would be strike jobs." The Molders went beyond warning members not to use the bureau. They picketed it for two years after its effective use against them in the 1905–06 foundry strikes, to "persuade" members not to frequent it. The union fined members who ignored this "advice" – $25, two weeks' wages for the average foundry employee in 1914, declining to $10 a decade later.[38]

When, despite the unions' opposition, the bureau became established, they became more sophisticated and also tried sabotage. Secretary McPherson reported in the boom year of 1906 that "A large number of men sent from the Bureau to our shops either failed to report, or if they did report and secure employment, never showed up for work, [which was] . . . a source of considerable annoyance and delay." One reason was the

concerted efforts of the Business Agents of the various local Unions, who made it a practice to send some of their unemployed members to the Bureau, and these men after securing cards to the concerns in need of help, would turn them over to the Business Agents, who would send some one to the shop the following morning, and the Bureau not having filled the job, being unaware that the man sent had not reported, the applicant sent by the Business Agent would frequently be hired.[39]

These tactics enjoyed some success in limiting the bureau's access to the local supply of skilled metal tradesmen, worsening the secretary's relations with the managers and foremen of member firms, and maintaining the unions' tenuous hold on the local skilled labor market. But their combined effect was irritating rather than seriously obstructive.

Despite the fact that the Labor Bureau clearly played a mainly anti-union role, Secretary McPherson claimed to have "overcome" union opposition "due to the fact union men have not been blacklisted, as they were lead (*sic*) to believe they would be, by the walking delegates, but have been given employment and no questions asked as to whether they were union or non-union men." The result, he thought, was that "the more intelligent

---

[38]   McPherson, SEC 1904, p. 1, and SEC Feb. 1905, p. 1; Morgan, in USCIR, *Final Report*, Vol. 3, p. 2913; ECM, 28 Oct. 1924, p. 5; Memoranda for Special Committee on Study of Employment Department Methods, 21 Feb. 1930, p. 5, MMAP II-3-46.
[39]   McPherson, SEC 1906, pp. 5–6.

Union men" had joined the nonunionists in coming to look for work. How do his claims square with his practice? Was he lying, or merely deluding himself?[40]

The answer is mostly a matter of usage. The MMA seems to have believed that blacklisting was what the big firms did – they were only nominally open shops, and were definitely closed to any man known to be a union member. The MMA was less absolutist and more discriminating: What it was engaged in was identifying, and alerting members to the presence of, active union members among job applicants, so that, as George Cresson put it, "undesirable help may in this way be diverted into other channels."[41]

The MMA's register of work histories of applicants for employment and of existing and former employees of member firms grew at an average rate of more than 3,000 new records per year from 1904 to 1916. From about 1912, a man's index card contained an explicit reference to his involvement in strikes. (Before then, such data were probably kept separately or in a coded form; they were certainly available, and communicated to members.) But the MMA persisted in asserting that this was not a blacklist because an adverse report on a man – even such a damning one as that he was what Secretary Morgan called "a disturbing factor . . . a slugger, or something of that kind" – did not necessarily bar him from employment. Of course, the bureau would not knowingly send him to fill a vacancy, but it only filled a fraction of those occurring in member firms; and if he applied at the shop door, and the firm took the trouble to check up on his past, the decision about whether to employ him or not remained the company's, not the bureau's.[42]

What this respect for a member firm's autonomy might mean in practice was illustrated in the fall of 1908. Lighting fixture manufacturers Sulzer & Co. "notified [the bureau] that they had hired a polisher known to be an agitator. They were given full particulars regarding strikes caused by this man in four Association shops during the past five years, but refused to discharge him, saying that inasmuch as they had his record he could do no harm in their shop as they would keep a strict watch on him."[43]

They did so by making him their foreman, perhaps hoping to turn the poacher into a gamekeeper and win favorable relations with the union into the bargain, by giving him control over hiring. This he proceeded to use in his union's interests when "a polisher who had refused to go on strike with the employees of the Bauer Gas Fixture Works applied for work at Sulzer & Co.'s shop." The "agitator" told him "that under no circumstances

[40] McPherson, SEC Dec. 1905, p. 2; Feb. 1905, p. 1.
[41] Cresson, PRES 1904, p. 1.
[42] Morgan, SEC 1916, p. 5; Morgan in USCIR, *Final Report*, Vol. 3, p. 2905.
[43] ECM, 14 Oct. 1908.

would he be allowed to work for Messrs. Sulzer & Co. while he, the said agitator, had charge of the shop." The Sulzers were informed, but "they did not credit the story."[44]

The association decided to persuade them not to "keep this man in their employ" by deploying its penultimate sanction. They were given "formal notice" that, if they did not let him go, they "could not conscientiously expect support . . . should they become involved in labor trouble." The firm had probably calculated on pursuing an alternative, conciliatory strategy for labor peace; the association responded by threatening to withdraw its insurance policy, should that plan fail. In this whole process the MMA confined itself to supplying information and leaving its member free to choose the action to take in response. The firm was given the option of running the risk of having to face an entrenched union without ready access to an alternative supply of skilled labor. The choice was real, but constrained. The Sulzers took the sensible course, firing the man, faithfully hewing to the association line through the great Chandelier Strike of 1910–11, and staying in the MMA for the next quarter-century.[45]

This case was the only one recorded in which a member had to be pressured into letting go an "agitator" whom the association had fingered. Evidently the MMA, while not maintaining what it thought of as a blacklist, was engaged in systematic and selective victimization, in which it usually enjoyed the members' willing support because, after all, most of them had joined it to weaken the unions in the first place. The MMA's targets were the minority of known labor activists, not the ordinary rank-and-file, unless the latter happened to be on strike, in which case the MMA's campaign to undermine organized labor required that other shops be closed to strikers. This policy, identical to the Cincinnati Metal Trades Association's, made unions' strike-support costs much higher. It denied their striking members the opportunity of getting temporary work elsewhere in the locality while only a minority picketed and got strike pay. It was also difficult to maintain a struck employer's will to fight if he could see competitors taking his business and giving refuge to his disloyal workmen. So barring shops to striking workmen was as essential to maintaining target employers' morale as it was to undermining their workers' morale.

In 1907, for example, the Autocar Company's Superintendent Pollard responded to Secretary McPherson's warning that Enterprise Mfg. Co.'s employees were out on strike, with the undertaking to "be very careful about employing any help without first referring them to you." Ordinarily, firms could quite safely hire at the shop door, and only a minority checked out all recruits with the bureau. But in seasons of strife, such precautions were essential to undermine unions and prevent problems such as those

[44]   Ibid.
[45]   Ibid.; database MMAYEARS.

occurring during the MMA's long foundry strike of 1905–06, when bedstead maker Bernstein Mfg., which was not involved in the conflict, inadvertently engaged some striking molders previously employed by James Barker, who was involved. The Bernsteins were called to account, and one of them had to make a statement about the unfortunate incident in a personal appearance before the executive committee. He "promised to write a letter, putting himself on record to the effect that hereafter no molder or coremaker will be hired by his firm without first telephoning this office. Mr. Bernstein also stated that his firm had not looked for any new business since the strike started, and at the present time they had idle floors." Employer solidarity, no less than that of their employees, needed to be policed; and the MMA did so quite effectively.[46]

The bureau was the key to the association's union-busting campaign; but there were limits to the tactics that it was able or prepared to use, some of them imposed by state law, more by self-restraint and by the qualified support of the membership. It seems that the MMA considered a totally union-free environment, while desirable in principle, neither necessary nor attainable at reasonable cost in practice.

The association did its best to weaken organized labor, to weed out "agitators," and to isolate and defeat strikers. But it was not altogether opposed to the employment of union members in its members' shops, provided that they were employed *as individuals* and under conditions that did not threaten a firm's freedom to operate as an open shop if it so chose. It also understood that the skilled man might need to maintain his union membership, even when working peaceably and obediently in a nonunion shop. He might at some future date need to look for work within the unionized sector, and he also had an investment in his union's benefit fund that he could protect only by continuing to pay his dues. So in 1909 the MMA extended its union substitution strategy beyond the hiring process into the benefits sphere, using its collective strength to negotiate insurance coverage at a discount "whereby the independent workman, who loses time through accidental injury, or sickness will receive some benefits, and in case of death his heirs will receive a certain amount."[47]

By this means, as President Langworthy argued, "we not only offset one of the strong inducements to membership in the union . . . , but render a real service to our employees and those dependent upon them." The association promised workmen who bought their insurance from the MMA's nominated carrier that it would pay their families $100 in the event that they died from natural causes while in a member's service, over and above the benefits that they had paid for. In other respects this was a

---

[46] MMAP II-3-4, Banquet file 1907; ECM 10 Sept. 1906.
[47] Langworthy, PRES 1909, p. 4.

contributory scheme – as indeed were the unions' – and participation was entirely voluntary. Firms had to take the initiative to help their employees buy into it. But very few did. The company-based, management-supported but employee-financed and -run mutual beneficial society, not the MMA's group insurance scheme, was the only poor alternative to union programs that most employers endorsed, if they took any action at all. As a result of the MMA's inability to sell its program to its members, unions retained a limited raison d'être because they continued to perform functions that even the MMA executive committee regarded as legitimate and necessary.[48]

Thus the MMA accommodated itself to a continuing union presence in its members' shops. Its attitude toward union membership was that it was "perfectly natural for the workman to take such action as regards union-ism or non-unionism as will, in his opinion, prove to be to his best inter-est individually," and that it could be unthreatening.[49] It was at least equally respectful of the independence of its members. As we saw in Chapter Four, some firms, particularly the smaller iron foundries, continued to recognize and deal with organized labor, either informally at the shop level or (from 1913 to 1923) in resumed citywide bargaining, a process that, they thought, gave them some protection against union pressure on wages and working practices. They were vulnerable because their particular product required the highest skilled craftsmen, of whom the Molders maintained a genuine monopoly, or because, despite their best endeavors, they had not managed to defeat their union adversaries once and for all.[50]

The MMA was opposed to formal recognition of trade unions in princi-ple but, rather than alienate the unionized sections of the foundry and other skill-dependent trades by making operating under open shop conditions a necessary qualification for association membership, it tolerated them and used the bureau to defend the open shops without denying the union shops access to its facilities. Under these circumstances the bureau could not have operated a general blacklist, even had the association been so minded.

What it did instead was to be discriminating, directing "card men" (ordi-nary union members) to the firms that dealt with unions, and to try to make sure that they never reached dangerously high proportions in the shops of members who were only prepared to put up with them so long as they kept their heads down. It let members know about potential employees' union affiliations, even if they were not "agitators" or "men who took an active part" in a strike and "made themselves objectionable by picketing and intimidating the independent workmen," but only "to make sure that they are employed in union shops where this is possible." As for the "agitators,"

---

[48]   Langworthy, PRES 1910, p. 4; Sparks, SEC 1919, p. 2; Schwacke in USCIR, *Final Report*, 3, p. 2892.
[49]   Langworthy, PRES 1909, p. 3.
[50]   Morgan, USCIR, *Final Report*, Vol. 3, p. 2913; Philadelphia Roll & Machine Co. vs. Molders, NWLB Case 316.

of course, no quarter was given or expected: In 1914, the Machinists' business agent, Edward Keenan, thought that the MMA knew "every man active in the organization" and simply expected that "when I get out of this job I will have to move out of Philadelphia."[51]

Labor Bureau activity peaked in years of tight labor markets and active strike-breaking. But what else did it do, particularly during what George Cresson called "such times when the employees are working to the mutual satisfaction of themselves and their Employer and the Labor Leaders are not stirring up strife"?[52] Supplying replacement workmen, and sapping away at the foundations of unionism by competing for control of the skilled labor market, were not the only services that the bureau supplied to MMA members, even in its earliest years.

First, it tried to limit competition for skilled labor between member firms. As Cresson explained, it was "not the general policy of the Manufacturers to take employees away from competitors, but this is sometimes inadvertently done." Secretary McPherson amplified his point, saying that, "Previous to the establishment of the Labor Bureau, wages were bid up continually by the manufacturers hiring each others (*sic*) men. The Labor Bureau has to a large extent put a stop to this evil."[53]

The bureau worked to limit individual skilled workers' ability to exploit their scarcity value by, first, only offering its facilities to unemployed workmen. Those who were already in a member firm's employ could not use it to look for a better or higher paying job, either to simplify the process of job search and reduce the risk and cost of coming onto the labor market, or to acquire a job offer for use in individual bargaining with their present employer. Even if they avoided it and relied on their own resources, they might still find their task made more difficult. If "the members who hire their help direct" agreed to "only telephone this office before offering employment to any man," the secretary could bar the factory gate to present employees by letting new potential employers know that they already "belonged" to another member.[54]

The bureau also made it harder for a man to talk his way into a better job than his skills and experience justified, by compiling an ever-growing record of the jobs that he had performed, the machines that he was competent to operate, and the actual rates that he had been paid. Skilled men rested their claims to a particular job and pay-classification on precisely this

[51] McPherson, SEC 1907, p. 11; Attorney Thomas Raeburn White's opinion on legality of Bureau, ECM 30 March 1920; Sparks, SEC 1917, p. 5, SEC 1919, p. 7 [screening out undesirables]; Keenan in USCIR, *Final Report*, Vol. 3, pp. 2882, 2883.
[52] Cresson, PRES 1904, p. 2.
[53] Ibid., p. 1; McPherson, SEC Dec. 1905, p. 2.
[54] McPherson, SEC 1907, p. 5; ECM, 23 Dec. 1924, p. 4, 27 Jan. 1925, p. 5, 24 Feb. 1925, p. 3.

sort of information, which, of course, they had an interest in falsifying. A Philadelphia machinist recalled in 1936 how he got his first job by "overrat[ing] myself. You don't get a job, you know, telling them how dumb you are." A firm was at risk of damage to tools and waste of raw material, as well as of paying a man too much, if it fell for an applicant's sales talk and only discovered its mistake later. A full résumé gave a firm the ability to make an intelligent choice rather than take a chance because, as exployment expert H. A. Worman explained, " 'Where have you worked?' . . . is a question not less important than 'Have you a trade?' " in assessing a man's degree of skill. The bureau also added to the employer's already considerable advantages in "individual bargaining" by providing him with accurate and timely data about the going rate in other Philadelphia firms, or in other metal-working centers, that he could use to rebut employees' claims.[55]

If the bureau had worked perfectly in the performance of all of these tasks, it would have attained an extremely impressive degree of influence over the hiring policies of member firms and over the employment prospects of their past, present, and would-be employees. But, to the oft-expressed chagrin of successive MMA presidents and secretaries, it did not come close to achieving the power and usefulness to which they aspired, and of which it was theoretically capable.

The fundamental reason for the yawning chasm between vision and reality was that most members only cooperated closely with the bureau when, and to the extent that, they needed its help in dealing with a union threat. Where such a threat did not exist, or was in abeyance, most of them could not be bothered to make the alterations to their normal informal employment policies that the bureau required of them, in order that its own centralized procedures should work efficiently.

Most basically, the bureau needed accurate information – regular updates on men hired, leaving, or discharged, including reports on the skill, performance, and character of former employees and the reasons for getting rid of them. Firms were expected to supply this on printed forms from which the data would be transferred to the cardfile, adding to an existing record or creating a new one.

Its first problem was that many firms in the 1900s and 1910s only kept the most rudimentary "personnel records" containing an irreducible minimum of data necessary to ensure that the right person got the right pay envelope. This minimum often did not include an employee's name, simply

[55] Testimony of Mr. George Drum, in Transcript of Proceedings, 25 Nov. 1918, p. 52, in Machinists vs. Smith-Drum and Co., NWLB Case 641; Respondent 618, Machinists Study, Palmer Papers, TUUA; H. A. Worman, *Building Up the Force: How to Get Help, Handle Applicants, and Fit Men into the Organization* (Chicago, 1913), pp. 24, 55.

his timecheck number! Even George Cresson, who stressed in 1904 that "Every manufacturer who has a record of his employees finds this information of great advantage and always ready for reference," added that "[m]any Manufacturers do not keep such records as they are expensive and the advisability is truly questionable in some instances." Firms in which the only "personnel record" was the one maintained by the time-keeper, and in which the management did not feel the need to spend money on the extra clerical assistance required to provide more data for itself or anybody else, had no means of generating the kind and quantity of information on which the Labor Bureau's system depended.[56]

President Hallowell emphasized in 1909 how easy, as well as essential, cooperation was: "Suitable blanks are furnished you for the purpose, which require but a moment to fill out, and this can all be done by ... whoever keeps records of your employees, it only devolves upon the member to give the necessary orders and to insist that this be regularly done, every day, all through the year." However, in 1910, only 15 percent of the MMA's members provided the full reports that the bureau required; by 1916, 40 percent of the members, employing two-thirds of the operatives, were cooperating, but the demands of wartime production, coupled with the shortage of clerical staff, meant that this improvement was not maintained.[57]

Predictably, it was the smaller firms that were unable and unwilling to undertake the investment in administrative capacity and systematic record-keeping that the MMA requested of its members. But these were also the companies that were most reliant on its services for helping them hire their labor, as their lesser size meant that they had less pulling power in the labor market, and their lack of records of past employees meant that they could not easily draw on the latter unless their foremen maintained personal contact with them. There was therefore an incurable structural flaw in the bureau's relations with the MMA's membership: Those firms best prepared to cooperate with it ordinarily had the least need of its help, while the section of the membership that turned to it most frequently for assistance was the root cause of its chronic problem of having to operate with incomplete information.[58]

The second problem was the quality of information that the member firms provided, even when they made the effort. "Employment

---

[56] Joseph H. Willits, *Steadying Employment: With a Section Devoted to Some Facts on Unemployment in Philadelphia* [Philadelphia, 1916; supplement to *The Annals* 65 (May 1916), No.154], p. 86; Cresson, PRES 1904, p. 1.

[57] Hallowell, PRES 1908, p. 7; Morgan, SEC 1910, pp. 4–5; Morgan, SEC 1916, p. 5; 1918, p. 5.

[58] Finance Committee Report, ECM 27 Apr. 1925, p. 1; Dorothea De Schweinitz, *How Workers Find Jobs: A Study of Four Thousand Hosiery Workers in Philadelphia* (Philadelphia, 1932), pp. 111–12.

management" in most firms was an informal, decentralized affair, in the hands of the foremen and superintendents, who often enjoyed close personal relations with their skilled subordinates. When a man quit voluntarily, or if he had to be let go, the foremen would often do their workmates the last favor of writing them a flattering report for submission to the Labor Bureau, to help them get another job. The result of this indulgent behavior was that, as Secretary Morgan complained in 1912, "good records are continually being furnished to men of indifferent qualifications, and instead of the record card always being of service in determining ability, it is oftentimes misleading and causes dissatisfaction. The Bureau can only be guided by the information furnished by the members, who could furnish confidentially the true character and qualifications of any employee who is laid off," but all too often failed to do so.[59]

What proportion of the tens of thousands of individual records that the bureau compiled contained the accurate, current, and complete data it needed can no longer be known. But the frequency of secretaries' complaints about members' unhelpfulness on this score, that they used to explain and excuse the bureau's repeated failure to provide members with the quality and quantity of manpower they asked for, leads one to suppose that it cannot have been as high as they might have wished.

The second thing the MMA asked of its members was that they should either hire through the bureau or at least check out the men they intended to hire direct, for the reasons noted above. Ideally, the MMA would have liked to see all of its members adopt the best practice of its most tightly run anti-union firms and deny employment to skilled men who did not carry the MMA's card. But here, too, the members' cooperation left much to be desired, mostly because such procedures infringed on the personal control over hiring that was the heart of their "foreman's empire." It also imposed costs and delays that there often seemed no good reason to bear. If enough labor of the right type was available through the usual informal channels, and there was no need to be particularly watchful against the infiltration of union agitators, then direct hiring was cheap, quick, and quite safe. Edward Keenan also observed in 1914 that employers' cooperation with the bureau "depends on whether they have got a great amount of work; if they have then they won't take the trouble, but they will hire them at the shop." He knew that they were supposed, in that case, to check men out with the bureau first, but "They might not phone right away; they would phone and find out within a short time." If they then discovered that a man was a unionist, what would they do? "That depends . . . ; if business is very brisk and men are very scarce they very often overlook that thing for the time being."[60]

The foreman's chief purpose when hiring men, particularly in rush times,

[59]   Morgan, SEC 1912, p. 6.
[60]   McPherson, SEC 1906, p. 5; Keenan in USCIR, *Final Report*, Vol. 3, p. 2882.

was to get them speedily to satisfy the pressing demands of production. To do this in the 1906 boom, firms "sent their representatives into shops of other members" and their foremen even telephoned men directly, while they were at work, to poach them away![61] But even when they were not so undisciplined, they were reluctant to rely on the bureau, or wait for it to satisfy their needs, with the harmful consequences that the secretary related in 1909:

Someone asks us to secure a mechanic; we follow our regular system and write the man to call here, this takes perhaps four or five hours; in the meantime a man calls at the factory door who can fill the position; the foreman hires him, and when our man calls a little later and the job is filled, in nine cases out of ten that man will never call again at the Bureau. He thinks it a fraud. This trouble to a large extent could be obviated if the foremen would anticipate their wants of mechanics and give the Bureau time to communicate with applicants registered.[62]

Constant pressure to get members to make their foremen toe the line had only a limited effect. In 1914, for example, 10 percent of the vacancies that firms asked the bureau's help in filling were occupied "before the Bureau had an opportunity to care for wants." This was more than merely frustrating for successive secretaries. It undermined their key strategy for weaning skilled men away from the trade unions and their employment service. As Secretary Passwaters explained, "Men are not going to call at any Bureau unless there are prospects of securing employment. They cannot secure employment at this Bureau unless our Members hire their men through same. . . . [T]he ability to obtain work for the mechanic is what will determine the career of usefulness of the Bureau."[63]

The bureau was not concerned if members hired their common labor directly, since the latter had no unions competing for their loyalties. Revealingly, when laborers did apply to the bureau, no effort was made to check on their references; they could not represent a threat, and had no skills or experience worth recording anyway. Its target was the "mechanics above the average in capacity" who would only "make use of the Bureau more frequently if positions can be secured for them promptly." Drawing these men in was difficult in any case, because they were often union members, and because "The good mechanic does not seek work very often, being valued where he may be employed"; whereas "the poor workman or those of only fair ability in many instances apply at the Bureau every two or three months."[64] But it was vital for the MMA to develop contacts with the cream of the Philadelphia metal trades' labor force, partly because

[61] ECM 11 Sept. 1906.
[62] Passwaters, SEC 1909, p. 3; cf. Morgan, SEC 1911, p. 5.
[63] Morgan, SEC 1914 p. 1, cf. 1913, p. 8; Passwaters, SEC 1909, p. 2, Morgan, SEC 1910, p. 4.
[64] McPherson, SEC Feb. 1905, p. 1; Morgan, SEC 1911, pp. 5–6; Morgan, SEC 1916, p. 5.

In copeing (*sic*) with union agitation and labor disturbances we must rely largely upon the service of those men who have received employment through the Bureau, and who through talking with the examiner have become familiar with the labor policy of the employers.

Many of these men know that the associations are protecting the independent workman from the usurping of their (*sic*) individual rights by the unions. It is therefore of paramount importance if your Association is to be of the greatest benefit to the members in times of stress, that the workers of the community be acquainted with the Bureau and its operation, by having obtained positions through its various channels.[65]

From the viewpoint of the association's officers, members' cooperation with them in building up a body of grateful independent workmen, willing stool-pigeons, and strike-breakers – "an acquaintance that is invaluable in the event of labor difficulties" – was never satisfactory. They knew that success in this endeavor relied on long-term commitment and the ability to trade favors. Philadelphia's independent workmen's "loyalty" to their employers and the MMA was calculated, and, in Gerald Zahavi's terms, "negotiated." The bureau was where much of the "negotiation" went on, so it needed to be able to persuade its skilled worker clientele to call in and keep in touch. In Secretary Morgan's phrase, it was "a bureau for the exchange very often between the mechanic and myself of sentiment." Such "sentiment" included reports from dissatisfied union members about intimate goings-on within the city's labor movement, which may have been one reason why the MMA did not have to pay for espionage services.[66]

The coin in which the MMA could pay for such "negotiated loyalty" was, however, mostly in the pockets of its members. Secretary Morgan claimed to have interceded on employees' behalf against oppressive foremen, but what he needed most of all was a corner on the job market. And this, because of the imperfect cooperation of member firms and their foremen, the bureau never acquired. In 1916 and 1917, for example, only 615 and 633 of the more than 10,000 workmen members hired each year got their jobs from the bureau.[67]

---

[65]   Sparks, SEC 1918, p. 6.

[66]   ECM 18 Nov. 1925, "The Basis for the Budget Estimate for the First Quarter of 1926" p. 2; Gerald Zahavi, "Negotiated Loyalty: Welfare Capitalism and the Shoeworkers of Endicott Johnson, 1920–1940," *JAH* 70 (1983–84): 602–20; Morgan in USCIR, *Final Report*, Vol. 3, p. 2904.

[67]   Morgan, SEC 1916, p. 5; Sparks, SEC 1917, pp. 5–6. The MMA's placement rate in 1914 was less than a tenth that for NMTA branches – 4.2 percent of the average number of operatives vs. an NMTA average of 49 percent (range 7–86 percent), emphasizing the strong hold of decentralized, informal employment practices in Philadelphia and the weakness of labor. Cf. Table 4.1, NMTA, *Synopsis of Proceedings of the 16th Annual Convention* (1914), pp. 47–48. But its ratio of applicants to operatives (0.9) was nearer the NMTA norm (1.6, range 0.1–3.6), emphasizing its acceptance by workers.

Eventually, the MMA gave up trying to persuade its members to use the bureau as anything other than a specialized service, to "furnish men in case of labor difficulties" and to recruit men of particular skills that firms could not locate for themselves. By the 1920s, the union threat had receded, so bureau screening became less important. Also, as the average size and administrative capacity of member firms grew, more of them acquired their own employment departments, and the ability to develop and implement their own hiring policies. The MMA therefore accepted that "more prompt recruiting c[an] be done by the plants themselves first drawing upon prospects from the neighborhood and that the use of a central employment department . . . would be an interference and retard recruiting rather than expedite it." Sparks eventually concluded that "[i]t is the natural thing for the membership when adding to their forces to recall their former efficient employees and to recruit from applicants at the shop who have been interviewed and apparently are desirable prospects."[68]

It is therefore plain that the MMA's Labor Bureau never achieved the power that its founders and early advocates desired to win, and in due course it trimmed its mission to suit the environment in which it worked and the role its members wanted it to fill. However, an institution does not have to operate perfectly to function well enough.

Clearly, the bureau did build up a clientele on whose services it could draw in emergencies in return for having helped them find employment. In 1905–07, the bureau placed in jobs about four-fifths of the men who registered for work with it. This success rate declined precipitously after 1907, to about one man in sixteen to twenty in the bleakest years 1908 and 1914, at the same time as the numbers of men using the bureau increased fourfold. But the extent to which men patronized the bureau depended more on their desperation than on its ability to guarantee them a job. In the depression of 1907, for example, hundreds of unemployed skilled men registered with the bureau, presenting it with an opportunity to "cause them to look upon [it] with favor" by finding them work. It could not help many – there were few jobs – but the fact that it was there, and that it tried, caused a distinct improvement in its reputation among the craft labor force, "some of the most skilled mechanics in the city having registered and gladly accepted employment through the office." So Philadelphia's metal tradesmen seem, from the reports of the bureau's operations, to have accepted it and to have added it to their repertoire of ways of looking for work.[69]

Unfortunately, data allowing us to break down the flood of applicants into skill categories, whose chances of finding a job through the bureau varied greatly, exist only for its first year (see Table 4.2). Thereafter, incom-

[68] Memoranda for Special Committee (1930), pp. 2, 4–5; Minutes of the Meeting of the Special Committee to Study Methods of Recruiting Labor, 24 Feb. 1930, p. 1, MMAP II-3-46; Sparks, SEC 1931, p. 8.

[69] McPherson, SEC 1907, p. 5, 1908 p. 3.

plete aggregate statistics are all that survive (see Table 4.1). But these permit us to see that, between 1910 and 1913, one-third to one-half of the men registering at the bureau as unemployed would at least be sent to a firm to be looked over by the hiring boss, and have a chance of learning about the terms on offer. About one-third of these in turn would end up securing their jobs through the bureau's introduction. It cannot be assumed that all those who did not take up a job were rejected by the firms that they went to. Men declined job offers if the terms did not suit them, or if they found their own, better, jobs before presenting their "cards of introduction" at MMA members' shops – or indeed after they had accepted employment, but before they started work. There were many reasons why an MMA introduction might not result in a man's receiving a job offer, deciding to accept it, and actually doing so, that did not involve his being turned down by a member firm or finding the job that he was sent to fill already occupied before he arrived on the scene. A skilled, radical machinist at Baldwin's, for example, "registered with the Metal Manufacturers Association for a job, but I never took one they offered. The size of the pay was an insult."[70]

But more of the skilled men were positive or neutral about the bureau than were antagonistic. A Tabor machinist, for example, recalled that "Some of the best jobs that he has gotten, he has gotten through the Phila Metal Manufacturers' Employment Agency." This man, and many of his fellows, accepted the dependent situation in which all but the most highly skilled found themselves in the Open Shop era. In this context, as President Schwacke argued only a little disingenuously in 1914, the bureau was "a very much greater advantage to the employee than it was to the employer," because it provided a free, centrally located place for one-stop job-shopping in "a very large city [whose] workshops are scattered all over . . . , so that a man out of work . . . in order to ascertain where he could find employment, might spend several days going around . . . to find a vacancy." It was not the only way in which workmen found work, or employers found "help," but it was rapidly accepted as a useful additional facility by both.[71]

The bureau soon built up a relatively stable clientele: In every year between 1908 and the first full year of war-induced prosperity, 1916, apart from the brief tight labor market of 1910, about 90 percent of the men who applied to it for work were already known to it. This was either because they had previously registered in person or because they had worked for one of the member firms that cooperated with the MMA's record-keeping. The MMA recirculated this portion of the city's settled skilled labor force among member firms, and, although it could never prevent the latter from

[70]   Sparks, SEC 1917, p. 5; Respondent 459, Machinists Study, Palmer Papers, TUUA.
[71]   Respondent 178, Machinists Study, Palmer Papers, TUUA; Schwacke in USCIR, *Final Report*, Vol. 3, p. 2890.

doing most of their hiring directly, it helped them find men of particular skills, who were often hardest to locate. It thereby acquired enough patronage from foremen to enable it to make it worth the skilled man's while to call at the bureau when he was out of a job; and by helping enough of them out, it built up its pool of resident strike-breakers and nonunion workmen on whom it could always call in seasons of difficulty.[72]

By 1914, the MMA was well established, with a decade's success behind it and a record of fairly steady growth. Its finances were sound, its leaders experienced and secure, and its administrative procedures thoroughly routinized. Its roots were firmly planted in a substantial section of the city's metal manufacturing community, whose interests it had served and whose loyalty it had won. It was just as well that it had achieved this much, because it was about to meet its greatest test, the most serious threat that the Open Shop would encounter before the 1930s.

[72] ECM, 10 March 1920, p. 3.

6

Riding the Storm, 1915–1918

The campaign to establish and maintain the Open Shop, in Philadelphia as in the rest of industrial America before the war, had been aided by recurrent periods of very high unemployment, and scarcely impeded by state intervention. Entrepreneurial liberty rested on sound foundations: Competition between firms for workers' services was rarely unmanageable; governmental involvement in the private relations of employers and employees was only occasional, and normally quite supportive – law-enforcement stiffened with the occasional injunction.

But as 1905–07 and 1910–11 illustrated, a tight labor market made the Open Shop somewhat more vulnerable. During cyclical upswings makers of producers' goods, in particular, experienced short-run but severe demand pressures that sharply increased the bargaining power of their skilled workers, the supply of whom was quite inelastic. And the political equilibrium of the Republican era was under strain in the prewar years. "Progressivism" infected the elected portions of city, state, and national governments, and threatened to increase the forces all three brought to bear limiting employers' freedom to manage.

So the foundations of the Open Shop were not, perhaps, quite as solid as they at first seemed. Workers were numerous, had votes, and had middle-class sympathizers; their unions had political options open to them providing a new forum within which to pursue the goals of industrial struggle even after meeting defeat on the picket line and shop floor. And prosperity, one day, must surely return, with its attendant organizing drives and strikes.

Because of these possibilities, insecurity pervaded the MMA's membership in the early 'teens, providing ever-present and growing reasons for collective self-defense. Chronic oversensitivity about threats to their independence and profitability translated into a durable commitment to the MMA, which responded to new challenges flexibly and successfully on their

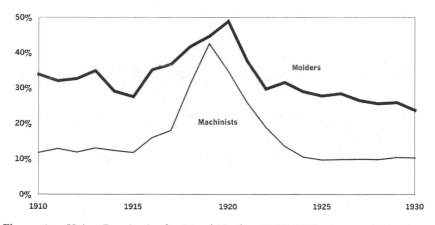

Figure 6.1. Union Density in the Metal Trades, 1910–1930. *Source:* As in Figure 3.1.

behalf. In these as in other respects, the MMA's members' outlook, rhetoric, and behavior mirrored that of their fellows in other industries and cities. A sense of continuing crisis was vital for mobilizing the rank-and-file of the Open Shop movement, and keeping it mobilized, but it did not have to be manufactured by the movement's leaders. It sprang from their supporters' everyday experience.[1]

The Open Shop movement thrived on struggle, but none of the challenges it had faced matched, in scale or duration, those presented by America's involvement in the Great War. The first and most basic challenge was that of full employment. In midsummer 1915, the Philadelphia and national labor markets tightened. Unemployment evaporated as fast as it had appeared the previous spring, and it would not return to anything approaching its normal prewar level for the next five years. How would the Open Shop fare during this long boom, which dwarfed the two brief upswings that the MMA had had to ride out since its creation at the end of the previous major expansion of 1898–1903? (Cf. Figures 3.3 and 6.2 for trends of output in the three key sectors underpinning the Philadelphia metal trades' prosperity, and Figure 4.1 for unemployment).

The challenge of full employment was exacerbated by the challenge of progressivism. For what made the Great War even more dangerous to Open Shop employers in the Philadelphia metal trades – and to their fellows in

---

[1] See Howard M. Gitelman, "Management's Crisis of Confidence and the Origins of the National Industrial Conference Board, 1914–1916," *BHR* 58 (1984): 153–77 at pp. 155–56; NMTA, *Synopsis of Proceedings of the 15th Annual Convention* (New York, 1913), p. 13, *16th* (1914), p. 21, *17th* (1915), pp. 18, 24.

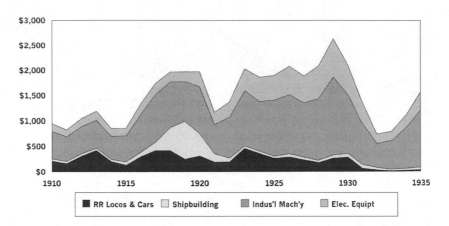

Figure 6.2. Output of Major Capital Goods Industries, 1910–1935, in Millions of 1913 Dollars. *Note:* Data as in Figure 3.3, with the addition of Electrical Equipment (Series P355). The 1914–15 and 1921 recessions, wrapped around the shipbuilding boom and collapse, and the stagnation of these traditional sectors through the 1920s shows clearly. Electrical equipment, Philadelphia's postwar growth sector, increased its output from about a third to a half as much as industrial equipment between 1920 and the middle of the decade, and maintained or exceeded that level until the Depression. The impact of the Depression (see Chapters 10 and 11) was stunning.

other cities and other industries around the country – than simply the labor shortages it caused, was that it occurred during a period of policy innovation by reformist state and federal governments. They had begun to devise their own industrial relations agendas and the institutions for carrying them out; and they were developing patron–client relationships with the unions of the AFL, which were their chosen instruments for the pursuit of social peace and the vague but compelling goal of "industrial democracy."

Finally, the war also coincided with, and helped stimulate, an upsurge of collective self-assertion by American industrial workers whose tactics and objectives developed in new, imaginative, and potentially threatening directions. They were both reacting to the heady environment of full employment and federal patronage, and helping to bring about the concessive government policy itself, one of whose objects was to channel and contain the force of workers' protests.

These tendencies, already visible in the last years of peace, would be magnified many times as America moved from being the theoretically neutral supplier of Britain and France and became their associate in war. Washington would rapidly supplant Harrisburg as the chief source of threats to Philadelphia employers' freedom, as well as of their new-found prosperity. The federal government would become, directly or indirectly, durable-goods producers' major customer, giving it enormous potential leverage over them. And that leverage would be exerted by the distended bureaucracy of a "war-welfare state" that had to appease and cajole organized and unorganized labor because it was restive and in short supply, and that wanted to in any case. The war would therefore provide both the means and the excuse for the attempted implementation of much of the prewar Democrat and progressive social agenda.[2]

This chapter and the next will chart the MMA's course as it battled through the manifold and interconnected problems presented to its members by full employment, workers' insurgency, and federal intervention. They describe the coming of the war emergency to industrial Philadelphia and the MMA's response to the ensuing difficulties. The prime focus remains on the business community, but due attention will also be paid to the strategies and behavior of two other important groups of protagonists in the wartime labor relations game – the leaders of the local metal crafts struggling to make the most of the best organizing and bargaining opportunities that they had ever seen, and the federal dispute adjusters who grappled with the most serious of the resulting conflicts.

The war – and certainly the "industrial war" – was not really over until the war-welfare state was dismantled in 1919–21, and "normalcy" returned on a tide of rising unemployment and anti-unionism. Therefore the time frame of these chapters is set at 1915–23, to include the collapse of labor's limited and fragile wartime gains, and what seemed at the time to be the final and total triumph of the Open Shop in the Philadelphia metal trades of the 1920s and indeed in the country at large.[3]

The MMA's membership, ideology, strategy, and tactics scarcely changed through the period covered by these chapters, except that the war fostered the development of more bureaucratic and systematic personnel management among some member companies. This created new demands for services, which the association hastened to supply, and wartime prosperity delivered the resources that the new program required. The result was that

[2] Melvyn Dubofsky, "Abortive Reform: The Wilson Administration and Organized Labor 1913–1920," in James E. Cronin and Carmen Sirianni, eds., *Work, Community and Power: The Experience of Labor in Europe and America, 1900–1925* (Philadelphia, 1983), pp. 197–220; Joseph A. McCartin, *Labor's Great War: The Struggle for Industrial Democracy and the Origins of Modern American Labor Relations, 1912–1921* (Chapel Hill, 1997); David Montgomery, *The Fall of the House of Labor: The Workplace, the State, and American Labor Activism, 1865–1925* (New York, 1987), esp. Chs. 7–8; Ronald Schaffer, *America in the Great War: The Rise of the War-Welfare State* (New York, 1991), esp. Ch. 5.

[3] See David Brody, *Labor in Crisis: The Steel Strike of 1919* (New York, 1965) and Colin J. Davis, *Power at Odds: The National Railroad Shopmen's Strike* (Urbana, 1997) for classic explorations of the two great national disasters that drew a line under workers' – especially metal workers' – hopes of a better world.

the MMA, like the business community in general, emerged from the war with its commitment to the Open Shop undiminished, and its strength and sophistication greatly enhanced.

6.1 CREATIVE DESTRUCTION: THE SHAPING OF THE WAR ECONOMY

In the summer of 1915, the Philadelphia metal trades began to benefit from the war that was already raging in Europe, and the insatiable appetite of Britain and France for ammunition, weapons, and industrial equipment. Over the next three years the city and its region became one of the most important war production centers for the United States and its European associates. As the Philadelphia Chamber of Commerce proudly boasted, "When Uncle Sam calls the roll of those who are furnishing most to wage this mighty war, he finds that th[is] district . . . leads all the rest. . . . Philadelphia counts in this war with the weight of a belligerent nation." And metalworkers were in the front line of its industrial army.[4]

The war's impact on Philadelphia's industrial structure was profound. Philadelphia experienced one of the largest rates of growth in manufacturing employment among major industrial cities, outpaced only by the smaller but even more dynamic Detroit and Los Angeles. Much of this increase was concentrated in the metal trades and, within them, in durable goods production. The war's peculiar demand patterns favored producers of the heaviest, hitherto most skill-intensive, capital goods – shipbuilding, transportation equipment, and armaments – bringing a welcome revival from prewar stagnation, and almost the last gasp of prosperity, to a number of the city's traditional metal-working industries and their established suppliers. The war meant overflowing order books, worsening labor shortages, and a strong bargaining position for the growing numbers of metalworkers to exploit. Pennsylvania state surveys reported a 37 percent increase in Philadelphia secondary metal trades employment (shipbuilding excluded) between 1915–16 and 1918–19 (from about 56,000 to 77,000). The numbers of workers classified as millwrights, tool-makers, and machinists rose even more sharply – from almost 20,000 to more than 30,000 – between the 1910 and 1920 censuses. This crowded, turbulent city, bursting with new businesses and migrant workers, would be the scene of unprecedented levels of conflict in the metal trades, and particularly on the part of machinists, between 1916 and 1921.[5]

---

[4]   Philadelphia Chamber of Commerce, *1918–1919 Philadelphia Yearbook* (Philadelphia, 1920), p. 19.

[5]   Gladys L. Palmer, *Philadelphia Workers in a Changing Economy* (Philadelphia, 1956), p. 22; PID-1640 database; Helen M. Herrman, *Ten Years of Work Experience of Philadelphia Machinists* (Philadelphia, 1938), p. 1.

Satisfying the war's demands involved both the conversion and extension of existing industrial facilities, and the construction of wholly new ones. In the first phase of growth, the city's firms and factories moved from recession in 1914–15 to full utilization of their facilities and rebuilding of their workforces. Some large companies became prime contractors to American and European governmental agencies; far more smaller ones benefitted too as subcontractors from the business that the city's industrial giants parcelled out among them.

Between 1915–16 and 1918–19 the largest rate of sectoral increase (151 percent), and 47 percent (9,919 workers) of the absolute increase in secondary metal trades employment, was accounted for by the greatest of these giants. Baldwin Locomotive restored its Philadelphia payroll to a little less than its prewar peak, and more than quadrupled its output of locomotives between the 1914–15 doldrums and the furious activity of 1918. Baldwin invested heavily in both the old downtown and the new Eddystone works, where it employed a further 8,500 workers by January 1918, and more than 11,000 by the fall. The two plants' combined capacity grew to almost 3,600 locomotives a year, shipped by the hundreds to America's allies or to meet the U.S. Railroad Administration's standardized requirements. Baldwin also built prodigious quantities of weaponry for the British, French, Russian, and eventually American war machines. Any initial reluctance to get into the munitions business was quickly overcome – partly, its chief executive, Samuel Vauclain, claimed, as a result of the death of the firm's Paris representative when a German submarine sank the *Lusitania* in May 1915. Thereafter, it threw itself into the business with a vengeance. Vauclain became chair of the Council of National Defense's Munitions Committee, and the company collaborated closely with J. P. Morgan & Co., the Allies' agents. Baldwin acquired a quarter of a billion dollars' worth of government and allied contracts by war's end, producing heavy artillery as well as locomotives in its two main plants. It also set up wholly owned subsidiaries at Eddystone, including an ammunition works dedicated to filling huge British orders for shot and shell that employed 5,500 workers in January 1918, and what was claimed to be the largest rifle factory in the world, employing 14,000 at the same time. (Both plants' peak employment was over a thousand higher.) In 1918 the rifle works was leased to and operated by a reorganized Midvale Steel company, ambitious to become America's Krupp. Midvale's own payroll at its North Philadelphia works increased from less than 4,000 in 1915–16 to about 11,500 employees in 1918, their product line shifting from a diverse range of heavy forgings and steel castings that met the needs of the railroad equipment and other domestic industries to concentrate single-mindedly on heavy ordnance.[6]

[6]   PID-1640 database; Paul T. Warner, *History of the Baldwin Locomotive Works: 1831–1923* reprinted in Fred Westing, *The Locomotives That Baldwin Built* (Seattle, 1961), Ch. 8 and p. 182; Samuel M. Vauclain (with Earl Chapin May), *Steaming Up!*

Other city firms were equally opportunistic. The Brill streetcar factory converted to war production for the Entente powers in 1914, and the smaller Hale & Kilburn (manufacturers of seats and other car-fittings) transformed itself into a military truck body maker. War-related exports were as much a blessing for these businesses as for Baldwin, because the end of the streetcar system building boom in 1912 had left them with excess capacity. Many local companies did not need to adapt their facilities so much. Edward G. Budd Mfg., only recently established as an auto body maker, found additional profitable trade in the manufacture of steel helmets and other specialist metal pressings, notably airplane wheels. Other firms simply exploited large-scale, war-created markets for their regular peace-time product lines. American Pulley's order book began to fill in the summer of 1915, and the firm soon exceeded all production records, pouring out goods way above its plant's rated capacity to meet war industries' needs for power-transmission equipment. Abram Cox Stove supplied heating and cooking appliances for military bases, as well as jobbing high-quality castings for other local firms. David Lupton's Sons, manufacturers of architectural sheet-metal work, found huge markets in equiping government and military buildings and new factories, and easily converted their plants to supplying heavy metal stampings for the shipbuilding program, too. Fayette R. Plumb was perhaps the luckiest of all, as the wartime construction program and the brutalities of trench warfare created an enormous demand for its standard line of hand tools – hammers, hatchets, picks, sledges, and axes – easily augmented with new specialties – trenching mattocks, wire cutters, and throat-cutting knives. The city's skilled surgical instrument, artificial limb, and wheelchair makers were also, of course, beneficiaries of the cruel but generous war economy.[7]

In the second phase, Philadelphia, with its large skilled labor force, its concentration of major suppliers and subcontractors, and its tidewater location, became a favored site for new investments by out-of-town big capital and by the federal government itself. Swedish bearing manufacturer SKF, desirous of satisfying the enormous American market without having to run the gauntlet of British naval blockades and German submarine

The Autobiography of Samuel M. Vauclain (San Marino, Calif., 1973; first published 1930), Chs. 17–20, esp. pp. 247–48; "Baldwin Locomotive Works" and "Midvale Steel & Ordnance Company" in Philadelphia War History Committee, *Philadelphia in the World War 1914–1919* (New York, 1922), pp. 417–23, 456; additional employment data from "Eddystone, Pa. Joint Rept. 8 Jan. 1918," p. 1, in Report from L. A. Herr to C. W. A. Veditz, "Subject: General View of the Situation of Territory Visited," in U.S. Housing Corporation, Office of the President, Project Books, 1918–19, Box 26, RG3, National Archives.

7   "The Industries of Philadelphia During the War," in Philadelphia War History Committee, *Philadelphia in the World War*, pp. 415–17, 426-28, 432–33, 439–52, 455 esp.; PID-1640 database.

attacks, bought and expanded the established Philadelphia firm of Hess, Bright. General Electric opened a big switchgear factory, and Westinghouse set up a steam turbine and heavy electrical equipment works with about 4,000 employees. The Frankford Arsenal and the Navy Yard added thousands to their workforces, which reached about 6,000 and 10,000, respectively, by the fall of 1918. The Navy Yard also became the home of a new aircraft factory with about 3,600 employees. Most important of all, the Emergency Fleet Corporation brought its almost 4,000 headquarters staff to Philadelphia in the summer of 1918 in recognition of the fact that the "American Clyde" was to play the central role in building the "Bridge to France."[8]

Cramp's, the smaller down-river yards in Chester and Wilmington and up-river yards at Bristol, and huge New York Ship across the river in Camden, were all expanded. Cramp's workforce rose from its normal prewar level of about 4,500 (but a mere 2,500 in March 1915) to almost 12,500, and New York Ship's from 4,500 in early 1917 to a peak of nearly 20,000 in 1920. Their vast joint capacities, heavily committed to naval contracts, were dwarfed by the enormous new government-owned Hog Island yard, dedicated to the production of standardized merchant vessels. By the end of the war there were almost 14,000 shipyard workers living within the city limits, tens of thousands more in the neighboring counties, and yet more thousands working for EFC subcontractors. The wages, hours, and working conditions of all of them were dictated by the EFC's liberal-managerial bureaucracy, which "affect[ed] so many workers that practically speaking they set the scale of wages for the entire district."[9]

This then was the local context of industrial relations in the Philadelphia metal trades through the busy years of defense preparedness, mobilization, and war – economic growth, industrial revival and restructuring, labor

[8] SKF Co., *The Story of SKF* (n.p., 1982), pp. 7–8; PID-1640 database; Anon. (EFC) to Philip Hiss, 9 Oct. 1918, p. 2; Conference on Philadelphia District – Frankford Arsenal, Held by the Bureau of Industrial Housing and Transportation, 26 Sept. 1918, p. 1, and R. B. Blake, "Report of Preliminary Survey of Housing Conditions in the Tacony, Philadelphia, Conshohocken and Chester Districts, 15–23 July 1918," p. 6, all in U.S. Housing Corporation, Office of the President, Project Books, 1918–19 Box 26; F. G. Coburn, "Aeroplane Construction," *J. ECP* 36 (1919): 121–26; William F. Trimble, "The Naval Aircraft Factory, the American Aviation Industry, and Government Competition, 1919–1928," *BHR* 60 (1986): 175–98 at p. 178; Bernard Mergen, "The Government as Manager: Emergency Fleet Shipbuilding, 1917–1919," in Harold Sharlin, ed., *Business and Its Environment* (Westport, 1983), pp. 49–80; Edward N. Hurley, *The Bridge to France* (Philadelphia, 1927), esp. p. 74, Ch. 9, p. 142.

[9] Philadelphia War History Committee, *Philadelphia in the World War*, pp. 421, 361–95, 404; Blake Report (July 1918), p. 4 [quote]. In the five-county metropolitan area there were about 58,000 shipbuilding workers in 1919 – Palmer, *Philadelphia Workers*, p. 35.

migration and restiveness, and the new importance of the federal government and its agencies as customer, employer, and regulator. In these and other respects, Philadelphia's experience once again encapsulated that of other industrial cities and districts; what happened to the MMA, its members, and their larger corporate neighbors during this period reflected quite faithfully the new challenges that war brought to continued success in American employers' decade-long struggle for hegemony.

6.2 GATHERING CLOUDS: 1915–1916

The effects of the return of prosperity in the summer of 1915 were immediately felt by the MMA, its member firms, and their employees. Philadelphia's experience mirrored that of other major metal-working centers, pithily summed up by the NMTA's president Herbert Rice:

Speaking generally this is the story. Everybody quiet and on short time. War breaks out and a semi-panic seizes business. Then . . . a resumption of trade in machinery lines – and lo, everybody is busy all at once. The big munitions plants begin bidding up the price of labor to rates unheard of in our day. Careless for the most part of the future, of principles, of hours, or of wages – everything is sacrificed for immediate gain and often in total disregard of other industries and manufacturers.[10]

In Philadelphia, overtime rapidly became the norm as both labor and product markets tightened. The Labor Bureau revived from its recession inactivity. Between 1914 and 1915, the number of applicants for work increased by 60 percent as their likelihood of finding a place improved; the proportion of new faces among these applicants, that is, men who were not already known to the MMA, more than doubled, as "Rumors of work being plentiful brought many mechanics to the City." Member firms called on the bureau for help in filling more than two-and-a-half times as many job vacancies, and the MMA sent them more than three times as many men in reply. Of these, more than a third were hired, a number two-and-a-half times as great as in 1914. Better than three-quarters of the notified vacancies were satisfactorily filled through the bureau (see Table 4.1). The absolute numbers were still quite small – member firms continued to hire about 90 percent of their men directly – but the trend was sharply upwards. This indicated how much more inclined members were to turn to the bureau, and how useful it could be for recruiting hard-to-find skilled workers, once unemployment began to disappear. Most of these increases took place in the second half of 1915, during which time the bureau did almost three-quarters of the whole year's business.[11]

[10] "President's Report," in NMTA, *Synopsis of Proceedings of the 18th Annual Convention* (New York, 1916), p. 24.
[11] Morgan, SEC 1915, pp. 2–3.

The year was a remarkably quiet one for labor relations. The high unemployment of the first half helped persuade the IMU to call off two machinery foundry strikes that had started three years earlier, but which had been lost long before the recession, the firms "hav[ing] needed no mechanics that were not readily available." (Pickets had been "obnoxious" at only one MMA member's works, where they had persisted for fourteen months, albeit with negligible discouraging effect on strike-breakers, until the company secured an injunction to remove their irritant presence.) As for the Machinists, their year-end listing of bargaining gains across the United States had none from Philadelphia to report. The MMA's Secretary Morgan congratulated his members on their good fortune, for which he had a ready explanation: "The 'Open Shop' policy so earnestly advocated by this Association during the twelve years of its existence is now bearing fruit. With labor disturbances at our very doors, not a metal shop in this City (busy as all lines of industry are) has had labor trouble of any sort."[12]

The MMA's members responded to the tightening labor market, and rising cost of living, by paying war bonuses, "where conditions warranted . . . in such a way that it would be considered an increase due to the war conditions." They wanted both to maintain competitive pay during what they expected to be a relatively brief period of high demand and labor shortage, and to protect what they thought of as their normal wage rates in anticipation of the return of peacetime markets. No one supposed that they had five years of insistent demand pressures, extraordinarily high employment, and steep inflation ahead of them. President Schwacke's confident advice to "stand firm" in the face of "unreasonable demands" from their men, to buy them off cheap, face them down, or take a strike, that is, to hold to established practice, was adequate and sensible during this first phase of the munitions boom.[13]

In the short term, in any case, their problem was not so much organized

---

[12] Morgan, SEC 1915, p. 3; SEC 1914, p. 2; ECM 13 May, 10 June, 8 July 1914; "Advantages Gained by Machinists in Contract and Manufacturing Shops During 1915," *MMJ* 28 (1916): 266; Morgan, SEC 1915, p. 1. For more about the Molders' bitter but futile strike, see the testimony of business agent Torpy in U.S. Commission on Industrial Relations, *Industrial Relations: Final Report and Testimony* (Washington, 1916), Vol. 3, p. 2920; for the situation in the metal trades in general in 1914–15, see "President's Report" in NMTA, *Synopsis of Proceedings* (1915), p. 20, and "Commissioner's Report," p. 25; "President's Report" in *Synopsis of Proceedings* (1916), pp. 22–25, and "Commissioner's Report," pp. 30–31.

[13] ECM 11 Aug., 13 Oct. 1915. Schwacke's advice was standard NMTA policy. For wage and price changes, see PHIL1439 database and U.S. Department of Labor, Bureau of Labor Statistics, *Bulletin No. 699*: "Changes in Cost of Living in Large Cities in the United States 1913–41" (Washington, 1941), p. 50. Inflation ran at 7 percent in 1915–16, 21 percent in 1917–18, 18 percent in 1918–19, and 15 percent in 1919–1921. The net effect on metalworkers' wages was to limit their gain between 1915 and 1920 to about 12.5 percent, in real terms, although money wages increased ten times more.

labor pressure, but rather increased turnover and "the blandishments of the labor agents engaged in securing help for concerns making war munitions," whose wage scale was "revolutionary." To "maintain the integrity of organization in the various shops,... it would be necessary to satisfy the employees at present engaged."[14]

Necessary, yes; but possible? Philadelphia in 1916 was a mixture of firms still producing for the American market, and operating according to normal competitive principles, and of early beneficiaries of cost-plus contracts, whose deep pockets gave them all of the advantages in the increasingly desperate and unregulated scramble for scarce skilled labor. As the NMTA's commissioner, John Hibbard, described the results of this common obstacle to the maintenance of employer unity, "[n]ever before has this Association witnessed such selfishness, short-sightedness, and cowardice on the part of employers in their efforts to take temporary advantage of existing conditions. Methods... just short of piracy and shanghaiing have been adopted... by supposedly respectable concerns to which they would not have stooped in ordinary times."[15]

The result of the unequal and divisive struggle between winners and losers in the emergent war economy could be seen in the bitter protest of MMA member W. H. Lutz, of the Lutz-Webster Engineering Co., whose firm employed about twenty people, to the general manager of the giant new Remington Arms plant in the spring of 1916. Lutz did not complain privately; he issued a broadside headed "Common Decency In Business" against the suburban rifle maker's violation of local employment norms by having its agents distribute handbills stating "There Is Money For You" at the doors of city metal-working plants.[16]

The strains within the business community between "insiders" and "outsiders," those who could afford to pay the new going rates and those who could not, were obvious, and would become even more severe before the war was over. Maintaining employer unity in the face of these divisive forces, in an unprecedentedly tight labor market, would be one of the greatest challenges that the MMA would encounter during the war; confronting it successfully would be crucial.

The year 1916 turned into one of growing union pressure on Philadelphia's metal trades employers. The MMA members and others bound by the Foundrymen's Club–IMU contract faced the prospect of conflict early in the year, because the Molders were demanding extensive changes to the previous year's agreement, including the introduction of the eight-hour day and the elimination of, or serious restrictions on, piece work. But the employ-

---

[14] ECM 11 Aug. 1915, Morgan, SEC 1915, p. 1.
[15] NMTA, *Synopsis of Proceedings* (1916), p. 31.
[16] Copy of letter of 7 March 1916, MMAP I-3-32.

ers were spared confrontation by the IMU's President Valentine, who made it clear to business agent James Cronin and the local Molders' negotiating committees that the national union "w[ould] not stand for strike in Phila. district." So the existing contract was extended for another year, at an acceptable price, under the circumstances – a 14 percent raise (to a $4.00 minimum for a nine-hour day) for the hourly paid, and a like increase in piece rates to maintain piece-workers' (higher) minimum.[17]

The foundrymen had got off lightly. Having already established a pattern of union–management relations before the war, they would see little but incremental change for the duration. They just had to pay their molders much more money for fewer hours' work, and more of them had to accept a greater degree of union intervention in employment matters and working practices.

As for the MMA, it kept a wary eye on developments in the organized portion of the trade. And it deployed its customary labor-replacement defense to fight molders' strikes in several machinery foundries that came under pressure to recognize the union that summer, as Cronin concentrated his resources on building the union. But for the first time in years, that defense was not wholly adequate in the face of the Molders' aggressive picketing and an acute labor shortage. A few more MMA members threw in the towel and came under the protection of the collective contract.[18]

Wartime labor relations in Philadelphia's foundries were continuous with and not qualitatively different from prewar. But elsewhere, revolution was beginning to break out. At Cramp Shipbuilding, 1,100 previously unorganized boilermakers, riveters, and caulkers, the all-important hull construction crafts, walked out in April. This was only the second strike that the firm had known in a generation, and the largest that the Philadelphia metal trades had seen since Baldwin's in 1911. The men were aggrieved about poor piece prices and unjust working rules. When one man was discharged for not accepting a job assignment that would not pay him a decent day's wage, the yard emptied. The shop committee that led the strike advertised it, correctly, as "One of the greatest struggles in the history of the Ship Building Industry in Philadelphia." Calling for support, they spoke for the first time in the confident, authentic, and unprecedentedly resonant lan-

---

[17]   Copy of letter from James Cronin, President Local 15, 3 Dec. 1915, Subject: Change in Agreement; General Report Philadelphia, 26 Jan. 1916; Philadelphia Foundrymen's Club, Memorandum of Agreement Between the PFC and IMU Locals 1, 15, and 111, Feb. 1916 – all in MMAP II-3-15, 16. The second document seems to be a report from an "inside operative"; as the MMA did not hire them itself, the information probably came from one employed by the NFA or a helpful local firm.

[18]   ECM 12 Apr., 10 May 1916; Morgan, SEC 1916, pp. 1–2.

guage that American labor was learning to use even before the nation joined the Great War for Democracy:

As workingmen we have asked for nothing but the American privilege of meeting our employer, man to man, to discuss our grievances. We have been refused this. . . .
    This Company demands that we surrender unconditionally. Are you, as working-men, going to assist them in their Un-American demands? We think not! The fight is now on. It is your fight, as well as our own and now is the time to win.[19]

The workers had a better strategic appreciation of the changed balance of power than did their employers, who acted as if they were still living in the prewar world of ample unemployment; a stagnant economy; quiescent or helpless workers; and a distant, indifferent government. Instead, Cramp's had to adjust to challenge and intrusion. Two of the federal Department of Labor's conciliators arrived quickly on the scene, to be met with the usual frosty welcome from an autocratic employer. As they reported to Secretary of Labor William B. Wilson, "we presented ourselves to the General Manager . . . , and were denied an audience; they claiming they had no dif-ferences to settle, and if they had they were perfectly capable of taking care of it (*sic*) themselves." The boss's attitude was especially hostile because an Industrial Relations Commission staff member had called earlier "and informed him that he had better make a settlement as [we] would be on the ground the next day, and rather in a threatening manner tried to persuade him" to reach an immediate agreement. His response was to stiffen his resis-tance and even refuse the mayor's offer to mediate, after the frustrated con-ciliators had asked the latter to try to get the company to talk.[20]

But within a fortnight, Cramp's changed their tune, as they contemplated the strike's solidity and the threat that it would spread to include their whole workforce, and perhaps the whole shipbuilding district. They met their men's representatives and the newly appointed AFL organizer, and gave them almost everything that they had asked for. The conciliators, clearly far from impartial, were delighted, wiring the AFL man their congratula-tions on a "splendid" victory after what he called a "Clean cut fight." "United action always wins when right and justice are on your side," they opined. The MMA's members, preparing for an organized assault on their own firms, cannot have been encouraged by this huge breach in one of the city's open shop citadels.[21]

[19] "NOTICE!" (n.d.) and anonymous letter of 11 Apr. 1916 in Records of the Federal Mediation and Conciliation Service, Case 33-197, RG280, U.S. National Archives (hereafter FMCS Case –). McCartin's *Labor's Great War* discusses the broader ide-ological developments that Philadelphia workers' rhetoric reflected.
[20] Letter of 19 Apr. from Commissioners F. G. Davis and William Blackman to General Manager Hand, in FMCS Case 33-197.
[21] Letter of 13 June from Blackman and Davis to Secretary William B. Wilson; telegram of 4 May from Chas. F. Scott, Organizer, to Blackman and Davis, and their reply of the 5th, all in FMCS Case 33-197.

The major challenge that the MMA faced came from the IAM, whose national membership increased by a third in 1915–16 (see Figure 6.1). In Philadelphia, the IAM had begun organizing vigorously before the war. Its local leader at the time, Edward Keenan, was very prominent in the city's labor world as the president of the Central Labor Union and secretary of the Labor Forward Movement. They had approached the task carefully, compiling a register of nonunion machinists and dividing the city into districts, each with its own local organizing committee, for a systematic canvass. But the recession had made progress impossible.[22]

When it ended, the union found that it had a new problem to deal with: the massive influx of workers drawn by the job openings in the shipyards and munitions plants. These outsiders were indifferent to union membership and discipline, and spoiled the best labor market that Philadelphia machinists had known for years; at least that was how the local IAM leaders explained away their problems and excused their organizing failures. Troublesome too were local men who "desire[d] . . . to work sixteen hours a day, if allowed," aiming to maximize their own earnings rather than to fight for the achievement of collective goals.[23]

Nevertheless, District One persisted with its struggle, until in the spring of 1916 it was confident enough to join the IAM's national campaign to achieve the eight-hour day through concerted strikes that were scheduled to begin on the first of July. Its new business agent, Thomas Wilson, claimed optimistically that the Machinists were "at least seventy per cent organized in the skilled departments," despite continuing discriminatory discharges by employers. Given the by-then prevailing conditions of a chronic skilled labor shortage, victimized workmen could always find another local firm that was willing to take them on. Open shop employers were "of the opinion that they have enough non-union men to stay with them so that they can defeat us, but we know better." So "they can not deny us this time. . . . [T]his city is going to be one of the best. We have the work; we have the men; we will get the money and the hours, and in addition we will have a local consisting of ten thousand men and another with as many more." (Wilson was referring to the IAM's booming Marine Erectors' Lodge.) Wilson was even prepared to consider the flood of out-of-towners as potential recruits, rather than just problems: "if you think you are a good man and an improvement to our city 'Come and be with us.' You . . . will make better wages here than in any other city on earth." "[I]f you have had experience in tool work, you can practically set your own rate. . . . [I]f you want work this city is full of it. . . . If you will stand for more pay and shorter hours, you are always welcome. Come and be a part of the parade."[24]

[22] "Local Machinists Will Combine," *Trades Union News* (22 May 1913): 1; "Union Machinists Now Reach All Districts," Ibid. (18 Feb. 1915): 1.

[23] Edward Keenan and Thomas L. Wilson, "Philadelphia, Pa.," *MMJ* 27 (1915): 1021, 1137–38.

[24] Wilson, "Philadelphia, Pa.," *MMJ* 28 (1916): 496–97, 607.

The IAM gave fair warning of its intentions, in its *Journal* and through advertisements. So the MMA had plenty of time to plan its defense before too many members followed Hugo Bilgram's bad example and compromised with their men on hours and wages. Concession was not just bad in principle, it did not seem to bring any lasting solutions either. Rather, it inspired their men to press for more, with demands for fifty-five hours' pay for forty-eight hours' work even hitting shops that had given 30 percent pay increases – twice as much as Bilgram – to try to hang on to their established production schedules. Companies seemed to be facing a growing rank-and-file revolt, with incidents like a mass walkout of more than 2,000 men at Standard Roller Bearing protesting the discharge of one man for union activities.[25]

Three weeks before the Machinists' D-Day, the MMA convened the first of a series of crisis meetings to coordinate the employers' response, reaching out beyond its own membership to the whole local industry. The aim was to work out a strategy having the broadest possible backing from the city's metal trades firms, and having forged that solidarity to decide appropriate tactics and raise adequate resources for the fight.[26]

At the first special meeting, firms employing over 13,000 workers were represented. Three large nonmember open shops, Cramp's, Brill, and Hale & Kilburn, made up over half the total. President Schwacke, the MMA's link to the NMTA, briefed his audience on the IAM's national strategy, the way other open shop employers had met the challenge already, and the situation faced by sister NMTA local associations across the country. The "sense of the meeting" against any reduction in working hours was unanimous, but employers were not so sure what to do next. Should they launch a headlong assault against the IAM's propaganda, or would that alienate their men, whom it would be better to deal with directly at the shop level? And how were they to cope with the unfortunate side effect of taking on lucrative federal government contracts – that they were compelled to accept the basic eight-hour day regardless of their workers' strength? A joint committee, uniting the MMA and the big open shops, was set up to discuss the next steps.[27]

A fortnight later the metal trades employers reassembled, with more important guests present, including Henry Disston, the Electric Storage Battery Co., and Standard Roller Bearing. Altogether, the big nonmembers employed over 8,500 of the more than 16,000 workers whose interests in

[25]   ECM 12 Apr. 1916, Special Meeting Minutes 23 June 1916.

[26]   Special Meeting Minutes 7, 23, 26 June 1916.

[27]   Special Meeting Minutes 7 June; employment figures from PID-1640 database; for NMTA advice, see "Experience Meeting," *Synopsis of Proceedings* (1916), pp. 52–53; cf. Howard M. Gitelman, "Being of Two Minds: American Employers Confront the Labor Problem, 1915–1919," *Labor History* 25 (1984): 189–216 at pp. 197–98.

not having their working hours cut, or pay increased, were being [mis]represented. There was, however, at least one significant absentee: Midvale. For the manufacturers' united front to be effective, they had to be truly united. But, Schwacke feared, with Midvale's new gun plant "requiring one thousand men on eight hour basis, and stating they would pay any price to obtain them, in the event of a general tie-up, Midvale Steel Company might take the opportunity of recruiting the idle men."[28]

Despite the risk of provoking a larger conflict, it was decided, partly at Link-Belt's local manager Staunton Peck's urging, to fight the IAM's campaign with "good sound economic reasons" and an unprecedented (for the MMA) barrage of advertising. Howard Chambers of machine tool makers Chambers Bros. stressed that "it was absolutely essential that the employers should publish their attitude, so that the non-union man could then know that the employing interests were anxious to sustain them in their desire to continue at work on existing basis of hours"![29]

This point deserves emphasis: The employers' principal preparation for, and novel weapon against, the IAM's summer offensive was to be sober public argument. It would be couched in terms of the presumed common interest of locally based manufacturers and workers in the city's continuing prosperity, and of the *employers*' right to declare what the protection of that interest required – no surrender to the eight-hour demand. Ideological leadership would demonstrate the employers' class unity to waverers in their own ranks as well as to their men, dissuading the former from self-interested defections and warning the latter that they would not be pushing at an open door.[30]

Just agreeing to say no was only the beginning of the battle, however; more important was to make that resolution stick. A preemptive publicity blitz was launched before the Machinists' mass walkouts began. All of the local papers were blanketed with half-page advertisements containing the employers' manifesto over a list of signatories, all of them MMA members. Supportive but reticent nonmembers contributed to the war chest in proportion to their payrolls, and the MMA paid out almost $2,300 for this campaign. (To put this figure in perspective, it amounted to almost one-half the previous year's total expenditure, and more than ten times the direct costs of strike-breaking in 1916.)[31]

After these preliminary skirmishes, the IAM still had to be beaten down, shop by shop. This turned out not to be too difficult. For when it came to

[28] Special Meeting Minutes 23 June 1916; employment figures from PID-1640 database; cf. Gitelman, "Management's Crisis of Confidence," pp. 167–68.
[29] Special Meeting Minutes 19, 23 June 1916.
[30] Ibid. Draft and final texts of the manifesto are included with the Minutes for June 23.
[31] Special Meeting Minutes, 10 July, ECM, 9 Aug. 1916; MMA Auditor's and Treasurer's Reports in MMAP III-4-3.

the crunch, the IAM could not deliver on its bold words. There were at least thirty Machinists' strikes in 1916, affecting firms employing about 12,000 workers. But the employers did not collapse in the face of these walkouts, nor did nonunionists join the IAM's parade in sufficient numbers; and most of those who did returned to work within a week. By the 10th of July, when the struck firms met to compare notes and plan their next moves, it was clear that the situation was well under control. United action was paying off. "[T]he sense of the meeting indicated a very general belief that the movement was dying out." None of the firms still affected was wavering or thought it would have to make concessions. Instead, they were confident that they could follow their usual approach to Machinists' strikes, that of "letting the movement die a natural death." This did not imply passivity: "Any cases of violence on the part of the strikers [were to] be followed up by the concern whose employees or property was involved and vigorously prosecuted," with the help of the Philadelphia police, which was "very good in the direct vicinity of the plants where pickets congregated." With this backing, the employers settled back for the long haul.[32]

By August, as far as the MMA was concerned, the strike seemed to be petering out: Picketing was tolerably ineffective, skilled labor shortages were annoying but manageable, and production was hampered, but they had the upper hand. IAM victories were confined to the smaller shops, its continuing struggle hampered by an injunction secured by Niles-Bement-Pond that was "wider in scope than ha[d] been granted . . . [for] years." Its overall failure against its prime targets, the machine tool manufacturers, was impossible to conceal. Business Agent Wilson was reduced by December to appealing to the national union's members to support his "faithful men. . . . Have a thought for them and help all you can." They did not. District One's petition for $20,000 to prop up its failing strike was turned down.[33]

The contrast in mood between the combattants at year's end could not have been greater. The MMA's secretary Henry Morgan's report to his members was "conspicuous for the superlatives . . . [it] discloses in every branch of its affairs. . . . The wages paid mechanics are the highest in the history of the trade; the strikes involved the largest number of men in the life of this organization; the report of operatives employed by the members

[32] Strike reports from Pennsylvania Department of Labor and Industry, *Third Annual Report of the Commissioner of Labor and Industry 1915* (Harrisburg, 1916), Part 2, pp. 567–68, 580–82; employment data from PID-1640 database; Special Meeting Minutes, 10 July 1916.

[33] Earl S. Sparks, "The Metal Manufacturers' Association of Philadelphia: A Review of Activities 1903–53," (typescript, Jan. 1954), p. 2, in MMAP I-1-2; Morgan, SEC 1916 p. 3; Wilson, "Philadelphia, Pa.," *MMJ* 28 (1916): 1004, 1106–7, 1196; "Machinist Labor Situation: Recent Strikes Called by Machinists' Union Have Fallen Flat," *The [Open Shop] Review* 13 (1916): 391.

is the largest; the expenditure the greatest, and the number of strikes and subsequent victories the grandest in our annals."[34]

Employers of about 26,000 people, three-quarters of them nonmembers (finally including, fortunately, Midvale), had attended one or more of the MMA's strike crisis meetings. Most of them had supported its strategy with money for publicity and their subsequent anti-union resistance. The MMA had established valuable connections with many of the city's larger firms and won more new recruits than it had seen since 1911–12. Its members' payrolls had increased by about a half, and its own regular revenue went up proportionally. This was just as well, as the Labor Bureau was, in absolute terms, busier than ever, whether measured in terms of numbers of job applicants (up 24 percent on the previous year), calls for help from members (up 41 percent), or successful placements (up 29 percent).[35]

The Eight-Hour crisis had had a unifying effect on the city's metal trades employers, and they had enjoyed useful backing for their fight from other sections of the city's business community as well. "Strikes thrive on publicity," Morgan noted, "[but] with twenty-eight shops involved, the newspapers did not . . . [with one exception] . . . make mention of it." This news blackout is inconvenient for the historian, and cannot have helped the strikers' morale either; so Morgan was confident "From information at hand" that "cold weather w[ould] bring necessary relief" at the five machine-tool makers, all of them MMA members employing about 1,000 men between them, where the rump of the summer's strikers were still picketing.[36]

6.3 THE EYE OF THE STORM: 1917–1918

In 1917, the Machinists changed leaders yet again but found no more success, stuck in "an endurance struggle" against implacable opponents and still hampered by the continuing influx of workmen intent on making an immediate buck for themselves rather than on effecting lasting changes in the conditions of employment in their trade. The new business agent, William Kelton, threw his helpless words against this flood: "Brothers, if you are figuring on coming to Philadelphia, please make up your minds that you are going to take off your coat and give us a lift in organizing this city; but if you are just coming for a stake, please stay away." He did not see this migrant stream as just a spontaneous response to job opportunities. Instead, he paid the MMA the compliment of blaming it for his troubles: "Philadelphia was progressing very nicely, wages being increased and we were taking in a very great number of members when the enemy awoke

---

[34]　Morgan, SEC 1916, p. 1.
[35]　Ibid., p. 5.
[36]　Ibid., p. 3; employment figures from PID-1640 database.

to the situation. . . . [T]he Metal Manufacturers' Association is . . . having the machinists from all over the United States who desire to make a change come to Philadelphia. Everyone knows . . . what happens when the supply of men exceeds the positions to be filled." Kelton must have been one of the few men who thought the 1917 labor market well supplied, but it was certainly in flux, which caused difficulties for employers and unions alike.[37]

The Machinists, unable to win with their own resources, abandoned voluntarism in favor of taking advantage of the new facilities for saving hopeless strikes that the state and federal governments provided. They asked for help from the Pennsylvania Department of Labor and Industry's Mediation Bureau, which quickly referred their case up to Washington. Secretary Wilson appointed a neighboring machine shop operator as a conciliator, and he brought Kelton and Schwacke together for seven fruitless meetings in February, before abandoning all prospect of a solution. He had been called in too late; "[t]he men who used to be employed in the shops, except those who have returned (of which there are many) have secured positions elsewhere, and the shops have secured men to take their place" – reasonably competent workers, and enough of them to rebuild firms' labor forces to above prestrike levels.[38]

The MMA handled the threat of federal intervention much more skilfully than Cramp's had a year earlier. Its officers treated the state and federal conciliators politely, praising them for being "earnest conscientious and impartial," but made sure to get their members' position on record alongside that of the union.[39]

Kelton argued that "Workingmen will be compelled to make many sacrifices during this war and owing to the enormous expense they are under, due to high prices, they should be given some consideration."[40] The employers replied by blaming the union for trying to exploit a tight labor market unfairly. They too linked themselves to the national interest – the country needed their machine tools and, given the shortage of skilled workmen, production targets could only be met through maintenance of the long day – and they condemned the union for its unpatriotic obstructiveness:

Men who would be disposed to take work with us are hindered and intimidated by outside interference, by picketing and blacklisting of our shops. Our present forces have been built up through personal solicitation and advertisement and by the

[37] William A. Kelton, "Philadelphia, Pa.," *MMJ* 29 (1917): 249, 767.
[38] Telegram, John Price Jackson to William B. Wilson, 21 Jan. 1917; Clifton Reeves (Commissioner) to J. S. Brand, 3 Feb. 1917; Preliminary Report of Commissioner of Conciliation, 22 Feb. 1917; Reeves to Wilson, 24 Apr. 1917 – all in FMCS Case 33-322; cf. ECM 14 March 1917.
[39] Executive Committee, Machine Shop Owners Association to Commissioners Clifton Reeves and James A. Steese, 21 Apr. 1917, in FMCS Case 33-322.
[40] Kelton to Congressman George W. Edmonds, 25 May 1917, in FMCS Case 33-322.

return, notwithstanding threats, intimidation and actual violence, of some men who previously worked for us. We are sure more of our old men would return if the hindrances referred to were removed. . . .

Our plants are open to all of our old men who have not been engaged in acts of violence and intimidation, and they will be given employment on application as opportunity presents as we prefer our old men. All we ask of our employees is that they shall work peaceably and harmoniously in our shops with other men, doing a fair day's work for a fair day's pay, and abide by the established rules of the shops.[41]

The employers expected that, with the American declaration of war in April, and the defense preparedness program's shift into high gear for actual combat, their ability to get the government to intervene on their side would be significantly increased too. Harry Champion, Newton Machine Tool's president, replied in May to a "hurry-up" request from naval ordnance procurement officers by attributing all delays in delivery to manpower shortages. These were, he wrote, caused by the enlistment in the armed forces of skilled men who were "certainly needed at home more than they are at the 'front'," and by the effects of the Machinists' continuing official strike. Although he had "a full force of men[,] . . . they are not efficient, and skilled machinists will not go to work in a shop where there is a strike." (For good measure, he blamed the strike itself on the Wilson Administration, too: It "would not have taken place if the Union leaders were not given encouragement on account of the attitude which Washington took in the 'eight-hour' question.")[42]

The next month, his plant manager reiterated his request for federal intervention to get the strike called off – "From every practical point the strike situation in Philadelphia has been over for some time, but pickets are being maintained by professional Unionists," who should be brought to heel. Instead, the firm found itself faced with a fresh conciliation effort, instigated by the IAM's national vice president, who believed that if they could be persuaded to break ranks, the rest of the employers would follow. But Newton had no compromise proposals to make, and there were none that it was prepared to accept. Rather than voluntarily concede the eight-hour day, they would prefer to see the federal government commandeer their shop and operate it, if it needed their tools so much; otherwise, they were "determined . . . to continue the fight indefinitely."[43]

They were as good as their word. Newton and the other struck toolmakers, although inconvenienced by the IAM's year-long strike, stuck to

---

[41] Executive Committee, Machine Shop Owners Association to Reeves and Steese, 21 Apr. 1917, in FMCS Case 33-322.
[42] Harry W. Campion (*sic*) to Lieut J. B. Staley, 4 May 1917, in FMCS Case 33-322.
[43] Nicholas P. Lloyd to Ralph Earle, 8 June 1917; IAM Vice President Anderson to Wilson, 26 June 1917; Commissioners E. E. Greenawalt and J. J. Hughes to Wilson, 30 June 1917 – all in FMCS Case 33-322.

their guns until they won what the MMA's secretary called a "complete victory." They had helped to preserve the Philadelphia metal trades' open shop character and long day in the process, spared themselves further trouble from the IAM for the duration of the war, and diverted its organizational efforts into the more promising territory offered by the shipyards and munitions plants.[44]

Having seen off the threat from the Machinists, and coped well with the first significant attempt by the federal government to intervene in its affairs, the MMA turned to face once again a challenge from a more familiar quarter – the IMU's Local 15. Prohibited from calling a strike in 1916, James Cronin concentrated his efforts on expanding his organization instead. He got his 600 members to accept a dollar a week assessment at a mass meeting that February, promising them a new union shop every week in return. He could not deliver on that pledge, but he made some progress, and the local's membership doubled within a year. He also "bulldoz[ed]" another meeting into voting an extra 10¢ a week per man to boost his salary to $100 a week (about four times their average wage, and more than twice as much as the MMA paid its secretary) for five years. This was against the Molders' constitution, but IMU President Valentine did not intervene, despite members' complaints about Cronin's dictatorial leadership and at having to pay total weekly union dues amounting to more than three hours' wages.[45]

Cronin dealt with his internal opponents brutally but effectively. His huge assessment income – by 1917, assuming that all of his members paid, it was about five times as large as the MMA's – for which he did not have to account to anybody, enabled him to employ what his critics called a "strong arm gang" of "non-producers" to thrash them into line. Local 15's tightening hold on the trade meant that he could pursue them from shop to shop, and deny them employment. Their only recourse, by the spring of 1917, was to take their grievances to the MMA, which consulted famed anti-labor lawyer Walter G. Merritt on their behalf, with a view to bringing a conspiracy suit against the IMU. The MMA was prepared to help them as they gave it a stick with which to beat the union, as well as because of a principled commitment to their "right to work." They were what one member foundryman, faced with Cronin's ultimatum to fire nine of his molders who had been expelled from the union, termed "free American cit-

[44] ECM 14 March 1917; Sparks, SEC 1917, p. 3 (note: all subsequent Secretaries' Reports are the work of Earl Sparks, so there is no more need to identify them by name); ECM 12 Dec. 1917; Kelton, "Philadelphia and Vicinity," *MMJ* 29 (1917): 943.
[45] John T. Beale to Henry Morgan, 26 March 1917 and Copy of Letter of Protest from Nine Members of Local 15 to Mr. Jos. F. Valentine, President, IMUNA, 16 Sept. 1916, in MMAP II-4-25.

izens" with the individual liberty "to do as they please" with respect to union affiliation.[46]

By the summer of 1917, Cronin was once again confronting many MMA members directly, trying to continue his union's expansion from the jobbing into the machinery foundries begun in 1913, and to compel a reduction in working hours. He had enough "enforcers" not to have to rely on actually having many men working in a shop, in order to be able to blockade it. Cronin did not believe in the niceties of collective bargaining – grievance procedures, negotiations, committing proposals and agreements to paper, only calling a strike as a last resort, ballots, and so on. As he explained the situation to a frustrated federal conciliator, "The law of the organization is that only one man can call a strike, and that happens to be me." Once he had presented his terms, pulled out his members, and sent in his troops, the issue was to be resolved by conflict – picketing, beatings, night visits to non-strikers' homes, threats that drove one of Philadelphia Roll & Machine's molders to suicide. Victory could come in either of two forms – acceptance of IMU terms or payoffs to his picket bosses – for example, $500 from the Cresson-Morris Co. – as the price of "persuading" them to shift their attention elsewhere.[47]

Altogether Local 15 started at least twenty-five strikes in 1917, and the MMA busied itself in fighting nine of them that affected members or applicants. Confrontations were rife. In July the Thompson foundry complained to the Pennsylvania Department of Labor and Industry about "being interfered with by men who call themselves pickets" and who "intimidate the men who work for us, and cause delay in getting out the work and other inconveniences." Schaum & Uhlinger were similarly threatened, despite the fact that "there is a large majority of our hands who have been with us since we started in this business, and who do not wish to join the union," and that they thought that the government's war labor policy of not disturbing "existing conditions" ought to protect them.[48]

---

[46] George Silcox [Molder], "To Who (*sic*) It May Concern," 29 May 1917; Copy of Walter G. Merritt to John T. Beale [Molder], 21 March 1917, MMAP II-4-25; ECM 16–18 May, 13 June 1917. There is a hint in the records that at least one of the leaders of Cronin's opponents may have been an NFA stool-pigeon – Morgan to C. W. Burgess, 28 May 1917, MMAP II-4-25. Foundryman quoted from Budd Grate Co. to Frank L. Garbarino, n.d., Preliminary Report of Commissioner of Conciliation 21 Aug. 1917, Final Report 18 Oct. 1917, all in FMCS Case 33-624.

[47] Budd to Garbarino, p. 1, and transcript of conciliation meeting 24 Aug. 1917, p. 7, FMCS Case 33-624; Report of Conference Between Mr. R. W. Seymour, Representing the War Labor Board, and Mr. Alfred Crook of the Philadelphia Roll & Machine Co., 23 Sept. 1918, pp. 2, 4, 5, in Records of the NWLB, Docket No. 316, RG2, National Archives (hereafter cited as NWLB Case –).

[48] SEC 1917, pp. 3–4; J. Thompson & Co. to Gentlemen, 13 July 1917, in FMCS Case 33-543; Otto W. Schaum to Samuel M. Vauclain [chair, Munitions Committee, Council of National Defense], 12 June 1917, in FMCS Case 33-511.

Cronin's biggest target was Niles-Bement-Pond, which had whipped the Molders ten years earlier and had just done the same to its Machinists. N-B-P provoked a walkout by discharging a man who had left the union on the collapse of the 1905–07 strike but who had just applied to rejoin. The company claimed that the man had been "smoking in the shop during working hours, indulged in conversation with his fellow-workmen that retarded output, and made himself otherwise obnoxious," but these were just pretexts; his very modest degree of IMU activism had made him "highly objectionable and . . . under no circumstances would they agree to reinstate [him]." Cronin wrote "an impertinent letter" demanding that they do that very thing, or face a strike. "Naturally" they refused, the company wrote to Secretary of Labor Wilson, demanding intervention on their side as important defense contractors; so the inevitable violent dispute followed. N-B-P pursued its usual course, employing "private detectives and also . . . the City police force to the full extent of making arrests and prosecuting wherever necessary," but this did not prove "as effectual as the necessity demands"; hence the appeal for intervention from on high.[49]

Neither Schaum & Uhlinger nor N-B-P secured the decisive federal backing that they desired, nor, in this case, did they need it. Instead the MMA, with the NFA's assistance, performed its usual labor replacement services, adding to their complements of loyal workmen and assisting in procuring injunctions until the strikes could be considered lost – that is, although picketing continued, and N-B-P was still employing guards four months after the strike began, production had been restored to normal levels.[50]

Philadelphia Roll & Machine was not so lucky, however, in dealing with a strike that Cronin called at about the same time to compel them to discharge steel molders who would not join his organization, on the grounds that "a Company must be all Union or all non-Union." The MMA replaced the strikers, who were lower skilled men, as well as nonstrikers who "quit and went to other plants . . . to avoid the trouble," and the company hired guards to protect its scab molders. Cronin responded by pulling out his skilled iron molders from the company's other plant – where the union had always been recognized – too. He did so against their express but powerless wish to be allowed to carry on working as they had no grievances of their own to justify a stoppage and despite the provisions of the Foundrymen's Club's contract. The MMA also replaced most of these men, and "Protection and transportation by automobile" got them to work safely. But for the most highly skilled molders no nonunion substitutes were available. So the strike settled down into guerrilla warfare, with Local 15 main-

---

[49]   Commissioner Greenawalt to William B. Wilson, 7 Sept. 1917, Preliminary Report 11 Sept. 1917, and Edwin M. Abbott to Wilson, 8 Aug. 1917, FMCS Case 33-616.
[50]   SEC 1917, pp. 3–4.

taining pickets for the next fourteen months. Neither the MMA nor, in due course, the National War Labor Board (NWLB) were able to do anything to weaken Cronin's resolve or provide the firm with the élite craftsmen that it needed.[51]

But the MMA fought Local 15's strikes to a standstill, if not in every case to a clear victory. Local 15 still listed twenty-six foundries as struck in December 1918 and instructed molders to "Stay Away"; but as the MMA's new secretary, Earl Sparks, reported to his members, "With satisfactory conditions prevailing in the shops 'boy-cotted', we hope that the class of men that read the [Molders'] *Journal* will heed the advice given."[52]

The IMU's resulting organizational gains were unimpressive. Nine firms that had still been "open" in 1915–16 recognized the union and accepted its terms over the course of the next two years. Three of the new catches were MMA machinery foundries with about 600 employees between them, which had conceded to the IMU in the summer of 1916 and raised the number of union shops that the association included to nine with about 1,700 workers in all. But the total union shop territory still only amounted to about thirty firms with almost 3,000 workers by 1918–19, the same as before the war. This was because at least seven shops – the three largest of which, with about 300 workers between them, were or became MMA members – were lost by the union over the same period. So on balance Local 15's advances, even during this exceptionally favorable period, were kept within narrow bounds, and most of the MMA's machinery foundry members kept their open shop status (twenty-two firms with a 1918–19 employment of about 5,000 people).[53]

The net effect was that the unionized section of the Philadelphia foundry trade had scarcely altered in size or character, save that it was even more strongly controlled by the IMU than ever. It included as before the "purely jobbing foundries" that were "very largely organized," as well as a minority of larger plants. Nevertheless, the Molders' wartime offensive was not without its effects. Union molders' wages increased a further 12.5 percent in 1917, 22 percent in 1918, 33 percent in 1919, and 20 percent in 1920, figures that compared well with changes for other skilled workers. Hours had been cut to eight per day, piece work had been eliminated, and output

---

[51] Ibid., p. 4; Alfred Crook to William Jett Lauck, 21 Aug. 1918, Report of Conference, 23 Sept. 1918, and I.A. Rice to Lauck, 28 Sept. 1918, in NWLB Case 316.

[52] SEC 1917, p. 5, SEC 1918, p. 10.

[53] Data on the extent of IMU recognition from sources cited in note 17, and in Memorandum of Agreement Between the Foundrymen's Club and Iron Molders Union of North America 9 Feb. 1917; copy of Agreement Between Philadelphia Foundrymen's Club and Iron Molders Union No. 15, 7 Feb. 1918; Agreements . . . 31 Oct. 1919, 8 May 1920 – all in MMAP II-3-17, 18, 19; all employment data from PID-1640 database.

had been restricted; but the major advances in organization had taken place before the confrontations of 1917–18, which bore few fruits.[54]

6.4 THE STORM BREAKS: 1918

The MMA and Local 15 remained locked in conflict for the whole of the period during which the United States was at war, but at least there was one problem that Cronin and the Molders spared the association and its members – government intervention. Although they railed against him as "autocratic, socialistic and anarchistic," he was really just a moderately successful combination of old-fashioned, voluntaristic AFL business agent and opportunistic racketeer. The only reason that state and federal conciliators and, eventually, the NWLB became involved in the Philadelphia Molders' labor disputes was because employers called them in. The Molders thought that they were strong enough to turn their backs on the government's developing labor relations apparatus, having nothing to gain or fear from it; the MMA's Open Shop machinery foundrymen, weaker than they were vis-à-vis the IAM, were prepared to take advantage of it, although state intervention (other than that of the local police and courts) does not seem to have helped them much.[55]

But in most of the strikes and disputes of 1918–19 the MMA's antagonist was once again the IAM, whose business agent Kelton saw in the war emergency "our golden opportunity . . . our life-time chance . . . [to] get Philadelphia organized." The IAM's rediscovered confidence resulted from the fact that, for the first time, it had managed to establish a large local membership base. Its new territory was not the machine shops, which were still overwhelmingly hostile, but the shipyards, where Cramp's in particular conceded everything, time and time again, in the face of sectional strikes by craft groups. The urgent business of shipbuilding and repair meant that the U.S. Navy was breathing down managers' necks if work was held up; the cost-plus basis on which they operated gave them no incentive to resist.

---

[54]   SEC 1919, pp. 5–6. However, the indirect effects of the IMU's continuing organizational threat may have had a measurable impact even on the foundries that escaped its embrace. Open shops seem to have at least matched union wages and hours as the price of freedom from the other restrictions of a union relationship. In the MMA's August 1918 wage survey, which drew on reports from large nonunion firms as well as from its own membership, iron molders' actual wages were second only to those of boilermakers, averaging 15 percent above the IMU's agreed minimum, and 51 percent above those of the average male metal-worker – machine operators and the like – Wage data from "General Wage Report: Philadelphia and Vicinity, Aug. 1918," in MMA 2-IV-42. Of course, it is debatable whether the nonunion firms' decision to match or beat union rates was a consciously anti-union strategy or simply the result of operating within the same tight local labor market.

[55]   Budd to Garbarino, p. 1, FMCS Case 33-624.

The federal government was also, of course, a large direct employer of ship-building labor under union-friendly conditions itself, at the Navy Yard and through the EFC, which further assisted the growth of Philadelphia metal trades unionism. The IAM established a brand-new Marine Erectors' Lodge at Cramp's in June 1918; by Labor Day that single lodge could put "4,000 uniformed men, five bands and four floats" onto the streets, of whom about a quarter were already paid-up members. The IAM had never enjoyed such strong support in Philadelphia. It now possessed a foundation from which to try to build up the union in its original industrial jurisdiction.[56]

Kelton's strategy, unlike Cronin's, depended on the availability of state and federal mediators and adjudicators, their generally pro-labor disposition, and their especial readiness to intervene in defense-related strikes. He no longer had to risk his new and fragile shop organizations in serious conflict with his tough employer targets; he could rely on the mere threat of a strike to win immediate government involvement instead. In 1918 he would take cases at about twenty firms, employing over 20,000 workers, to the U.S. Conciliation Service and National War Labor Board. He had some success, winning formal recognition for the IAM at a few, and pay increases at rather more.[57]

Kelton was a native Philadelphian, thirty-seven years old when he won his office after working in one of the city's few big safe havens for an actively pro-union Machinist, the Bureau of Water. Politically he was conservative or at least conformist – to hold a city job he must have been a Republican "machine" loyalist. He took wholehearted advantage of the opportunities that the war bureaucracy offered a cooperative union man: He became a member of the local labor advisory committee of the Council of National Defense and of the board overseeing the work of the U.S. Employment Service in the state, an agent of the U.S. Public Service Reserve, and an

[56] Wm. A. Kelton, "Philadelphia and Vicinity," *MMJ* 29 (1917): 943 [quotes] and "District Lodge No. 1 – Philadelphia and Vicinity," *MMJ* 30 (1918): 246–47; Strike at Wm. Cramp & Sons Ship & Engine Building Co., May 1917, FMCS Case 33-453; Exhibit A listing 122 strikes since 1916, with Commissioners Charles J. Fury and John A. Moffitt to Director of Conciliation, 16 March 1921, p. 3, in FMCS Case 170-1345.

[57] *Companies and cases involved, and month of beginning of dispute*: American Engineering, FMCS 33-1094, March; Merchant & Evans, FMCS 33-1268, Apr.; Budd Wheel, FMCS 33-1296, May; Hess-Bright, NWLB Case 63, Midvale Steel & Ordnance, NWLB Case 129, and H. W. Butterworth/Hale & Kilburn, FMCS Case 33-1514, June; Arthur Brock, J. G. Brill, Carlson-Wenstrom, Curtis Publishing, Fox Motor, Harnett & Co., Hess-Bright, Kingsbury Bearing, Savage Arms, Standard Roller Bearing, Wildman, NWLB Case 400, Brill [separately], FMCS 33-2388 and Savage Arms [separately], NWLB Case 434, Sept.; Smith, Drum, NWLB Case 641 and H. W. Butterworth, NWLB Case 946, November; David Lupton's Sons, FMCS 33-2943, Dec. Employment data from PID-1640 database.

ardent peddler of Liberty Bonds to his members. His ambition was to become a Department of Labor staffer with responsibility for overseeing welfare and personnel work at area war plants, a job that would have enhanced his ability to be of service to his union by giving him status and an *entreé*.[58]

Kelton may well have been genuinely patriotic. He was certainly prepared to harp on about his and his members' Americanism. This he compared favorably with the doubtful loyalties of some of their employer opponents – like MMA executive committee member Adalbert Fischer, somewhat embarrassingly arrested for rowing out at night to smuggle goods off German merchant ships interned in the Navy Yard, and deprived of his freedom and control of his machine works for the duration on the basis of that offense and his nationality.[59]

One-hundred percent Americanism was both an offensive and a defensive tactic for Kelton to employ, but the latter use was the more important. He was fighting to protect his own position and his union's against his usual employer opponents, who were ever-ready to condemn the strikes that he called, or that his members engaged in, as acts of treason. He was acutely aware that behind his enemies loomed the repressive potential of parts of the wartime state that were less favorable to labor than were the U.S. Conciliation and Employment Services or, later, the War Labor Board.

But he could not afford simply to act as an agent of government policy, because he owed his office to his members, who might desert him in favor of more radical and aggressive leadership if he took his patriotic responsibilities too far. Kelton's election victory had been very narrow – a single vote separated him and his defeated opponent – and disputed; as a national union officer wrote at the time, although "it was agreed to bury the hatchet [, i]t looks to me as if the handle is still sticking up."[60]

Kelton was therefore caught between two fires. The Plant Protection Service of the Military Intelligence Division (MID) kept him under close scrutiny from midsummer 1918, accusing him of being "influential and active in stirring up trouble in labor circles" in a way "calculated to hinder production." They tried "on several occasions . . . to call his hand" in strike situations but reported that "His alibi is that the men intend to strike and he does all he can to keep them on production." A member of the federal Grand Jury similarly denounced him as an agitator whose "activities . . . [were] directed to cause discontent among the laborers when, in fact, no

---

[58] Report, Agent Edward Oechsle, 4 Oct. 1918, notes on interview with Kelton, pp. 2–3, in Military Intelligence Division (MID) Correspondence, Box. 3540 F. 10634-258, RG 165, National Archives (hereafter Kelton File).

[59] Kelton to Hon. Geo. W. Edmonds, 25 May 1917, in FMCS Case 33-322.

[60] SEC 1918, p. 7 [treason accusation]; discussion of Kelton's perspective drawn from transcripts of his interviews with federal agents and undercover operatives' reports on his comments at membership meetings, in Kelton File; "Report of Board Member J. J. Keppler," *MMJ* 29 (1917): 150 [quote].

dissatisfaction was felt," and called for him to be investigated for possible violation of the Sabotage and Espionage Acts. A member of the minority faction within his own local, a machinist at MMA member Savage Arms who was angling to become business agent himself – but was also a Pinkerton operative – reported his "disloyal" remarks at lodge meetings to the MID, which then sent in its own informants to listen for evidence to use against him. The MID eventually called Kelton in to answer for his actions and his words, so that by the fall of 1918 he certainly knew that he was in jeopardy, and he thought he knew who was to blame: The MMA "will stoop to anything to try and have my organization activities stopped. I am firmly convinced that this is some of their dirty work, and I would like to meet the man who would dare say that I am not a true American." To do so, he would simply have had to go see MMA Secretary Sparks, or any of his members.[61]

While guarding his front against attacks from the familiar enemy, he also had to watch his back. Not all of his internal union opponents were mere personal rivals or employers' stool pigeons; the more serious political threat he faced came from a new breed of radicalized machinist brought to Philadelphia by the war boom and swept up by the widely shared hope for fundamental social transformation. They aimed to use the union as an instrument for achieving that project, and they were certainly impatient with Kelton's cautious approach and limited achievements.

Fortunately for Kelton, he was able to turn his doubly embattled position, at least temporarily, to his own advantage. He himself became an agent of the employer-supported American Protective League, which extended the arm of the federal government's political police into the industrial world and, as befitted a good A.F. of L. man, denounced his radical opponents to the national security apparatus as Wobblies and One Big Unionists. By supplying information leading to the conviction of several of them as "leading agitators," he was able both to demonstrate his patriotic *bona fides* and to get the better of some of his internal critics. And by treading a fine line between disciplining his raw, untried members and encouraging them to have confidence in their new-found power, he was able to make his strike threats somewhat credible while not alienating the federal dispute adjusters on whom his strategy ultimately depended.[62]

[61] Col. M. Churchill to Maj. W. C. Rogers, 17 July 1918, in FMCS Case 33-1296; Special Reports, Agents Todd Daniel and Edward Oechsle, 15 and 16 Sept., 4 Oct. 1918, in Kelton File.
[62] On the insurgent spirit in the wartime machinists' trade, see esp. Cecelia Bucki, "Dilution and Craft Tradition: Bridgeport, Connecticut Munitions Workers, 1915–1919," *Social Science History* 4 (1980): 105–24; McCartin, *Labor's Great War*; Montgomery, *The Fall of the House of Labor*, Ch. 8. Clinton Golden, leader of the Philadelphia insurgents, reflects this spirit in "The Militants of the Metal Trades – the Machinists," in Amalgamated Clothing Workers of America, *Amalgamated Illustrated Almanac, 1924* (New York, 1924), pp. 142–44.

In the chilly climate of wartime America, Kelton felt that he needed to wrap the flag tightly about himself, if he was to remain free to function at all. He boasted about having "assisted the Government in quieting labor difficulties. . . . It has always been my custom to notify the U.S. Dept. of Labor, War or Navy Dept. just as soon as I discovered anything brewing in any shop. It grieves me to see any loss of production, and I have always tried to have the trouble settled while the men were working." His record of cooperation, he believed, would "vouch for my American Spirit." This man, necessarily two-faced given the unenviable position in which he found himself, bore the chief responsibility for trying to make the most of his union's and its members' wartime strength.[63]

His problems in this regard were worsened by the IAM's own recently won members' uncertain loyalties. When some went out on strike at war plants, he had to prevent others from taking their place, and he was bitter that "we seem to be having more trouble keeping our own men out . . . than non-Union men." Once he had won the eight-hour day in a shop, he had to defend it against "card men" quitting if they did not get enough overtime to keep their pay up. "[L]et me tell you that it is one of the principles of Unionism to get an eight-hour day and now that you have it you want to ruin it by working ten just to get more money."[64]

He had to inspire his men with the belief that "the working man is going to come into power and it won't be long," and also get them to share his own, somewhat contradictory, sense of urgency that "There is going to be an industrial war in this country and we must get ready for it. . . . [T]he poor man will have to pay for this War and it is up to us to get the money now." He had to get them riled at the injustice of the unequal distribution of gains and sacrifices resulting from the war, and to see their employers as rightful targets – "we want some of the money these fellows have made and we are going to get it too or know the reason why." He had to persuade new members not to "be afraid to let it be known in your shop that you are a card man," and to reassure them that "there is no law to stop you from striking for more money. I know the bosses are sowing the seed and some of it is getting ripe, that if you strike or quit your job, they will throw you right in the army, but don't pay any attention to that."[65] But he also had to counter their patriotic doubts about the rightness of strik-

---

[63] Col. M. Churchill to Maj. W. C. Rogers, 17 July 1918, in FMCS Case 33-1296; Kelton to Oechsle, 16 Sept. 1918, pp. 2–3, with Oechsle Report of same date, Kelton File. See Joan M. Jensen, *The Price of Vigilance* (Chicago, 1968), for the A.P.L., a business-sponsored organization that cooperated very closely with local law enforcers and civilian and military federal investigators to root out alien and other radicals.

[64] Informants' Reports, 20 Sept. p. 2, 15 Nov. p. 1, in Kelton File.

[65] Oechsle memorandum, 16 Sept. 1918, including informant's report on 2 Aug. lodge meeting, p. 2, Informant's Reports, 15 Nov., p. 1, 6 Sept., pp. 3–4, in Kelton File.

ing against the war effort, as employers, the government, and the press represented it:

Don't be afraid that you are endangering the boys on the other side by sticking up for your own, for if they come back and find that you have not made conditions good for them, they will call you a coward, but they won't call me one for I am going to fight these bosses so that when they do come home, this country will be worth living in, and it can be done and it is up to you men to do it. . . . Go in your shop to-morrow, throw out your chest, hold your book high in the air and say I am a union man and damn glad of it, and every man in this shop ought to be one. The time of being afraid is past as you are the dictator now and not the boss.[66]

Kelton's words might have been what one manufacturer he dealt with called "revolutionary talk," but his practice was quite otherwise. He tried to persuade reluctant businessmen to recognize his union and to "harmoniz[e] real or imaginary differences that might exist between employer and employees" by drawing up a contract, whereby "harmony among the workmen will be promoted and production stimulated." But in Philadelphia such soft words turned away little wrath, so the appeal to "Dear Sir and Brother" – Secretary of Labor Wilson or, from June onward, NWLB secretary W. Jett Lauck – was his usual next or even first step.[67]

Kelton launched the Machinists' normal spring offensive in 1918, calling rather optimistically for a membership of 25,000 and $1 an hour by the first of July. He appealed to nonmembers' better natures, trying to persuade them of the legitimacy and utility of collective action –

FOLLOW THE CROWD AND JOIN THE IAM! EVENTUALLY, WHY NOT NOW? BE IN THE VANGUARD AND DO SOMETHING FOR YOUR CRAFT; DON'T SIT IDLY BY AND LET OTHERS GET CONDITIONS FOR YOU. DO YOU KNOW THAT HUNDREDS OF MACHINISTS ARE JOINING EVERY WEEK TO HELP MAKE PHILADELPHIA A GOOD PLACE FOR MACHINISTS TO LIVE IN? UNION MEN ARE BEING RESPECTED BY ALL CLASSES! (*sic*) OF SOCIETY – ARE YOU ONE OF THEM? IF NOT, WHY NOT? WHAT'S YOUR ANSWER?[68]

– and his campaign did make some progress, particularly among the élite tool-and-die makers, who were almost as well paid as the city's boiler-makers and molders.[69]

What Kelton demanded on their behalf was formal recognition and a written, fixed-term contract implementing the War Labor Conference Board's principles: no strikes or lockouts, acceptance of the right to organize, maintenance of existing conditions (i.e., no official closed shop) and of the "customs of the locality," and a joint commitment to maximum pro-

[66]   Informant's Report, 6 Sept. 1918, pp. 4–5, in Kelton File.
[67]   Informant's Report, 15 Nov. 1918, p. 2, in Kelton File; Kelton to Gentlemen, 27 May 1918, in NWLB Case 63; Kelton to Wilson, 27 Dec. 1918, in FMCS Case 33-2943; telegram, Kelton to Lauck, 9 Sept. 1918, in NWLB Case 400.
[68]   Copy of handout, 29 May 1918, in FMCS Case 33-1268.
[69]   MMA General Wage Report Aug. 1918.

duction. Hours were to be cut to forty-eight per week, overtime paid at time-and-a-half till midnight, double time after (or on Sundays and seven specified public holidays), and minimum wages for first- and second-class toolmakers raised to the Navy Yard scale (at the time 72.5¢ and 62.5¢ an hour).[70]

At least one firm, which was pressured by its own men, by the threat of sympathetic action from strongly unionized construction crafts who used its products, and by military procurement agencies, did agree to the IAM's terms. But, more frequently, the IAM ran into the roadblock of unyielding employer opposition. Edward G. Budd, for example, paid the employees at his aircraft wheel works far less than the going rate – 17¢ for women assemblers, up to 55¢ for straw bosses, plus a 10 percent "war bonus" that was arbitrarily fixed by himself. His skilled machinists walked out, asking for a cost of living increase, so Kelton called in the feds. However, particularly because the firm was an important ordnance contractor, the conciliation commissioner's primary object was not justice for the strikers, but an immediate end to the dispute. He advised the men to send their representatives to see Budd and offer to go back to work in a body, and then to "depend upon [Budd's] assurances that wages would be readjusted." He "impressed upon [them] the necessity of remaining at work and endeavoring in every way to facilitate production as a duty they owed the government in this time of stress." They followed his guidance, but Budd "declined their offers *in toto*, saying he would employ them again on his own terms and deal with each individually." He was "utterly opposed to any form of collective bargaining and absolutely w[ould] not allow his employees to even offer a tentative wage scale." He was equally "bitter toward the representatives of the Government . . . [who] were evidently in sympathy with the workers."[71]

The suspicion was usually justified and the employers' reciprocal hostility perfectly understandable. But it made the conciliators' work frustrating unless they had some more powerful outside agency standing threateningly back of their efforts. When they did not, they were liable to meet the "welcome" that David Lupton gave them when his machinists struck: He failed to keep an appointment *in his own office* and later told the powerless dispute adjusters "that he needed no help from us."[72]

Kelton's strategy thus depended for its success on federal officials whose

[70] Copy of agreement and case summary, June 1918, in NWLB Case 63.
[71] John R. Alpine (President, United Association of Plumbers and Steam Fitters) to Hugh L. Kerwin, 15 Apr. 1918; Preliminary Report of Commissioners of Conciliation Greenawalt and Rodgers, 25 Apr. 1918; James D. Evans to George Creel, 29 May 1918; all in FMCS Case 33-1268; James L. Rodier to Greenawalt, 11 May [quotes], in FMCS Case 33-1296.
[72] Special Representative Charles Fury to John J. Casey [Labor Administrator, Industrial Relations Bureau, Emergency Fleet Corporation], 18 Jan. 1919, in FMCS Case 33-2943.

agenda was not necessarily the same as his own, and whose powers were somewhat limited. Nevertheless, he put his trust in them; he had little real choice. Days before the Armistice, he told his members what had become of the bold target of 25,000 union machinists by the first of July – "we are still only 20 percent organized and we must get at least 50 percent more in order to hold up our end."[73]

Meanwhile, given his union's weakness, the determination of his employer opponents, and the dangers of actually mounting strikes in wartime, he came to bank on the NWLB rather than the utterly powerless U.S. Conciliation Service as his ace in the hole. The threat of its intervention persuaded a few employers to settle with him directly, on condition that he withdraw cases affecting them from the board. The board's officials were irritated at the way he used them "as a whip," but there was nothing that they could do about it. For the majority of employers who remained obdurate, and against whom he had little bargaining power anyway, he was prepared to await an NWLB ruling to settle the affair.[74]

The great advantages of the NWLB were that it had the authority to issue orders and administer awards, rather than just trying to bring disputing parties together; and that the Philadelphia IAM had already incorporated its declared policies as the basis of its own desired standard contract. The great *dis*advantage of the board, however, was that it was snowed under with work, and moved slowly; and to get it to pay serious attention to a group of workers' grievances, it helped if they were strategically located and offered a credible strike threat. So it was, at best, a supplement for union organization and direct action, not a substitute.[75]

By the war's closing months, the IAM had two big new groups of recruits in Philadelphia who were in a position to demand federal intervention on their behalf. The first, and largest, were the skilled gunmakers of the huge Shop No. 7 at Midvale's Nicetown works; the second group consisted of tool-and-die makers who were scattered through several smaller plants.

In April of 1918 the IAM had presented Midvale with its proposed model agreement, but received no response. Organizing activities continued, as did Midvale's discriminatory discharges, until the situation came to a head with two mass strikes in June. The first was sparked off by the company's continuing refusal to negotiate with the IAM – the specific grievances around which the gunmakers mobilized had to do with having to train and work alongside inexperienced women workers. This anti-dilution struggle was called off in return for the promise of high-level meetings between union

[73] Informant's Report, 8 Nov. 1918, p. 3, in Kelton File.
[74] Report of Examiners to W. Jett Lauck, 9th Oct. 1918, p. 2, in NWLB Case 400.
[75] For the NWLB, see esp. Valerie J. Conner, *The National War Labor Board: Stability, Social Justice, and the Voluntary State in World War I* (Chapel Hill, 1983).

and company representatives, under the U.S. Conciliation Service's auspices. There is no record of these having happened; there was hardly time, as another mass walkout occurred almost as soon as the return to work began, in protest at the company's breach of faith by refusing to take back all of the strikers. The Department of Labor passed the parcel to the WLB, stating that conciliation's possibilities had been exhausted, and another temporary truce was brokered by the Ordnance Department. Midvale once again violated its terms: Some strikers were turned away at the plant gates; but as soon as the bulk of his men were working again, President Alva C. Dinkey "emphatically denied the existence of any trouble, and therefore denied the right of the War Labor Board to assume jurisdiction."[76]

The summer months passed, with Midvale's machinists waiting patiently for the promised federal adjudication of their case and the company standing pat. It took Secretary of the Navy Josephus Daniels's September demand – implicitly backed by the threat of federal seizure – that Midvale submit, to get it to agree to cooperate with the WLB. It was the end of October before a hearing could be arranged, only to be aborted as "counsel for the employers had no knowledge as to the nature of the complaint which was to be heard." In the meantime, Midvale had experienced an eleventh-hour conversion to the virtues of collective bargaining whose sincerity did not pass unquestioned. It set up a company union or "Plan of Representation" that was firmly under management control: Only the machinists of Shop No. 7 voted to be represented by anyone other than their foremen; and once their chosen spokesmen discovered what kind of organization the "works committee" was going to be, they resigned.[77]

Midvale's success in getting its men back to work and, by masterful delay, staving off federal intervention and winning itself valuable time to effect a pioneering preemptive settlement of its problems tied up Kelton's attention and the IAM's limited resources throughout the summer. It also gave its smaller neighbors a fine lesson in how to behave when other local firms, in their turn, faced the aggrieved presence of significant numbers of Machinists in their shops.[78]

[76] President A. C. Dinkey to John F. Perkins (employer member, National War Labor Board), 23 Aug. 1918, in NWLB Executive Session Minutes, 28 Aug. 1918 a.m., pp. 4–6, in Melvyn Dubofsky, ed., *Research Collections in Labor Studies: The Wilson Administration and American Workers: Papers of the National War Labor Board* (Frederick, 1985), microfilm ed., Reel 8; Employees vs. Midvale Steel & Ordnance Co., case summary pp. 2–4, NWLB Case 129.

[77] Ibid.; Gerald G. Eggert, *Steelmasters and Labor Reform 1886–1923* (Pittsburgh, 1981), Ch. 5; McCartin, *Labor's Great War*, p. 164; Informant's Report 27 Sept. 1918, p. 1, in Kelton File. For the text of the plan, see A. B. Wolfe, *Works Committees and Joint Industrial Councils* (Philadelphia, 1919), pp. 207–12.

[78] The delaying tactics and arguments deployed in the Philadelphia Machinists' cases were becoming common, and may also have been inspired by the successful example of the Bethelehem Steel Co. – McCartin, *Labor's Great War*, pp. 162–64.

In the first two weeks of September, walkouts occurred or mass meetings voted to strike at a dozen firms, employing almost 11,000 workers altogether. In most cases, the tool-and-die makers were at the heart of the workers' insurgency. Only two of the companies affected – Smith, Drum, a small textile machine shop, and Savage Arms, an out-of-town corporation that had located in Philadelphia for the war – were MMA members, but Savage was the association's biggest, with about 1,400 employees. Dominating the struck nonmember firms were bearing makers Hess-Bright and Standard Roller, with about 1,300 and 2,400 workers, respectively, and carbuilders J. G. Brill, with about 5,500. The Ordnance Department's Industrial Service Section tried to work out settlements, but failed utterly as "Firms refuse to confer with employees." Accordingly, the best that could be done was to get an immediate return to work where men had actually walked out, and to persuade those who had voted to strike to delay their action, on the promise of a speedy resolution by the WLB and retroactive payment of any award made.[79]

Despite the fact that only two of its own members were in the direct line of fire, the MMA nonetheless served this group of mostly middling to large firms, as it had in the 1916 Eight Hours crisis, as their strategic advisor and the coordinator of their defensive maneuvers. Before the WLB hearing in October, their representatives met with the MMA's executive committee to compare notes and agree on a position, which President Schwacke suggested: that "satisfactory settlement having been made with their employees [i.e., the men were back at work] they had no points at issue to submit to the Board for adjustment, however they would appear before the Hearings and state their case."[80]

And appear they did, to deny charges of anti-union discrimination and to use the NWLB in an attempt to deal with their own manpower problems. What these firms had in common, apart from employing unionized Machinists, was the fact that they were mostly Ordnance Department contractors or subcontractors. They were prevented by their client's rules or by the fixed-price contracts that they were working on from exceeding or even matching Frankford Arsenal, Navy Yard, or Emergency Fleet rates of pay.

The department's logic was impeccable – it was acting in accordance with

[79] Examiners' Report, 9 Oct. 1918, p. 1 and Case Report 12 Nov. 1918, pp. 1–4, both in NWLB Case 400; IAM vs. Employers, Philadelphia, Pa., Digest of Case No. 400, in Dubofsky, ed., *Papers of the National War Labor Board*, microfilm ed., Reel 22.
[80] Informal Meeting, ECM 30 Sept. 1918. Three MMA members had experienced brief strikes during the "spring offensive," but they had overcome them in the usual way – holding out, waiting for the men's resolve to crack, labor replacement, and judicious wage adjustments – rather than submitting to USCS mediation or NWLB rulings. See SEC 1918, pp. 8–10, FMCS Cases 33-1094, 33-1097, and NWLB Case 641. Only the last was troubled again that fall.

the War Labor Policies Board's attempt to prevent government agencies and their contractors from bidding against one another for scarce labor, by working out and enforcing areawide standards. The difficulty was that the Navy and EFC rates had become, in effect, minima: Both agencies turned a blind eye to bonus systems that allowed them and their contractors to pay far more. The EFC, in particular, was a law unto itself in the way it set about its huge, urgent task of assembling and keeping a workforce. It had the resources and the inclination to build housing and improved public transportation facilities, advantaging its contractors, as well as to encourage them to pay their men top dollar. The Sun Shipbuilding Corporation, for example, provided its employees with housing, commissaries, and restaurants to spare them the horrors of wartime Chester, PA; it offered free express train service from Philadelphia for commuters; it paid up to 96¢ an hour for the highest skilled labor and 80¢ for first-class machinists (10 percent above the Ordnance Department rate), with comparably attractive rates for the less skilled. It wanted "Husky Men to Operate All Kinds of Machines; No Experience Necessary"; it promised them all "Big Money. . . . Plenty of overtime and lots of Sunday work."[81]

Firms working for a more stringent government agency or, even more unfortunately, as subcontractors on a fixed-price rather than cost-plus basis, could not hope to compete with these blandishments. Representatives of companies that could not afford, or were not permitted, even to match EFC basic rates therefore testified to the fact that there was

the greatest necessity in the Philadelphia district for a uniform rate. Nothing else will get results. . . . The trouble in Philadelphia is that some of us obey the fiat of the Ordnance Department not to increase the rates, while other companies on government work are permitted to ignore that command and pay any rate they wish. This is unfair and is destroying our labor market.[82]

As they saw it, they had no grievances with their men – Fox Gun "want[ed] our men to get what is coming to them" – but only with their direct or indirect customer, the government, whose restrictive and confusing practices had caused all the trouble in the first place. They just wanted a level playing field, and for the government to do and pay for the leveling – thus retroactivity, for example, was not a problem: "That is a matter for the procurement division of Ordnance. The rates will affect them and they will have to pay." Having submitted to, or appeared before, the WLB, they could then sit on their hands and wait, knowing that a settlement would depend on the achievement of consensus and coherence in the war mobi-

[81] Clipping, "Wanted Wanted Wanted Wanted Wanted Today – Any Time – Today And All Week," *Philadelphia Public Ledger*, 1 Nov. 1918, in U.S. Housing Corporation, Office of the President, Project Books, 1918–19, Box 26.
[82] Case Report 12 Nov. 1918, pp. 18, 15, NWLB Case 400.

lization bureaucracy that would solve some of their problems, should not cost them a cent, and that a WLB recommendation might hasten.[83]

By late October, therefore, Kelton's strategy appeared at last to be paying off. There seemed every chance of a favorable award in the Machinists' cases, and Midvale was, at long last, being forced to submit to the WLB's authority. To Kelton, Midvale's was "the principal case and the most important. . . . [T]he rest here will not be so hard, for once we get the Midvale we will have scored a victory on the Steel Trusts." But, seeing the war's end looming, this "manager of discontent" was actually teetering between desperation at the continuing delay and optimistic (or pacifying) reassurances to his members about the certainty of eventually favorable outcomes. He called on them "in every shop to get busy before it becomes too late and get in their greivance (*sic*) so [I can] put same before the War Labor Board, as this is going to be a big victory for the hard work of the men who organized Philadelphia's machinists." In an apparently buoyant mood, he told them "to start to count up what is due to them." He placed his confidence in former President William Howard Taft, the board's co-chair, to vote the right way on his cases, "and expects a retroactive settlement in most of the plants." His "only wish" was that he "had thirty-three more shops that I could slap at the Labor Board. I wish you fellows would get together and come see me and I will go with you and get it for you. . . . We have put Philadelphia on the map and that is where we want to keep it and we ought to have a labor board here all the time, in peace as well as in war."[84]

Unfortunately for Kelton and his men, when he gave them that encouragement the Midvale hearings had only just finished, and the war had just three days left to run. It would be another six weeks before an award was made in the Machinists' cases and three months in the Midvale affair. The breakthroughs that Kelton thought the war promised had been repeatedly stymied, first by MMA-coordinated resistance to the Eight Hours strikes through 1916–17 and more recently by the employers' fabian tactics of the summer and fall. So the outcome of the Machinists' continuing weakness in Philadelphia was that, by the time they did receive the largely favorable WLB awards that they had been promised, those long-delayed gifts came too late. For, as the MMA's Secretary Sparks realized a week after the Armistice, "now would be an opportune time to endeavor to operate the Labor Bureau on a normal basis." The storm was blowing over.[85]

[83]   Ibid., pp. 15, 18.
[84]   Informants' Reports, 1 Nov. pp. 1–3, 8 Nov. pp. 2–3, in Kelton File.
[85]   Award and Findings in re *Machinists vs. Certain Employers of Philadelphia, Pa.*, Docket No. 400, Serial No. A-136, 20 Dec. 1918; Findings and Award in re *Employees vs. Midvale Steel & Ordnance Co., Nicetown, Philadelphia Pa.*, Docket No. 129, Serial No. A-205, 11 Feb. 1919; both in Dubofsky, ed., *NWLB Records*, microfilm ed., Reel 5; ECM 19 Nov. 1918.

6.5 TOWARD A NEW ERA: WAR AND THE MODERNIZATION OF PERSONNEL MANAGEMENT

For the sake of narrative clarity, this chapter has concentrated on the history of wartime labor relations thus far. But underlying all of the MMA's and other Philadelphia metal-working firms' employment management problems, particularly in 1918, was the unprecedented tightness of the labor market. The MMA members' most serious difficulties were the result of this shortage of job-seekers and the consequent desperate competition between companies, rather than of organized labor pressure or federal intervention per se.

Between January 1917 and the summer of 1918, area war plants' employment grew by about 90,000 workers; plans for further growth at just twenty key establishments called for 28,000 more male workers by January 1919. Philadelphia had turned into the center of a grossly overcrowded, overheated industrial region. The great suburban munitions works strained the housing and other facilities of nearby small towns to the breaking point. The region's public transportation system could barely cope with the new burden of commuting that it had to bear. Housing costs, even in the city, soared. Workers faced with slow journeys to and from work at either end of long workdays naturally responded with high rates of absenteeism, quitting, and simple nonappearance to take up job offers – they were forever on the lookout for better pay or work nearer home. The resulting turnover could be astronomical. Midvale's Eddystone Rifle plant never attained its planned workforce of 14,500, despite hiring between 4,000 and 5,500 men and women every month of 1918 from spring until the Armistice, a level of turnover that prevented the plant from achieving more than about three-quarters of its target production. Similar problems were reported by Baldwin, and at the Tacony Ordnance works turnover hit a crippling 350 percent in September 1918.[86]

In this desperate situation, firms bid against one another for employees, and as we have seen they were encouraged in this practice – or at least not prevented – by the widely differing policies of the federal agencies that were their most important customers. The resulting hemorrhage of workers to the ship-building industry and its suppliers, as well as the impact of the draft and the end of immigration on their prime adult male labor supply,

---

[86] Blake Report (July 1918), pp. 2–6; Payson Irwin to Maj. W. C. Rogers, "Housing Conditions in the Philadelphia District," 16 June 1918; Satterthwaite (Eddystone Rifle) to John C. Jones, 21 May 1918, and attached "Digests" of Eddystone Munitions Co. and Baldwin Locomotive Works; John Nolen to F. L. Olmsted, 31 July 1918; Interview with Walter F. Mulhall (Tacony Ordnance), 4 Oct. 1918; C. H. Schlacke (Midvale) to Charles S. Herzig, 1 Nov. 1918 – all in U.S. Housing Corporation, Office of the President, Project Books, 1918–19 Box 26, RG3, National Archives.

therefore placed many Philadelphia employers in severe difficulties. The MMA's members were particularly badly affected, as 1917 and 1918 were "The greatest of all years in the manufacture and sale of metal-working machinery . . . . 1918 business was for many manufacturers several years rolled up into one."[87]

The MMA did what little it could to help its members in this crisis. It had ample financial resources – the increase in membership, and the rise in members' payrolls, meant that its revenues were outpacing inflation – but its supply of job-seekers was stretched to the breaking point. The number of men who called at the Labor Bureau looking for work dropped by 10 percent between 1917 and 1918, from a figure that was already 29 percent below the 1916 level, at the same time as the members' workforces and manpower needs were rising sharply. An increasing proportion of these applicants – 32 percent in 1917 and 38 percent in 1918, up from just 19 percent in 1916 – were previously unknown to the bureau. This resulted from the large number of out-of-towners in the city's war labor supply and the fact that the bureau's old local clientele had less need to use it when they could easily walk out of one job and into another. The quality of applicants was poor too, and their asking price was often higher than employers were able or willing to offer, so it became more and more difficult to make successful placements. And even if the men were adequately skilled, and accepted job offers, increasing numbers of them simply failed to turn up to start work, having made their own better bargains elsewhere in the meantime. So by the summer of 1918 the bureau was barely functioning, relying "almost entirely on the calls of the men who were acquainted with . . . [it], managing to secure a few desirable mechanics from those leaving the employ of one or another of our members," and trying to recirculate these few to other members before they were "lost" to nonmember firms.[88]

Part of the reason for the bureau's reduced activity was that it deliberately lowered its profile. In June 1918 the MMA stopped its increasingly costly and counterproductive help-wanted press advertising and succeeded in getting practically all of the other metal trades employers in the city to do so too, in an effort to slow the pace of job-shifting and the bidding-up

---

[87] Philadelphia Coppersmithing Company and Roberts Filter Mfg. Co. responses in War Industries Board, *Progress Reports on Army and Navy Contracts*, Oct. 1918, Boxes 373-5, U.S. Housing Corporation Records (John J. McCloskey, a blanket manufacturer, replied very simply to the questionnaire about his labor supply problems: the kind of workers he needed were just "Male and Female"); Philadelphia Chamber of Commerce, *1918–1919 Philadelphia Yearbook* (Philadelphia, 1919), p. B-7 [quote]. Employment in the manufacture of metal-working equipment in the state as a whole (mostly in Philadelphia) more than doubled between 1914 and 1918 – see Fred H. Colvin, "The War and the Machine Tool Industry," *American Machinist* 50 (1919): 1167–69 at p. 1169.

[88] For Labor Bureau figures, see Table 4.1; ECM 9 July 1918, SEC 1918, pp. 3–4.

of wages. But the larger explanation was that the MMA and other labor placement agencies found themselves up against new and powerful competition, the U.S. Employment Service, which in July acquired a legal monopoly over the common labor supply and offered skilled men an alternative, and genuinely impartial, source of job information. The service was initially welcomed, but the MMA's members, like most other employers, soon turned against it when they discovered how seriously it took its obligation not to refer workers to jobs in struck plants.[89]

The MMA took two significant steps to attempt to offset its members' manpower problems. The first was to help and encourage them to hire women workers to make up the shortfall (see Introduction). The second, and more important, was to try to attack the turnover problem directly. The root cause – excess demand for workers – was of course beyond the MMA's or its members' control; but, at least potentially, one of the major causes of job-shifting, the huge disparities between rates of pay for comparable jobs among the city's employers, was not; at least, not entirely. However, before they could begin to reduce the incentive for employees to quit in search of improvement, they needed to know what the going rate was for workers of particular types and degrees of skill. In the rapidly changing local labor market, comprehensive, accurate, and reliable pay information was in chronically short supply. Wartime inflation and the bidding-up of wage rates had rendered accumulated informal knowledge almost valueless. Managers of large firms that were new to Philadelphia lacked it in any case. But employers absolutely needed what the MMA's new young secretary, Earl Sparks, called "authentic figures on which to base contemplated changes" so that they could confront the turnover problem by bringing their wages into line with area norms without running the risk of offering too much and further stoking the inflationary fires.[90]

Increasingly urgent requests for just this kind of information created a new opportunity for the MMA to meet its actual and potential constituents'

[89] For the USES, see Samuel Mathers to Federal Director, 23 Jan. 1919, and Special Representative to the Director General to Director General, USES, "Report on Allegation of Striking Workmen of the Firm of David Lupton & Sons, Phila., Pa., that Service Was Supplying Laborers to the Lupton Concern," 24 Jan. 1919, both in FMCS Case 33-2943. The fact that a local USES official had broken its rules by supplying unskilled workers to a firm, even when only its skilled workers were on strike, resulted in an IAM protest, a rapid and forceful investigation by higher officers, and a dressing-down for the local man. This demonstrated how seriously the USES took its effectively pro-labor official doctrine of neutrality. For resulting hostile employer reactions, see SEC 1919, p. 5; "The United States Employment Service: Resolutions adopted May 2, 1919, at New Orleans by the Southern Metal Trades' Association," *Industry* 1 (15 May 1919): 5; E. Jay Howenstine, Jr., *The Economics of Demobilization* (Washington, 1944), Ch. 9.

[90] SEC 1918, p. 6.

needs, and to build on the closer relationship with large nonmembers that the 1916 Eight Hours crisis had created. The MMA, with its detailed knowledge of area firms' labor requirements and wide confidential contacts, was "able to furnish information that probably could not be obtained through any other source." In August 1918, 121 metal-working establishments employing over 17,500 men and women took part in a massive data-gathering effort reporting the exact hourly earnings (including incentive pay) for every single one of their workers in forty-six male and seven female job categories. This was, as Sparks proudly told his members that December, a "more complete" compilation of wage data "than had heretofore been attempted." It was made available to the managers in participating firms – at least half of them nonmembers – in the form of a large spreadsheet allowing them to see the precise distribution of earnings for workers of a particular skill and identify mean, median, and modal rates.[91]

This information is useful for the historian, both for its own sake and because of the improvement in companies' administrative capacities and strategic awareness that it bespeaks. Tight labor markets, the growth in the labor forces of existing city firms and the arrival of managerially "modern" outsiders, the federal government's example and encouragement, and the easy profits and comparatively high taxes that eroded companies' previous reluctance to invest in administrative overhead had conspired to begin a quiet revolution from *personal* to *personnel* management.[92]

Firms participating in the MMA's surveys had to have payroll records sufficiently detailed that they could report, for example, how many cupola tenders received 44¢ an hour. To do that, they had to have had a belief that the information was worth gathering in the first place. To be willing to share it with competitors, they had to be convinced of their common dependence on labor markets and that it was in the general interest to understand and manage better. They also had to have managerial structures in place that would allow them to use the data that the MMA made available. To do all of these things they needed administrative staff, a degree of centralized control over their wage structure, and an awareness of the importance of employment problems and the possibility of dealing with them "scientifically," all of which had been quite rare in prewar Philadelphia.

[91] Ibid., pp. 1, 6; the spreadsheet survives in fragments in MMAP II-4-42.
[92] For the employment management movement, see Daniel Nelson, *Managers and Workers: Origins of the New Factory System in the United States, 1880–1920* (Madison, 1975), esp. Ch. 8; Sanford M. Jacoby, *Employing Bureaucracy: Managers, Unions and the Transformation of Work in American Industry, 1900–1945* (New York, 1985), esp. Ch. 5; cf. James N. Baron *et al.*, "War and Peace: The Evolution of Modern Personnel Administration in U.S. Industry," *American Journal of Sociology* 92 (1986): 350–83. In the Philadelphia metal trades, at least, explaining the timing and reasons for the formalization of personnel policy is relatively straightforward – cf. Walter Licht, *Getting Work: Philadelphia, 1840–1950* (Cambridge, Mass., 1992), Ch. 5.

Rare, but not unknown. Chapter 2 emphasized that Philadelphia metal working was both the birthplace of Taylorism and an entrepreneurial community largely committed to nonbureaucratic management practices, with regard to employment as well as other matters. Even before the war, however, that commitment had begun to erode. One of the principal agents of change was Frederick Taylor's closest collaborator, chief publicist, and Germantown neighbor, the engineer Morris Ll. Cooke (born 1872); the other was Cooke's protégé, a young instructor in the University of Pennsylvania's Wharton School of Finance and Commerce, Joseph H. Willits (born 1889). Explaining their message for and their influence on the city's employers requires some backtracking.

Cooke had entered the public arena in 1911 as the city's director of public works in a short-lived reformist administration. The massive industrial upheavals of 1910–11 had strained the political loyalties of Philadelphia's working classes, and accentuated divisions within the Republican machine and between it and its middle-class critics. As a result, "the Old Dutch Cleanser," Rudolph Blankenburg, a retired textile manufacturer, won the mayoralty as an independent and Philadelphia found itself with a "progressive" local administration promising clean, economical, and efficient government.[93]

Cooke's department was the centerpiece of the mayor's assault on endemic graft and poor service provision. Blankenburg had tried to recruit Frederick Taylor to run it, but Taylor, approaching the peak of his national fame as the "father of scientific management," had declined and recommended Cooke in his stead. Cooke's policies at the head of his large, labor-intensive department, with its lax, patronage-riddled employment practices, reflected those of the relatively liberal wing of the local business community from which he came, and which constituted the Blankenburg administration's core support. They blended anti-unionism, a determination to reassert managerial control, and genuine reformism. He canceled union contracts, extended working hours, and got rid of 1,000 workers (about a quarter of the total) from the politically padded payroll. But, to benefit those who remained, he also introduced a pension program, an "open

[93] Lloyd M. Abernathy, "Insurgency in Philadelphia, 1905," *PMHB* 86 (1963): 3–20; Lucretia L. Blankenburg, *The Blankenburgs of Philadelphia: By One of Them* (Philadelphia, 1928), esp. pp. xviii, xx, 60–76; Donald W. Disbrow, "Reform in Philadelphia under Mayor Blankenburg," *Pennsylvania History* 27 (1960): 379–96; Bonnie R. Fox, "The Philadelphia Progressives: A Test of the Hofstadter-Hays Thesis," *Pennsylvania History* 34 (1967): 372–94; Daniel I. Greenstein, "Urban Politics and the Urban Process: Two Case Studies of Philadelphia" (Oxford, England, D.Phil. Thesis, 1987), esp. Chs. 4–6; Peter McCaffery, *When Bosses Ruled Philadelphia: The Emergence of the Republican Machine 1867–1933* (University Park, 1993), esp. pp. 179–80.

door" consultation system, and employment policies modeled on those of private-sector personnel pioneers.[94]

Cooke entered office with a normal (for a Taylorite) technocratic disdain for democracy and trust in his own expertise. But his experience of public-sector management, his response to the Progressive *zeitgeist*, and his reaction to the conflicts and crises of the prewar years caused some rethinking. He acquired a new, more politically sensitive understanding of the importance to the manager of gaining his subordinates' cooperation and consent. Taylor's former acolyte became one of the leading proponents of the Taylor Society's successive conversions to consultative and participative management, and eventually to cooperation with organized labor and the endorsement of collective bargaining. All of these developments were wholly unpredictable while the Old Man lived, and are sure to have set him spinning with impotent fury in his grave. More immediately important, though, Cooke also became convinced that chronic unemployment, resulting from managerial failures and a disorganized labor market, was a far more influential impediment to the realization of efficiency than workers' obstructiveness and "soldiering," as The Boss had preached. So Cooke made use of his brief period of authority to try to persuade Philadelphia employers to revolutionize their everyday personnel practices.[95]

What gave this mission its urgency was the severe recession of 1914–15, the greatest trial with which the Blankenburg administration had to cope. It was wholly unprepared to deal with such a crisis, whose scale and duration overwhelmed the community's feeble, voluntaristic unemployment relief mechanisms. So its response included an attempt by Blankenburg

[94] Blankenburg, *Blankenburgs of Philadelphia*, pp. xx, 48, 60–62; Jean Christie, *Morris Llewellyn Cooke: Progressive Engineer* (New York, 1983), pp. 23–27; Morris Ll. Cooke, "Impressions of an Engineer in Public Office," *Procs. ECP* 33 (1916): 1–15 and *Our Cities Awake: Notes on Municipal Activities and Administration* (Garden City, 1918.); Frank B. Copley, *Frederick W. Taylor: Father of Scientific Management* (New York, 1923), Vol. 2, p. 394; Kenneth E. Trombley, *The Life and Times of a Happy Liberal* (New York, 1954), Ch. 2. Cooke's models were the pioneering Filene's department store in Boston and Dennison Manufacturing Co. of Framingham, Massachusetts, for which see esp. Kim McQuaid, "Henry S. Dennison and the 'Science' of Industrial Reform, 1900–1950," *American Journal of Economics and Sociology* 36 (1977): 79–98, esp. pp. 80–82.

[95] Cooke testimony in USCIR, *Final Report and Testimony*, Vol. 3, pp. 2674–86; Cooke, "Impressions of an Engineer in Public Office," pp. 1–2, 6, "Who Is Boss In Your Shop?" *Annals* 71 (May 1917): 167–85, and *Our Cities Awake*, p. 72. See also Edwin T. Layton, Jr., *The Revolt of the Engineers: Social Responsibilty and the American Engineering Profession* (Baltimore, 1986; first published 1971), esp. pp. 148–49, 160–62; Milton J. Nadworny, *Scientific Management and the Unions 1900–1932: An Historical Analysis* (Cambridge, Mass., 1955), esp. Chs. 7, 8; Hindy L. Schachter, *Frederick Taylor and the Public Administration Community: A Reevaluation* (Albany, 1989), pp. 73–86; Donald Stabile, *Prophets of Order* (Boston, 1984), pp. 78–79, 103.

and Cooke to use their influence to persuade Philadelphia's major employers to alter their own employment policies to mitigate the effects of this and future recessions. The city's industrial leaders were unable or unwilling to do anything new themselves, at least in the short term. But they agreed with Cooke that any intelligent planning for future action must rest on better knowledge and understanding of the problem than any of them then possessed.[96]

Cooke had realized that an adequate intellectual basis for efficient social management of the city's unemployment problems was lacking, even before the recession brought others to share his concern. As Guy Alchon emphasizes, Cooke, like a number of other prominent Taylorites, had begun to concentrate on "human relations and the wastes . . . associated with labor turnover, absenteeism, and workers who were ill suited to their jobs" rather than on production engineering and administrative restructuring per se. He was an active member of the American Association for Labor Legislation (AALL) that, even before the recession struck, held its first National Conference on Unemployment in Philadelphia in February 1914. He had written a pamphlet under the auspices of the Wharton School's radical economist, Simon Patten, a founding member of the association, arguing that

> it would be a great and good thing if some citizens or group of citizens would establish at the University of Pennsylvania a chair on unemployent, the function of which would be to organize a study of the causes of both the chronic and the exceptional types of unemployment and make suggestions to our manufacturers and workers as to the best means of reducing it.[97]

No pockets were opened in response to this suggestion, but the city's industrial leaders were at least prepared, at the conclusion of their December meeting with Cooke and Blankenburg, to endorse his proposal that the city should pay for an investigation. As the employing interests would not fund and coordinate the research and reform initiative, the city had a responsibility to take the lead.

Cooke's strategy for social change was fully in keeping with his brand of technocratic progressivism – "intensive study . . . accompanied by proper publicity." Cooke recruited a junior faculty member at the Wharton, Joseph H. Willits, to carry out the research project. The University of Pennsylva-

[96] Philip Klein, *The Burden of Unemployment: A Study of Unemployment Relief Measures in Fifteen American Cities, 1921–22* (New York, 1923), p. 138; Philadelphia Emergency Aid Committee, Home Relief Division, Bureau of Employment, *Special Report* (Philadelphia, 1915), esp. pp. 3–13; Joseph H. Willits, *Steadying Employment: With a Section Devoted to Some Facts on Unemployment in Philadelphia* (Philadelphia, 1916; supplement to *Annals* 65 [May 1916]), pp. 3–4, 127–29.

[97] Guy Alchon, *The Invisible Hand of Planning: Capitalism, Social Science, and the State in the 1920s* (Princeton, 1985), p. 16; for Patten, see Daniel M. Fox, *The Discovery of Abundance: Simon N. Patten and the Transformation of Social Theory* (Ithaca, 1967); Cooke Exhibit No. 2 in USCIR, *Final Report*, Vol. 3, p. 2719.

nia was Cooke's usual source of expert assistance with technical problems – and to the optimistic Cooke, most social problems were just that. Wharton gave Willits a leave of absence during which he did the research that Cooke requested and wrote up his findings and policy recommendations, and it gave him his doctorate on the strength of that work.[98]

Willits was the product of a high-status rural Quaker family from the western outskirts of Philadelphia. He graduated from the Hicksite college, Swarthmore, in 1911, stayed on for a year as an instructor in city government to get his Master's, and then moved to Penn for his doctoral work in social science under Patten and other progressive tutors. Wharton's young instructor in geography and industry was not just the lucky recipient of Cooke's commission. He had actively sought it, having decided to make the new field of "employment problems" his own, and having spent the last two summer vacations "in trips over the country, going through . . . over 200 manufacturing plants from Massachusetts to Georgia" to equip himself.[99]

Willits, like Cooke, was "progressive" and "civic minded." His findings were empirically novel, but the recommendations that they underpinned were already parts of the conventional wisdom of labor reform. Willits and his liberal Republican mentor were less radical than the AALL itself, which advocated countercyclical public works planning and unemployment insurance as the keystone of its program. Cooke's roots were deep in the private sector, and he was fully aware of the fiscal and political constraints under which the city government operated. He was convinced that public works could merely mitigate unemployment; Willits quantified the direct employment-creation role that they ascribed to the city government at no more than 800–1,000 jobs, far fewer than Baldwin could lay off in a day.[100]

Yet though they offered only half-hearted support for the most statist planks in the AALL's program, Willits and, to a lesser extent, Cooke, did want the government to take on new responsibilities. Their principal goal

---

[98] Cooke, *Our Cities Awake*, pp. 86, 153–54; Cooke, "Responsibility and Opportunity of the City in the Prevention of Unemployment," *American Association for Labor Legislation Review* (hereafter *AALLR*) 5 (1915): 433–36.

[99] Steven A. Sass, *The Pragmatic Imagination: A History of the Wharton School 1881–1981* (Philadelphia, 1982), p. 178; "Willits High Up in Aircraft Plant and at University," *The Phoenix* (Swarthmore, Pa.), clipping, 1919, in Joseph Willits files, Box 5, F. 52, Rockefeller Archives Center (RAC) Accession IV-2A-39; "Personal Facts of Joseph H. Willits, October 30 1916," Box 7, F. 68.

[100] Sass, *Pragmatic Imagination*, p. 178; Alchon, *Invisible Hand*, p. 17; John B. Andrews, "A Practical Program for the Prevention of Unemployment in America," *AALLR* 5 (1915): 171–92; cf. (New York) Mayor's Committee on Unemployment, *How to Meet Hard Times: A Program for the Prevention & Relief of Abnormal Unemployment* (New York, 1917); Cooke, *Our Cities Awake*, p. 292; Willits, *Unemployed in Philadelphia*, p. 8.

was a system of free public employment bureaus established by the city and state governments to make the labor market work more fairly and efficiently. But because the Blankenburg administration was nearing the end of its political tether, the city could play no part. So they had to fall back on the no less ambitious, but, to taxpayers at least, much less costly option of using the municipal administration's influence to exhort and assist the city's employers toward their secondary objective, the modernizing of personnel policies in the private sector.

Cooke had a vision of "A City Planned for Industrial Competency," its enlightened bureaucrats performing the same kind of services for the local economy – research, consultancy, and the coordination and stimulation of change – as Herbert Hoover's Department of Commerce would later attempt to deliver at the national level in the maturing "associative state" of the New Era. Cooke believed that "In the one word 'Unemployment' is summed up a problem of tremendous importance to any industrial city ... [and an] obstacle to our growth as an industrial nation." But he was optimistic that "No one of the unfortunate conditions of our industrial life is more susceptible to control than this one, if manufacturers, educators, the labouring (*sic*) class, and others interested will so view it." He thought "that, say, 90 per cent. of all the unemployment, which makes men and women suffer and which demoralizes and degrades them, can be eliminated by proper organization within our factory walls." His engineer's utopian vision of the future was of each establishment having "a definite number of employees each working full time – without overtime – and at maximum wages and with no changes in the personnel." He admitted that "This 100 per cent. result is not possible of achievement," but it was nonetheless useful as "a standard with which to compare such results as are obtained." It was also a position from which to attack present errors, particularly the newly discovered phenomenon of the almost unbelievably high levels of turnover in the industrial labor force, which he considered "perhaps the worst malady of American industry."[101]

Willits amplified Cooke's ideas, like him uniting the twin concerns – efficiency and welfare, productivity and social justice – of the emergent personnel management movement. He too believed that "Unemployment is primarily a question of industry and industrial organization." He was not prepared to accept it as an inevitable accompaniment of a capitalist economy, nor to conclude with the Socialists that only a revolution could solve the problem, since "the introduction of a new industrial system is a proposition so doctrinaire that it can scarcely be counted as offering any

[101] Cooke, *Our Cities Awake*, pp. 301, 286–89 [quotes]; Ellis W. Hawley, "Herbert Hoover, the Commerce Secretariat, and the Vision of an Associative State, 1921–1928," *JAH* 61 (1974): 116–40, for the bigger picture of the marriage of technocracy and voluntarism; for the discovery of turnover, see Jacoby, *Employing Bureaucracy*, pp. 115–17.

immediate practicable hope." Willits's object was reform of the *existing* system.[102]

Willits and Cooke did more than just sermonize about business's responsibilities: Before the Blankenburg administration's mandate expired, they set about forming a new kind of local employers' association to promote enlightened practice. In June 1915, at Cooke's invitation, a select group of about forty companies with relatively well-developed employment and/or welfare policies met to form the Philadelphia Association for the Discussion of Employment Problems (PADEP), one of the first personnel managers' organizations in the United States. It was an experience-sharing forum, as its name suggested; "a *purely voluntary* association for purposes of study, involving on the part of the members, *no joint support of each other in labor troubles* or of any outside course of action" (emphasis added). Unlike the MMA, it was an organization of executives in firms that devolved responsibility for employment work to salaried managers rather than of business principals. Willits became its secretary – a part-time job combining the roles of recruiting-agent, convenor, strategist, and publicist.[103]

No full list of PADEP members survives, but it included some of Philadelphia's largest companies, notably Curtis Publishing, the city's two great department stores, Wanamaker's and Strawbridge & Clothier, and the huge hat-maker, the John B. Stetson Co. From the metal trades it recruited the giant New York Ship, the Taylorite showpiece Tabor, American Pulley, Leeds & Northrup (instrument makers), Miller Lock, and others. A Fayette R. Plumb Co. manager reported in 1916 on how membership in the association had led them, as Cooke and Willits intended, to formalize their personnel policies, centralize responsibility for their conduct in an employment department, and overthrow the "foreman's empire." With the creation of PADEP, Philadelphia had acquired a local focus for managerial efforts to rationalize company employment practices. This occurred even before the insistent demands of war production and a federal war bureaucracy staffed with the proselytizing pioneers of personnel management strengthened the forces making for modernization which the corporate system itself generated.[104]

---

[102] Willits, *Unemployed in Philadelphia*, pp. 68–69.

[103] Ibid., pp. 91–2, 169; "Employment Associations," *Engineering Magazine* 52 (Oct. 1916): 110–11; J. H. Willits, "The Philadelphia Association," *Industrial Management* 52 (Feb. 1917): 725–26; "Development of Employment Managers' Associations," U.S. Bureau of Labor Statistics *Monthly Review* 5 (Sept. 1917): 85–87.

[104] Willits to E. M. Hopkins (ex-Curtis Publishing), 6 Dec. 1915, reporting on monthly meetings, Box 7, F. 68, Willits Papers, RAC; A. H. Williams (Assistant Sec., PADEP) to J. Irvin Behney, Assistant Employment Manager, Lukens Steel, 1 Dec. 1919, in Charles Lukens Huston Papers, Box 1997, Folder 12, Lukens Steel Collection, Accession 50, HML; John M. Williams, "An Actual Account of What We Have Done to Reduce Our Labor Turnover," in Willits, ed., *Stabilizing Industrial Employ-*

Willits also argued for the extension and institutionalization of the temporary program to study the labor market that Cooke had promoted and he had carried out. He urged the Wharton School to "take the lead, in the community's efforts to study the problem" by organizing a program of training and research to produce a pool of expertise and a fund of useful knowledge. Willits could not realize his dream immediately; he was still a mere instructor, but he had made valuable contacts through the PADEP, and his career was well launched. He became Wharton's expert in this important new field, teaching a course on "Personnel and Employment Problems in Industrial Management," strengthening his connections with the liberal wing of the Taylor Society, and acquiring consultancy contracts of his own. By the end of 1915 he was confident that "the Employment Management work here ... is to be my pet, to feed, clothe, water and cherish, so that it may grow as my abilities and the possibilities of the subject warrant."[105]

Willits was an honest, ambitious academic entrepreneur. He admitted to one of his managerial patrons that he was more interested in the furtherance of his career and the opportunities opening up "than in the altruistic motive of bringing about the recognition of the employment management field." Happily for Willits, he was able to advance himself precisely through his early attachment to this new specialty. As an anonymous supporter of his wrote in 1920, "Everyone seems to like him and nearly everyone who has the opportunity offers him a job." But Willits declined all invitations to leave Wharton for the next two decades: "Frankly, with the already organized laboratory which Philadelphia furnishes, I should be loath to leave such an environment." For a student of labor markets, the city was a challenging but rewarding place to work, and the PADEP provided Willits with access to data and an ability to influence practice that no other less organized community could offer.[106]

Then the war came, transforming his laboratory into America's greatest center of munitions production, and heightening the importance of improved personnel management, whose objective changed from minimizing the wastage produced by unemployment into maximizing the utilization of labor, a newly scarce resource. His patrons moved into positions of power within the war machine – Cooke as chair of the Purchase, Storage, and Traffic Division of the Council of National Defense, where he was

ment, pp. 51–70 (read at the second national employment managers' conference, organized by Willits at Philadelphia in April 1917 – see U.S. Bureau of Labor Statistics, *Bulletin* No. 227 (1917) for full proceedings).

[105]   Willits, *Unemployed in Philadelphia*, p. 63; "Personal Facts of Joseph H. Willits"; "Willits High Up in Aircraft Plant and at University"; Willits to E. M. Hopkins, 5 Nov., 2, 6, and 27 Dec. 1915, Box 7, F. 68, Willits Papers, RAC.

[106]   Willits to Hopkins, 5 Nov. 1915; JRS to Edgar S. Smith, 30 Dec. 1920; Willits to Hopkins, 17 Feb. 1917, Box 7, F. 68, Willits Papers, RAC.

among the first to propose that the government get into the business of training employment managers; then on to the Army Quartermasters' Department, where he was instrumental in promoting General Order No. 13, which set out a liberal employment code for contractors; and finally with Link-Belt's Charles Piez at the Emergency Fleet Corporation. Willits himself became industrial relations manager at the huge Aircraft Factory in the Philadelphia Navy Yard, practicing what he had hitherto only preached.[107]

Which is where he was when the MMA's able new young college-educated secretary, Earl Sparks, replacing the seasoned old strike-breaker, Henry Morgan, began attending PADEP meetings in the spring of 1918. The 1916 Eight Hours crisis had strengthened MMA contacts with the larger local firms; the 1918 manpower crisis deepened them, forging new alliances between organizations, companies, and individuals developing a broader and more sophisticated approach toward the problems of employment management than had ever been displayed before the war. The MMA moved beyond the limited range of employment-related issues that had preoccupied its members during the fight to establish the Open Shop. The challenge of labor had already persuaded firms to cooperate through the Labor Bureau and to modify some hiring practices. On this foundation Sparks and a new generation of MMA leaders would soon be able to build, once the troubles of war were behind them.[108]

6.6 CONCLUSION

The war period had brought the MMA and other metal trades employers new challenges, but none they could not handle. The essence of their wartime strategy was containment. The driving force of the MMA's and NMTA's policy, besides their unchanging ideology, was the belief in the absolute necessity of retaining the competitive advantage that the Open Shop represented. Their leaders expected a relatively short period of war-derived prosperity, to be followed by a return to "normal" (i.e., prewar)

[107]   Trombley, *Life and Times*, Ch. 6; Christie, *Morris Llewellyn Cooke*, pp. 35–57; John K. Bangs, Jr, ed., *"As You Were": Reminiscences of the General Supplies Division of the Purchase, Storage, and Traffic Division, General Staff, U.S. Army* (New York, 1919), pp. 117–18; Willits to E. T. Clayton (Assistant Director, U.S. Employment Service), 1 June 1918, p. 2, in Box 7, F. 68, Willits Papers, RAC.

[108]   ECM, 13 Feb. 1918, for the MMA-PADEP linkup. Morgan, whose secretaryship ended in a bitter and confused quarrel with the MMA executive, put his anti-union expertise to good use in service to the local Cloth Manufacturers Association, which also had major strikes to fight – see Philip Scranton, *Figured Tapestry: Production, Markets, and Power in Philadelphia Textiles, 1885–1941* (New York, 1989), pp. 303–12.

conditions of domestic stagnation and instability, made worse by heightened international competition from European economies whose industries
had been fattened and modernized by total war.[109]

In 1915–16, the challenge had been primarily one of full employment.
Labor market conditions strongly favored their union opponents, but the
latter – particularly the IAM – were much more weakly organized than the
Open Shop employers, with less experienced and secure leaders, and much
less committed members. During the Eight Hours crisis the MMA demonstrated the advantages of having a clear strategy and the machinery for
implementing it, even to those large local companies that had never before
seen much advantage in cooperating with the association. The result was
that it went into the second phase of the emergency in an extraordinarily
strong position – with the IAM beaten, its inability to rely on its own
resources clearly demonstrated, its leadership and strategy once again in
flux. The MMA's situation mirrored that of the metal trades generally,
which was summed up by the NMTA's president W. H. Van Dervoort on
the brink of war: "It has cost us much in money, work, and anxiety, but,
gentlemen, we still control the situation, and the members of this Association are privileged to operate their own plants. We have kept the situation
tolerable."[110]

In the second phase of the emergency, 1917–18, medium-term concerns
were submerged by the immediate problems of getting and keeping workers,
and staving off the pressures of an enormously expanded, somewhat pro-
labor federal government. But here, too, both the MMA and its national
affiliates were in a strong position. As Van Dervoort emphasized to the
NMTA in the spring of 1918, "all the expense of effort, time and money
made by our members during the past twenty years . . . has been amply
repaid in its efficient operation during the past few years of exceptional
stress." The Open Shop associations had lost few of the normal peacetime
advantages of organized capital. They found new ones to set against labor
and its allies in the political economy of war.[111]

First, the Wilson administration's chief priority was maximum and continuous production; its great object was national unity and social cohesion,
to be achieved by persuasion if possible, but by force if necessary. The result,
as we have seen, was that its agenda and that of even the most conformist
sections of the trade union movement were not necessarily the same. In fact,
organized labor – as a "disturber of the peace" – was often suspect, and
open to the fatal accusation of disloyalty. This meant that employers gained
an even stronger sense of the legitimacy of their authority, of the congru-

---

[109] NMTA, *Synopsis of Proceedings of the 19th Annual Convention* (New York, 1917),
        pp. 27, 30–32; *Synopsis of Proceedings of the 20th Annual Convention* (New York,
        1918), p. 28.
[110] NMTA, *Synopsis of Proceedings* (1917), pp. 22–23.
[111] NMTA, *Synopsis of Proceedings* (1918), p. 28.

ence between their personal interests and the national interest, and one with which much of the middle-class public and many of the state's coercive agencies agreed. The MMA, just as much of the rest of the employer community, incorporated the rhetoric of patriotism and the assistance of the wartime loyalty police into its defensive armor and offensive weaponry. The postwar "American Plan" anti-union offensive was already taking shape even while labor and its liberal allies thought that they were participating in a Great War for Democracy.[112]

Second, the Wilson administration became increasingly dependent on the active cooperation of the business community, whose members colonized most of the new and enlarged federal agencies. However, their cooperation came at a price – it increased the receptivity of the government to capital's demands; it even gave businessmen a direct and powerful voice in the making and implementation of national policy itself. The logic of "voluntarism" meant that the federal war labor relations policy, in particular, could be nothing other than a compromise agreeable to them. They took much of the credit for wresting control over it out of the untrustworthy hands of Secretary Wilson and giving it to a War Labor Board, on which they and the "responsible" unions were equally represented, under joint chairmen – Frank Walsh and former-President Taft – acceptable to the respective contending parties. The National Industrial Conference Board a new consortium of employers' associations that was formed to meet the political challenges of the Wilson years – had pressed hard for this outcome, and turned itself into what the NMTA's president Van Dervoort termed "the recognized representative of the employer" as a result. He led its delegation at the conference in March 1918, which worked out the terms of the truce that was supposed to govern labor relations for the duration and set the parameters for federal intervention when that truce broke down.[113]

As far as Open Shop employers were concerned, the crucial condition was that the National War Labor Board would lack the power to require them to recognize and bargain directly with the trade unions. The basic principle that neither capital nor labor should be able to take advantage of the national emergency to alter existing conditions was, Van Dervoort explained, as much of a protection for open shops as for closed. With this

---

[112] See esp. Jensen, *The Price of Vigilance.*

[113] NMTA, *Synopsis of Proceedings* (1918), pp. 26–27, 33 [quote]. For the political economy of war and the war labor program, see esp. Conner, *The National War Labor Board;* Robert D. Cuff, *The War Industries Board: Business-Government Relations During World War I* (Baltimore, 1973) and "The Politics of Labor Administration During World War I," *Labor History* 21 (1980): 546–69; Melvyn Dubofsky, "Abortive Reform" and *The State and Labor in Modern America* (Chapel Hill, 1994), Ch. 3; Sidney Fine, *"Without Blare of Trumpets": Walter Drew, the National Erectors' Association, and the Open Shop Movement, 1903–1957* (Ann Arbor, 1995), esp. pp. 143–44, 146–48, 154–55, 161–64.

understanding of its purpose, he went on to chair the employer representatives on the NWLB, and attempted to see to it that the policy did not
depart too far from industry's objectives.[114]

In fact, as we have seen, the NWLB's policy did seem to develop a
momentum of its own, and by the fall of 1918 the MMA was heavily
engaged on behalf of the members and nonmembers with cases before it –
trying to squeeze favorable outcomes to their problems with the procurement agencies that were their paymasters, and playing for time. It is impossible to know how things might have turned out if the timetable of
American mobilization had been different – if, as Taft had instructed the
NMTA in April, they had had three more years of conflict to which to look
forward. But of course, they didn't. By the fall of 1918, Philadelphia's
Machinists seemed on the verge of a breakthrough: Midvale Steel and other
large companies were making their own more or less reluctant compromises
with the NWLB's agenda of industrial democracy; nationally, the AFL was
organizing for a concerted attack on the steel industry, the citadel of the
Open Shop. But it was all too late. Although no one seems to have recognized it at the time, the failure of the Ludendorff Offensive on the Western
Front months earlier, and the ensuing collapse of the *Kaiserreich*, had guaranteed the survival of the Open Shop Order even as it doomed the *anciens
régimes* of Central Europe to destruction. And, thanks to the war experience, metal trades employers would enter the postwar world far better prepared to attack than labor was to defend its limited and insecure wartime
gains. Labor only had aspirations. The employers had fierce commitment,
strengthened organizations, more sophisticated political and industrial
relations strategies than ever, and substantial clout. The outcome was
scarcely in doubt, but the path to total victory would still involve years of
struggle.[115]

---

[114]   NMTA, *Synopsis of Proceedings* (1918), p. 27. Cf. Statement of Principles and Policies Submitted by the Representatives of the Employers, 6 March 1918, Memorandum Respecting the Interpretation of the "Principles" of the National War Labor
Board As Applied to the So Called "Non-Union Establishment," submitted by Loyall
A. Osborne, n.d., and Osborne to William Howard Taft, 31 May 1918, all in Dubofsky, ed., *NWLB Records*, microfilm ed., Reel 20.

[115]   NMTA, *Synopsis of Proceedings* (1918), p. 89.

7

The War After the War, 1918–1923

What follows war is not necessarily peace. In this chapter, we will examine the waning of the war labor program and the disintegration of the war economy, and the resultant withering of Philadelphia labor's prospects for a change of fortune. In 1919–20, while the Great Steel Strike and the President's Industrial Conference mapped out the collapse of wartime hopes for a fundamental transformation of the landscape of U.S. labor relations, the Philadelphia metal trades witnessed their own smaller scale tragedies as the liberal state withdrew, unemployment returned, employers unsheathed their swords, and their union adversaries began to implode.[1]

The reconstruction of the labor relations Old Order in the Philadelphia metal trades was not a tidy process. It required struggle. Strangely enough, Philadelphia metalworkers and their families did not all seem to understand that what was required of them was once again obedience and gratitude. Instead, they had to be retaught the lesson of their powerlessness. Echoes of the wartime insurgency therefore rumbled on for three more years, until the victories of the city's and nation's Open Shop employers in their "American Plan" anti-union offensives, and the short but savage recession of 1920–21, ushered in the Republican "New Era." At the end of this period, labor was shattered. The MMA, its members, and their allies appeared at last to have the field to themselves. The major question facing them would be an ironic result of their success: What future faced an anti-union employers' association after the death of its opponents?

7.1 THE AFTERMATH, 1918–1921

Machinists leader Bill Kelton and his members were doomed to disappointment. They had put their trust in the federal government, but its ability

---

[1] See David Brody, *Labor in Crisis: The Steel Strike of 1919* (Philadelphia, 1965); Burl Noggle, *Into the Twenties: The United States from Armistice to Normalcy* (Urbana, 1974), esp. Chs. 4–5.

and willingness to respond to their grievances started to evaporate almost as soon as they began to scent victory. By late November he urgently wrote NWLB co-chairman Taft requesting a quick decision, as "The Company's (*sic*) are discharging the active union men in these shops and are on the verge of serious trouble as the men will not stand this discrimination much longer."[2]

For while the NWLB deliberated, employers and workers were squaring off against one another. The trouble center was the Brill streetcar works, very recently unionized, which had dealt with the initial toolmakers' strike threat in September rather cleverly. It had called a mass meeting of the entire workforce, including unorganized semi-skilled workers and laborers, who outvoted the skilled minority and accepted a pay offer below the IAM's target (possibly because they made more money under a lax bonus system than they could expect if they were paid time rates, as the Machinists demanded). Kelton tried to get the plant committee to call a strike vote among the toolmakers anyway, but only two of its seven members supported him.

Taking advantage of the divisions among its workforce and the union's uncertainty, Brill then circulated a "Loyalty Petition" (a no-strike pledge) that, in the heated conditions of wartime, when dissent was both unpopular and dangerous, every employee signed. Getting their endorsement was all the easier because the first names on the petition were the union's leaders, whom Brill persuaded to abandon office and become company men. According to Kelton, "The day Stewart (*sic*; presumably steward) was taken out on a joy ride with some of the fair sex of the manufacturer's hire, and they roped him and the next day he was taken for a conference in the office with the night Stewart and they both signed their names in ink. You know how good a fellow feels after a joy ride, so the trick worked."[3]

As a result of the company's skillful exploitation of the situation, the IAM's position in the second-biggest plant (after Midvale) where it had established a presence was now precarious. Brill refused the rump of the works committee an audience until ordered by the Ordnance Department and began intimidating the remaining activists, a senior manager promising one that "as long as I live you will not get a job in this shop or in any other shop in Philadelphia if I can possibly stop you from doing so." Brill was the worst of the poisonous labor relations situations from which Kelton hoped the NWLB could rescue his union by a favorable award.[4]

[2]   Kelton to Taft, 27 Nov. 1918, NWLB Case 400 (the Philadelphia Machinists' case).
[3]   Edward Oechsle memorandum, 16 Sept. 1918, in Military Intelligence Division (MID) Correspondence, Box. 3540 F.10634-258 (hereafter Kelton File); Clinton Golden et al. to R. B. Liddell, Superintendent, Brill Corp., 16 Sept. 1918, in FMCS Case 33-2388; Report of Examiners, 9 Oct. 1918, pp. 19–22, in NWLB Case 400; Informant's Report 20 Sept., p. 3, [quote], in Kelton File.
[4]   Report of Examiners, 9 Oct. 1918, p. 22, in NWLB Case 400.

But the Armistice in Europe led to a small war in Philadelphia. On the 15th of November, a scant week after the end of the board's hearings, the War Department began canceling Brill's contracts. The company responded with mass dismissals that were scheduled to affect 1,000 men (about one-fifth of its war-inflated workforce), allowing it to start weeding out surplus and undesirable workers at the rate of over 100 a week. In these circumstances Brill's organized machinists did not feel that they could afford to await the NWLB's ruling. Instead, they had to use immediately whatever waning strength they still possessed. According to their new leaders, thirty-four-year-old Clinton Golden (previously a locomotive fireman, Brotherhood officer, and member of the executive committee of the New York State branch of the Socialist Party, who had only been in the city since 1916) and Harry Shaner (a former printer), "the men struck because they feared or felt that if they didn't strike they would all be discharged," so on the 21st of November they jumped before they were pushed.[5]

There was no love lost between Kelton and the Brill strike leaders, men who had no roots in his city, no background in his craft, and a far more militant style than his own. Golden and Shaner were thorns in Kelton's side that he was happy to see removed. In a slackening labor market, Brill easily replaced the strikers, estimates of whose number varied between 180 and 350, and who were reduced to making angry demands that the NWLB intervene to save their bacon. But, as far as the board's local administrator, John O'Brien, was concerned, they were "really outlaws" who had "projected themselves out of the case . . . [by] violating their agreement . . . to remain at work pending an award." He was encouraged in this indifference to their fate by Kelton, who told him their leaders were "under Union scrutiny and 'stand an excellent chance of being chucked out.' [He] . . . says they are a 'pair of fakers.' "[6]

Employer action therefore temporarily relieved Kelton of some of his intraunion difficulties, but in most respects the return of the manufacturers' freedom to manage that came with the end of hostilities in Europe was a disaster for him. His entire strategy was predicated on the continuing existence of a largely passive union membership, a tight labor market, insistent demand pressures and negligible cost constraints on employers, and an interventionist federal government tieing their hands and paying their bills. One by one the legs were knocked out from under his seat.

[5] O'Brien to E. B. Woods, 16 Jan. 1919, pp. 2–6 and 6 March, pp. 1–2 [quote], in NWLB Case 400. For Golden, see his autobiography in Solon De Leon, ed., *The American Labor Who's Who* (New York, 1925), p. 88.

[6] Thomas R. Brooks, *Clint: A Biography of a Labor Intellectual* (New York, 1978), p. 44, gets the strike's year and outcome wrong; O'Brien to E. B. Woods, 16 Jan. 1919, pp. 2–6 [quote, p. 6]; Shaner to W. Jett Lauck, 4 Mar. 1919; O'Brien to Woods, 6 March, pp. 1–5 [quote, p. 1], 1–2, all in NWLB Case 400.

Kelton obtained his award, for what it was worth, on the 20th of December. It did not affect working hours or union recognition, and only granted retroactive pay increases to those categories of workers that the IAM had managed to organize – in most cases, just toolmakers and first-class machinists. It brought pay levels up to Frankford Arsenal standards, but the Ordnance Department would not allow them to match the Navy Yard/ Emergency Fleet rates. Worse still, the NWLB could only recommend that firms receive extra government money to compensate them for having to pay higher wages than they had expected when they took their contracts, but there was no guarantee that the procurement agencies would comply.[7]

And, of course, making an award was one thing; enforcing it was quite another. Four firms (including Brill) had declined to submit to the board's jurisdiction, although they had presented their cases before it, and it had been unable or unwilling to compel them. The result was that it could only deliver "findings" in their cases, which it considered morally binding but the companies regarded as simple recommendations with no particular force. Also, in theory, as board secretary W. Jett Lauck wrote Standard Roller Bearing, the award was valid for the period of the war, defined as ending only "when the President proclaims peace under a treaty ratified by Senate." But in practice the entire war economy and its labor relations machinery was winding down, and everyone knew it. Firms only had to stall long enough to be able to escape the effect of the board's orders; they did not need to oppose it outright. And it had handed them a nice excuse for prevarication: Saying that first-class machinists should receive the first-class rate was fine, but who was to determine what skill category a man actually belonged to or deserved? There were endless possibilities for haggling and delay.[8]

Kelton could deploy no credible strike threat to resolve these difficulties. And in response to his request for the board to send an administrator to enforce its awards for him, the disintegrating NWLB could only offer the services of one man. John O'Brien had to deal with the tangle of employer–union and intraunion hostilities created by the Brill strike, the extraordinary complexities of job-classification issues in eleven very different and widely scattered plants, and employer resistance masterminded by the MMA. As if these were not enough troubles, after the 11th of February he had to oversee the implementation of Midvale's shop committee system too!

[7] NWLB, Award and Findings in re *Machinists vs. Certain Employers of Philadelphia Pa.*, Docket No. 400, Serial No. A-136, 20 Dec. 1918 in Melvyn Dubofsky, ed., *Research Collections in Labor Studies: The Wilson Administration and American Workers: Papers of the National War Labor Board* (Frederick, 1985), microfilm ed., Reel 5.

[8] O'Brien to Woods, 18 Jan. 1919, pp. 3–4; Lauck to W. D. DeWolfe, 2 Jan. 1919; all in NWLB Case 400.

Understandably, there was little that O'Brien could do. As Kelton complained to his boss, "Seventy-five percent of the firms involved have said they desire to keep quiet until the time is up [i.e., the award, and the board's authority, expired], this seems to be the metal manufacturers association (*sic*) orders as they all have the same answer when their employees request an interview." In the unsettled conditions of America's unregulated reconversion, they had good reason to hold back from "paying war wages on peace profits," and as their volumes of business and employment were both declining they could well afford to wait. Meanwhile, they exploited their strong hand by "striving to duck the award, but [being] careful not to admit it," "covertly trying to skin the award by placing men in lower classes than they belong in," and dismissing union activists under the cover of general reductions-in-force. At MMA member Savage Arms, although not all members of the shop committee were discharged, they were "afraid to press [their] demands lest that action be made a pretext for closing the works," which had shed 80 percent of its employees since the Armistice.[9]

So when O'Brien quit Philadelphia at the end of March, the situation he left behind was, from Kelton's point of view, dire. Nothing good had come of his state-dependent strategy. Midvale had its company union in place, and Standard Roller Bearing had introduced one *at O'Brien's suggestion*. Brill, too, had its own fake "employee representation system," whereby employees were "represented" by their foremen. Only one of the eleven firms covered by the December award was complying with it in full.[10]

What Kelton did have was plenty of unemployed and embittered members – he estimated that there were 15,000 jobless machinists in the city by the end of February, about one-half of the total. He told members denied the NWLB awards that they had expected "to let well enough alone for the present," but patience with his counsels of moderation had run out. Instead they found new leaders in the shape of the "firebrands" Clint Golden (who had gotten work at the new Westinghouse plant) and Harry Shaner. They were soon to be joined by Emil J. [Jack] Lever, a twenty-five-year-old Philadelphia machinist of Russian immigrant origins who was just back from military service in France.[11]

The incumbent local leadership was not without resources for their desperate fight against the "progressives," denouncing them as Wobblies and

---

9   Kelton to Woods, 8 Jan. 1919; O'Brien to Woods, 24 Jan. 1919, p. 4; O'Brien to W. B. Angelo, 27 Jan. 1919, p. 1; O'Brien to Woods, 6 Jan., pp. 2–3, 18 Jan., p. 4, 7 Feb., 15 Feb. 1919; all in NWLB Case 400.

10 On the importance to O'Brien of establishing some kind of representation system, with or without a union, see O'Brien to Woods, 1 Feb. 1919, pp. 1–3 [Standard], in NWLB Case 400; 20 March 1919, pp. 5–6 [Brill] in NWLB Case 129.

11 O'Brien to Woods, 20 Feb. 1919, p. 6, in NWLB Case 129; Kelton to Commissioner Greenawalt 20 March 1919, in FMCS Case 170-6; O'Brien to Woods, 6 March 1919, p. 2, in NWLB Case 400; for Lever, see his autobiography in De Leon, ed., *The American Labor Who's Who*, p. 135, and his "Tribute to a Friend," *Golden Lodge News* 10: 4 (Apr. 1962), p. 3.

One Big Unionists, "members of a soviet" who "constantly advocated their doctrines" and tried "to win the organization over to their views." For their sins, which included trying "to get members to attend meetings" and to gain support for a sympathy strike on behalf of the imprisoned Socialist leader Eugene Debs, Lever and three comrades were expelled from the IAM on the 27th of November. This was a desperate last-ditch attempt by the national president to save his local henchmen's skins before the union elections the next month.[12]

But the attempt failed. Golden was overwhelmingly elected to replace Kelton and try to salvage the union from what he called the "demnition bow-wows." So in 1920, just at the time when the Philadelphia metal trades stood on the brink of an economic precipice, the Machinists finally acquired the imaginative, committed leadership that might have done them some good over the previous few years, but could now do little more than oversee their fragile organization's heroic collapse.[13]

As for the MMA, it too experienced leadership turnover in the immediate postwar period. But there was no drama, no contest, and little immediate change in strategy. Instead, what took place was an orderly process of succession, which the war had delayed and the postwar situation required.

The MMA had depended heavily on the continuity of management provided by a few men active in it since its origins. By the end of 1917, the old-timers were growing tired. Former president Edward Langworthy thought that "it was not fair to continually ask the same men to devote so much of their time to the business of the Association." However, "the present conditions . . . make it necessary to have in charge . . . men of experience in its history." So, under pressure of crisis, and for the common good, the elderly team continued, with the assistance of one relative youngster, the fifty-three-year-old Staunton Bloodgood Peck, Philadelphia manager of materials-handling specialists Link-Belt, who became a councillor. Peck had played an active part in developing the MMA's strategy in the 1916 Eight Hours Crisis, and his company was one of the MMA's largest members, ranking third in 1918 and first in 1921, so he was well qualified for high office.[14]

---

[12] "Labor Unions Oust Reds; Open War on Radicals by Expelling Four Machinists," *Philadelphia Bulletin* 26 Nov. 1919; "Union Ousts Radicals; Action of Machinists' Association Expected to be Followed" and "Machinist Union Reveals Red Plot to Control Labor," Ibid., 27 Nov. 1919. For other radical labor activities in the city in 1919, see Philadelphia War History Committee, *Philadelphia in the World War 1914–1919* (New York, 1922), p. 350.

[13] Golden, "Philadelphia, Pa.," *MMJ* 32 (1920): 637.

[14] ECM 12 Dec. 1917; for Peck, see Hartwell Stafford, ed., *Who's Who in Philadelphia at the Time of the Sesquicentennial* (Philadelphia, 1927), pp. 192, 332; for Link-Belt, see PID-1640 database.

The next December came, and once again the incumbent officers only consented to carry on for another difficult year "with much reluctance" that was not just ritual modesty. They expressed a "strong ... desire" to "be relieved of the burden." President Schwacke "trust[ed] his wishes [to retire] would be respected at the next election, as he had been endeavoring to relinquish some of the many responsibilities which entailed the sacrifice of much of his personal time." Vice President Robert Biddle, proprietor of a middle-sized (c. 120 employees) lighting-fixture plant, offered a more interesting reason for needing to be replaced: He no longer felt up to the job. He believed that the MMA's vice president should be "a man who could be groomed for the higher office later, one of larger interests and who was affiliated with national problems a good deal more than he. ... [T]he time had arrived when new thoughts should be put into our Board." He recognized that he was yesterday's man, not suited to navigate the MMA through the rapids of reconversion or to meet the future's demands.[15]

But they were persuaded to stay in harness through 1919, partly by counterarguments about the especial importance of continuity during a period of turbulence when "the conditions confronting industry were without precedent ... [which] made it particularly desirable for [the] Association ... to have ... officers ... who were in close touch with [its] sentiment and feeling." Stronger even than this reason was the simple fact that they were at least available, and their preferred successors were not. Staunton Peck could not accept the MMA's presidency yet because he was still fully occupied running the whole of Link-Belt while its chief executive was doing his patriotic duty trying to bring order out of chaos at the Emergency Fleet Corporation. Scientific instrument manufacturer Morris Evans Leeds, who was the longest serving council member not already an officeholder, and was thus a logical choice for the vice presidency, was also otherwise engaged (see Chapter 8, Section 3), and therefore withdrew his name from candidacy too. So Biddle, like Schwacke, agreed to soldier on: "until some man could be obtained ... he would do all that he could."[16]

At last, in December 1919, the MMA's leadership began to change; but not all at once. The arguments for continuity were once again voiced – but this time by the incumbents, perhaps less exhausted now that the war emergency was over, and unwilling to be put out to pasture once the prospect became imminent. William Hallowell, MMA treasurer and still district chairman of the NFA, emphasized "the necessity that [officers] be somewhat familiar with the work of the Association so that it may be kept running smoothly and efficiently." Schwacke thought that it was "highly desirable ... to retain ... a sufficient number of representative men ... , so that when other establishments in town are solicited for membership, we

15   ECM 10 and 11 Dec. 1918.
16   Ibid.; MMA-EXEC database.

can name men who carry with them sufficient weight to give confidence." In any event, Peck remained unavailable for the presidency as he still had to spend much time at his firm's midwestern plants, and did not yet feel "sufficiently familiar with the intimate nature of the problems of our association to accept." So Schwacke had to carry on, but Peck changed places with Biddle to prepare himself to take over.[17]

Finally, in December 1920, Peck became president. Schwacke's departure was marked by a massive turnout at his farewell dinner, the biggest that the MMA had ever hosted, in recognition of his services to the membership and "indirectly to the entire metal industries of Philadelphia." During seventeen years on the executive comittee he had "tenaciously . . . contributed . . . to the steadily increasing growth, popularity, efficiency, and high standing of the Association." He remained an active member of the association's council, but he no longer set the tone of its policies.[18]

The MMA that Peck inherited was an organization in good shape. The war and, even more, the immediate postwar periods brought a significant boost in membership and employment – up from 58 companies employing 7,774 men and women in 1915–16, to 66 employing 10,472 in 1918–19 (1,354 in a munitions plant just outside the city limits) and 73 employing 14,702 in 1921–22. This growth reflected a big increase in the average size of MMA firms, which resulted both from fast-rising payrolls among some established members and the recruitment of a couple of new, large, branch plants of national corporations, particularly General Electric, by 1921 the MMA's second-biggest member.[19]

Given that this growth occurred during a period of surging metal trades employment, it needs to be set in context for its relative importance to be properly appreciated. In the Philadelphia secondary metal trades (excluding shipbuilding), the labor force had increased by 37 percent between 1915–16 and 1918–19. Postwar adjustments – the collapse of the munitions business and declines in traditional durable goods production – trimmed the rate of growth to less than 3 percent between 1918–19 and 1921–22; over the whole six-year period, it went up by 41 percent. The MMA grew at only half the rate of the local industry as a whole during the first triennium – by just 18 percent – but more than twenty times more rapidly during the second (by 61 percent), resulting in a 90 percent increase over the six years. Its share of local metal trades employment therefore rose by almost a half, from less than 14 to nearly 19 percent.

The MMA's increasingly impressive performance can be attributed partly to the presence of substantial numbers of dynamic firms among its mem-

[17]   ECM 10 Dec., 11 Nov. 1919.
[18]   ECM 8 Dec. 1920.
[19]   Figures from PID-1640 database.

bership whose growth far exceeded the city's metal trades norm and partly to the solidarity-building industrial relations crises of the war and immediate postwar years. There was a steady flow of new members in every year between 1915 and 1919, with the largest gains during the periods of greatest stress. Gains were partially offset by a very few resignations, but the number of these declined throughout, to almost none in 1919–20 (see Figures 5.1 and 5.3). Prosperity between 1915 and 1920 meant no departures through business failure or retrenchment; inflation reduced the real cost of membership, to about 0.1 percent of the blue-collar wage bill; and the cloud of dangers gave its members good reason to sustain the MMA as their shield, sword, and insurance policy.[20]

Philadelphia metal trades employers' growing commitment to collective action was therefore the direct product of the environment in which the association operated. Crises created an increased demand for the services that the MMA offered; and a growing membership, including firms with rising workforces, meant that its income and reserves boomed at a rate that outpaced both inflation and the costs of service provision. The contrast in fortunes between the MMA and its organized labor opponents as they faced the trials of postwar readjustment could not have been greater.[21]

7.2 THE GOLDEN YEARS, 1920–1923: THE END OF METAL TRADES UNIONISM

When Clinton Golden took over, the Machinists still had a substantial membership in the area's declining shipbuilding industry and in railroad repair shops but were otherwise confined to the "contract shops" (machine repairers and auto mechanics), a few other highly skilled trades (meter mechanics, surgical instrument and dental equipment makers), and installation and maintenance workers in strongly unionized industries (construction, brewing, printing). The IAM hardly impinged on the MMA's territory at all. Even during the war, its presence in the middle-sized and larger machine shops had been tenuous at best; by the end of 1919, it had already been evicted.[22]

But Golden was not discouraged. He behaved as if he believed that he and his members were facing an opportunity, not a disaster. His first step on the road ahead was necessary house-cleaning: "Careful investigations"

[20] Membership costs estimated by dividing average wage (from PHIL1439 database) by annual dues per operative ($1.20).
[21] The NMTA experienced a similar postwar membership surge – see *Synopsis of Proceedings of the 21st Annual Convention* (New York, 1919), pp. 34–35, *22nd* (1920), p. 24, *23rd* (1921), p. 24.
[22] Brooks, *Clint*, pp. 45, 52; Golden, "Philadelphia, Pa." *MMJ* 32 (1920): 636, 754, *MMJ* 35 (1923): 25, 147.

were followed by "fearless exposures" of "the activities and destructive tactics of some former officials of the District," and the IAM was "rid . . . of at least one man whom it could well spare" – the unlamented Bill Kelton, whose unacceptably close relationship with the American Protective League was revealed. Even after the old guard had been purged, continuing vigilance against employers' finks and stool pigeons was required. But a strong defense was only the beginning of Golden's strategy. Most of his efforts were put into building and revitalizing the union. He quickly established a Joint Organizing Committee of the twenty-one locals, and welcomed Jack Lever back into the IAM, as District Organizer.[23]

Golden's whole approach was different from his predecessor's, focusing on developing membership participation through the "active cooperation of real workers" dedicated to building "a solid effective organization capable of expanding and promoting the interests of the rank and file." He immediately established a trade union education program for inexperienced local activists, and set up a weekly labor newspaper, the *Metal Worker*, under Harry Shaner's editorship, to produce an informed membership. He also took further steps designed to turn the IAM into the focus of metal trades unionism throughout the city. The Machinists acquired premises in the heart of the Spring Garden district that were large enough to accommodate the offices of most of the metal trades crafts, including the Boilermakers, Metal Polishers, and Molders. This "Temple" was more than just an administrative headquarters – it was a social center where membership meetings of the various organizations were held; classes, lectures, amateur theatrical performances and movies put on; and workers could drop in to play basketball or pool, get a cheap lunch, buy a radical paper, or borrow a book.[24]

There was a great similarity between Golden's "program of reconstruction" and the "new unionism" of Sidney Hillman's Amalgamated Clothing Workers, both of which aimed to make the union the center around which its members' lives revolved, as a way of meeting their various needs and strengthening their commitment to it. Golden lent the ACW his organization's help as it tried, unsuccessfully, to break into the open shop citadel of the Philadelphia clothing industry. The ACW reciprocated by putting him on its staff from 1921 to 1923 at the same time as he was trying to save his own by then embattled and near-bankrupt union from final defeat.[25]

[23] Golden, "Philadelphia, Pa." *MMJ* 32 (1920): 636–37.
[24] Article II., "Object," in *By-Laws of District Lodge No. 1, IAM* (Philadelphia, 1923), p. 5; Golden, "Philadelphia, Pa." *MMJ* 32 (1920): 636–37, 755. No copies of the Philadelphia *Metal Worker* seem to survive.
[25] Golden, "Philadelphia, Pa." *MMJ* 32 (1920): 754. The *Report* of the General Executive Board and *Proceedings of the 7th Biennial Convention of the Amalgamated*

For the fact is that, although Clint Golden could write boldly about "the workers . . . taking greater interest than in the past in political matters" and the "crystalliz[ing]" of "progressive sentiment in the Central Labor Union," and although he could promise that in the developing struggle against the city's open shop employers "the forces of organized labor will be welded closely together with the result that the master class will get a full taste of the workers' solidarity" – he was actually up against a wall. The withdrawal of the federal government's support for organized labor, the severe postwar depression, and the launching of the employers' "American Plan" anti-union offensive formed the background to his four strenuous years as the Machinists' business agent.[26]

The end of full employment was probably the most important of all of these changes. Employment levels in U.S. metalworking fell by between 30 and 40 percent in 1921 alone; overall, they shrank by more than one-half between the start of the economic contraction in 1920 and its trough in the third quarter of 1921. Philadelphia participated fully in this general deflation, and the metal trades were particularly badly affected: The index of local metal trades employment fell by more than two-thirds, or about one-half if shipbuilding is excluded from the reckoning. Metalworkers' annual average earnings declined from over $1,500 in 1920 to less than $1,200 two years later. These years of mass layoffs, short-time working, and chronic joblessness and destitution wrought havoc in the Philadelphian and national metal trades unions. What was left of their limited war-won gains evaporated more quickly than they had been created in the first place (see Figures 6.1 and 7.1).[27]

Clothing Workers of America, Montreal, 10–15 May 1926, pp. 111–13, review the ACW's problems and limited progress in the Philadelphia market, brilliantly captured in Elden LaMar, *The Clothing Workers in Philadelphia: History of Their Struggles for Union and Security* (Philadelphia, 1940), esp. Chs. 1, 2; "Biographical Sketch of Clinton S. Golden, September 21, 1944," p. 1, in Emil John Lever Papers, Pennsylvania Historical Collections and Labor Archives, Pennsylvania State University Box 4, File 17. J. M. Budish and George Soule, *The New Unionism in the Clothing Industry* (New York, 1920) and Steve Fraser, *Labor Will Rule: Sidney Hillman and the Rise of American Labor* (New York, 1991), esp. pp. 215–23, discuss the ACW's strategy.

[26] Golden, "Philadelphia, Pa." *MMJ* 32 (1920): 754.

[27] Vincent W. Lanfear, *Business Fluctuations and the American Labor Movement 1915–1922* (New York, 1924), p. 60; Willford I. King, *Employment Earnings and Hours in Prosperity and Depression: United States 1920–1922* (New York, 1923), pp. 35, 48, 53–54; Leo Wolman, *Growth of American Trade Unions 1880–1923* (New York, 1924), pp. 39–43; Anne Bezanson et al., "A Study in Labor Mobility by the Industrial Research Department Wharton School of Finance and Commerce, University of Pennsylvania," Supplement to *The Annals* 103 (Sept. 1922): 164–225, at pp. 183–84, 187; Anne Bezanson et al., "Four Years of Labor Mobility: A Study of

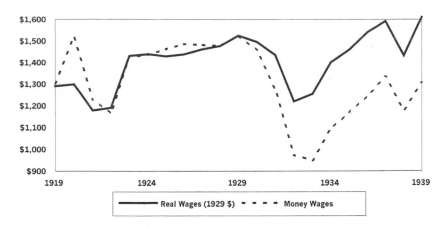

Figure 7.1. The Philadelphia Metal Trades: Average Earnings, 1919–1939. *Note:* Male workers' earnings averaged about 4 percent above the all-employee average, females' about 40 percent below. *Source:* PHIL1439 database (1925 interpolated), adjusted using price index in U.S. Department of Commerce, Bureau of the Census, *Historical Statistics of the United States, Colonial Times to 1970* (Washington, 1976), series E-135.

The Machinists and Molders were incapable of responding successfully to this crisis. In 1921 and 1922, about four-tenths of the IAM's shrinking revenue went on strike benefits alone, as it tried – generally unsuccessfully – to defend its representation rights and its members' pay and working conditions. It ended up impotent and penniless. As for the Molders, in those two bleak years union members received, on average, seventeen and ten weeks of unemployment benefit each, figures two or three times worse than in the very worst prewar year, 1908, up from about three days in 1916–18. The union temporarily abandoned its thirteen-week limit on eligibility for this benefit in a desperate but hopeless attempt to hold on to members. Its financier reported that "the conditions which existed during the period from October, 1920, to April, 1923, have never been duplicated in the history of our organization, nor as a matter of fact, in the history of American industry." The much smaller Pattern Makers' League's experience was similar: Unemployment increased by a factor of almost six between August 1920

Labor Turnover in a Group of Selected Plants in Philadelphia, 1921–1924," Supplement to *The Annals* 119 (May 1925), pp. 1, 7–11; Philip Klein, *The Burden of Unemployment: A Study of Unemployment Relief Measures in Fifteen American Cities, 1921–22* (New York, 1923), pp. 25–26, 35–36, 94, 138–39; PHIL1439 database for money wage changes. In real terms, the decline was much less – 8.5 rather than 23.5 percent.

and December 1921, until almost one-half of the shrinking union's members were out of work.[28]

The first sign of how hard a row Golden had to hoe was the resolution of one of the disputes that he had inherited from Kelton at MMA member Schutte & Koerting, one of the tool shops that had defeated the IAM's eight-hour strikes in 1916–17. S & K was in the peculiar position of being in a sense government property, since it had been seized in 1918, placed under the control of the Alien Property Custodian, the Pennsylvania Democrat (and Hicksite Quaker) A. Mitchell Palmer, and was operated thereafter by his nominees. This was because its proprietor, MMA executive committee member Adalbert Fischer, had been – according to an IAM national officer – "one of the most seditious among all the enemy aliens interned during the period of hostilities." So if there was any firm against which the IAM could expect federal intervention to prove useful, even after the NWLB disappeared, it was surely S & K.[29]

Events of 1919 seemed to bear this out, because in August–September Kelton had been able to get the firm's appointed administrator to reach a satisfactory agreement after a short strike and intervention from the Department of Labor. The firm reduced standard working hours from fifty-five to forty-eight, with no cut in pay (i.e., almost a 15 percent increase on hourly rates), and promised a further increase to close the gap with shipyard rates within a month. However, no such increase was forthcoming, so the men struck again in late November, asking for 20 percent more. To MMA

[28] Mark Perlman, *The Machinists: A New Study in American Trade Unionism* (Cambridge, Mass., 1961), pp. 220–21; "Officers' Reports and Proceedings of the 26th Session of the International Molders Union of North America," Supplement to *IMJ* 59:12 (Dec. 1923): 132–33; "Report of the General President to the Fifteenth Convention," *PMJ* 37:7 (July 1926): 5. NMTA presidents' and commissioners' reports for these years highlight the key struggle in which the MMA's parent organization was involved – an enormous (c. 70 firms and 7,000 strikers), prolonged (four and a half months) IAM strike in the NMTA's Cincinnati stronghold beginning April 1920, which was "by far, the greatest attempt ever made by that organization to unionize and control any large metal trades center" and the largest in which the NMTA had ever been involved. Victory was a matter of "vital importance" and was achieved by the fall of 1920, i.e., even before the recession and large strikes, like Cramp's and that of the railroad shopcrafts, finished off the IAM in 1921–22. It was followed by a peace as profound as that already enjoyed by the MMA. See NMTA, *Synopsis of Proceedings of the 23rd Annual Convention* (New York, 1921), pp. 21, 23–24 [quotes] and *24th Annual Convention* (New York, 1922), pp. 19, 25, 27. What was distinctive about the MMA was not victory and subsequent peace, but the absence of struggle required to obtain it, which points to the singular failure of metal trades unionism in wartime Philadelphia.

[29] Robert Fechner (General Executive Board member, IAM) to William B. Wilson, 26 Aug. 1920, in FMCS Case 170-950. For Fischer's crime, see Chapter 6, Section 4; for Palmer, see Stanley Coben, *A. Mitchell Palmer: Politician* (New York, 1963).

Secretary Sparks, this, the only Machinists' strike that he had to deal with that year, proved "the oft-repeated assertion, that where men are under the domination of unscrupulous leaders, who never are satisfied, conceding to demands is simply a stepping stone to further drastic demands until a break occurs, and the Company proceeds to 'clean house.' " Sparks had inside knowledge that the workforce was divided and correctly anticipated an early return to work.[30]

The strike collapsed, two activists were not re-hired, and the remaining IAM members at S & K seethed with discontent. Golden found himself under pressure from the Department of Labor conciliators on the case to "hold the men in line a little longer" – which he did by promising them a settlement soon, from February until October 1920 – although the conciliators privately believed that the situation was actually hopeless. No settlement could be reached. The Board of Directors played hard to get, and Palmer was unable – or unwilling – to compel them to negotiate.[31]

It turned out that the appointed administrators, "men of large and multiplied financial interests, closely connected with the Manufacturers' Club, the Union League, Metal Trades Association (*sic*) and in a degree influenced by their attitude on many matters," had other plans. They included the president of a prominent local bank, the vice president of the local Federal Reserve Board, and Palmer's assistant general counsel himself, whose public responsibilities and private interests were evidently a little confused. The frustrated conciliator believed that these "active and influential Republicans . . . [did] not wish an increased or high wage rate established." The Wilson administration had turned the plant over to men who, on election night 1916, had joined a march from the Union League up Broad Street singing that they were going to "Hang Woodrow Wilson to a sour apple tree," and who by midsummer 1920 included one of the leaders of Philadelphia's open shop movement. They were "one of the worst crowd (*sic*) of 'autocrats' we have ever had to deal with." The last thing they wished to see was the federal government's power used to snatch a victory for the IAM from the jaws of defeat, thereby setting a bad example and increasing the operating costs of a company that would soon be back in the private sector, and in which they would hold a stake.[32]

30 Kelton to William B. Wilson, 10 Sept. 1919, and Preliminary and Final Report of Conciliation Commissioner Jno. J. S. Rodgers, 15 Sept. 1919, in FMCS Case 170-788; SEC 1919, pp. 8–9.
31 William C. Liller to Hugh L. Kerwin, 12 Feb. 1920; 28 Aug. Conciliator Fury to Director of Conciliation, 28 Aug. 1920; Golden to Kerwin, 26 Oct. 1920 – all in FMCS Case 170-950.
32 Liller to Kerwin, 12 Feb. 1920, p. 2 and crossed out "Confidential Notes"; Calwell to Kerwin, 20 Feb. 1920; Liller to Kerwin, 7 Apr. 1920, pp. 2–3; Fechner to Wilson, 26 Aug. 1920; all in FMCS Case 170-950; *Proceedings of the Business Revival Luncheon of Philadelphia Industrial and Business Leaders, September 13, 1921*, p. 29, identifies the "autocrats" among the leaders of the Open Shop movement.

And they had time on their side: As the economy slid in the summer of 1920, and the Wilson administration visibly decomposed, the S & K machinists could not risk a strike. Instead they found themselves handed back to the tender mercies of the "particularly vicious" Adalbert Fischer, who proceeded to resume control of his plant with the administrators' full cooperation and without having had to reach the settlement that his men had long been promised.[33]

The Schutte & Koerting case showed that the writing on the wall spelled disaster. Philadelphia employers were gearing up for battle, emboldened by the rising tide of unemployment that set in with the severe recession. Workers and unions could not resist the pay cuts that businessmen felt they had to have. In May the Philadelphia Chamber of Commerce (PCC) established an Industrial Relations Committee, on which the metal trades were well represented. The MMA supported it with a $500 donation, the backing of many individual members, and close cooperation in its first battles to make Philadelphia once again a citadel of the Open Shop. They "publicly announced that they intended to bring pressure upon all bankers to refuse credit to employers doing business with organized labor or conducting a union shop," and worked more quietly through the local Iron League to persuade major construction firms to resist the city's building trades, the hard core of the local labor movement.[34]

In November the Democrats crashed to defeat in the national elections, and Philadelphia businessmen celebrated the impending emasculation of those remaining federal agencies that had stood in the way of the developing American Plan crusade. The MMA wired the incoming President Harding asking for "the appointment of a Secretary of Labor who by reason of experience and understanding shall be qualified to represent all labor and not merely organized labor." And on 1 December, PCC Industrial Relations Committee member Harry Mull, president of Cramp's, gave his 8,000 men a month's notice that the company was unilaterally terminating all of the collective agreements that it had been forced to sign over the previous five years by their unions and the

[33] Fechner to Wilson, 26 Aug. 1920 in FMCS Case 170-950. Schutte & Koerting is still (September 1999) in business, and still an MEA member – see http://www.s-k.com

[34] ECM 13 July 1920; *Annual Report of the Board of Directors of the Philadelphia Chamber of Commerce for the Year 1920*, pp. 47–48; Golden, "Philadelphia, Pa.," *MMJ* 32 (1920): 754; for the origins of the Iron League, see ECM 8 July and Sidney Fine, *'Without Blare of Trumpets': Walter Drew, the National Erectors' Association, and the Open Shop Movement, 1903–1957* (Ann Arbor, 1995), pp. 188–89. For the "American Plan" itself, Robert W. Dunn's *The Americanization of Labor: The Employers' Offensive Against the Trade Unions* (New York, 1927), esp. Chs. 1–5, has scarcely been bettered.

federal government, and would proceed to reestablish the *status quo ante bellum*.[35]

The great Cramp Shipyard strike of 1920–21 was a response to this declaration of war. Cramp's was in a strong position – about 1,500 of its men were already laid off because of the slowing down of new naval orders, and there was massive unemployment in the metal trades locally and nationally of which it could take advantage. But it was also faced with a real – and, as it turned out, insuperable – problem of corporate survival that inspired its anti-labor offensive. It was overwhelmingly dependent on naval contracts and had grown fat during the war on this business. It had caved in to every one of the 122 recorded strikes of its sixteen skilled crafts since 1916; it had lost control of discipline, time-keeping, payment systems, and production standards; its labor costs had increased by 178 percent; and none of that had mattered, because it had still been massively profitable, declaring for example a 150 percent stock dividend in 1920. But it could not look forward to enough naval contracts to utilize its expanded capacity, and the firm's new owners (Averell Harriman's American Ship and Commerce Corporation) had an – as it turned out, impracticable – plan to enter the wholly different business of merchant shipbuilding. To do so in a glutted market entailed an attack on labor costs, which required breaking with the unions and breaking free of their job controls.[36]

Cramp's ultimatum was greeted with an unauthorized walkout of hundreds of men, even before its deadline. The company responded by the summary dismissal of union committeemen, and more and more crafts joined the strike movement in the latter part of January, until only the patternmakers were still working. The strike was not pre-authorized by the fifteen national unions involved: It was a local, spontaneous affair and was directed by "a central strike committee, composed of one worker actually on strike from each one of the trades involved. . . . This committee has sole control over the actoins (*sic*) of the various groups. . . . Business agents and other salaried officers of the various organizations are permit-

[35] ECM 22 Dec. 1920; C. S. Golden, "The Strike at Wm. Cramp & Sons' Ship and Engine Co., Philadelphia, Pa.," *MMJ* 33 (1921): 264–65; "Cramp's Break Off All Relation With Labor Federation," *Public Ledger* (hereafter *PL*) 16 Jan. 1921, pp. 1, 13, for Mull's ultimatum. Thomas R. Heinrich, *Ships for the Seven Seas: Philadelphia Shipbuilding in the Age of Industrial Capitalism* (Baltimore, 1997), pp. 206–09, complements the following account.

[36] Commissioners Charles J. Fury and John A. Moffitt to Director of Conciliation, 16 March 1921, p. 3, in FMCS Case 170-1345; Golden, "Strike at Wm. Cramp," p. 264; Exhibit A listing 122 strikes since 1916, with Fury and Moffitt letter; William Cramp & Sons Ship & Engine Building Co., *Cramp's Shipyard War Activities* (Philadelphia, 1919), p. 19; George McCormick to Secretary of Labor Davis, 24 March 1921, p. 1, in FMCS Case 170-1345; Rudy Abramson, *Spanning the Century: The Life of W. Averell Harriman, 1891–1986* (New York, 1992), pp. 123–38.

ted a voice but no vote in the committee meetings." Rank-and-file, quasi-industrial unionism had at last come to Philadelphia, but not in the best of circumstances.[37]

Although they had not initiated it, the national unions backed the strike with official endorsements, money, and requests for Department of Labor intervention. The conciliators arrived on the scene in late January and immediately reached the conclusion that the situation was "practically hopeless." Nothing that would happen over the next eight months, until the Machinists finally voted to end their strike, rendered that initial assessment inaccurate. Within a month Mull had replaced the strikers, whom he stigmatized as "almost without exception of that body of employes who drifted to our shipyard in an effort to evade military service during the war." He could rely on executives and foremen and on "men who have been with the shipyard for many years . . . [who] have saved their money and many of [whom] own the homes in which they live." With these local loyalists and out-of-towners accommodated at the yard he could keep the business running until hell froze over. "[A]s far as I am concerned, this matter is finished. I am through with the unions and I shall let matters rest just as they are." It was a matter of basic principle as far as he was concerned: "No concern can long endure if its employes (*sic*) attempt to serve two masters."[38]

The strike was exceptionally large and violent. Huge crowds of strikers and their sympathizers assembled on the streets of Kensington, picketing the yard closely. When a massive police presence made that impossible, they shifted their attention to streetcar transfer points far from the yard itself, where "scabs" could be assaulted with less danger and difficulty; and "entertaining parties" visited the homes of strike-breakers at night "to knock Hell out of every one they catch," daub their front doors, and break their windows. The whole northeast of the city was in a state of near civil war, as the Cramp's strike came on top of bloody and bitter textile workers' strikes that were already dividing the same neighborhoods. In the resulting disorder, Cramp's private police shot one striker dead and injured many more.[39]

[37] Golden, "Strike at Wm. Cramp," p. 264.
[38] C. S. Golden, "The Cramp Strike – Final Chapter," *MMJ* 33 (1921): 909–10, for chronology; James O'Connell (president, Metal Trades Dept., AFL) to Hugh L. Kerwin, n.d., Preliminary Report of Commissioner of Conciliation Charles J. Fury, 21 Jan. 1921, in FMCS Case 170-1345; "Cramp's Will Not Arbitrate Strike, Says Plant Head," *PL* 21 Feb. 1921, pp. 1, 4; "Rotan Will Prosecute Rioters," *PL* 19 Feb. 1921, p. 1; "Police Quell Hot Riot of Shipyard Strikers," *Philadelphia Record* 20 Jan. 1921, pp. 1–2; Mull statement of 14 Feb. in Fury and Moffitt to Director of Conciliation, 16 March 1921, p. 2.
[39] "Cramp Workmen Beaten in Streets," *PL* 21 Jan. 1921; "1000 Police Sent to Enforce Order in Strike District," *PL* 11 Feb. 1921; "Wives of Cramp's Workers Living in Fear and Worry," *PL* 19 Feb. 1921, pp. 1, 6; "Beaten Workers Tell of Brutality in

The Cramp strike remained remarkably solid. About 4,000 men had walked out in December and January; of these, only 25 had returned to work by the 11th of March (apart from the Molders, who were ordered back by their business agent, James Cronin, a fortnight after they had joined the walkout). They were, as Golden put it, "all standing shoulder to shoulder with no other thought except victory and the right to retain the meager measure of industrial democracy won as a result of organization during the war." They had a strong sense of the rightness of their cause: On their marches and parades their flags and banners proclaimed that "we are good Americans," and their supporters repeatedly referred to their contributions to the late war effort as justification for their right to resist the return of industrial autocracy.[40]

Golden was deeply committed to the strike, as befitted the local leader of the second-largest group of workers involved (after the Boilermakers). He became bitter against the "plute" or "prostitute press" for its misreporting of the strike, against Philadelphia capitalists for their countersolidarity, against "the murderous tactics of the police" and the "Cossacks" (state troopers). He was also angry with the Harding administration, whose Navy Department was still Cramp's all-important customer. The administration was "apparently fearful lest they invite upon themselves the wrath of the sponsors and supporters of the nation wide, open shop campaign . . . [and] willing to bow its head and take its commands from the Organized Masters of Industry."[41]

But Golden, revolutionary optimist that he was, could see a silver lining to this cloud of troubles – the educative effect of experience on the workers affected. "The class lines were never so apparent as at the present time," and "Slowly but surely they are awaking to a realization that the powers of press, state and all government are being controlled by their enemies and that sooner or later they must combine their forces and forever abolish a system that makes the workers the victims of the insatiable lust for profits of a small minority."[42]

Strike," *PL* 20 Feb. 1921, pp. 1, 5; "400 Cops Battle Strikers in Trolley Car Attack; 200 Women, With Babies in Arms, Join Melee," *Philadelphia North American* 8 March 1921, pp. 1–2; "City-Wide Plot to Maim Cramp's Workers Charged," *PL* 21 Apr. 1921; Mrs. M. Klauser (wife of a strike-breaking molder) to Secretary Davis, 19 March 1921, pp. 2–3, in FMCS Case 170-1345; Philip Scranton, *Figured Tapestry: Production, Markets, and Power in Philadelphia Textiles, 1885–1941* (New York, 1989), pp. 359–66; Heinrich, *Ships for the Seven Seas,* pp. 207–08.

[40] Commissioners Fury and Moffitt to Director of Conciliation, 11 March 1921, pp. 1–2; Golden, "Cramp Strike – Final Chapter," p. 910; Golden, "Strike at Wm. Cramp & Sons," p. 264; "400 Cops Battle Strikers," p. 1; McCormick to Davis, p. 4, and Mrs. T. Nicholson to Secretary Davis, 18 Apr. 1921, both in FMCS Case 170-1345.

[41] Golden, "Gigantic Strike of Allied Crafts at Cramp's Shipyard Still On," *MMJ* 33 (1921): 420; Golden, "The Strike at Cramp's Shipyard," Ibid., p. 500.

[42] Golden, "The Strike at Wm. Cramp & Sons' Ship and Engine Co., Philadelphia, Pa.," *MMJ* 33 (1921): 265; Golden, "The Strike at Cramp's Shipyard," Ibid., p. 500.

Golden concentrated his attention on his own members, most of whom were striking or unemployed. He prepared mailing lists and sent them educational literature at least twice a month. The strikers' commitment was further maintained by daily meetings and by a relief effort that ended up costing almost $174,000. Most of the money came from the national union, but much was gathered locally by "Minstrel shows, block parties, river excursions, drawing contests, dances and entertainments," which raised cash and the strikers' spirits at the same time. A pioneering Woman's Auxiliary was set up to make sure that the "wives, mothers and women folks" understood the issues and supported the men of their community. The auxiliary played an important role on mass pickets, too, as the police did not use their firearms when women "with babies in arms" were present.[43]

The strikers began, out of necessity, to create their own separate cooperative economy. They and their families were sustained by the organization of a commissary system that was capable of supplying food to over 1,000 households a week, much of it directly purchased from local farmer members of the All American Cooperative Commission. The hostility of local bankers to the strikers (they would not even cash union checks) also led to the formation of a cooperative Producers and Consumers Bank, under organized labor control. Golden was therefore hopeful that the strike was bearing valuable fruit of lasting significance, whatever its attendant hardships: "The talent for administering relief, legal aid, commissaries, publicity, etc., that has developed during this gigantic strike is ample proof that the workers have all the potential abilities to successfully manage their business once they are given an opportunity for expression."[44]

He laid plans to make the commissaries "permanent institutions on a cooperative basis when their service as a strike relief agency is completed," and to establish "a course of lectures and entertainment for the coming fall and winter months," to meet his unemployed members' zeal for knowledge. "If a better understanding of the labor movement and the present industrial system develops as a result of the dissemination of constructive information regarding it during this period of industrial stagnation, then all the suffering and sacrifices being made will not have been in vain."[45]

Golden was clearly writing partly to maintain his own and his readers' morale, but there were real signs of a new spirit among Philadelphia's workers and labor movement, which surprised even their more radical

---

[43] Golden, "Philadelphia, Pa.," *MMJ* 33 (1921): 594; Golden, "The Present Status of the Cramp's Strike," p. 825; Golden, "Cramp Strike – Final Chapter," pp. 909–10; Golden, "Strike at Cramp's Shipyard," pp. 500–01; "400 Cops Battle Strikers."

[44] Golden, "The Cramp Strike and the Commissary," *MMJ* 33 (1921): 649–51 [quote from p. 651]; "Philadelphia, Pa.," Ibid., p. 823; "The Cramp's Strike After Seven Months," Ibid., p. 772; "Philadelphia, Pa.," Ibid., p. 771.

[45] Golden, "Philadelphia, PA.," *MMJ* 33 (1921): 771.

leaders. "Few of us imagined that any group of workers in this section had within it the potential leaders, managers, executives or even the determined thousands of the rank and file that this strike has developed." The building trades, printing trades, longshoremen, and textile workers all mounted huge strikes against wage reductions and attempts to break their unions, and at the same time gave the Cramp's strikers what help they could. Labor Day saw the biggest workers' demonstration that the city had ever witnessed, with 25,000 marchers, a third of them from the metal trades. Harsh policing by what was supposed to be a "reform" administration – which had indeed attempted to settle the strike through early mediation by Morris Ll. Cooke – "aroused the workers of the city to the necessity of united workers political action." This led to the launching of a local Labor Party that gathered about 32,000 votes for its candidates in the fall elections, despite the concerted refusal of the Philadelphia press even to report its existence. Golden concluded that "When the happenings of the past year are reviewed one cannot help but feel that while we may have been groping about in the past without aims or an objective, the workers are now thinking and acting along constructive lines, and that a new scheme of things is being developed within the shell of the old."[46]

The strike clearly had a great effect on Golden himself, convincing him, among other things, that "The chief lesson to be had from these . . . struggles with an organized master class is the fact that there is not the degree of unity and cohesion essential for success in the present form of craft organization. . . . [W]e find the most damnable crimes committed against the workers; in some instances by their own leaders, and all in the holy name of autonomy." He became an advocate of industrial unionism, a movement whose potential he saw reflected in the Cramp's dispute and which he attempted to extend by establishing a "really effective Metal Trades Council" in Philadelphia, pending agreement to craft amalgamation at the national level by the "labor faking delegates of other metal trades unions."[47]

However, despite the quality of the strikers' leadership, their own solidarity, and the substantial community support they enjoyed, they could not prevail. Cramp's was powerful and determined; it enjoyed the full support of the local press, the city administration, and the forces of order; and it was able to recruit sufficient strike-breakers from among its established workforce and the ranks of the unemployed.

Nor could the strikers rely on the federal government to redress the balance. Secretary of Labor James J. "Puddler Jim" Davis and his concil-

---

[46]   Golden, "Cramp's Strike After Seven Months," p. 772; Golden, "Philadelphia, Pa.," *MMJ* 33 (1921): 823–24, 989 [quotes]; for Cooke's mediation atttempt, see "Conciliator Named in Shipyard Dispute" and "Cramps' Will Not Arbitrate Strike, Says Plant Head," *PL* 19 Jan., 21 Feb. 1921.

[47]   Golden, "Philadelphia, Pa.," pp. 770, 823.

iators attempted to speed the end of the strike soon after the Harding administration assumed power. He could not get the firm to accept a form of union recognition, though he tried. And the best return-to-work scheme he could negotiate with Cramp's was rejected by the strikers, as it would have given the company a free hand to discriminate against activists and absolutely excluded those convicted of strike-related crimes. The strikers' objective was for all to be taken back, which was impossible, because the company simply did not need all of its former employees. It needed even fewer after the summer of 1921, when naval disarmament plans and general retrenchment resulted in a cutting of naval appropriations, and Cramp's was ordered to cease work on some of the warships that it was building, and to slow down completion of the rest. The company even had to lay off 1,000 of its loyal "scabs" and impose a pay cut on those it kept on in the aftermath of that blow, from which it would in due course succumb.[48]

The national officers of the metal trades unions, who had supplied the bulk of the strike funds, saw that Cramp's was a lost cause. Heavy unemployment and a mass of other failing strikes meant that their revenues were severely depleted. So they pulled the plug on their Philadelphia members in late August; and a fortnight after receiving their last strike pay, the Machinists voted to go back to work, if they could. They had done everything right, and they had lost utterly.[49]

Golden had to make the best of a bad job and refocus his and his members' energies on self-help activities – soup kitchens, unemployment relief, and a Tenants' Protective Association to fight evictions. His program for 1922 was a masterpiece of the power of positive thinking:

Even though industrial conditions may be such that we cannot go out and organize on a large scale, we can assist in developing the intelligence of those tried and true members who have stuck to the organization through thick and thin, and devise ways and means of not only getting back what we have lost in the frequent attacks of the masters of industry, but to make still further progress towards industrial freedom and justice in the future.[50]

But in fact he had to cope with a period of more than eighteen months, during which over three-quarters of his declining membership were unem-

---

[48]   Transcript of telephone conversation between Secretary Davis and J. H. Mull, 8 Apr. 1921, and attached return-to-work offer; Harry G. Murray (Pres.) and Edward Keenan (Sec.), Delaware River Ship Builders Council, A. F. of L. Metal Trades Department, to Davis, 11 Apr. 1921; counterproposal with Jas. O'Connell (Pres., Metal Trades Department) to Davis, 12 Apr. 1921; Golden, "Gigantic Strike of Allied Crafts," pp. 420–21; Davis to John W. Ford, 16 June 1921; Fury and Moffitt to Director of Conciliation, 19 July 1921 – all in FMCS Case 170-1345.

[49]   Golden, "Present Status of the Cramp's Strike," p. 825; Golden, "Cramp Strike – Final Chapter," pp. 909–10.

[50]   Golden, "Philadelphia, Pa.," *MMJ* 33 (1921): 895, 34 (1922): 42 [quote].

ployed and activists were systematically blacklisted, while his union, locally and nationally, was dealt the *coup de grâce* through the massive, bitter railroad shopcrafts strike. By the start of 1923, those of Golden's members who remained at work had had to accept steep wage reductions, even in the limited job shop territory where their union was still recognized. In the rest of the city's machine shops, nonunion skilled men took the lower rates set by the MMA. The Machinists' strongest local had lost about 85 percent of its members since 1920, and overall, by the end of 1924, fewer than 4 percent of Philadelphia machinists were left in the IAM.[51]

By that time Golden was long gone: The union could no longer afford to pay his salary after 1923. But the Labor College that was the outcome of his commitment to workers' education lived on, sustained by the Clothing and Textile Workers as a vital institution in the city's proletarian culture and a nucleus around which surviving radicals could gather. As for Golden, he had pursued that commitment on an errand into the wilderness, following Jack Lever to Brookwood Labor College in Katonah, just north of New York. There and in the ACW's service he would eke out a living for the rest of the decade until, in the 1930s, the Philadelphia metalworkers' premature "dress rehearsal for the New Deal" could be restaged by a larger, more experienced and enthusiastic cast before a more receptive public and supportive government, with Golden and Lever, by then with the Steel Workers Organizing Committee of the CIO, once again offering direction.[52]

Golden's departure from the scene was an honorable one, but not so that of James Cronin, boss of the Molders. Local 15's strength ebbed steadily after 1919. The first brush between it and the MMA occurred in November of that year, when Cronin tried to extend his organization's reach beyond the city limits to protect its position in Philadelphia jobbing shops against nonunion competition from nearby. This was increasingly serious because of wartime industrial development in the hinterland and the coming of motor-truck transportation. The MMA helped the first firm that the IMU targeted, sending strike-breakers from the Labor Bureau even though the company was not a member. The strike failed quickly, and the

[51] Golden, "Philadelphia, Pa.," *MMJ* 35 (1923) 25, 147; Colin Davis, *Power at Odds: The National Railroad Shopmen's Strike* (Urbana, 1997); SEC 1922, p. 6; SEC 1924, p. 1.
[52] Golden, "Philadelphia, Pa.," *MMJ* 33 (1921): 896; Brooks, *Clint*, pp. 61, 64; Richard J. Altenbaugh, *Education for Struggle: The American Labor Colleges of the 1920s and 1930s* (Philadelphia, 1990), on Brookwood; Steve Fraser, "Dress Rehearsal for the New Deal: Shop Floor Insurgents, Political Elites and Industrial Democracy in the Amalgamated Clothing Workers," in Michael H. Frisch and Daniel J. Walkowitz, eds., *Working Class America* (Urbana, 1983), 212–55, for the phrase, which of course meant something very different in the garment trades context.

union-building movement collapsed, not to be revived for almost twenty years.[53]

Thereafter, Local 15 went into steep decline, losing recognition at five foundries that went over to the open shop cause and – because of severe unemployment – two-thirds of its dues-paying members by the end of 1922. The MMA assisted with this process whenever possible, providing replacement labor for members who discharged union molders for organizing during working hours, or who imposed wage reductions and were met with the predictable short and unsuccessful strikes. All of this time President Peck did his damnedest to persuade the Foundrymen's Club to abandon their collective contract with Local 15, which had turned into its protection, not theirs, and which was the one surviving bad example of relatively harmonious labor–management relations in the city's metal trades.[54]

However, there were still limits beyond which the MMA's anti-Molder campaign would not go. In January 1921 the innocuously (and misleadingly) named "Bureau of Industrial Research" of New York City made a proposal "for improving the situation as it now exists in the Union foundries," which the MMA executive committee rejected with contempt. But some members were interested in the assistance that the bureau could offer, so ex-President Justus Schwacke and Secretary Sparks both raised the issue again once the economy, and the Molders, began to revive. Finally, in February 1923, acceptance of the bureau's services was decisively rejected: "While some of the gengtlemen (*sic*) thought they would like to have such information it was the unanimous opinion of those present that they condemned the source as well as the method by which this information might be obtained."[55]

Just what was the bureau offering? All was revealed when its officers fell out and their quarrel spilled over into the New York courts, where the IMU discovered that "The business of this agency was the selling of service to employers, and conveying to [them] the information that they were in the confidence of people connected with labor organizations, and that with such knowledge they were able to . . . enforce reductions in wages, prevent increases in wages and prevent or handicap labor organizations from getting better conditions for their members."[56]

The bureau was exceptionally well placed to serve Philadelphia foundrymen, because its agent since at least 1921 had been none other than James

---

[53] SEC 1919, p. 8.
[54] SEC 1922, p. 5; ECM 11 May 1920; SEC 1921 p. 10; ECM 18 Oct. 1921, 19 Jan. and 22 May 1923.
[55] ECM 25 Jan., 18 Oct. 1921, 27 Feb. 1923.
[56] "The Special Trial Committee" in *Officers' Reports and Proceedings of the 26th Session of the IMU*, p. 271. Cronin's motive is unclear; one could speculate that the decline in union membership would have reduced his personal income so he had to look to alternative sources.

Cronin himself! The Molders' early desertion of the Cramp's strike, and Cronin's uncharacteristically pessimistic announcement in September 1921 that they had no choice but to accept whatever wage reductions the local foundrymen imposed, took on a new meaning. Cronin himself was expelled from the IMU in September 1923, but the damage that his self-seeking treachery had caused would not begin to be undone for at least a decade. As Sparks reported in December, Local 15 had "lost about 40 percent of its membership [since 1920], but its weakness today is probably more in the loss of morale" resulting from the "gross disloyalty" of its leader. The MMA exploited the situation to the full, finally persuading the jobbing shops in the Foundrymen's Club to abandon their ten-year-old collective contract with the IMU and destroying the last vestiges of formal union recognition in the industry that had once been the center of craft union power. The task had taken twenty years, but now, at last, it was complete.[57]

Of course, the MMA and its members were damaged by the recession, too. But for them it was not all bad news. On the one hand, it removed all but the last traces of labor strength and led to "a more reasonable attitude on the part of the mechanic," that is, desperation for employment on almost any terms as turnover plummeted and wage rates and hours were both cut by over a fifth, with scarcely a strike to hinder the deflation. The war and postwar periods had seen the wage bill swallow up an ever-growing share of the Philadelphia metal trades' sales dollar. Now the process was reversed, and companies that survived the recession were in a position to rebuild efficiency and profitability (see Figure 7.2). On the other hand, it damaged the MMA's finances. Revenues declined by a quarter between 1920 and 1921; reported operatives fell by 38 percent between March and December 1921 alone. The association remained financially weak even after the return of prosperity in 1922–23, because members emerged from the recession with drastically slimmed workforces, which translated directly into lower dues payments. Total employment in the sixty-six companies that were members in both 1921 and 1924 declined by about a quarter between those two survey dates. Until new recruits could be won, the MMA therefore found itself with an income that did not cover its expenses.[58]

Still, compared with its shattered opponents, the MMA's position was enviably strong. By 1923 the association was entering the sunlit uplands of the Republican New Era, and had finally shaken itself free of the travails of labor insurgency, government intervention, and excessively high employment that had disturbed it from 1915 through 1919, with modest aftershocks of decreasing intensity over the next four years. As Sparks reported with delight, there had been "Not a strike in the shops of any

---

[57] ECM 27 Sept. 1921; SEC 1923, p. 11.
[58] SEC 1921, pp. 4, 6, 8 [quote]; SEC 1931, p. 1; PHIL1439 database and Figure 6.2; ECM 9 March, 14 Dec., 1921; PID-1640 database.

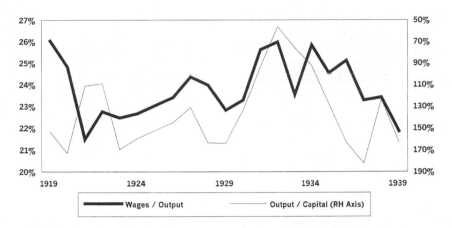

Figure 7.2. Operating Ratios in the Philadelphia Metal Trades, 1919–1939. *Note:* The ratio of output to capital is displayed using an inverted scale because the ideal situation, from a business perspective, is a low ratio of wage costs to product value, and a high ratio of product value to capitalization, so that the closer both of these measures were to the horizontal axis, the better. The best interwar years were 1923–25, 1928–29, 1936–37, and of course 1939. *Source:* PHIL1439 database.

of our members during the year – a record we've made before and increasingly frequently lately, but never with so large a membership." Between 1920 and 1924 only nine member firms – five of them the foundries reestablishing open shop conditions – experienced strikes; 97 percent of the MMA's "hands" did not launch a single overt collective challenge to their employers.[59]

The MMA had emerged from the war and its aftermath with its labor relations strategy remarkably intact; unionism in the Philadelphia metal trades had been abandoned by the federal government, weakened by its own internal divisions, then crushed by determined employer onslaughts, and finished off by massive unemployment. Now prosperity was returning, but labor was in a worse position to do anything to take advantage of it than at any time since 1900.[60]

7.3 THE CHANGING OF THE GUARD

The MMA had led a relatively untroubled existence through the years during which "Normalcy" returned to the Philadelphia metal trades. There was enough of a sense of crisis to build membership commitment to the organization and boost recruitment, but most of the decisive action took

[59] SEC 1923, p. 11.
[60] SEC 1924, p. 1.

place elsewhere – in other cities or, within Philadelphia, in confrontations between labor and the giant open shops. As a result, the MMA had not had to pay much of a price for victory. But the very conditions that under-pinned its members' apparent security *vis-à-vis* their workers contained within them challenges to its future, not just to its finances.

First, the postwar shakeout produced dramatic changes within the city's metal-manufacturing community. The Philadelphia metal-working indus-tries that emerged from the war, and prospered until the recession, included most of the same firms, or the same kinds of firms, that had dominated the sector since at least the outset of this study. At the 1918 state industrial census, Baldwin Locomotive still stood head and shoulders above the rest of the metal-manufacturing community, employing on its old city-center site almost twice as many workers (16,500) as all 127 machine builders, whose 8,290 employees made them the second most important local metal indus-try. Three years later Baldwin's workforce had more than halved, and the decline was irreversible. By mid-decade Baldwin had evacuated its vast red-brick works, which stood empty as a symbol of the power of technologi-cal change and industrial restructuring. By then Cramp's Shipyard was also closed, apart from an engineering department with a few hundred workers that was converted to manufacturing hydroelectric turbines. Weeds grew in the empty acres that had once launched so many ships and employed thou-sands of men. At Midvale, c. 11,000 employees were laid off between the 1918 peak and 1922 trough, leaving only about 1,000 old-timers. By June 1921, the company was "practically down and out." Midvale survived, in shrunken form, regaining its independence of the shortlived steel-to-arma-ments combine to which it had lent its famous name, but it would take another war to rebuild its labor force to pre-1917 levels. Brill, too, clung on, but only as a division of a national corporation. Niles-Bement-Pond's Bement-Miles Works, on the other hand, was rationalized out of existence as its cash-strapped parent tried to stem massive losses. Traditional indus-trial landmarks were collapsing. Adding insult to injury, urban renewal – the building of the Parkway and the Ben Franklin Bridge – devastated some of Philadelphia's old metal-working neighborhoods, removing all traces of the plants that had supported them from a cityscape being reshaped for the automobile.[61]

Massive forces of destruction were therefore on the loose in the Philadel-

---

[61]   PID-1640 database; Philip Scranton and Walter Licht, *Work Sights: Industrial Philadelphia, 1890–1950* (Philadelphia, 1986), pp. 198 [Baldwin], 235 [Cramp]; "Your Picture in the Safety Bulletin" and "Present Industrial Conditions," *Midvale Safety Bulletin* 9:9 (Sept. 1922): 5 and 8:6 (June 1921): 3 [quote]; Sylvester K. Stevens, *Pennsylvania: Titan of Industry* (New York, 1948), Vol. 2, pp. 2–5 [Brill]; Cecil E. Fraser and George F. Doriot, *Analyzing Our Industries* (New York, 1932), pp. 185, 207 [N-B-P] – return on capital was minus 14.6 percent in 1921 and –19.9 percent in 1922.

phia metal trades in the postwar years. Giant companies identified with the first industrial revolution of steam and iron, and many of their smaller suppliers, were being taken out. There was a net loss of over 9,000 metalworking jobs between the 1921 and 1924 censuses, almost 7,800 more disappeared by 1927, and another 2,300 by 1930 – altogether, a near 24 percent decline in sectoral employment in nine years, more severe in the old skilled trades. Between the 1920 and 1930 federal censuses, the city registered a 27 percent decline in the number of metal polishers and falls of 28 percent for molders, 29 percent for their brother patternmakers, 33 percent for machinists, 46 percent for blacksmiths, and 55 percent for boilermakers – the latter two crafts were devastated by the disappearance of Baldwin and Cramp.[62]

The catastrophic short-term unemployment that resulted, and the chronically weak skilled labor market that persisted through the twenties, helped establish and maintain the Open Shop's final victory. But there were costs here, too. Baldwin, Cramp, Midvale, Brill, and N-B-P had been the rocks on which the Philadelphia metal trades unions had repeatedly dashed themselves to pieces. Although only N-B-P had ever joined the MMA, the association and its members had prospered under the cover provided by the giant firms. Now they were gone, or much reduced. In a future crisis, the old allies would no longer be around to help.

The second, and more immediate, major problem facing the MMA in the early 1920s, as the ironic consequence of the Open Shop's victory and the way it had been achieved, was this: If there is no longer a labor movement to offer a credible threat, and if governmental intervention is scarcely a problem, why bother to maintain an employers' association at all? How could the MMA survive the death of its raison d'être? Staunton Peck recognized that "in times when industry was quite (*sic*) . . . the members [were] inclined to lose sight of the value of the organization as a preventive and combative agency." But the association's activists had a larger, longer term vision. Experience taught them that labor kept getting up off the floor, however many times it was knocked down. So there was a need to maintain the organization as an insurance policy. Also, the MMA and its parent organizations, the NFA and the NMTA, had already demonstrated that they could perform many useful functions for their members besides union-busting and lobbying. Even before the war, the latter had "devolved themselves into constructive institutions" with relatively uncontroversial programs for promoting skills training and health and safety at work. Perhaps this was a way in which the MMA too could broaden its appeal and reposition itself for continued membership service in a new era of labor peace.[63]

---

[62] PID-1640 database; census data as in Table 1.1.

[63] ECM 7 Dec. 1920; cf. the NMTA president's very similar remarks to its 1920 Convention – "we cannot stress too much the importance of continuing and expanding

On closer examination, the MMA's twin crises of the early 1920s therefore turned into an opportunity. The association already had the bases of an alternative program on which to build – the ordinary employment services provided by the Labor Bureau and its secretary. And, among the existing and potential membership in the Philadelphia of the early 1920s, there were managers and entrepreneurs who shared its leaders' strategic vision that, the unions having been defeated, hopefully for good, the association could now proceed to strengthen the foundations of lasting industrial peace and profitable production. The association had a purpose and a future – rationalized, humanized employment management – the pursuit of which could hold existing members and attract new ones, including giant firms that would support the benign new union-free order just as effectively as Baldwin et al. had backstopped the Open Shop during its militant heyday.

Progress in this direction had begun in 1918, when Earl Sparks joined Joseph Willits's Philadelphia Association for the Discussion of Employment Problems (PADEP) and inaugurated the MMA's regular semi-annual earnings surveys. To these he had added monthly reports on turnover, which remained high through 1919 and the first half of 1920, and "operating conditions, changes in hourly schedules, and wage adjustments." By 1921 these reports covered 132 metal plants with a normal employment of over 96,000 people, about two-thirds of the metropolitan district total. They were sent out to all members and cooperating nonmembers to provide them with information for intelligent decision making that was particularly essential during both the inflationary period up until spring 1920 and the deflation that followed. ("[L]iberal dissemination" to nonmembers was partly in return for their help in supplying data, but it was also intended to "inculc[ate] a realization of [the MMA's] value that when conditions improve will be reflected in a gratifying addition to our present roll.") Sparks took pride in the NMTA's adoption of the data-collection forms and

our constructive program. No organization of any kind can permanently continue on a purely negative basis, and it behooves every employers' association to study and introduce practical advanced measures." – *Synopsis of Proceedings of the 22nd Annual Convention of the NMTA* (New York, 1920), p. 20. For the prewar origin of the NMTA's and NFA's "constructive" programs, see Robert Wuest, *Industrial Betterment Activities of the National Metal Trades Association* (pamphlet, n.p., n.d. – c. 1912) and its convention proceedings, which reflect its enduring preoccupation with industrial education and workplace safety; and Magnus Alexander, *Safety in the Foundry* (Chicago, n.d. – c. 1916). The report of the NMTA's Committee on Industrial Relations, *Industrial Relations in the Metal Trades* (Chicago, 1929), sums up developments in policy and practice among the association's membership through the 1920s that parallel those in Philadelphia – not accidentally, as Morris Leeds, the MMA's president for the second half of the decade, was a member of that committee.

procedures he had devised as the models for its national program. Now he was eager to do more.[64]

The "able and active" Sparks was the man principally responsible for the MMA's day-to-day operations. His job satisfaction, pay, status, and career prospects – all depended on its survival and growth. As Morris Leeds later approvingly put it, he was

not only vigilant . . . in marshaling our resources to meet unwarranted aggression when those qualities are called for, but . . . also, when opportunity offers, uses his ability and resourcefulness to accumulate facts, develop understanding and work out plans and policies which shall minimize the chance of future conflict.[65]

The MMA was fortunate to have a forward-looking secretary, and Sparks was equally lucky to have a similarly progressive new executive committee with whom to work. For the early 1920s witnessed a thorough changing of the guard here too, as the MMA's tough old leaders withdrew from office and retired from business. A generation of stalwarts departed and were succeeded by younger activists who were determined not to become as immobile a group of fixtures as the men they replaced. The MMA altered its political character with this change of régime, as the new leadership laid greater emphasis on membership participation and an openness to fresh ideas than on the time-served experience that their Victorian predecessors had valued above all else. They wanted to add "new members to the Executive Committee year by year so that the feeling might not go abroad that the Association was in the hands of a few men." They wanted "new blood [to] . . . be introduced . . . and . . . amongst the membership . . . an increasing number of those who have served intimately in directing the Association's affairs." The business population of Philadelphia metalworking, the managerial personnel of member firms, and the problems they had to confront, all were changing, and the MMA had to change with them.[66]

As Joseph Schumpeter reminds us, capitalism is a process of *creative* destruction. The picture of industrial decline presented earlier was incomplete. At least some of the lost firms and jobs were replaced, by local capital and entrepreneurship as well as by national and international companies. Dynamic firms making new kinds of electrical and mechanical products for growing national markets filled some of the gaps left by industrial restructuring among the business population and its labor force. The most notable examples of inward investment were by both of the giant electrical equipment manufacturers, General Electric and Westinghouse. These brought

[64]   ECM 23 Sept. 1924, 27 Feb. 1923; Leeds, PRES 1928, p. 4; SEC 1921, pp. 7–8, 12.
[65]   Leeds, PRES 1928, p. 4.
[66]   ECM 8 Dec. 1920, 25 Apr., 13 Dec. 1922, 23 May 1923, 8 Dec. 1926 (retirements); 28 Nov. 1922, 25 Nov. 1924, 8 Dec. 1926 (rotation).

their cosmopolitan managerial philosophies and practices into what had been a quite self-contained business community and shifted the locus of strategic decision making right away from it into the hands of distant strangers.[67]

As a result of these changes, the composition of the metal-working sector was transformed. Between 1918 and 1921 the city's electrical machinery, equipment, and appliance makers took on almost 3,400 workers – Westinghouse, in the city's southwestern suburbs just across the county line, added as many more – and moved from seventh to second in the ranks of Philadelphia's metal manufacturers. They employed another 5,300 by 1924, overtaking machine builders as the city's leading metal industry, a rank that they would not surrender for the remainder of the interwar period. By 1930, profiting in particular from the booming new industry of radio manufacture centered in Philadelphia and Camden, they would employ almost a quarter of the city's metal trades labor force – nearly 15,000 men and women, not far short of Baldwin at its prewar peak – 80 percent of them in four giant plants (Atwater-Kent, Exide, G. E., and Philco) with over 1,000 workers each. Westinghouse and, across the Delaware, the Victor Talking Machine Co. added almost another 10,000 to the metropolitan district total. Automobile body and parts makers experienced similar if less sustained growth, gaining more than 3,000 workers between 1918 and 1921, and as many more again by 1924, establishing themselves in a solid third place behind the electrical equipment and the machinery builders. Budd was the only major player, its 4–6,000 employees accounting for between 62 and, in 1930, 79 percent of the city total, making it Philadelphia's largest metal-working plant and a worthy successor to Baldwin. Finally, an industry whose size had been almost insignificant at the end of the war – the scientific instrument makers, employing a mere 1.8 percent of the metal trades labor force in 1919 – rose into fourth place by 1930, albeit on the strength of just under 4 percent of the total, two-thirds of whom worked in just two large proprietary enterprises, Brown Instrument with 517 employees, and Leeds & Northrup with 1,113, both of which were national market leaders in their respective fields. So, although most of the old giants of the first industrial revolution had been felled, new ones had arisen from developing industries to take their place.[68]

---

[67] See Ronald Schatz, *The Electrical Workers: A History of Labor at General Electric and Westinghouse 1923–1960* (New York, 1983), Ch. 1, for the best account of these companies' policies.

[68] All figures from PID-1640 database save RCA-Victor, which is from Philip Scranton, "Large Firms and Industrial Restructuring: The Philadelphia Region, 1900–1980," *PMHB* 116 (1992): 419–65 at 432–33. The net change in employment between 1921 and 1930 (78,882 falling to 59,809) concealed massive turnover in the business population: The 531 survivors from the 920 establishments providing 1921's jobs total only employed 49,278 people in 1930 (7 percent fewer than they had nine years

The sectoral composition of the metal trades was changing dramatically, as was the character of constituent firms. G. E. and Westinghouse were local branches of multinational bureaucracies run by professional managers according to "scientific" principles. The smaller, dynamic, still locally owned, specialized machinery and instrument makers also employed large proportions of white-collar and technical staff, because their entire growth strategy depended on their ability to continuously develop and patent new products and to manufacture them to the highest quality standards. Finally, some of the larger traditional local enterprises had learned the advantage or even the necessity of a certain amount of systematic management, too, notably of the newly recognized personnel function, during the war.

All of these changes meant that the type of firm and proprietor-manager typical of prewar Philadelphia, and thus of the MMA, was being pushed from center stage, partly displaced by more "modern" institutions, executives, and practices. Existing MMA members were changing their character, and the constituency of potential new members was being transformed. Much of the history of the MMA's growth and development through the 1920s would represent its successful institutional response to this more bureaucratized, managerial environment with its new needs and preferences.

The MMA's new leaders exemplified the forces for change within the metal-manufacturing community outlined above. Staunton Peck, unlike Justus Schwacke, was not a provincial Philadelphian. Schwacke had joined Sellers two years before Peck was born, had learned on the job, had worked his way up, and had never left. Peck was a New Yorker, a Columbia-trained engineer and professional manager who had spent much of his career in Link-Belt's midwestern plants. His company was renowned as a testbed of Taylorism, its Philadelphia plant alone almost twice the size of William Sellers (993 to 547), with almost four times as many white-collar workers and a growth-rate more than six times greater between 1918 and 1921 (99 vs. 15 percent).[69]

Most of the men on whose support he depended, and who would become the core of the leadership group for the next decade, came from firms that were similarly distinguishable from those of their predecessors: Even if they were local proprietary enterprises, they were more bureaucratically "modern" and more dynamic, technologically and otherwise. Peck's key

earlier); the 389 casualties had taken 26,143 more jobs with them (a third of the 1921 total), while 15 percent (8,956) of 1930's jobs were at 320 companies that had not existed in 1921.

[69] Biographical details on Schwacke in U.S. Commission on Industrial Relations, *Industrial Relations: Final Report and Testimony* (Washington, 1916), Vol. 3, p. 2889; information on MMA executives and firms from databases MMA-EXEC, PHILCHAP, and PID-1640.

associates included Stogdell Stokes and Charles Evans of Stokes & Smith (manufacturers of packaging machinery – high-value, customized, internationally marketed products), another early Taylor client, which more than doubled in size between 1918 and 1921, employing 416 workers in the latter year; Bob Yarnall of Yarnall-Waring (specialized, patented pipe fittings used particularly in electrical generating plants), who had supervised the Taylorization of Stokes & Smith early in his engineering career, and whose own company had a similarly impressive recent growth performance; Morris Evans Leeds of Leeds & Northrup, whose firm more than tripled in size over the same period (129–412) and almost half of whose employees were white-collar workers, including a substantial scientific research staff; and G. A. Elder, manager of General Electric's newly established, mushrooming Philadelphia plant (76–946). Only one of Peck's close collaborators, Howard Chambers of machine-tool builders Chambers Bros., represented an old-style proprietary firm of modest size, traditional product-line and technology, limited administrative capacity, and little dynamism (132–169 employees) – the backbone of the prewar MMA and still numerically predominant among the membership.[70]

New men brought new measures. Peck was hardly a liberal – most of his attitudes, particularly toward unions and government intervention, were scarcely distinguishable from his predecessors', and were firmly rooted in the Open Shop creed and rock-ribbed Republicanism. He remained attached to Link-Belt's individualistic tradition, opposing, as too collectivist and paternalistic, the new ideas of employee representation and welfare capitalism that won an increasing measure of support among some of his more liberal colleagues. He still believed in the fundamental importance of hard work, long hours, and payment by results. But he and Link-Belt had learned some lessons from the personnel management movement, and he was prepared to support and implement programs designed to remove what he and others took to be the root causes of labor unrest.[71]

His basic object was to "endeavor to bring about. . . . that contentment which comes from the sense of fair treatment." This would depend on continuing managerial activism to eliminate "the warfare in Industry" that was "ever present in greater or lesser degree." Such conflict was damaging and

[70] See biographical detail in Chapter 8, esp. Section 1.
[71] For Peck's ideas, see the very individualistic "Efficiency," in NFA, *Proceedings of the 16th Annual Convention* (New York, 1912), pp. 146–53; the more liberal "The Workmen's Compensation Law of Illinois," in NFA, *Proceedings of the 17th Annual Convention* (New York, 1913), pp. 110–17; and PRES 1921, 1924–25. Peck's ideological development was rather limited. PRES 1921 was his fullest statement on personnel policy; by 1924–25, he was emphasizing employee stock ownership and economic education as the solution to the labor problem, rather than further changes in working conditions. For the liberal managerial program, see esp. Sanford M. Jacoby, *Modern Manors: Welfare Capitalism since the New Deal* (Princeton, 1997), Ch. 1.

senseless, "analogous to that worst of all wars, civil war, because between those whose larger interests are mutual and not conflicting." Any solution required "the recognition of the worker as a human being and not a mere machine." To this end, management should pay the "strictest attention" to continuous improvement in physical working conditions, occupational health and safety, training provision, and even morale-boosting recreation programs.[72]

Management must also take action to improve human relations at work, and to cater for workers' demands for fairness and security, which Peck recognized as legitimate entitlements. His – and Link-Belt's – program for improved human relations began with removing sources of injustice and poor communications within the organization. "Hiring and firing are taken to a considerable extent out of the hands of immediate foremen, often quick tempered and prejudiced, and delegated to trained employment managers. Foremen are taught to be trainers and co-operators rather than drivers." Once front-line management had had its teeth drawn and manners improved in this way, the traditional "open door" policy could be expected to work.[73]

Peck was a transitional figure within the MMA, his presidency more preoccupied with completing the union-busting project and weathering the recession than with deciding what should come next. For that the association would depend on his collaborators, who moved into key positions on the executive comittee between 1920 and 1924, and by the end of that year were ready to take over. In the next two chapters we will examine their motivations, their program, and their achievement.

---

[72] Peck, PRES 1924, pp. 2, 4, 1921, pp. 2, 4, 5.
[73] Peck, PRES 1921, pp. 4–5.

8

Pacific Passage: Quaker Employers and Welfare Capitalism, c. 1905–1924

The argument of this book has been that Philadelphia in the 1900s through early 1920s was actually a good, rather than simply a convenient, place in which to study the dynamics of labor–capital relations in the metal trades. What happened in the metal manufacturing industries of other major cities usually happened in Philadelphia too, generally at much the same time, and for many of the same reasons. The business communities, labor unions, and skilled workers who are the protagonists in this story were all reacting to the same great national events – particularly changes in the business cycle and the balance of political power, and the war. Local developments took place in a context shaped by national institutions, and the information and experience they circulated within and among themselves. The MMA thus stands as a representative for its two dozen sister associations that gave the NFA and the NMTA a grass-roots presence and prosecuted the Open Shop war on the ground. It was cheaper than any of them, more conservative than some, less combattive than others, and more successful than most. But its ideology, strategy, and practice were quite commonplace.

In another sense, too, Philadelphia looked like a microcosm of metal-trades labor relations nationwide: Great corporations held up the umbrella under which mid-sized businesses could find shelter from the rain. The metaphor is not exact and the protection was incomplete, but the successes of the NFA, the NMTA, and the local employers' associations are best understood alongside the anti-union climate created and maintained by the likes of U.S. Steel, International Harvester, and others. The MMA had its Baldwin, Brill, Cramp, Midvale, and Niles-Bement-Pond allies; mid-sized businesses in other metal manufacturing communities had similar local champions, like Allis-Chalmers in Milwaukee, whose great strike beginning May 1906 was the IMU's largest challenge before the war and its biggest defeat, and was crucial in establishing Open Shop conditions in the metal trades of that industrial city.[1]

It would be possible to construct this chapter and the next simply as an extension of the above argument. It could be couched in David Brody's classic terms, as just another example of the "Rise and Decline of Welfare Capitalism" or, following Sanford Jacoby, of "Moderation in the 1920s."[2] As the closing sections of Chapters 5 and 6 made clear, much of the explanation for the MMA's new departures in personnel management in the decade between the recovery from the postwar depression and the final collapse of Herbert Hoover's dream of managed prosperity can indeed be produced from standard ingredients. The near death of the metal trades unions took the heat off the MMA and the NMTA, and allowed and required both to moderate their rhetoric and seek a new raison d'être. Generational change within the business community, and the rise of professional, proactive, and more bureaucratic management styles, created pressures and possibilities for more sophisticated, systematic, and comprehensive approaches to the solution of human resource problems.[3]

So far, so normal – and so bland. To serve as the basis for an examination of the Open Shop in general, the Philadelphia and MMA case study can indeed be treated as more or less representative. But one of the attractions of the case-study approach is the likelihood of turning up something different. The historian has to be open to the uniqueness of his or her historical actors, research materials, and the story enfolded within them. It would be possible, and it is certainly necessary, to explain how the MMA developed and what it did in the 1920s as a local reflection of larger processes of change within the national business community. But it is not sufficient, for many of the key figures who dominated the MMA in the 1920s were not just entrepreneurs and professional managers responsive to the *zeitgeist* of modern managerialism. They were members of a peculiar subcultural group – the Orthodox minority within the small but influential Philadelphia Quaker community – and their religious commitments shaped their everyday behavior, moreso after the searing experience of the First World War than before. Much of what they did within their own companies, and most of what the MMA did under their influence, was not especially distinctive – techniques and programs were borrowed and imitated from the NMTA and from other

---

[1]   Walter Peterson, *An Industrial Heritage: Allis-Chalmers Corporation* (Milwaukee, 1978), pp. 118–21.

[2]   Brody's 1968 essay is reprinted in his *Workers in Industrial America: Essays in the Twentieth-Century Struggle* (New York, 1993), pp. 48–81; Jacoby, *Employing Bureaucracy: Managers, Unions and the Transformation of Work in American Industry, 1900–1945* (New York, 1985), Ch. 6.

[3]   Cf. Allen M. Wakstein, "The National Association of Manufacturers and Labor Relations in the 1920s," *Labor History* 10 (1969): 163–76.

pioneers in the personnel management movement – but some of the motivation was unique.

In this chapter we examine this group, and some of its individual members, to discover why a handful of men developed such a particular outlook on industrial relations and other social problems, and such a strong commitment to remedial action within their own firms and in the other circles in which they moved, between the late 1900s and the early 1920s. In the next chapter, we will pursue them into the MMA, as they strove to turn an Open Shop employers' association into a force for positive good within the city.

In a sense, this liberal interlude was a mere interruption in the MMA's institutional history, leaving few lasting traces. The Great Depression and the New Deal, and the explosion of workers' collective action in the 1930s, overwhelmed religious and secular liberals' versions of union- and conflict-free employment relations as surely as they did the conservative and combative. But this particular book would not be complete without them; their story permits us to see in all their complexity the manifold forces that shaped employers' changing policies toward their employees. The Orthodox Quakers among Philadelphia's metal manufacturers were a peculiarly progressive and conscience-driven bunch; but the history of American business's engagement with the labor problem is in general a history of changing values, not simply of changing calculations by narrowly economic men, and of the shifting patterns of social forces setting some of the constraints within which they operated.

8.1 A PECULIAR PEOPLE

Morris Evans Leeds, Charles Evans, and Stogdell Stokes, together with the younger Orthodox Quaker proprietor-managers and engineer-entrepreneurs like Arthur C. Jackson of Miller Lock, or D. Robert Yarnall of Yarnall-Waring, who moved into controlling positions within the MMA in the early and mid-1920s, had far stronger and deeper bonds among themselves than most Philadelphia metal manufacturers. They came from a small, ingrown, and inbred middle to upper middle-class sect numbering scarcely 4,000 people in southeast Pennsylvania and southwest New Jersey, of whom about a third lived within Philadelphia itself. The Philadelphia Orthodox were the traditionalist remnant of original Quakerdom, still suffering in the 1900s from the divisive and demoralizing consequences of a doctrinal controversy in the 1820s that had fissured their community and left them alienated from, and heavily outnumbered by, their Hicksite neighbors.[4]

[4] PHILCHAP and MMA-EXEC databases; William P. Vogel, *Precision, People and Progress: A Business Philosophy at Work* (Philadelphia, 1949) [Leeds]; Francis J. Stokes, Jr., *Stokes Cope Emlen Evans Genealogy: Genealogical Charts of Four Closely Associated Germantown Families* (Philadelphia, 1982) [Stokes]; C. Elliott Barb, *The*

Orthodox Quakers clustered in the same few suburbs – particularly Chestnut Hill and Germantown – and, within them, in what were, in effect, extended-family compounds. Most of their socializing was with other Friends who, because of the sect's rules of endogamy, were also relatives, sharing the same limited stock of surnames. They were well educated in their own Orthodox schools, where teachers, pupils, and the supportive alumni who financed and controlled them were drawn from the same narrow group. When they left school, the boys could go on to Haverford, deepening the ties among them, or to Penn, where they were also assured of finding many Friends and relatives. And for that minority who pursued careers within existing family businesses or in entrepreneurship, religious connections provided employment, opportunity, and financial backing.[5]

Work, leisure, and charitable activities all overlapped so much that it was rarely necessary for the Orthodox to look outside the comfortable confines of their small world for companionship. Whatever they did, they kept bumping into one another, more by choice than by accident. In the 1880s and 1890s, for example, alumni of Westtown, the premier Orthodox boarding school, set up two associations to renew valued friendships as well as to raise money for a building program. The first president of the Old Scholars' Association was farm equipment maker Samuel Leeds Allen (b. 1841), the patriarch among Orthodox metal manufacturers; when that association and the older Alumni Association eventually combined, its first president was electrical instrument maker James G. Biddle and its vice president the mechanical engineer Robert Yarnall, his cousin (b. 1878). One of the humanitarian associations in which old Westtonians were particularly active was the Friends' Freedmen's Association, which was dedicated to bringing practical and educational assistance to African Americans in the southern states at a time when such benevolent white attention was singularly rare. Morris Leeds (b. 1869), also active in the Old Scholars' Associ-

Yarway Story: An Adventure in Serving (Philadelphia, 1958). [Yarnall and Waring]. The basic source on their community is Philip S. Benjamin, *The Philadelphia Quakers in the Industrial Age* (Philadelphia, 1976). For the broader religious background, see Howell J. Harris, "War in the Social Order: The Great War and the Liberalization of American Quakerism," in David Adams and Cornelius van Minnen, eds., *Religious and Secular Reform Movements in American History* (Edinburgh, 1999), pp. 179–204.

5 Stokes, *Stokes Cope Emlen Evans Genealogy*, p. 3 [co-residence]; Margaret Hope Bacon, *Let This Life Speak: The Legacy of Henry Joel Cadbury* (Philadelphia, 1987), pp. 3–4 [sociability]; *Friends' Journal* (1 March 1986): 28 [endogamy]; Watson W. and Sarah B. Dewees, *Centennial History of Westtown Boarding School 1799–1898* (Philadelphia, 1899), Helen G. Hole, *Westtown Through the Years* (Westtown, 1942), Isaac Sharpless, *The Story of a Small College* (Philadelphia, 1918), and Rufus M. Jones, *Haverford College: A History and an Interpretation* (New York, 1933) [education]; Occupational Census in Social Order Committee (hereafter SOC) Minutes 10 Jan. 1921, Quaker Collections, Haverford College (hereafter QC-HC) [c. 15 percent of the Philadelphia Orthodox in paid employment, and with known occupations, were managers and proprietors].

ation, was its secretary, a position that brought him into close and friendly relations with Bernard G. Waring, Yarnall's school friend and future business partner – and another old Westtonian.[6]

These Friendly endeavors were not always so serious in purpose. In January 1901, Samuel Allen organized the Friends Golf Union (later the Ozone Club) so that, when Quakers wished to join in the growing Philadelphia middle-class passion for that sport, they could do so separately, in their own congenial company. Members included other S. L. Allen Company executives, James Biddle, Morris Leeds, and packaging machinery manufacturer Stogdell Stokes – the last three had all entered Westtown in the same year, 1883, and Leeds and Stokes were also together at Haverford – together with executives from other Quaker firms in the Philadelphia region like Warren Webster & Co. (steam fittings) and the Esterbrook Steel Pen Manufacturing Co., of Camden. In 1912, Morris Leeds and his brother Arthur – the latter a textile company executive – and another packaging machinery manufacturer, Frank Stokes (also an old Haverfordian), founded the Four Way Lodge on the Great Egg Harbor River near Mays Landing, New Jersey. There, middle-aged men could get away from the city's sticky summer to spend time canoeing and relaxing with similarly high-minded friends and relatives, and with their old tutors – "Master Thomas" Brown, Westtown's principal, and Rufus Jones, the scholar, mystic, and social activist into whose guidance they had passed when they moved on to Haverford, and who remained their inspiration and external conscience for the rest of his and their lives.[7]

The Orthodox metal manufacturers' business lives were also interwoven, and separate from their schismatic Hicksite cousins'. It was not just individuals who were Orthodox or Hicksite, it was firms. The Harrison Safety Boiler Works, for example, had Hicksite partners; Haines, Jones, & Cadbury (brass founders) were Orthodox. Given the personal and familial bases of Philadelphia capitalism, it could scarcely have been otherwise.

---

[6] Dewees and Dewees, *Centennial History,* esp. pp. 192, 196, 203; Hole, *Westtown Through the Years,* pp. 271, 304–05; "Personnel Security Questionnaire," Morris Evans Leeds Papers, Box 12, QC-HC; Barb, *Yarway Story,* p. 79.

[7] *"Down the Fairway" and In the Rough with the Ozone Club from 1901 to 1927* (Philadelphia, n.d.), pp. 7, 9, 101, 105, 110, 112, 117, 127, 131, 132, 139, and Fiftieth Anniversary Meeting Photograph, both in Leeds Papers, Box 9, F. 5, QC-HC; Watson W. Dewees, compiler, *A Brief History of Westtown Boarding School With a General Catalogue of Officers, Students, etc.* 4th. ed. (Philadelphia, 1888), p. 205; Committee of the Haverford College Alumni Association, *A History of Haverford College for the First Sixty Years of Its Existence* (Philadelphia, 1892), pp. 670, 678; John Van Schaick, Jr., "Cruising Cross the Country, V: The Four Way Lodge," *Universalist Leader* (31 Jan. 1925): 6–7; for Jones, see his memoir *The Trail of Life in the Middle Years* (New York, 1934), esp. pp. 154, 170, 212, 218–9, and Elizabeth G. Vining, *Friend of Life: The Biography of Rufus Jones* (Philadelphia, 1958), esp. pp. 81, 116, 144–45, 147.

When Morris Leeds went looking for long-term financing for his growing scientific instrument business in 1906, he raised it from an Orthodox venture capitalist, J. Henry Scattergood. Leeds's vice president – and partner in office within the MMA – William C. Kimber, lived with four intermarried Orthodox families, including J. Henry's brother Alfred and the Frank Stokes already mentioned, on the same Germantown estate. Bernard Waring's and Robert Yarnall's careers also benefited from their ability to exploit these dense Orthodox networks. Waring's first job on leaving Westtown was with the sales department of Ozone Club member Esterbrook Steel Pen. Yarnall, an engineering graduate from Penn, where he and Arthur Jackson had become friends through rowing together on the Schuylkill, found employment at Stokes & Smith, where he assisted with the "Taylorization" of the growing company. When Yarnall and Waring launched out with their own venture to manufacture patent pipe-fittings, Stogdell Stokes bankrolled the business, took a one-third interest, and became its vice president and "sleeping partner." Yarnall's applied research to develop the young company's product line depended on collaboration with Warren Webster, another Ozone Club member. And when Yarnall-Waring needed to refinance its business in 1920, Alfred Scattergood helped them out.[8]

8.2 QUAKERS AND THE LABOR PROBLEM

Philadelphia Quaker metal manufacturers, Orthodox and Hicksite, played a full role in the associational life of the city outside of their more or less restrictive sectarian networks. Morris Leeds was an active member of the Franklin Institute, its electrical section in particular. Robert Yarnall and Arthur Jackson were leaders of the local engineering community. Quakers threw themselves into repeated, temporarily successful, efforts to clean up

---

[8] PHILCHAP database; Hicksites identified from signatories to "Some Particular Advices for Friends and A Statement of Loyalty for Others: Being the Views of Some Members of the Society of Friends Regarding Its Attitude toward the Present Crisis. Third Month, 1918," File 99-35, Box 137, MID Corr., RG165, National Archives; Bacon, *Let This Life Speak*, p. 4; M.E. Leeds to Executive Committee, May 1920, Report No. 44: Finances of Expansion, and C.S. Redding to Executive Committee, 13 Dec. 1922, Report No. 90: Proposed Payment to Scattergood Estate, Leeds & Northrup Co. Papers (hereafter L&N Papers), HML; E. Digby Baltzell, *Philadelphia Gentlemen: The Making of a National Upper Class* (Glencoe, Ill., 1958), pp. 268–70 [Scattergoods]; Stokes, *Stokes Cope Emlen Evans Genealogy*, p. 3; Barb, *Yarway Story*, pp. 11–21, 79–82; remarks of Arthur C. Jackson in verbatim transcript, "Memorial Meeting for Worship for D. Robert Yarnall, Seventh Day, Ninth Month Sixteen, 1967," p. 19, in D. Robert Yarnall (hereafter DRY) papers [copies in author's possession, supplied by D. Robert Yarnall, Jr.]; Yarnall and G.A. Binz, "Recent Development in V-Notch Weir Measurement," *J. ECP* 34 (1917): 314–20; Yarnall to Waring, 7 June 1920, DRY Papers.

city government in the 1900s and early 1910s, alongside their bourgeois Protestant suburban neighbors. And, as we have seen in Chapter 4, they also made an important contribution to the Open Shop crusade. Hicksites were leading figures within the MMA and PMA. The Orthodox were less numerous, initially less influential, and less combattive, but they too were not altogether averse to the more respectable techniques of union-busting, particularly at the outset. Samuel Allen, whose stated interests were "The welfare of the community and his employees," a skilled, versatile bunch for whom he provided stable and highly paid work, turned to the MMA for replacement metal-polishers in 1905; Warren Webster made no such public commitments, but he was at least equally ready to use the Labor Bureau against his machinists that same year; Morris Leeds served on the MMA executive committee from 1905 to 1907, through the bitterest years of the anti-labor struggle.[9]

The older generation of Orthodox employers shared the usual sentiments of their class toward proprietary rights and labor relations. In Philip Benjamin's opinion, "Friends' love of pacific relations strengthened their anti-labor predisposition." Strikes threatened public order as well as the proper relationship between employers and employees. Philadelphia Quakers gave some support to the idea of arbitration, a common middle-class panacea for industrial conflict, but this was at best lukewarm. When Rufus Jones joined an interdenominational group recommending an arbitrated settlement to the PRT strike in 1910, Joshua Bailey of paper-box makers Brown & Bailey, one of the "weightiest" Orthodox elders, countered that the PRT had the same right as he had to "employ anyone it wished and discharge workers whenever it thought necessary. . . . [His] employees were not permitted to dictate how he ran his business; if they tried, he would quickly replace them." His junior partner, Henry Tatnall Brown, later admitted to having had "rather feudalistic notions concerning [their business]; that is, he regarded the factory as their family castle and the workers as their retainers."[10]

But some of the younger generation of Quaker manufacturers were markedly more liberal. In the 1900s they began to adopt a new theology (new to them, at least, although it was already a generation old among

9 "Committee Memberships," *JFI* 153 (1902): 80 [Leeds]; A.S.M.E. Annual Dinner Program, 3 Dec. 1941, pp. 5–10 [Yarnall]; Philip S. Benjamin, "Gentleman Reformers in the Quaker City, 1870–1912," *Political Science Quarterly* 85 (1970): 61–79 [insurgent Republicanism]; *"Down the Fairway" and in the Rough*, p. 102; testimony of company treasurer Llewellyn in Transcript of Proceedings in Case No. IV-C-44, S. L. Allen and Co., Inc. and Federal Labor Union No. 18526, 9 March 1936, pp. 18–25, 41–42 in Records of the NLRB, RG25, National Archives; ECM 12 Apr. 1905 [Allen]; McPherson, SEC Dec. 1905, p. 3 [Webster]; MMA-EXEC database.

10 Benjamin, *Philadelphia Quakers*, pp. 89–90; Lester M. Jones, *Quakers in Action: Recent Humanitarian and Reform Activities of American Quakers* (New York, 1929), p. 176.

transatlantic Protestantism). The Social Gospel emphasized that individual Christian commitment must translate into active striving for what Rufus Jones called in 1912 "one of the most impressive undertakings of the Twentieth Century, the conquest of unnecessary disease, the banishment of unnecessary poverty, the transformation of environments which breed and foster disease and sin, the spiritualizing of both capital and labor and the recovery of faith in the actual coming of the Kingdom of God in the world." Joining Progressive crusades for social justice became a religious obligation on a par with Orthodox Quakers' traditional philanthropic concerns for the weak and defenseless.[11]

Morris Leeds adopted this outlook by the late 1900s. It would be pure speculation to wonder what part his experience as a close spectator of the industrial conflicts and economic disruption of 1905–07 may have had in his conversion. He and his liberal associates had secular as well as religious inspiration for their newfound progressivism. Leeds also echoed the technocratic optimism of Simon Patten, a professor at the Wharton School and an intellectual leader for the city's reformers. The application to industrial production of inanimate sources of power, and of scientific knowledge, was creating a revolution in economic and social organization and ushering in an age of abundance and of limitless possibilities for improvement. But this materialistic analysis led Leeds back to a moral conclusion: Since poverty was no longer inevitable, "economic justice and the best interests of the race as a whole, demand that every individual who is willing at the proper age to do his fair share of the world's work, should always be in a position to earn at least the necessities of life, in exchange for a reasonable amount of work performed under healthful conditions." This condition of affairs was now feasible, and it was desirable, but it was not normal. Bad housing, poor education, child labor, low and irregular wages, excessive hours, industrial accidents, and seasonal and cyclical unemployment, all of these blighted workers' lives. Leeds did not blame the poor for their poverty, and had moved beyond the old certainty that it resulted from their "idleness and vice"; rather, the moral failings of the poor, as well as their material insecurity, were the result of "lack of opportunity." Leeds had become a thoroughgoing environmentalist, not at all given to the individualistic-moralistic or hereditarian explanations of poverty and inequality so common among his entrepreneurial contemporaries.[12]

Leeds's egalitarianism was unequivocal – "the existence of pressing need for a more equitable distribution of the world's wealth needs no argument"

[11] Paul T. Phillips, *A Kingdom on Earth: Anglo-American Social Christianity, 1880–1940* (University Park, 1996); Vining, *Friend of Life*, p. 144 [quote].
[12] Daniel M. Fox, *The Discovery of Abundance: Simon N. Patten and the Transformation of Social Theory* (Ithaca, 1967). Quotes from "The Attitude of Friends Toward Industrial Conditions," unpaginated typescript c. 1909, Leeds Papers, Box 9, QC-HC.

– and sincere, but it did not lead him down the path toward socialism that was trodden by some of his female Quaker contemporaries. He was a reformer, not a radical; a voluntarist, not a collectivist; and he was, after all, an employer. He saw the solution to problems of poverty and inequality in making more good jobs available within the existing capitalist system. State regulation had a role to play, particularly protective legislation for women and children. But so too did employers like himself. Welfare capitalism and improved personnel management became, for Leeds and his friends, a moral imperative.[13]

Within the conservative context of the Philadelphia Orthodox business community, Leeds was a pioneer. But he and his associates moved in and were open to ideas from a much larger world of reform, which provided them with practical models for action. Real pioneers were already well down the road that they would begin to tread. Leeds had traveled to Germany in 1892–93 to do graduate work at the University of Berlin and to study the *Reich*'s science-based industries. One visit in particular, to the Carl Zeiss Werke at Jena, a pioneer in welfare capitalism, made a profound and lasting impression on him, and would help to guide his own business conduct. The Philadelphia Orthodox, particularly (in the 1900s) the liberals among them, also looked to British Friends, a community still joined to them by visiting and intermarriage, for intellectual leadership. Leeds was thus unusually aware of, and impressed by, the innovations in employment relations and employee welfare associated with the English Quaker confectionery manufacturers – the Rowntrees of York and Cadburys of Bournville – who had turned the 1900s into a Chocolate Age in the development of British personnel management. Leeds was also interested in home-grown experiments by American personnel pioneers, notably the Filenes (department stores) and Henry S. Dennison (container manufacturing) of Boston and Framingham, Massachusetts – perhaps coincidentally, the same models that Morris Ll. Cooke followed in his renovation of the City of Philadelphia's personnel policies in 1911–15.[14]

Mention of Cooke should remind us that there were also forces for the

[13]   Leeds, "Attitude of Friends"; Carol and John Stoneburner, eds., *The Influence of Quaker Women on American History: Biographical Studies* (Lewiston, Maine, 1986), esp. pp. 329–408.

[14]   Letter to Hadassah Leeds, 26 June 1923, in Leeds Papers, Box 5, QC-HC; typescript ms., "Ernst Abbe and the Karl Zeiss Stiftung," n.d. (1912 latest date within document), p. 4, Leeds Papers, Box 9, F. 3; Leeds, "Attitude of Friends." Iolo A. Williams, *The Firm of Cadbury 1831–1931* (London, 1931); Charles Dellheim, "The Creation of a Company Culture: Cadburys, 1861–1931," *American Historical Review* 92 (1987): 13–44; Anne Vernon, *A Quaker Business Man: The Life of Joseph Rowntree, 1836–1924* (London, 1958), Elfrida Vipont, *Arnold Rowntree: A Life* (London, 1955); Asa Briggs, *Social Thought and Social Action: A Study of the Work of Seebohm Rowntree 1871–1954* (London, 1961) – for the two remarkable families at the heart of Quaker "progressivism" in Britain.

reform of employment policy coming from within the scientific management movement itself, another Germantown- and Chestnut Hill-based circle with which Leeds, Stogdell Stokes, and Robert Yarnall overlapped. Yarnall and Waring's Nelson Valve plant (c. 200 employees) had benefited from the services of H. J. F. Porter, like Cooke a Lehigh engineering alumnus, and a former associate of Frederick Taylor's at Bethelehem Steel. Porter had gone on to become a management consultant, too, but unlike Taylor his solution to the labor problem involved advanced welfare policies and employee participation schemes.[15]

As for Leeds, in 1915 he responded to the dictates of his conscience by beginning to share ownership of his medium-sized firm (c. 100 employees) with his associates. He did this by commissioning America's pioneer consultant in personnel problems, Robert Grosvenor Valentine (1872–1916), to analyze his company and make recommendations for improvement. Valentine was a progressive with a varied career behind him – professor of English and settlement-house worker, banker and railroad executive, and finally a reforming Commissioner of Indian Affairs under President Taft. For his efforts he won notoriety and plenty of political enemies, leaving office (before he was thrown out) to fight for Teddy Roosevelt in 1912. After the end of the Bull Moose campaign he had to find a new career, so, with minimal experience to draw on, he invented one: "industrial counselor," impartial advisor to employers and unions alike on the just and peaceable solution of their difficulties. He was a member of the Taylorites' Society to Promote the Science of Management, but with unusual attitudes and priorities: According to one obituary, he had a "conception of the unity of industry, in which both workers and management have a common interest in healthy human relations, not for the advancement of efficiency merely, which he regarded as subsidiary, but for the sake of the soundness of industrial conditions as a whole."[16]

Valentine's four years as an industrial counselor – during which time he also found time to be first chair of the Massachusetts Minimum Wage Board, chair of its State Committee on Unemployment (whose work par-

---

[15] H. J. F. Porter, "The Democratization of Industry, or Enlightened Methods of Treating the Employed," *JFI* 161 (1906): 161–78 and "Labor Efficiency Betterment," NMTA, *Synopsis of Proceedings of the 13th Annual Convention* (New York, 1911), pp. 60–78; Joseph Caccavajo, "Welfare Work: A Typical Example of the Interest Leading Manufacturers are Taking in Their Employees' Welfare," *Procs. ECP* 34 (1917): 121–26 [Nelson Valve]; Jacoby, *Employing Bureaucracy*, p. 307.

[16] Vogel, *Precision, People and Progress*, pp. 38–41, 44, on the partnership scheme and Valentine's role; Diane T. Putney, "Robert Grosvenor Valentine 1909–12," in Robert M. Kvasnicka and Herman J. Viola, eds., *The Commissioners of Indian Affairs 1824–1977* (Lincoln, Nebr., 1979), pp. 233–42; Obituary reprinted from *Seventh Report of Harvard College, Class of 1896*, p. 3; cf. Felix Frankfurter, Remarks . . . at the Memorial Meeting, . . . 7 Jan. 1917 in Felix Frankfurter Papers, Box 108, LCMD.

alleled Cooke's and Joseph Willits's in Philadelphia), and to work with the Molders' leader John P. Frey and the economist Robert Hoxie in the U.S. Commission on Industrial Relations's investigation of scientific management – were full of drama. He sought out conflict, offering his services to help settle labor–management disputes; and he did not avoid controversy. He confronted the anti-labor orthodoxy of the Taylorites within their own firms and meetings, promoting an alternative vision of the pursuit of efficiency with the cooperation and organized consent of the workers themselves, unionized and otherwise. In the short term, his colleagues rejected him: He was, as Willits explained, "too generally regarded as a visionary," too close to the outsider Hoxie, and too subversive of managerial hubris. But he was a "pioneer who will rush to the skirmish line willing to sacrifice his own existence and the concrete amount of good he accomplishes so that people will at least think about the problem." Soon, they did; and Valentine's radicalism would become the Taylorites' – particularly Morris Ll. Cooke's – new orthodoxy after his, and Taylor's, death.[17]

This was the exceptional person to whom Leeds turned for advice. Valentine's technique was to conduct what he termed an "industrial audit" – a survey that another satisfied Taylorite client, Henry P. Kendall of the Plimpton Press, detailed as covering both physical working conditions and the organizational environment, including "means for venting grievances and little troubles which always cause greater troubles in a mill or factory, and the development of the personnel side of industry, which gives to the worker at least as great care as to the mechanical and production side of business." Valentine had a grand vision of the possibilities of building a rational, efficient, humane, and just employment relationship within the firm. This broad agenda was in tune with Leeds's own.[18]

The result of their collaboration was a series of innovations in personnel policy including a profit- and equity-sharing scheme inspired in general

[17]   Obituary, p. 1; Howell J. Harris, "Industrial Democracy and Liberal Capitalism, 1890–1925," in Nelson Lichtenstein and Howell J. Harris, eds., *Industrial Democracy in America: The Ambiguous Promise* (New York, 1993), pp. 43–66 at pp. 57–58; Jacoby, *Employing Bureaucracy*, pp. 103–4, 109; Alex Keyssar, *Out of Work: The First Century of Unemployment in Massachusetts* (New York, 1986), pp. 265–70; Jean T. McKelvey, *AFL Attitudes Toward Production: 1900–1932* (Ithaca, 1952), pp. 22–24; Willits to E. M. Hopkins, 6 Dec. 1915, in Joseph Willits Papers, Box 7, F. 68, Accession IV-2A-39, RAC; cf. F. L. Lamson (Norwalk Tire & Rubber Co.) to Henry P. Kendall (Plimpton Press), 7 Dec. 1916, on the frosty reception of Valentine's groundbreaking paper, "The Progressive Relation Between Efficiency and Consent," by the Taylorites – Frankfurter Papers, Box 108, LCMD.

[18]   Kendall quoted in Obituary, p. 4; Frankfurter, "Robert Grosvenor Valentine, '96," *Harvard Alumni Bulletin* 19 (1916): 228–30; cf. Valentine, Tead and Gregg ("Industrial Counselors, Labor Problems, Industrial Auditors"), *The Industrial Audit: What the Industrial Audit Is* (pamphlet, n.d.), in Ordway Tead Papers, Box 18, F.10, LMDC; Ordway Tead, "The Labor Audit: A Method of Industrial Investigation," *Federal Board for Vocational Education Bulletin* 43 (Jan. 1920).

terms by the Carl Zeiss *Stiftung* and directly modeled on Henry Dennison's, that is, it only extended as far as managers and other equivalent "contributors" (e.g., senior salesmen). It was designed to enable Leeds to motivate, reward, and include his executive co-workers as co-owners of a growing company that was evolving away from being a small, simple proprietary enterprise. Management and controlling ownership would broaden out and remain united in the same persons; absentee capital would be deprived of any right to anything more than a fair return. In particular, unsympathetic outside investors would be deprived of any power to subvert the company-based "cooperative commonwealth" that Leeds was intent on creating. Yarnall and Waring introduced a profit-sharing scheme within their own business at the same time, but theirs included all of their employees.[19]

As a result of these innovations, by 1915 these Quaker proprietors had moved within a few years from the fringes to the front line of managerial efforts to address the "labor problem" by the application of techniques that were radically different from those of their MMA fellows. Within the MMA, the Orthodox minority were no longer to be found among the active union-busters. Instead, they confined themselves to the promotion of one new and nonconflictual subject in which the MMA became interested, following the NMTA's strong lead: technical and vocational education. This suited them because of the skill-dependency of their own dynamic firms, and their commitment to investment in human capital, and also because of their experience in running a variety of Quaker educational institutions.[20]

---

[19] Daniel Nelson, "'A Newly Appreciated Art:' The Development of Personnel Work at Leeds & Northrup, 1915–1923," *BHR* 44 (1970): 520–35, and "The Company Union Movement, 1900–1937: A Reexamination," *BHR* 56 (1982): 335–57, are generally reliable, although they slight Leeds's essentially religious motivation. More surprisingly, so does C. Canby Balderston, Jr., *Executive Guidance of Industrial Relations: An Analysis of the Experience of Twenty-Five Companies* (Philadelphia, 1935), pp. 141–154 – Balderston was the son of Leeds's old math teacher, and former colleague, at Westtown. He was a fellow-Haverfordian, wartime volunteer on AFSC work in France and Belgium, and close collaborator with Leeds in applied personnel research through the 1920s – Balderston Personnel File, University of Pennsylvania Archives; Jones, *A Service of Love*, p. 267; Vogel, *Precision, People, and Progress*, esp Ch. 3; Leeds, "Democratic Control of Business" 8 May 1917, in SOC Records F4.18, QC-HC; C. Canby Balderston, Jr., "Profit-Sharing – An Incentive Plan for Executives," pp. 181–87 and Leeds, "Paying Executives for Results," pp. 211–12, in Hugo Diemer, ed., *Wage-Payment Plans That Reduced Production Costs* (New York, 1930); Kim McQuaid, "Henry S. Dennison and the 'Science' of Industrial Reform, 1900–1950," *American Journal of Economics and Sociology* 36 (1977): 79–98. pp. 80–82 esp.; Charlotte Heath, "History of the Dennison Manufacturing Company: II," *Journal of Economic and Business History* 2 (1930): 163–202 esp. pp. 176–78; Barb, *Yarway Story*, p. 52.

[20] MMA-EXEC for committee roles; Langworthy, PRES 1912, pp. 2, 4 and ECM 10 July 1912, 11 June 1913, 14 Jan., 11 Nov., 9 Dec. 1914, detailing growth of interest in training; NMTA, *Synopsis of Proceedings of the 13th Annual Convention* (New

8.3 A SERVICE OF LOVE

It is impossible to know how far and fast, and in what directions, the Orthodox metal-manufacturers' managerial progressivism would have developed
had there been no war. The war was a particular challenge to their community, because their core religious value – the commitment to the avoidance of conflict and coercion in human relations – was tested as never before
by the pressure to participate in the war effort. The Hicksites succumbed,
or enthusiastically embraced, what they termed the "Cause of Civilization."
The Orthodox did not. Draft-age Quaker males were most at risk in the
ensuing crisis. To provide them with a publically acceptable form of service
as an alternative to conscription or imprisonment, and to demonstrate that
Quaker pacifism was an active and respectable endeavor, not cowardice or
pro-Germanism, the Philadelphia Orthodox threw themselves into organization-building and fund-raising for relief work among civilians in the
devastated areas of France and Belgium. The community's spiritual and
intellectual leaders – Thomas Brown from Westtown, the theologians Rufus
Jones and his brother-in-law, Henry J. Cadbury (who was also Brown's son-
in-law), and Isaac Sharpless, from Haverford, all of whom felt a particular
concern for their former pupils and students – joined with their usual partners in leisure and philanthropy to establish the American Friends Service
Committee (AFSC) in April 1917. As a result, Orthodox Quaker metal
manufacturers and their business associates had far more on their minds
from 1917 through 1920 than promoting vocational training through the
MMA, or helping the ageing Hicksites and other warhorses on the executive committee to bear the burdens of office. Morris Evans Leeds joined J.
Henry Scattergood, his company's financial backer, on an exploratory visit
to France and England in June 1917. They returned with a firm plan of
action for the AFSC, whose implementation in the field was overseen by
Charles Evans, Leeds's colleague on the (necessarily inactive) MMA Education Committee, while Leeds handled the Philadelphia end of operations.
Nor did the altruistic capitalists' commitent decline with the end of the war:
Robert Yarnall abandoned his own business in 1920 to help J. Henry's
brother Alfred, his own financial backer, with the *Kinderspeisung*, the
AFSC's great child-feeding effort in a starving Germany. He was joined in
that enterprise by his old crew companion from Penn and successor as

York, 1911), pp. 21–37, *14th* (1912), pp. 31–48, *15th* (1913), pp. 35–75, *16th*
(1914), pp. 71–97, *17th* (1915), pp. 30–40 – industrial education was one of the
NMTA's two main prewar preoccupations, alongside workers' compensation. For
Quaker firms' activities, see Benjamin Cadbury, "A Plan for Educational Work in a
Small Corporation," *National Association of Corporation Schools Bulletin* 4 (June
1914): 33–37 [Haines, Jones & Cadbury]; Report No. 84, 30 Sept. 1922: Appren-
ticeship Course; W.M.C. Kimber, Report No. 14, 20 Aug. 1919: Production Course;
L&N ECM, 22 Nov., 3 Dec. 1918 – L&N Papers, HML.

leader of the Philadelphia engineering community in the 'teens, Arthur C. Jackson of Miller Lock, who had already served as the AFSC's purchasing agent. In 1924, when the Friends' Germany–Austria program was coming to an end, Yarnall and box-manufacturer Henry T. Brown, married to another Scattergood, went to organize its wrapping-up.[21]

Leeds, Evans, Yarnall, and others absented themselves from businesses that were booming because of the war economy, thereby imposing a burden on their partners and associates who were left managing the shop. This was a real sacrifice by proprietors of firms with at most a handful of policy-making executives. Companies like theirs could not avoid benefiting from the war, even though they were not directly involved in munitions making. Giving freely of their time to the AFSC, and of their money, too, was one way for their owners to deal with their resulting sense of guilt.[22]

But it was not enough. The AFSC represented, as Philip Benjamin wrote, "the culmination of the trend toward activism already at work in Philadelphia meetings" before the war and "generated an excitement in the Quaker community which had not been felt since the programs for Indians and the freemen" after the Civil War. However, the aroused consciences of the Philadelphia Orthodox were not satisfied with merely palliative action to help the victims of war. Instead, they turned a sharp critical attention on their society to discover why it had produced such a calamity in the first place.[23]

8.4 WAR AND THE SOCIAL ORDER

In 1917 a group including Leeds, Yarnall, Waring, Alfred Scattergood, Henry Brown, and other executives petitioned the Philadelphia Yearly Meeting stressing the growing "realization . . . that we should more completey live up to [our] ideals" and that Quakers "should seek more fully to recognize what is implied by our stand against all war."

[21] Harris, "War in the Social Order"; Hicksite support for war effort in "Some Particular Advices for Friends" [quote]; Bacon, *Let This Life Speak*, Ch.3; Mary H. Jones, *Swords Into Ploughshares: An Account of the American Friends Service Committee 1917–1937* (New York, 1937), esp. pp. 3–5, 7, 16–17; Rufus M. Jones, *A Service of Love in Wartime: American Friends Relief Work in Europe, 1917–1919* (New York, 1920), esp. pp. 8, 12–15, 17–27, 62, 65–66, 72, 119–20; Jones, *Quakers in Action*, esp. pp. 18–19, 47–48, 59, 66; Jackson remarks, 1967, in DRY Papers; Brown entry in *Dictionary of Quaker Biography* (typescript, QC-HC).
[22] Vogel, *Precision, People, and Progress*, pp. 35–36, 98. Leeds & Northrup shipments increased from $149,000 in 1914 to $1,015,000 in 1919 – "Estimate of Production Capacity," L&N ECM 25 July 1919, L&N Papers, HML; Yarway's went from $91,000 to $428,000, 1914–20. "Shipments 1908–1959," DRY Papers.
[23] Benjamin, *Philadelphia Quakers*, pp. 202–03.

The war in Europe has laid bare the fact that Twentieth Century Civilization falls far below the standard of Christ in industrial and national as well as in international life. We have discovered the seeds of war in our social order. If Love can and should be trusted to the uttermost and made the ruling principle of action in international affairs it follows it can be and should be made supreme in social and industrial life. It seems therefore, that part of the great task before us is to discover what practical steps the Society of Friends should take in applying Christ's teaching of love and brotherhood in business, in the home, in politics and in all other relations of life.

They were "baffled and perplexed," but also surprisingly hopeful:

We believe that a great opportunity lies before us at this time. The world is in deep need of light and leadership. . . . If with the sin and agony of the world pressing on our hearts, with the vision of so many men and women in Europe laying down their lives for the right as they see it, we also are willing to give our time, our possessions, our lives to establish the Kingdom of God on earth, who can say what great work God may accomplish.[24]

The Yearly Meeting responded by setting up a "Committee on Social and Industrial Problems" (soon shortened to the Social Order Committee), whose active membership and that of the AFSC overlapped, and which was full of all the usual suspects. Bernard Waring was its chair, and Morris Leeds its secretary. Their agenda was quite explicit: the critical analysis of the competitive and wage systems, that is, of basic capitalist institutions that were deemed to be at variance with Friends' beliefs, but on which their prosperity depended.[25]

The committee was divided about how, and how far, to proceed. Two members, moved by the millennarian spirit common on the secular as well as the religious left, argued that fundamental social change was possible because of the war, and that it was "surely more necessary to avert war between classes than between nations." Others were not so radical. Samuel Allen suggested that they should explore possibilities for change *within* the existing social order. It was "impossible to eliminate all troubles, but let us commence by hoping they may be alleviated." The patriarchal Allen recommended a mix of state and private actions – legislation for minimum wages and maximum hours; provision of public work when the market economy could not sustain full employment; and welfare work conducted in a Christian spirit by employers. Haverford's president Sharpless responded to the group's evident uncertainty by advising Leeds to pursue an open-ended investigation of "the various efforts that have been made in the past to correct [capitalism's] evils, or replace it entirely with a better order

[24] "To the Yearly Meeting," March 1917 (month names used in footnote references, not in originals), in SOC Minutes, SOC Records F4.18, QC-HC. Jones, *Quakers in Action*, Ch. 14, gives a full account of the SOC's work.

[25] Extract from the Minutes of Yearly Meeting, 26/30 March 1917, SOC Records, F4.18, QC-HC.

of society," aided by "lectures on the subject by people who know more about the subject than you do, if that supposition is possible."[26]

The committee accepted Sharpless's suggestion. It divided its work among several different interest groups that discussed matters most directly concerning them. The groups in turn organized programs of lectures by a roll-call of social reformers, enlightened businessmen, trade union leaders, educators, and others from the progressive center and nonrevolutionary left, which became a regular feature of the social and intellectual life of Philadelphia Quakerism thereafter.

But it would be wrong to dismiss the Social Order Committee as having resulted in little more than the creation of a series of talking-shops. This was a quite effective program of voluntary political re-education, which produced (for example) a renewed, active, and thereafter unbroken commitent to the cause of racial equality and other civil liberties, and a somewhat less full-blooded commitment to "industrial democracy," which was of immediate practical significance. For one of the Social Order Committee's largest, most active groups of supporters, whose wealth and generosity underpinned the rest of its work, was its Business Problems (originally Managing Employers) Group, set up in October 1917.[27]

The creation of the Business Problems Group was a natural response to the class backgrounds of the Philadelphia Orthodox and to the social criticism in which some of them were so deeply engaged. The community was overwhelmingly composed of members of the comfortable middle class, doing rather well out of the very social order of which some of them were now so critical. The uneasiness that this caused many of them rarely resulted in political radicalization, but there was a more moderate response possible, which their leaders pointed out. As the committee summed it up,

When [the Society of Friends] has perceived wrongs in institutions in which it has been involved it has tried first of all to clear itself of complicity in those wrongs. It has believed that permanent good to society can best be brought about by the influence of conviction and example which spreads from the individual to the group and from the group to the community. This was Jesus' teaching and method of work.[28]

The Son of God's method of social change – with which who could disagree? – was "an appeal to the conscience and the arousing of a sense of duty in the favored class, not a call to rebellion or to an assertion of their

---

[26] Charles A. Ellwood and Agnes Tierney to SOC, 24 Apr. 1917; SOC Minutes, 8 May 1917; Sharpless to Leeds, 20 Apr. 1917 – SOC Records, F4.18, QC-HC.

[27] Benjamin, *Philadelphia Quakers*, pp. 208–12; Minutes of the SOC, 13/14 Oct. 1917, F4.18; SOC Report to the Yearly Meeting, Third-Month 1920, p. 2, F4.13; Minutes of the SOC, 15 June 1922, p. 1, F4.18 – SOC Records, QC-HC.

[28] SOC, Second Annual Report, 1919, p. 5, in SOC Records, F4.18, QC-HC.

rights on the part of the poor." And, Henry J. Cadbury pointed out, "As the membership of the Friends lies almost wholly in the favored class it is all the more important that we observe this technique of Jesus." The employing capitalists among them bore a specially heavy responsibility to "stir our own consciences and appeal to our own sense of duty." Out of this stern self-examination concrete results could follow, because they owned and controlled the firms that they ran. Leeds, Allen, Yarnall, Waring, the Scattergood brothers, Stogdell Stokes, Charles Evans, Arthur Jackson, and other AFSC activists were the Business Problems Group's leaders or among its founding members.[29]

8.5 MORRIS LEEDS AND THE PURSUIT OF THE KINGDOM, 1918–1924

One of the fruits of Leeds's visit to England on AFSC work in 1917 was the personal contacts that he made with Quaker employers there. They were grappling with the realities of industrial conflict in a heavily unionized wartime Britain, and with the mandates of their own War and the Social Order Committee (the model for Philadelphia's) to reduce or eliminate strife and injustice in the companies that they ran. Out of their deliberations, at some of which Leeds was present, came a series of well-publicized social experiments, including company-based employee consultation programs at Cadbury's and Rowntree's cocoa and chocolate works.[30]

Leeds's understanding of what employee representation entailed was advanced by this British experience. Before he left America, all he supported was profit- and equity-sharing designed to erode sharp distinctions of power and reward among owners and employees within businesses. But when he came back, he reported himself "much impressed with the spirit in which these responsible businessmen, many of them representing large interests, approached the problems; and the freedom with which they discussed any suggestions brought forward for more equitable arrangements between workers and employers." He now understood that management decisions could be divided into "Financial or Commercial" questions (strategic issues – e.g., investment, pricing, sales) and "Industrial" ones, including "Engagement and dismissal of Employees; Hours of work; Rates of pay, bonuses,

---

[29] SOC Annual Conference (1926), p. 5; SOC Minutes, 13/14 Oct. 1917, p. 6, 11 March 1918, p. 1, 9 Apr. 1918, p. 2 – SOC Records, F4.18, QC-HC.

[30] J. E. Hodgkin, ed., *Quakerism and Industry: Being the Full Record of a Conference of Employers, Chiefly Members of the Society of Friends, Held at Woodbrooke, near Birmingham, 11–14 April 1918, Together with the Report Issued by the Conference* (Darlington, 1918), reports the major conference that followed on from the smaller preparatory meetings which Leeds attended; John Child et al., *Reshaping Work: The Cadbury Experience* (Cambridge, 1990), Ch. 2; Briggs, *Social Thought and Social Action*, Ch. 5.

etc.; Shop discipline; Welfare Work; Relations with Trades Unions." Employee consultation became a less threatening idea once this distinction was appreciated, because the worker was not

immediate[ly] concern[ed] . . . with regard to the Financial or Commercial sides, but he is directly and continuously interested in the Industrial . . . , and . . . as a preliminary step in establishing closer relations between employers and employed, the setting up of Works Councils was suggested to assist in the industrial side of business, on which councils the laborers would have a representation equal to that of the employers.[31]

Over the next few months he directed the Business Problems Group to think about "all relations between employers and employees in industry, such as problems involved in the democratization of business," and showed the way by introducing a representation plan, the Leeds & Northrup Co-Operative Association, within his own firm. The Jackson brothers did the same at Miller Lock. Unlike Midvale Steel's, these schemes were not designed to compete with or preempt organized labor, or to forestall an NWLB ruling. There were no such clouds on the horizon for these firms, both of which had workforces with high proportions of white-collar and female employees. Their programs were purely the result of managerial conviction and initiative. Leeds was concerned about the effects of wartime growth on the close personal relations that had prevailed in his company when it was much smaller, and the plan was in part a response to that problem. But it was not a necessary response; the details of the plan were in no way affected by these temporary conditions, and the company remained committed to it even when they had passed.[32]

Leeds quickly made sure that the new association had significant business to deal with, including the introduction of a minimum wage and improved overtime pay; reduction of office workers' hours to eight per day; and putting the plant onto a five-day, forty-four hour week, initially as an experiment. Onto a firm with an already well-developed welfare and benefit program (including employee-administered sick relief and athletic associations, a lunchroom, a dispensary, vacations with pay, loans to employees to help them buy their homes, a co-operative marketing scheme for employees, and community gardens) Leeds and his executive associates grafted a culture of rights. Vacation entitlements, for example, were strictly tied to length of employment, and workers' acquired seniority rights were protected even if they had left the company on military service.

---

[31] Leeds, "Democratic Control of Business."

[32] SOC Minutes, 13–14 Oct. 1917, pp. 1–2, in SOC Records F4.18, QC-HC; Meeting of the Business Problems Group Held at the Plant of the Miller Lock Co., June 8, 1920, in Charles Lukens Huston Papers, Box 1989, F. 25, Accession No. 50, HML; PID16–40 database; Nelson, "'A Newly Appreciated Art'" and "The Company Union Movement."

Most significantly, Leeds and his associates gave up their and their subordinates' unilateral right to discipline employees without redress. Department heads lost the right to fire even in cases of insubordination and gross incompetence. Senior managers alone had the power to initiate a discharge; the employment supervisor was responsible for looking into the case and trying to find alternative employment elsewhere in the plant for workers who had fallen out with their bosses; a joint management-association appeal board had final authority.

Leeds and his colleagues were not engaged in a cosmetic exercize in consultation: Even before he formalized the procedure, the discharge of a foreman, for example, was referred to a jury of his peers for decision, with Leeds and his works manager "present at the meetings only to state the case and hear the conclusion." By 1924 they had "established the general policy of handling through [the Co-Operative Association] all matters of interest to the employees in which there are negotiations between the employees and the management." The agenda of negotiations was much broader than in adversarial union–management relationships, and involved a full and frank interchange of views and information, joint decision making, and shared administrative responsibility.[33]

Leeds used the Business Problems Group as a means of disseminating his company's new approach to labor relations and personnel problems to a wider circle of Orthodox proprietors and executives, which by the beginning of 1920 included over 100 men from about fifty companies. (The two-thirds of them who replied to a questionnaire employed 12,204 people.) In October 1918, they decided that "real progress [in employer–employee cooperation] could probably best be brought about by the group employing a qualified expert to study carefully and report on all experiments along these lines" who would be "available for consultation by members of the group and others who desire to inaugurate such co-operative movements themselves." Leeds chaired the committee charged with hiring and working with the "Expert Investigator"; Stogdell Stokes and Robert Yarnall joined him.[34]

They ended up securing the services of the New York–based Bureau of Industrial Research (BIR). Confusingly, this shared the name and home town of the industrial espionage agency that was simultaneously hiring the Molders' James Cronin as a fink; but in every other respect it could not have been more different. It was the successor to the pioneer industrial

[33]   L&N ECM, 29 July, 12 Dec. 1918, 16 June 1919, 15 June 1920, 6 June 1918, 20 Aug., 10 March 1919, 2 Apr. 1921, 27 May 1920, 17 Nov. 1919, 8 Sept. 1920, 3 Apr. 1919 [quote]; 28 Jan. 1924 for the statement of principle codifying six years' practice – L&N Papers, HML.

[34]   SOC Minutes, 9 Feb. 1920; 5 Oct. 1918 p. 3, 30 Dec., 13 Jan. – SOC Records, F4.18, QC-HC.

counseling outfit set up before the war by Robert Valentine and was now headed by Robert Bruère, a noted progressive and friend of organized labor, and Herbert Croly of the *New Republic*. It had a distinguished staff including Valentine's old partner, personnel expert Ordway Tead, and Tead's collaborator, Henry C. Metcalf. It made propaganda against the open shop (but for employee representation) and was sufficiently radical to merit investigation by New York's red-baiting Lusk Committee, which was surely to its credit.[35]

Leeds did not just head the "Expert Investigator" committee: He, Stogdell Stokes, Henry Brown, and two other manufacturers brought the BIR inside their own businesses to conduct audits and make recommendations, root out what Brown termed "various unchristian and undesirable" practices, and set an example that they hoped the rest of the Business Problems Group's membership would follow.[36]

Brown gained a great deal from his audit; but Leeds was less pleased with his more ambitious experiment that involved, in effect, the delegation of much staff and line responsibility to the BIR and its protégé in the factory, the new personnel manager, who turned out to be an unnecessary and unwelcome intrusion. Tead and Bruère were hostile to the growing policy-making and executive powers of the Co-Operative Association, which limited theirs; they were so committed to the goal of employment stabilization at all costs that they opposed overtime working that was necessary to deal with an order backlog in 1919 (they also complained "that it would considerably interfere with the studies they were making," using Leeds & Northrup as a testbed for their theories); their conception of supervisors' duties emphasized the personnel function at the expense of managing production; their vision of the personnel manager, an outsider, as co-equal with the group of stake-holding Friends who made up the rest of the Executive Committee, was the last straw. So, although they made some contributions to the development of Leeds & Northrup's personnel program between

[35] SOC Minutes, 10 March, 12 May, 19 June 1919; for Bruère, see Melvyn Dubofsky, *When Workers Organize: New York City in the Progressive Era* (Amherst, 1968), p. 25, Steven Fraser, *Labor Will Rule: Sidney Hillman and the Rise of American Labor* (New York, 1991), esp. pp. 136, 173, 217–20; for Tead's and Metcalf's views, see their text, *Personnel Administration: Its Principles and Practice* (New York, 1920); for Bureau publications, see Savel Zimand, *The Open Shop Drive: Who Is Behind It and Where Is It Going?* (New York, 1921); BIR, *American Company Shop-Committee Plans: A Digest of Twenty Plans for Employees' Representation* (New York, 1919); for their politics, New York State Legislature, Joint Committee Investigating Seditious Activities, *Revolutionary Radicalism: Its History, Purpose and Tactics* (Albany, 1920), Vol. 1, pp. 1120–21.

[36] Jones, *Quakers in Action*, p. 177; PID16–40 database; U.S. Bureau of Labor Statistics, "Unemployment-Benefit Plans in the United States," *Bulletin* No. 544 (July 1931), pp. 51–54.

1919 and 1921, and although their presence was Leeds's idea, eventually they and their man had to go.[37]

The disagreements that occurred at Leeds & Northrup between production- and sales-oriented executives and the BIR replicated what was happening in U.S. industry more generally after the war. Self-aggrandizing personnel managers were cut down to size or ditched altogether once the recession of 1920–21 bit. But there was this difference: When Leeds and his associates were forced to cut costs, they did not backtrack on their commitments to their workforce. Instead, they carried on with the task of turning their company into an "attempt to realize some portion of God's Kingdom on earth," in line with their basic religious principles, always paying attention, as Leeds put it, to "the standpoint of good business and the happiness of the people who work with us."[38]

By 1921 the Co-Operative Association was a going concern, no longer an experiment. But, apart from Miller Lock – also an early PADEP member – no other Business Problems Group members created employee representation schemes. Interest in industrial democracy waned rapidly after the war; what took its place in 1921 was a renewed concern about unemployment, a response – like Leeds's termination of the BIR's contract – to the severe recession.

The Social Order Committee remained publicly committed to promoting "Team Work in Industry," the "opportunity to lead a self-directed life and to share in determining the conditions under which one should live and work" which was "supremely valued by free men." In the context of the American Plan open shop offensive, they were sympathetic to "Labor's revolt against the exclusive control of industry by capital" and the resulting "attempt to meet power with power." But they gave a higher priority to the promotion of "The Creative Instinct" by cutting hours and redesigning work (echoing socialist feminist Helen Marot's analysis; Marot was born and brought up a Philadelphia Quaker, but there is no evidence of her participation in Social Order Committee affairs); to the pursuit of a higher standard of living and the more equitable distribution of income; and most of all to the search for employment security, to liberate workers from "the shadow of fear" that blighted their lives.[39]

[37] Nelson, "'A Newly Appreciated Art'," pp. 526–30, reads this story differently, but see L&N ECM 16 Sept. 1919 p. 7, 21 Nov. 1919 p. 13, 12 Dec. 1919, 21 Jan. 1920, 11 Feb. 1921, 27 May 1921, 21 July 1921, 20 Dec. 1921; Reports No. 17, 13 Sept. 1919, No. 67, 13 July 1921, L&N Papers, HML.

[38] Jacoby, *Employing Bureaucracy*, Ch. 6, esp. pp. 171–80; for the quotes, SOC Minutes, 13–14 Oct. 1917, p. 1, SOC Records, F4.18, QC-HC, and Leeds remarks on Report No. 17.

[39] Leading PADEP members, though not strictly Quaker firms, Fayette R. Plumb [axes and edge tools], for whom Willits's young Orthodox associate C. Canby Balderston, Jr., served as employment manager, and American Pulley, in which the Scattergood

The committee adopted a two-track strategy to promote its commitments. The first was to take its message beyond its own circle. The way it did this was to sponsor part of a lecture tour by probably the best-known exponent of managerial liberalism in the English-speaking world, Seebohm Rowntree himself, British Quakerism's chocolate conscience personified. Rowntree was invited to the United States to lend his prestige to the pro-labor campaign of Social Gospel Protestantism. He battled zealously, lecturing widely and making highly publicized attacks on the Open Shop movement.[40]

According to liberal personnel man Robert E. Wolf, Rowntree, with his "Plea for Industrial Disarmament," was a "'lone voice crying in the wilderness'." This may have been true of his American tour in general, but not of the largest part of it. Rowntree lectured at least fourteen times in Philadelphia, where a Business Problems Group steering committee under Morris Leeds, including his MMA associates Arthur Jackson, Charles Evans, Bernard Waring, and, from the Wharton School, Joseph Willits, arranged an intensive program.[41]

Willits's presence reflected more than his closeness to these men because of his secretaryship of the PADEP. It was also a result of the way in which joint support for the work of the AFSC had begun to erode the Hicksite/Orthodox divide within Philadelphia Quakerism, a process that the Social Order Committee had accelerated after the war by inviting Hicksite representation. We know less of what his religion meant to Willits than we do about his professional and academic credo, but he was an active member of his branch of the Society of Friends, and common beliefs as well as secular ties were clearly strengthening his connections with the Orthodox Quaker group within the MMA.

Rowntree had never been to Philadelphia before, but he was not a

brothers had a major stake, also had employee representation schemes, but there are no further details – Meeting of the Business Problems Group Held at the Adelphia Hotel 18 December 1922, Huston Papers, Box 1989, F.26; Statement by the SOC, Oct. 1921, in SOC Records, F4.18, QC-HC; Helen Marot, *The Creative Impulse in Industry: A Proposition for Educators* (New York, 1918).

[40] Briggs, *Social Thought and Social Action*, esp. Ch. 6; Donald Meyer, *The Protestant Search for Political Realism, 1919–1941* (Berkeley, 1960), esp. Chs. 3–4; Dennison to Rowntree, 15 Aug. 1938, Dennison File; *Cocoa Works Staff Journal* 2:1 (Sept. 1922), clipping in File America 1921; IMHS, "Memorandum: B. Seebohm Rowntree in America 1921–1951," p. 9, and Journals 1921, 6 Nov. 1921 p. 2, 12 Nov. 1921 pp. 2–3 – all in BSR Papers, JSRT; "Attack and Defend the Trade Unionist," *New York Times* and "Large Empoyers Clash in Speeches on Trade Unionism," *New York World*, both 2 Nov. 1921, clippings in File Lectures 8/4, 8/8, BSR Papers, Borthwick Institute, York, England.

[41] Wolf to Alvin E. Dodd (president, American Management Association), 20 Feb. 1937, extract in IHMS, "Memorandum"; Rowntree, "A Plea for Industrial Disarmament"; Journals 1921 – all in BSR Papers, JSRT; SOC Minutes, 21 Oct. 1921, p. 4, 10 March 1919, SOC Records F4.18, QC-HC.

stranger. His older brother, John Wilhelm, the key figure in the liberalization of Anglo-American Quakerdom's theology and social commitments,
was buried at Haverford; his younger brother's daughter – like their friend
Rufus Jones – had married a Philadelphia Cadbury; and, more prosaically,
his Cocoa Works in York was full of Stokes & Smith packaging machines,
so there was an established business connection, too. He made lasting
friendships with Willits and Leeds. And he had a galvanizing effect on the
Business Problems Group, which had become somewhat demoralized by
the limited impact that it was having, even within its own circle, because
of the recession:

He helped to put driving-power into the interest which the Group was beginning
to take in the subject of unemployment. His message on this topic, backed by his
experience, his scientific knowledge, and his engaging personality, convinced his
hearers that unemployment is a menace hanging like a black cloud over the workingmen, that it is a menace which we can remove, and that we ought to have done
so long ago.[42]

And this, indeed, was the second track of the Business Problems Group's
strategy. Rowntree's message was directed as much at themselves as at the
broader business community. After he left, they organized a subcommittee
to discuss the issues of the regularization of business and unemployment
insurance, which they recognized as "a difficult one" on which "it did not
seem likely that any general joint action ... would be practicable." The
most that some members would do was "to keep records of employees laid
off for lack of work" on forms that the group provided "so that more adequate information might be gathered as the basis for future action." But a
handful went further, with Leeds & Northrup, as usual, at their head.[43]

The brutal and wholly unexpected inventory recession of 1921 hit Leeds &
Northrup hard. Their first step was to slash overhead expenses by sacking
middle mangers, and to spread available work by cutting everybody else to
a thirty-two hour week; but it soon became clear that this could not be

---

[42] IMHS, "Memorandum," p. 5 (Rowntree's Christmas card list); BSR to Chudleigh,
3 Dec. 1923, Chudleigh File, America 1923–8, and Dennison to Rowntree, 2 Dec.
1936, Dennison File; both in BSR Papers, JSRT; *Social Order Bulletin* 1 (Feb. 1923),
in SOC Records F4.17, QC-HC [quote].

[43] SOC Minutes 6 Feb., 1 May, 4 Dec. 1922, SOC Records, F4.18, QC-HC. See also
Industrial Relations Counselors, Inc., *Unemployment Compensation Plans in the
United States*, Vol. I: Company Plans, Preliminary Report (New York, processed
report, 1928), p. 87, on the Group's work. Of fifteen company-based unemployment
benefit plans that the U.S. Bureau of Labor Statistics could discover in 1931, four
were in Philadelphia – Leeds's own, Henry Tatnall Brown's (introduced 1927), and
two at the Bromley family's Bromley Mfg. and Quaker Lace mills, which operated
in a unionized industry and, uniquely, with union cooperation – "Unemployment
Benefit Plans in the United States," pp. 46–49, 51–54.

afforded, as it reduced productivity (which was already unacceptably low). There was no choice but to let go the least efficient 20 percent of the workforce, and to cut the wages of those who were left by a flat 10 percent. This strategy was negotiated with and modified by the Co-Operative Association, but layoffs were nevertheless galling. As the association's secretary explained, there was an implicit contract between Leeds & Northrup and its employees: They accepted wage levels below the going rate in expectation of job and income security. Market conditions were forcing the company to renege on its promise.[44]

Members of the Executive Committee were also troubled, especially when the cuts affected long-service employees. Their company had grown without serious interruption for twenty straight years, and they had no experience of mass layoffs. They met the men and women they had to let go, face to face, to tell them the bad news, because "we should at least understand the human consequences of our acts." As Leeds later recalled

these talks showed us how serious a crisis we were bringing into their lives. Those who had no savings were confronted with real physical want. Others had to give up partly purchased homes, discontinue the education of children, and the like. All of these commendable plans had been undertaken because of the expectation of continued employment. Thus the social harm that comes from the sudden interruption of employment became obvious to us. We saw why . . . Carl Zeiss said that industry had an obligation toward those whom it dismissed to see that they were provided with means of support during a reasonable time in which to relocate themselves, and that this obligation bore some relation to the length of their employment. We examined with renewed interest the provisions he made for discharging this obligation and resolved that we would make similar provision if a return of prosperity permitted.[45]

In the short term, all they could do was offer limited lay-off allowances (three months' pay to those with more than ten years' service) because they had no reserves to draw on. But they became committed to not being caught similarly unprepared again. This was the situation in which Leeds & Northrup's executives found themselves when they joined in planning Seebohm Rowntree's inspirational visit.[46]

The year 1922 was a time of preparation, using the Business Problems

[44] "Working Hours," L&N ECM, 29 Dec. 1921; Executive Committee to Wages Committee, 16 Aug. 1921; Executive Committee to Board of Councillors, Report No. 70, 19 Aug. 1921: Cost Reduction; Thomas R. Hill to Executive Committee, 25 Aug. 1921; Executive Committee to Council, 30 Aug. 1921: Overhead Payroll in Relation to Cost Reduction – L&N Papers, HML.
[45] Leeds, "President's Report" (1929), MMAP; Leeds, "Unemployment Benefits," in U.S. Department of Commerce, *Unemployment: Industry Seeks a Solution. A Series of Radio Addresses given under the auspices of the President's Emergency Committee for Employment* (Washington, 1931), p. 16.
[46] C.S. Redding to Executive Committee, Report No. 68: Lay Off Allowances, 29 July 1921; L&N ECM 3 Aug. 1921 – both in L&N Papers, HML.

Group as a forum for the exchange of experience with Henry Dennison, who had been prompted by the 1914–15 recession to start his own unemployment insurance fund under joint company–employee control. Dennison had been able to pay his laid-off workers 80 percent of their normal pay (if they had dependants; 60 percent otherwise) through the recent collapse in business. Leeds & Northrup resolved to be able to do the same in the future, working out the details with the Co-Operative Association through the fall of 1922 as prosperity returned, and giving it charge of the fund once it was set up in 1923.[47]

At the same time the company embarked on a product development and diversification strategy, together with careful inventory control, market forecasting, and production planning, to enable it to anticipate (and minimize the gravity of) future recessions that might put pressure on the fund. It also adopted a clear countercyclical policy of inventory increase, work-sharing, and reequipment in such circumstances, "with the expectation that we will at no time have to make greater decreases in our force than natural shrinkage and the elimination of inefficients will bring about." This was a sophisticated and many-sided approach to guaranteeing income and job security for the company's growing workforce. Finally, in 1924, a company-financed, employee-administered group life insurance and pension scheme, together with a much broader employee share-ownership program whose purpose was explicitly to reward and encourage commitment to the business by its highly skilled workforce, were added. These benefit programs were the capstones in the structure of advanced personnel policies that Leeds & Northrup had begun to build almost a decade earlier.[48]

---

[47] SOC Minutes 6 Feb., 1 May 1922, in SOC Records, F4.18, QC-HC; Dennison, "Reserves Against Unemployment," in U.S. Department of Commerce, *Unemployment: Industry Seeks a Solution*, p. 11; Personnel Division, Dennison Mfg. Co., "Plan in Use By an American Industry for Combatting Unemployment," *ALLR* 11 (1921): 53–58; L&N ECM, "Unemployment Insurance," 17 Oct. 1922; Joint Committee on Unemployment Benefit Project, 28 Nov. 1922; L&N ECM, 16 and 27 Feb. 1923; Executive Committee to Council, Report No. 97: Unemployment Benefit Fund, 16 Feb. 1923 – L&N Papers, HML; Jones, *Quakers in Action*, pp. 175–76 and Industrial Relations Counselors, *Unemployment Compensation Plans*, pp. 85–96, for details.

[48] C. Reed Cary to Executive Committee, 31 Aug. 1923, Report No. 115: Resale Business, 12 Dec. 1923, Report No. 118: Advertising Policy, 3 Jan. 1923, Report No. 93: Business Conditions and Their Relationship to Our Sales, and discussion, L&N ECM 10 Jan. 1923; W.M.C. Kimber to Executive Committee, 20 Aug. 1923, Report No. 111: Production Schedule; L&N ECM 30 Sept. 1924, Maintenance of Force During Periods of Small Incoming Business; C.S. Redding to Executive Committee, 6 March 1924, Report No. 129: Building Expansion; C.S. Redding to Executive Committee, 31 Dec. 1923, Report No. 123: Group Life Insurance, and discussion, L&N ECM 28 Jan. 1924; 31 Oct. 1924, Pension Plan; 6 July 1923, Report No. 103: Investment Shares – L&N Papers, HML.

One can read the significance of Leeds's widely reported experiments in a number of different ways. One could be cynical and say that, as a controlling proprietor (despite his partnership scheme, his ownership share only fell from 83 percent in 1915 to just over half by 1932), he simply had an unusual degree of freedom to express his deep personal convictions in his actions. One could add that Leeds & Northrup was also peculiarly favored as a market leader in a dynamic industry whose customers were not very price-sensitive (because the devices that it sold, particularly industrial control equipment, were so massively productivity-enhancing). A research-based growth strategy also meant that, in most product lines, Leeds & Northrup had an effective monopoly protected by patents or sheer expertise.[49]

Leeds could also afford his forty-four-hour week, his benefit programs, and his commitment to employment security for his workers, because of his company's peculiar economics: Production employees' wages represented less than one-eighth of his costs. It was therefore feasible to build commitment among his organization's skilled employees, and it also made good business sense because the company had made a major and long-term investment in their human capital. Careful investigations revealed that men continued to improve in ability and productivity for at least ten to fifteen years after hiring. They were assets that were not to be squandered.[50]

None of the above factors, nor his religious convictions, should be left out of any explanation of why it was that Leeds's "holy experiment" could be so successful. But they combined to make his company's policies difficult for others to imitate, even had they been so minded. So one could write him off as a benign freak. This was certainly the way Israel Mufson of the Philadelphia Labor College thought about him in 1929, lumping him together with other ethically driven pioneers in welfare capitalism as "introspective individuals, dominated by a Great Father complex." They were "on the fringe of industry rather than in it. And their experiments are paternalistic rather than democratic. Their workers are isolated from the problems pertaining to industry in general." Even Leeds's admirers, like economist Paul A. Douglas, recognized how exceptional he was in his "fine intelligence and social imagination." He and other managerial liberals, like Owen D. Young of G.E., were "as much above the rank and file of management as Jane Addams and Lillian Wald are to the average social worker,

[49] Vogel, *Precision, People and Progress*, p. 40; Stuart Bennett, " 'The Industrial Instrument – Master of Industry, Servant of Management': Automatic Control in the Process Industries, 1900–1940," *Technology and Culture* 32 (1991): 69–81 at pp. 70–72, 76–77.

[50] "Estimate of Production Capacity," 25 July 1919; C. S. Redding to Executive Committee, 19 July 1922, Report No. 83: Overhead Rate, p. 3, all L&N Papers, HML; Leeds, PRES 1929, p. 3, MMAP.

and as Michelson and John Dewey are above the garden variety of college professors."[51]

But Morris Leeds and his fellows enjoyed great prestige in the New Era, and even erstwhile labor-liberals and future New Dealers attached their realistically limited hopes for social progress to them and their projects. In John Fitch's words, progressive employers "constitute[d] merely an oasis in a great desert. But it is an oasis that is very cheering and full of promise. I have faith to believe that it will grow."[52]

By 1924, Leeds and his close associates had, as the Social Order Committee's original strategy required, done their utmost to "clear [themselves] of complicity" in the evils of capitalism. They had "believed that permanent good to society can best be brought about by the influence of conviction and example which spreads from the individual to the group and from the group to the community." They were now ready to spread their influence beyond their own companies and co-religionists, through an apparently improbable channel: the Metal Manufacturers' Association of Philadelphia, an organization looking for new leaders and new purposes. Leeds believed that it was through such organizations that "thoughtful business men can probably exert their greatest influence for good." Soon he and his friends would find out how effective that influence could be.[53]

---

[51]   Mufson, "Why a Conference on New Relations Between Capital and Labor," p. 5, in Philadelphia Labor College, *Proceedings of Conference on New Relations Between Capital and Labor* (Philadelphia, 1929); Douglas, "Can Management Prevent Unemployment?" *ALLR* 20 (1930): 273–81 at p. 276.

[52]   Fitch, " 'An Oasis That is Full of Promise'," *ALLR* 17 (1927): 242–43 at p. 242.

[53]   SOC, Second Annual Report, 1919, p. 5, in SOC Records, F4.18, QC-HC; Leeds, "Political Economy and the Industrialist," *Annals* 204 (1939): 72–79 at p. 78 – an article summarizing a lifetime approach.

9

A Liberal Interlude:
The Modernization of the MMA,
c. 1924–1931

This chapter describes how and why the MMA responded to some of the liberal currents that had swept through the awakened consciences of some of its members. The progressive impulse was necessarily diluted as it spread from proprietor-managers, who were convinced of the rightness of their program, through the Business Problems Group, few of whose members were able to accompany them very far down the welfare capitalist road, and into the MMA, where the Orthodox were never more than a small but influential minority. The MMA remained a voluntary association with an increasingly diverse membership whose needs it existed to serve. In this context, the impact of managerial liberalism could not but be limited. However, Leeds and his associates had allies who might not share their religious perspective but could agree to their specific policy recommendations. These allies were professional managers (particularly personnel specialists) of the MMA's new recruits, including some of Philadelphia's largest metal products companies and branch plants of both of the giant electrical manufacturers, General Electric and Westinghouse. The electrical manufacturers in particular were at the forefront of the employee representation and other movements for the reform of capitalist employment relations *by enlightened capitalists themselves*. In addition, the reformers found support outside of the local business community, in the new world of foundation-backed, university-based applied social science, represented in Philadelphia by Joseph Willits and the Wharton School's Department of Industrial Research (DIR), which he created and ran. The story of managerial reform among the Philadelphia metal trades in the later 1920s is therefore a complicated one, dependent on alliances between proprietary capitalists and managerial professionals, among academics, businesspeople, and some government agencies, and between local and cosmopolitan influentials. It is a story that is emblematic of the larger program of moderate, voluntaristic, cooperative reformism associated with the liberals'

309

hero, Herbert Hoover. Like his, it is a story of limited achievement that ended in disaster.

9.1 THE ORTHODOX TAKEOVER

Leeds and his close associates made relatively little impact on the MMA up until the early 1920s, despite serving on its executive committee. They were not recorded as participants in any big strategic discussions, nor did they act as link-men between the MMA and other local and national employers' organizations. They held none of the key offices before Charles Evans became vice president in 1920 and Leeds treasurer in 1922. They were evidently respected – in March 1919 Evans was the keynote speaker at the quarterly meeting, when he returned from fourteen months in France on AFSC work and received "a hearty rising vote of thanks"; Robert Yarnall was similarly honored the next year, addressing the massive annual banquet that marked President Schwacke's retirement about his child-feeding experiences in Germany. They were also trusted, as their selection as auditors or finance committee members indicated. But they were not central to the design and implementation of the MMA's anti-labor policy. At the most they, and the Hicksite William S. Hallowell, moderated it, notably because of their reluctance to be directly involved in the "labor spy racket."[1]

These men's relative unimportance within the MMA ended in the early 1920s. As the older generation of belligerent activists (if Quakers, predominantly Hicksite) retired, the younger, second-level officers (predominantly Orthodox) moved up to take their place. The established processes of leadership succession and cooptation brought them to the fore and enabled them to advance their associates and their causes through the MMA.

Staunton Peck had been reluctant to take up the presidency in 1920, and he soon wished to be relieved of it. He was prevailed upon to stay in 1922 and 1923, but by 1924 he was determined to resign. He "had a very strong feeling that the conduct of an Association such as this ought not to be held too closely within a little group and that rotation in the officials of the Association would tend to stimulate the general interest." He believed that "one of the finest things that could happen to the Association was having Mr. Leeds as President."[2]

---

[1] MMA-EXEC database; ECM 13 Jan. 1920, 12 March 1919, 7 Dec. 1920; Leo Huberman, *The Labor Spy Racket* (New York, 1937), for the phrase; Sidney Howard and Robert Dunn, *The Labor Spy* (New York, 1924), and Jean E. Spielman, *The Stool-Pigeon and the Open Shop Movement* (Minneapolis, 1923), for studies of contemporary practice.

[2] ECM 13 Dec. 1922, 12 Dec. 1923, 25 Nov. 1924.

This is, on the face of it, strange. Peck and his vice president (the office Leeds held by 1924) disagreed about collective bargaining and employee representation, about the desirability of maintaining or shortening employees' hours of work, and also about the dangers of paternalism inherent in company welfare schemes. They also had a series of disputes on the MMA executive committee itself. For example, Leeds would always recommend that a liberal speaker be brought in to address the assembled members at dinner meetings; Peck's choices were characteristically conservative. In 1923, Leeds preferred Henry Dennison over John Leitch, author of the Leitch Plan for a restricted form of employee representation, and also opposed inviting Walter G. Merritt of the League for Industrial Rights. The next year, he wanted Morris Ll. Cooke to talk about the "Giant Power" proposals for the planned development of Pennsylvania's electrical generating resources, whereas Peck suggested a spokesman from Sherman Service, an industrial detective agency branching out into anti-union personnel consulting.[3]

The most serious disagreement between them was about the MMA's financial support for a viciously anti-labor monthly magazine, *Industry*, which was an extension of the American Plan offensive into the field of propaganda. This was the pet project of Justus Schwacke himself, who had long believed in the importance and efficacy of "public education" campaigns to weaken labor's support, and had run the NFA–NMTA Joint Publicity Committee through the 'teens. *Industry*, its vehicle, was full of oversimplification and distortion, and was a thoroughly discreditable publication. Its intended readership was state and federal legislators, editors, and particularly educators, ministers of religion, and other liberal opinion-makers who were thought to harbor dangerously pro-labor views. Peck was troubled by their "tendency. . . . to see only the side of labor in any controversy" that resulted largely from their "dense ignorance and lack of interest in industrial matters," which *Industry* might correct, as well as from "the sympathy of naturally sympathetic dispositions, towards the supposedly under dog."[4]

Peck was not as obsessed as Schwacke by the importance "of creating sane public opinion on industrial questions," or as convinced that *Industry*'s attacking approach to the task was the best. He supported "the dissemination of information of an instructive and educational nature but . . . . he was not in favor of circulating information of a strongly controversial (*sic*) nature." Nevertheless, he did not block Schwacke's plans, and the MMA poured out hundreds of dollars between 1919 and 1924, even

[3] ECM 24 Apr. 1923, 1 Apr. 1924.
[4] Schwacke, "President's Annual Report," NMTA, *Synopsis of Proceedings of the 13th Annual Convention* (New York, 1911), esp. pp. 8–9 and regular reports in annual proceedings thereafter; Peck, PRES 1921, p. 3.

while it was in deepening deficit, to sponsor the circulation of *Industry* (captioned M.M.A.) to opinion-formers in the Philadelphia metropolitan area.[5]

Leeds and his friends became determined to disassociate themselves from this magazine, one of whose chief focuses of attack – Social Gospel Protestantism – was, after all, their personal credo. In 1924 they launched a frontal assault on it within the executive committee, resulting in fierce discussions that Earl Sparks recorded far more fully than usual, and still remembered thirty years later as an important incident in the MMA's development. Robert Yarnall reported that he only "glanced at it occasionally" and that "his Superintendent had recently said. . . . that it was simply another pamphlet whose articles would not bear careful scrutiny and smacked of propaganda." William Sauter of American Engineering, an Orthodox ally on industrial education issues for over a decade, though not himself a Quaker, "did not think much of it" either. Karl Legner of Haines, Jones & Cadbury dismissed it as "very partisan. . . . both sides of the subjects covered should be presented." Leeds himself was scathing – "it would not carry very much weight with anyone really familiar with what they are reading." But Staunton Peck retorted that "the purpose. . . . was to present the employer's side and quite naturally it would seem partisan but. . . . its articles were mild indeed when contrasted to the material that is circulated by the radical and union organizations." The most he would do was to canvass members' opinions, and meanwhile write the editor to try to get him to tone down his rhetoric and balance his arguments a little.[6]

Given all of these disagreements about politics and values between the machinery foundrymen Peck and Schwacke and their more liberal Republican associates, why then did Peck have such a good opinion of Leeds and think him so well suited to be his successor? Any answer must be speculative, but the beginning of it is surely that everyone who knew him thought well of Leeds. He lacked charisma, but he possessed great personal authority and a quiet, persuasive wit.[7] Leeds was respected for his achievements as well as his character – for building a successful, dynamic company; for

[5] ECM 17 Jul. 1923, 27 Sep. 1921.
[6] Sparks, "The Metal Manufacturers Association of Philadelphia: A Review of Activities 1903–53," p. 5, MMAP I-1-2; ECM 13 May, 2 June, 29 July 1924.
[7] Rowntree to Chudleigh, 3 Dec. 1923, p. 2, in Chudleigh File, America 1923–8, BSR Papers, JSRT; *Dictionary of Quaker Biography*, QC-HC; Editorial, "The Immortality of Ideas," p. 1 and "Morris Evans Leeds 1869–1952," *The Cooperator* 9:11 (March 1952): 3, 15; "Morris Evans Leeds 1869–1952," *Instrument Manufacturing* (March–Apr. 1952): 40; Stanley R. Yarnall, "Morris E. Leeds," resolution adopted by Science and Art Club of Germantown, 25 Feb. 1952, copy in DRY Papers. The correspondence between Leeds and Charles Lukens Huston, manager of the Lukens Steel Co., who had abandoned his family's Quaker roots in favor of a sanctimonious evangelicalism, illustrates the determined yet not argumentative way in which he dealt with his more conservative peers – see, e.g., letters of 7 Jan. and 4 May 1920 in Huston Papers, Box 1989, F. 25, Accession 50, HML.

his work for a range of Philadelphia civic institutions, as well as a varied assortment of Quaker educational and philanthropic activities. He had given his services to the MMA over almost twenty years, and had proven his ability to run a businessmen's association by helping to found the Scientific Instrument Manufacturers of America in 1920 and becoming its first president, an office that he held until 1926. Nobody else left on the executive committee by 1924 matched his qualifications and experience. An alternative candidate would have had to have risen through the MMA's committee structure, but by 1924 the only men with service records similar to Leeds's were William Sauter and Stogdell Stokes, who were his allies, and W. J. Hagman of Niles-Bement-Pond, who was not. Hagman might have been able to stand for the old guard's interests, but for the fact that his company pulled out of Philadelphia in 1924 as part of a retrenchment program forced on it by heavy losses.

Leeds also had a program for the organization's survival and growth in the face of the challenges posed to it by the end of the Open Shop war, the recession and industrial restructuring winnowing the ranks of its members and their workforces, and the simple fact that inflation and the MMA's war and postwar expansion of activities had outpaced the growth of its income over the same period. Leeds drew members' attention to the fact that MMA dues had not changed since 1903, "although its usefulness had enlarged considerably." The MMA had operated on a shoestring for too long: By 1925, its dues were only between a third and a sixth of the amounts charged by comparable NMTA branches, with those running employment departments costing the most. MMA members had grown too used to low-priced services, which its cheap and bloodless victories over organized labor had permitted it to sustain.[8]

Leeds was the architect of the MMA's survival strategy in this difficult situation. As treasurer in 1922 and 1923, and vice president in 1924, he stood for a policy of maintaining and even expanding the association's personnel management-related services, even though in the short term that might worsen the problem of operating with an accumulating deficit. For the MMA, just as much as for his own company or, later, the U.S. economy as a whole, Leeds believed in countercyclical action rather than aiming at year-to-year budget balancing. The way out of the hole was not to cut services, but to finance them out of reserves and to aim to increase income by expanding the membership that, "especially if it embraced the very large firms, would not only increase our revenue, but increase our prestige and our usefulness" and reverse the spiral of decline. The strategy paid off. In 1923 and 1924 the MMA made a net gain of eighteen members, from seventy-five to ninety-three companies – the most successful recruitment

---

[8]   ECM 6 June 1922; 12 Dec. 1923; 28 Oct., 10 Dec. 1924; Finance Committee Minutes, 31 March 1925.

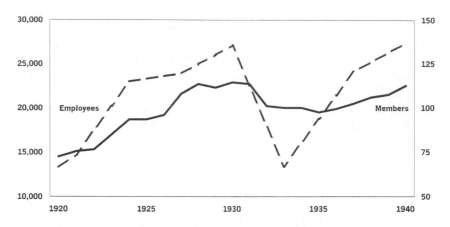

Figure 9.1. Growth of the MMA, 1920–1940. *Note:* Employment figures between survey dates have been estimated by interpolation. Reported "operative" totals were not used because they reflected actual employment increasingly poorly after the introduction of graduated assessments in 1924–25. *Source*: PID-1640 database.

drive since 1911–12 and 1919–20, and unlike them in not being attributable to the mobilizing effects of previous labor conflicts (see Figure 9.1). Two of the new recruits were giants, bringing the MMA additional resources and Leeds and his associates powerful support for their program of reorienting the MMA toward positive and progressive action in the whole human resource management field.[9]

Why did the Henry Disston saw, tool, and steel works with its 3,050 employees, and Westinghouse Electrical and Manufacturing Co.'s turbine plant with 3,546 respond to the MMA's recruitment attempts in 1924, when they and their like had always refused in the past?

The first part of the explanation is financial. The MMA had been in negotiation with Westinghouse since 1921, having helped it through "foundry trouble," but the problem was that the company was not sure that the benefits it would derive from membership would be worth its massive share of the association's dues. (It would have paid about one-fifth of the total in 1921.) Westinghouse required that there should be either a maximum amount of dues a member must pay, irrespective of size, or that assessments must be graded – the more operatives a firm employed, the less it would have to pay on each above a certain threshold. In 1921 the MMA would not accept these terms – what would the effect of such a

[9]   ECM, 1 Apr. 1924; cf. Leeds's comments at Finance Committee meeting, 18 Nov. 1930, during next depression, and in Henry S. Dennison et al., *Toward Full Employment* (New York, 1938), Pt. I.

concession be on firms that were large compared with other MMA members but too small to qualify for Westinghouse's special deal? They would certainly be resentful that "tho (sic) paying dues relatively less [it] would receive practically the same benefits." There was also fear of the possibility, "in the event of a number of large establishments enrolling with us, of their obtaining control to further their own interests." Offsetting these reservations was the desire "to reach out further and probably accomplish our purposes more broadly, as well as, to better control and stabilize the labor conditions here." But Peck came down decisively against giving Westinghouse or any other large company cut-rate membership, so the matter was shelved.[10]

What happened in 1924 was that the finance committee, led by Leeds and his replacement as treasurer – G.E.'s plant manager! – worked out a plan for graduating assessments to meet the big firms' requirements. They did this in a way that did not need to be submitted for the members' approval because they claimed that it did not involve a change in the constitution, merely in its interpretation. Members employing women had already negotiated special rates on these operatives, so there was an available precedent for varying the rate of assessment in line with the amount of "service" a member was liable to require on a particular class of "help"; the clear implication was that big companies would make less of a call on the MMA because they already possessed their own employment departments, which did indeed turn out to be the case.[11]

This was the first stage in the solution of the MMA's financial and structural problems; the second came in Leeds's first year as president, when the constitution was amended to formalize what had already been done on an ad hoc basis. Dues were raised on the first 500 employees by 20 percent (to 12¢ per operative per month), cut to 5¢ on the next 500, and limited to the female rate of 1¢ on all employees, of either gender, above 1,000; initiation fees were similarly capped at one month's dues. These actions in 1924 and 1925 enabled the MMA to break free of the financial and recruitment problems that afflicted it during Peck's presidency.[12]

The second part of the explanation for the sudden attractiveness of MMA membership to firms with ample independent resources and well-developed personnel and welfare programs of their own is the statistical and other research services that Sparks could offer them. Westinghouse and G.E. operated a clear policy of matching or exceeding the going rate in communities

[10] Paper on Sparks's activities, ECM 27 Jan. 1925; ECM 9, 21 March, 26 Apr., 24 May 1921; PID-1640 and MMAYEARS databases.
[11] ECM 29 Jan. 1924; 11 Feb., 11 March 1919.
[12] Statement Regarding Changes in Constitution and By-Laws, 7 Feb. 1925; Finance Committee meeting, 27 Apr. 1925; ECM 27 Oct. 1925; Memorandum for Mr. Stokes, Chairman of Finance Committee, as basis for recommendation of the assessment to be levied for the Quarter Beginning June 1, 1928.

where they had plants. The MMA's maintenance of its regular data gathering through the postwar recession and its period of deficit financing meant that it was in a position to give them access to information necessary for their sophisticated union-free employment systems. Disston was probably motivated to join because a manpower crisis caused by massive turnover in a hitherto-stable workforce, which had resulted from the development of alternative employment opportunities in its hitherto-isolated Tacony neighborhood, had forced a rapid development in personnel policy. It was already a member of Joseph Willits's PADEP; joining the MMA, with its focus on the turnover problem, was a logical next step.[13]

The third reason for the MMA's sudden access of strength involved Disston alone, but, given that that single company employed 15 percent of the 1924 total, it is worth mentioning. Disston's hand tools found their market among construction workers – especially carpenters – who were still some of America's most highly unionized craftsmen. The end of large-scale industrial conflict and the beginning of the progressive régime in the MMA freed Disston to join without having to worry about the impact that this might have on its corporate image.[14]

What was the effect of the accession of Leeds and his group to power within the MMA, and of the change in its support base toward larger, managerially if not necessarily politically progressive, companies?

A part of the difference reflected the distance in political values between the new and old régimes, which the *Industry* fight in 1924 had already highlighted. *Industry* itself did not survive long: It was axed in midsummer 1925, ostensibly on financial grounds, and Schwacke – who emerged from retirement to protest the decision – was palmed off with a single $100 payment "for educational purposes to counteract radical propaganda." Leeds and associates now had their way in the choice of keynote speakers at MMA banquets, too – for example, Henry Dennison on "Employees' Participation in Management and Profits"; industrial psychologist Elton Mayo on "Fatigue and Obsessions in Industry"; the vice president of Bell Telephone on "Human Relations"; Sam Lewisohn, chair of the American Management Association, on "The New Leadership in Industry"; Arthur H. Young of John D. Rockefeller, Jr.'s Industrial Relations Counselors on the regularization of employment.[15]

These choices were significant, because they indicated which wing of the

---

[13] Ronald Schatz, *The Electrical Workers: A History of Labor at General Electric and Westinghouse, 1923–60* (Urbana, 1983), pp. 18–19; Harry Silcox, *A Place to Live and Work: The Henry Disston Saw Works and the Tacony Community of Philadelphia* (University Park, 1994), Ch. 6.

[14] ECM 27 May 1929.

[15] ECM, 23 June, 29 July 1925; 13 May, 9 Dec. 1925, 8 Dec. 1926, 1 June 1927, 27 May 1929.

business community the MMA was siding with, and they laid out its leaders' agenda for the instruction of the membership, not all of whom were by any means so liberal. So too did the refusal to cooperate with the NAM Fuel Supply Committee, which was attempting to weaken the United Mine Workers by encouraging the purchase of coal from nonunion producers; Leeds's opposition to the Pennsylvania Manufacturers' Association, on the grounds of its president Joseph Grundy's autocratic, isolationist, and reactionary stance; his turning down Walter Merritt's request for support for the League for Industrial Rights; his argument against his members' reflexive demand for tax reduction, that "the State must have taxes" to perform its necessary functions; and his general position on advances in social welfare policy, that the MMA should not "always be in a position of opposing legislation."[16]

This is not to say that the MMA, even under Leeds, was wholeheartedly "progressive": It opposed the federal Child Labor Amendment, on the grounds that the matter was one for state-by-state action, although worthy in principle; on behalf of its hard-pressed foundrymen members, it continued to resist pressures for stringent occupational safety regulations; and it remained firmly against the AFL's ultimately successful campaign to limit the courts' power to issue injunctions in labor disputes. Nevertheless, there was a marked change of tone and policy as compared with anything that the MMA had seen before. The association was now prepared to work with government agencies for the solution of commonly perceived problems (notably in the areas of vocational training, employment stabilization, and improving the working of the labor market) and would even lobby on behalf of increased funds and powers for the agencies whose programs complemented its own.[17]

Leeds's basic preference was not, however, for an enhanced role for the state. He remained essentially a voluntarist, albeit a more positive and liberal one than any previous MMA president. His basic welfare capitalist assumption was that "if management assumed the responsibilities that were rightly theirs . . . . the likelihood of large increases in labor influence was remote."[18]

How did these principles translate into a program of action within the MMA itself? Actions to improve workers' satisfaction within a nonunion employment system – and, at the same time, to meet members' needs – concentrated in three areas: updating the policy and reputation of the Labor

[16] ECM 23 June 1925, 26 March 1926, 27 March 1928, 24 Jan. 1928, 31 March 1925, 27 May 1930.
[17] ECM 27 Jan. 1925; 23 Feb., 26 March, 27 Apr., 5 Oct., 23 Nov., 28 Dec. 1926; Report of the Law and Legislative Committee on Senate Bill S-3151, 22 May 1928; ECM 27 May 1930.
[18] ECM, 9 Dec. 1925.

Bureau (renamed the Employment and Personnel Department); research and remedial action to deal with the continuing turnover problem; and vocational education and training, to counter the skills shortage that troubled Philadelphia metal manufacturers by mid-decade.

One of the first steps taken by the Leeds–Sparks team in 1925 was to revitalize the association's labor bureau, and to change its emphasis and image among members and their workers alike. This was both possible and necessary because of its decisive shift away from having to engage in occasional striker replacement – because there were hardly any strikes – toward acting purely as a specialized recruitment agency.

For the first time, an explicit policy was worked out to govern the bureau's work, based on the principle that it "would function most successfully and fulfill the objects of the Association . . . . if [its] conduct was such as to inspire confidence in the applicants that they would receive a square deal." And, in a way that reflected the executive committee's liberal values and would otherwise have been out of place in the nativist 1920s, its formal policy of nondiscrimination with respect to membership or non-membership "in any organization of workmen lawfully organized and conducted" was strengthened and extended to cover "their religious belief, color or nationality." This went much further than the old claim not to operate a strict blacklist, and recognized that the association still included some union establishments and more, including G.E. and Westinghouse, that tolerated individual union members, and would even bargain informally with their own skilled workers. The MMA proclaimed that it would treat all jobseekers even-handedly. It still could not guarantee that individual members would do the same, and it did not attempt to except by issuing statements of policy; but nonetheless its claim to be acting "for the mutual benefit of the applicant and the prospective employer" was now stronger than ever before.[19]

This is not to say that the MMA's primary dedication to serving its members' interests was subordinated. The mission of the Employment Department, which absorbed two-thirds of the association's total expenditures, was "to cultivate sources of labor supply, to secure willing and effective workers, and endeavor to maintain a stable, reliable and cooperative body of workers in the plants of the member companies." But Sparks and the managerial liberals saw that this was a much larger task than the old anti-union role, and one that needed to engage the best efforts of companies and any community agencies that would work with them.[20]

The next priority was to address the problem of employment stability.

[19] ECM 24 Feb. 1925; "Resolution of Policy Governing the Conduct of the Association's Employment and Personnel Department," 17 March 1925, with ECM 31st. Mar. 1925.
[20] ECM, 28 Apr. 1925; Treasurer's Report, 1925; "Resolution of Policy."

Turnover was no longer a general preoccupation of American personnel specialists in the way it had been during and immediately after the war, but in the Philadelphia metal trades it remained a major concern. Among the plants that the MMA surveyed, amounting to about one-half of the local industry, it reached 170 percent per annum in 1923. Then, after falling by the end of 1924 to a figure that the Wharton's Anne Bezanson's continuing study demonstrated to be "not only low, but. . . . low beyond all precedent in the last decade" – on an annual basis, a "mere" 100 percent – it recovered to 150 percent in 1926.[21]

These levels were higher than those observed in any other major metal trades center apart from Detroit, where the automobile industry was characterized by rapid growth and massive seasonal variations in employment. They are hard to explain except by referring to some continuing structural characteristics of the Philadelphia metal trades' product and labor markets. Many local companies were still engaged in contract and small-batch manufacture, and the extension of hand-to-mouth buying by their customers after the 1920–21 inventory recession accentuated their entrenched habit of frequent hiring, layoff, and recall. Also, the unregulated, union-free labor market resulted in wide variations among firms in rates of pay for workers of comparable skill. The net effect was that workers were compelled, or had every reason, to keep on the look out for the marginally more secure or better-paid job rather than sticking with one employer; and that metal trades employers were the most frequent and active help-wanted advertisers in the city, paying local newspapers $107,000 for this purpose in 1926. There was, as Sparks told his members, "an army of one hundred and fifty thousand men and women. . . . march[ing] in and out of the metal plants in the Philadelphia district" every year, costing manufacturers an estimated $3,000,000 for "recruiting, introduction, training and additional supervision, spoilage and retarded production."[22]

[21] SEC 1926, pp. 3–5; Bezanson et al., "Four Years of Labor Mobility: A Study of Labor Turnover in a Group of Selected Plants in Philadelphia, 1921–1924" (Supplement to *The Annals* 119 [May 1925]), p. 8.

[22] Bezanson, "Labor Market Comparisons: Turnover Rates in Four Metal Manufacturing Centers," *Journal of Personnel Research* (hereafter *JPR*) 5 (1927): 387–401; Respondents 201, 295, 496, Machinists Study, Palmer Papers, TUUA; Hummel LaRue Frain, *Factors Influencing the Collection of Wage Data: An Examination of the Relation Between Some Influences Relevant to Earnings of Workers in Certain Standard Machine Tool Occupations as Shown by Data Supplied by a Group of Plants in Philadelphia* (Philadelphia, 1928), pp. 6, 33, 37–38 and *An Examination of Earnings in Certain Standard Machine-Tool Occupations in Philadelphia* (Philadelphia, 1929), pp. 1–7, 62, 66, 78–79; Bezanson et al., "Four Years of Labor Mobility," pp. 3, 39; Bezanson, *Help-Wanted Advertising as an Indicator of the Demand for Labor* (Philadelphia, 1929), pp. 31, 78–79; SEC 1926, pp. 3, 4. Department of Industrial Research, *Industrial Progress and Economic Research: Twenty-Five Years of Research Accomplishment* (Philadelphia, 1946), pp. 14–15, shows turnover of the metal trades' male workforce, 1923–29, by industrial category, and

This mobile labor force helps account for the MMA's increased attention to its Employment Department, which members used to fill specialized needs when normal methods had failed. But it also explains another new departure for the MMA: the development of a close, collaborative relationship with Joseph Willits and his associates from the Wharton, a cooperation that was designed to provide the knowledge base for progressive personnel management.

9.2 JOSEPH WILLITS AND THE IDEA OF COOPERATIVE RESEARCH

Joseph Willits had returned to the Wharton School from his job as employment superintendent at the Aircraft Factory in the Philadelphia Navy Yard in 1919. His prewar colleague, Alfred Williams, was demobilized from that haven of liberal Taylorism, the U.S. Shipping Board, at the same time. These men, thirty and twenty-six years old, respectively, had enjoyed considerable administrative responsibility during the war emergency, including in Willits's case entire charge of the hiring and firing of a workforce of up to 3,600 men and women. Now they were reduced to being mere junior academics, with careers to build in a utilitarian institution dedicated to practical research and the training of managers and professional specialists.[23]

Willits fit in comfortably. He was enticed back by a promotion to Assistant Professor, a small prize he preferred to the lucrative business consultancy he was offered at the same time. The university valued him partly because of what an anonymous sponsor called his "middle-of-the-road position" within the personnel management movement. He could "work with employers," as his secretaryship of the PADEP demonstrated. And because of his wartime connections, he promised to bring Penn a special bonus as it strove to establish a position of "leadership. . . . in the science of employment management. . . . [which] turns out men for wants that are as definite and as acute as the want for a dentist," and was thus in keeping with the university's utilitarian and vocational role.[24]

Willits had been chair of the committee of local employment managers' associations that created the National Association of Employment

indicates that the highest rate occurred among heavy equipment makers, whose product markets were exceptionally unstable. It peaked at almost 300 percent in the last quarter of 1926.

[23] Career and Military Service Records, Willits Biographical File, and Williams Biographical File, University of Pennsylvania Archives; Steven Sass, *The Pragmatic Imagination: A History of the Wharton School 1881–1981* (Philadelphia, 1982), esp. Chs. 6–7.

[24] Anonymous letter to Provost Edgar S. Smith, 30 Dec. 1918, in Joseph Willits Papers, Box 7, Accession IV-2A-39, RAC.

Managers in 1918, and was that organization's national treasurer, so he was incomparably well connected. But his unique selling point, so far as Wharton was concerned, was his closeness to the group of applied psychologists under Walter Dill Scott who had made up the Army's Committee on the Classification of Personnel. When they returned to civilian life they formed the Scott Company, of which Willits became an associate, to sell their services to industry. It based itself in Philadelphia, home of Scott's close collaborator, Robert Clothier, employment manager at paper-goods maker A. M. Collins and Curtis Publishing before the war and a founding member of the PADEP. The university was interested in the Scott group's skills because of their presumed usefulness in student testing and placement. They were "sought by nearly every university in the country," and with Willits's help Penn could "probably get them on terms which are exceedingly advantageous."[25]

The anticipated direct benefits of rehiring Willits were therefore obvious enough. The indirect benefits were also thought to be considerable. Wharton's, and the university's, relations with its trustees, alumni, and local clients had been strained by political controversies in 1915–17 that resulted from the anti-capitalist and anti-war stance of prominent (and quickly dismissed) faculty member Scott Nearing. Willits could help restore them: He would make Wharton "solid with the leading citizens of Philadelphia," his contacts with the Scott group would "put the University on [their] tongues. . . . and will make them think that after all the [Wharton] is of particular as well as general value."[26]

Willits's sponsors' hopes were to be fulfilled in general but not in detail. Willits was no psychologist, and his work would have little to do with this new field of applied science. But he did build on his PADEP contacts to promote outreach into the business community, notably in 1920, when he

---

[25] "Historical Sketch of the National Association of Employment Managers," pp. 4–6 in *Proceedings of the First Annual Convention of the National Association of Employment Managers* (Newark, 1919). For the Scott group, see Loren Baritz, *The Servants of Power: A History of the Use of Social Science in American Industry* (New York, 1965 ed.; first published 1960), pp. 45–52; Daniel Kevles, "Testing the Army's Intelligence: Psychologists and the Military in World War I," *JAH* 55 (1968): 565–81; Edmund C. Lynch, "Walter Dill Scott: Pioneer Industrial Psychologist," *BHR* 42 (1968): 149–70, esp. pp. 166–68; James P. Mulherin, "The Sociology of Work and Organizations: Historical Context and Pattern of Development" (Ph.D. diss., University of California–Berkeley, 1979), esp. p. 116; Donald S. Napoli, *Architects of Adjustment: The History of the Psychological Profession in the United States* (Port Washington, 1981), Ch. 1; Michael M. Sokal, "James McKeen Cattell and American Psychology in the 1920s," in Josef Brozek, ed., *Explorations in the History of Psychology in the United States* (Lewisburg, 1984), pp. 277–79, 284–88; Michael M. Sokal, "Origins of the Psychological Corporation," *Journal of the History of the Behavioral Sciences* (hereafter *JHBS*) 17 (1981): 54–67 at pp. 56, 62; Letter to Provost [quote].

[26] Letter to Provost.

and Williams organized Wharton's Industrial Service Department to place its students and graduates in appropriate jobs with local firms. He was rewarded with a rapid promotion to full professor in 1920 and chairmanship of his department; the receipt of a job offer from the Harvard Business School cannot have harmed his chances.

Instead of Willits going to Cambridge, the traffic was the other way. In 1921 he recruited from Harvard a woman who would turn into his key collaborator, Anna (later Anne) Bezanson. Together they founded a new Industrial Research Department designed to further develop Wharton's program of service to its manufacturing neighbors. Bezanson's career path was not as straightforward as her two male colleagues'. She entered Radcliffe College only after several years as an employment manager at the Gillette Safety Razor Company in Boston, but then ascended the academic ladder fast. She came to Philadelphia during the war to help organize personnel courses for women at Bryn Mawr College under federal government auspices, and then returned to a position at Harvard as a member of its Committee on Economic Research. She was a superb statistician and a highly original economic historian, and most of the best work done by Willits's department would be hers or that of her Bryn Mawr protégée, Gladys Palmer.[27]

But, in many respects, Willits would deserve the credit he gained for it. He articulated the rationale for the joint research program, he raised the funds, and he ran the show. He was a research manager at ease in the new world of organized knowledge of the 1920s. As an influential advocate of his plans argued in a letter to Provost Smith in 1920, he was "unique in combining an unusual group of qualities – likeableness, understanding of men, a creative intellect, and unusual ability to attract and hold associates, and develop outside connections of value to the University."[28]

Willits's ability to establish his new research empire depended, as had so much of his career, on knowing the right people. The contact of most use to him was Beardsley Ruml, who, in Robert Hutchins's words, was "the founder of the social sciences in America." At Dartmouth, Chicago, and Carnegie Tech, Ruml had worked under the founding fathers of applied psychology – Walter Bingham, James Angell, and Scott himself. He had nat-

[27] For overviews of the DIR's work, see its *Industrial Progress and Economic Research*, Pt. II; Former Members of the Staff, *A Research Program in Retrospect: A Review of the Work of the Industrial Research Department 1921–1953* (Philadelphia, Dec. 1955, processed); Sass, *Pragmatic Imagination*, pp. 175, 179, 188, 208–09; Willits to Dean Walter B. Donham, 9 March 1920, Willits Papers, Box 7, F. 68, RAC; Willits to Ruml, 9 Nov. 1926, LSRM Papers Ser. III-6, B. 75, File 792 (Bezanson c.v.), RAC; Biographical Files for Willits, Williams, Bezanson, and Palmer, University of Pennsylvania Archives.

[28] Copy of Anon. to Smith, 21 Jan. 1920, in Willits Papers, Box 7, RAC.

urally followed them into the War Department, where he served as director of the Division of Occupational Tests, and then out into private consultancy. He became the Scott Company's secretary and was in charge of its statistical work. He was a close associate of Willits both there and in the National Research Council's Conference on Personnel Research, which was designed to promote and coordinate activity in this new field.[29]

Out of that conference came the Personnel Research Federation, of which Ruml was Acting Director, and Willits was an executive member. But Ruml's tenure there was short: He followed his patron Angell to New York in 1920 when the latter became president of the Carnegie Corporation. And when Angell moved on to become president of Yale in 1921, Ruml's independent career really took off. At the age of twenty-seven he was appointed Director of the Laura Spelman Rockefeller Memorial, established in 1918 in honor of John D. Rockefeller, Sr.,'s late wife. It had an endowment of more than $70,000,000 and only the vaguest objectives, which it had unsurprisingly failed to do much to fulfill before his arrival.

Ruml was perhaps a "stopgap choice" intended to perform as "'an influential office boy'" until the Rockefeller Foundation trustees could reunite the memorial's funds with their own. But Ruml had other ideas, and he persuaded the trustees to let him carry them into action. For the next eight years he would enjoy an extraordinary degree of freedom in dispensing Rockefeller money for the advancement of applied social science research in the United States.[30]

As Franz Samelson observed, a "network of bright and influential people, sharing interests, plans, and visions of the future, was emerging." Ruml would provide many of the resources and much of the guidance that they needed to bring their ideas to fruition. "The war had given them a taste of the future, of entrepreneurial research, with large-scale projects, ... research time freed from teaching, and a big supporting apparatus, all financed by huge sums of money." With the winding-down of the Wilsonian war economy, they were suffering what Stanley Coben termed "'withdrawal' pains," and Ruml with his Rockefeller millions arrived on the scene just in time to fill the hungry gap.[31]

[29] Mulherin, "Sociology of Work and Organizations," pp. 110–19 [quotes from pp. 110, 117].

[30] Alfred D. Flinn, "Development of the Personnel Research Federation," *JPR* 1:1 (May 1922): 7–13; Waldemar A. Nielsen, *The Big Foundations: A Twentieth Century Fund Study* (New York, 1972), Chs. 3, 4; David M. Grossman, "American Foundations and the Support of Economic Research, 1913–1929," *Minerva* 20 (1982): 59–82 at pp. 79–82; Martin and Joan Bulmer, "Philanthropy and Social Science in the 1920s: Beardsley Ruml and the Laura Spelman Rockefeller Memorial, 1922–29," *Minerva* 19 (1981): 347–407 at pp. 350–58.

[31] Franz Samelson, "Organizing for the Kingdom of Behavior," *JHBS* 21 (1985): 33–47 at pp. 38–41; Stanley Coben, "Foundation Officials and Fellowships: Innovation in the Patronage of Science," *Minerva* 14 (1976): 225–40 at p. 233.

Ruml's support for Willits's work was of fundamental importance. When it was set up, the Department of Industrial Research was funded jointly by the university, the PADEP group, and the Carnegie Corporation. Carnegie's grant made up half of the DIR's income, was guaranteed for five years, and was the key to getting the other half pledged from local sources, in that it was conditional on their matching it dollar for dollar. With this degree of financial security, Willits, Bezanson, and their growing team were able to embark on a quite ambitious program of long-run research. When the Carnegie seed-money ran out Ruml, the "Maecenas" of applied social science, would be able to fund the DIR's work even more adequately.[32]

Having established the department and secured sponsorship, Willits and Bezanson still had to define its role. But while they were developing their strategy they busied themselves with service to Willits's PADEP contacts, responding to local businesses' immediate perceived needs in accepted Wharton style rather than pursuing their own lines of inquiry. The PADEP had divided its work among four separate groups, all meeting regularly, as it had grown – employment managers, works managers, industrial editors, and supervisors. The two latter groups reflected the fact that many firms had established plant newspapers to deal with their morale problems and supervisory training programs (under Willits's direction) to improve lower level personnel and production management. By 1921 the first flush of enthusiasm for the personnel movement was passing, and during the head-long deflation companies wanted to be able to gauge and improve the effectiveness of these once-fashionable, but unproven, activities. The DIR willingly obliged.[33]

But this reactive, wholly practical applied research was designed to demonstrate its immediate usefulness rather than to be the core of an ongoing program. It was "not established as a service station for industrial plants," although this secondary function would remain one of its characteristic relationships with its local community. Despite the fact that Willits was emphatic that the department was "not in a consulting business," nevertheless because the "area of understanding and sympathetic contact in the community must. . . . set a limit to the possibilities of effective research," it

[32]   Irving S. Sayford, "'No More Square Pegs' in Round Holes," *Philadelphia Public Ledger*, 24 Sept. 1922; Ruml memorandum, 17 Jan. 1923, p. 1, in LSRM Papers, Box 75, F. 790, RAC; Willits, "Need for Cooperative Research in an Industrial Community," *Engineers and Engineering* 75 (1922): 403–08 at p. 404; Coben, "Foundation Officials and Fellowships," p. 233, for the appellation.
[33]   Sayford, "No More Square Pegs"; Willits to Donham, 9 Mar. 1920, p. 2; "Research Program of the Industrial Research Department" (April 1927), Appendix A, "The Work of the Department of Industrial Research to Date," pp. 1–3, in LSRM Papers, Box 76, F. 797, RAC.

was worthwhile and necessary to engage in a certain amount of this sort of customer-led work.[34]

Willits's grand objective was to build on the foundations that he and Morris Cooke had laid before the war with his pioneering study of the Philadelphia labor market. Cooke remained devoted to the promotion of research and action designed to foster grass-roots employment stabilization:

Only as we study the every-day and all-the-year-around variety of unemployment, and learn to cope with it within the individual manufacturing plant will we able to prevent or at least to minimize the effects of those great waves of unemployment which we have come to look upon as necessarily associated with periods of business depressions.[35]

Cooke continued to believe that what was vital was microlevel action by managers of individual firms to eliminate irregular and underemployment, rather than a state-led countercyclical macroeconomic policy designed to affect the aggregate level. "The burden of proof is upon every employer who lays any claim to industrial leadership to show that he has availed himself of every possible device for providing steady employment." Such voluntarism was the moral, the self-interestedly enlightened, and, in the context of the postwar reaction, the only politically practicable course.[36]

Willits still shared with Cooke his prewar convictions about the need for more knowledge about the facts of unemployment and the promise of employment stabilization. But, as befitted a man embedded in the personnel movement pursuing his career in a business school, his emphasis was now rather different from that of his old mentor.

Cooke was a patrician reformer of independent means who had been somewhat radicalized by conflicts with conservative business interests during the Blankenburg administration and after. His preferred weapons were the old progressive's – moralistic argument and publicity. He saw a role for research, but it was of the kind that he helped promote through the Federated American Engineering Societies' celebrated *Waste in Industry* study – research as an adjunct to a high-profile campaign. The Philadelphia metal trades were the subject of one of the field studies that *Waste* researchers carried out, designed to demonstrate the human and

[34] Willits, "Industrial Research: A Virtually Unexplored Field," (1925), p. 2, typescript, Willits Biographical File, University of Pennsylvania Archives; Willits, "The Department of Industrial Research," *The General Magazine and Historical Chronicle* 32 (1929): 89–94 at p. 90; "Research Program" (1927), Appendix A, p. 1.
[35] Cooke, "A Measuring Stick for Unemployment," *ALLR* 11 (1921): 170–72 at 170.
[36] Ibid.; Daniel Nelson, *Unemployment Insurance: The American Experience* (Madison, 1969), Chs. 1–3 esp.; John A. Garraty, *Unemployment in History: Economic Thought and Public Policy* (New York, 1978), Ch. 8, esp. p. 150.

economic costs of irregular employment in an "irrational" free-market system.[37]

Willits chose to work with rather than against the grain. His temperament, his personal politics, his ambition, his institutional affiliation, and his dependence on research grants, all argued in favor of a "scientistic" rather than a moralistic approach, and an orientation toward seeing "problems" from a business decision-makers' perspective. At the very time that Cooke was forging enduring links with leaders of the labor movement, and consummating the unlikely union between Taylorite technocratic reform and the idea of "industrial democracy," Willits was launching off in a decidedly more promising direction.[38]

Willits's holy grail was useful knowledge: empirically verifiable, academically respectable, and managerially acceptable "facts" about "the man in the job rather than the man out of the job." The facts that he and Bezanson decided to concentrate on for their "first fundamental study" were those related to labor turnover, than which "No problem in personnel management had received more attention between 1915 and 1921." Turnover was widely deemed costly to employees and injurious to business. Reducing it was the chief object of most employment departments set up during the war boom, and their success (or otherwise) in so doing was an accepted yardstick of their effectiveness.[39]

But Bezanson and Willits were impressed by how sloppily this key phenomenon had been defined, and how little systematic attention had been given to its measurement, explanation, and significance. Academics and practitioners had to rely on isolated research, aggregate data, and anecdotes. "No subject was discussed more loosely and no careful scientific study of the subject. . . . had ever been made." As a result, all that the meetings of groups like PADEP amounted to were opportunities to "get acquainted and profit by mutually helpful experience, talk over a few platitudes and leave most of the problems still unsolved." This situation was wholly unacceptable to social scientists in the New Era, positivists to a man and woman, convinced that organized research could provide definite answers, eager to demonstrate their disciplines' applied, problem-solving potential and put them on the same level as the natural sciences.[40]

---

[37] For Cooke and the FAES episode, see esp. Donald Stabile, *Prophets of Order* (Boston, 1984), pp. 107–14; Kenneth Trombley, *The Life and Times of a Happy Liberal: A Biography of Morris Llewellyn Cooke* (New York, 1954), pp. 91–100; for the study itself, see Committee on the Elimination of Waste in Industry of the Federated American Engineering Societies, *Waste In Industry* (New York, 1921), Ch. 9 esp.

[38] For Willits's commitment to Hooverite "cooperative individualism," see "Unemployment" (1930), in Willits Papers, Box 5, F. 52, RAC.

[39] Willits, "An Industrial Personnel Research Program," *JPR* 3 (1924): 125–8 at p. 126; "Research Program" (1927), Appendix A, p. 3.

[40] "Research Program" (1927), Appendix A, p. 4 [quote]; Bezanson et al., "A Study in Labor Mobility by the Industrial Research Department Wharton School of Finance

The DIR was in a position to do something about those deficiencies and thereby establish its own reputation with both its managerial and its academic constituencies at the same time. It would be investigating a subject in which firms were genuinely interested, delivering reports of which they could hope to make use, and for which they would therefore cooperate in supplying data. And it would be producing work that was based on original research quantitative in character and directed at the solution of basic social problems, thereby satisfying the professional requirements of Willits's and Bezanson's peers and grant-givers in the emerging social science research community. Members of the PADEP group had been gathering and comparing turnover data for years, and they knew and trusted Willits. The presence of so many Penn and, specifically, Wharton alumni in executive positions facilitated the relationship. The Scott Company provided help and advice with developing a standard definition of turnover and data-collection forms that firms were willing to adopt. And, thanks to the DIR's ample funding, Bezanson and Willits could afford to recruit a dozen research assistants who went out to plants and introduced the new forms, and to buy calculating machinery to help them gather and process the information.[41]

The result was that – as an admiring reviewer put it – "the reporting and tabulation are more accurate than is the case in any but very few personnel offices," and crucially that the data were supplied even though the DIR began its work "during a depression in which most business heads considered the keeping and analysis of labor records below the margin of necessary expenditures." But the PADEP group's commitment to employment management antedated the war and postwar bubble of enthusiasm, and was quite deeply rooted. They therefore constituted an ideal group of research subjects and collaborators who were already "moderately well equipped with adequate record systems." They were not going to scrap them as a short-term cost-cutting measure, particularly as the DIR held out before them the promise of practical guidance on improved policy-making in return for their aid.[42]

and Commerce University of Pennsylvania," supplement to The Annals 103 (Sept. 1922), p. 167; Willits, "Need for Co-Operative Research," p. 405 [quote]; for positivist manifestos, see Emory Johnson [Dean, Wharton School], "Can Business Be Made a Science?" Engineers and Engineering 46 (1929): 73–76; James R. Angell, "Reasons and Plans for Research Relating to Industrial Personnel" and Robert M. Yerkes, "What Is Personnel Research?" JPR 1 (1922): 3–6, 56–64. Guy Alchon, The Invisible Hand of Planning: Capitalism, Social Science, and the State in the 1920s (Princeton, 1985), is excellent on this zeitgeist.

41 "Research Program" (1927), Appendix A, pp. 4–5; Bezanson et al., "A Study in Labor Mobility," p. 166; Bezanson et al., "Four Years of Labor Mobility," pp. 128, 130–31.

42 For Z. C. Dickinson's review, see JPR 1 (1922): 249–52 at pp. 250, 249; Bezanson et al., "A Study in Labor Mobility," pp. 166–69.

The DIR's research program was distinctive in three respects. It was collaborative, and not just in the sense that it was a pioneering example of a "big science," team approach to social investigation. The PADEP group were anything but passive suppliers of data: They owned it, it cost them to produce it, they only cooperated because they expected to learn something useful, and they were experts in making sense of the results and suggesting directions in which the research should develop. The DIR's collaborators also, of course, put up some of the department's money and provided Wharton students with employment opportunities and faculty with consultancy work. The DIR reported its findings to them in regular bulletins (originally called *The Latest Curve*, emphasizing the quantitative nature of the data and the heavy reliance on graphics for reporting it), and they commented, critically or appreciatively. The feedback relationship between the DIR and the firms that were at one and the same time its research subjects and co-workers, its patrons and its clients, was intensive. Bezanson described how this relationship worked in the context of a study that she made of the local foundry industry:

Scarcely a month goes by without some foundry executive's questioning our figure of prices, our ratio of production to capacity, the representative character of the data or the applicability to the varying conditions of the foundry trade. In answering these friendly inquiries we are given every opportunity to visit plants and discuss specific problems.[43]

The other two features of Bezanson's and Willits's research strategy strengthened this relationship. They confined their scope, most of the time, to the Philadelphia city-region, which – Bezanson argued – facilitated the development of "continuous contact . . . . as well as background . . . . knowledge concerning community factors." This was useful in refining the research design and interpreting their findings; it was especially important in turnover studies. A key question to be resolved was how much of the turnover was determined by the individual plant's own policies (and therefore, potentially, under its control), and how much was simply a reflection of wider trends in the local and national labor and product markets.[44]

---

43 Isolated copies of *The Latest Curve* survive in LSRM Papers, Box 76, File 801 (Vol. 1:1, third quarter 1922) and Box 75, File 790 (Vol. 1:3, first quarter 1923). There are excerpts from DIR reports in Willits, "Need for Cooperative Research," and Sayford, "No More Square Pegs," and findings are summarized in Bezanson et al., "A Study in Labor Mobility" and "Four Years of Labor Mobility." For examples of feedback showing cooperating firms' use of the reports to guide personnel policies (e.g., raising wage rates or installing training programs), see Willits, "Industrial Research" (1925), pp. 1–2; Bezanson and Robert Gray, *Trends in Foundry Production in the Philadelphia Area* (Philadelphia, 1929), p. v [quote].
44 Bezanson et al., "A Study of Labor Mobility," p. 167 [quote]; Bezanson et al., "Four Years of Labor Mobility," p. 2.

The DIR's community orientation was more than just a matter of research convenience, however. It had a deeper purpose, too, in that Willits was eager to affect decision-makers' behavior, to promote "progress" and "rationality" in the best Hooverite way:

> We ... have an opportunity ... to "seek the largest common ground of ascertainable truth": to contribute fundamentally to mutual understanding[,] to industrial disarmament, and to social cooperation by turning attention from "the antagonisms of opinion to agreement upon facts." ... Working in one industrial center year after year, close to the sources of materials, and in interested, practical cooperation with those who are actively in contact with the situations being studied, makes for a deep penetration of community life and for an increasing interdependence between the community and the research department. Slowly but surely the part of the community influenced by the department's work comes to look at its own problems in a spirit of research and to turn to research for a disinterested analysis of them.[45]

Concentration on the richly varied Philadelphia region therefore did not imply provincialism; rather, it was the way for these cosmopolitan social scientists to produce the most satisfying and broadly applicable answers to general questions of interest to their academic peers, and to promote solutions to the "social problems" that they examined. Philadelphia was "one of the most complex labor markets in the country" and "represent[ed] a cross-section of industrial and social America." So the DIR "considered that it would best serve the cause of national research by constituting itself a regional experiment station." It could develop and exploit the unique research opportunities that the Philadelphia region, and Willits's contacts, afforded. And it could begin to deliver on the promise of applied social science in the New Era – that it could contribute to the rational solution of problems affecting the general welfare – by stimulating the voluntary cooperation of men and women of good will and the local, private sector institutions they controlled.[46]

Third, Bezanson and Willits aimed to develop a research program, targeting one subject (turnover) and studying it continuously over a period of years, across different phases of the business cycle; broadening out their group of research collaborators to include an increasingly large, diverse, and representative sample of firms and industries (and an increasingly multidisciplinary team of social scientists); and encouraging new phases of the collective research project to grow out of an accumulating body of knowledge and questions. They were creating a "moving picture" rather than a "photograph," to use Willits's revealing metaphor. (See Figure 9.2 for an

---

[45] "Research Program" (1927), pp. 2–3.
[46] "Research Program of the Industrial Research Department of the University of Pennsylvania," Dec. 1926, Sec. III, p. 2, in LSRM Papers, Box 76, F. 798, RAC and "Research Program" (1927), pp. 2–3.

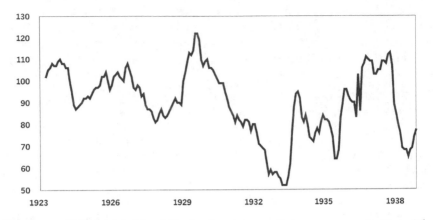

Figure 9.2. Philadelphia Metal Trades Employment Index, 1923–1938. *Note:* The MMA/DIR sample was not unchanging, hence some short-term fluctuations reflected a loss or gain of collaborating companies as well as an increase or decrease in respondents' workforces. *Source:* April 1923–June 1933, original returns in Box 170, unprocessed Records of the DIR, University of Pennsylvania Archives, and 1933–38, NMTA *Labor Barometer.*

example of the results of this approach.) They were not interested in what he derided as "Merely spraying a community with a large number of disconnected studies." Such work could only be episodic and superficial: The DIR promised to produce an "industrial X-ray revealing basic causes and fundamental conditions."[47]

They were almost as good as their word. In the fall of 1922 they were persuaded to shift their attention away from Philadelphia for one year. They answered the call of the U.S. Coal Commission to take charge of its inquiries into "labor relations, wage rates, irregularity of employment, absenteeism, and labor turnover" in the anthracite and bituminous fields. (Willits covered labor relations while Bezanson and her associates handled the more statistical questions.) The Coal Commission work retarded the progress of their research program, but it brought them broader national recognition and, perhaps not incidentally, a share of the commission's lavish $600,000 budget during a recession that dried up other sources of consultancy

---

[47]   Willits, "Industrial Personnel Research Program," p. 126; Willits, "The Work of the Industrial Research Department and Its Educational Significance" (c. 1929), p. 1, in Willits Papers, Box 8, F. 75, RAC. For an interesting parallel with Willits's strategy, see Martin Bulmer, "The Early Institutional Establishment of Social Science Research: The Local Community Research Committee at the University of Chicago, 1923–30," *Minerva* 18 (1980): 51–110.

income. It was also an unmissable opportunity for Willits to join the growing ranks of Secretary of Commerce Hoover's social science "experts," and to assume a position of "public . . . responsibility" from which he could preach the virtues of rational and humane employment management to the leaders of one of America's (and especially Pennsylvania's) most important, disorderly, and conflictual industries.[48]

But by the middle of 1923 that interruption was over, and they took up their Philadelphia research where they had left off. Her turnover study had convinced Bezanson that much of the received wisdom of the early personnel movement about the irrationality of constant job-shifting was grossly oversimplified. It was "not the disordered floating from place to place that the war writings deplored." Instead, it served many purposes from the employee's point of view, particularly in an unstable and disorganized labor market where disparities between earnings in different plants were considerable and frequent job shifts were inevitable.[49]

Bezanson also made some important discoveries – again, contrary to the conventional wisdom – about the continuing importance of skill in much industrial work. She came to understand the essential contribution that having held a wide variety of jobs made to a skilled man's possession of "all-round" experience, with its resulting high status among employers and workmen, high wages, and employability. She realized that much turnover was therefore functional, from the perspective of the man and his employers, particularly in a labor market where there were many firms of modest size but with a high dependence on skill and few formal training facilities.[50]

For Bezanson, then, the DIR's strategy was certainly paying off. Intimate contact and conversation, particularly with the PADEP's foremen's group in her first stopgap research project, had given her an appreciation of some of the facts of contemporary manufacturing industry that other "experts" lacked. (The mechanical engineers behind the *Waste in Industry* survey, for example, hewed strictly to the "turnover bad, stability good" doctrine.) The turnover study provided her with ongoing contact with a growing group of go-ahead, modernizing, and well-managed firms, and suggested new lines for profitable inquiry.

How important "skill" still was, how it could be defined, and how it was

---

[48] "Research Program" (1927), Appendix A, pp. 8–9 [quotes]; M. B. Hammond, "The Coal Commission Reports and the Coal Situation," *QJE* 38 (1924): 541–81; Edward E. Hunt et al., eds., *What the Coal Commission Found: An Authoritative Study by the Staff* (Baltimore, 1925), Part I, esp. Chs. 3, 6.

[49] Bezanson et al., "A Study in Labor Mobility," pp. 223–24 and "Four Years of Labor Mobility," esp. pp. 3, 69–73.

[50] Bezanson, "Promotion from Without" and "Skill," *QJE* 36 (1922): 154–61, 626–45 and "The Advantages of Labor Turnover: An Illustrative Case," *QJE* 38 (1924): 450–64.

acquired, became key questions for her and the DIR in 1923 at the end of the Coal Commission episode. Answers "would be of great value in testing the generalizations in common circulation, in making for a more enlightened community policy in respect of trade training, and the preservation of craft skill, whether in school or in industry." So the department embarked on a new project, and focused on one of the most highly skilled groups of workers employed by firms in Bezanson's survey group, tool-and-die makers. Cooperating firms supplied men's employment records, questionnaires were sent to craftsmen themselves, and their answers were followed up by small group conferences involving researchers and workers together. Bezanson's initial hunches were confirmed, but – unusually for the DIR – no results were quickly published. This was because the study "opened up so much opportunity for intensive work in metal plants in the area" that researchers pursued their ever-widening investigations instead.[51]

What was this opportunity? It was cooperation with the MMA. The MMA had collaborated with the PADEP for five years; the MMA and the DIR had complementary interests in the gathering, interpretation, and use of labor market data; the MMA's new executive committee was dominated by firms that shared the DIR's commitment to rationalized employment management, and some of them were already in Bezanson's survey group; and, for its own reasons, the MMA was intensely interested in questions that had to do with skilled labor supply.

As for the DIR, working with the MMA fit in with its strategy of extending its range of contacts with firms and institutions in industrial Philadelphia. The MMA gave it an opening to smaller and less well-managed firms than those with which it had cooperated since 1921, notably the foundry sector, broadening its research base considerably and extending the possibilities for exerting constructive influence. They were in industries that:

suffer[ed] from a dearth of information as to what each firm is doing, from unintelligent competition, and from lack of imagination. . . . The management technique throughout such an industry seems likely to be improved by the educational process of working with an impartial agency which collects and interprets the figures for the industry as a whole.[52]

This was obviously a marriage that was made in heaven. The MMA's and DIR's agendas were compatible, and each side had something that the other one wanted – data and expertise, respectively.

There was just one impediment to the consummation of the union. The

[51] "Research Program" (1927), Appendix A, pp. 12–13.
[52] Report of the Department of Industrial Research, University of Pennsylvania to the Laura Spelman Rockefeller Memorial for the Year 1930–31, p. 18, in LSRM Papers, Box 76, F. 796, RAC.

MMA was renowned as an anti-labor organization. This mattered to Willits and Bezanson because, quite apart from their liberal inclinations (evidenced in their Coal Commission work), their research strategy needed the cooperation of skilled workers and their organizations, too. In Philadelphia's largest industrial sector, textiles, trade unions were going concerns with and through which they wished and had to work. The national academic organizations – the Personnel Research Federation, the Social Science Research Council – in which Willits was prominent were also corporatist in form and pluralist in character, extending formal recognition and representation to the AFL. Finally, the charitable bodies to which the DIR looked for funding, particularly the Rockefeller foundations, were determined to avoid controversy and the appearance of partisanship in matters of class conflict. The result was that, although Rockefeller money underpinned the development of the personnel movement and the academic study of industrial relations in the 1920s, it was supplied in a cautious and very discriminating fashion.[53]

By 1923 Joseph Willits had hooked the Rockefeller fish, but he had not securely landed it. John D. Rockefeller, Jr., personally financed one curious sideline of the DIR's work, bringing the antipodean charmer and charlatan Elton Mayo to Philadelphia between 1923 and 1926, where he did some field work and established his reputation as a combination of industrial psychiatrist and guru. Mayo was Ruml's protégé, and Willits accommodated him to oblige Ruml and to enable the DIR to improve its credentials as a center of interdisciplinary social science research. (So long as it was just a group of economists and statisticians, the Spelman Memorial would not fund it.) But the DIR's main program remained dependent on the Carnegie grant, the university, and local contributors. Willits could not afford to jeopardize his excellent chances of getting his snout in Beardsley Ruml's overflowing trough once the Carnegie money ran out.[54]

[53] "Research Program" (1927), Appendix A, pp. 16–17, for work undertaken with and for the Upholstery Weavers' Union; Samuel Gompers was vice chairman of the PRF, and Matthew Woll on the editorial board of the *Journal of Personnel Research* – see Flinn, "Development of the PRF," p. 13, inside front cover, *JPR* 3 (1924–25); Florence Thorne of the AFL and Leo Wolman of the Clothing Workers joined Leeds, Willits, and Henry Dennison as members of the SSRC's Advisory Committee on Industrial Relations – see Herman Feldman, *Survey of Research in the Field of Industrial Relations by The Advisory Committee on Industrial Relations* (New York, 1928), p. 1. For Rockefeller caution, see Bulmer and Bulmer, "Philanthropy and Social Science," pp. 379–81; Howard Gitelman, *Legacy of the Ludlow Massacre: A Chapter in American Industrial Relations* (Philadelphia, 1988); Grossman, "American Foundations and the Support of Economic Research," pp. 71–76; Nielsen, *Big Foundations*, pp. 54, 57.

[54] Richard C. S. Trahair, *The Humanist Temper: The Life and Work of Elton Mayo* (New Brunswick, 1984), Chs. 9, 10; Richard Gillespie, *Manufacturing Knowledge: A History of the Hawthorne Experiments* (New York, 1991), pp. 100–16; document headed "University of Pennsylvania Department of Industrial Research," 17 June

At last, in 1925, the one remaining obstacle to close the DIR–MMA cooperation, and danger to Rockefeller funding, was removed. Staunton Peck
retired as president of the MMA, and his place was taken by Morris Leeds,
"with the condition that certain activities which had characterized the Association in the past should be discontinued and that a substitute program of
a positive and socially constructive character be developed." To do so, Leeds
and Sparks looked to the DIR for help. The "progressive" takeover of the
MMA by executives who had worked closely with the DIR for years was
complete. The way was clear for Willits and Leeds and their associates
to bring their organizations even closer together. As Willits wrote Ruml,
"One of the best things that could happen to the Research Department has
happened."[55]

9.3   KNOWLEDGE AND POWER

The MMA–DIR relationship had begun in the winter of 1923–24, when
Earl Sparks persuaded Willits's associate, Alfred Williams, to undertake a
study of future skilled labor requirements and the adequacy of training provision in the local foundry industry. The MMA supplied contacts, its
members offered data, Williams got his doctorate, and the association paid
a publication subsidy for a report intended to affect its members' readiness
to invest, individually and collectively, in their human capital requirements.
Bezanson's studies of turnover and skills acquisition deepened the relationship. Now, because of the Orthodox Quaker takeover, and the MMA's
abandonment of open-shop militancy, Willits was prepared to consummate
it. And the MMA was ready to make more use of his department's services
to try to discover how to control the costly turnover, not just count the
entrances and exits. This was a central element in Sparks's and Leeds's
pursuit of a program of constructive membership service to take the place
of the anti-unionism that was no longer necessary, and which the executive
committee no longer wished to highlight.[56]

The MMA wanted "a study of the effect of personnel activities, wages
and hours upon Labor Turnover," and Willits in return "desire[d] . . . to
have the sympathetic cooperation of the Association and a Committee to

---

1923, in LSRM Papers, Box 5, F. 790. The Rockefeller grant for Mayo's work alone
matched the Carnegie grant, and represented a third of the DIR's income – Minutes
of the Trustees of the University of Pennsylvania, file A-18, pp. 462, 517, 639, 698.
Mayo did some of his early fieldwork at Miller Lock.

[55]   "Research Program" (1927), pp. 4–5; Willits to Ruml, 17 July 1925, in LSRM
Papers, Box 75, F. 791, RAC.

[56]   Alfred H. Williams, *Study of the Adequacy of Existing Programs for the Training of
Journeymen Molders in the Iron and Steel Foundries of Philadelphia* (Philadelphia,
1924). See also ECM 27 March, 30 Nov. 1923, 26 June, 23 Sept., and 22 Dec.
1924.

advise with them on the matter." Stogdell Stokes gave the proposal his hearty backing: It had the additional argument in its favor that it "would entail practically no expense upon the Association," as the university, the Carnegie Corporation, and, after 1927, the Laura Spelman Rockefeller Memorial were picking up the tab. By way of comparison, the MMA's total operating budget in 1927 was slightly less than $17,000, rising to almost $20,000 in 1930; the DIR's was about three times as large in 1927, and more than six times greater in 1930. Wharton evidently had the resources to carry out research on a level that the MMA could not match; but the MMA's members owned the data and controlled access to it, so it is not obvious which party was more dependent upon the other.[57]

The result was a succession of studies identifying which types of companies, in which divisions of the metal trades, were the most and least affected by the turnover problem; what effect the presence of a company cafeteria or group insurance plan had on turnover rates; and what connection there might be between turnover and accident rates among the MMA's members, or (anticipating the Hawthorne research) between supervisory styles and employee satisfaction as, presumably, revealed by turnover.

This research was circulated only to cooperating companies, and no copies seem to have survived. But there were other, larger projects that resulted in published monographs – including Hummel LaRue Frain's on wage rates and payment systems for skilled metalworkers; Anne Bezanson's on turnover trends and advertising for labor; Dorothea De Schweinitz's on recruitment methods; and Bezanson's and Robert Gray's on foundry production, which was a follow-on to Williams's on foundry training, and provided market research data for the MMA's attempt to affect its members' competitive behavior. These joined the DIR's lengthening shelf of case studies turning the Philadelphia labor market, and particularly its textile and metal trades, into the best-analyzed in the country.[58]

What effect all this collaboration between applied social scientists and practical manufacturers had on the latter's behavior is hard to judge, particularly because what the researchers discovered was how complex the "total situation" was. One inconclusive study pointed to the need for another in the joint quest for the knowledge that might eventually bring the ability to predict and control. Honest research also had the annoying

[57] Memoranda for the Special Committee on Study of Employment Department Methods, with ECM for 21 Feb. 1930, esp. pp. 3–4; Dorothea De Schweinitz, *How Workers Find Jobs: A Study of Four Thousand Hosiery Workers in Philadelphia* (Philadelphia, 1932), pp. 111–13; MMA Treasurer's Report 1927; Minutes of the Trustees of the University of Pennsylvania, A-19, p. 197, A-20, p. 358.

[58] "Research Program" (1927), esp. Sec. I, pp. 4–5, 7–9, II, pp. 4–6, V, and Appendix A, pp. 13–16; Minutes of the Meeting of the Committee to Study the Effectiveness of Personnel Activities, ECM 10 Oct. 1927, p. 1. There is a full list of studies and reports in Industrial Research Department, *Industrial Progress and Economic Research*.

tendency to throw up "disconcerting" findings, for example, that "some plants without any formal employment technique continually and normally maintain a lower turnover than plants with highly developed technique." Even so, the DIR and the MMA persisted with their efforts for more than a decade.[59]

What was interesting about the work of the joint Committee to Study the Effectiveness of Personnel Activities (renamed the Advisory Research Committee on Labor Relations in 1928) was how it operated and whom it involved, as well as why and with what (limited) direct effect. Academics and managers – increasingly, personnel specialists from the larger member firms, rather than controlling executives in the smaller proprietary businesses – met together to plan and review the program. The research acquired a momentum of its own, and became somewhat disconnected from the practical business of supplying "factual information that would bear upon the problems of industrial relations" and "enable management to maintain fair standards in its relations with employees," which Leeds had hoped for in the beginning.[60]

Nevertheless, the MMA deepened its own commitment to research through its collaboration with Wharton, and Sparks began to turn his office into an agency for precisely the kind of focused, problem-oriented consultancy work that the DIR disdained to perform. Special surveys were carried out and bulletins issued about matters including "wages, hours, incentives and penalties in enforcing punctuality and attendance, holiday observance, extent and method of administration of personnel activities." Whenever it became clear that enough members were interested in a subject and wanted the guidance on standard and best practice that the MMA could supply, Sparks did his best to offer it. Wharton's work was somewhat abstract in comparison. Sparks, on the other hand, could not afford to stray very far from supplying services that his members needed, or that he thought they ought to have. So the Wharton connection was just a part, and perhaps not the most important, of the MMA's expanding sphere of activities in the late 1920s, as Sparks turned his office into a focus for the practical encouragement of positive personnel management.[61]

9.4 BUILDING HUMAN CAPITAL

The MMA's other main new area of emphasis in the 1920s was skills training – for the machine shop rather than the foundry trades, where, despite

---

[59] "Research Program" (1927), Sec. V, p. 3.
[60] ECM 24 Jan. 1928; Activities for 1927 and Committees, 25 Jan. 1927; ECM 19 May 1926.
[61] SEC 1925, p. 4, SEC 1926, pp. 7–8, SEC 1927, p. 8, and SEC 1929, p. 8, chart the growth of Sparks's research and consultancy work.

Sparks's urging, Alfred Williams's research, and the efforts of a committee, not much was achieved. But in the machining and fabricating divisions of the Philadelphia metal trades, there was real progress.

The machine-shop operators' growing interest in skills training may surprise readers who think that "de-skilling" was well-nigh ubiquitous in American industry in the 1920s, the decade *par excellence* of standardization, electrification, and mass production. This misapprehension was equally common at the time. As William H. Woodruff of machine-builders Ingersoll-Rand put it, "Now that the machine has absorbed the skill of the old-time mechanic, so that a laborer with a C- or D mentality can start, feed and stop the automaton devised to do the difficult mechanical job, some people have the impression that high-grade skilled machinists are no longer necessary." Even an "expert" like Paul A. Douglas believed that "Modern industry does not require a large percentage of all-round skilled workmen. The vast majority of jobs can be learned in the space of a few days or at the most, in a few weeks. . . . In modern industry, machines produce other machines, steel gives birth to steel." According to this dehumanized technocratic vision, the mass of the industrial labor force no longer possessed or required much skill: Modernization had acted like a giant cream separator, reducing most workers to the metaphorical equivalent of skimmed milk, and concentrating ability and knowledge in fewer heads amid a Taylorite élite. "A large number of highly trained and competent engineers are needed in the drafting room. For the other workmen, however, muscle and endurance rather than skill and dexterity are required." The only blue-collar workmen whom Douglas thought still required all-round training were machine repairers: "The skill which was formerly spread out thin over the whole mass of workers has been concentrated in these men. They are distinctly the aristocracy of the labor-force."[62]

The fact was, however – as Douglas himself had to recognize – that surveys of actual employment practices and perceived training needs, as well as of labor force composition and pressure points in the labor market, revealed a distinctly different picture. Skilled workmen were not measurably declining as a proportion of the blue-collar labor force, and their strategic importance was not falling as they moved out of direct production and into essential support roles – in fact, rather the reverse was true. As employment expert H. A. Worman put it in 1913, they "form[ed] the backbone of the factory organization, set the pace for the whole machine, h[e]ld the reputation of the company in their hands." In the metal trades they were in chronically short supply, because of America's lack of an efficient skills

[62] Woodruff, "The Machinist Apprentice I. Recruiting, and Costs," *JPR* 6 (1927): 173–75 at p. 172; Douglas, *American Apprenticeship and Industrial Education* (New York, 1921), pp. 109, 111, 113; cf. Forrest Crissey, "The Disappearing Apprentice," *Saturday Evening Post* (1923), offprint in Box 132, Department of Industrial Research Records, University of Pennsylvania Archives.

training system; and their status and pay reflected this reality, as did the attention that employers in the machine-building and -using industries gave to attempts to devise better ways of utilizing, and adding to, this vital resource.[63]

The Philadelphia metal-machining trades reflected this general picture. In the late 1930s, Wharton researcher Irving L. Horowitz discovered that through the 'twenties approximately a third of their factory labor still required an all-round craft training that took four to six years, on top of a high school–equivalent education. These tool and die makers, instrument mechanics, maintenance men and repair machinists, layout and setup men, erectors, and versatile craftsmen, from whom foremen and supervisors were recruited, were joined in the shops by a further c. 20 percent of skilled but specialized machinists. They lacked the former groups' wide experience but still had to be capable of setting up their own work and carrying out simple engineering calculations. They typically required six months to two years' on-the-job training to become proficient, and a good general education if they were to be able to follow written instructions and be taught to read blueprints and figures.[64]

A firm's ability to train skilled specialists – as well as to make use of semi-skilled machine operators who could not set up their own work – depended on its cadres of all-around craftsmen. The problem of the Philadelphia machine trades in the early 1920s was that the means of training fully skilled men were quite inadequate to the task.

The difficulty did not lie in any bad fit between the city's occupational structure and its educational facilities. The Philadelphia public school system was ready to play its part in preparing working-class boys for skilled jobs through its general and industrial curricula. Local private institutions

---

[63] U.S. Department of Labor, Bureau of Apprenticeship, *The Skilled Labor Force: A Study of Census Data on the Craftsman Population of the United States, 1870–1950* (Washington, Apr. 1954), processed report, pp. 15–16 esp.; Andrew Dawson, "The Paradox of Dynamic Technological Change and the Labor Aristocracy in the United States, 1880–1914," *Labor History* 20 (1979): 325–51; Philip J. Leahey, "Skilled Labor and the Rise of the Modern Corporation: The Case of the Electrical Industry," *Labor History* 27 (1986): 31–53; Douglas, *American Apprenticeship*, p. 119 and Chs. 8, 9, 11; Worman, *Building Up the Force: How to Get Help, Handle Applicants, and Fit Men into the Organization* (Chicago, 1913), p. 41; Berenice Fisher, *Industrial Education: American Ideals and Institutions* (Madison, 1967), pp. 110–19, 128–37. For the national strategy, see NMTA, Committee on Industrial Education, *Apprenticeship in the Metal Trades* (Chicago, 1922) and the resulting *Apprenticeship Plan of the Metal Trades Industries* (Chicago, 1926). By 1929, 83 percent of NMTA members had training programs for skilled and semiskilled workers, reflecting the high priority that they gave to this issue – Committee on Industrial Relations, *Industrial Relations in the Metal Trades* (Chicago, 1929), pp. 15–16.

[64] Irving L. Horowitz, *The Metal Machining Trades of Philadelphia: An Occupational Study* (Philadelphia, 1939), pp. 13–14, 32–36, 40–45, 48–61, 68–72, 78, 91–93 esp.

(Girard College, the Williamson Trade School, and the Philadelphia Mechanical and Electrical Schools and Shops) produced a small but valuable number of youths who were theoretically and practically very well equiped to take advantage of shop experience and advance rapidly into highly skilled work. And the Spring Garden Institute and School of Industrial Arts offered postapprentice courses for skilled men ambitious for promotion.[65]

The major cause of the problem was instead industry's reluctance or inability to provide the in-house training that even well-educated and well-motivated working-class youths required. Employers were agreed that they absolutely depended on having a third of their workforce with the kind of structured, varied experience and instruction best offered through an apprenticeship system. But they seemed unable to sustain one. In 1923, there was one apprentice to about eighteen craftsmen, less than a third of the number required to reproduce the skilled labor force as "promotion, illness, . . . retirement, death, and change in occupation" took their toll. The problem was particularly acute because the company that had been Philadelphia's largest local supplier of skilled metal tradesmen, Baldwin Locomotive, had slashed its payroll during the postwar depression and closed its old inner-city plant for good. At the same time, it was no longer possible, because of immigration restrictions, for Philadelphia firms to depend on a steady stream of skilled young men from northwestern Europe. (A fifth of the three-quarters of Philadelphia machinists surveyed in 1938 who reported a formal apprenticeship had learned their trade before coming to the United States.)[66]

The year 1923 was the first really prosperous one that the Philadelphia metal trades enjoyed after the severe recession. The frantic advertising for skilled men that resulted, the poaching, increased turnover, and consequent increases in wages, which recovered much of the ground lost since 1920, served as a powerful inducement to Philadelphia machine-shop operators to turn their attention toward the fundamental problem of an inadequate labor supply. By the time of the next busy year, 1926, they were ready to act.[67]

The revitalizing of the MMA's vocational education work was one of the

[65] Richard A. Varbero, "Philadelphia's Southern Italians in the 1920s," in Allen F. Davis and Mark H. Haller, eds., *The Peoples of Philadelphia: A History of Ethnic Groups and Lower-Class Life, 1790–1940* (Philadelphia, 1973), Ch. 12, p. 256, on the vocational priorities of the School Board; Philadelphia Chamber of Commerce Industrial Relations Committee, Sub-Committee on Apprenticeship, *Report and Recommendations* (25 Sept. 1923), pp. 2–3, 6, 8–19, for details on provision. This is in marked contrast to Henry W. Spangler's earlier study – "Training in the Engineering Trades in Philadelphia," *J. ECP* 26 (1909): 113–34.

[66] Horowitz, *Metal Machining Trades*, pp. 99, 124; Helen Herrmann, *Ten Years of Work Experience of Philadelphia Machinists* (Philadelphia, 1938), p. 17.

[67] Bezanson, *Help-Wanted Advertising*, Ch. 7, esp. pp. 78–80; see Figures 7.1 and 9.2.

first fruits of Morris Leeds's presidency. His own company's situation gave him an acute awareness of the causes of the general skilled labor shortage, because it was expanding rapidly but unable to draw on the German and Austrian instrument mechanics it had traditionally relied on. Accordingly, L & N had had to introduce its own apprenticeship scheme, and was therefore ready to lead the rest of the MMA toward an action program.[68]

This had three parts. The first was resisting the penchant for narrowly vocational education among the professionals running the city's public schools. Educationalists believed in channeling working-class boys into working-class jobs and aimed to truncate, simplify, and vocationalize the curriculum in high schools in blue-collar neighborhoods. The MMA lobbied hard for the maintenance of a full four-year academic curriculum, understandably so as detailed studies would soon reveal that there was a closer connection between a good general education and skilled performance among MMA members' workforces than there was with trade training per se. Employers' preference for senior high school graduates as craft apprentices reflected their knowledge of what their jobs required, rather than their cultural conservativism.[69]

The second result of the improved liaison with the public school system that began in 1925 was even more constructive. Philadelphia metal trades employers believed that part of their problem was that they could not recruit enough youths of the right caliber for the apprenticeships that they did offer, because of ignorance among teachers and pupils about the attractiveness and potential of the manufacturing jobs available. They sought to overcome this by organizing plant visits (initially only to the more modern and better-managed factories, like Link-Belt) for school superintendents, principals, and teachers of "shop" courses, and eventually for thousands of high school students; and by producing and distributing pamphlets ("A Future in the Metal Trades" and "Your Future – What Next?") to eighth-graders to attempt to influence course and career choice.[70]

The third part of the program was the most obviously effective. It involved constructing a cooperative training course – cooperative in two senses: It involved collective action by a number of firms adopting a common apprenticeship system with a standard curriculum, and it combined work experience with Saturday morning classes given in and by the public schools, at their expense. It was, the Vocational Education committee reported, "a feasible, economical solution of the problem."[71]

[68] Mildred Fairchild, "Skill and Specialization: A Study in the Metal Trades," *JPR* 9 (1930): 128–75 at p. 144.
[69] ECM 31 March 1925, pp. 5–6 and 26 Jan. 1926, p. 2; Secretary's Report for the Committee on Vocational Education, with ECM 9 Dec. 1925, pp. 1–2; Fairchild, "Skill and Specialization," p. 133; Horowitz, *Metal Machining Trades*, pp. 55–59.
[70] First Annual Report of the Vocational Education Committee, 9 Dec. 1925, pp. 5–6, with ECM.
[71] Ibid., pp. 1–4 [quote at p. 2].

It had many advantages: Systematic instruction would improve the quality of the training provided; it would standardize the basic skills of Philadelphia machinist apprentices irrespective of the plant that trained them; and it would increase their commitment, reducing their tendency to quit because they could earn more in the short term as specialized machine operators on piece work. They would know that they were getting something of value in return for the sacrifice of immediate earnings. Everything was done to increase the apprentices' sense of being junior members of an artisan (or even future manager or entrepreneur) élite, including annual formal dinners with their employers and graduation ceremonies at the end of the course. "The American boy is quick to sense the difference between education and exploitation. He is strong for education." So that was what he would be given.[72]

The cooperative program would also, of course, be cheaper for the participating companies than if they had to devise their own schemes and hire their own instructors, something that was in any case beyond the resources of all but the largest firms. Philadelphia was also lucky that the city's public schools were prepared to do their part – eager to negotiate details of curricula, provide the required equipment for school workshops, and discuss all other matters, with collaborating employers. "[W]e have the successful agencies of instruction on the one hand and the great laboratories of production on the other. Let each one do that portion of the job for which they are best fitted." Otherwise, "From where are you going to get your skilled workers of the future? You won't get them unless you make them. This is not a case of letting George do it, but of every firm doing its share and doing that to the best of its ability." Together the companies and the schools could produce "the future bulwark of industry."[73]

Philadelphia was not alone among American metal-manufacturing centers in devising such an industry-school approach to vocational education. Its ideas and rhetoric were commonplace. But the MMA's work was impressively effective. A combination of enhanced activity by individual firms (like Westinghouse and L & N) and the cooperative program increased the number of apprentices from about 6 percent of the fully skilled labor force in 1924–26 to about 10 percent in 1927–30 (from about 300 to almost 500 young men). The result was to close the gap between the number of recruits that the industry needed to replenish its craftsmen and the numbers actually in training. The first class of MMA apprentices graduated after three years' work-study in 1930, the

---

[72] Ibid., p. 2 [quote].

[73] Ibid., p. 4. For other details, see ECM 26 Jan. 1926, 23 Feb., 27 Apr., 25 May and Proposed Joint Report to the Executive Committee (same date), for course content and organization, 26 Oct., Second Annual Report of the Vocational Education Committee, 8 Dec., and SEC 1927, pp. 6, 8, SEC 1928, pp. 4–5; ECM 3 May 1927; 27 March, 26 June, 25 Sept., 27 Nov. 1928; 16 Jan., 25 June 1929; 16 Sept. 1930; 17 March, 21 Apr., 19 May 1931; 16 Feb., 17 May, 20 Sept. 1932.

following cohorts grew steadily larger, and it seemed that the chronic train-ing problem was well on the way to a solution. Intra- and interfirm coor-dination, and partnership with a cooperative city administration, had done the trick.[74]

The MMA did not confine itself to apprentice training alone. Personnel and management experts in the 1920s had become convinced, largely through experience gained during the wartime boom, that the quality and efficiency of production and of "human relations" in industry depended crucially on skilled and consistent supervision. Companies, local em-ployment managers' groups including Willits's PADEP, educational in-stitutions, and government departments accordingly developed programs for systematically producing the correct attitudes and behavior among front-line managers. These programs were sustained through the postwar upheaval and recession, and expanded in the 1920s; the NMTA gave them particular encouragement as part of its preventive labor relations strategy. In the summer of 1927 the NMTA seconded its education direc-tor to help the MMA set up its own scheme; the State and Federal Boards for Vocational Education provided expert staff and financial support. What they created was a small but state-of-the-art course for the intensive training of group leaders selected from MMA members' experienced supervisors. Once instructed in best practice and the approved pedagogical technique (employing discussion groups manipulated toward the "correct" conclusions), these went on to lead conferences among hundreds of their peers drawn from foundry or machine-shop foremen and different sections of the MMA's membership (e.g., machine tool and repair plants).[75]

The effectiveness of this program may be doubted – subsequent research indicated that the conference method produced verbal acceptance of the rules of the "new supervision," and a stronger ideological identification with management rather than the craft community from which foremen were drawn, but little enduring behavioral modification. Nevertheless, its introduction showed how closely the MMA had become aligned with managerial best practice by the late 1920s, adapting the techniques of large, autonomous corporations to the needs and resources of its wider

[74] For the pioneering American example of the plan the MMA implemented, see C. C. Sharkey, "The Co-Operative Industrial High School and the Part-Time Extension Trade School for Apprentices," *American Machinist* 51 (1919): 1105–08; Horowitz, *Metal-Machining Trades*, pp. 100, 124.

[75] Clarles R. Allen, *The Foreman and His Job* (Philadelphia, 1922); ECM 3 May 1927 p. 1, 22 June p. 1, 27 Sept. p. 2; SEC 1927, p. 7; 24 Jan. 1928 p. 2, 28 Feb. p. 4, 26 June p. 3, 25 Sept. p. 2, and SEC 1928, p. 4; 16 Jan. 1929 p. 2, 26 Feb. p. 1, 22 Oct. p. 2, and SEC 1929, p. 7; 28 Jan. 1930 pp. 2, 4, 24 June p. 2, 16 Sept. p. 1, 29 Oct. p. 2. For NMTA encouragement, see Committee on Industrial Relations, *Industrial Relations in the Metal Trades*, p. 16 – by 1929, about a third of members had formal supervisory training programs.

membership, and organizing them in a distinctively collective and corporatist fashion.[76]

9.5 THE MMA AT HIGHWATER, 1929–1930

The remaking of the MMA took place in the context of a reshaping of the Philadelphia metal-manufacturing community itself and resulted in a transformation of the MMA's place within it. The old patterns of industrial distribution and MMA recruitment had still been visible at the 1921 state industrial census: The association still had no members with more than 1,000 workers; and the eight with more than 500 only represented 14 percent of the total labor force of the twenty-five companies in that size category in the city (6,085 of 42,015 workers). Link-Belt, the largest member, only ranked tenth overall, behind the old open-shop giants (Baldwin, Midvale, Disston, Brill, Hale & Kilburn) and the newer, more dynamic firms (including Budd, Westinghouse, and Electric Storage Battery [Exide]). General machinery and machine-tool builders still made up about half of the MMA's membership, and companies with fewer than 500 workers still employed about 60 percent of its total workforce.

Thereafter, the old patterns changed rapidly (see Figure 9.3). By 1930, the association recruited eleven of eighteen metal-working companies with more than 500 workers, and employed 55 percent (17,216 of 31,068) of their combined labor force. It recruited about 40 percent of the city total, twice as large a proportion as at the start of the decade. Budd was now the city's largest metal-working plant, with 4,174 employees, but the MMA recruited the second through fourth biggest (G.E., radio makers Atwater Kent, and Westinghouse), all with more than 3,000 workers. The fifth through seventh (Exide, Philco, and a downsized Midvale, all employing 2,000-plus) remained nonmembers, as did the shrunken remnants of the old transportation equipment makers (Brill, the I. P. Morris & De La Vergne subsidiary of Baldwin), but otherwise the city's larger establishments were now MMA members, and employed 55 percent of its total labor force. In addition, the MMA's two largest members, G.E. and Westinghouse, were branch plants. Managers at Link-Belt and Hess-Bright/SKF, its seventh and ninth biggest members, enjoyed considerable local autonomy from their corporate headquarters (in Chicago and Sweden, respectively), but even so the MMA's character as an association of mid-sized, local, and proprietary

[76] Howell J. Harris, *The Right to Manage: Industrial Relations Policies of American Business in the 1940s* (Madison, 1982), pp. 267–68; Karen L. Jorgensen-Esmaili, "Schooling and the Early Human Relations Movement: With Special Reference to the Foreman's Conference, 1919–1939" (Ph.D. diss., University of California-Berkeley, 1979), Chs. 2, 3.

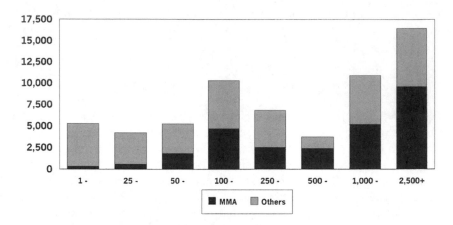

Figure 9.3. The MMA at Highwater: Philadelphia Metal Trades Employment, 1930, by Size of Firm and MMA Membership. *Note:* Westinghouse is included with other MMA members although its main plant was just outside the city limits. The chart makes plain that the MMA's growth in the 1920s superimposed a new pattern of recruitment on an old one (cf. Figures 2.1 and 5.2). The MMA's strongest presence was now among companies with 500–999 employees (where its members accounted for 64 percent of the total employment), more than 2,500 employees (59 percent), and 1,000–2,499 employees (48 percent). Giant plants with more than 2,500 employees contributed 36 percent of its total workforce. *Source:* PID-1640 database.

companies had changed irrevocably. Branch plants now employed 31 percent of its members' total workforce.

Of the city's ten largest metal-working industries, only three (auto parts, iron and steel forgings, and railroad cars) showed a negligible to nonexistent MMA presence, reflecting its lack of appeal to Budd, Midvale, and Brill, which did not participate in the managerial reformation of the 1920s. In contrast, the MMA dominated all of the other important sectors, including the technically and managerially progressive electrical, radio, instrumentation, and bearing makers; and these were now the industries that contributed the bulk (46 percent) of its labor force and resources. The MMA had not lost its old members in the process of growth (unless they had gone out of business), but the general machinery and machine-tool builders and repairers were now responsible for less than a quarter of its employees. G.E. and Westinghouse were bigger than all forty-two members put together from what had, until Leeds's accession, still been the heart of the association.[77]

---

[77]   All data from PID-1640.

But this transformation does not seem to have caused the MMA any major problems of disaffection among the old proprietary members. This is partly because the MMA's new activities were grafted onto the old; they did not displace them. The MMA was thus successful in serving an old and a new constituency, with different needs and priorities, at the same time. In 1925, for example – shortly after the beginning of Leeds's recruitment drive and the MMA's diversification away from the old Open Shop and into human resource management – the eleven largest members already employed almost half of the association's total labor force, but were responsible only for a quarter of the Employment Department's placement work; the other eighty-six members gave it three-quarters of its business. The smaller firms still wanted occasional help in union-busting, regularly turned to the MMA when the usual informal recruitment mechanisms for skilled workers failed to produce the right men quickly enough, and also took advantage of the cooperative training programs on offer. The large firms were interested in wage, hour, and turnover data; in the joint research program; and in pooling the experience of their employment and personnel managers (a group first mentioned in the records in May 1923, when the MMA began to organize informal fortnightly meetings of these men), who ran their own recruitment and training activities. The MMA's old and new programs were therefore complementary, not conflicting.[78]

The second explanation for the MMA's success in holding together as it reinvented itself was that Leeds and his associates transformed its political character. With the growth in membership, the increasing disparity in size and resources among members, and the widening cultural and ideological gulf between the cosmopolitan professionals who staffed the dynamic firms and the diminishing contingent of shop-bred local proprietors, there was an obvious potential for a breakdown in the commitment of the latter. There were worrying signs of this – for example, their reluctance to come to the now alcohol-free dinners, from which the old conviviality had disappeared together with the rousing reactionary rhetoric that had been staple fare during the Open Shop crusade.[79]

The leadership combatted this tendency by adapting the MMA's leadership structure to reflect the increased size and diversity of the membership, allowing far more avenues for direct participation in association business. In 1924, for example, the association only involved eleven men in its work as officers and councillors, plus a handful more as members of the nominating committee (largely an honorary position) and as nonexecutive members of its two working committees (education and foundry training).

<hr/>

[78] Finance Committee 27 Apr. 1925, ECM 22 May 1923.
[79] ECM 12 Dec. 1927 (74 percent of members were present at dinner; they employed 91 percent of operatives, and a far higher percentage of actual workers.) See also 21 Dec. 1928, 22 Jan. 1929, on nonattendance.

By 1929, the inner core was no larger, and – apart from G.E.'s plant manager and Staunton Peck – still consisted of representatives of large (Disston) and small (a nonferrous foundry with just ninety-one employees) locally controlled companies. Policy was still in the hands of middle-aged Philadelphia entrepreneurs; G.E., Westinghouse, and SKF were not throwing their weight about, as had been feared. Furthermore, the core was now surrounded by a cluster of working groups fully reflecting the growth in the MMA's sphere of activities and the new diversity of its membership. These involved a further thirty representatives of member companies and dealt with membership recruitment and retention, the collaborative training programs, collaborative personnel research, and – for the foundry sector – problems of safety regulation, cost-comparison, and production control (i.e., fighting state agencies and rigging the market). Professional managers from the larger companies dominated the personnel-related committees that they were interested in, proprietors from the older members and sectors ran most of the rest. It was a natural, mutually acceptable arrangement.[80]

It must also have helped that the new-model MMA that emerged under Morris Leeds's and Earl Sparks's direction had ample resources, thanks to its own growth, the Wharton connection, and city, state, and federal education budgets, to service its traditional and its "progressive" members at the same time. Revenues grew by 63 percent between 1925 and 1930, and expenditure by only 34 percent, so that the association was able to rebuild its reserves from a low point equivalent to six months' income until they exceeded a whole year's.[81]

On the brink of the Great Depression, and after five years of renovation, innovation, and growth, the MMA was therefore, or so it seemed, in better shape than ever before. Its bloodless and, by the early 1920s, near-total victory in the Open Shop crusade had not left it fatally lacking in a raison d'être. Interest in a new program of "constructive work in the betterment of labor relations" that was far less "exacting" and more "agreeable" than its old "defensive" purposes had been quietly growing up within it since at least 1915. The near-death of the metal craft unions, the retirement of the old pugilists who had led it since its birth, and the structural transformations within the business community itself turned out to have been, not a terminal crisis for the MMA, but the opportunity for a thoroughgoing renaissance. Almost everything seemed for the best in the best of all possible worlds. Almost, but not quite: Morris Leeds was still eager to lead his members in a struggle against the last old enemy left for progressive capitalism to vanquish.[82]

---

[80] MMA-EXEC database.
[81] Auditor's Report, MMAP III-4–5/6.
[82] Resolution Unanimously Adopted at the 23rd. Annual Meeting, 8 Dec. 1926, with ECM – to mark the retirement of Schwacke and Hallowell.

9.6 HUBRIS AND HIGHMINDEDNESS: THE CONQUEST OF UNEMPLOYMENT

In December 1928 the MMA celebrated its twenty-fifth anniversary, and a reflective Morris Leeds addressed his members about its past, its present activities, and the basic philosophy that – he thought – should underpin them. Its goal was constructing "the very basis of right human relations" at work, which depended on providing equitable payment, continuity of employment, and good supervision. The MMA and its Wharton partners were providing member firms with the factual data and expert guidance that they needed to achieve these objectives and establish "permanent peace, based securely on justice, coöperation, and mutual understanding."[83]

But there was more to be done. America's was a dynamic economy, and Leeds thought it "clear that our working people should have their share of our increasing prosperity," on the grounds of "justice between ourselves and our employees, which is essential to good relations; and . . . because industry can only be expected to flourish in a country of good wages and regular employment."[84]

Leeds was reaching toward the underconsumptionist understanding of the causes of America's economic fragility that would turn him, in the next decade, into one of the advance agents of Keynesianism in the United States. He was doing so from his familiar positions, including a concern for "the cause of industrial peace" and a preoccupation with the "grave anomaly" of unemployment, "the outstanding shortcoming of our industrial system." He challenged his members to study and understand it, and to do everything within their power, individually and collectively, to seek to control it. As a voluntarist and a principled welfare capitalist, he thought that they had no alternative:

We of the owning and managing class ask for a free hand in managing industry and that we shall be little interfered with either by organized labor or the State. We believe that we can thus best serve the interests of all classes. To a large degree we have been accorded that freedom, and so in all fairness we must face the task . . . of reducing unemployment to the minimum, and the further task of making proper provision for those who, through no fault of their own, are the victims of the still remaining unemployment which cannot be obviated. We must face these tasks and stay with them until we master them. We run much risk of legislative and other intervention if we do not.[85]

---

[83] Leeds, PRES 1928, pp. 4–7 [quote at p. 7], 10 [quote].
[84] Ibid., pp. 7, 8, 10.
[85] Ibid., pp. 7–10. For a fuller and more accessible version of Leeds's wage theory, see Morris E. Leeds and C. Canby Balderston, Jr., *Wages: A Means of Testing Their Adequacy* (Philadelphia, 1931), esp. pp. 9–13, on Leeds & Northrup's unique needs-based review of individual employees' earnings; for the later development of his

Readers who still think of the 1920s as a time of high, general, and stable prosperity may be surprised at Leeds's continuing preoccupation with the unemployment problem, which was, he believed, "attracting more attention among thinking people than any other aspect of our industrial situation" even before the Depression hit. The explanation is that the surprised reader is misinformed, and that Leeds knew what he was talking about.[86]

In the Philadelphia metal trades, for example, most of the improvement in workers' real living standards that took place in the decade was the result of the collapse of food prices between 1920 and 1922, and their failure subsequently to recover. There was no great increase in male earnings, which took until 1929 before slow growth restored them to 1920 levels, in money terms, for those lucky enough still to have a job (see Figure 7.1). The sector provided a livelihood to about 19,000 fewer workers at the end of the decade than it had at the beginning (79,000 in 1921, 60,000 in 1930). This downward trend was compounded by seasonal and cyclical fluctuations (see Figure 9.2), by persistent high turnover and an increase in short-term job tenure, and by the pockets of long-term unemployment resulting from the collapse of traditional industries.[87]

When Leeds spoke, the city's manufacturing economy was in a mild recession. In the metal trades, employment had declined by almost a third, touching bottom in the summer of 1928 (see Figure 9.2). Employment in the Philadelphia metal trades was both less buoyant and more volatile than either the rest of the city's manufacturing industries' or the average for the American metal-working sector. This was the background against which Leeds argued the necessity for further research and constructive action.[88]

With the help of his usual collaborators, Joseph Willits and Henry Brown of Brown & Bailey and the Social Order Committee, Leeds began trying to energize the city's leading businessmen for a concerted attack on the problem. They seized on the Chamber of Commerce's concern that Philadelphia's growth rate through the 1920s was below the national average, and turned its Industrial Relations Committee – whose argument had once been that the Open Shop would guarantee prosperity – into a vehicle for their purposes. Together they convened a conference at The University of Penn-

collectivist, countercyclical views, see Dennison et al., *Toward Full Employment*, Pt. 1; Robert M. Collins, *The Business Response to Keynes, 1929–1964* (New York, 1981), esp. pp. 63–67.

[86]   Leeds, PRES 1928, p. 7.
[87]   PID16–40 database; Bezanson, *Help-Wanted Advertising*, Ch. 8; Burton R. Morley, *Occupational Experience of Applicants for Work in Philadelphia* (Philadelphia, 1930), esp. pp. 48–49, 86–87, 102; Herrmann, *Ten Years of Work Experience*, pp. xiii, 4–5.
[88]   NMTA, *The Labor Barometer* (December 1929): 1, 3; Palmer, *Recent Trends in Employment and Unemployment in Philadelphia*, esp. pp. 4, 40.

sylvania in April of 1929 that was attended by many of the leading national figures in labor economics and industrial relations as well as representatives of interested local institutions. Leeds made his customary plea for more facts and "Analyses of the Total Situation," and with Willits's support proposed the establishment of an "Institute of Regularization." This would educate businessmen in the part that they should play in the collective assault on avoidable instability that Leeds and Willits proposed. "The people to be dealt with in this connection are managers, nobody else. It is they who manage either poorly or well." Leeds and his committee laid out as their ideal

that every person who is honestly seeking should be able to find work that is suited to his capacities, under conditions that are reasonable; and that when he has to change from one job to another, it should be possible for him to do so without reducing himself and his family to living conditions that will deteriorate them. Before this ideal can be achieved employers generally will have to feel so strong a sense of responsibility toward all those employed that they will not lay off an employee without making sure that he has some provision against the hazard of poverty during the time he is seeking new employment. They will have to feel that a failure to meet this responsibility is a failure of management's obligation, something like failure to earn dividends or interest on bonds.[89]

The task was urgent   "There is today no test of the capacity of industrial leadership so searching as its capacity to deal with this situation. If industry fails, political leaders . . . will be forced by public opinion to take up the task." But industry had the opportunity to forestall such a development by providing " 'an American way out' " – voluntarist, decentralized, dependent on the enlightened self-interest, private initiatives, and cooperation of business men and organizations, social scientists, and local government. And Philadelphia, because sections of its business community, the Wharton, and city and state authorities had begun to work together, had a special opportunity to take the lead in this quintessentially Hooverite project. As AMA president Sam Lewisohn enthused, it could "work out intensively a laboratory . . . to conduct as we say in mining, 'a pilot mill,' for the entire country."[90]

Ironically, Leeds and Willits launched their program – the end point of fifteen years' work that had begun in the 1914–15 depression – just as the Philadelphia metal trades labor market and the national economy were about to go crazy in ways that destroyed forever the prospects of real-

[89]   Proceedings of a Conference Devoted to Regularization of Employment and Decreasing of Unemployment in Philadelphia held at The University of Pennsylvania Christian Association Building April 30, 1929 (typescript, mimeo.), pp. 3–4, 7, 9, 46, 56.
[90]   Program for the Regularization of Employment and Decreasing of Unemployment in Philadelphia: Report of a Sub-Committee to the Industrial Relations Committee of the Philadelphia Chamber of Commerce (1929), pp. 7–8, 11 esp.

izing their dreams of orderly progress through voluntaristic, community-based action.

While Leeds's conference was meeting, and his committee reporting, man-ufacturing employment in the city was recovering fast, almost regaining its 1926 peak. In the metal trades, it raced ahead 20 percent between January and July, reaching the same high point. All of a sudden, the problem was a lack of workers – particularly skilled men – not jobs. Toolmakers in par-ticular were unobtainable locally. Poaching and turnover rose astronomi-cally, and the Employment Department found itself trying, fruitlessly, to recruit men from other higher wage cities – while out-of-town employers were advertising more successfully in Philadelphia, despite the MMA's attempts to persuade the local press to refuse their business. The MMA coordinated its members' response to this crisis, recommending the re-engineering of products to reduce toolroom work, re-emphasizing training as the only long-term solution, and advising members whose wage rates were out of line to raise them toward the norm revealed by the most recent wage survey.[91]

Then, even faster than it had boomed, demand for the local industry's products, and thus its need for workers, collapsed. So began a sickening but unsteady slide interrupted by brief and weak recoveries that would take the employment index below the pit of the 1927–28 trough by the early months of 1931. By the time of Franklin D. Roosevelt's election it would be 50 percent below the summer 1929 peak, and by the time of his acces-sion 10 percent lower still. The old Baldwin works, long vacated by the last of its thousands of workers, would find its final, symbolically appropriate use before being razed in 1937 – as a shelter for thousands of destitute homeless men.[92]

However, realization that what they had to deal with was a catastrophe, not a normal cyclical correction bringing relief from an overheated labor market, took some time dawning on the MMA's leaders and members. Leeds persisted with his "Regularization" scheme, winning the city Chamber of Commerce's endorsement in December, and advising his members on how to cope with the "mild business depression" that faced them. He was "profoundly impressed with the leadership and proposals of President Hoover" and "presume[d] that most of us will want to follow . . . to the limit that sound business will permit." They would act like L & N and "hold up wage rates," "retain on our payrolls, forces as large as we

91 Bezanson, *Help-Wanted Advertising*, pp. 42–46; ECM 4 Apr., 2 May, 15 May, 27 May, 25 June, 1 Sept. 1929; Leeds, PRES 1929, pp. 3–4.
92 Bonnie M. Fox, "Unemployment Relief in Philadelphia: A Study of the Depression's Impact on Voluntarism," *PMHB* 93 (1969): 86–108 at p. 99; Federal Writers' Project, *Philadelphia: A Guide to the Nation's Birthplace* (Philadelphia and Harrisburg, 1937), p. 459.

can possibly employ advantageously," build up inventories, and "stimulate other business by using this time of slackness for repairs, and for any plant extension that we may have planned – in preparation for the next time of business activity, which will certainly come."[93]

Leeds appealed to his members to go against what most of them thought of as sound, conservative practice so that they could play their collective part in Herbert Hoover's grand countercyclical program for mobilizing American governments, large corporations, and associated businesses against the forces of deflation. "Although as individual concerns we may not be able to do much, if all of us in such groups go along to the extent of our powers, the sum total will be great and will be a real influence for better conditions."[94]

Leeds, as usual, led from the front. It helped that his own company was comparatively unaffected by the first eighteen months of the depression – they were actually still hiring through the early part of 1930, employing 13 percent more people than in 1929. Once the depression caught up with them, L & N eliminated overtime, and then cut their forty-hour week, making up their employees' lost wages from the unemployment benefit fund, before laying off an eighth of their workers. When that distasteful step finally had to be taken, there was at least the consolation that most of them were protected against want by payments from the fund, and a substantial minority of Leeds's highly skilled workers succeeded in finding work before their benefits ran out. His seven years of preparation for such a crisis were paying off; company reserves seemed adequate for what was still expected to turn out to be a recession whose depth and duration could not exceed that of 1920–21, before the New Capitalism had taken hold. The next two disastrous years would wipe them out and demonstrate the impotence of even the best-laid welfare capitalist plans. Nemesis would follow hubris in time-honored fashion.[95]

[93] Leeds, PRES 1929, pp. 4–5.

[94] Ibid., p. 4. Leeds's influence by this time was national rather than local in scale: As one of four members of the NMTA's Committee on Industrial Relations, he won that once conservative organization's support for the business liberals' program too – Committee on Industrial Relations, NMTA, *Stabilizing Metal Trades Employment* (Chicago, 1931). For the Hoover program and the strictly limited successes of the nationwide business response, see Jacoby, *Employing Bureaucracy*, pp. 208–23.

[95] U.S. Bureau of Labor Statistics, "Unemployment-Benefit Plans in the United States," *Bulletin* No. 544 (July 1931), pp. 28–29; Leeds, "Unemployment Benefits," in U.S. Department of Commerce, *Unemployment: Industry Seeks a Solution. A Series of Radio Addresses given under the auspices of the President's Emergency Committee for Employment* (Washington, 1931), p. 18; Balderston, *Executive Guidance*, p. 146; SEC 1931, p. 1; Nelson, "The Company Union Movement," p. 355.

10

The Deluge: The Great Depression and the End of the Open Shop

In the 1920s innovative employment policies, and the institutional changes within the MMA that accompanied and facilitated them, resulted from local, private initiatives by the association and those of its member companies that gave its managerial progressivism their support. The only important outside forces that impinged on it were the cosmopolitan communities of businessmen and social scientists who devised and implemented the progressive agenda and the national corporations, G.E. and Westinghouse, whose local managers lent it their assistance. What businessmen and their allies did was all that mattered; public policy rarely affected their decision making. They could take their political environment more or less for granted – a distant, inactive federal government, whose rare interventions supported the progressives' programs; a state government of similar character; and a city government on whose help they could utterly rely, whether for vocational education or, if necessary, policing strikes. The labor movement almost vanished from view; workers figured only as a mass of disconnected individuals with sometimes awkward behavior, particularly the tendency to move from job to job.

But, in the 1930s, this cozy world turned upside down. What mattered about the thirties was what other people and institutions did, and how businessmen responded. They were battered, as never before or since, by forces that were national or even international in scope – the Depression, the development of interventionist governments and a pluralistic polity, and the rise of working-class militancy and of new forms of working-class action and organization. What happened in Philadelphia in the 1930s was a performance in a national drama, scripted and produced elsewhere, but acted out locally (see Figures 10.1 and 10.2 for key national indicators of the labor relations climate).

In the twenties, businessmen's (and academics') voices and actions were the only ones that counted. In the thirties, the academics almost disappeared

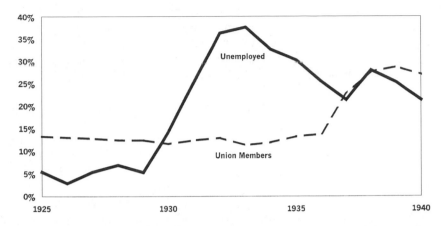

Figure 10.1. Unemployment and Union Members as Percentages of the Nonfarm Labor Force, 1925–1940. *Note:* The shape and timing of labor's breakthroughs were the same in Philadelphia as in the nation at large – 1936 was the decisive year. *Source:* U.S. Department of Commerce, Bureau of the Census, *Historical Statistics of the United States, Colonial Times to 1970* (Washington, 1976), Series D9, D10, D951, D952.

Figure 10.2. Strikes and Man-Days Lost (×1,000), 1925–1940. *Note:* Philadelphia metal working's major strikes – SKF and Budd in 1934, the sit-downs in 1937 – took place at the crest of major national strike waves. *Source:* U.S. Department of Commerce, *Historical Statistics*, Series D977, D982.

from view, except in their new roles as servants of the New Deal state and acceptable neutral mediators in Philadelphia's organized, often violent class conflicts. And the businessmen who have been the moving spirits in this story so far found themselves reduced to objects of historical change, reactors rather than actors. The measure of success in industrial relations policy making in the 1930s was the speed, good grace, and intelligence with which they eventually – like their fellows in other industries and cities – adjusted to a new reality. Charting the road to this unexpected destination will be the purpose of this chapter and the next.

In writing these chapters, I found myself moving into territory that is both familiar to me, and contested among historians. In *The Right to Manage* (1982), on American manufacturers' response to what we can now call, following Steve Fraser and Gary Gerstle, the "New Deal Order," I developed a simple threefold typology of the spectrum of corporate industrial relations policies that greeted the rise of organized labor: "persistent anti-unionism" (resisting the new legal framework that the New Deal state erected, opposing unions with all the traditional coercive techniques or, after 1937, those that were less crude and obvious but no less effective); "realism," by which I meant a pragmatic, often belated acceptance of the new legal-institutional order in the spirit of making the best of a bad job, and with the purpose of defending or recovering the essentials of management's "right to manage"; and a "progressive alternative" (rapid accommodation to the new laws, a willing embrace of unionism, especially industrial unionism, as an adjunct to business's existing personnel programs and a solution to pressing problems of economic stabilization and ensuring social peace).[1]

This typology was neither original, elaborate, nor wholly satisfactory. But it was useful, and it has survived employment by others, notably Daniel Nelson, who have tested it against the behavior of individual companies. So in one respect what I am doing in these chapters is not simply completing this book on the birth and life of the Open Shop, by attending to its death and transfiguration; I am also reencountering my own earlier work and seeing how well its derivative notions, garnered entirely from secondary sources, assist with the telling of a new, hitherto untold story growing from deep primary roots.[2]

It turns out that in the thirties Philadelphia metal-working firms can be found occupying all parts of my (1982) spectrum, moving from one end to another because of the forces to which they were subjected. The MMA itself

[1] Howell J. Harris, *The Right to Manage: Industrial Relations Policies of American Business in the 1940s* (Madison, 1982), pp. 23–36; Steven Fraser and Gary Gerstle, eds., *The Rise and Fall of the New Deal Order, 1930–1980* (Princeton, 1989), esp. Fraser, "The 'Labor Question'," pp. 55–84.

[2] Richard Willcock, "Industrial Management's Policies Toward Unionism," in Milton Derber and Edwin Young, eds., *Labor and the New Deal* (Madison, 1957), pp. 277–315; Nelson, "Managers and Non-Union Workers in the Rubber Industry: Union Avoidance Strategies in the 1930s," *Industrial and Labor Relations Review* 43 (1989): 41–52. Sanford Jacoby's critique in his *Modern Manors: Welfare Capitalism since the New Deal* (Princeton, 1997), pp. 33–34, is entirely persuasive.

went from a position of 1920s managerial liberalism, through a phase of acceptance of the early New Deal, to dogged opposition, and finally toward accommodation and adjustment. One of the purposes of these chapters is therefore to describe and explain the policy choices made, to situate them in time, and thus to enrich my own earlier work.

So far, so agreeable. But in the process of accounting for the triumph of a realistic consensus within the Philadelphia metal-manufacturing community by the late 1930s, and explaining the exceptions, I encountered a variety of social actors and forces: state and federal legislators, bureaucrats, and judges; and labor activists and the institutions they created. The historical profession is far more engaged with their behavior and its consequences than it is with businessmen's. The literature is far more abundant, the debates lively and sometimes fierce. There are three essential, closely intertwined questions to address:

First, was the renewal of the American labor movement that occurred primarily a result of grass-roots militancy that new institutional forms – the New Deal collective bargaining policy, industrial unionism, the increasingly elaborate contracts of employment that resulted from labor–management negotiations – captured and contained? Or was the creation and survival of a stronger labor movement critically dependent on, and unthinkable without, supportive institutions and imaginative but pragmatic leadership? Despite the attractions of what one must still call the "New Left" position, although it is now more than a generation old, I have long been convinced by David Brody, Melvyn Dubofsky, Daniel Nelson, Robert Zieger, and others that it is misleading and untenable.[3]

Second, how is one to understand the role of "The State" in this process? "New Left" historiography had little substantial to say about this question, but "critical legal historians" have more than made up for any neglect ever since Karl Klare's seminal essay in 1978 – if, at least, one's definition of "The State" is confined to the federal judiciary and the administrative agencies that implemented federal labor relations policy. Did the Wagner Act, as the best of the "crits," Christopher Tomlins, argued, offer workers a mere "counterfeit liberty"? Or is there room for the reassertion of another old liberal conclusion: Without Section 7(a) of the National Industrial Recovery Act (hereafter NIRA), the Wagner Act, the La Follette Committee, and the National Labor Relations Board (hereafter NLRB), then workers'

[3] Brody, "The Emergence of Mass-Production Unionism," "The New Deal and the Labor Movement," and "The CIO After Fifty Years," in *Workers in Industrial America: Essays on the Twentieth Century Struggle* (New York, 1993), pp. 82–119, 120–28, 135–56; Dubofsky, "Not So 'Turbulent Years': Another Look at the American 1930s," *Amerikastudien/American Studies* 24 (1979): 5–20; Nelson, *American Rubber Workers and Organized Labor, 1900–1941* (Princeton, 1988); Zieger, *American Workers, American Unions* (Baltimore, 1994), Ch. 2 and *The CIO 1935–1955* (Chapel Hill, 1995), esp. Chs. 2–4.

individual freedom, collective strength, and capacity for a degree of self-liberation at work would have been in short supply in the 1930s.

I have given my answer to this question elsewhere and see no reason to alter it. But, to move the argument on, in the story that follows readers will encounter a more complex working definition of "The State" than is customary. It will give proper attention to local and state, as well as federal, government; to the critical contributions of unseen and unsung state and federal dispute adjusters to the creation of the new labor relations system rather than to legislators, judges, or even NLRB administrators; and to the importance of law enforcement (or the lack of it) in permitting labor's organizational triumphs.[4]

Third, how should one understand what the "victory" of organized labor amounted to? Were official recognition by management, a representative status that could, if necessary, be certified by the NLRB, and the achievement of a written contract specifying the union's role and some of the workers' employment rights, the triumphs that militants thought they were at the time? Did they offer security at the end of hard struggle, or were they perhaps false goals, in part entrapment devices? Was there a credible "road not taken"?[5]

In the account of the transformation of Philadelphia from "scab city" to union town that follows, my argument is that workers' self-activity, that reached hitherto unheard-of levels in the Philadelphia metal trades in the 1930s, followed rather than preceded state encouragement and endorsement. The New Deal did not alone cause it, but determined its timing, its language, some of its goals, and much of its success. Militancy was a response to the Depression, certainly, but it is also important to note that it was concentrated in two periods of swift economic recovery, the summers of 1933 and 1936–37, which improved its chances of a quick payoff and therefore of securing something temporarily approaching mass participa-

---

[4] Klare, "Judicial Deradicalization of the Wagner Act and the Origins of Modern Legal Consciousness," *Minnesota Law Review* 62 (1978): 265–339; Christopher L. Tomlins, *The State and the Unions: Labor Relations, Law, and the Organized Labor Movement in America, 1880–1960* (New York, 1986), p. 326; Howell J. Harris. "The Snares of Liberalism? Politicians, Bureaucrats, and the Shaping of Federal Labour Relations Policy in the United States, ca. 1915–1947," in Steven Tolliday and Jonathan Zeitlin, eds., *Shop-Floor Bargaining and the State: Historical and Comparative Perspectives* (Cambridge, 1985), pp. 148–91; see also Melvyn Dubofsky, *The State and Labor in Modern America* (Chapel Hill, 1994), esp. Chs. 5–6.

[5] See the debate between David Brody, "Workplace Contractualism in Comparative Perspective" and Nelson Lichtenstein, "Great Expectations: The Promise of Industrial Jurisprudence and its Demise, 1930–1960," in Nelson Lichtenstein and Howell J. Harris, eds., *Industrial Democracy in America: The Ambiguous Promise* (New York, 1993), pp. 176–205, 113–41; see also Staughton Lynd, ed., *"We Are All Leaders": The Alternative Unionism of the Early 1930s* (Urbana, 1996), for a forceful but unpersuasive restatement of the old "New Left" sentiments.

tion and support. Its immediate objects were limited to winning improvements in working conditions, in which it was quite successful, within the limits of what an underperforming economy and the ground rules of private ownership allowed.

To achieve this much, militancy required strategy, direction, and discipline; to keep what it won, it required institutionalization. In the Philadelphia metal trades, these were mostly provided by the organizations that became the United Electrical, Radio, and Machine Workers of the Committee for (later Congress of) Industrial Organzization (hereafter UE and CIO) and by the Communist cadres and other progressives within its leadership. By 1936–37, that is, from the very beginning of Philadelphia labor's breakthrough, formal recognition and written contracts were the UE's necessary goals. To win them, and to preserve them through the recession that followed, it was prepared to compromise and to share in designing a new labor relations system that MMA members found acceptable and even, in some respects, advantageous.

The UE therefore helped the companies it dealt with toward a pragmatic accommodation with the new system of "workplace contractualism." But the ascendancy of managerial realism in and after 1937 was not primarily the result of political sophistication or ideological flexibility within the metal-manufacturing community. Rather, it was the consequence, and a recognition, of defeat.

Insofar as the New Deal affected the politics of Philadelphia metal manufacturers, it revived and deepened their bedrock conservatism. The MMA and its members put more effort into defending the Open Shop in 1934–36 than they had for a generation; they spent more money, and used more violence than ever in the past. They lost. Workers began to win organizational strikes again in 1936, helped by a sympathetic city administration, the diplomatic efforts of state and federal mediators, and by divisions in the ranks of capital itself. The Roosevelt campaign and victory that fall increased militant workers' self-confidence and the resonance of their message. Workers supported one another: Individual crafts, plants, and unions were no longer fighting alone. And they adopted a bold tactical innovation: the sit-down strike, which the city police tolerated. In the face of this overwhelming pressure, the Open Shop crumbled.

The structure of this chapter is a simple narrative. The first section details the impact of the Depression on the MMA, its members, and their workers. The second describes the coming of the National Recovery Administration (NRA), the MMA's positive response, and the restorative effects of the New Deal on the economic fortunes of Philadelphia metal manufacturing and on the MMA as an institution. The third reveals the fly in the ointment: the unanticipated rise of worker militancy in a favorable political environment, and the establishment of a union beach-head in the Philadelphia metal trades in the summer of 1933. This was largely because of the "progressive" (in my 1982 terms) response of the managers of the city's largest company, the radio manufacturers Philco, to the challenge of labor. The fourth section discusses the counterattack spearheaded by the second largest metal manufacturer, vehicle body maker Edward Budd, and followed up by the MMA itself, which helped produce a stalemate that lasted through 1934–35. And the fifth deals with the showdown year, 1936, in which the MMA invested in violent, law-defying union-busting attempts that either failed immediately or "succeeded" at such high cost as to be unrepeatable, and in any event were reversed in due course. By the winter of 1936–37 the MMA had reached a strategic dead-end, from which the only way out would be a major policy reversal: enforced abandonment of the Open Shop; reluctant acceptance of the New Deal Order in labor relations; adjustments in attitudes and behavior to assist members with the difficult tasks of accommodating themselves to unwanted change, and the association itself with survival in a new, potentially hostile, climate. Chapter Eleven will detail the ways in which these complicated but unavoidable strategic maneuvers were carried out.

These chapters recount a drama of conflict ending in a new stability. It is, of course, primarily a story about Philadelphia. But, give or take a few details of timing and specific policy choices by particular managements, what happened in the Philadelphia metal trades in the 1930s happened in every large industrial community. At the end of a decade of being steamrollered by the nationalizing institutions and universalizing experiences of the Depression and the New Deal, the Philadelphia metal trades' distinctiveness was almost obliterated.

10.1 SEASONS OF DESPAIR

How did the Depression affect the MMA, and how did its members respond? The most obvious effects were on the total number of members, on the size of their workforces, and thus on its revenues. Membership continued to increase, but at less than half of 1929's rate, through 1930, until it reached an interwar high of 118 firms. Then an inexorable toll of bankruptcies, receiverships, and resignations by companies unable to afford or unwilling to pay their dues cut it back below 100 over the next two years. Their total employment declined further and faster from 1929's record level of 28,472 – it fell 25 percent in 1930, another 30 percent in 1931, and a further 35 percent in 1932, when the figure for members' total combined workforces bottomed out at less than 10,000, making an overall contraction of two-thirds (see Figures 9.1 and 9.2).[6]

---

[6] MMAYEARS database; SEC 1929–1932.

Revenues followed a similar downward path, but less steeply: Because of the graduation of assessments, as large (500+) and very large (1,000+) firms declined, the average amount they paid per employee actually rose. At the other end of the scale, the minimum dues level meant that even when a company shrank almost to vanishing point, it still had to pay at least $25 a quarter, or resign. Three times as many members were caught by that rule in 1933 as in 1929. The net result was that the MMA's income only fell about 50 percent, from the 1929 peak to the 1933 trough. Given that most of it was spent on wages and salaries, which could be cut hard in a deflationary period before affecting staff living standards, or rent, which could be negotiated down in a slack property market, the MMA actually experienced little real reduction in its purchasing power. It only had to "let go" the most recently hired clerk. When expenditures did exceed revenue in 1932–33, there was a reserve equivalent to almost two years' income on which to draw, so there was no need to cut back on services.[7]

As an institution, therefore, the MMA weathered what Morris Leeds's successor as president, his friend Stogdell Stokes, called "the distressing three years" 1930–32, "remarkably well." Economies had to be made – in staff holiday entitlements, in the entertainment allowance at the annual banquets – but costs were also falling "naturally" because of the reduction in business activity. For example, in 1929 the MMA spent a large amount ($1,216, 7 percent of its total expenditure) on help-wanted advertising – in the following years, little or nothing.[8]

But the MMA that was surviving was a shriveled husk whose basic functions had been gouged out. Its original core activities – anti-unionism and running a labor market for skilled men – were unimportant in a period of massive unemployment; and its new programs of personnel research, skills training, and the promotion of welfare capitalism were irrelevant, or unattainable.

The year 1929 had seen stirrings of movement among the metal crafts – toolmakers had struck the giant Philadelphia Storage Battery Company (Philco), radio manufacturers, in defense of their customary noon and evening washup time, and to protest an offensive foreman. The IAM lent these unorganized men help, "in the hope that the result will be that they will become members," reported the first U.S. Commissioner of Conciliation to intervene in a Philadelphia metal trades strike since 1924. But the Machinists were quickly disappointed: The commissioner's attempts to persuade the company to compromise were unsuccessful, the strikers drifted

---

[7] Financial Reports in ECM 19 Nov. 1929, 18 Nov. 1930, 14 Oct. 1931, 20 Sept., 2, 20 and 21 Dec. 1932.
[8] ECM, 30 Dec. 1932.

away, "all secured employment elsewhere, and the strike . . . died a natural death."[9]

Once the slide began, the labor front quietened down almost completely – there were a couple of lockouts of Molders at small foundries that the MMA helped to establish open-shop conditions in 1929–30, and a short, this time successful strike by Philco machinists against speedup and rate cuts. Nothing else happened, except for the first signs of a troubling future – Philadelphia's Communists became "more than usually active," holding plant-gate meetings and even handing out "considerable inflammatory literature" inside them! Local radical groups that had not rated a mention through the 1920s all of a sudden became worth watching closely. But they did not seem too much of a threat – the Philadelphia police had a tough "red squad" to keep them on the run; and by the end of 1931 Sparks could report that their "efforts to establish shop nuclei . . . [had] met with practically universal failure." In 1931 and 1932, while elsewhere in the United States desperation was sparking a hopeless militancy, the MMA had no strikes at all to deal with: Contrary to the experience in the 1920–22 recession, "by and large the workers with commendable good grace have accepted the readjustments in their time and pay which have been essential."[10]

Believing this surely made Sparks and his audience feel better, but it was not wholly true: There may not have been much activity inside their plants, but there was more on the streets than there had been for twenty years. Local Socialists and the League for Industrial Democracy, aided by radical students from Penn, Bryn Mawr, and Swarthmore, set up an Unemployed

[9] L. R. Thomas to Hugh L. Kerwin, 9 Jan. 1929, Preliminary Report 10 Jan. and Thomas to Kerwin. n.d., all in FMCS 170-4756.

[10] Lockouts: ECM 22 Oct. 1929, 26 Nov., 7 Jan. 1930, 28 Jan., 16 Sept., 29 Oct., Kerwin to J. F. Dewey 24 May 1930, FMCS 170-5662. Philco: Summary of Final Report of Commissioner of Conciliation and Thomas to Kerwin, 15 Jan. 1930, FMCS 170-5462. Communists: ECM 25 Feb. 1930 [quote]; Thomas H. Coode and John F. Bauman, *People, Poverty, and Politics: Pennsylvanians During the Great Depression* (Lewisburg, 1981), pp. 56–61; Frank Donner, *Protectors of Privilege: Red Squads and Police Repression in Urban America* (Berkeley, 1990), pp. 41–42, 52–53; SEC 1931, p. 2 [quote]. Industrial Peace: SEC 1932, p. 6 [quote]. There was a fortnight-long toolmakers' strike against rate cuts at Disston, but it seems to have escaped Sparks's notice – Summary of Final Report of Commissioner of Conciliation Homer J. Brown, 12 April 1932, FMCS 170-7138; Harry C. Silcox, *A Place to Live and Work: The Henry Disston Saw Works and the Tacony Community of Philadelphia* (University Park, 1994), p. 146. The MMA's experience was not – for Pennsylvania – exceptional; the state's mediation service recorded no metal trades strikes between 1929 and 1933. See A. Norman Gage, "Pennsylvania Labor and Industry in the Depression: A Record of the Four-Year Period, 1931–1934," Commonwealth of Pennsylvania, Department of Labor and Industry, *Special Bulletin No. 39* (Harrisburg, 1934), p. 38.

Citizens League to fight evictions in March 1932; its rival, the Communists' Unemployed Council, was similarly active, notably in organizing the brutally repressed center city demonstration in August 1932 that went down in history as the "Battle of Reyburn Plaza." Even while Philadelphia workers were failing to strike, and failing to vote – or still voting Republican – they were beginning to make connections with local militants and other progressives on which the labor movement would soon be able to build.[11]

Strike-breaking had been a marginal activity for the MMA for years, but the Employment Department was at the center of its program of service to members and their skilled workers. The first effect of the Depression, and of Leeds's commitment to organized local effort to mitigate it, was to enhance the department's importance. A committee of employment managers from the larger member companies examined its work to see how its role could be expanded. Members also cooperated by sending laid-off men to report and by notifying it of vacancies. The result was that more than three times as many job-seekers applied as in prosperous 1929 (37,523 as against 11,828), and one in twenty of them could be placed (1,986 vs. 926). But the next year, less than a third as many were placed, and discouraged job-seekers stopped calling – 26,720 in 1931 (29 percent down), only 8,500 in 1932 (another 68 percent cut), at which point Secretary Sparks stopped bothering to report his negligible success rate.[12]

The MMA's ability to place workers was undermined by a change in the way the glutted labor market functioned, as well as by the simple dearth of jobs. As Sparks put it, "Employers, much concerned as they have been with the distress of their businesses, have been more concerned than ever before with the plight of their workers." The norms of welfare capitalism, with its stress on employers' obligations, affected companies' behavior to such an extent that the impact of the Great Depression was qualitatively different even from that of 1920–22. Reductions in wage rates were belated and modest – about 15 percent between 1929 and 1932, while the cost of living index slumped by more than 20 percent. Earnings fell much more steeply because of layoffs and short time, of course – the average annual male wage in the metal trades dropped from almost $1,600 in 1929 to

[11] "Jobless Union Is Organized," *Union Labor Record* (hereafter *ULR*) 25 March 1932, p. 10, "Jobless Fight Evictions," 19 Aug., p. 1, "Labor Backs Unemp. League," 2 Sept., pp. 3, 10; "The Unemployed Citizens League of Philadelphia," *Monthly Labor Review* 36 (1933): 495; Robert Drayer, "J. Hampton Moore: An Old-Fashioned Republican" (Ph. D., University of Pennsylvania, 1961), p. 311.
[12] ECM 7 Jan. 1930, Memoranda for Special Committee on Study of Employment Department Methods and Minutes of the Meeting of the Special Committee to Study Methods of Recruiting Labor, 21 and 24 Feb., ECM 24 June; SEC 1929 p. 8, SEC 1931 pp. 8–9, SEC 1932 pp. 5–6.

barely $1,000 in 1932; but, after taking into account changes in the cost of living, it was still higher than at the end of the postwar recession (see Figure 7.1).[13]

The effect of this nondeflationary wage policy on the economics of the metal-working sector was quite profound: Quantitative evidence supports Sparks's judgment that it entailed "the sacrifice of efficiency." As a proportion of the collapsing output, the wage bill rose from less than 23 to more than 26 percent, back to the unsustainable heights of 1919, but in a vastly different market climate (see Figure 7.2). The effect on its workers was equally significant, raising the value of having and holding on to a job, and affecting their labor market behavior and the priority they attached to fairness and predictability in the way employers allocated the inadequate supply of jobs that they had available.[14]

MMA members did what they could to follow Leeds's advice, and provided work for as much of their core skilled labor force as possible. Before they cut wage rates or made layoffs they cut hours, to fewer than thirty-six a week by the end of 1932, and in many cases below thirty by the time of Roosevelt's inauguration. They let go the "less efficient" and retained valued employees in less skilled jobs. To cope with temporary surges in demand, they boosted working hours rather than hiring anybody new. If they did need extra workers, they "recall[ed] their former efficient employees" or recruited from applicants at the plant with whom their foremen and employment managers were acquainted.[15]

The result was that the formerly fluid citywide labor market was "balkanized" into a collection of sluggish, plant-specific labor pools. The voluntary resignation rate was down to a twentieth of its 1929 level by 1932, and the discharge rate to a fifteenth. As Sparks reported, "only the cream of the working force now remains." This inner core of established employees was surrounded by a middle ring of laid-off workers with priority in re-hiring and an outer circle looking for the first vital break. Companies did not need to look any further to meet their labor needs – supply comfortably exceeded demand, even for skilled men. And the sense of obliga-

---

[13] SEC 1932, p. 6; PHIL1439 database. Richard Jensen, "The Causes and Cures of Unemployment in the Great Depression," *Journal of Interdisciplinary History* 19 (1989): 553–83, offers the best overview of this change in employment and wage policies, though his explanation differs from mine.

[14] SEC 1931, p. 1; PHIL1439 database; cf. Sanford M. Jacoby, *Employing Bureaucracy: Managers, Unions, and the Transformation of Work in Amerian Industry, 1900–1945* (New York, 1985), pp. 216–18; Ronald Schatz, *The Electrical Workers: A History of Labor at General Electric and Westinghouse, 1923–60* (Urbana, 1983), pp. 61–62.

[15] ARCLR Report, 30 Oct. 1930, "A Suggestion for Temporary Application to Reduce Unemployment," and ECM 18 Nov.; Leeds to annual meeting, 17 Dec. 1930, and details of members' plans for employment regularization, 18 Dec.; SEC 1931 pp. 4, 8–9 [quote].

tion that they were encouraged to feel toward "their" workers further militated against any resort to the MMA. They still controlled the hiring and firing process unilaterally; and insofar as any rules governed it, those rules were of their making – notably job reservation for adult men with family responsibilities, and the allocation of job opportunities among them on grounds of "merit." But the stage was set for incumbent workers to struggle to control the new labor market, and to impose their own preferred allocative criterion – seniority.[16]

The MMA's other functions were also affected by the Depression. Its training schemes were early casualties – foreman training was suspended in 1931, while the cooperative apprenticeship program tailed off gradually. As Sparks explained, apprentices were "outsiders" in the new labor market: "Plants unable to provide sufficient work for long service employees did not feel justified in further limiting their work" to accommodate them. By 1933 so few were enrolled that the Saturday morning school was barely viable. But, as the demand for fully skilled labor had fallen from about a third to barely a fifth of available jobs in the metal machining trades (probably because smaller firms and traditional capital goods manufacturers, with their higher skill requirements, suffered worse than the large consumer goods makers, particularly the radio builders), then the collapse of the MMA's quite successful attempt to increase its supply seemed a matter of regret rather than alarm.[17]

Finally, what of the alliance with the Wharton for personnel research? This continued, but it too declined in importance, for both parties. First, Willits lost his main financial sponsor. In 1928 Beardsley Ruml left the Laura Spelman Rockefeller Memorial, which was wound up. The Rockefeller Foundation resumed full control and retreated from Ruml's ambitious programs for the support of applied social science research centers. Willits himself moved on to higher things in 1930, becoming a member of Pennsylvania Governor Pinchot's Committee on Unemployment and President

---

[16] SEC 1932 pp. 4–5, ECM 16 May 1933, SEC 1933 p. 6. Irving L. Horowitz, *The Metal Machining Trades in Philadelphia: An Occupational Study* (Philadelphia, 1939), p. 124, on changing demand for skilled labor; Helen M. Herrmann, *Ten Years of Work Experience of Philadelphia Machinists* (Philadelphia, 1938), Sec. III, for their relative job security and stability; Dorothea De Schweinitz, *How Workers Find Jobs: A Study of Four Thousand Hosiery Workers in Philadelphia* (Philadelphia, 1932), p. 105, demonstrates workers' preference for seniority – hosiery workers, admittedly, but there is no reason to think them exceptional; while De Schweinitz pp. 111–12 and Horowitz, pp. 63–66, 76–77, 79 show how hiring and allocation decisions were actually made. Cf. Nelson, *Rubber Workers*, pp. 114–15, and Schatz, *Electrical Workers*, pp. 105–11.

[17] SEC 1931 p. 5, ECM 21 Feb. 1933, 1 9 June 1934; Horowitz, *Metal Machining Trades*, pp. 96, 100, 124 – the number of apprentices declined by more than two-thirds, to between a fifth and a sixth of the replacements needed in the long term. Cf. Jensen, "Causes and Cure of Unemployment," p. 575.

Hoover's Advisory Committee on Employment Statistics, and then the Director of Development of Plans of the Emergency Committee for Employment. Thereafter, Wharton, while still interested in the Philadelphia labor market and continuing to enjoy the MMA's help in gaining access to company data, reoriented itself toward the needs of new patrons and research clients – the city, state, and federal governments – all of which had acquired an understandably pressing interest in unemployment.[18]

As for the MMA, the dream that research would produce knowledge that could be turned into power to manage the employment relationship in a rational, efficient, humane, and harmonious fashion turned into a sour joke. The guidance it could produce was now scarcely relevant, powerless against the overwhelming forces of the market. When Sparks told his members in December 1932 that the "large reductions in the rates of voluntary turnover ... substantiate the opinion that [it] is much influenced by conditions outside the plant," they may have agreed that the banal answer to this question had been bought at too high a price.[19]

So what was there left for the MMA to do? The answer was simple: pursue the logic of voluntarism to the extent possible; and then descend into fruitless argument and pointless lamentation when the limits of the association's and its members' resources were reached, and it became clear that solutions to the problems of the economy must entail a vast extension of state activities.

Morris Leeds retired from the presidency in December 1930, moving on to a broader career of public service. He pursued his struggle against the Depression alongside Willits as a member of the Pennsylvania Committee on Unemployment and President Hoover's Organization for Unemployment Relief. The first, a classically liberal-corporatist body, made all of the usual suggestions and brought Leeds together with many of the people who would, like him, go on to staff the New Deal state's labor relations agencies. To implement one of its central recommendations – the improvement of public and private employment bureaus – Leeds became chair of the State Employment Commission, with Willits chair of its Technical Advisory Committee and Sparks a committee member. They raised money from liberal local sponsors, and from the Rockefeller Foundation, to turn the Philadelphia employment office into a model for the state as a whole.[20]

18 Willits Personnel File, Univ. of Pennsylvania Archives; Martin and Joan Bulmer, "Philanthropy and Social Science in the 1920s: Beardsley Ruml and the Laura Spelman Rockefeller Memorial, 1922–29," *Minerva* 19 (1981): 347–407 at pp. 397–99; Steven A. Sass, *The Pragmatic Imagination: A History of the Wharton School 1881–1981* (Philadelphia, 1982), pp. 223–24.
19 SEC 1932, p. 4.
20 Pennsylvania Committee on Unemployment, *Alleviating Unemployment: A Report ... to Gifford Pinchot, Governor* (Harrisburg, 1931), pp. 5–11 esp. Leeds's and Willits's fellow committee-members included Morris Cooke and Clinton Golden; for

Stogdell Stokes was also deeply involved in voluntarism's anti-depression campaign. While he was MMA president he acted as the metal trades "captain" in the city's United Campaign to raise relief funds from the voluntary contributions of companies and those in work. It was quite successful – and the city government was as parsimonious as ever – with the result that Philadelphia stood out as a triumph, of a kind, for the Hoover anti-depression program. In 1931 the private sector contributed 55 percent of the relief budget, twice the national average. But by the next spring it was exhausted. Stokes retired after only two years, pleading the burden of his community responsibilities.[21]

With the failure first of the economy and then of voluntarism, businessmen had to cope with the political fallout. The result was that the one growth area in the MMA's activity after 1931 was lobbying, as its old conservatism reasserted itself. The 1930 elections had brought maverick Republican Gifford Pinchot back as Pennsylvania's governor, and increased Democratic representation in the state legislature. Even the machine Republicans of Philadelphia and Pittsburgh began to respond to constituency pressure, and the threat that the Democrats posed, by becoming unprecedentedly ready to entertain radical notions. As a result Harrisburg became a threat for the first time in fifteen years, as well as an ally for the MMA's progressives.

Bills were introduced in 1931 to reduce hours of work for women and children, to outlaw "yellow dog" contracts, and to prepare the ground for an old-age pension system. The MMA and the Pennsylvania Manufacturers' Association were able to fight them to a standstill. But the next year Pinchot appointed a State Committee on Workers' Security to plan a compulsory, employer-financed unemployment scheme, and began an assault on other elements in the state's previously lax employment laws. In particular, the Workmen's Compensation system, thoroughly rigged against workers' rights, and its inadequate benefit levels came under scrutiny.[22]

the Philadelphia experiment, see Pennsylvania State Employment Commission, *30,000 in Search of Work* (Harrisburg, 1933), esp. p. 3; "State Opens Model Agency," *ULR* 25 Mar. 1932, p. 3; Gage, "Pennsylvania Labor and Industry in the Depression," pp. 25–27; and Richard M. Neustadt (director) to Lewis G. Hines, 23 March 1933, in Box 1, F. 5, Hines Papers, LCMD; for Leeds's first prominent public role, as an arbitrator (with Cooke) in the great Aberle hosiery strike of January–April 1930, see Philip Scranton, *Figured Tapestry: Production, Markets, and Power in Philadelphia Textiles, 1885–1941* (New York, 1989), pp. 444–45.

21 ECM 17 Nov., 15 Dec., 1931; Daniel Nelson, *Unemployment Insurance: The American Experience* (Madison, 1969), p. 135; Bonnie M. Fox, "Unemployment Relief in Philadelphia, 1930–1932: A Study of the Depression's Impact on Voluntarism," *PMHB* 93 (1969): 86–108 at p. 102; Ewan Clague and Webster Powell, *Ten Thousand Out of Work* (Philadelphia, 1933), p. 87; ECM 18 Oct. 1932.

22 ECM 17 Feb., 17 March 1931.; SEC 1931, p. 7; SEC 1932, pp. 7–9. For workmen's compensation, see: John P. Horlacher, "The Results of Workmen's Compensation in

When businessmen turned their eyes from Harrisburg to Washington, they found no relief. Congress, too, had been transformed by the off-year elections, and its responsiveness to AFL lobbying similarly increased. The most serious result was the passage of the Norris–La Guardia Anti-Injunction law, that led old-guard Pennsylvania Republican Congressman James M. Beck to warn MMA members that it represented "a long march away from that Philadelphia where the Constitution of the United States was framed and in the direction of Moscow." It "enthroned the possible rule of the proletariat in free America."[23]

How did the MMA respond to these threats? The fact that the executive committee invited Beck to be the keynote speaker at the December 1932 annual meeting provides the answer. With Leeds's departure, and the developing crisis of American conservatism, chill winds of reactionary anxiety quickly snuffed out the MMA's fair-weather managerial liberalism. At the same time as members struggled to maintain the commitment to their own employees, which was the heart of the welfarist program, they embraced the comforting certainties of traditional Republicanism ever more tightly. Beck told many of them what they wanted to hear, as did the city's "Old-Fashioned Republican" Mayor, "Hampy" Moore, who promised that "everything possible would be done to make Philadelphia [a] desirable place for manufactures, to protect the citizens on the streets and employees in their right to work." But these reassurances were of limited value.[24]

Discussions about politics took place increasingly frequently through 1932, but their prevailing tone was one of bleak hopelessness. The association wired Hoover urging him to veto Norris–La Guardia, and requested members to do the same, while acknowledging "that this action was not likely to be effective." The executive committee coordinated a letter-writing campaign to try to persuade local congressmen to support cuts in government programs, as "the country can no longer support Governmental extravagances or the current Congressional policies." But it could not actually agree on any cuts to recommend and regretted some of those that Congress proposed – notably the slashing of the Federal Board for Vocational

Pennsylvania: A Study of the Pennsylvania System from the Point of View of the Injured Worker," Commonwealth of Pennsylvania Department of Labor and Industry, *Special Bulletin* No. 40-Pt. I-b (Harrisburg, 1940); C. A. Kulp, "Workmen's Compensation in Pennsylvania," *ALLR* 24 (1934): 170–74; J. Roffe Wike, *The Pennsylvania Manufacturers' Association* (Philadelphia, 1960), p. 121. See also M. Nelson McGeary, *Gifford Pinchot: Forester-Politician* (Princeton, 1960), pp. 360–81; John Wilson Furlow, Jr., "An Urban State Under Siege: Pennsylvania and the Second Gubernatorial Administration of Gifford Pinchot, 1931–1935" (Ph. D. diss., University of North Carolina at Chapel Hill, 1973), pp. 329–34.
23 ECM 20 Dec. 1932; SEC 1932, p. 7 [quote]; Morton C. Keller, *In Defense of Yesterday: James M. Beck and the Politics of Conservatism 1861–1936* (New York, 1958).
24 ECM 15 Dec. 1931; Drayer, "J. Hampton Moore," esp. Chs. 18–20.

Education's budget, on which the foreman training program had largely depended.[25]

President Stokes sounded a note of tired defeatism at the mid-year dinner. "Sometimes we wonder what good is accomplished by our letters to Congressmen. . . . We are victims of well organized minorities who so often secure what they want." As the elections approached, the concern with politics became obsessive. Machinery foundryman Fletcher Schaum thought that somebody should "tabulat[e] the vote on important measures by our Congressional Representatives . . . in order to vote intelligently when these representatives are up for re-election," and his executive colleagues supported him. They worked with the PMA and the Taxpayers' League of Philadelphia to that end, but decided that there was little point – it was too late to mobilize manufacturers and their employees, the candidates were already chosen, and the issues decided. It was "becoming increasingly important to return Mr. Hoover to the Chief Office and if possible increase Republican representation in the Congress," but in the political circumstances of 1932 they thought that an open endorsement by manufacturers could be the kiss of death to a candidate.[26]

In this bitter winter, the MMA's liberals (notably the large electrical manufacturers) and the Advisory Research Committee on Labor Relations, which they still controlled, fought a rearguard action. The issue was the future of welfare capitalism: Should not employers persist in making a positive response to the crisis, rather than simply opposing whatever Harrisburg or Washington proposed? The committee had been the driving force behind the work-sharing program. In 1931, it had also begun examining the American Association for Labor Legislation's proposals for companies to establish unemployment reserve funds, just like Leeds's. Given General Electric's prominence, it was also natural that they should support and circulate the Swope Plan for industry-level employment regularization and unemployment relief.[27]

But these corporate liberals were swamped by the defensive, cost-conscious, rearguard Republicanism that was now in the ascendant. When they finally brought forward a coherent plan after the election, so that industry could take "an intelligent and constructive part" in shaping the coming state system by acting in accord with the "trend of the times," embattled machine tool maker William Sellers opposed it, on the PMA's behalf. "[I]f it became known that a substantial group of manufacturers

[25] ECM 15 March 1932, 19 April, 17 May.
[26] ECM 18 May 1932, 21 June, 20 Sept., 18 Oct., 15 Nov. In fact, Philadelphia still voted Republican in 1932, to the extent that it voted at all – turnout was almost a third lower than 1928's. See John Shover, "The Emergence of a Two-Party System in Republican Philadelphia, 1924–1936," *JAH* 60 (1974): 985–1002 at pp. 990–93.
[27] "A Suggestion for Temporary Application to Reduce Unemployment," ECM 30 Oct. 1930; 17 March 1931, 21 Apr., 6 May, 20 Oct.

were willing to go a certain distance in the consideration of unemployment reserves . . . the bargaining power of the employer would be weakened and the proponents, having learned that the opposition would go so far, would attempt to force further concessions."[28]

The liberals fought back, but were finally defeated. The conservatives' arguments were pragmatic, not ideological: The committee was proposing a ten-week limit on benefits in any one year, so in "a prolonged depression" like the present they would be "inconsequential." But once the manufacturers had sold the pass and accepted a role in a state initiative, "benefits would be liberalized," and the "percentage of payroll contributed . . . would need to be substantially increased." This "would place another fixed charge upon the employer and unless something like uniformity existed in the legislation of the other States would tend to put the Pennsylvania employer at a competitive disadvantage." Administering a joint public–private scheme would also "necessitate the extension of public employment offices . . . and would authorize a politically appointed committee to determine the suitability of work offered and the equity of the wages being paid." So there was the awful prospect of having unemployed workers maintained at their expense, while pro-labor public employment officers refused to send people from the jobless rolls to work in struck plants or those that did not or could not pay what bureaucrats thought a fair minimum.[29]

On the threshold of Franklin Roosevelt's inauguration, and with the Pennsylvania state legislature threatening to take action on unemployment insurance, workmen's compensation, and the control of working hours, the MMA, like the rest of the state's business community, was reduced to a condition of angry opposition. In the short term they could still block state-level action, but they had lost the initiative and would soon lose their veto. And once Washington replaced Harrisburg as the focus of change, they would have even less influence. The political system was out of control and the economy in free fall.[30]

---

[28] "A Preliminary Statement on Unemployment Reserves," 7 Dec. 1932; ECM 21 Dec. 1932.

[29] ECM 17 Jan. 1933. The MMA's conservatives were faithfully echoing the arguments of the business representatives (including the boss of Baldwin) on Governor Pinchot's committee investigating the plan – see Pennsylvania State Committee on Unemployed Reserves, *Report*, pp. 7–46 – a well-informed, massively hostile document. This opposition scuppered the proposal – see "Pennsylvania Again Runs True To Form," *ALLR* 23 (1933): 101; Furlow, "An Urban State Under Siege," pp. 261–62; Nelson, *Unemployment Insurance*, p. 189. For evidence that opponents' fears were justified, see Chapter 11.

[30] ECM 21 Feb. 1933 and petition to state legislators (document headed "Whereas," filed with minutes); "Important State Legislation Necessitating YOUR Action," 28 Feb. (notice to members); "Pennsylvania Comes Back!" *ALLR* 24 (1934): 40;

The Open Shop employment system survived, in the sense that the Philadelphia metal trades were still almost union-free (apart from the few employee representation plans that the managerial liberals had launched). But it was sustained only by inertia and crippling unemployment. All of its positive content had been gutted out and its supportive institutions – Sparks's Employment Department almost as much as Leeds's benefit programs – drained of resources. By the spring of 1933 companies had finally had to cut wages and hours to such an extent that even their remaining core employees were beginning to protest rather than submit gratefully. The city was ripe for change.[31]

10.2 DELIVERANCE: THE BLUE EAGLE YEARS, 1933–1935

When Earl Sparks reviewed the "sweeping changes" of 1933 for his members that December, he concluded that it had been the most important in the MMA's thirty-year history.

The New Deal brought salvation to the MMA and the industry whose interests it defended. Its most important effects were economic. The employment index for the Philadelphia metal trades surged from barely 50 to more than 90 percent of the 1925–27 average between April and December of 1933, about twice the rate of increase recorded in the nation at large. Sparks reported that the recovery "matched, if it did not surpass, any improvement of the past many years, not excepting the War period." However, it was not sustained – the index slumped to about 80 in the spring of 1934, stayed there for a year, then fell another 15 points in the summer of 1935, before beginning a 50 point advance that almost took it back to 1929's heights, until the "Roosevelt recession" of 1937 saw another sickeningly rapid 30 point collapse (see Figure 9.2).

Despite the overall failure of recovery, its unevenness and instability, its impact was nevertheless dramatic and its contribution to the business and labor history of the Philadelphia metal trades in the 1930s fundamental. The industry was brought back from the brink of disaster, and – unlike the 1920s – its performance through the 1930s matched or exceeded that of most of the other major metal manufacturing centers, principally because of the buoyancy of the automobile, bearing, radio, and electrical industries.

Other vital signs also demonstrated a restoration of economic health:

Furlow, "An Urban State Under Siege," Ch. 4, Pt. 2; Richard C. Keller, "Pennsylvania's Little New Deal," (Ph. D. diss., Columbia University, 1960), Ch. 2; Wike, *Pennsylvania Manufacturers' Association*, p. 142.

[31] ECM 16 May 1933 [earnings survey], 30 Aug. [upsurge of discontent].

With the increase in activity, the Output:Capital and Wage Bill:Product Value ratios recovered from the catastrophic levels that they had reached by 1932–33, reflecting a solid rebuilding of efficiency, profitability, and cost control (see Figure 7.2). The New Deal meant that the Philadelphia metal trades, and therefore the MMA, saw their material foundations reconstructed. But it also, of course, massively increased their workers' bargaining power.[32]

The other benefits that the New Deal brought the MMA were the paradoxical results of its severe political costs. The crises of regulation and labor relations that the New Deal thrust on the industry gave the MMA a renewed raison d'être, and local firms every cause to maintain their membership or to join up.

The NIRA itself gave companies previously indifferent to organization a powerful incentive to join together and seek common counsel to exploit the opportunities that the act offered, and to defend themselves against the threats it contained. In making and administering "Codes of Fair Competition," the NRA listened to *organized* interests. Small, independent businesses knew that, by themselves, they would be left out in the cold. Accordingly, groups of jobbing foundrymen, tool-and-die makers, and heat-treaters joined the MMA en bloc. Earl Sparks would represent them in the code-making process and in the national trade associations that the NIRA brought into existence in these bitterly competitive industries, and the MMA would see to the local implementation of the resulting codes. Thereby the MMA gained new members in sectors of the local industry where it had always found difficulty recruiting, income (to carry out local tasks for the national code authorities, which had the right – stronger in theory than in practice – to demand compulsory subscriptions from firms within their jurisdiction), and some power to deal with its members' problems resulting from excessive competition. Finally, companies could also easily afford MMA dues again, and the rebuilding of their labor forces automatically increased its resources. So a stagnant institution found itself unexpectedly revitalized by the federal government that was the ultimate source of both its salvation and of the immense problems that it had to face.[33]

[32] SEC 1933, p. 1; NMTA, *Labor Barometer* (Chicago, 1933–1938); PHIL1439 database.
[33] ECM 30 Aug. 1933; Statement from the Finance Committee as Basis of Its Recommendation of a Budget, ECM 15 Nov. 1933; SEC 1933, p. 5; ECM 20 Feb. 1934, 20 March, 25 Sept. for examples of the MMA as interface between members and their respective code authorities; SEC 1934, p. 4, for their dawning realization that the NRA had not worked out as they hoped. The theme of the unfulfilled promise of the NRA for competitive businesses is best explored in Donald R. Brand, *Corporatism and the Rule of Law: A Study of the National Recovery Administration* (Ithaca, 1988), esp. Ch. 6.

The National Industrial Recovery Act that emerged from negotiations between the administration, Congress, the AFL, and business groups in the early summer received, on balance, a cautious welcome from the MMA as from much of the nation's business community. Earl Sparks served as a "Major" in the city's Blue Eagle drive to persuade companies to accept the terms of the President's Re-Employment Agreement (as the MMA had itself). He congratulated his members that they and their fellows were "in sympathy with the objectives of the President and ha[d] shown by and large a spirit of wholehearted co-operation with him in his stupendous efforts."[34]

This was partly because the federalizing of industrial regulation offered Pennsylvania manufacturers protection against a perhaps less controllable state legislature. It therefore freed them, they thought, from the threat of competition from less-regulated, lower wage states. It also gave manufacturers a voice in drawing up and administering the NRA's codes of fair competition for their own industries. There were doubts among the executive committee about the NIRA's constitutionality, the quality of its administration, and the limits to which regulation might extend. But these were subordinated to the hope that it would be effective: "in this emergency some control that would prevent further cut-throating of prices and stop the vicious spiral of deflation in values, of wages particularly, would be desirable." The law was also perceived as a way of delivering on the work-sharing program to which the MMA had been committed for four ultimately disappointing years, as well as creating employment and restoring profitability.[35]

The NIRA's impact was remarkable. As Sparks reported that December, it "appear[ed] to have modified ... the natural laws of supply and demand," in that those workers in jobs benefitted hugely, even while unemployment remained high. Working hours in the local metal industry dropped to 26 percent below 1929's, but hourly earnings rebounded 21 percent, almost recovering their 1929 levels. Real living standards of employed metalworkers matched those last seen in the prosperous year 1926, for thirteen and a half fewer hours' work a week. These gains were not simply the results of NIRA and its accompanying surge in economic activity. They were also the fruits of struggle or, more frequently, of employers' attempts to preempt any challenges to their authority. Up until the adoption of the NIRA there was no mention in the executive committee's

[34] ECM 30 Aug. 1933; SEC 1933, p. 4.
[35] ECM 18 Apr. 1933; Special Meeting, 26 Apr. For an eloquent expression of the doubters' position, see address of James A. Emery (counsel, NAM) on "The Industrial Crisis," ECM 9 May. Even he acknowledged that the New Deal had rescued industry from a "deadly spiral" and that "The President's bold and vigorous steps ... transformed our public psychology to a new faith in vigorous leadership" (p. 1).

discussions about any possible impact it might have on labor relations. Afterwards, there was little else.[36]

10.3 FIRST BLOOD: 1933

Philadelphia metal trades labor, funereally peaceful for a dozen years, stirred out of its hopeless quiescence in the summer of 1933. All of a sudden, the MMA was caught in an unexpected crisis. The AFL craft unions, the [Communist] Metal Workers Industrial Union, and even employee representation plans, all protested depressed wage rates. They were emboldened by the rapid economic recovery and by the NIRA itself, whose Section 7(a) gave employees the right to form and join unions of their own choosing for collective bargaining purposes, free from employer interference and in particular free from any obligation to join a company union. As interpreted by labor organizers, the NIRA's one-sided defense of workers' rights – against employers and their agents *only*, not against the possible abuse of union power – turned into a moral obligation to join. Even the AFL Metal Polishers clothed their drive to rebuild their union, and stabilize their industry, in patriotic language: They were "anxious that steps be taken to conform with the mandates of the Government."[37]

Workers responded by, as the Socialist-inclined *Union Labor Record* editorialized, "flocking to the banner of unionism" in an "amazing landslide," newly confident that self-organization was safe, legitimate, and could be effective.

Workers WILL organize into unions when given some promise of governmental protection. . . .

Men and women who work want the aid and sense of security that a union offers them but unless they feel that the agencies of society are on their side will be reluctant to avail themselves of their rights in this respect.

The new attitude of the Federal authorities towards the question of collective

---

[36] SEC 1933 pp. 3–5.

[37] ECM 30 Aug. 1933; Sparks Memorandum [on union activities], ECM 22 Sept. 1933; Industrial Recovery Committee, Metal Polishers International Union, Local No. 90, to all employers in the electroplating industry, Philadelphia, 14 June 1933, in Hines Papers, Box 1, F. 5. For Hines and the Metal Polishers' campaign, see esp. National Labor Board (hereafter NLB) Case 77, 22 Sept. 1933–16 Apr. 1934; NLB Case 29, 31 Oct.–1 Nov. 1933; FMCS 162-1068, 8 Dec. 1933–25 May 1934; NLB Case 106, 2 Jan.–16 Jul. 1934; NLB Case 98, 31 Jan.–26 Feb. 1934; NLB Case 168, 21 March–12 Jul. 1934 (NLB and NLRB holdings in RG 25, U.S. National Archives). The NRA's Fabricated Metal Products code authority and the NLB were unable to secure the industry for the AFL, despite Hines's best endeavors. For the consequence, see Chapter 11.

bargaining has made a profound difference in the psychological situation among workers. . . .

The important factor is that the impression has been created that it is national policy to have workers unionized.

It is too early to say that the present drift will result in the establishment of solid and permanent labor organization; but it is not too early to say that only when government is favorable to the idea of having labor organized can organization on a really large scale be brought about.[38]

By late July, the city was "In Organizing Fever," with militant and effective leadership coming from the Communists, Socialists, and even, most surprisingly, the long-dormant AFL metal crafts, led by the Metal Polishers' former business agent, Lewis Hines. Hines, an old-guard Republican loyalist, had suffered for his politics by losing his job as a state labor mediator on Gifford Pinchot's accession. His patron, former Secretary of Labor, now Senator, "Puddler Jim" Davis, got him a federal position to replace it, as director of emergency employment work in the state. But Roosevelt's accession put Hines out of that job, too, thereby making his services available to his old craft brethren and to the masses of the never-organized in Philadelphia's metal trades. Utilizing the almost-forgotten medium of the federal labor union, Hines – "the self-styled 'Mussolini of the American Federation of Labor'" – and his associates brought thousands of Philadelphia workers into labor unions for the first time.[39]

How should the MMA meet this crisis? Sparks sought advice from the NMTA, attending its emergency conference in Chicago on the 22nd of August. This recommended that "every possible step should be taken to prevent unionization, particularly keeping close to one's own employees" and that labor's misinterpretations of the NIRA's Section 7 be corrected by posting notices of President Roosevelt's and NRA administrator General Hugh Johnson's "clarifications." In the MMA's case, "keeping close" would include the unusual step of bringing in an NMTA undercover agent (John McElgin, "Special Contract Operative No. 419") to keep an eye on organizing developments, so sudden, numerous, and serious were the problems that beset it. Executive committee members were not optimistic about their prospects in a fight: The NIRA "encouraged union labor and it was quite likely that industry to a very large extent would be obliged to deal with

[38] Editorial, "Workers Will Organize," *ULR* 7 Jul. 1933, p. 8.
[39] "Bullets Fly in Lansdale; City in Organizing Fever," *ULR* 21 July 1933, p. 1; for Hines's career, see political correspondence re 1930 campaign in Box 1, Folder 1, and Neustadt to Hines, 23 March 1933, John A. Phillips to William Green, 24 Jul. 1933, in Folder 5, Hines Papers; "Metal Trades in Huge Drive," *ULR* 21 Jul. 1933, pp. 1, 3; "30,000 in Federal Unions; Ritchie-Hines Lead A.F.L.'s Successful Union Drive," 3 Nov. 1933, p. 1. Quote from J. Werb to RLB, 16 Apr. 1934, p. 2, in NLB Case 77.

[its] representatives." Still, "every effort should be made to avoid the closed shop."[40]

That hot summer, however, not all Philadelphia employers were any longer able or willing to do so. Labor's greatest triumph was in the city's largest mass-production plant of its booming radio industry. Two locally owned companies, Philco (5,178 workers in 1933) and Atwater Kent (1,211), an MMA member, were among the nation's leading radio manufacturers. Philco in particular – the industry's largest producer – was, in relative terms, thriving through the Depression: Its workforce more than doubled between 1930 and 1933, while Atwater Kent's more than halved. However, the industry's young labor force was not very well paid, and its male majority (70 percent of the total) had suffered particularly severely from rate-cutting and irregular work. They had seen their annual average wages drop from $1,534 in 1929 to a low of $884 in 1933.[41]

Philco responded to the NIRA by forming a company union, but this did not protect it against labor troubles. Instead, 350 testers, assemblers, and repairers – mostly male, and from the skilled section of the labor force that had challenged management before – struck in protest against a temporary increase of working hours on 11 July. The rest of the workforce soon followed them out, and a young leadership group, some with previous craft union experience, and including Socialists who had been working for over a year among the city's unemployed, rapidly emerged.

Astonishingly, the company conceded quickly – possibly to end the interruption to the rush of orders that had caused it to try and impose the increase in the first place; partly, too, because the strikers had the mass support of the Kensington neighborhood's powerful, Socialist-led Hosiery Workers' Union. In addition, Philco's proprietor-managers, notably Executive Vice President George Deming and chief industrial engineer John Pehlert, president of the Philadelphia Engineers' Club, who devised the company's strategy, were pragmatic liberals. Deming, in particular, made it clear that he would welcome unionization, so long as it was on an all-inclusive plant rather than craft basis, and had no objections to the union shop, if the NIRA did not prohibit it.[42]

[40] ECM 30 Aug. 1933 [quotes]; for NRA labor policy, see Brand, *Corporatism and the Rule of Law*, pp. 232–48 [on Johnson]; [La Follette] Subcommittee of the U.S. Senate Committee on Education and Labor, *Violations of Free Speech and the Rights of Labor: Hearings* (Washington, 1937), Vol. 3, pp. 1046–48, 1054, 1088 [Elgin].

[41] PID-1640 and PHIL1439 databases. Philco employment was extremely volatile – 3,300 in July, 8,000 by October – but the figures are probably acceptable averages – Fred Keightly to Hugh L. Kerwin, 1 Oct. 1933, in FMCS 170-9063. See also Gladys L. Palmer and Ada Stoflet, *The Labor Force of the Philadelphia Radio Industry in 1936* (Philadelphia, 1938), pp. 2–4 esp.

[42] Irving Bernstein, *Turbulent Years: A History of American Workers, 1933–1939* (Boston, 1969), pp. 102–03; Patricia Cooper, "The Faces of Gender: Sex Segregation and Work Relations at Philco, 1928–1958" in Ava Baron, ed. *Work Engendered:*

Philco's settlement matched or bettered the terms of the President's Re-Employment Agreement, removed major grievances (abolishing penalties for faulty work, introducing payment for waiting time between jobs), and recognized the right of shop committees to handle others. It also granted the fledgling local, which was chartered as the Radio and Television Workers Federal Labor Union (FLU) of the AFL on the 3rd of August, official recognition. A fortnight later Philco went an extraordinarily long step further and signed a union shop contract, once NRA administrator Johnson's approval had been secured, hoping thereby to stabilize its labor relations situation and to bolster its already strong competitive position. It expected the industry to become rapidly unionized, and that the AFL would quickly succeed in imposing Philco's wage rates across the board. The contract obliged the AFL to do just that.[43]

Atwater Kent, in contrast, tied up by a strike of another new Radio Workers federal local from the 5th of August to the 25th, won a return to work for a wage settlement markedly less than Philco's (the male minimum was 13 percent lower). It promised new time studies to counter protests against speedup, settled the same outstanding grievances as had Philco, and acknowledged its workers' rights to collective bargaining "through representatives of their own choosing" on other grievances and wage rates. But, crucially, it did not grant the union shop, and only about 15 percent of its workers actually joined their union, which, lacking contractual protection,

Toward a New History of American Labor (Ithaca, 1991), Ch. 13, esp. pp. 327–29; Milton Derber, "Electrical Products," in Harry A. Millis, ed., *How Collective Bargaining Works: A Survey of Experience in Leading American Industries* (New York, 1942) Ch. 14, esp. pp. 782–83; Ronald L. Filipelli and Mark D. McColloch, *Cold War in the Working Class: The Rise and Decline of the United Electrical Workers* (Albany, 1995), pp. 17–19; Schatz, *Electrical Workers*, pp. 96–97 – are the sources for this account, supplemented by contemporary accounts and activists' recollections – "Radio Workers on Strike," *ULR* 14 Jul. 1933, p. 1; "2,500 Philco-ites in Union; Strikes Stir Every Craft," 21 Jul., pp. 1, 3; "Workers Wages Boosted, Union Closed Shop, Employment Gains; Company Wins Much Too," *People's Press* (hereafter *PP*) 7 March 1936, p. 8; "Philco Contract Shows Firms See Union Worth," *PP* 18 Apr. 1936, p. 4 – and federal conciliators' reports: Fred Keightly and Homer J. Brown to Hugh L. Kerwin, 13 Jul. 1933 and Preliminary Report, same date; Brown and Keightly to Kerwin and Summary of Final Report, 15 Jul.; Keightly to Kerwin and Preliminary Report, 1 Oct. 1933, and Keightly to Kerwin, 3 Oct. 1933, all in FMCS 170-9063. These reports are valuable commentaries on the "business like cooperative spirit shown" (15 Jul.) and on the company's efforts to "lean over backwards . . . to cooperate with the new union" (1 Oct.). Cf. Stanley Vittoz's discussion of managerial attitudes in his *New Deal Labor Policy and the American Industrial Economy* (Chapel Hill, 1987), pp. 150–52.

43 "Courage and Pep Put Over Philco Closed Shop," *PP* 29 Feb. 1936, p. 5. Philco was also supposed to be protected against any further wage demands unless secured from its competitors first or incorporated in the industry's NRA code – James Matles and James Higgins, *Them and Us: Struggles of a Rank and File Union* (Englewood Cliffs, 1974), p. 52.

and subject to continuing discrimination against members and officers by the management, soon went into terminal decline, along with the company itself.[44]

Philco had made a strategic mistake of enormous importance for the future of labor relations in Philadelphia metalworking. It did not *need* to have paid such a price for peace. Labor could not keep its side of the bargain – radio workers' unionization scarcely spread beyond the Philadelphia–Camden area for another three years – so Philco's wage rates and working conditions stood way above the rest of the industry's. As the industry's leading producer, enormously profitable through the radio boom of the early to mid-1930s, shifting smoothly from the domestic to the automobile business as one market matured and a new one opened up, in the short term Philco could easily afford to pay. But the costs piled up, and the consequences of its precipitate surrender spread well beyond its own huge plant. As a result of its combination of idiosyncratic liberalism, self-interested pragmatism, and simple inexperience in labor relations, it had succeeded in establishing a large industrial union with contractual security and a big, regular dues income at the heart of the city's largest and most dynamic metal products industry.[45]

Philco's response to the summer labor relations crisis would cost it dearly in the long run. It would also, by laying the foundations for what became one of the UE's key strongholds, increase the pressure on smaller Philadelphia companies to concede when they were up against that organization as it muscled into their own plants after 1936. So the consequences of Philco's unnecessary abandonment of the Open Shop ramified throughout the local metal-working sector for the rest of the decade.

The MMA's biggest immediate problems occurred, not at Atwater Kent, nor at Westinghouse, where a group of old "Wobblies" set up an FLU a little later, but at one of its oldest and one of its largest members – respectively, S. L. Allen & Co. (farm equipment makers) and Hess-Bright Mfg. Co. (bearing makers), owned since 1916 by the Swedish multinational SKF and in the throes of rationalization as the parent company drove to consolidate its scattered manufacturing outposts.[46]

[44] "Atwater Kent Workers Strike," *ULR* 11 Aug. 1933 p. 1 and "Kent Strikers Spurn Pittance," 25 Aug. p. 5; Agreement of 24th August 1933 and Summary of Final Report of Commissioner of Conciliation Anna Weinstock, 31 August 1933, FMCS 176-213; Lewis G. Hines to Stanley W. Root (secretary, Philadelphia RLB) 20 May 1935, in NLB Case 880; Sparks Memorandum, ECM 22 Sept. 1933. Atwater Kent closed down completely in 1936 – John N. Ingham, *Dictionary of American Business Biography* (Westport, CT, 1983), Vol. 2, p. 708.

[45] Derber, "Electrical Products," p. 784.

[46] For Westinghouse, see Matles and Higgins, *Them and Us*, pp. 35, 54; Kerwin to Joseph T. Miller, 14 Sept. 1933, FMCS 176-424; SKF Co., *The Story of SKF* (n.p., 1982), pp. 7–8, 11.

S. L. Allen & Co. had been devastated by the Depression, cutting its workforce by about 60 percent until only a hard core of about a hundred long-service, skilled workmen remained. Its old Orthodox Quaker proprietor-managers had had to cede control to a tough outside capitalist formerly associated with Bethlehem Steel, with its utterly different labor relations *mores*, as the price of a financial bail-out. The resulting lay-offs, speedups, rate-cuts, and insecurity violated the terms of the old compact between Allen and its workers, and there was no personal loyalty to the new absentee owner Matthew Scammell to moderate their anger. The summertime recovery, and the NIRA, gave them confidence to form an FLU and seek redress by striking in mid-September.[47]

It took two weeks of difficult negotiations for U.S. Commissioner of Conciliation Fred Keightly to broker an agreement with Scammell and the local management (the old proprietors). Keightly got the angry, inexperienced strikers to abandon their demand for a closed shop, and substituted exclusive recognition and a 22 percent wage increase through the abolition of piece work. There was no contract between Allen and the local – instead, these terms were incorporated in a "Memorandum of Understanding" signed by the conciliator, a way of getting around Scammell's quite normal refusal to sign a legal document recognizing a union as the other party. The agreement was explicitly limited in validity to the duration of the NIRA, its only legal support. What mattered in the short term, however, was not the form but the substance of the new relationship. Although there was no official union shop, one existed in effect. The union built up 100 percent membership, and for the next two years the FLU and its shop committee of radicalized skilled workers were effectively, though informally, consulted in the running of the works.[48]

S. L. Allen was a troubling, swift defeat. The Hess-Bright/SKF strike, which happened at the same time, was much larger in scale, involving more than 500 workers, and was more threatening still. It was not just a rebellion by an isolated work group, it was the result of the takeover of an employees' association in one of the MMA's leading progressive firms by a militant cadre with visions of building an industrywide union. "[S]marting under the indignities and injustices which have been inflicted upon the workers of their industry" during the Depression, as they later reported,

---

[47] For the similarly mobilizing effect on his men of the Depression and welfarist Quaker proprietor Richard Brown's sale of his Instrument Co. to Minneapolis-Honeywell, see Richard A. Lester and Edward A. Robie, *Constructive Labor Relations: Experience in Four Firms* (Princeton, 1948), Ch. 4, pp. 42–43 esp.

[48] Keightly, Preliminary Report 16 Sept. 1933; Keightly to Kerwin, 24 Sept. 1933; Summary of Agreement and Keightly to Kerwin, 3 Oct. 1933 – all in FMCS 176-501. For subsequent bargaining history, see "In the Matter of S. L. Allen & Co., Inc., a Corporation, and Federal Labor Union Local No. 18526", Case C-60 decided 13 May 1936, 1 NLRB (1936), pp. 717–18.

"they decided that the only solution to the whole problem lay in industrial unionism. With the helpful knowledge that the NIRA guaranteed 'Collective Bargaining' as a constitutional right, they set about to organize their fellow workers."[49]

First they won their own quick strike, securing a six-month truce including a closed shop agreement, the right of the union to supply new employees, the right to challenge discharges, and their business agent's right to visit the plant at any time. All of this took a ten-day shutdown. After the return to work, SKF foremen and managers had to cope with an aggressive, organized opposition right within their own plant. As federal conciliator P. W. Chappell later reported, "it was but natural a feeling of resistance should have been built up" among them. But they had to bide their time, while demand continued strong, the industry's NRA code was being hammered out in Washington, and the union tried to spread its organization into the factories of other bearing manufacturers in Philadelphia and elsewhere, and to influence the code-making process. The MMA decided to attempt to reverse this defeat as soon as the contract expired.[50]

What helped put iron into the MMA's soul was the experience of the costs of concession, on the one hand, and the realization of the possibility of successful resistance, on the other. Philco was an example of what not to do; another of the giants of the local industry, financially troubled auto body maker Edward G. Budd Mfg. Co., still run by Edward G. himself, pointed in an apparently more promising, as well as more ideologically acceptable, direction.

Budd faced an attempt to organize an FLU in August 1933 at the same time as the radio manufacturers, S. L. Allen, and SKF, but he met it with staunch, clever opposition. Budd both defeated the AFL and highlighted the impotence of the National and Regional Labor Boards (RLBs) that were supposed to implement the NIRA's labor provisions. He had to confront the New Deal itself, because the NIRA was the heart of the AFL's organizational pitch. The union campaigners claimed, according to Budd, "that the President of the United States wanted them to join the A. F. of L.; that the NRA would compel them to affiliate themselves with that organization." Almost half of his blue-collar labor force of about 3,500 attended a mass meeting on the 30th of August, and unanimously – according to their

49   ECM 30 Aug. 1933, Sparks Memorandum 22 Sept. 1933; quote in telegram, George H. Kitson (President, SKF Employees Association) to Frances Perkins, 29 Aug. 1933, in FMCS 176-257; posters, AN APPEAL TO ALL WORKERS ENGAGED IN THE MANUFACTURE OF ANTI-FRICTION BEARINGS and COLLECTIVE BARGAINING, both in NLB Case 93, Messenger Bearings Co. (Jan.–Jul. 1934). The strike can be followed in the *ULR*, 25 Aug.–15 Sept. 1933.
50   Chappell to Benedict Wolff (NLB), 23 May 1934, in FMCS 170-9668; ECM 24 Oct. 1933.

AFL organizers – agreed to join the AFL, many of them signing individual applications for membership.[51]

Budd would not stand idly by and see his authority taken away like this. Although he admitted that there was "no request from the shopmen" for the company to offer them a different, more acceptable union, he determined to do so anyway. Notices were posted on timeclocks and attached to individuals' time cards advertising a snap election, by secret written ballot, just before the NRA auto code came into effect on 5 September. Workers could vote for nominees pledged to the AFL, "no company union," or an "independent" plan. According to the frustrated AFL organizers, in the ensuing confusion many of those who voted for the latter thought that they had been voting for the federal local they had already joined![52]

In any event, as a result of what he termed "normal relations and innocent communication which are a part of all friendly intercourse, albeit between employer and employee," rather than coercion, which he denied, Budd secured his majority. Seventy-nine percent of his workers designated their representatives on the 5th of September, and on the 7th 92 percent of the latter accepted, with little amendment, a constitution that Budd had written. They set up a quintessential employee representation plan, officered by company "trusties" – its first chairman was promoted assistant foreman after the election, and the constitution was amended to permit other workers to be represented by their supervisors too. The officers claimed that they were dedicated to serving as "liaison agents in cases where the men had, or thought they had, grievances against the management." Their association was "a going concern, performing for its members a real service. Some of these grievances are adjusted and some are not."[53]

After creating his own union, Budd did everything necessary to support it, including discharging AFL loyalists. The AFL, unsure of its position and never eager for a fight, finally had to respond, issuing a strike call on 14 November after all of its requests for mediation had been rejected. About 500–600 workers responded – one-seventh or one-eighth of the labor force. Budd quickly replaced them. There followed what its organizers called a "heroic struggle ... against tremendous odds. ... Tactics worthy of the most bitter labor hating employers throughout the history of organized

[51] Transcript of hearing before NRA National Compliance Board, 24 Jan. 1934, pp. 1–8 [quote p. 6], in Box 19, Hines Papers. Sidney Fine, *The Automobile Under the Blue Eagle* (Ann Arbor, 1963), pp. 194–212, is the fullest account of the Budd case.
[52] Budd Transcript, p. 7.
[53] Ibid.; Fine, *Automobile Under the Blue Eagle*, p. 476 n30 for the constitutional change; for the broader context, see U.S. Bureau of Labor Statistics, *Characteristics of Company Unions 1935* [*Bulletin* No. 634, June 1937] (Washington, 1938) – illustrating Budd's typicality.

labor [were] resorted to by the Company, . . . including spies, gunmen, stool-pigeons, police intimidation and starvation."[54]

The distinctively new feature of the strike was that it was not just a bloody knock-down, drag-out struggle between Budd and the forces of order on one side, and hundreds (eventually thousands) of his former employees, their sympathetic neighbors and fellow-workers, and Philadelphia's radicals, on the other. It also involved the New Deal state directly – it would, indeed, prove to be one of the fatal trials to which the NIRA-period labor relations machinery was subjected.

Philadelphia's new Regional Labor Board (RLB), set up as a local agent of the federal strategy for dealing with the upsurge of industrial conflict that the NIRA had unexpectedly provoked, swiftly recommended a "Reading Formula" settlement – a return to work, with no discrimination by the company, and a new, supervised election. Budd refused, so the dispute was referred up to the National Labor Board (NLB), which quickly endorsed, and strengthened, the Philadelphia Board's ruling.

But Budd was immovable. By now he was a fervent convert to the merits of employee representation, and an upright defender of the rights of the "fine men and their representatives who have been so steadfastly loyal to us" by crossing mass picket lines. So he refused to let go of any newly hired strikebreakers to make room for his old employees (who included "the very conspirators" who had tried "to injure our business"). He would not break his faith with the men who had stood by him in his hour of need – a principled position for which he received the MMA executive committee's unanimous support that December, when his confrontation with the NLB was reaching its climax.[55]

Nor would he re-hire without discrimination. "Any of our former employees whom we are satisfied remained away either from fear or intimidation by the real strikers and whom we believe wish to come back, not for the purpose of making trouble for us but honestly to help us make automobile bodies for our customers, we will be glad to re-employ as fast as our expanding business makes the use of additional men necessary." But the company had the right to screen would-be returners, on grounds of self-defense, and to exclude any who were "playing a game," that is, intending to bring the union back inside the plant. Budd had become a "peaceful industry" once again, at great cost, and had "to be careful" to keep it that way. While it was still under attack by "outsiders" it had "to keep our guard up for a while." What this meant was that only fifty-nine strikers got

54 Letter from AFL organizers Lewis Hines and Joseph M. Richie and officers of FLU No. 18763 to the Officers and Members of all Unions affiliated with the A F of L, n.d. [Dec. 1933], in Hines Papers, Box 19.

55 Keightly to Kerwin, 24 Sept. 1933, in FMCS 170-9358; Budd Transcript p. 5; ECM 19 Dec. 1933.

their jobs back in the first several weeks after the board's ruling and the AFL's decision to call off the strike.[56]

Budd's obdurate defiance of the Regional and National Labor Boards resulted in the reference of the case to the NRA's National Compliance Board, which substituted a "compromise" proposal strongly favorable to the company and unacceptable to the strikers. With the strike continuing, General Hugh Johnson became personally involved in seeking a settlement; he, too, was ignored. Eventually, as a by-product of the settlement of a threatened widespread automobile strike at the end of March 1934, Budd agreed to rehire a proportion of his ex-employees who had gone out on strike four months earlier. But after the partial return to work his representation plan remained in firm possession of the plant, while their union collapsed. Budd's victory illustrated that the New Deal labor relations policy had no future unless and until it acquired the statutory power to compel the obedience of adherents of what the AFL termed the "baronial conception of [the] relationship between employer and employee."[57]

Budd's lead was quickly followed by companies large and small. When American Can's local plant was struck in October, for example, by most of its 300 men and women workers protesting discriminatory discharges for union activity and low piece rates, and demanding union recognition and a raise, the management refused to negotiate and closed the works. That same month Brill (railroad car and bus builders) responded to an AFL organizing drive by attempting to reverse a majority vote for the "outside" union against its own recently reestablished employee representation plan. It organized a second ballot where the voting cards were given out by its departmental foremen, who "stood over the men while the men marked their choice and signed their names," which the anonymous worker who complained to AFL organizer Joseph M. Richie rightly "consider[ed] coercion and intimidation of the worst type."[58]

The MMA and its members, too, were inspired by Budd's success in fighting the good fight. At the Klein Stove Co., for example, Julius Klein told his men in February 1934 that he was "going to put on whom I want to," that is, refuse to rehire in line with seniority, as he had informally agreed the previous year. "Nobody is going to tell me who to put on."

[56] Budd Transcript, pp. 5, 8–9 [quotes], 3.
[57] Undated [early 1934] Statement Issued by the Philadelpia Office of the A F of L and the United Automobile Workers Union No. 18763, in Box 19, Hines Papers. For the wider significance of the Budd case, see Fine, *Automobile Under the Blue Eagle*, pp. 201–02.
[58] Preliminary Report of Commissioner of Conciliation 6 Oct. 1933 and Chappell to Kerwin, same date, both in FMCS 176-614; copy of Anon. to J. M. Richie, 10 Oct. 1933, Richie to Sen. Robert Wagner 11 Oct., and Kerwin to Chappell, 18 Oct., in FMCS 176-728.

The previous October his company had been quite conciliatory. Now he was confident that "the NRA doesn't mean a thing. 'Who is going to know you are working over 48 hours a week?'" The government's Labor Boards and the NRA's code authorities were paper tigers he could defy with impunity.[59]

These developments of the summer through early winter of 1933 – the collapse of Philco's management in the face of the first challenge, the establishment of what would become one of the mainstays of the UE, the beginnings of a Communist presence among Philadelphia's skilled metal crafts, significant defeats for some MMA members in their contests with their own employees, and then the inspiring example of Budd's successful resistance – set the stage for the next, and most confrontational, period in the troubled evolution of the local metal manufacturing industry's labor relations from the Open Shop toward collective bargaining.

10.4 COUNTERATTACK: 1934

The first blow was struck in January when the bearing workers attempted to expand beyond MMA members SKF and Nice Ball Bearings into the third important local plant, a fiercely independent proprietary firm with about 200 workers. Messinger Bearings nipped the movement in the bud, discharging all of the union's officers and its handful of active members and leaving them with no recourse other than the NLB. It also followed Budd's example in seeking its continuing employees' endorsement of its authority.

They were asked, in a "secret ballot" conducted by Messinger on company premises, "Are you contented with your working conditions, and are your interests served to your satisfaction by the management?" One hundred and thirty-three voted Yes, twenty-one No. Thirty supported what President Messinger called the "Foreign Organization," while 124 rejected it. One hundred and forty-six professed themselves happy with the continuation of their old beneficial association as the sole recognized bargaining vehicle, only six wanting something different. Heartened by what he termed, revealingly, "Ratios of Fidelity," which he reported to his workers correct to one decimal place, apparently taking comfort in a mathematically precise resolution to his troubles, President Messinger dug in his heels and resisted everything that the union, and eventually the Philadelphia RLB, could do against him – which was nothing. He had his incumbent employees behind him, grateful for work on any terms now that 1933's false recov-

[59] Adam Pietrowicz to "Gentlemen," 23 Feb. 1934, cf. Walter Brown to John L. Connor, Commissioner of Conciliation, NLB, 20 Oct. 1933, in NLB Case 129.

ery had petered out, and unwilling to share it with the men who had been so foolish as to think that the government's guarantee of the right to join a union of their own choosing actually meant what it said.[60]

Where Messinger led, proving the union's powerlessness, SKF quickly followed. Their six-month agreement was due to expire in early March, and negotiations to continue it began in good time. Federal conciliator Chappell reported that they went smoothly enough for almost a month until, with four days to go, the company's president William L. Batt, whom some historians would probably term a "corporate liberal," and "who had not taken direct part in the negotiations, submitted an agreement to the employees (*sic*) committee which wiped the slate clean of all of the points agreed upon up until then and out lined (*sic*) what the men claim was a typical Company Union." The closed shop, the union's rights in hiring and firing, and the business agent's access rights would all be deleted. Understandably, the men voted in a secret ballot 92 percent in favor of going out on strike until a satisfactory agreement could be reached, and 800–900 men hit the streets.[61]

The Philadelphia RLB quickly intervened. Its labor member Emil Rieve, president of the Hosiery Workers, and employer member Morris Leeds, Batt's colleague on the Department of Commerce's Business Advisory Council, recommended that the strike be suspended, the *status quo ante* temporarily restored, the parties resume negotiations, and that any issues not resolved within a fortnight should be referred to the board for resolution. Batt agreed. So did the Anti-Friction Union's president Kitson. But his striking members insisted that Batt should negotiate while their strike continued. This attitude was quite understandable – they wanted to maximize their bargaining power. But by taking it they put themselves on the wrong side of the question, and freed Batt to pose as the injured party and proceed to replace them.[62]

Batt had played a very clever hand, winning the support of Rieve, who understood the etiquette of orderly negotiations, that the men should "Go Back First"; and of Leeds, who thought that the RLB was in danger of becoming a mere tactical expedient for parties to industrial conflict if

[60] ORGANIZE! To the Men of the Messinger Bearing Co. [announcement of meeting, 14 Jan. 1934 by Executive Council, Anti-Friction Bearing Workers Union]; statement of case to Philadelphia RLB, 20 Jan. 1934; memorandum, 8 Feb., and transcript of hearing, 17 Feb.; ballot form, 22 Jan. 1934 and President W. Messinger "To My Fellow-Workers," 23 Jan. 1934; Attorney John J. Mitchell, Jr., to Philadelphia RLB, 17 Feb., 17 March, 7 Apr., 9 Apr., 10 July 1934 – all in NLB Case 93.
[61] Chappell to Wolff, 23 May 1934, pp. 1–2, in FMCS 170-9668 [quotes]; Statement of W. H. Goldstein, Attorney for the Union, 30 Mar., 1934, in NLB Case 157.
[62] Memorandum of conversation between Philadelphia RLB public member Jacob Billikopf and Batt, 20 Apr., report on hearing of 17 March, press release No. 5319 24 May, and Stanley Root to Gentlemen (PRLB members), 19 May, all in NLB Case 157. For Rieve, see Scranton, *Figured Tapestry*, pp. 439, 480.

it did not insist on acceptance of its recommendations and penalize those who declined by refusing them further mediatory assistance. Otherwise they "could refuse to go along, relying on being called in at a future time. . . . Allowing people to appeal to the strike and then come back to the Board again is just an encouragement to strike." The RLB's evolving but embattled status as a source of authoritative rulings on the law of labor relations would be undermined if it became just a pawn in the contestants' games.[63]

Ten days after the men rejected the RLB's recommendation, SKF gave notice that it would reopen the plant, and there followed almost four months of bitter, violent conflict. There were, as the *Public Ledger* reported at the strike's conclusion, "frequent riots in which scores were injured, shots fired and automobiles overturned and burned." Paint, acid, and phosphorus bombs were thrown at the houses of union leaders and backsliding strikers alike. The fighting spread far from the plant gates, to the neighborhoods where strikers lived and onto the mass transit system that many of them still used to get to work, as the police prevented pickets from gathering within four blocks of the plant. The hundreds of strikers and, sometimes, thousands of their sympathizers were met with hundreds of city police mounted on horseback and motorbike. The latter's brutal "Cossack" tactics – which even the local press described as riotous themselves – resulted in unsuccessful appeals by the union to Governor Pinchot to send in State Troopers to guarantee even-handed order. This was an unusual request to be coming from Kensington radicals, illustrative of the strikers' desperation and of the extent to which Philadelphia city and Pennsylvania state politics were now out of step. To Batt, thanking Mayor Moore for his services, the lesson of the strike was which "if other cities had a police force governed by the same principles as that of Philadelphia there would be less violence and unrest." For Philadelphia workers, the lesson was that they needed a new local administration.[64]

The strike was, from SKF's point of view, a strategic triumph. As one of the company's managers told RLB public member Jacob Billikopf, "You know, the strike did not come at an inopportune time. It gave Mr. Batt a chance to rid the plant of an undesirable and disturbing element . . . at a time when necessary repairs had to be made." The six-month truce had taken the company through the end of their busy season. As its attorney, famed anti-labor lawyer Walter G. Merritt, accurately stated, "our business

[63] Rieve in report on hearing, 17 March and, with Leeds, in memorandum on RLB members' discussion, 20 Apr. 1934, in NLB Case 157.
[64] *Evening Public Ledger* (EPL), 11 Jul., 12 Apr.; *Philadelphia Record* (PR), 24 May; EPL 5 May, 16 June, 18 June; PR 10 June, 11 July – clippings in NLB Case 157. For reporting from the labor viewpoint, see *ULR* 16 March–29 June 1934. Batt's letter is cited in Drayer, "J. Hampton Moore," p. 313.

was such that there was a time when we wanted a settlement at all costs, and ... knowledge of this ... made the other side overplay its hand." The company, with plants in Connecticut, Sweden, England, France, and Germany, could then afford to ride out a strike during a period of weak demand and slowly rebuild its workforce as its former employees were beaten and starved into submission. Their replacements were, as one of them, Calvin Hill, wrote General Johnson, mostly "on relief ..., consequently all broke," and easily exploited with rate-cuts and speed-ups. Hill surely spoke for many, that though "not a union man" he did not "enjoy scabing, but after starvation and loosing all I posess for three years, I like a drownding man grabbed the job."[65]

However, SKF's victory was neither quick nor easy. The MMA helped, by spending more on striker replacement than it had since 1916; the NMTA assisted, too. But the strikers' inexperience and strategic errors helped more. First they rejected the lifeline that the RLB threw them in March. When it repeated the gesture in May, proposing a return to work, work-sharing between "new" and "old" employees, except those from either side "proven guilty of substantial violence," and arbitration of future differences, they spurned it again. The RLB then became deadlocked between employer and labor members, each taking sides, so the case was handed up to Washington. Senator Wagner, NLB chairman, himself renewed essentially the same proposal, further sweetened by a company agreement to reinstate at least 250 men within ten days, with the rest of the strikers to be the exclusive source of rehires until they were all placed. But they rejected that, too, fearing a plot to divide them. As the board noted, "the 250 men who will be immediately replaced are the most highly skilled men in the plant – the die makers. ... They are the key men. Without them the company will continue to be seriously handicapped. They are the hardest men of all those in the company's employ to replace, and they are sticking with the strikers."[66]

<hr />

[65] Billikopf to Root, 30 May 1934, Merritt statement in NLB press release 5319, 24 May, Hill to Johnson? 5 Jul., all in NLB Case 157. "Starved into submission" is not a hyperbole – the independent union had no resources to support its members, and the local Associated Charities adopted an unsympathetic attitude to strikers' calls for relief, particularly once the RLB's hostility toward their strike was understood. Memorandum of conversation between Stanley Root, RLB secretary, and Miss Dorothy Kahn, 12 Apr.

[66] ECM 25 Sept. 1934; NLRB Case C-60, S. L. Allen & Company, Inc. and Federal Labor Union No. 18526 Affiliated with the American Federation of Labor, Formal File, Hearings Transcript, pp. 196–97; Proposition Submitted by the Regional Labor Board to SKF Industries, Inc., and the Representatives of the Anti Friction Bearing Workers Union, Local No. 1 on March 17th., 1934, in FMCS 170-9668; "US Labor Board Enters SKF Case," *PR* 24 May; report in NLB Case 251, 31 May; memorandum of proposals, 21 May 1934 and memorandum of discussion at Board meeting, 8 June, in NLB Case 157 [quotes].

So the rejection made sense, but it was nonetheless fatal. The Regional and National Boards just walked away from the strike. According to federal conciliator Chappell, Batt "told them that he had the union licked and did not want any more outside interference." So Chappell inherited "A nice job washing up their dirty linen. . . . [P]erhaps we may be able to save something from the wreckage." That "something" clearly did not include the union, or its strong contract. By late June it was clear that "this strike . . . was about shot. . . . The bulk of the workers would like to go back to work under any conditions." Chappell had no sympathy with the union activists' self-defeating militancy, nor did local AFL organizer Lew Hines. "[A]nything we would do now would merely prolong useless warfare," so the best policy was to sit on the sidelines and wait for the strike to collapse. At least some of the strikers would then be able to get their jobs back. Batt promised that "he woud let by-gons be by-gons and he thought in a very short time most of the men woud be back on the job but that he was not going to fire any of the men he now had on to make room for them." Two weeks later the strike was over, SKF's employment office was open for normal business, and those strikers to whom the company did not object were free to file their individual applications for reinstatement.[67]

The 1934 SKF strike eliminated the second-largest union shop in the Philadelphia metal trades, and far and away the largest and most militant in the MMA's territory. But its scale, duration, cost, and attendant violence, which dwarfed anything the MMA had previously encountered, illustrated that anti-unionism, even when successful, was a more daunting project in the New Deal years than ever before, even for a company of the size, sophistication, and resources of SKF.

And, once the Budd and SKF strikes were over, what had been gained? Earl Sparks could tell his members that December, with some relief, that "No such gains in union membership in Philadelphia's metal-working industry were made this year as last and at the moment the labor situation is quiet with many instances indicating that the spontaneity and enthusiasm with which union membership was embraced has considerably subsided." But, unlike in the aftermaths of the 1905–07 Molders' strike, or the 1911 Baldwin strike, or the 1920–21 Cramps Strike, employer victories and high unemployment did not leave Philadelphia workers cowed, disorganized, and friendless. Instead, many of the organizational gains of 1933 were still in place; defeat had created an even more sympathetic hearing for Communists and other militants among skilled metalworkers than they had enjoyed before; a huge program of patient "workers' education" in trades unionism was being carried on, funded by the Federal Emergency Relief Administration, to train shop-floor activists in the new, insecure organiza-

---

[67]   "SKF Strikers Defy Labor Board Ruling," *PR* 7 June; Chappell to Kerwin 14 May, 20 June 1934, in FMCS 170-9668 [quotes].

tions; alliances of mutual support had been forged across occupational lines among the city's working classes, particularly in the strike-torn northern industrial neighborhoods; and, crucially, the lesson that the federal government (particulary Senator Wagner) learned from the Budd strike was about the need for clearer, more authoritative intervention than ever before.[68]

10.5 SHOWDOWN: 1935–1936

By spring 1935 it seemed as if the worst of the New Deal trauma was over. The NIRA was found unconstitutional by the Supreme Court, and the MMA managed to salvage what was worthwhile from the Blue Eagle period. Its groups of ferrous and nonferrous founders and tool and die shops that had formed in the previous two years continued to work together, exchanging credit information on customers, trying to fix prices, and cooperating in dealing with labor. It also counseled its members not to exploit the advantage that the Schechter case gave them, but rather to maintain established wages, hours, and working conditions. MMA president George Morehead, general manager of Link-Belt, explained that

the spokesmen of industry had been going to Washington and claiming that if the restrictions imposed . . . were eliminated confidence would be restored and the return of normal times hastened while industry would show a capacity for self-government; that compulsory regulation on the part of Government for the maintenance of fair labor standards would be unnecessary. . . . [I]t was the obligation and a great opportunity for industry to show that it can govern itself without impairing the fair standards of labor.[69]

The MMA's surveys showed that members – encouraged by the strong recovery of business and employment in the pre-election boom that began that July – followed his good advice.[70]

By the end of 1935 the MMA seemed to have adjusted quite well to the new regulatory and labor relations environments created by the Depression and the New Deal. Sparks thought that "Trends in labor relations" were

[68] SEC 1934, p. 3; for the workers' education program, see "Labor Classes Booming in Quaker City," *ULR* 23 Feb. 1934, p. 3 and "Organization Through Education," 23 March, p. 6; Elizabeth Fones-Wolf, "Industrial Unionism and Labor Movement Culture in Depression-Era Philadelphia," *PMHB* 109 (1985): 3–26 esp. pp. 10, 16, 25.

[69] Secretary's Report on Summer Activities, ECM 4 Oct. 1935; SEC 1935, p. 3; Sparks to Gentlemen, 31 May 1935, in MMAP 2-IV-34; Morehead in Special Meeting of the Executive Committee, ECM 31 May 1935.

[70] Employment surged 29 percent in the third quarter of 1935, and by the end of 1935 it was just 9.5 percent below the 1929 peak – Secretary's Report on Summer Activities, p. 1; SEC 1935, p. 1.

"encouraging, the exciting situations of a short time ago have been lacking." AFL strength in the local metal-working industry was not much greater than it had been in the spring of 1933. It had failed to make a breakthrough at the G.E. plant in 1934, and its surviving FLUs were having difficulties with dues collection. The "industrial unions," principally the radio locals at the giant Philco plants and RCA–Victor in Camden that would help form the UE in March 1936, were "level pegging." Organized labor's only significant growth area was the smaller machine shops where the [Communist] Metal Workers, renamed the Machine, Tool, and Foundry Workers' Union (MTFWU), and led by James Matles, had found an unprecedented degree of support among some of Philadelphia's most skilled metalworkers. As a machinist at Baldwin's De La Vergne diesel engine division proudly reported in 1936, "We got our own union. . . . [I]t ain't no company union, it's rank and file. . . . [I]t's not very old, but it did plenty for us already, they tried to give us a wage cut, well we didn't let it go over." He neither mentioned the MTFWU's politics nor appeared to care. What mattered was that it was militant and effective. But the MTFWU was the exception. Otherwise, the MMA and its members seemed to have weathered the storm.[71]

Little occurred to disturb the MMA's growing confidence. Only two of the five small strikes recorded in the Philadelphia metal trades in 1935 affected MMA members, and they were easily dealt with by compromises not involving formal recognition of the unions concerned. The result was that at the end of the year Sparks could still boast that there was "not one written agreement between a member firm and a labor union."[72]

Sparks and his members, like their employees and the latter's unions, were more impressed by the vital significance of official recognition, expressed in a written contract, as a symbol and support of union status and strength than some labor historians of the past generation.[73] He had to admit that

---

[71]   Secretary's Report on Summer Activities, p. 3; SEC 1935, p. 4. For UE and G.E., see ECM 25 Sept. 1934; for RCA, see Derber, "Electrical Products," pp. 790–93 esp.; for the MTFWU, see Filipelli and McColloch, *Cold War in the Working Class*, pp. 21–5; Matles and Higgins, *Them and Us*, pp. 30, 35, 41; Schatz, *Electrical Workers*, p. 63; Respondent 459, Machinists Study, Palmer Papers, TUUA.

[72]   Schneider-Bowman v. Molders, NLB Case 886, June 1935; S. L. Allen Case, Oct.–Dec. 1935, FMCS 182-925. The other strikes were at nonmembers Enterprise Mfg. Co. (over a Molders' wage demand, resulting in the closure of the firm's foundry); Janney Cylinder Co. (over the MTFWU's demand for recognition, which was denied because Mr. Janney would not deal with "this communistic outfit," and which ended with most of its members drifting back as individuals); and William & Harvey Rowland, auto spring makers (over wage cuts, led by a shop committee unaffiliated with the AFL and resulting, uniquely, in the formation of a new federal local and a one-year comprehensive contract brokered by state and federal mediators). See NLB Case 881 and FMCS Case 182-358 (March–June 1935); FMCS Case 182-576 (Sept. 1935); NLB Case 945 (Aug.–Sept. 1935). SEC 1935 p. 4 [quote].

[73]   As labor intellectual J. B. S. Hardman explained about Philadelphia's clothing workers' Depression-era union breakthrough, "the great majority recognized the

seven member foundries were closed union shops, as far as their skilled Molders were concerned; that seven tool and die makers organized by the MTFWU had unofficial union shops; and that, at S. L. Allen, the AFL remained entrenched, despite the fact that its informal agreement had expired when the Blue Eagle crashed to earth. But the key strategic questions of formal recognition and bargaining had almost nowhere outside Philco been decided in the unions' favor, and it still seemed possible to win on them.[74]

The MMA, like much of the American business community, had been politically mobilized by the New Deal experience, and in a firmly reactionary direction. President Morehead came, like almost all of the mid-1930s executive committee, from the machine-shop and machinery-foundry heartland of the MMA that had run it until the mid-1920s and now resumed control. Senior Orthodox Quakers withdrew from participation in the MMA's counsels, just as they quit the NMTA when its belligerently anti-union old proclivities reasserted themselves. Their managers remained active in the MMA's personnel and education committees, but the proprietors pursued other fields of service. Morris Leeds moved in national circles now, serving as a member of Franklin Roosevelt's Advisory Council of the Committee on Economic Security that designed the Social Security Act; and Bernard Waring busied himself organizing relief efforts for destitute coal miners and their families. When D. Robert Yarnall revisited Germany with Rufus Jones in the late 1930s, their mission would be the attempted rescue of Jews from the impending Holocaust. But when President Morehead went to Europe, he came back proclaiming that "Germany was in better shape than any country which he visited" and that "Mussolini has done a splendid job of cleaning up in Italy."[75]

Understandably, the association that he headed thought that its time had come for a final showdown with labor. There was every prospect that the Wagner Act would suffer the same fate at the Supreme Court's hands as

---

union only after their employers were made to recognize it" [editor's Introduction to Elden LaMar, *The Clothing Workers of Philadelphia* (Philadelphia, 1940), p. 10]. Without a contract, a union's victories were very reversible; its standing with the mass of cautious, instrumental, and undecided or apathetic potential members forever in doubt; and its ability to deliver on its own and their objectives minimal. To believe otherwise one has to be a labor historian of a certain kind. See National Labor Relations Board, Division of Economic Research, *Written Trade Agreements in Collective Bargaining* [*Bulletin* No. 4, Nov. 1939] (Washington, 1940), summarizing the conventional wisdom of contemporary industrial relations experts.

[74] SEC 1935, pp. 1, 4.

[75] MMA-EXEC and NMTA9936 databases; Nelson, *Unemployment Insurance*, Ch. 9; C. Elliott Barb, *The Yarway Story: An Adventure in Serving* (Philadelphia, 1958), pp. 79–80, 83–84; "Hoover Gives Quakers Money for Miners' Relief Funds," *ULR* 11 Sept. 1930, p. 2, for the beginning of the program – Willits was a member of the AFSC subcommittee Waring headed; Morehead quote, ECM 7 May 1935.

had the NIRA, and therefore no reason to take serious notice of it. It seemed likely (to optimistic reactionary Republicans) that the Roosevelt adminis- tration was on the way out, too. So the MMA began to spend thousands of dollars on what Sparks euphemistically described as "extraordinary expense . . . to keep himself informed on labor relations after the elimina- tion of Code provisions." The archives are understandably coy about what this arrangement meant in detail. But "extraordinary expense" was a bud- getary item that only became significant in 1934, the year of the SKF strike. It more than doubled in 1935 and increased again in 1936, before tailing off. So it seems likely that Sparks was spending far more heavily than ever before on espionage, strike-breaking collaboration with the NMTA, and other preparations for war.[76]

The slack winter season presented the ideal time for lockouts, with freez- ing weather to add to pickets' woes. The MMA attacked – at the S. L. Allen Co. works, outside Westinghouse the biggest remaining center of union strength within the MMA's territory, and among the tool and die shops before Matles's radicalized skilled followers could become too deeply entrenched.

Trouble had been brewing at S. L. Allen since the Schechter decision on 27 May ended the two-year truce between workers and management by terminating their agreement. The local responded to its loss of status by trying to negotiate for formal recognition, a closed shop, and a signed con- tract. Bargaining fruitlessly sputtered on through the fall, punctuated by a threatened strike when the company discharged union president Alex Ross for attending the AFL convention. That issue brought the AFL's local orga- nizer Hines and the U.S. Conciliation Service into play, and they helped secure his reinstatement and even, at the end of a series of bad-tempered, frosty meetings, a draft contract. But, as Allen's president Matthew Scam- mell stressed to Ross and the state and federal mediators at their last meeting on 3 January, "You can draw up this memorandum of agreement but I haven't signed it yet."[77]

Nor would he. Scammell and general manager W. T. Llewellyn (an MMA activist) had strung out negotiations through the company's busy period. Then on 9 January they provoked their men to a concerted defiance of man- agerial authority when they ordered one department to work a night shift

---

[76] Secretary's Comment on Financial Transactions for the Year Ending November 30th, 1935, and Explanation of Suggested Budget and Financial Transactions for 1936, ECM 7 Jan. 1936; Statements for the Finance Committee as Basis of Its Recom- mendation of a Budget, ECM 13 Nov. 1934, 6 Jan. 1936, 14 Dec. 1939.

[77] FMCS 182-925, for the threatened strike and subsequent negotiations; Official Report of Proceedings Before the NLRB, in NLRB Formal File, Case No. C-60 – the draft agreement is Exhibit No. 8; Transcript of Hearings, p. 256; NLRB, "In the Matter of S. L. Allen," p. 720 [quote].

with no extra pay from the start of the next week. They claimed that this was normal practice in the local metal trades, as evidenced by MMA surveys, but the basic issue was one of authority, not just conformity to open-shop custom. Scammell told Ross "I am going to put a night shift on. . . . You are going to like it. The union is not dictating terms to me." But the men concerned turned up at their usual clocking-in time on Monday the 13th regardless, and were sent home, factory superintendent D. R. Richie telling them "until they can report for work at the time we want them to they need not report at all."[78]

The entire factory labor force supported their locked-out brothers the next day, and the shutdown became total. The company was obviously ready for a fight: As Llewellyn told Ross, "if you can take it we can." Federal conciliator Rose Forrester and state mediator Charles Kutz both thought that "the employees walked into a trap and that Mr. Scammell welcomed the chance not to further consider an agreement. The Union is a Federal union and its committee has more valor than judgement."[79]

Continuing attempts to talk to the management by Hines, Kutz, Forrester, and the shop committee were rebuffed. A fortnight into the dispute, Richie sent every striker a letter advising them that by "absent[ing] yourself from your work, without notice to the Company and without permission" they had ended their employment and "severed their relations with the Company." The dread word "strike" was not even mentioned; the fiction of individual communication denied the collective nature of the men's action. After an average of twenty and a maximum of fifty-two years in the same plant, it was all over; they had three days, until the end of the month, in which to call and pick up their tools. The men replied that as far as they were concerned they were still S. L. Allen employees, and all they wanted was to return to work after a satisfactory agreement could be negotiated with their committee. Richie answered that "further negotiations would be useless" and "We have accordingly made other plans."[80]

S. L. Allen was going to play hardball: When neither the threat of mass dismissal nor individual efforts at persuasion by foremen visiting strikers' homes cracked their unity, it was ready to restart production with an entirely new crew. To do so, it would use the MMA, its usual hiring agent, but also – signifying that this was no ordinary dispute, it was the decisive battle – the full strike-breaking services of the NMTA. Earl Sparks coordinated his tactics with the NMTA's Eastern Representative, L. A. Stringham. They placed an experienced "fink captain," Robert

[78] NLRB, "In the Matter of S. L. Allen," pp. 721–2 [quotes].
[79] NLRB, "In the Matter of S. L. Allen," p. 722; Forrester to Kerwin, 27 Jan. 1936, p. 3, FMCS 182-925.
[80] NLRB Case C-60, Formal File – Richie to Alexander Trubin, 27 Jan. 1936, Exhibit No. 11; Walter Holtsmith et al. to Richie, 30 Jan. 1936, Exhibit No. 10; Richie to Alex. J. Ross et al., 1 Feb. 1936, Exhibit No. 9.

Mann (or Mannette/Manent), last seen in Philadelphia during the SKF strike two years earlier, into the Allen plant as "assistant superintendent in charge of employment." Sparks and Stringham proceeded to recruit replacement workers from out of town, seasoned with thugs with criminal records, to brave the pickets and break the strike. Never in thirty years had the MMA stooped so low. Old Samuel Leeds Allen, Quaker patriarch and friend to his employees, must have been squirming despairingly in his grave.[81]

At the same time, and again unprecedentedly, the MMA prepared for legal combat with the union. Probably anticipating that the lockout could turn into an NLRB case, the MMA executive committee entered into a retainer arrangement with the prominent local law firm of Brown & Williams, whose reactionary senior partner, Ira Jewell Williams, Sr., impressed them with his "viewpoint and . . . vigor and enthusiasm." The aim was to procure "competent legal advice" to underpin a uniform policy of determined anti-unionism. The Allen management's behavior showed what the MMA's response to the new legal environment created by the Wagner Act would be: They had met with their workers repeatedly, keeping a verbatim transcript of the fruitless, frustrating, stonewalling sessions, to use as evidence before the board; they had "bargained" to an impasse; and they had provoked their men into a walkout, and thereafter steadfastly denied that they had locked them out. They thought that they had complied with the letter of the law, and could now get down to the serious business of union-busting with clean hands.[82]

Sparks appeared to look forward to the battle with confidence and relish. As he told Hines, "We are not going to attempt to [break this strike]. We are going to do it, and we are going to put that union out of business." Once all of the preparations were in place, the issue was forced – as Sparks reported to his executive committee, "on February 4th the shop was opened with ten men and . . . on the evening of February 5th there was a fracas, bricks thrown through cars, attempts to overturn one car and fist fights." Until then the plant had been shut, picketing peaceful, and policing minimal, but armed with the evidence of striker violence – a predictable reaction to an attempt at reopening that was clearly just a maneuver – Sparks was able to approach the city authorities asking for a much heavier

[81] NLRB, "In the Matter of S. L. Allen," p. 723; U.S. Senate, La Follette Committee *Hearings*, Vol. 1, pp. 172–73; Vol. 3, pp. 903–09; NLRB C-60, Formal File – hearings transcript, pp. 196–97; ECM 12 Feb. 1936.
[82] Special ECM 16 Jan. 1936; ECM 12 Feb. 1936; NLRB C-60, Formal File – Respondent's Objections and Answer, pp. 4–5; pp. 204–306 of the Transcript of the Hearing of 10 March 1936 consist of attorney Ira Williams, Jr. taking Alex Ross through the the details of every "negotiating session," quoting from or summarizing the company's record, which they had refused to disclose to their workers or lay before the board.

presence in preparation for the start of full-scale strike-breaking. The show-down had arrived.[83]

And not only at S. L. Allen. The tool and die makers of Local 203 of the MTFWU were on the point of merging with the IAM, as the Communist Party ended its "Third Period" strategy of strictly independent action and began to feel its way toward the "Popular Front." Once the Communists had come in from the cold they would be more formidable opponents. Work was slack, the weather was ideal for a lockout, so – as the *People's Press* put it – "A couple of hard-boiled bosses," of MMA members Atlantic Mfg. and F. C. Castelli, "[o]bviously in co-operation with one another, . . . forced strikes on their men. . . . [S]omeone thought it a good time to break the union."[84]

Atlantic and Castelli were not large firms – they employed about fifty men apiece – but they were the biggest in the MMA's tool and die manu-facturers group. On 5 February, just as S. L. Allen's strike-breaking was about to begin, twenty-two of Castelli's men walked out over his attempts to lengthen the working week and refusal to recognize their union. Castelli told the MMA "that he expected to fight the thing through" and was promised "all the assistance possible." Two days later Atlantic laid off its second shift, conveniently including all active MTFWU members, claiming "lack of work." The union countered with a demand for the equal division of available work, and – as at Castelli and Allen – it became difficult to tell whether what was occurring was technically a strike or actually a clever lockout, where the men had been provoked to walk. The layoff followed a dispute, like Castelli's, about the company's attempts to slide out of NRA-era working conditions and restore parts of the *status quo ante*. Atlantic had tried to reinstitute a Saturday half-day in place of the normal (since 1933) five-day week, and to reduce overtime payments for Sunday work – inevitable in the seasonal, feast-or-famine jobbing business – from double time to time and a half. They told Sparks that "as business was slack . . . [they] expect[ed] to sit tight for a while," and he called a meeting of the MMA's Tool, Die and Machine Shop Group to coordinate the industry's behavior in this crisis that it had created.[85]

Castelli was an upwardly mobile machinist who had built his shop from nothing through the worst years of the Depression, a strong character

---

[83] NLRB C-60, Formal File – Transcript of Hearings of 9 March 1936, p. 94; NLRB, "In the Matter of S. L. Allen," p. 724; ECM 12 Feb. 1936; transcript, pp. 156–60, 172, 179, 182–84 (evidence of police officers).

[84] ECM 7 Jan. 1936; "Independent Metal Locals Join I.A.M., Radio Not In," *PP* 29 Feb. 1936, p. 4.

[85] "Radio Workers Help Win Sweeping Victory for Machinists at Atlantic," *PP* 4 Apr. 1936, p. 4; PID16-40 database; ECM 12 Feb. 1936. On the Atlantic strike and the rhythms of the jobbing trade, see Respondent 669, Machinists Study, Palmer Papers, TUUA.

described by federal conciliator Rose Forrester as "a very interesting colorful person who must be handled with great patience and tact." He vowed that he would "go out of business before recognizing the union" and "refused to meet any but his own employees," that is, he would not negotiate with their business agent, Young Communist League organizer Dave Davis (Dubensky), a bookkeeper by training. Castelli was adamant that he would not accept "the rule of seniority rights as applicable to layoffs in slack time; and that he would under no circumstances compromise his absolute right to hire and fire anyone whom he pleases." Atlantic did not take quite such a firm line, but its sticking points were the closed shop and formal recognition: It was quite prepared to promise not to discriminate against union members, and to deal with their representatives, but balked at signing a contract, insisting that a "'gentlemen's' agreement" was enough. This was perhaps because its proprietor had given the MMA his word that he would hold out, as a condition of receiving help.[86]

These three lockout/strikes, all coming to a head during the first weekend of February, were, as Rose Forrester reported to her boss, "outstanding not on account of the large numbers involved but for the bitterness on both sides." The MMA and its members provoked these conflicts and entered them with confidence and resolution. So far, so normal in the history of the Philadelphia metal trades' Open Shop campaigns. What the employers did not appreciate was that times had changed.[87]

The first big difference was that the strikers maintained a degree of solidarity among themselves, and between themselves and other, more powerful local unionists, which was unprecedented in the history of the Philadelphia metal trades. What should have happened was that these three small groups of men should have been weakened by the defection of the desperate or the uncommitted; dire poverty in a hard winter should have

[86] PHILCHAP database; PID16-40 database; Forrester to Kerwin, 30 Apr. 1936, p. 1; Preliminary Report, 11 Feb. 1936; Summary of Final Report, 26 March; George L. McGuigan (president of what was by then IAM Lodge 1555) to Castelli, 16 Apr. 1936 – all in FMCS 182-1179; 26 March Preliminary Report, 27 March Final Report, FMCS 182-1296; "Radio Workers Help Win Sweeping Victory." For Davis, see Sherman Labovitz, *Being Red in Philadelphia: A Memoir of the McCarthy Era* (Philadelphia, 1998), pp. 16, 21, 144. Friends of Dave Davis from the 1940s and 1950s remembered his height (short), weight (puny), temper (hot), honesty (total), and effectiveness (high), but were hazy about his background outside the party, which he had served from 1928 onwards, and whether he had *any* machineshop experience – conversations with Vince Pieri, Haldor Reinholt, and Jack Zucker, Philadelphia, September 1994. The FBI archives doubtless contain the answers – as Davis rose in prominence within the UE, and became a member of the Communist Party's central committee, they recruited at least one close associate to spy on him. Davis ended up as a defendant in the Philadelphia Smith Act trial.
[87] Forrester to Kerwin, 30 Apr. 1936, p. 3.

driven them back to work or off to jobs in other shops. But it did not. That was in part because they were well organized, and in the MTFWU's case led; but it was also because they could draw on the resources of a burgeoning local labor movement.

The AFL gave little practical assistance to its struggling federal local, but the Allen strikers were helped instead by the two big Philco locals, foundation-stones of the new UE, strongest organizations in the proto-CIO Joint Council of Labor, to which the Allen local's Alex Ross had been a delegate. Philco unionists started a "10¢ a Week Club" to sustain the "hard pressed . . . Allen crowd," confident, as local president and former railroad brotherhood officer Martin Cassidy put it, that "when a gang like ours puts its shoulders to the wheel something is bound to happen." The Allen strikers were enabled to hold out for months because they had strike pay and funds and the knowledge that they were not alone. Philco workers joined in mass pickets of the Allen plant, forming up outside their works and "parad[ing] through the streets of Northeast Philadelphia" to join their comrades so that "The neighborhood was jammed." Cassidy, "official parade marshall," egged his members on: "Keep it up, brothers, and we'll be going places."[88]

The MMA had never had to meet such large-scale, organized, persistent resistance – not even in the 1905–07 Molders' strike, because the Molders only fought their own battles, neither asking for nor offering solidarity action. The SKF strike had been larger, but so was the company, and it, not the MMA, had borne most of the burden; nor had the independent Anti-Friction Workers enjoyed much support from other workers or unions. In the Allen strike, the MMA was more or less on its own, and the strikers and their sympathizers did not just picket the plant – they took the fight to the enemy. Earl Sparks, middle-aged pillar of the community, had "his home . . . visited by a squad of strong arm men" as if he was a common scab, and needed police "protection throughout the night." Obviously shocked at this new development, the MMA took out insurance on his house (against "riot and civil commotion"), automobile – at risk of being rammed, turned over, or having a brick through the window as he drove to inspect the industrial battlefields – and person. The worm had turned, and grown teeth.[89]

The Allen strikers' *élan* demonstrated that the MMA had made a strategic miscalculation in raising the stakes: Philadelphia metalworkers now held enough good cards in their deck, and collectively had deep enough pockets, to stay in the game for several long, nerve-wracking rounds.

[88] "Philco Locals Help Organize, Win Strikes," *PP* 7 March 1936, p. 8; "Philadelphia Joint Council Has First Birthday," 4 Apr., p. 5; Cassidy, "18369 Ramblings," 25 Apr., p. 9; Cassidy, "Local 102 Ramblings," 9 May, p. 8; "Philco Workers See Craft Union in Action," 16 May, p. 4.
[89] ECM 12 March 1936.

Eventually, the MMA and the company "won" – after five months the union acknowledged defeat, and about half the strikers were taken back – but the price had been intolerable. The MMA had broken its last strike. Members would still sit out others, but its militant attempts to restart production were over.[90]

The fate of Atlantic and Castelli was even worse than that of Allen. All that the Electrical Workers could offer the Allen strikers was money and moral support. But Atlantic and Castelli were both subcontractors to the organized radio plants. Philco local president Cassidy explained the consequences: the small "sweatshops," unencumbered by Philco's thirty-six-hour week and lavish wages, were "doing our work." "[T]he job has been forced upon us at last – the job of plugging up the cut-throat machine shops and press shops. . . . How long do you think we are going to be able to compete with that situation?. . . . LET'S GIVE IT TO THEM. PUT A UNION IN THEIR SHOP." As George Berry, secretary of the UE's first new local in the competitive radio parts sector, explained, "These steps will put a crimp in the boss' argument that he can't compete with other companies because of higher labor costs – they'll all have the same higher labor costs when the U.E. & R.W. gets through with them."[91]

So the ties that bound the UE's radio locals to the small tool-and-die shops were numerous and strong; the fact that the former were staunchly anti-Communist and the latter were red strongholds was at this time of no importance. The Philco locals had a "'no scab goods'" clause in their contracts that allowed them to refuse to work on parts produced under strike conditions without suffering any sanctions from their management. The RCA local did not have the same formal right, but it had the power. "That was that – and their biggest customers were gone."[92]

Usually in Philadelphia subcontractors had been constrained to follow the same open-shop policies as their big customers, for fear of losing business. Now the world had turned upside down. Philco removed its dies from the struck plants, and their owners were left twisting in the wind while their striking workers were supported by the giant radio locals' generosity, and enabled to keep all their men on daily mass pickets outside their gates. Cassidy's message to the proprietors of small jobbing shops was clear: "F. C. Castelli Co. has gone to the cleaners. . . .

---

[90]   Scammell to Ross, 27 Feb. 1936, Exhibit 12, and Answer [of company] to Petition for Enforcement of an Order of the NLRB, Oct. 1937, p. 3 in NLRB C-60, Formal File.

[91]   "Cassidy Elected 18369's President; Three Are Re-Elected," *PP* 7 March 1936, p. 4; Cassidy, "18369 Ramblings," 25 Apr., p. 9; Cassidy, "Local 102 Ramblings," 2 May, p. 8; "Local 102 Ramblings," 16 May, p. 8; Berry, "Local 105 List Demands as Strike Holds Tight," 23 May, p. 4.

[92]   "Cassidy Elected 18369's President"; "Radio Workers Help Win Sweeping Victory."

The bosses will either pay a living wage or else they themselves will go back to work."[93]

The second side of the new triangle of forces bearing in to crush the Open Shop was represented by government agencies – local, state, and national – that were newly responsive to organized labor and staunchly committed to the New Deal collective bargaining policy.

Perhaps most important was a revolution in the city administration's and police's attitude toward unions, and behavior during strikes. As Cassidy reminded his members before the 1936 elections, "Philadelphia has always taken care of the powers that be." As late as 1932 the Republican machine could still deliver the votes in inner-city wards, producing a Hoover majority and a reliably reactionary, tight-fisted, anti-labor mayor. But the old loyalties and habits soon broke down, partly because of the growing contrast between the city's inactivity against the Depression, and repressive strike policing, and the behavior of the Pinchot and Roosevelt administrations. In 1933 the Republicans split between regulars and reformers, and some Democrats were elected to local office. In 1934 the old machine collapsed, and renegade Republican George Earle, the Democrats' first successful gubernatorial candidate since 1890, came within an ace of winning a majority in Philadelphia. So in 1935, faced by a serious Democrat challenge in the mayoral race, the Republicans followed a twin-track strategy: counting the Democrat out, as usual, but also offering a Pinchot Republican, S. Davis Wilson, to attract wavering voters.[94]

To his backers' amazement, once in office Wilson adopted a La Guardia-esque policy toward the New Deal and the labor movement. He established a Labor Board with tripartite representation – including only employers who recognized unions, and labor leaders including the AFL's Lew Hines and the UE's Harry Block. This supplemented the state and federal mediation services, and replaced the defunct RLB. He made the Hosiery Workers'

---

[93] cf. Chappell to Kerwin, 15 Oct. 1933, explaining the Heintz Mfg. Co.'s reluctance to sign an agreement because of the likely effect on its ability to secure credit and contracts – FMCS 176-138; "One Down and One To Go," *PP* 18 Apr. 1936, p. 1; Cassidy, "Local 102 Ramblings," 2 May, p. 8.

[94] "Let's Not Eat Sunflowers, Cassidy Advises Members," *PP* 17 Oct. 1936, p. 4 (the sunflower was the symbol of Kansas Republican presidential candidate Alfred Landon's campaign); Keller, "Pennsylvania's Little New Deal," pp. 6, 113, 152, 304; Shover, "Emergence of a Two-Party System," pp. 990, 992–96 esp.; Russell Weigley, ed., *Philadelphia: A 300 Year History* (New York, 1982), pp. 621, 623–25. See esp. David Montgomery, "Labor and the Political Leadership of New Deal America," *International Review of Social History* 30 (1994): 335–60, for the interaction between working-class mobilization and a supportive or responsive liberal state, and David Plotke, *Building a Democratic Political Order: Reshaping American Liberalism in the 1930s and 1940s* (New York, 1996), esp. Chs. 4–5.

attorney the City Solicitor, who went on to play a large role in negotiating strike settlements and exposing and attacking employer anti-unionism. And he altered policing and other law enforcement behavior, to the Open Shop's detriment. The MMA had not reckoned on the effects of these new policies on its ability to break strikes.[95]

In the Allen strike, for example, the mayor intervened personally to try to get Scammell to talk even before the strike-breaking began. When it did, the strike-breakers were at first accommodated inside the plant to shield them from the pickets, but after two days the union brought this to Wilson's attention and he required the Health and Fire Departments to order the company to cease and desist – from violating building and sanitary ordinances! The company responded by hiring Pullman cars to house them, which it parked on its railroad spur, but this proved too expensive as the strike dragged on. The city police, now openly sympathetic to the strikers, refused the protection required to convoy the strike-breakers in by car. In accordance with the mayor's policy that "Orderly mass picketing will be permitted . . . and imported strikebreakers will be denied police protection," they would no longer ride shotgun, merely following at a safe distance. A company executive who was a Major in the Pennsylvania National Guard tried to ferry the strike-breakers in his own car, behind the shelter of his uniform and weaponry, but a protest to Harrisburg stopped this stratagem, too. Finally there was no alternative but to bring them in by regular passenger train, enabling the strikers to buy tickets and exercize their persuasive powers in an environment relatively free of police surveillance, and where the strike-breakers could not easily escape. This resulted in a running fight between strikers and the NMTA's thugs, one of whom turned out to be handier with his knife than with a micrometer. Frankie Alvaro's was certainly a vicious attack, but scarcely, as the NLRB reported, unprovoked.[96]

Mayor Wilson went well beyond neutrality, doing his utmost to implement the Wagner Act's restrictions on the more flagrant unfair labor practices of employers. For example, he promulgated a city ordinance closing down "detective agencies" that employed ex-convicts, formerly one of the service sector's Depression-era growth industries. In the Freihofer Baking Co. strike, "Acting on the union's complaint, the police entered the plant and removed eighteen thugs hired as strikebreakers. The management didn't

[95] "Leader Heads City's Labor Advisory Board," *ULR* 13 Dec. 1935, p. 1; "City Labor Board set Up; Cops' Policy Changed," 17 Jan. 1936, pp. 1, 6; "Wilson Picks Labor Board," *Trades Union News*, 7 Feb. 1936, p. 3; "Block on Mayor's Labor Committee," *PP* 7 March 1936, p. 5; SEC 1936, p. 1.

[96] U.S. Senate, La Follette Committee *Hearings*, Vol. 1, pp. 172–74; "Philco Locals Help Organize, Win Strikes"; "Block on Mayor's Labor Committee"; NLRB, "In the Matter of S. L. Allen," p. 725; NLRB C-60, Formal File, transcript of hearing of 10 March 1936, pp. 154, 165–69, 184–92, 198–99 (police evidence).

have a chance in the world to claim that these were 'loyal employees.'" The city authorities didn't all sing from the same hymn-sheet – Judge "Injunction Harry" McDevitt of the Court of Common Pleas did his best to preserve the old order – but the vital facts were these: The Mayor was extending the cloak of public legitimacy over the labor movement; and the police were either leaving the parties to get on with their struggles or, once a conflict threatened to cross their revised tolerance threshhold, actually intervening even-handedly to preserve public order. In this respect, too, the world had been turned upside down.[97]

This behavior by the politically responsive city government was vital in 1936, when the labor movement was still insecure, and the hiatus between the Schechter and Jones & Laughlin cases meant that the NLRB lacked the power to intervene decisively to protect workers' and unions' statutory rights. Its importance was highlighted by the contrasting performance of the Camden city and New Jersey state authorities at the other end of the Ben Franklin Bridge, who used all of the old brutality in an attempt to crush UE Local 103's strike at RCA that summer. This happened at precisely the same time as the Philadelphia locals of UE and Matles's machinists were free to use mass pickets and other solidarity actions to build their unions out from their original bases. Local politics mattered; as Cassidy exulted after the elections, when Philadelphia returned a New Deal majority, "times have changed." It was no longer "a scab town. . . . November 3rd showed that labor is running the policies."[98]

This emphasis on the local state should not lead us to overlook the fact that the Pennsylvania and federal governments were also, though with less immediate and dramatic effect, on the workers' side. Federal conciliator Rose Forrester and state mediator Charles Kutz were deeply involved in all attempts at settlement in the Allen, Atlantic, and Castelli strikes – which they clearly perceived as one conflict, not three. They were partisans, not neutrals, "jubilant" over the settlements that they brokered in the two smaller strikes, "instrumental" in the successful conclusion of the merger talks between the MTFWU and the IAM, and right behind the union's

[97] U.S. Senate, La Follette Committee *Hearings*, Vol. 1, pp. 172–74; "Philly Police Cop 18 Thugs in Freihofer Strike," *PP* 11 Apr. p. 5; Cassidy, "Finks, Nobles Are Starving," *PP* 19 Oct. p. 3.

[98] Derber, "Electrical Products," pp. 793–94, "How RCA Fought the Strike," *ULR* 24 July 1936, p. 2; "New Jersey CIO Flays Camden Cops for Acts Senate Probe Revealed," *PP* 3 Apr. 1937, p. 4; Cassidy, "Philco Locals Set Up Co-Op," *PP* 28 Nov. 1936, p. 4 [quote]. Electoral mobilization between 1932 and 1936 in Philadelphia was stunning – turnout increased from 42.1 to 60 percent – as was the transfer of voters into the Roosevelt camp. Shover, "Emergence of a Two-Party System," pp. 990, 996. For the strategic importance of city politics and police behavior in shaping the outcome of social conflicts, cf. Barbara W. Newell, *Chicago and the Metropolitan Labor Movement: Metropolitan Unionism in the 1930s* (Urbana, 1961), esp. pp. 47, 147, 149–50.

policy "that before long every machine jobbing shop in Philadelphia will be operating under a union agreement." Their commitment was to "peace in this area" and the New Deal collective bargaining policy rather than to union growth *per se*, but in 1936 the nuances of difference between these two approaches were barely distinguishable to the naked eye.[99]

Nor did the fact that the NLRB was weakened by the Wagner Act's status – as something whose constitutionality was contested by employers – mean that it was inactive, or did not figure in the combattants' reckoning. It did not intervene in the tool-and-die strikes, because they were too small and did not affect interstate commerce directly enough. But the Allen case was an obvious collection of compounded unfair labor practices in a national-market company. Lew Hines filed his charge on the 3rd of February, after the mass dismissal had taken effect and in the last few desperate days of trying to persuade Allen's and the MMA not to carry their "other plans" into effect. The NLRB swung quickly into action, issuing a complaint on the 26th alleging that the company had attempted "to dissuade its employees ... from continuing their membership in the union, and ... refused to bargain collectively."[100] The company replied within a week, in tones of Republican outrage:

Respondent explicitly denies the right and the power of the National Labor Relations Board to assume or exercise power or jurisdiction over it in any way whatever. It challenges the power and jurisdiction of said Board over it; and files these objections and answers under duress, under protest, and solely *de bene esse*, only because the National Labor Relations Act provides that objections not made by answer are foreclosed, and it is conceivable that said Act may be held to be constitutional as applied to respondent.

In truth, the act was unconstitutional through and through, and "null and void": S. L. Allen was a manufacturing firm, and was not "engaged in interstate commerce"; the duty to bargain was a deprivation "of liberty and property without due process of law" for the company and its individual employees; the prohibition of company attempts to dissuade "its employees or persons who might be its employees from joining or remaining members of any union ... abridges respondent's freedom of speech"; the NLRB's status as prosecutor and judge "denies ... the right of trial by jury"; the Wagner Act violated the Tenth Amendment because it invaded states' rights; it violated the Third Amendment, too, because it delegated judicial and legislative power to the board; and, finally, it was "so vague and ambiguous as to be meaningless in so far as providing any certain standard of conduct whereby those intended to be subjected thereto may be governed." What was a "unit appropriate for purposes of collective bargaining"? What was the "duty to bargain collectively?" After assaulting the

[99]   Forrester to Kerwin, 30 Apr. 1936, pp. 2–3, in FMCS 182-1179.
[100] Complaint in NLRB C-60, Exhibits.

act, Allen's attorneys attacked the board's "facts" – particularly whether their client's dealings with its employees fell within the law's prohibitions. It had "the constitutional right to discourage its employees, by any means short of intimidation, from joining or remaining members of the union." It had negotiated with its employees, and remained willing to – on its own conditions – but "reserve[d] its right at any time to decline to deal with any person or persons with whom it does not wish to deal."[101]

The board wasted no time, ordering a hearing the day after receiving Allen's reply. It started four days later while the strike was still in progress, and witnesses' wounds from the assaults of Allen's thugs were still fresh. Allen's attorney kicked off proceedings by asking trial examiner Robert Gates "to grant me the benefit of my objection to every act performed by you during this hearing. . . . I want my constitutional objections to apply to every act sought to be performed by the Board or any of its agents. Then I shall not have to renew them with each question and answer." Throughout the hearings he was hostile and insulting to union witnesses, and barely civil toward Gates, accusing him, for example, of committing "a piece of the grossest inhumanity that any tribunal could commit" if the proceedings helped the union identify strike-breakers. The company introduced no witnesses of its own, because "it seemed so clear . . . that the Board ought to pass on a motion to dismiss before putting us to the expense and trouble of giving testimony." And it did not even put in an appearance before the board itself when the trial examiner's report was being reviewed.[102]

Given the facts as presented, the law as the NLRB meant to interpret it, and the company's ideologically and emotionally satisfying, but rather perfunctory, defense, the outcome was predictable. On the 13th of May the board ordered S. L. Allen to dismiss as many strike-breakers as were required to make room for the reinstatement of all of the strikers in order of their seniority. Any who could not be immediately accommodated were to be kept on a preferential hiring list that would be the exclusive source of employees until all who wanted their jobs back had got them.[103]

On the face of it, this was total vindication for the strikers. In fact, it was useless. Within a month the strike would end in defeat, and neither the AFL nor the NLRB would make any attempt to enforce the order until after the Supreme Court had ruled on the Wagner Act's constitutionality. It would simply have been a waste of time and resources, and contrary to the board's

---

101 Objections and Answers in NLRB C-60. Attorney Williams also advised Sparks to ignore the board's subpoena, thereby depriving at least one historian of some potentially interesting testimony. ECM 14 May 1936.

102 NLRB C-60, Formal File: Transcript, pp. 3–4, 148.

103 NLRB C-60, Formal File: Ira J. Williams, Jr., to Robert A. Gates, 15 May 1936, Exhibit A, and Petition for Enforcement of an Order of the NLRB, March Term 1937, p. 3; NLRB, "In the Matter of S. L. Allen," p. 729.

legal strategy of fighting a few big and absolutely clear-cut cases through
to the court, and stalling all the rest.[104]

Clearly, the federal government did not yet have the power to make a
recalcitrant employer conform, but nevertheless Allen and the MMA had
received a salutary lesson in the price of ignoring or opposing the new law.
It had cost the MMA itself an unprecedented amount of money merely to
retain Brown & Williams for legal advice. Allen's own legal fees, over and
above the costs of the strike itself (on an issue that would have cost $66 a
week to settle on the men's original terms, although they were ready to compromise on $40), must have been huge, and dragged on for another two
years. The MMA had been essentially law-abiding in its thirty-year battle
for the Open Shop, and it (and Allen) were extremely uncomfortable with
their deviation from that norm. Treasurer Llewellyn, for example, asked the
police if any of the strike-breakers that the NMTA supplied really did have
criminal records, as the union alleged, because "he did not want men like
that in the plant."[105]

Nor was the crisis over once the board had made its decision. Even
though the board could not enforce it, another branch of the federal government – the La Follette subcommittee of the Senate Committee on Education and Labor – had the unquestioned power to follow up on the unfair
labor practices that the board uncovered. Later that year its investigators,
who had exposed the MMA's role in the Allen strike in the course of their
examination of the NMTA, rolled up in Philadelphia and subpoenaed
Sparks himself and all of the MMA's records. There was no escape. In
January 1937 the committee's agents were "welcomed" into the MMA's
offices and given every cooperation, which was preferable to having the files
carted off to Washington.[106]

The cumulative effect of these experiences at the hands of the city, state,
and federal governments was to make the MMA rethink the wisdom of the
belligerent course it had pursued, with increasing vigor and expense and
decreasing returns, for the previous three years. Optimism about any

---

[104]   ECM 17 Sept. 1936; Peter Irons, *The New Deal Lawyers* (Princeton, 1982), Chs.
        12–13.
[105]   ECM 12 Nov. 1936 – Brown & Williams advised Sparks that $1,000 a year was
        "the smallest retainer which they would accept . . . and . . . in fact they thought it
        quite nominal." Nominal for a law firm, but not for its client: legal expenses rose
        from nowhere to 6.4 percent of the MMA's total expenditures, third in importance
        after $9,707 on salaries and $1,374 on rent – Statement to the Finance Committee,
        ECM 2 Dec. 1936. NLRB C-60, Formal File, Transcript p. 151 [quote].
[106]   Jerold S. Auerbach, *Labor and Civil Liberties: The La Follette Committee and the
        New Deal* (Indianapolis, 1966), on its role as an unofficial enforcement arm for the
        New Deal collective bargaining policy; "La Follette Smokes Out Metal Trades
        Finkdom," *PP* 30 Jan. 1937 p. 2; ECM 12 Nov., 9 Dec. 1936, SEC 1936, p. 5; ECM
        7 Jan. 1937; SEC 1937, p. 7.

prospect of deliverance disappeared after the shock of the 1936 elections, which also gave Governor Earle the House and Senate majorities that he needed to enact his "Little New Deal," and caused MMA president Morehead to predict more "rough times ahead" in his retirement address that December.[107]

By that time, individual members had already begun to make their peace with the new order. Atlantic Manufacturing was the first hole in the dyke, accepting a settlement on 27 March that George McGuigan, Lodge 1555's president, accurately saw as "a victory for the entire organized Labor movement, and a defeat for the Metal Manufacturers' Association . . . who were determined to crush all Unions in the Metal Industry." Castelli followed a little over a month later; other tool and die shops soon came into line. They were "persuaded" by all of the forces referred to above, and also by a third that proved decisive in cracking the Open Shop and producing "the first agreement signed in a machine shop, or in a strictly metal industry, since 1916." That final factor was division in the ranks of capital itself.[108]

The immediate pressures on them to settle did not simply result from the UE's solidarity actions. They were accentuated by Philco itself, whose executive vice president, George Deming, was an employer member of Mayor Wilson's Labor Committee. He was denounced by the NMTA's I. A. String ham as "the A.F. of L.'s strongest organizer" for his work in championing the growth of unionism, and "'yes man' for the labor racketeers on the board." Through 1936 Philco was still pursuing its extraordinarily cooperative labor relations policy. It gave company products as prizes for Local 102's "Gala Picnic," its entire senior executive team attended the union's annual dinner, and UE members who had never worked for Philco were given preferential hiring rights over nonmember applicants, an enormous incentive to join the union for other Philadelphia metalworkers.[109]

Local 102 reciprocated, arguing that collective bargaining "stabilizes the working force, eliminates individual haphazard action through group representation on a planned basis, and simplifies personnel problems. . . . Unwarranted and unlooked for stoppages and conflicts are outlawed by the Union agreement." Grievances could be dealt with by orderly negotiation

[107]   Keller, "Pennsylvania's Little New Deal," Chs. 8–10; FCM 9 Dec. 1936.

[108]   'Memorandum of Understanding,' FMCS 182-1296; McGuigan to "Dear Sirs and Brothers," 15 Apr. 1936, in UE District Council No. 1 Minutes, Harry Block Collection, University of Pittsburgh (hereafter UE Minutes); 'Memorandum of Understanding,' FMCS 182-1179; "Radio Workers Help Win Sweeping Victory"; SEC 1936, p. 1.

[109]   U.S. Senate, La Follette Committee *Hearings*, Vol. 3, pp. 1080–81, Exhibit 449, Stringham to NMTA commissioner H. D. Sayre, 8 March 1936; "Philco 102 Plans for Gala Picnic, June 20," *PP* 23 May 1936, p. 8; Charles Van Housen (Secretary, Local 102), "Speeches Make Way for Fun at 102 Dinner" and Cassidy, "Philco Recognizes UE & RW Book as Guide for Hiring," 12 Dec., p. 5.

and the main terms of the employment relationship fixed by long-term contracts. "We are primarily interested in minimum wage rates, maximum hours, and a minimum number of hours per week per man." Most of the key elements of the managerial prerogative remained undisturbed.[110]

A union like Local 102 could be a force for uniformity and order, and if it was good enough for Philco, it was good enough for its suppliers too. Philco did not simply *not resist* UE members' refusal to work on products from struck plants, it drove home the message. Atlantic buckled first; Castelli held out, but Deming "pulled his work from Castelli's shop, hailed Castelli before the Mayor's Labor Board and insisted that Castelli settle with the strikers, run a union shop with a union agreement, or he would never receive another dollar's worth of Philco work. Castelli told him to go to –, he would not sign a union agreement if they took the shop from him."[111]

But that was bluster and bravado: If his chief customer insisted that he had to settle, in the interests of citywide labor peace and an end to the consequences of disputes in suppliers' plants for Philco's own ability to satisfy without disruption the enormous demand for its radios, then he had to swallow his pride and sign. In the end he had little choice. Stringham moaned that Deming "should be broken down. Can you suggest anything that we can do to off-set his activities?" NMTA Commissioner Homer Sayre's answer, if any, is unrecorded. A Trojan horse the size of Philco was uncontrollable; and thanks to Deming, the Greeks were now inside the gates. The Open Shop citadel was lost.[112]

---

[110] "The Observer," "Philco Notes: Local 101," *PP* 9 Jan. 1937, p. 9; Cooper, "The Faces of Gender," pp. 332–33. However, Derber, "Electrical Products," pp. 785–86, notes "Sources of Irritation" in everyday labor relations.

[111] Stringham to Sayre, p. 1081.

[112] Ibid. and testimony, p. 911.

11

The New World: Accommodation and Adjustment, 1936–1939

The crumbling of the MMA's Open Shop policy was no more the result of an ideological conversion to the possible merits of collective bargaining than were the comparable changes taking place at the same time in the business community at large. The Open Shop was simply overwhelmed by a conjunction of mutually reinforcing hostile forces that made the prospects of victory too uncertain, and the costs of resistance too high. The pressure of an apparently unstoppable labor movement enjoying widespread public support, increasingly effective governmental backing, and even some corporate encouragement continued unabated through 1936 and 1937. The time for adopting a new approach that was more in keeping with the requirements of this unwanted New Deal Order had come.

11.1 THE ROAD TO REALISM

The process of coming to terms with a new reality was a protracted one. Government agencies played a key role in easing the transition and educating Philadelphia metal-trades executives to the rules of the new game. The Atlantic and Castelli agreements are illustrative here.

First, neither of them was called an agreement, although this was the union's preferred title. They were just "Memorandums of Understanding," the same term as had applied to the S. L. Allen settlement from 1933 to 1935. In the Atlantic case, neither of the parties concerned was required to sign anything – the state and federal agents alone signed, "attest[ing] to the fact that they were present." As Rose Forrester wrote her boss, "We are very happy over the outcome as we hope that . . . . we may be establishing a way out for other disputes into which the metal trades association injects itself. It gives the employees what they want and saves the face of the employer." It might not be called a contract, but a record of "understandings" between a company and the acknowledged union of its employees, witnessed by two government officials, came close enough. By the time Castelli settled, he was prepared to add his signature to those of Forrester and Kutz, and alongside those of Lodge 1555's tough Communist business agent and the shop committee. Subsequent local agreements progressively abandoned the fiction that they were anything other than formal contracts in which the union was a or the principal.[1]

Other careful, soothing language was found to further disguise the reality of what was happening. Neither firm conceded the union shop in so many words, but both stated that they had "no objection that all employees . . . . shall be members of the . . . . Union." Atlantic agreed "to reaffirm this statement of policy in the presence of the Shop Committee to any employee who may refuse to join the Union"; Castelli went further, agreeing to do the same with every new employee. Both companies agreed to recognize the union as a source of labor supply on a par with all of the others including, of course, the MMA. This was not as strong as the union wanted – they aimed for a preferential shop – but it gave them much of the substance.[2]

Granting recognition to the union as such, and agreeing to deal with its officers rather than with one's own employees, had always been sticking points. Atlantic glossed over them by recognizing the union as the sole collective bargaining agency for its employees, and agreeing to deal with "any of the elected or appointed representatives" so long as the union kept majority support. Castelli found solace in giving his departmental shop committees pride of place in the grievance procedure, and graciously "according them the privilege of naming another representative who may or may not represent the International Association of Machinists, and who may or may not be an employee, and who may assist them in bargaining with the Company." It would have been shorter but harder just to write "Dave Davis," but the meaning was the same.[3]

Once the companies had accepted the basics of an ongoing relationship, and had agreed to reinstate all of the strikers (and, in Castelli's case, discharge all of the strike-breakers), they found the union quite accommodating on other matters. In these unstable jobbing shops, fairness in distributing available work, and then in making layoffs and recalls, was a key issue for workers. But they seemed prepared to recognize the employers' need to maintain a skilled, competitive labor force. At Atlantic, work was to be shared among members of a work group until they only had

---

[1] "Memorandum of Understanding," FMCS 182-1296 and FMCS 182-1179, cf. Copy of Agreement (proposed by Union) in FMCS 182-1179; Forrester to Kerwin, 27 March 1936, FMCS 182-1296; cf. 1937 agreements referred to in note 19.
[2] "Memorandum of Understanding," FMCS 182-1296 and FMCS 182-1179.
[3] Ibid.

three eight-hour days a week each, and then layoffs could be made "on the basis of competency without discrimination for Union activity." Recalls were to be on the same basis, and throughout the company was acknowledged "as the sole judge" – but only "after discussion with the Shop Committee." Where competence was equal, decisions would be made in line with seniority, and no new hiring would take place until the laid-off workers had been offered a chance to return, at the same pay as they had been receiving in their previous jobs. The Castelli agreement was less explicit but substantially the same. In both cases the essence of job reservation for incumbent workers, and seniority as the fundamental basis for movement in and out of the current labor force and from night to day shifts, had been accepted.[4]

Both companies also agreed to limitations on their right to fire. Any proposed discharge, even "for cause" – that is, because of violation of acknowledged shop rules that were written into the agreements – could be appealed immediately, and must be discussed with the shop committee. They also accepted the union members' right not to do any "scab work" without penalty. Other outstanding grievances – call-in pay and weekend overtime – were also settled, basically on the union's terms.

What did they get in return, other than an end to their strikes? Atlantic was promised that strike breakers and noncommunists would not be subjected to "any annoyance, be refused co-operation or threatened"; any workers violating this agreement could be disciplined and, on the second offense, discharged. Castelli won a pledge that no union activities would take place during working hours, and no coercion would be used to compel employees to join the union, with the same progressive sanctions for offenders. If labor lived up to these agreements, post-strike turbulence should be minimized. Furthermore, the union promised Atlantic "three full working days' notice before declaring any strike, in order that an attempt can be made to adjust any grievance," while Castelli's agreement provided that the state and/or federal dispute adjusters must be given a chance before any strike or lock-out.[5]

The foundations of a new stability in labor relations were being constructed on the wreckage of the old order. Atlantic's memorandum was open-ended; Castelli's was to run for one year. Grievances had been settled, explicit minimum wages spelled out, company rules accepted, and procedures to govern difficult circumstances (e.g., compulsory weekend overtime on emergency work) agreed. Both companies also knew that the local would be attempting to impose the same or better conditions on all of their competitors, and Castelli agreed that if the union won higher wages from them,

4   Ibid.
5   Ibid.

then it would come into line. Neither the AFL nor the NRA had succeeded in producing competitive equality among Philadelphia's jobbing machine shops. Now the Communists would have their chance.[6]

11.2 LABOR'S HIGH TIDE

The pressures on the MMA itself built up throughout the closing months of 1936 and early 1937. Reflection on the Atlantic, Castelli, and other job shop defeats, and on the pyrrhic victory at S. L. Allen, was given further point by the endless succession of blows dealt to the old order.

RCA, for example, was robbed of victory over UE Local 103 in the bitter summer strike by the Philco locals, which paid their union brothers' and sisters' legal and other costs while they kept on working and allowed their employer to steal an intolerably high market share. The strike was terminated on RCA's agreement to let the NLRB carry out a representation election. The company's strategy – its labor relations specialist was none other than the hamfisted General Hugh Johnson – was to advise employees, including members of a well-entrenched company union and of the rival AFL Electrical Workers, not to vote. As a result the UE only received 3,016 ballots out of 3,163 cast in an election where 9,752 workers were eligible. The NLRB simply ignored the nonvoting majority and certified Local 103 as the exclusive bargaining agency for the whole production workforce. It could not enforce its judgment, but UE members were emboldened and the plant endured "industrial guerrilla warfare for months and months" until, once the Supreme Court had spoken on the Wagner Act, management eventually saw sense, fired Johnson, and started to negotiate in earnest.[7]

Within the MMA, workers at G. E. were encouraged by developments elsewhere in the city and the corporation, and began to join the UE and agitate against the company union. Shortly after the Roosevelt landslide the

---

[6] For a surviving example of one of the second phase of contracts that was also brokered by Forrester and Kutz, see "Wilkening Manufacturing Co. June 25, 1936. Memorandum of understanding terminating strike and promoting harmonious relations" – in some respects (e.g., strict seniority) more far-reaching, but in most less so than the above. Uncatalogued District 1 Records, UE Archives, Archives of Industrial Society, Univ. of Pittsburgh.

[7] "Regional Labor Body Backs UE & RW as Official RCA Union," PP 5 Sept. 1936, p. 3; "Labor Board Ruling Historic Doctrine for American Labor," 12 Sept., p. 9; "Radio Union at RCA Sole Bargaining Unit, Labor Board Decides," 14 Nov., p. 2; Milton Derber, "Electrical Products," in Harry A. Millis, ed., *How Collective Bargaining Works: A Survey of Experience in Leading American Industries* (New York, 1942), pp. 794–97; James Matles and James Higgins, *Them and Us: Struggles of a Rank and File Union* (Englewood Cliffs, 1974), pp. 55–59 (quote at p. 58).

huge Westinghouse South Philadelphia FLU joined the UE, too, and employees at its smaller center city plant, who had "merely been waiting for the organized group to make the first step," quickly followed suit. The UE joined the CIO, and at the Steel Workers Organizing Committee's regional director Clint Golden's suggestion SWOC brought his fellow Machinist and old comrade Jack Lever back from his retirement as a struggling small farmer to make him their, and the CIO's, local representative. These members of what Lever called "the small but case hardened army of union men" headed up the second prong of labor's assault on the Philadelphia metal trades Open Shop, winning recruits in the nonelectrical heavy machine works where neither the UE nor the Communists had made much effort or progress.[8]

By the end of the year Philco Local 102's correspondent, operating under the pseudonym "Yip-Yip-Yippee," which gives some flavor of the consistently upbeat tone of his reports, could write confidently in the *People's Press* that "Philly is getting to be more nearly a 100 percent union town than ever in its history." The UE, by far the strongest CIO organization in the area, determined to seize the time "to make the city of Philadelphia the best organized city in the country."[9]

The national and local political contexts were singularly threatening to the survival of the old systems of employer control; so too were new tactical developments within the world of labor. Inspired by the example of the United Automobile Workers' (UAW) sit-down strikes sweeping through General Motors in the first week of January, members of the AFL federal local at Exide Battery occupied the plant – with 2,469 employees, the fifth largest in Philadelphia metalworking, and the obvious next target after Philco (7,655), Westinghouse (c. 3,500), and G. E. (2,965) – to force the company to bargain on their demand for a 15 percent wage increase. The battery workers' tactics were also influenced by the reaction that they, incor-

[8]   "Union Forging Ahead in Philly-Camden Area," *PP* 31 Oct. 1936, p. 4; "UE & RW Parade in F.D.R. Rally Wins Cheers for Fight on RCA," 7 Nov., p. 3; "So. Philly Westinghouse Now Local 7, UE & RW" and "UE & RW in CIO," 14 Nov., pp. 4–5; Harry Block (vice president, District 1), "New Westinghouse Local Looming in District 1," 21 Nov., p. 9; copy of Golden to Garfield Lewis [SWOC Director, Eastern Pennsylvania], 24 Sept. 1936 and Golden to Lever, 11 Nov. 1936, Box 4, F.16, E. J. Lever Papers, Penn State University; quote from "Excerpts from Report of Field Director E. J. Lever at the Philadelphia District Convention, Saturday, December 10, 1938" in SWOC Lodge 1839 paper, n.d., p. 3, in Box 13, F.11, Lever Papers. For more on Golden and the SWOC drive, see Robert R. R. Brooks, *As Steel Goes: Unionism in a Basic Industry* (New Haven, 1940), p. 182.

[9]   Yip-Yip-Yippee, "Philco Notes: 102 Ramblings," *PP* 28 Nov. 1936, p. 9; "District Council 1 Takes Leading Part in Phila. CIO," 30 Jan. 1937, p. 2; UE District Council No. 1 Minutes, 19 Nov. 1936, Harry Block Collection, University of Pittsburgh (hereafter UE Minutes).

rectly, anticipated from their employers. As UE District One Vice President Harry Block explained, "[a]gainst the well-known strike breaking methods of the Manufacturers Association" – of which, ironically, Exide was not a member, and which certainly no longer had the stomach for a fight – "the sitdown strike was the best method of showing the employer the solidarity of the organized local."[10]

The strike lasted seven weeks, during which the UE offered unstinting support while the AFL's officials stood carping on the sidelines. The strikers – male, and mostly middle-aged – occupied themselves with games and cleaning up the plant: Their only casualty injured himself slipping on a bar of soap in the showers. They were firmly in control, briefly restarting production at the request of veteran Taylorite Morris Ll. Cooke, by then head of the Rural Electrification Administration, to rush out huge batteries needed for disaster relief in the Ohio Valley. Jack Lever was the intermediary who negotiated this deal, stressing to Cooke that "it is to be clearly understood that your relations as a government official is (*sic*) directly with the striking battery workers union and not with the employer." Cooke accepted those terms, and thanked these men, whom others called law-breakers, for their public spirit. "It goes to prove that when confidence is placed in organized workers, they will do the right thing every time."[11]

The Exide sitdowners had nothing to fear from the city and state governments. There was no disorder, no provocative policing or judicial intervention. Instead, Mayor Wilson's Labor Committee settled the strike by a three-month truce on the men's terms – an immediate wage increase, a week's paid vacation, recognition of their union as sole bargaining agency, a joint committee to adjust wage rates on any disputed job, and an agreement that the vote on the lasting settlement to be negotiated during the truce period must be taken while the men were at work, so that they could resume the sitdown if necessary. The strike ended with the union much more strongly organized than it had ever been – it claimed 90 percent membership – and ready to join the UE by a unanimous vote.[12]

So by the end of February 1937 the UE was in possession of three of the

[10] "All Battery Production Halts in Pay-Rise Move," *ULR* 8 Jan. 1937, p. 1; Harry Block, "Exide Strikers Sit Tight: Refuse Company Offer to Talk If Men Get Out of Plant," *PP* 13 Feb. 1937, p. 9.

[11] Block, "District 1 Pledges Unqualified Support to Exide Battery Strike," *PP* 16 Jan., p. 8; Block, "American Federation of Labor Holds Off on Granting Benefits for Exide Sitdown Strikers," 23 Jan., p. 4; Martin Cassidy, "UE & RW Organizer Eats His Supper With Exide Boys," 13 Feb., p. 9; "Exide Strike Model of Efficiency and Discipline," 20 Feb., p. 6; "Exide Strikers Ship Emergency Order for Use in Flooded Area" and "Sitdowners Aid," 6 Feb., pp. 9, 2.

[12] "Exide Strikers Agree Of (*sic*) Increase Promise to Truce Within Wages," *PP* 20 Feb., p. 9; "Exide Strikers Win! Get 5¢ Raise and Vacation With Pay," 27 Feb., p. 4; "Exide Joins UE & RW By Unanimous Vote," 20 Mar., p. 4.

five largest plants in the Philadelphia metal-working industries, with an aggregate labor force of c.14,000. Budd, the second largest with 6,338 employees, was an Open Shop holdout, and the UE still had a hard road ahead of it at G. E.; but otherwise the commanding heights had been won. The SWOC was organizing the sixth through ninth largest plants, Disston Saw (2,450), Midvale Steel (2,431), SKF (1,835), and Brill (1,557), working to take over company unions or to revive dormant federal locals. At the tenth largest plant, Crown Can (1,310), the UE was once again active and showing Philadelphia workers' unaccustomed, confident militancy: Martin Cassidy, now district organizer, put his pickets on roller skates so that "Even the cops couldn't say those birds didn't 'keep moving.'" As the *People's Press* exulted, "Unionism [is] Sweeping America," and for once Philadelphia metalworkers were in the vanguard of what Cassidy called "the mighty army of labor . . . . building a New America."[13]

11.3 CHANGING TACK, SAVING FACE

What could the MMA, most of whose members were rather attached to the old America, do about this? General Motors had settled with the UAW; the SWOC was on the point of winning recognition from U.S. Steel. City, state, and federal governments backed labor's cause. Workers were confident, aggressive, and in short supply. The economy was booming, and strikes were accordingly expensive as well as risky. The MMA executive committee's anxious observation of the Exide sit-down, and fear that the tactic would become general with no local law enforcement to stop it, compelled a reexamination of strategy and tactics.

The way in which this was done recalled the change of direction toward "progressivism" in the early 1920s. New times required new policies, and the best way to get them was with new leadership. Link-Belt's general manager Morehead, still unreconciled to the New Deal dispensation, was succeeded as president by George Benzon, Jr., an industrial engineer and vice president of William Sellers, who had served on the MMA executive committee since 1927 and been a long-time member of the progressives' committee on personnel matters. And an entirely new man was brought in, Clarence Tolan, Jr., vice president of the Dodge Steel Co. (a division of Link-Belt), to head a new high-level committee on labor relations meeting every month before the executive committee itself. At the committee's inaugural meeting Tolan made the most remarkable personal statement

[13] Cassidy, "Philadelphia Workers Turn to CIO For Aid," *PP* 30 Jan., p. 9; "Radio Club Makes Hit With Candidate Nites," 6 Feb., p. 6; front page headline, 13 March; Cassidy, "Philadelphia GE Workers Fight Company Unionism," 20 March, p. 4. Progress in organizing at Disston and Brill was thoroughly reported in the *ULR* 29 Jan.–21 May, 1937.

recorded in the MMA's papers, underlining the fact that he was setting a new course:

> At the outset I think I should tell you that I am a New Dealer, and accepted the offer to become a member of your Council, and of this Committee, only after this was clearly understood by those who sponsored me. However, I am not a radical – I favor a fair deal for both employer and employee. I am against Sit-Down Strikes and unscrupulous labor racketeers. I strongly favor an open-minded and intelligent study of Employer–Employee relations, and the adoption of a concerted plan of action that will enable us to anticipate the activities of labor agitators, and by this I do not mean all labor leaders. . . .
>
> [L]et us do those intelligent and fair things for our employees that have not always been done in the past, and the failure to do [which] has given the worst element of labor leaders the opportunity to agitate. Our job is to beat them to it.[14]

Belligerent anti-unionism must be abandoned; in its place the association should return to the strategy of 1920s progressivism, the adoption and pursuit of positive personnel policies, but with a vigor and general commitment not seen when there was no rival state and labor movement to compel them to do the right thing. Members should "review what we are doing about hours of work, overtime, unemployment, minimum wages, living wages, wage dividends, and develop together ideas and plans that would strengthen our position with our employees, and the general public."[15]

So much for the long term. But what of the immediate crisis? At the committee's second meeting, just after the end of the Exide sit-down, the Disston representative reported that they "had received from employees in their several departments a request in the nature of a 'round robin' for a 25 percent increase in wages, an eight-hour day, forty-hour week." Jack Lever had telephoned asking for an appointment to introduce his bargaining committee. The company had declined, attempting to hold to the appearance of unilateral control by deciding "that they would that afternoon post on their bulletin board an announcement of a general 10 percent increase in wages." The company was under pressure: It had already experienced a short sit-down in one department and feared more.[16]

Without drama, three decades of Open Shop policy were discarded in an

---

[14]   MMA-EXEC and PHILCHAP databases; Minutes of the First Meeting of the Committee on Labor Relations and "Mr. Tolan's Statement," ECM 1 Feb. 1937.

[15]   "Mr. Tolan's Statement"; cf. Memorandum on Employer-Employee Relations, 3 March 1937, MMAP II-4-21.

[16]   Second Meeting of the Committee on Labor Relations, ECM 24 Feb. 1937; Harry C. Silcox, *A Place to Live and Work: The Henry Disston Saw Works and the Tacony Community of Philadelphia* (University Park, 1994), p. 147, states that "There was never a threat of a strike during the three weeks of talks leading to the agreement," but this begs the question of the role of the earlier strike in getting the company to the bargaining table, and of implicit but credible threats in keeping it there.

instant. Ever since the Pattern Makers' League's business agent had asked for a meeting in 1905, the MMA had adhered to NFA–NMTA wisdom: "Ignore the officials."[17] The tool-and-die settlements of the previous year showed, by their convoluted language, the last desperate attempts to main tain the fiction of nonrecognition. Now Earl Sparks himself counseled that Disston should accept reality:

if they thought Mr. Lever represented a group of their employees . . . . it seemed to be the wisest course for them to meet him . . . . [I]t had been the policy of the Association that as an organization they did not recognize labor unions and that the Secretary should not meet labor union representatives . . . . [I]n view of developments of recent months . . . . it might be this policy should be modified somewhat and . . . . if he could be useful he might be present as an agent for member companies when they are discussing their employer–employee relations.[18]

Sober negotiations, organization to organization, professional to professional, with the MMA in its usual service role as advisor, strategist, and coordinator, were better than disorderly, unpredictable, and unregulated conflict. This point was swiftly underlined when the proceedings were interrupted by news of a quickie strike in another member's machine shop. He asked for work to be resumed until he could meet his men's representatives, and left in a hurry.

And that, more or less, was that. In April, IAM Local 1555 began to renegotiate the path-breaking tool-and-die and machine shop contracts at the end of their first year. The resulting documents were much fuller and less tentative. They were not completely standardized – the "production" shops bargained hard, and in any case their larger and more heterogeneous workforces required more complex, detailed provisions – but the job shops signed up to almost exactly uniform terms.

This time, every agreement was called an agreement – the days of "Memoranda of Understanding" were gone for good. The parties were the companies and the union, which joined its more natural associates in the UE as Local 155 in June and was recognized as a principal rather than just as its members' agent. The union's full-time officers, with or without the shop committees' chairs, signed on the workers' behalf.

The previous year's gains were built on, and the concessions that had had to be made then (e.g., on emergency work, regard for competence in layoffs and recall) were eliminated. The jobbers agreed to operate formal union shops. The union was to be their primary source of labor; only if it could not meet their needs were they allowed to hire on the open market, and workers so recruited were to join the union within a week. Wage and hour provisions were spelled out in detail, as were controls on the status, pay,

---

[17] See Chapter Four; O. P. Briggs, "Ignore the Officials!" *Open Shop* 6:1 (Jan. 1907): 21–22.

[18] Second Meeting of the Committee on Labor Relations, ECM 24 Feb. 1937.

and numbers of apprentices – one for every ten journeymen and one for the shop, the old craft union standard. Toolmakers' minimum wages were raised to the union's $1 an hour goal. Seniority became the only guide to layoff, recall, and shift allocation decisions, and "just and sufficient" cause the only grounds for suspension or discharge, of which the shop committee must be advised.[19]

In the production shops, union security was not unknown, but exclusive recognition combined with a nondiscrimination pledge was more usual. Toolmakers' and journeymen's minimum wages were set at the jobbing shop rate, and their differentials over machine operators, assemblers, and laborers (and, within the latter categories, of one job over another, and men over women) were spelled out to produce precise, published pay scales. Piece and premium workers were promised that their rates would be set at incentive levels that would allow them to earn at least 15 to 25 percent above the minimum for their job. Apprenticeship provisions followed the job shop model, as did those for layoff and recall, save that "Knowledge, training, ability, skill and efficiency" were still sometimes supposed to count, after seniority had been given the greatest weight.[20]

The most significant differences between the job and production shops were that the latter, with their more complex managerial hierarchies, several departments, and interrelated operations, devised formal multistage dispute resolution procedures to minimize sectional strikes. These required grievances to be put in writing, specified the maximum length of time allowed at each stage, and began to provide for impartial arbitration as the last resort. The Mitchell Specialty (auto parts) contract emphasized the "contracting parties'" absolute agreement "that there shall be no stoppage of work, no interference with the functions of the plant until all of this procedure has been exhausted." The UE was becoming "responsible"; the industrial jurisprudence of "workplace contractualism" was rapidly taking shape.[21]

All of these agreements stressed, as their overall purpose, the establishment of "equitable conditions for collective bargaining," the promotion of "cooperation and harmony" between employer and employees, and maintaining "the utmost teamwork between fellow employees" the better to advance, as the Wilkening Mfg. (piston rings) agreement put it, "the success of the Employer's enterprise."[22]

These agreements, which were all negotiated with a militant but disci-

[19]   ECM 23 Apr. 1937. Agreements – job shops: C. A. Spaulding, 14 Apr.; Penn Instrument Co., 3 May; Philadelphia Metal Stamping Co., 8 June; production shops: Mitchell Specialty 30 June, Ocean City Mfg., 13 Aug., Wilkening Mfg., 22 Oct. – all in uncataloged UE District 1 records, UE/Labor Archives, Univ. of Pittsburgh.
[20]   Agreement, Mitchell Specialty.
[21]   Ibid.
[22]   Agreements cited in note 19.

plined, Communist-led, craft-based union aiming for inclusive coverage of Philadelphia's small- and mid-sized metal-working firms, promised employers a stable, predictable, and tolerable future. Uniform conditions governing basic working conditions for all local competitors for business and labor would henceforth be negotiated at annual intervals and adhered to in the meanwhile. All might have to run the risk of a strike at contract renewal time, but none would find himself placed at a disadvantage in the final settlement. At the cost of a certain loss of flexibility, they had gained much; and the MMA, in its new guise as labor relations counselor, would help them as a group with their bargaining difficulties.[23]

The process of adjustment for the MMA and its members was hastened by continuing governmental pressures, among which the Supreme Court's decisions in the Wagner Act cases in April were key: As the *People's Press* proclaimed, they removed the "Last Barrier to Labor's Triumph." The MMA's legal strategy of 1936 – trusting to the electorate or the courts for deliverance, and ignoring the law in the meanwhile – was dead and buried. Even before *Jones & Laughlin*, the MMA Executive was becoming tired of Brown & Williams's predictable, useless opinions. Clarence Tolan, Jr., wondered whether "the Association's legal advice might better be secured from some attorneys with a more liberal viewpoint and reputation." Good counsel was vital, because the net of regulation was ever tightening: First came the La Follette Committee investigation; second, Pennsylvania's "Little New Deal," enacted in the General Assembly's historic January-to-June session; and, third, the Supreme Court's green light to New Deal economic and social policy. The MMA and its members had to adapt to operate within this new framework. Evasion was still possible, but not escape.[24]

11.4 TOWARD A NEW ERA

The most important effect of these pressures on the MMA itself was to compel it to reform and reevaluate the role of its Employment Department. The MMA had succeeded in persuading the La Follette Committee's investigators that it was doing "a legitimate business in a lawful manner"; but nevertheless, after that scrutiny, the Wagner Act cases, and the enactment of new state laws, it was forced to eliminate information about union affiliation and activities from its individual records, and to stay out of the strike-

---

[23]   Loss of flexibility: Charles J. Post to John Steelman, 29 Nov. 1939, and "In the Matter of the Arbitration Between F. C. Castelli Co. and Machine Tool and Die Local No. 155 UERMWA-CIO," 27 March 1939, in FMCS 199-4758.

[24]   "Court Removes Last Barrier to Labor's Triumph," *PP* 17 Apr. 1937, p. 3; Minutes of the 2nd. Meeting of the Labor Relations Committee, 2 Feb. 1937, p. 2.

breaking business. The National Industrial Council's advice after the Wagner Act cases was that keeping information that might be used for anti-union discrimination by member firms could "be construed by the Board as interference with the right to organize." At the same time state regulation of employment departments was tightened up, and striker replacement recruiting was generally prohibited. The MMA changed its record-keeping and lived within the law.[25]

Pressures on the Employment Department did not end there. Pennsylvania had also set up an unemployment insurance system to comply with the requirements of the Social Security Act. Advising members on how to cope with these (and other) laws added to the MMA's role as a source of authoritative counsel. But they also further undermined the association's old core function of labor market management. It was under attack in any case, from the development of firm-specific internal labor markets and layoff/rehire systems that the welfare capitalist response to the Depression had begun, and the spread of unionization further encouraged and formalized. Competition from unions like Local 155, whose contracts specified that it should be a or *the* source of new labor, and from the state, finished the job.[26]

In October 1937 the Roosevelt boom peaked. Philadelphia area metal trades employment exceeded the 1929 maximum by 6 percent. Thereafter employment collapsed by about 42 percent over the next ten months (see Figure 9.2). Providentially on 1 January 1938 workers became eligible to receive their first state unemployment compensation benefits. But to do so they first had to register with the state employment service. This revolutionized the range and quality of workers that it had on its books and turned it into the city's best-placed recruitment agency, with which the MMA decided to cooperate rather than compete. The service operated under strict rules: As its director, William Collier, told the district Unemployment Council Meeting,

The law will not allow anyone to be forced to take employment under the following conditions: 1. when a strike or lock-out is in progress; 2. when conditions of employment: i.e., wages, hours, and working conditions are less satisfactory than those prevailing in the industry [which usually meant union rates]; 3. where, as a condition of employment, the worker will be forced to join a company union, or to refrain or be restrained from joining and participating in a bona-fide labor organization.[27]

[25] SEC 1936, p. 5; SEC 1937, pp. 4–6; Memorandum of the Meeting of the National Industrial Council at the Biltmore Hotel, ECM 22 Apr. 1937.
[26] SEC 1937, p. 3; SEC 1938, p. 4; ECM 19 Dec. 1939, p. 3; SEC 1939, p. 5.
[27] Ruby Weil, "Job Insurance – At Last," *PP* 15 Jan. 1938, p. 7; Unemployment Council Meeting, 29 Nov. 1937, pp. 1–2, in UE Minutes. In the state as a whole, employment service registrations increased from about 50,000 a month in August 1936–October 1937 to 160,000 per month in January 1938 – Pennsylvania Department of Labor and Industry, *Biennium Report 1937–1938* (Harrisburg, 1939), p. 55.

Unions' strike-support costs would also be greatly reduced: Strikers were to receive unemployment compensation, though after double the waiting period for the "normal" unemployed. And unions were granted an explicit role as advocates of their members' interests if there was any dispute over eligibility for benefit. Pennsylvania's was thus a remarkably union-friendly unemployment insurance law. It underpinned the state's other 1937 reforms (including the "Little Wagner Act" for companies doing intrastate business, the anti–strike-breaker recruitment law, limitations on the carrying of weapons by industrial police, and an anti-injunction law) to create a regulatory environment comprehensively supportive toward the labor movement. As the *People's Press*'s Fred Gendral enthused "Something's Happening in Pennsylvania; Coal and Steel Barons Quake" – "You Wouldn't Know Pennsylvania Now."[28]

Adjustment for the larger MMA members that still had open shops or company unions was harder than for the smaller fry covered by Local 155, because they had more to lose, less to gain, and more options. The full meaning of the Wagner Act remained unclear in 1937, and Philadelphia firms, even those reconciled to union recognition, were unsure how far they had to go, or needed to.

Westinghouse, for example, did not dispute the representative status of its UE locals, and even accepted the inclusion of salaried workers within the UE bargaining unit. But it refused to sign any collective agreement until compelled to do so by the NLRB in 1940. Instead, the company summarized the results of bargaining in "Statements of Policy" that it posted in its plants, and to which it adhered – sometimes, of course, because the UE compelled it to by "disciplinary" strikes – until it wished to alter them. Westinghouse claimed that this gave it flexibility and other benefits; the NLRB ruled that it deprived the UE of the full status that it deserved, and stood in the way of the development of a "set procedure for the peaceful determination of grievances and other disputes" that would "fulfill the purposes of the Act by insuring industrial peace and stability."[29]

As for the companies that were wholly unreconciled to the new law, they

[28] *PP* 13 Feb. 1937, p. 7, 3 July, p. 1.
[29] For the parent corporation, see Derber, "Electrical Products," pp. 763–65, 771–2; "In the Matter of Westinghouse Electric & Manufacturing Co. . . . ," 22 NLRB 147-183 (1940) [quotes]. For local developments, see "Westinghouse Yields Sole Bargaining Right to Philadelphia Local," *PP* 29 May 1937, p. 5; "Westinghouse White Collar Workers Join," 10 July, p. 8; "Westinghouse Refuses Fair Play to Workers," 21 Aug., p. 5; Tom Wright, " 'We Are Dealing With Mental Corpses'," 11 Sept., p. 8 [on Westinghouse's attitude]; "Westinghouse Sets Up Law Evasion School," 23 Apr. 1938, p. 8; Preliminary Report and Progress Report of Commissioner of Conciliation P. W. Chappell, 29 June 1938, copy of M. H. Goldstein (UE Attorney) to Bennett F. Schauffler (NLRB), 30 June, Progress Report, 1 July, all in FMCS 196-673; "UE Moves Ahead in Three Westinghouse Plants" and "Labor Forced to Take Disciplinary Measures Against Westinghouse," *PP* 29 Oct. 1938, pp. 1, 3.

had some nasty shocks in store. S. L. Allen, for example, found that, under the new dispensation, you could win a strike, at great cost, destroy a union, and rehire acceptable former employees as individuals – and still, months later, discover that the union you had smashed continued to enjoy representative status! You had to agree to "cease and desist" from your "unfair labor practices," bargain collectively with an organization that barely existed, rehire remaining former strikers who remained unemployed, and post notices agreeing to obey the law! George Pilling discovered that you could undermine a weakly established union by threats and blandishments, persuade your employees to abandon it without a fight – and still be compelled to recognize and bargain with it. And even the giant RCA came to understand that, as the *People's Press* exulted, "It's Expensive to Fire Members of UE–CIO."[30]

There were shifting sands beneath labor law in the late 1930s but, to mix the metaphor, the tide was mostly flowing in one direction. It took a great deal of determination and resources to delay change, like Westinghouse, or to positively obstruct it, like Link-Belt and G. E. Link-Belt encouraged the establishment of its first "Employee Independent Union" after the Wagner Act cases were decided, and sustained it through years of legal challenge, until the Steel Workers' final victory in 1946. G. E.'s Philadelphia management steered its established company union toward independence as the "Independent Switchgear Organization," fighting the UE's organizational efforts to a standstill at the same time as G. E. nationally was sitting down to bargain.[31]

Most MMA members and other area metal-working firms, however, were

[30] NLRB C-60, Petition for the Enforcement of an Order of the NLRB, 27 Aug. 1937; Answer of Company, Case No. 6558, October Term 1937; Stipulation [Consent Decree], 12 Jan. 1938; "In the Matter of George P. Pilling & Son Co. and Dental, Surgical and Allied Workers Local Industrial Union No. 119, Affiliated With the CIO," 16 NLRB 650-66 (1939); Matles and Higgins, *Them and Us*, p. 59; PP 26 March 1938, p. 6.

[31] Kathy Burgess, "An Unprecedented Endeavor: The Employees' Independent Union of the Link-Belt Company," unpublished essay, Univ. of Pennsylvania, 1985, esp. pp. 21–26, and "Heading Off the CIO: The Employees' Independent Union of the Link-Belt Company," unpublished essay, n.d., esp. pp. 12–19 [copies in author's possession, gratefully used with author's permission] – a version of these is available in her "Organized Production and Unorganized Labor: Management Strategy and Labor Activism at the Link-Belt Company, 1900–1940" in Daniel Nelson, ed., *A Mental Revolution: Scientific Management Since Taylor* (Columbus, 1992), pp. 130–55; Martin Cassidy, "Philadelphia GE Workers Fight Company Unionism," PP 20 March 1937, p. 4; "Stooges Duck at Philadelphia GE," 21 Aug., p. 5; "GE Company Union Is Folding Up" and "GE Jottings," 4 Sept., pp. 4, 5; "UE & RW Files Charges Against Company Union in Philadelphia GE," 2 Oct., p. 8; George McGinn, "Crowd Overflows Philadelphia Hall" (detailing employees' concerns about the effects of unionization), 23 Oct., p. 10; Carl Bersing, "I.S.O. End Opens Door for Real Collective Bargaining at GE Co.," 5 March 1938, p. 9 and "GE Workers Spurn New Attempt to Set Up Company Union," 12 March, p. 9; "GE Local Is Ready to Seek Certification," 19 March, p. 9; "Philadelphia GE Workers to Vote UE This Week – GE Con-

not so resolute. In the face of a union presence in their shops, and an NLRB that won almost every case a company appealed, they gave way reasonably gracefully – like Fayette R. Plumb, which held its own secret ballot election once it learned that the SWOC was organizing in its plant, and called in Jack Lever after its company union lost; or even RCA itself, which fired General Hugh Johnson after the Jones & Laughlin decision, hired Assistant Secretary of Labor Ed McGrady in his place, and proceeded to put its relations with the UE on a settled footing. Surrender was not unproblematic – companies found themselves trapped in jurisdictional disputes between the AFL and CIO, or in intra-union disputes that took some Philadelphia locals from the AFL into the CIO (or, more rarely, vice versa), or from both into an independence of which the NLRB was justifiably suspicious. But the achievement of a new stability, rather than resistance, principled or otherwise, quickly became the principal object that companies pursued, and the MMA fostered.[32]

11.5 STASIS AND EQUILIBRIUM

The solidification of the realist consensus was fostered by two further developments of 1937–39. First, the labor relations policies of the premier expo-

tract Growing as Plants Organize," 23 Apr., p. 1 (detailing the last-minute intervention of a Rev. Naugle and the anti-Communist Minute Men and Women of America); "GE Employees Building Union for Final Victory" and James Matles, "The National Office Says," 30 Apr., p. 2 – the election was lost 595 to 772, the first UE defeat, but one that was soon reversed – Derber, "Electrical Products," pp. 752–53. Leeds & Northrup's Cooperative Association also became an independent union – William P. Vogel, *Precision, People, and Progress: A Business Philosophy at Work* (Philadelphia, 1949), p. 43.

32   "Smart Firm Polls Workers Then Calls in SWOC to Bargain," *ULR* 7 May 1937, p. 5; "RCA and UE&RW to Open Negotiations This Week," 1 May, p. 4; "RCA Contract Milestone in Radio Organization," 16 Oct., p. 3; "RCA Pact Pulls 'Em In at Camden," 6 Nov., p. 1; Irving Bernstein, *Turbulent Years: A History of American Workers, 1933–1939* (Boston, 1969), p. 610; Matles and Higgins, *Them and Us*, p. 59; "Union Seeks Writ Against NLRB – Molders Ask Injunction To End CIO Recognition in Hatboro Plants," *Philadelphia Evening Bulletin* (hereafter *PEB*) 12 Sept. 1938; "In the Matter of Roberts & Manders Stove Co., Hatboro Foundry Co. and International Molders' Union of North America," 16 NLRB 943-50 (1939) [the SWOC narrowly secured representation in a consent election and forced the company to bargain and to grant a closed shop in successive sit-downs; the Molders protested the violation of their historic jurisdiction, without success]; "In the Matter of Henry Disston & Sons, Inc. and Steel Workers Organizing Committee, Lodge 1073" 21 NLRB 856-62 (1940) and 22 NLRB 959-60 (1940) [the SWOC, insecurely rooted, called for an election to guarantee its representative status, was challenged by a newly established AFL federal local, and lost; see also Silcox, *A Place to Live and Work*, pp. 150–51]; "In the Matter of Heintz Manufacturing Company and United Automobile Workers Federal Labor Union No. 18454, Affiliated with the American Federation of Labor," 24 NLRB 1011-17 (1940) [see below].

nents in Philadelphia of an alternative, concessive approach exploded in their faces. Second, the economy went over a precipice; the New Deal stalled; labor's onward march was halted; and employers were given a strengthened bargaining position, renewed self-confidence, and time to complete their adjustment to new ways.

Mayor Wilson's hand-picked "representatives" of the metal-working industries on his Labor Board were George Deming of Philco and William J. Meinel, president of Heintz Mfg. Co., a large jobbing pressed metal shop with almost 800 employees. Meinel (b. 1893) was a Philadelphia success story to compare with the men we met in Chapter Two. A local boy, he had studied mechanical engineering at the Franklin Institute and business administration at Temple Evening School while pursuing an apprenticeship in a small (c. 30 employees) machine shop that was an MMA member. He joined the Erectors' Union but did not stay a journeyman for long, rising fast to become shop superintendent by the time he was twenty, and leaving when he was twenty-three to supervise Edward Budd's machine shop, and eventually work as Budd's vice president and operations director. He left Budd in 1932, finding his independence at Heintz, a ten-year-old auto body parts supplier that was devastated by the Depression and headless because of the death of its founder, Leo Heintz, one of Budd's original cadre of skilled metal-benders. Heintz had been an MMA member, but its succession crisis and near-bankruptcy had forced it to withdraw.[33]

When Meinel took over, the company had only nineteen employees, less than a twentieth of its pre-Depression average. Meinel built it back up, slashing wages and desperately chasing business wherever he could find it. But when in August 1933 his men formed an AFL federal local and struck for union recognition, a raise, and the reduction of working hours from 49½ to 40, Meinel dealt with them very differently than his old boss Budd. He "agree[d] to adjust . . . . differences in dispute in a just and equitable manner so far, and as quickly, as is possible to do so." The company and the union appointed a mutually acceptable arbitrator to decide any unresolved issues, whose judgment was to be final and binding on both sides and awards fully retroactive. Heintz management later "acknowledge[d] their plant is unionized and that they are dealing with union shop committees" and told federal conciliator Chappell, who helped them toward this settlement, that "they have no intention of trying to change this condition." Concern for the company's standing with its creditors and open shop customers alone prevented them from going public and signing a contract at the time, but a durable private relationship was established nonethe-

[33] For Heintz, see PID16-40 and MMAYEARS databases; for Meinel, "William J. Meinel Dies At 68; Industrialist, Civic Leader," *PEB* 17 Nov. 1961; "Heintz Co. Squeezes Shells Out of Steel Like Toothpaste," *PEB* 5 Oct. 1952; Meinel testimony in Formal File, Heintz Mfg. Co. Case C-1316, NLRB Records.

less. From 1935 on – that is, after the Wagner Act was passed but before Jones & Laughlin – the company recognized FLU No. 18454 as the exclusive bargaining agent of its employees.[34]

Meinel had thus earned his place on Mayor Wilson's Labor Committee, like Deming, for his early embrace of unionization. Heintz was a model employer; Meinel congratulated himself on the fact that "Being a man from the ranks myself I have an appreciation of the workers (*sic*) problems." But in early 1937 the United Automobile Workers–CIO began organizing in his factory. By that time, he had secured solid financial support for his now-booming firm – from Eugene Grace of Bethlehem Steel, whose son was installed as vice president and treasurer. Meinel's tough response to the CIO challenge may have been affected by the need to conform to his backer's policies while the "Little Steel" strike was at its height.[35]

To settle the rivalry between the UAW and the federal local, Meinel agreed to a secret ballot election in his plant in June, which the UAW won by 389 votes to 380. But after their narrow victory the Auto Workers overplayed their hand, demanding the discharge of four FLU officials in their struggle to take over the local's funds as well as its bargaining rights. Meinel refused, discharged two UAW officers, and was hit from both sides, with the CIO sitting down against him and the AFL men sitting down against the CIO! After a five day occupation the men left the plant, on the understanding that Meinel would reinstate the two men that he had fired and negotiate a contract. But Meinel's attorney – Ira J. Williams – denied that there was any such agreement; and Meinel declared that he would "not enter into a written contract with a group which is not responsible, is undependable, and has not the interest of the employees at heart."[36]

A violent and prolonged mass picket followed in which the UAW brought in other CIO supporters from Philadelphia and its suburbs. Meinel witnessed two strikers thrashing their opponents with lead pipes concealed in paper bags. Dominic Sacco "was beaten so badly that his memory was partially destroyed and he [wa]s unable to identify his assailants" – a hard-earned wisdom. Meinel himself was threatened. A picket stuck his head through the window of Meinel's car and told his chauffeur "'Take your boss back to the factory. Take him right away, and bear in mind the

[34] Meinel testimony; Meinel to Homer J. Brown, 21 Aug. 1933; Preliminary Report of Commissioner of Conciliation, 23 Aug.; Chappell to Hugh L. Kerwin, 15 and 17 Oct., all in FMCS 176-138.

[35] Meinel to Hines, 3 Apr. 1937, Box 1, F. 7, Hines Papers; "In the Matter of Heintz Mfg. Co.," p. 1014; "Grace Named Head of Heintz – Meinel to Remain as Board Chairman," *PEB* 15 June 1955.

[36] "Union Faction Sues for $3,000," *PEB* 24 June 1937; "'Sit-Down Protest' Held," 14 Jul., "Sitdowners Close Heintz Plant," 15 Jul.; "350 Heintz Workers End 5-Day Sitdown, Strike Not Settled," clipping, 18 Jul., FMCS 199-162; "Heintz President Charges Threat," *PEB* 29 Jul.

boss' car isn't bullet proof'." Meinel responded to the crisis with lasting anger and an unsuccessful attempt to secure an injunction. The federal district court denied his request and in the end Meinel had to rely on Mayor Wilson, who had the UAW leader and many of his violent followers locked up.[37]

After about two months the strike collapsed, and the UAW with it; and so had the second-longest attempt at cooperative labor relations in the Philadelphia metal trades. When UAW activists – who had by that time seceded to the AFL – began to organize again in 1939, Meinel would emulate Budd and encourage straw bosses and disillusioned former CIO loyalists to found an independent union, the Heintz Employees Protective Association, which survived the AFL's challenge, an NLRB investigation, and successive representation elections against the UAW–CIO, for the next fifteen years.[38]

As for Philco, there too the story of union–management harmony would end in tears in the summers of 1937 and 1938. Its three locals and the strategically vital Teamsters, about 8,500 men and women in all, struck in May 1937. They were protesting the company's refusal of their wage-and-hour demands and complaining about "speed-up and discrimination" by management, slow grievance settlement, an unsatisfactory seniority system, and – significantly – the company's increasing tendency to subcontract work rather than relying on its own expensive workforce, with their generous thirty-six-hour week. A good-humored, self-confident, mile-long picket line surrounded the plant, with the strikers' banners proclaiming "We Share the Work, Let's Share the Profits." Finally, after a four-week strike, the strikers won, defending the four-and-a-half day week, raising average wages about 9 percent, getting a guaranteed 25 percent bonus from what had started out as an incentive pay system, and forcing management to improve grievance handling. Philco had been getting "somewhat hardboiled" – now the UE had "showed that it could be hardboiled too, if necessary." Philco could not hold out – the busy season was about to begin and RCA was negotiating with UE, not fighting it, and stealing a march in the market.[39]

---

[37] "Two Strikers Held in $10,000 Each," *PEB* 4 Aug. 1937; "Auto Bodies – 10 Men Arrested for Attack on Dominic Sacco, 5934 Norwood St., Aug. 12th.," clipping, n.d., FMCS 199-162; "Heintz President Charges Threat"; "Injunction Denied Heintz Company," *PEB* 30 July; "3 Heintz Strikers Jailed by Mayor," 6 Aug., "CIO Chief, 20 Men Held for Assault in Heintz Strike," 19 Aug.

[38] Investigation by John E. Johnson, Field Examiner, 22 March 1939 and Bennett F. Schauffler to Nathan Witt, 4 Apr. 1939 in Office File, Case IV-C-623, NLRB Records; Brief of Intervenor Contra Exceptions to Intermediate Report, Formal File, Case C-1316, NLRB Records; "In the Matter of Heintz Mfg. Co.," pp. 1014–17; "Heintz Workers Keep Independent Union," *PEB* 27 June 1954.

[39] "Drivers Back Up UE & RW" and "Philco on Strike; Four Locals Out," *PP* 8 May 1937, pp. 2, 4; "Philco Conference 'Collective Arguing' – Union Stands Fast," 15 May, p. 4; "Philco Settlement Seen Near; Company Ready to Raise Pay," 22 May,

The company was understandably sore, unleashing Boake Carter, commentator on its popular sponsored radio show, to fire some of the opening salvoes in the red-baiting propaganda war against the CIO that, together with the coming recession, would help stop labor in its tracks. Clearly, there had been a sea change in the quality of Philco's relationship with the UE: It was now something that was shaped by the workers' power, not the company's largesse.[40]

Philadelphia labor was at its zenith after the "Greatest Half-Year in History," and the UE was at its center. Matles's machinists ended their brief and unnatural alliance with the IAM and rejoined their separated brethren, Matles becoming the UE's director of organization; the accession of Lodge 1555, renamed Local 155, nudged District One, and therefore the Philadelphia CIO, sharply leftward. Dave Davis's members were on the march: When Tucker Tool and Die made difficulties about renewing its agreement, unlike all of the other machine shops that were "now doing a splendid job," it was struck and penalized for its foolishness by being required to pay its workers for their lost time as a condition of settlement! By the fall, Davis reported that all of his members were working under effective closed shop contracts, and the UE had a dues-paying membership of about 15,000 in the district. District President Harry Block claimed a total membership of about 25,000, almost all of them working "under a signed agreement that gives them either a union shop or sole bargaining agency."[41]

That September the UE held its convention in Philadelphia, its strongest center. The delegates were greeted by Mayor Wilson and Pennsylvania's Lieutenant Governor Thomas Kennedy, the United Mine Workers' Secretary-Treasurer. Their own secretary-treasurer, Julius Emspak, reported on their union's momentous, record-breaking year. Six times more members, ten times more locals, "one period of three months in which the membership of the union doubled . . . one month in which as many locals

p. 4; "9,000 Pickets Prove Union's Strength to Philco Bosses," 29 May, pp. 4, 8; "Philco Union Wins 36-Hour Week – UE&RW Victory Inspires Labor in Quaker City" and "Union Drive Brings More Than Pay Boost to Philco Strikers," 5 June, pp. 2, 5. See also Derber, "Electrical Products," pp. 784–86.

40 "Shut Carter Up Or Insure Jobs, Is 101 Demand," *PP* 24 July, p. 5. Given that the Philco locals were the heart of the UE's right wing, red-baiting them, even at the height of the Popular Front, was decidedly unfair – see Ronald L. Filipelli and Mark D. McColloch, *Cold War in the Working Class: The Rise and Decline of the United Electrical Workers* (Albany, 1995), p. 141.

41 "Labor Ends Greatest Half-Year in History," *PP* 10 July 1937, p. 2; "10,000 Machinists Join – 50,000 More On Way," 12 June, p. 1; "Machinists Local Wins Closed Shop, 5¢ Raise, Strike Pay in Walkout," 17 July, p. 9; Organizers' Reports and Financial Statement, 4 Nov. 1937, UE Minutes; Block, "District One Doubled Membership in 1937," *PP* 25 Dec. 1937, p. 1.

were chartered every week, as the International had a few months ago." It could not continue.[42]

And of course it didn't. The labor unity of the previous year, when even lifelong Republican Lew Hines had supported Labor's Non-Partisan League and joined the Democratic 100 Club, quickly broke down as the AFL–CIO rivalry ripped it apart. In Philadelphia and nationwide, the reaction to labor's threatening triumphs was already under way. In the Apex sit-down, the Hosiery Workers could rely on the city police standing aside, but their action sparked the beginnings of the federal judiciary's rollback campaign against organized labor's "excesses." While the Philco workers were celebrating their victory, Chicago police were committing the Memorial Day Massacre. While Local 155 was humbling Tucker Tool & Die, the UAW's drive on Heintz was collapsing. And as the UE registered its last organizational gains that fall, the recession was about to hit.[43]

Within weeks, the union's preoccupation was self-defense, which its president Harry Block euphemistically termed "consolidation." District One shifted its focus away from continued organization and toward demonstrations against unemployment, lobbying for increased federal work relief, and cooperating with state authorities to get its laid-off members the unemployment benefits or relief payments and WPA jobs to which they were entitled. Local 155, a third of whose c. 800 members were jobless by Christmas 1937, and about 40 percent by the next summer, opened a games center for them to pass their time playing pool, bowls, ping pong, or darts – hardly the stuff of militant unionism.[44]

At Philco, the minimum twenty-eight-hour week could not long be maintained, so huge layoffs began, quickly affecting workers with four years' seniority – that is, all those hired since unionization – and demoralizing the union. By the spring of 1938 about three-quarters of its laborforce were

[42] "Delegates Cheer UE & RW Gains" and "Emspak Reports Membership Soars," *PP* 4 Sept., pp. 1, 2.

[43] Thomas T. Spencer, "Labor is with Roosevelt: The Pennsylvania Labor Non-Partisan League and the Election of 1936, " *Pennsylvania History* 46 (1979): 3–16; M. H. McCloskey, Jr. to Hines, 24 Oct. 1936, in Box 1, F.6, Hines Papers; "A Tragic Error," *ULR* 26 Mar. 1937, p. 8 [on Hines's purge of CIO supporters from the Central Labor Union]; Philip Scranton, *Figured Tapestry: Production, Markets, and Power in Philadelphia Textiles, 1885–1941* (New York, 1989), pp. 491–92; SEC 1937, p. 2; "Phila. Battery Industry Nears 100% Organization," *PP* 4 Sept. 1937, p. 5; "Lamp Strike Ends as 8 Shops Sign Up," 2 Oct., p. 9; "RCA Contract Milestone in Radio Organization," 16 Oct., p. 3.

[44] President's Report, UE Minutes, 4 Aug. 1938; "District Plans Demonstration Against Layoffs," *PP* 11 Dec. 1937, p. 9; Organizers' Reports, 7 July 1938, President's Report, 2 Dec. 1937, 3 Feb. 1938, Financial Statement 4 Nov. 1937, Local Reports 6 Jan. 1938, UE Minutes; Per Capita Reports, July–August 1938, Local 155 Records, UE/Labor Archives; "Machinists Local Opens Game Center," *PP* 22 Jan. 1938, p. 10.

unemployed, the company's rivers of profit had dried up, and its management determined to reverse the previous year's defeats and get their wage costs and working conditions back into line with the rest of the industry. If they could not force the Philco locals to accept their terms, they were prepared to decentralize production to nonunion areas, and to hugely increase the proportion of brought-in components that even Philadelphia-assembled radios contained.

There followed a bitter strike (or lockout) four months' long, which tested Mayor Wilson's pro-labor commitment to the limit when he saw the city threatened with the departure or downsizing of its biggest industrial employer. The financial heart was ripped out of District One just as it faced its first great challenge: It had to fight this battle on the verge of bankruptcy. Dues-paying membership collapsed to about 5,500 by July, and the district's bank balance to $10.33. Philadelphia G.E. workers, in part responding to anti-Communist propaganda and the climate of insecurity, rejected the UE in the first representation election that it had ever lost. This was a vital defeat because it destroyed the union's ability to demand national recognition from the company and left it with little choice but to accept G.E.'s terms.

Philco workers, too, were forced to concede, despite impressive displays of solidarity and an imaginative campaign to promote a nationwide consumer boycott of the products that they only wanted the opportunity to make. The thirty-six-hour week and lax bonus system were surrendered, the company gained the unprecedented stability of a two-and-a-half year contract, and even so most of the jobs lost were not regained. This was partly because of the free hand that the company now had to subcontract work, but also because, with changes in demand and the rise of new competition, it had lost the market leadership that had underpinned its four years of labor peace.[45]

An extraordinary period in the Philadelphia metal trades' labor relations had come to an end. Philco, the biggest surviving obstacle to the victory of the realist consensus among major employers, had seen the error of its ways. The Philco locals, labor's spearhead in 1933, the force behind the machinists' breakthrough in 1936, and the UE's and city CIO's backbone in 1937, had been blunted and broken. The CIO was on the defensive – against unemployment and insecurity; against a resurgent AFL, exploiting employer favoritism, divisions within the workforce, and the CIO's vulnerability on the Communist issue; against the federal courts, ending the period of offi-

---

[45]   Richard Roberts, "Local 101 Acts to Protect Seniority," *PP* 13 Nov. 1937, p. 1; the course of the Philco lockout/strike can be traced in UE Minutes, 3 March–4 Aug. 1938, and *PP* 19 Mar.–1 Oct. 1938, its causes and results in Derber, "Electrical Products," pp. 786–90.

cial toleration during which the sit-down strike had flourished; and against
the Dies Committee of the House of Representatives, which began to give
business and AFL critics, and other redbaiters, a platform for their attacks,
and of which the UE was a prime target.[46]

The Earle administration, and with it Pennsylvania's "Little Wagner Act,"
did not survive the 1938 elections. Labor's gubernatorial candidate, the
Mine Workers' Thomas Kennedy, ran hard in the Democratic primaries but
was thoroughly beaten in both of the state's big cities. Mayor Wilson abandoned his notional Republicanism and ran against Earle for the Senatorial
candidacy of the bitterly divided and discredited Pennsylvania Democratic
Party. He too crashed to defeat in the primaries, but in November the
Republicans won both races handily anyway and reestablished their customary majorities in the state legislature. They quickly and effectively rolled
back the "Little New Deal," cutting employers' costs and weakening
workers' and unions' rights, which had been so recently and tenuously
established. Lew Hines, by now absolutely embittered against the radicals
and industrial unionists with whom he had worked for four years, regained
his old Republican faith and reentered state government as Secretary for
Labor and Industry, a position from which he could very effectively do them
down. At the national level, the Fair Labor Standards Act would be the
last new regulation to which the MMA and its members would have to
adapt. After the off-year elections, the NLRB would be thrown onto the
defensive, and pressure from the Smith Committee established by the dominant conservative coalition in the House, and from the White House,
would begin to change its personnel and to moderate its pro-labor (and
pro-CIO) bias.[47]

Readers might think that what this account of the restoration of a "normal"
– that is, hostile – environment for organized labor is leading up to is a pessimistic conclusion: Nothing much had changed. But they would be wrong.
There is all the difference in the world between reaction, or restabilization,
and restoration. The old order of the Open Shop could not be restored. All
of the leaders of the metal-manufacturing community realized this, and
none of them made an attempt to reverse the course of history. None had
wanted the New Deal collective bargaining system, but all more or less
accepted it. Continuing resistance came from large, once "progressive"
firms – G.E. and Westinghouse – with traditions of employee representa-

[46]   Robert H. Zieger, *The CIO 1935–1955* (Chapel Hill, 1995), Ch. 5 esp., for the
       national context.
[47]   In the state as a whole, metal trades strikes fell to about a third of their 1937 level
       in 1938 – Department of Labor and Industry, *Biennium Report*, p. 61; Richard C.
       Keller, "Pennsylvania's Little New Deal," (Ph.D. diss., Columbia University, 1960),
       Chs. 11, 13, 14; Hines to William Green, 7 June 1939, in Box 3, June 1939 folder,
       Hines Papers.

tion and definite personnel policies, parts of which they tried to sustain in the face of the UE; from Link-Belt, with its ingrained commitment to the defense of its own managerial authority which had distanced it from employee representation in the 1920s and made "independent" unionism the only compromise that it was prepared to make with the Wagner Act even after Jones & Laughlin; and from Heintz, with its singularly bitter experience – for workers and managers – of interunion rivalry.

Elsewhere the story, even at the depths of the 1937–38 recession, was of accommodation to the new order. The remarkable feature of it was not the Philco strike, it was the relatively peaceful bargaining and contract renewal that happened everywhere else in the UE's territory. The tool-and-die shops, for example, did not exploit Local 155's weakness to attempt to get rid of it. Instead, they deepened their relationship by drawing up a single master agreement covering thirteen firms, relying on Local 155 to extend its terms to other companies in the area, agreeing explicitly to do their hiring through the union office, and winning a no-strike pledge in return. During a recession, the union's stabilization service, which took wages, hours, and working conditions out of competition, was particularly valuable for these labor-intensive enterprises. Using the same logic, Dave Davis even succeeded in organizing new territory, the lamp and shade manufacturers, successors to the old chandelier shops, winning an industrywide agreement by the end of the year. This must have been deeply irritating to the Metal Polishers' former business agent, Lew Hines, who had repeatedly tried to achieve the same result from the 'teens through the early 1930s and never succeeded.[48]

By the end of the 1930s there was thus the apparently paradoxical situation of a Communist-led craft union operating as a multiplant local within the UE, finally creating the kind of managed labor market and union–employer association cooperation in metal-working job shops for which their AFL predecessors had worked in vain for decades. The bitter union and employer antagonists of 1936 became, if not exactly amicable, then certainly reconciled. Tensions survived and strikes remained a serious, only partly predictable, possibility. But they occurred within a durable, civilized, mutually beneficial relationship. In 1939, for example, when the economy began to revive, Local 155 pushed for a wage increase. The employers stalled, and James Matles called in the federal conciliators. Charles Post reported to his boss John Steelman with evident amazement on the negotiations that resulted:

[48] "Every Contract Renewed But One," *PP* 13 Aug. 1938, p. 3; "Local 155 Signs City-Wide Pact With Tool and Die Jobbers," 16 Apr., p. 3; "Tolen Signs Closed Shop Contract With Lamp Local 126," 22 Oct., p. 3; "Contract at Eagle Lamp Speeds Local 126 Drive," 3 Dec., p. 3; Local Reports, 5 Jan. 1939, UE Minutes (Local 126 shared the same business agent and strategy as 155).

This conference was unique by reason of the entire lack of acrimony. Discussion was of the frankest and friendly character. (On a previous strike the employers served coffee to the strikers and pickets – it was in the winter. The employers jokingly stated that this time they would serve lemonade owing to the warmer weather. They are quite likley (*sic*) to do it, too.)[49]

The strike occurred, but it was short and peaceful. The owners knew that they could not escape the union – Sparks advised them that the days of strike-breaking were over. They could not stand a long strike – he told them that their major unionized customers would not give them contracts if they had labor trouble. So they had better get used to bargaining, do it as conveniently as they could, and get as much out of it as possible.[50]

The situation in the larger factories was different, but there too stabilization, not conflict, was the theme. At Exide, for example, the contract won after the long sit-down was renewed peacefully at its first anniversary. The company secured a wage cut to tide it through the recession, a no-strike pledge, and binding arbitration by a panel of impartial umpires (including our old friend Joseph Willits) as its *quid pro quo* for not taking too much advantage of its opponent's weakness. "Workplace contractualism" was well and truly established, its roots deepening and extending with every passing year. At the end of 1935, Earl Sparks had seen no formal union agreements within the MMA's territory. Two years later they were ubiquitous. Two years after that, what had so recently been completely unacceptable had become utterly routine.[51]

11.6 A PATH TO THE FUTURE

What role was there for the MMA in this new regime? Some adjustment was required, but not too much. Earl Sparks summed up its new philosophy in his 1937 end-of-year address, arguing that the costs of strike-breaking had become intolerable, and that in any event state and federal law established collective bargaining as a right. Living within the law would eliminate strife on questions of union organization and representation, and open the way to resuming the pursuit of the association's fundamental objective – " 'the promotion of such arrangements between members and their employees as will be to their mutual benefit' ":

Collective bargaining is but a means to an end. The ends sought by employees are proper working conditions, reasonable hours of work, good wages, continuity of

---

[49]   Progress Report, 15 Apr. 1939, FMCS 199-3457.
[50]   ECM May, 6 June 1939.
[51]   "Exide Signs Union Contract With 113," *PP* 6 Aug. 1938, p. 3; SEC 1938, p. 3, SEC 1939, p. 3, reporting a survey of 222 of the larger companies in the area indicating that almost half of their 67,000 employees were covered by agreements with national unions.

employment. It is upon these factors that emphasis has been placed and in furnishing to the members advice and information in this field that your Association has endeavored to be of greater service.[52]

The end of strike-breaking and the withering of the Employment Department did not mean the death of the association. Instead, they freed it of a costly, embarrassing departure from its rationalizing course through the 1920s and released its staff from the everyday routine of placement work and record-keeping. This allowed them to concentrate on providing information and strategic advice of which members had an increasingly urgent need in the new and complicated world of union–management relations and state and federal regulation that the thirties had created and the forties would extend. Furthermore, the MMA was not entirely preoccupied with organizing drives and strikes to the exclusion of more mundane personnel matters, even in the hottest years of the mid-1930s. Thus there was continuity and bureaucratic growth on which Sparks could keep building.

For example, foreman training was resumed in 1934, in cooperation with Penn State's extension service. As companies pursued efficiency in the harsh markets of the early 1930s, strove to cut unit labor costs while real wages were rising, attempted to minimize avoidable labor trouble of their supervisors' making, and tried to keep the latter's loyalty, which unions contested, they had ever more reason to be concerned about the skill, knowledge, and morale of their front-line managers. The MMA was able to answer their needs.[53]

Second, cooperative training programs for machinists and other craftsmen almost disappeared in the early 1930s. Almost, but not quite. By the middle of the decade, Sparks was again noticing, and members were complaining about, a relative shortage of skilled men. So the cooperative program was revived and enrollments rebounded, until by the late 1930s they were exceeding the levels they had reached before the Depression, and it was supplying a larger proportion of Philadelphia metal manufacturing's skilled labor needs than ever before.[54]

[52] SEC 1937, p. 1.

[53] SEC 1935, p. 3 and Report on Summer Activities, p. 1, 1936, p. 4, 1937, p. 5, 1938, p. 5, 1939, p. 2. Cf. Sanford M. Jacoby, *Employing Bureaucracy: Managers, Unions, and the Transformation of Work in Amerian Industry, 1900–1945* (New York, 1985), pp. 229–32, 235–36, 251–53, for similar arguments about the development of personnel management in individual firms in the later 1930s.

[54] SEC 1933, p. 5, 1934, pp. 2–3, 1935, pp. 2–3 and Report on Summer Activities, pp. 1, 3, 1936, p. 3, 1937, pp. 4–5, 1938, p. 4, 1939, p. 2. Cf. Gladys L. Palmer, *Trends in the Philadelphia Labor Market in 1934* (Philadelphia, 1935), p. 4; R. F. Evans (Director, Industrial Bureau, PCC), "To Firms Cooperating in Our Recent Survey of Philadelphia Reemployment and Skilled Labor Shortage," p. 1, in Box 170, DIR Papers, Univ. of Pennsylvania Archives; Irving L. Horowitz, *The Metal Machining Trades in Philadelphia: An Occupational Study* (Philadelphia, 1939), pp. 96, 100, 124.

Third, in the inflationary, unsettled climate of the 1930s, companies with or without personnel departments found that they had a greater need for statistical and factual information and advice about employment policy than ever. How should they pay and treat their ever-more-numerous white-collar workers? What was standard practice? What did they need to do to avert discontent among these staff members? How much differential should foremen receive over the workers they supervised? What should they do about the employment of married women, and what was everybody else doing? How about saving administrative costs by transferring from payment in cash to payment by check? What record systems did you need to comply with the federal and state social security systems and wage-and-hour laws? What other changes in practice did the laws require?

The Philadelphia metal trades' answer to these and other questions turned out to be, increasingly, the MMA. As Sparks put it in 1941, "It offers the opportunity for discussion of problems. It has the information for critical analysis of developments. It has the contacts and can make the approach for consideration of policy. It has the confidence of the industry." Sparks had started to turn it into an information and research bureau in the late 1920s. The Depression blew him off course, but the members' needs were growing, and the MMA was nothing if not responsive to the demands of its clientele and the environment in which it and they operated.[55]

Fourth, if you were involved in collective bargaining, where could you turn for authoritative strategic advice about, for example, whether what the union was asking of you was an acceptable, indeed a commonplace, provision? Where and with whom could the Tool and Die Manufacturers' Group, for example, meet to plan their response to Local 155's demands in the spring of 1939? Who would coordinate information about collective bargaining contracts to make sure that 155 really was imposing the same terms on all competitors? The answers were, respectively, the MMA's offices, and Earl Sparks and his staff. As the MMA later reported,

The really damaging kind of pressure for higher wages [is] based on what is done by other local companies of the same kind. . . .

Unions naturally try to exaggerate the size of competitive wages, tending to produce a distortion which can at least partially be offset if the company produces an accurate comparative wage picture for a substantial group of similar local companies, such as can be obtained from the local trade association. . . .

[Unions play] the concessions of one company against the offers of others, and . . . consequently every company has a deep and logical interest in what is being done by the rest.[56]

[55] SEC 1934, p. 2, 1935, p. 2 and Report on Summer Activities, p. 2, 1936, pp. 2–3, 1938, p. 3, ECM 18 Dec. 1941.

[56] Special Meeting, May 1939, with ECM 6 June; Contract Analysis, UE-MMA, 1946, and Inter-Company Conference on Collective Bargaining, 14 Aug. 1946, pp. 1–2, MMAP II-3-13 and II-4-24.

The bigger members' defenses against union intrusions were still largely of their own devising, but there was one tactic best pursued collaboratively among them and together with their smaller neighbors. This was the analysis of job titles and descriptions, payment systems, and wage rates, and the interchange of information about them, with the object of producing a broadly uniform areawide wage structure in which labor could not deploy "comparability" arguments in pursuit of sectional gains. Here, too, the MMA was active, bringing in Willits's successor at the Wharton School, C. Canby Balderston, to make a detailed study of the problem, organizing experience-sharing between the larger firms (G.E., Westinghouse) with well-developed job evaluation systems and the rest, and introducing NMTA experts to advise on the adoption of standard procedures. And here, too, the UE assisted, convinced that such rationalization was in its members' interests as well as their employers', because a reign of rules could guarantee them the rate for the job, and protect them against favoritism by foremen and the other vagaries of plant-level decision making.[57]

Finally, the growing volume of state and federal intervention required a response in the form of mediation between members and the government bureaucracies that affected them, as well as of lobbying. When the Pennsylvania maximum-hours law was passed in 1937, for example, the MMA negotiated exemptions for members who needed them; when the political tide turned in 1939, it channeled members' bad experiences at the hands of the NLRB to the Smith Committee, which was looking for precisely this kind of ammunition.

Thus, far from the New Deal Order being fatal for the MMA, it actually provided the association with a continuing raison d'être, even after the destruction of the Open Shop. Most importantly, it compelled the Labor Relations Committee to work out and enunciate in 1938 the MMA's first full statement of fundamental principles that should govern its members' behavior vis-à-vis their employees. "More acutely than ever before all industry is being measured by the effectiveness of programs of employer–employee relationships." So, whether judged from the standpoint of efficient operation or the need to contribute to the recovery of the business community's public standing, it was vital that member companies adopt minimum standards of good practice. In this new climate, the collective interests of the Philadelphia metal trades as a whole were given

[57] ECM 6 Feb. 1939. Job rating was the MMA's main project for 1939 – Minutes of the meeting of the Labor Relations Committee and of the Sub Committee on Job Rating, 20 Feb., 23 Mar., ECM 4 Apr., 1 June, 31 Oct.. See NMTA, *Job Rating Program* and *Job Rating Plan* (Chicago, 1938); C. Canby Balderston, *Wage Setting Based on Job Analysis and Evaluation* (New York, 1940); George S. Roy, "Securing Union Cooperation in the Establishment and Operation of Job Evaluation Programs" (MBA Thesis, University of Pennsylvania, 1948), p. 22.

greater weight than the autonomy of individual members, a relic of the
Open Shop era that could not be allowed to survive unscathed.[58]

The return of prosperity in 1939, the resumed growth of organized labor,
the development of a managed economy after 1940 – they all multiplied
members' needs, the pressures for greater uniformity and collective action,
and the MMA's opportunities – to intercede with the Regional War Labor
Board, the War Manpower Commission, or the Office of Price Administration on their behalf, to advise, and to interpret. As Clarence Tolan told
his members on his election to the presidency in 1944,

These are critical times we are passing through, and the future is fraught with uncertainty. To steer our course successfully through the shoals that surround us and lie
ahead will take all our wisdom and cooperation. . . . Never before was there greater
necessity for business to work together.[59]

Members and potential recruits in the Philadelphia metal trades evidently
agreed. The association's membership, solidarity, resources, range of activities, and overall importance in devising a uniform yet flexible labor relations strategy, which mattered more now than it ever had before, all
increased. So the New Deal Order turned into an opportunity rather than
a crisis for the MMA, one it survived and from which it emerged massively
strengthened. By the end of the war, the MMA included 202 firms employing 61,713 workers, approximately double the size it had attained at the
peak of the Hoover boom, in the last golden age of the Open Shop. Of
these, less than 10 percent were nonunion, 13 percent were in independent
unions, and 14 percent were AFL members. The other two-thirds were in
the CIO – 25 percent UE, 19 percent Steel Workers, and 18 percent UAW.
Two-thirds of the entire MMA workforce were also employed under union
security agreements of some sort – 43 percent under maintenance of membership, 23 percent in union shops, and 1 percent in closed shops. These
figures show how the political economy of war had profited the MMA as
well as its workers' unions. But that is another story.[60]

[58] Special Meeting, 2 Sept. 1937, with ECM; ECM 7 Mar. 1939; Policy on
Employer–Employee Relations, 4 Aug. 1938, p. 1. Key provisions of this uniform
policy included the assignment of the employment function to a designated officer
or department, conformity with state and federal wage and hour laws, and the establishment of "orderly and systematic" grievance procedures. See James N. Baron et
al., "War and Peace: The Evolution of Modern Personnel Administration in American Industry," *American Journal of Sociology* 92 (1986): 350–83 at pp. 354–57 and
Jacoby, *Employing Bureaucracy*, pp. 232–36, 250–53, for the broadly similar
national context of managerial renovation in personnel policy.
[59] Acceptance speech of C. Tolan Jr. on election as President of the Assoc (*sic*) 1-28-
44, MMAP II-4-37.
[60] "Member Companies of the Metal Manufacturers' Association of Philadelphia:
Collective Bargaining Recognition, 28 Aug. 1946" with Inter-Company Conference
report, MMAP II-4-24.

12

Afterword: "We'll Still Be There. We're Not Going Away"[1]

One of the regular features of the *American Heritage of Invention and Technology* is editor Frederick Allen's article, "They're Still There," in which some heroic lump of nineteenth- or early-twentieth century machinery is shown still clunking away and churning out profits, operated by people who still embody traditional manual, engineering, and entrepreneurial skills. The attraction of Allen's reports to the industrial antiquarian is obvious, but there is a serious point too: "Progress" does not entirely eliminate or obliterate the past; institutions can survive and adapt; the present is a composite in which things and behaviors we have been taught to disregard, as unimportant or *passé*, continue alongside what we like to consider normal, or significant, or the wave of the future.

The title quote, taken from the membership development director of a midwestern employers' association's report on a conversation with a hesitant recruit, echoes Allen's charming evocation of the survival of traces of the past in the present. But it meant something different to the woman who uttered it. The message that she intended to pass to her prospective member was that the employers' association movement, as it stood on the brink of its second century, had become a permanently useful and necessary feature of the environment in which managers and entrepreneurs operate. If the prospect did not want to join this year, fair enough; there would be plenty of time to reconsider.

Employers' associations today are not mere charming survivals. There are about seventy of them in the Employers' Association Group (EAG) of the

---

[1] Participant, employers' association staff seminar, Philadelphia, 25 Sept. 1998. In return for access to this meeting, and the documents distributed there, I agreed not to identify any participant or his/her association, except for the MidAtlantic Employers' Association, our host, in the use I made of the information that I gathered. Any apparently inadequately sourced claims in this Afterword are based on this unattributable material.

433

NAM's National Industrial Council. Their focus is primarily local – a metropolitan region or part of a state.[2] The largest of them count their members by the thousands and have annual revenues – from membership dues and members' fees for services rendered – exceeding $10 million. They can deploy staff members by the gross and lawyers by the score to attend to their members' human resource (HR) problems. Although labor relations scholars know little or nothing about them, the fact is that they have not, contrary to general academic assumptions, been eliminated from the post–New Deal industrial relations system. They have not been marginalized by the development of company-specific policies, administrative capacities, and (in a diminishing number of cases) collective bargaining relationships.[3] On the contrary, with labor union membership in the private sector lower now than it has been at any time since the 1920s, the employers' association movement looks forward with confidence to an expanding sphere of membership and activities.[4]

The postwar history of the MMA itself illustrates what employers' associations have been up to, and up against, through the decades when, according to the conventional scholarly wisdom, they have been thoroughly unimportant, if indeed they have existed at all. It is undeniable that associations, like the unions they dealt with, have had a hard task of adapting to changing circumstances. The MMA and its sister associations were all rooted in one cluster of industries – metal manufacturing – located in discrete industrial districts. They all drew on a membership base of propri-

---

[2] There are also manufacturers' associations in most states whose emphasis is more on lobbying than membership service in the human resource field, and single-industry associations, for example in construction and trucking, that are much more focused on anti-unionism.

[3] Milton Derber, "Employers' Associations in the U.S.A.," in John P. Windmuller and Alan Gladstone, eds., *Employers Associations and Industrial Relations: A Comparative Study* (Oxford, 1984) summarizes industrial relations scholarship on this subject. A tendency to minimize the importance of U.S. employers' continuing use of collective means to address human resource management problems seems to have resulted from the habit of looking for the wrong thing, not finding it, and not noticing what is actually going on. It is true that U.S. employers have not joined together very much for national or even industry-level collective bargaining with the unions (if any) of their workers in the "collective-bargaining era," contrary to what scholars impressed by experience in European and in some AFL-unionized industries thought they should have (see Keith Sissons, *The Management of Collective Bargaining: An International Comparison* [Oxford, 1987], pp. 174–79). As scholars could not find what they expected, and were interested in, they seem to have failed to spot the very significant non- or anti-union collective action that is everywhere to be seen. A search of the ArticleFirst™ and Wilson Business Abstracts™ databases revealed only two articles on employers' associations in this decade, both minor news items in trade rather than scholarly journals.

[4] Employers' associations typically recruit an additional 11 percent of members per year and retain about 90 percent of existing members, that is, they are stable or growing slowly.

etary and closely held firms and corporations, tied together by bonds of neighborliness and contractual interconnections. They have had to cope with dramatic changes in the structure of the American economy and the composition of the corporate sector – diversification of members beyond their original industrial focus; relocation of members from their old inner-urban industrial neighborhoods, tied to railroad transportation corridors, toward the postwar automobile suburbs and edge cities; merger movements and corporate consolidations, which have further fractured the old linkages between a particular company and any particular industry or locality; the decline of traditional industries, and the transformation of their technologogical bases. The MMA and its sisters have seen members and potential members go bankrupt, or just expire, or indulge in "downsizing," or get swallowed up by remote corporations deciding policy in another city or country, or move their factories across county, state, and regional or even international boundaries. The relative stability of the 1900s through 1930s has entirely disappeared.[5]

The MMA and its sisters have also had to cope with an increasingly competitive environment for the supply of the services that they can offer. Members' readiness to pay dues is still a matter of instrumental calculation rather than of ideological commitment. Firms of a size that, up until the 1930s, would have had no formal employment policies or personnel staff, now routinely have their own HR departments, lessening their dependency on association aid. HR specialists have their own networks and their own professional societies to provide them with ideas and information.[6] They can do more for themselves, or they can buy assistance elsewhere. For there is also a huge service industry – which scarcely existed before the 1940s – to supply companies with all of their various needs in the HR field: cor-

---

[5] The names of contemporary employers' associations often reflect the resulting weakening of their linkages with a particular industry or place – indeed, they often deliberately disguise the fact that most of them are still focused on a single metropolitan region, or part of a single state, which is one of their real strengths. Thus, the Chicago Metal Trades Association is now called the Management Association of Illinois, a territory it might appear to contest with the Peoria-based Employers' Association of Illinois (1917–), but in fact both are still centered in their respective city-regions; the Milwaukee Metal Trades Association (1901–) has evolved into MRA – The Management Association and recruits across Wisconsin, but it is still strongest in greater Milwaukee, and shares its state with Kenosha and Racine-based associations; the Employers Association of Detroit (1902–) now calls itself the American Society of Employers, although its focus is still southeast and mid-Michigan; the Cincinnati-based association serving the southern Ohio–Indiana–northern Kentucky tri-state area is called the Employers Resource Association, while its northwestern Ohio–northeast Indiana–southern Michigan equivalent simplifies matters by claiming to be *The* Employers' Association. Generic names like this seem to be increasingly common.

[6] See, for example, the websites of the Society for Human Resources Management (including the Employment Management Association), http://www.shrm.org/, and the National Human Resources Association, http://www.humanresources.org.

porate law firms with specialist labor and HR departments, publishers of manuals on every phase of employment policy and practice, private, for-profit consultancies delivering specialized services (e.g., fighting and winning union recognition and decertification election campaigns) or wide-spectrum advice and assistance.[7] Finally, the decay of the connection between an employers' association and any particular industry or city also threatens to bring them into competition with one another, as locally based associations fight it out with other business groups, all of them now potential suitors for the same limited pool of members. Turf wars threaten between local employers' associations and chambers of commerce, between state and national bodies and their local affiliates, and even between once geographically separate local associations themselves (because their territories have expanded to overlap with one another, and most recently because the Internet offers a new means of service- and information-delivery that respects no frontiers, and tempts the largest and most sophisticated local associations to fish in everybody else's ponds).

The times have indeed been challenging; but the MMA and its sisters have survived, and even thrived. The MMA itself adapted to the postwar deindustrialization of the city and the decline of the metal trades by changing its name in 1960 to the Manufacturers' Association of Greater Philadelphia, welcoming makers of other things besides metal products and extending its territory to include the whole metropolitan region – eight Pennsylvania counties plus five in New Jersey and even one in Delaware. That brought it into competition with the Manufacturers' Association of Montgomery County, which had originated in the textile industry's opposition to Progressive Era state legislation but had evolved in a way that paralleled the MMA's. In 1971, the two organizations merged to form the Manufacturers' Association of the Delaware Valley which, in the 1980s, opened membership to nonmanufacturing firms, expanded the range of services it offered, marketed them outside its own territory – as far afield as Maryland – and merged again, with the Manufacturers and Business Association of Southern New Jersey. In 1993, to reflect these developments, it

---

[7] Employers' associations emphasize their advantages in this competitive environment: HR professionals suffering from information overload can use their local association as a "one-stop shop"; the association offers its members full service and a long-term commitment, so that they do not have to enter into a succession of short-term contracts with a variety of untried consultants and providers; there are the added, intangible advantages of a long-term, "relational" contract with an organization that gets to know its members' needs; and there are also the free benefits of mutual support and advice from other members. Given the current tendency to "outsource" businesses' "noncore activities," members can also use their associations' professionals on a regular basis to extend the capabilities of their "lean" and overstressed managements: each full-time HR professional is typically responsible for about 100 employees (ranging from 58 in utilities and 75 in manufacturing, to 140 in nonmanufacturing enterprises and over 200 in the service sector).

changed its name once more, to the MidAtlantic Employers' Association, the title under which it will enter its second century.[8]

The MEA now has about 800 members, employing more than 100,000 workers, and after some difficult years is growing fast. Few of its members are left in the city. The North Philadelphia neighborhoods where most of them were to be found between the 1900s and 1940s are now thoroughly deindustrialized and depopulated, the remaining inhabitants' lives blighted by environmental degradation, poverty, family breakdown, and drug-related crime.[9] The vast majority of members are drawn from the suburbs and exurbs in southeastern Pennsylvania or southern New Jersey. There are still far more of them (71 percent) engaged in manufacturing than in any other activity, reflecting the MEA's historical orientation, but the growth sectors are the retail, wholesale, and distribution industries, together with service industries and professional and financial service providers, which already make up about a quarter of the total.

The industrial makeup of member firms, and the composition of their workforces (including, for example, twice as many chemical engineers or systems programmers as metal polishers and buffers), has therefore changed radically and is becoming ever further removed from traditional patterns. The size distribution of members is, however, much more familiar. A combination of the collapse, departure, or at best downsizing of the great industrial plants that began to join the MMA in the 1920s; of a renewed reluctance by large firms with substantial HR departments to join employers' associations; and of the much smaller average size of new recruits – means that it is once again an organization primarily of small- to medium-sized, locally based, proprietary or closely held corporate enterprises. Forty percent of the members have fewer than 50 employees, 65 percent fewer than a hundred, and 90 percent fewer than 250. In these respects, too, the MEA is closely comparable with other associations, which have evolved a long way from their common metal trades, Open Shop beginnings (see Tables 12.1 and 12.2).

What do modern employers' associations do for their members in order to hold their loyalty and justify the dues and fees they charge? There are variations among them: Some place more emphasis on lobbying, while others

---

[8] See Ken Fones Wolf, "What's Good for Business: the Records of Manufacturers in the Delaware Valley," *Urban Archives Notes* 22 (Feb. 1982) and James H. Soltow, "Small City Industrialists in the Age of Organization: A Case Study of the Manufacturers' Association of Montgomery County, Pennsylvania, 1908–1958" *BHR* 33 (1959): 178–89. This account is also informed by Diane E. Reed's brief internal staff history, "The History of MEA 1903–Present," February 1995 (copy in author's possession, supplied by Association).

[9] Steve Lopez, *Third and Indiana* (New York, 1994), is a fictionalized but only slightly sentimental description of this war zone at the height of the crack epidemic.

TABLE 12.1 Industrial Distribution of
Members, Ten Employers' Associations,
1998

SECTOR	Percent	Cumulative
Manufacturing	51%	
Services	17%	68%
Financial	6%	74%
Retail/Wholesale	5%	79%
Professional	3%	82%
Distribution	3%	85%
Health Care	3%	88%
Construction	3%	91%
Others[a]	9%	100%

[a] *Others* include Transportation, Communications, and Public Utilities; Public Sector and Non-Profit; Agriculture and Mining.

Source: Ten associations, 9,200 members, c. 1.7 million employees, located in the Mid-Atlantic, East North Central, and Mountain states.

TABLE 12.2 Size Distribution of Members, Ten Employers'
Associations, 1998

Employees	Share of Members	Share of Employment
1–25	14%	1%
26–50	21%	4%
51–100	20%	8%
101–250	28%	26%
251–500	10%	20%
501–750	4%	12%
751–1,000	2%	11%
1,000+	3%	18%

engage in collective bargaining on behalf of groups of their members (and also provide more anti-union services); but there is a common core of activities. Here again, the MEA is quite typical. Labor relations is not a major priority: Less than an eighth of its members are unionized, and only 3 percent of the members report any recent union organizing activity, which resulted in the calling of a representation election in less than half of those cases. Less than a third of such elections resulted in union victory, whereas half of the decertification elections (about half as frequent) have resulted in union defeats. In the diminishing minority of unionized plants, formal union security provisions are near-universal, but these and other vestiges of the New Deal labor relations system only linger on within a shrinking perimeter: They have lacked dynamism, and the capacity to fascinate or threaten, for decades.

The heart of the MEA and its sister associations in the 1990s lies elsewhere – as it did for the MMA and the NMTA and its branches in the 1920s. Labor bureaus, of course, have disappeared – although specialized placement services are once again quite common. But all associations still deliver the kinds of services pioneered by Earl Sparks in the 'teens, twenties, and thirties. Eighty years on, the MEA and its sisters are still carrying out the regular surveys of wage rates that Sparks began in 1918, together with detailed studies of other employment policies of the kind he added in the following decades.[10] This pooling of experience is still the local employers' association's key benefit to its members, whose own HR managers thereby gain unique access to confidential and authoritative reports on pay ranges and standard practices in the labor markets that matter most to them. This is all – to use the MEA's slogan for one of its regular bulletins to members – "News You Can Use," practical information as a guide for managerial policymaking and behavior.

The other core activity of the MEA and its sister associations is employee training – in particular, supervisory and management training tied to the objectives of enhancing staff effectiveness, improving total quality, and minimizing problems of compliance with the mass of state and federal regulations of which companies must be aware. This last, indeed, seems to be the big growth area in association work. Associations also support their members in handling regulatory risk by the publication of comprehensive, highly valued law manuals and compliance guides. Like the associations' wage, salary, benefit, and other personnel practice surveys, these are not normally available for commercial sale, even at a very high unit price, but they are free to members or available at a nominal cost. They explain

[10] Surveys have been extended to include administration and office support staff, data processing, engineering, scientific and technical workers, sales, supervisory, managerial, and even executive grades, alongside production, maintenance, and service employees.

to the harassed HR professional or front-line supervisor in practical terms how s/he can cope with ADA and ADEA and COBRA, EEOC, and FMLA, OSHA and other members of the monstrous regiment of acronyms.[11] When these publications and associated training activities do not suffice – where, for example, a manager in a member company wants an immediate answer to a question, without having to wade through hundreds of pages – there is in every association the telephone, or more recently e-mail or voice mail, hotline. Executives and supervisors can gain speedy access to comprehensive reference libraries, targeted advice, and the accumulated years of varied experience of teams of seasoned professionals. These are all resources that they could not provide for themselves, particularly in small and medium-sized enterprises, and are obtainable at a quality and price with which for-profit consultants can generally not compete. In addition to the practical value of the advice they receive, they gain reassurance: They are not alone.[12]

Without necessarily having read their Mancur Olson, employers' association executives have evidently mastered the arts of putting together packages of exclusive benefits sufficiently attractive as to persuade members to join, and stay. They can demonstrate to members the association's advantages of "repeat play" – its possession of a stock of specialized knowledge and expertise not otherwise available. They lack one thing, however, as compared with their Open Shop forebears. The modern movement is a professional and utilitarian affair. It lacks the personal commitment and the

[11] The Americans with Disabilities Act, Age Discrimination in Employment Act, Consolidated Omnibus Budget Reconciliation Act (providing for continuation of health care coverage), Equal Employment Opportunities Commission, Family and Medical Leave Act, and Occupational Safety and Health Act. The MEA's current law guide (Pennsylvania edition) lists fifteen major state statutes plus many other lesser regulations (covering, for example, the rights of volunteer firefighters), all of which need to be understood and applied, plus twenty-five federal statutes (including, for example, the Employee Polygraph Protection Act) and more administrative codes of particular agencies (notably the Internal Revenue and Immigration and Naturalization Services). Labor relations law represents only a very small fraction of this all-encompassing legal framework; violations of it are much less costly than those that can result in large fines and/or individual and class-action suits for compensation or redress. Two-thirds of surveyed HR professionals reported that their companies had been involved in employment-related lawsuits over the previous five years; compensation awards (excluding punitive damages) had averaged between $100,000 and $500,000 per claimant, depending on the statute violated, plus $100,000 of legal fees per case.

[12] Other services normally provided include: on-site audits of HR policy, ADA, EEO, and OSHA compliance, and of Affirmative Action plans; employee opinion surveys; assistance with production of employee handbooks and introduction of new HR policies; the supply of temporary HR staff – even whole departments – to monitor existing programs, install new ones, and respond to crises, e.g., mass layoffs. Associations also engage in group purchasing, particularly of health care, pension, savings, and other insurance and benefit programs for their members' employees.

ideological fervor – the awareness of enemies, the sense of a cause – so common in the period dealt with in this book.

Contemporary associations, in the first place, are much better endowed with staff and resources than the older organizations ever were. And, by and large, it is the staff who manage them. This is inevitable: The increase in association size and territory and the decrease in membership homogeneity mean that they are no longer connected with distinct employer communities like the old MMA, for example, always was. Running associations can no longer be an after-hours activity for elected officers, all of whom could be expected to know one another, to do business with one another, and to live nearby. CEOs of member firms still provide the elected policy boards of modern associations, which meet occasionally, and may play some role in recruitment and other activities. But they leave management and service delivery to the descendants of Earl Sparks, the full-time, career professionals – most commonly with an HR background themselves – who are the associations' CEOs.

Associations have generally, and deliberately, evolved beyond what they term the old "membership model" of organization – in which companies paid their dues, after which all services were effectively free – to the present "service model." What this means is that dues are tiered, as in the MMA since the early 1920s, with a minimum and a maximum level. The very numerous and comparatively dependent smaller members pay relatively more for what they get; larger firms, with more of their own administrative resources, pay relatively less; and there is a cap on maximum dues, typically at around 900 employees. This is a dues structure that is much less mutualistic than the old per-capita flat-fee system. For their dues, members receive the common core services – the law manuals, the employment practice surveys, the hotline support. Everything else, particularly training, they pay for, so that the relation of the association to its members is increasingly that of a "captive consultant." Members and recruits are considered, not as collaborators in the pursuit of employers' class interests, but much more prosaically, as customers who will enable the associations' staff to generate the business and the profit on which an association's financial health, and individual staff members' compensation, increasingly depend.[13]

Social ties among the members have also become attenuated. The clubbiness of the old local and national associations no longer exists. Traditions of dinner meetings and annual banquets are barely remembered. But a new kind of personal connection does link associations and their members

[13] Typically, membership dues represent a third of an association's income nowadays, as against the whole lot in the 1900s through 1930s; "billable services" to individual members make up the rest. The total cost works out at c. $20 per employee per year. Where publications and services are also offered for sale to nonmembers, there is a stiff price differential – enough to persuade a satisfied customer of the benefits of membership.

together – networking, by face-to-face meeting or phone or e-mail conversation, between associations' staff professionals and the managers, supervisors, and HR personnel with whom they interact in site visits, training
seminars, and over the hotline; business breakfasts and daylong "Round
Table" meetings for groups of member CEOs with a common interest based
on industry or locality, or peer groups of staff specialists in member companies; experience-sharing seminars for staff from collaborating associations, held at hotels near major airline hubs; bi-annual conferences of the
CEOs of the dozen largest associations, most of them former NMTA
branches, which group together under the name of the Management Association of America, at Palm Springs or some upscale Florida resort.[14] These
more or less informal connections, and their research collaboration through
the EAG, mean that one can still speak of an employers' association *move-*
ment, rather than simply of a number of separate but similar organizations;
but there is no single, clear, common objective with the mobilizing force of
the Open Shop creed.[15]

Perhaps there does not need to be. There is no enemy, not even the state,
which is a bureaucratic inconvenience and an accepted complication of
modern life, rather than a deadly foe. The modern employers' association
movement lacks a cause because – as a contributor to, and a beneficiary of,
the third bloodless victory in this book, that over the New Deal labor relations system – it has won.

---

[14] There is also an interesting change in the gender composition of the movement: Association *staffs* are increasingly female, reflecting the professional groups – HR personnel, educators, marketing and sales specialists – from which they are recruited.
CEOs, of member companies and of associations, are still generally male.
[15] This "end of ideology" is reflected in associations' rather banal slogans and mission
statements – "Progress Through Association," "Helping Employers Thrive," "Excellence in Human Resources," "Human Resources Solutions for Employers," "Your
Business Partner Since 1901," "Resources to Make Your Vision Soar – Ascend Above
the Competition," "A Business Resource for Employers," "We Strive to Strengthen
the Employer–Employee Relationship." A good selection of links to employers' association websites, which contain valuable source material, is available at "Employers'
Associations in the USA Today," http://www.dur.ac.uk/~dhiøhjh/RESEARCH/
ersassns.htm.

Appendix

Databases Referrred to in Text:
Nature, Sources, Use

The first database developed was MMAYEARS, a reconstructed member-ship list for the MMA. The records contained lists for a few individual years and an incomplete list of member companies and when they joined.[1] These sources were extended by a systematic examination of all records (particu-larly the Executive Committee Minutes and Presidents' and Secretaries' reports) for all company name occurrences to create a comprehensive listing of all members, 1904–40 (285 in number). The company is the record unit and the basic data units ("fields") are the years 1904–40, so that for every company, in every year, one can tell its status, if any – joining the MMA, leaving, in membership or not. From these data information about acces-sion, resignation, and turnover rates was calculated, and the identification of the MMA's stable membership core became possible.

The first logical extension to MMAYEARS resulted from a need to know how member companies compared with and related to the whole popula-tion of metal-working firms in the district. This was done by creating the databases 1902FACT (692 company records), from the Philadelphia returns in the 1902 state factory inspector's report[2] – the last one to give individ-ual company details (name, industry, address, male, female, youth, and total employment); and PID-1640 (2,333 records), from the state industrial direc-tories, which began publication in 1913 and became reliable and fairly consistent in 1916.[3] Between 1916 and 1922 directories contained infor-mation about the gender breakdown of the laborforce, as well as dividing

---

[1] In MMAP II-4-28/31.
[2] Commonwealth of Pennsylvania, *Thirteenth Annual Report of the Factory Inspector 1902* (Harrisburg, 1903), pp. 52–397. Forty-four percent of company records, rep-resenting 81 percent of 1902 employment, linked through to 1916.
[3] Commonwealth of Pennsylvania Department of Internal Affairs, Bureau of Statistics and Information, *Second* through *Tenth Industrial Directory of the Commonwealth of Pennsylvania, 1916–1940* (Harrisburg, 1916–40).

443

it between production and clerical/administrative categories. From 1924 on, only total employment was given. In addition, the early directories listed *all* of the main product categories reflected in a company's output, but from 1924 on mixed-output companies were classified according to their major product only, and industries were assigned three-digit codes. I applied the same procedure and coding system retrospectively to 1902 and 1916–22, in the interests of comparability – the original data were not discarded, but rationalized. The data were also supplemented by conservative interpolation – budget and staffing cutbacks harmed data collection in the early 1920s in particular,[4] and the procedures were never 100 percent foolproof, so if there was a return for years A and C, but not B (or industry data but no employment figure), I assumed that B's figure was halfway between A's and C's, and that industrial location was stable. Derived data of this kind were clearly distinguished from original data, and rarely made up more than 5 percent of employment totals. The justification of this procedure was that the resulting datasets gave a slightly better indication of the population of firms and their employment in any particular year than the original returns had. Neither was wholly accurate.

Because of the common field (company name), data from 1902FACT and PID-1640 could be used to extend MMAYEARS by providing information about the industrial location and employment of member companies at any survey date. PID-1640 was also extended by adding comment fields recording companies' involvement with labor union organizing and strike activity, so that the crises of 1916–18 and 1933–37, in particular, could be located and contextualized. Information for this purpose came from all relevant U.S. Conciliation Service, National War Labor Board, National Labor Board, and National Labor Relations Board files, as well as from the MMA papers and the labor press.

The second logical extension to MMAYEARS was to investigate individual executives' careers, both as activists within the MMA and in the companies where they worked. This resulted in two further datasets, both linked by company name to MMAYEARS, 1902FACT, and PID-1640, as well as to one another: MMA-EXEC (165 records), which gathered together all information from the MMA papers about its officers and committee members, and permitted the identification and location of its active minority and an understanding of its internal political processes; and PHILCHAP (1,043 records), which contained data about member firms' senior executives at four survey dates – 1903, 1913, 1925, and 1936. City directories

---

[4]   Secretary James F. Woodward, "Foreword" in Commonwealth of Pennsylvania Department of Internal Affairs, Bureau of Statistics and Information, *Report on the Productive Industries of the Commonwealth of Pennsylvania for 1924* (Harrisburg, 1925), p. 1 and 1927 (1928), p. 1, for the effect of budgetary restrictions, staff cuts, and enforced procedural changes, on the quality of his department's data collection.

and other sources[5] permitted the classification of companies by ownership and management type – individual proprietary, partnership, family, close corporation, and managerial corporation. There were very few of the latter, and distinctions among the former were often imprecise. Nevertheless, these data were helpful in demonstrating the gradual change in the composition of the MMA activist community – from being *exclusively* owners and/or senior executives in locally owned and controlled proprietary companies through the early 1920s, until it included a minority of corporate managers and staff personnel specialists by and after the late 1920s.

The final important dataset, PHIL1439 (1,141 records), is different in character from those previously mentioned in that its basic record unit is not an individual or the company he belonged to, but the industry. It consists of all data on the metal-working industries of the city of Philadelphia gathered by the Commonwealth of Pennsylvania's Department of Labor and Industry in 1914 and 1915, and by the Department of Internal Affairs from 1916 through 1939, together with the "All Manufacturing" totals for the same years.[6] Because these industries are classified using the same system and three-digit codes as those employed in PID-1640, it was possible to link up (for example) summary data on the proportion of an industry's total employment represented in the MMA in any survey year with descriptive information about that industry for the same year. This is the basis of most observations about the character of the MMA's membership and speculations about their reasons for affiliation.

All returns break the workforce down by gender, age (above/below 16), nationality (American/other), and race (African American/other), and provide figures for total wage bill and product value. From 1919 the wage bill is divided into male and female components, and a value for capitalization is included. Between 1921 and 1923 a figure is given for product value exported beyond state boundaries – which could include trade with parts of the metropolitan regions in New Jersey and Delaware. After 1929 there are also data for installed horsepower, which is a convenient proxy (alongside capitalization) for the extent of an industry's dependence on non-labor inputs. The principal use made of these data has been to examine changes in average earnings and the composition of industries' laborforces over time, and to calculate crude indicators of industrial character and per-

---

[5] Principally *Gopsill's* [1903], *Boyd's* [1913], and *Polk's* [1925, 1936] *Philadelphia City Directory* (Philadelphia, dates as stated) and *Moody's Industrials* (New York, 1922), together with the "company biographical" data sources employed in Chapter 2.

[6] Commonwealth of Pennsylvania Department of Labor and Industry, *Second* (1914) and *Third Annual Report of the Commissioner for Labor and Industry* (1915) (Harrisburg, 1915, 1916), and Commonwealth of Pennsylvania Department of Internal Affairs, Bureau of Statistics and Information, *Reports on the Productive Industries of the Commonwealth of Pennsylvania* 1916–1919 (Harrisburg, 1920); 1921 (1923); 1922–23 (1924); 1924 (1925); 1926 and annually through 1939 (published in year following survey.)

formance – output:capital ratios, and wage bill as a proportion of product value. State data were used in preference to federal census information, because they shared a common classification system with the industrial directories, were collected annually, and had broader detailed coverage. Federal census data *were* analyzed, and employed in Chapters 2 and 4, despite their limitations – including five- or ten-year gaps between surveys, and concealment by aggregation of the returns for some of the city's major metal-working industries – because they were the best that was available for the pre–World War period.

Finally, two further membership list datasets akin to MMAYEARS, though less complete, were compiled. These are NFA9805 and NMTA9936, for the NFA from its origins through 1905 and for the NMTA from its origins through the end of the Open Shop era in 1936. Sources were surviving membership lists for particular years and details of companies represented at annual conventions and on committees – there is therefore an overcount of activist firms.[7] The principal use made of them here was to locate MMA members' national affiliations. But they were also vital for buttressing the conviction that, especially in the character of its member companies, the MMA was reasonably representative of the metal trades' Open Shop movement at large.

[7] Sources include the very detailed reports on annual conventions in the *Iron Age* and *Iron Trades Review* – the NMTA met in April, the NFA in November – for 1899–1905; the NMTA's own *Bulletin* for 1903 and 1904; its published *Synopsis of Proceedings* for 1907 and for 1910 through 1922; published membership lists for 1909, 1910, and 1912 [NMTA, *Members* (Cleveland, 1909, 1910, 1912)] and 1922 [*The NMTA Organized 1899 – The History, Scope and Purpose of the Association: Roster of Officers and Members July 1, 1922* (Chicago, 1922)], and full membership and subscription details for 1933–36 compiled by the [La Follette] Subcommittee of the U.S. Senate Committee on Education and Labor, *Violations of Free Speech and the Rights of Labor: Hearings* (Washington, 1937), Vol. 3, pp. 980–94. For a preliminary analysis of these data, see my "Research Note: The Open Shop in the Metal Trades," http://www.dur.ac.uk/~dhiøhjh/nfa&nmta.htm.

Index